"Original and thought-provoking . . . likely to have a profound impact on studies of globalization."

Patricia Fernández-Kelly, Professor of Sociology, Princeton University

"Few books on Central America have drawn the relationship between transnationalism and its economic, social and political effects on people in the region . . . Robinson offers an important tool to academics, policy analysts, and those interested in case studies on globalization."

Manuel Orozco, Program Director for Central America Inter-American Dialogue

"*Transnational Conflicts*, a comprehensive case study of Central American transformations in the global political economy, is a model examination and conceptualization of transnational processes. Robinson extrapolates from contemporary world history to show convincingly that development is now a transnational project, and Central America is a dramatic laboratory."

Philip McMichael, Professor of Sociology, Cornell University

"This is a major study of a region that has long been marginalized from international analysis. Radical and revisionist, closely informed and lucid, Robinson's interpretation of the political economy of Central America is rooted in theory but never loses sight of the importance of named individuals."

James Dunkerley, Director of the Institute of Latin American Studies, University of London

"A new generation of entrepreneurs, mainly from the financial elite, are the agents of a transnational project in Central America that until now has gone largely unstudied. William Robinson's impressive work is the first academic attempt to take up the contemporary character of social struggles in the region in the context of globalization. His fine scholarship has brought success to the endeavor. This is an indispensable study."

Edelberto Torres Rivas, United Nations Development Program

Transnational Conflicts

Central America, Social Change, and Globalization

WILLIAM I. ROBINSON

VERSO

London • New York

First published by Verso 2003
© William I. Robinson 2003
All rights reserved

1 3 5 7 9 10 8 6 4 2

Verso
UK: 6 Meard Street, London, W1F 0EG
USA: 180 Varick Street, New York, NY 10014–4606
www.versobooks.com

Verso is the imprint of New Left Books

ISBN 1-85984-547-9
ISBN 1-85984-439-1 (pbk)

British Library Cataloguing in Publication Data
Robinson, William I.
   Transnational conflicts: Central America, social change, and globalization
   1. Social change – Central America – History – 20th century
   2. Globalization – Social aspects – Central America
   3. Globalization – Economic aspects – Central America –
   History – 20th century 4. Globalization – Political aspects
   – Central America – History – 20th century 5. Central
   America – Social conditions – 1979–   6. Central America –
   Economic conditions – 1979–   7. Central America – Politics
   and government – 1979–
   I. Title
   303.4′4′09728

   ISBN 1859844391 PB
   ISBN 1859845479 HB

Library of Congress Cataloging-in-Publication Data
Robinson, William I.
   Transnational conflicts : Central America, social change and globalization / William
Robinson.
      p. cm
   Includes bibliographical references and index.
   ISBN 1-85984-439-1 (pbk) — ISBN 1-85984-547-9 (cloth)
   1. Social change—Central America.   2. Central America—Social conditions—
1979– 3. Central America—Economic conditions—1979– 4. Structural adjustment
(Economic policy)—Central America.   5. Central America—Foreign economic
relations.   6. Globalization.   I. Title.

HN123.5.R6 2003
305.4′09728—dc21
                                                                    2003053502

Typeset in 9.5/11 Baskerville by SetSystems Ltd, Saffron Walden, Essex
Printed in the UK by Bath Press

Contents

Foreword and Acknowledgements

It is Autumn 2002 as I write these lines; political tensions are reaching a pinnacle around the world as conflict rages far and wide. The US government and its allies appear poised to unleash a war of unforeseen consequences in the Middle East, a region already aflame, from Afghanistan to Palestine. One crisis after another has broken out in scores of Latin American countries with a rapidity beyond anyone's prediction just a year ago. Aborted coup d'états in Venezuela and Haiti, street uprisings in Paraguay, Uruguay, and Peru, all-out war in Colombia, a mounting power vacuum in Argentina as that country slides into chaos—these are the order of the day. Sectarian clashes in South Asia are threatening a war between India and Pakistan. The UN summit on sustainable development in Johannesburg ended with a couched endorsement of further transnational corporate plunder, and in Washington, D.C., an army of police is violently repressing anti-globalization protesters. The so-called "war on terrorism" launched in the wake of 11 September 2001 was the inauguration of what my colleagues and I—in a "global crisis working group" that we formed earlier this year under the auspices of the Transnational Institute in Amsterdam—term the *new war order*, an outgrowth of the crisis of globalization.

It is this order into which Central America is becoming ever more enmeshed. The structural underpinnings of the storm clouds that are gathering globally are the same as those which have shaped Central America's destiny during the period examined in this book. It is my hope that this book may help to provide some novel theoretical, analytical, and global perspectives for Central Americans, and for all those concerned with the Isthmus, as they attempt to come to grips with the region's enmeshment. I aspire for this work to reach Central and Latin American scholars as well as those engaged with globalization issues: critical theorists of political economy, policy experts in the field of development assistance (NGOs, aid agencies, foundations), university students, and leaders and activists from the diverse movements for social justice in and beyond the Isthmus. I hope more generally that the book makes a lasting contribution to the economic and political history of Central America. It will be for my readers to arbitrate how successful I am in these aspirations.

Let me say to my readers that this is a lengthy book. I have tried to make it "user-friendly" and resourceful by preparing the manuscript in such a way that different chapters and subsections can be read on their own.

Chapter one may be read on its own by readers interested in my general theories on globalization. Those concerned with my reinterpretation of Central America's recent political history in light of globalization may read chapter two, or any individual country section in it, on its own. The subsections in chapters three and four covering specific dimensions of change in twenty-first-century Central American and world society may be accessed on their own.

Many friends and colleagues have been expecting the publication of this book for some time. The book is indeed long overdue. I first began work on it in 1995 but had to suspend this the next year due to a number of pressing personal and professional commitments. I was able to resume work, off and on, during 1998–2000 and finish a first draft, only to have to place on hold until 2002 the final preparation of the manuscript in the face of circumstances beyond my control. I wish to thank the many people and institutions who have contributed to this work in diverse ways, which range from reading parts or all of the manuscript or related essays, to engaging in stimulating intellectual discussions, providing financial support or institutional backing, offering collegial support, or contributing to my own intellectual, personal, and political development in manifold respects. I also want to thank them for their patience. They include, in alphabetical order: Tariq Ali, Paul Almeida, Giovanni Arrighi, John Booth, Roger Burbach, Sherry Cable, Christopher Chase-Dunn, Norma Chinchilla, Tim Clark, Wilmar Cuarezma and the Fundación Millenio in Managua, David Dye, Gioconda Espinoza, María Patricia Fernández-Kelly, Adam Flint, Jerry Harris, Donald Hasting, Jon Haynes, Asafa Jalata, Boris Kagarlitsky, the late Miguel Korzeniewicz, George Lambie, James R. Maupin, Marielle Mayorga, Jeffrey Mitchell, Abelardo Morales, Craig Murphy, Alison Newby, Manuel Orozco, N. Ysabel Passalacqua, Kees van der Pijl, Alejandro Portes, Kevin Robinson, Mark Rupert, Amandeep Sandhu, Denise Segura, Kathleen Shwartzman, David Skidmore, Leslie Sklair, Hazel Smith, Richard Stalher-Sholk, William Stanley, Edmundo Urutia, Sally Willson Weimer, and Howard Winant.

Many thanks as well to my friends and scholars at the Costa Rican and Guatemalan branch of the Facultad Latinoamericana de Ciencias Sociales (FLACSO) in San José and Guatemala City, at the Universidad del Valle in Guatemala City, the Universidad Centroamericana in Managua, the Coordinadora Regional de Investigaciones Economicas y Sociales (CRIES) in Managua, to my friends and former and current colleagues at the University of Tennessee, the University of New Mexico, New Mexico State University, the University of California at Santa Barbara, and the Latin America Data Base at the University of New Mexico. Apologies to anyone who I may have inadvertently left out.

I owe a very special debt of gratitude to my long-time friend, Kent Norsworthy, my wonderful friend Tomas Leal, and my children, Amaru Alejandro and Tamara Yoconda; to them, *un abrazo fuerte*.

I gratefully acknowledge the College of Arts and Sciences at the University of Tennessee, the College of Arts and Sciences at New Mexico State

University, and the Center for International Studies, also at New Mexico State University, for funding different portions of the research. While intellectual production is always a collective endeavor, I assume as a matter of course sole responsibility for the content of this study, including its inevitable shortcomings.

Santa Barbara
October 2002

Acronyms and Abbreviations

ACORDE	Association of Costa Rican Development Organizations
AID	Agency for International Development
ALIPO	Liberal Alliance of the People (Honduras)
ANEP	National Association of Private Enterprise (El Salvador)
APEC	Asia-Pacific Economic Cooperation
APENN	Association of Non-Traditional Producers and Exporters of Nicaragua
APROH	Association for Honduran Progress
ARENA	Nationalist Revolutionary Alliance (El Salvador)
ASIES	Association for Research and Social Studies (Guatemala)
ASOCODE	Association of Peasant Organizations for Cooperation and Development
BANADES	National Development Bank (Nicaragua)
BANDESA	National Agriculture Development Bank (Honduras)
CAAP	Private Council on Agriculture and Industry (Costa Rica)
CACIF	Chamber of Agriculture, Commercial, Industrial and Financial Organizations (Guatemala)
CACM	Central American Common Market
CAEM	Entrepreneurial Chamber (Guatemala)
CBI	Caribbean Basin Initiative
CENPRO	Center for the Promotion of Exports (Costa Rica)
CEPAL	Comision Economica para America Latina y el Caribe
CIA	Central Intelligence Agency
CIC	Costa Rican Chamber of Industries
CINDE	Coalition for Initiatives in Development (Costa Rica)
CIP	Commodity Import Program (Nicaragua)

CLE	Free Market Chamber (Guatemala)
CNAA	National Chamber of Agriculture and Animal Husbandry (Costa Rica)
CODESA	Costa Rican Development Corporation
COHEP	Honduran Council of Private Enterprise
CONAFEXI	National Council to Promote Exports and Investment (Honduras)
CONAPEX	National Council for the Promotion of Exports (Guatemala)
COSEP	Superior Council of Private Enterprise
CSN	National Defense and Security Council (Honduras)
DIVAGRO	Agricultural Diversification Program
EAP	Economically Active Population
ELD	Export-Led Development
EPS	Sandinista People's Army
EPZ	Export Processing Zone
ESAF	Enhanced Structural Adjustment Facility (IMF Facility)
ESF	Economic Support Funds (AID Facility)
EU	European Union
FDI	Foreign Direct Investment
FEDEPRICAP	Federation of Private Sector Entities of Central America and Panama
FIDE	Foundation for Investment and Export Development (Honduras)
FINTRA	Transitional Investment Trust (Costa Rica)
FIS	Social Investment Fund
FMLN	Farabundo Martí National Liberation Front (El Salvador)
FSLN	Sandinista National Liberation Front (Nicaragua)
FTZ	Free Trade Zone
FUSADES	Salvadoran Foundation for Social and Economic Development
G-7	Group of Seven
GATT	General Agreement on Tariffs and Trade
GCC	Global Commodity Chain

GDL	Global Division of Labor
GEXPORT	Guatemalan Non-Traditional Exporters' Association
HDI	Human Development Index
IDB	Inter-American Development Bank
IFIs	International Financial Institutes
ILO	International Labor Organization
IMF	International Monetary Fund
INGO	International Non-Governmental Organization
ISI	Import-Substitution Industrialization
MAS	Solidarity Action Movement (Guatemala)
MLN	National Liberation Movement (Guatemala)
MONARCA	Rafaél Callejas Nationalist Movement (Honduras)
MST	Landless Rural Workers Movement
NAC	New Agricultural Countries
NAFTA	North American Free Trade Agreement
NED	National Endowment for Democracy
NEM	New Economic Model
NGO	Non-Governmental Organization
NIC	Newly Industrializing Country
NIDL	New International Division of Labor
NTAE	Non-Traditional Agricultural Exports
OAS	Organization of American States
OECD	Organization of Economic Cooperation and Development
PAN	National Advancement Party (Guatemala)
PARLACEN	Central American Parliament
PCN	National Conciliation Party (El Salvador)
PDC	Christian Democratic Party (El Salvador)
PDCH	Honduran Christian Democratic Party
PED	Private Enterprise Development (AID program)
PID	Democratic Institutional Party (Guatemala)
PL	Liberal Party (Honduras)
PLN	National Liberation Party (Costa Rica)

PN	National Party (Honduras)
PRI	Institutional Revolutionary Party (Mexico)
PRIDEX	Investment and Export Promotion (El Salvador)
PUSC	Social Christian Unity Party (Costa Rica)
SAP	Structural Adjustment Program
TNC	Transnational Corporation
TNS	Transnational State
UN	United Nations
UNCTAD	United Nations Conference on Trade and Development
UNDP	United Nations Development Program
URNG	Guatemalan National Revolutionary Unity
WB	World Bank
WTO	World Trade Organization

Introduction:
Development and Social Change

The truth is in the whole

Hegel

Towards a Globalization Perspective

The present study has several interwoven objectives. One is to explore recent Central American history and the current state of affairs, highlighting the globalization dynamics that I believe are central in an understanding of the region. The second is to explore several issues of general sociological and social scientific import, among them globalization, development, and social change. The third is to make a contribution through intellectual production to the struggles of poor majorities in Central America, and around the world, in their quest for social justice and emancipation. These three endeavors are intimately interwoven. A proper understanding of Central America's recent history rests on an analysis of globalization and is essential to the twenty-first-century political protagonism of the region's poor majority.

Central America was in the spotlight of world attention from the 1960s into the 1990s and a major site of revolutionary challenge to international order. The appearance of guerrilla movements, the breakdown of the prevailing agro-export economic model, and mounting civil strife in the 1960s, ushered in a period of dramatic change. By the 1980s the region was engulfed in a general crisis: full-scale civil wars of revolutionary insurgency and US-organized counterinsurgency; the collapse of the regional economy; and the demise of dictatorial forms of political authority. The 1979 Sandinista revolution in Nicaragua and near revolution in El Salvador thrust the Isthmus onto the center stage of what Fred Halliday called "the Second Cold War."[1] No less dramatic, the late 1980s into the 1990s saw peace and demilitarization processes under the mediation of international organizations, "transitions to democracy," and economic restabilization under a new model of free market capitalism. And as the region fell from international purview in the wake of pacification, and the social fabric deteriorated, poverty, marginalization, and a pandemic of crime, drug abuse, and interpersonal violence spread, symptomatic of structural contradictions in the social order that had not been resolved. Was this apparent post-bellicose social breakdown a vestige of the regional conflict? Or were explanations to be found in a set of new historical circumstances?

The Central American crisis generated an extraordinary amount of rich scholarship, too vast to reference here, much of it focusing on one or another aspect of change. As a Latinamericanist whose own research has led me to stray in recent years, from specific area studies to a broader inquiry into globalization and transnational phenomena, I became convinced in a review of recent literature that a globalization perspective sheds enormous light on, and provides needed correctives to interpreting, the region's recent history, including revolutionary movements and their outcomes. Likewise, it became clear that a retrospective reinterpretation of the 1960s–1990s upheaval tells us a great deal about emergent twenty-first-century global society and provides important elements for a renewal of research into the sociology of development, world political economy, and transnational studies. I undertake this reinterpretation here through a methodological approach that sees globalization as offering a macro-historical-structural perspective on social change. In this approach, structural analysis frames and informs behavioral analysis and relational accounts. The development of a macro-historical-structural perspective provides a view of the "big picture," allowing the interconnections that weave different levels and seemingly disparate elements of change into a coherent whole to be uncovered. It is useful to consider a metaphor: If we were to stand a few inches from a full-sized mural on a city building, we would see seemingly unconnected spots of paint. Taking a few paces back, we could discriminate colors and perhaps certain variations among the spots. Another several paces back and we would distinguish *pattern*. Further back yet, these patterns would begin to form a picture. By the time we reached the other side of the street, what started out as disconnected spots in a milieu that allowed us no perspective would come into full view. An *understanding* of the reality depicted by the mural would now be possible. We would not want to carry the metaphor too far: social reality is a historical process, in which change and tendency in social structure is more important than the static snapshot, even when seen in full view. Yet the social world is in certain respects understood in a way similar to the reality captured in the full view of the mural: when we focus very close up to a historical process we are often unable to discern anything but atomized detail. As we step back and acquire perspective, essential contours of *social structure*, or recurrent patterns of social interaction and of change, come into focus. But to gain a fuller view of the phenomena we wish to understand, and therefore to *conceptualize* them, we need to "move across the street" and see them in proper macro-historical-structural perspective.

This "big picture" is globalization. I believe it is not possible to understand the world today without a systematic understanding of globalization as the defining macrosocial dynamic of our epoch. Around the world, with few exceptions, the underlying structural dynamic of each country and region in recent decades has been the breakup of national economic, political, and social systems—reciprocal to the breakup of a pre-globalization nation-state based world order—and the emergence of new economic, political, and social structures as each nation and region becomes integrated into emergent transnational structures. This proposition is applied in the present study to advance the thesis that globalization has exercised underlying structural causality in Central America's recent history. The crises that befell revolutionary projects that were launched as alternatives to international capitalism should be theoretically situated within globalization as the world-historic context of national developments in the late twentieth and early twenty-first centuries. The transitions in Central America are best viewed from this structural perspective rather than through an analysis of the surface political dynamics of the end of the Cold War or more temporal considerations of strategies of revolution and counterrevolution. Economic globalization, and the transnationalization of states, classes, political processes, and civil society that it involves, signals elemental change in the referent points of each national society and in the boundaries between the national and the transnational. As the region has experienced globalization it has undergone a transition to a new transnational model of society reciprocal to changes that have taken place in the global system. The old conflicts between dictatorships and disenfranchised masses, between competing Cold War ideologies, between feudal oligarchies and capitalist modernizers, have been superseded by a new set of problems bound up with the region's integration into the emergent global economy and society. Central America thus provides a case study of transnational processes that are now underway in every corner of the globe. Study of the processes in Central America can contribute to an understanding of the dynamics of change elsewhere in emergent global society.

Origin of this Study and Methodological and Epistemological Concerns

As all good social analysis requires, I am concerned with the general in the particular and the particular in the general. On the one hand, therefore, the present study focuses on Central America and its recent history with reference to the more general subject of how globalization has transformed, and transnational processes have penetrated, one particular region. On the other hand, the ongoing period of change in Central America is also grounded in the region's particular history and in the unique behavioral response of different agents to globalization and its repercussions. Social, economic, and political structures bear the imprimatur of particular national and regional histories and these histories shape the terms under which each society enters the new global order. A structural determinacy, however, lies in the global side of the dialectic. Globalization has increasingly broken down the autonomy of national actors and structures and integrated them into broader transnational ones. Accounts that attribute structural causation to specific national variables in the age of globalization reflect the persistence of nation-state centered approaches among scholars whose objects of inquiry are actually transnational phenomena.[2] On the other hand, debates regarding whether nomothetic accounts of social processes, which refer to the logic of statements of generalization, are preferable to ideographic accounts of these processes, which refer to the logic of the explanation of the unique, are misplaced. The general is only revealed in the unique, in an infinite variety of empirical and historical circumstances and variations. Knowledge requires a synthesis of nomothetic and ideographic accounts.

Closely linked to this epistemological concern is the dialectic between structure and agency, and between the objective and the subjective dimensions of social reality. This study is concerned with social forces in struggle as determinate in historic outcomes. Social forces are shaped by historic structures and their activities are structurally continent. But in dialectical interplay social forces also shape and reshape these structures. The distinction between structural and behavioral accounts of social processes and historical phenomena is not one of "right" and "wrong" but of the level of explanation we wish to provide. The greater the level of abstraction in our analysis, the greater the historic explanation we will provide. *Deep structure* refers to the most underlying historical processes at work, such as the laws of the development of capitalism, and globalization as the current stage in the development of world capitalism. It is the foundation of the most explanatory level in social science, bound up with metatheory. Whether it is the starting point, or even figures in the analysis at hand, depends entirely on the objective of our study. *Structure* refers to the patterns and processes that become fixed on top of the foundations of deep structure, such as the social structure in Central America and the region's changing articulation to world capitalism. "Below" structure is deep structure; "above" it is *agency*. The particular historical structures that emerge are not predetermined. They are shaped by the dynamic, manifold, and ongoing interplay of agency with the underlying historical processes that constitute deep structure. How particular social structures emerge and change can only be understood, therefore, by combining structural and behavioral analysis. Behavioral analysis requires great skill on the part of the social scientist, who must capture the infinite nuances, ambiguities, cultural idiosyncracies, unpredictability, contradictory influences, chance happenings, and so on, that influence individual and collective behavior and frame historic contingency, and relate all these manifold factors to each other and to structure in explaining the dynamics of social change. There is also a third level of analysis, what I have termed elsewhere *structural-conjunctural* analysis, which focuses on the point of convergence of structure and agency, on consciousness and forms of knowledge as reflection on social structure and consequent social action as the medium between structure and agency.[3]

I am largely concerned in this study with structural analysis undertaken through a historical approach, which should not be confused with structural*ist* analysis, or *structuralism*, which denies a role for human agency in history. Human beings *are* the authors of history, in this case, of the transitions to global capitalism in Central America and of the larger process of globalization into which these transitions fit. I attempt in the present study to document change at the structural level and am most concerned with structural change as it interacts "downward" with movement in deep structure and "upward" with movement at more circumscribed behavioral and conjunctural levels. My disciplinary tool in this endeavor is political economy. Good political economy as a disciplinary instrument searches for the causal rather than the incidental nature of phenomena, and establishes the locus of analysis and explanation in system-level, macro-structural features rather than in disaggregated micro-level and individual features. The issues of agency, of behavioral analysis and relational accounts, are therefore of great importance and are interwoven into the study.

An examination of Central America is therefore a *point of entry* for a deeper discussion on these issues of globalization, development, and social change. Globalization studies are at the cutting edge of social science research and of vital importance to twenty-first-century public agendas. This book forms part of my long-term research agenda involving theoretical inquiry into transnational society.[4] With the explosion of literature on globalism, I felt it imperative to undertake a new study in which to ground my own theoretical claims on the subject in a detailed empirical and historical examination of transnational processes in one region. If it is not possible to demonstrate propositions regarding the structure and motion of a larger global totality in such concrete historical studies then there is the risk of reifying the global system. Globalization theory has been faulted on this point.[5] Indeed, the dangers in globalization theory are the problems of reification, teleology, and functionalist explanation, insofar as connections between the local and the global, or micro and macrosocial processes, are not identified and specified. It is my hope to draw out such linkages by exploring social change in detail in one relatively small region of the global system, and to identify agents and their intentionalities wherever possible. I aspire in this way to advance globalization theory in a way that avoids functionalist analysis and teleological arguments.[6] This means being attentive to the relationship between theoretical categories and empirical phenomena. I strive to present a study in which theoretical categories advanced on globalization are shown to be abstractions derived from empirical and historical phenomena discussed in the text.

Organization of the Book

Times of momentous social change such as the early twenty-first century
force us to examine the epistemological assumptions that guide our thinking. We "see" only as much as our methodologies allow. Very often the
way forward is to reformulate the questions we are asking, with the aim of
shifting the frame of inquiry in ways which allow us to see things in a new
and more explanatory light. In chapter one I suggest how we may shift
our frame of inquiry by acquiring a globalization perspective for analyzing
development and social change. This chapter summarizes and synthesizes
theoretical propositions I have advanced in recent years in several journal
articles on the transition from a world to a global economy, on transnational class formation, the rise of a transnational state, and on a reconceptualization of development.[7] I argue that globalization is a qualitatively
new stage in the history of world capitalism. It is characterized by the rise
of transnational capital and by the supersession of the nation-state as the
organizing principle of the capitalist system. This new stage conditions
development and social change in novel ways. These propositions are then
applied to the case of Central America in subsequent chapters.

Chapter one also lays out my theory on transnational processes and
transitions to global capitalism, conceived as the diverse processes of structural, institutional, and organizational changes associated with each
country and region's incorporation into emergent global economy and
society. The chapter presents a model of transnational processes and identifies Central America as a major site of such processes. It discusses the
relationship between globalization and regional development, including
the notion of new regional profiles in the global division of labor. Chapter
one thus provides the theoretical framework for the study, operationalizes
theoretical precepts, and provides an analytical framework for what
follows.

Chapters two, three, and four form the empirical and historical core of
the study. These chapters document and analyze the transformation of
Central America through global integration, including the social forces that
drove the transitions from the 1960s into the 1990s, as well as the diverse
social, economic, and political restructuring that has taken place and the
region's changing articulation to the global system in light of transnationalization. They take a fresh look at the region from the critical new vantage
point of the transnational social, economic, and political processes that have
swept Central America and have been thoroughly transforming it *since* the
end of the wars. Common themes running through these chapters are: the
demise of the old oligarchies and revolutionary movements; the rise to
hegemony of transnational fractions among local elites; the emergence of
new class groups through economic restructuring; the introduction of
dynamic new economic activities linked to the global economy; a reconfiguration of civil society; and the central role of transnational actors in all

these processes. Each theme is discussed in more general terms as it pertains to globalization and social science research, such as global civil society, transnational migration, and so on, and then treated in relation to Central America. I draw on mid-range theories from the social sciences in examining the manifold subprocesses bound up with the region's integration into the emergent structures of the global system. The chapters build on earlier research into these themes presented at professional and public forums and published in academic journals.[8]

Chapter two provides a political analysis of the transitions. It reconstructs the struggle of the distinct social forces in each of the republics in historic and comparative perspective and shows how globalization dynamics conditioned the outcomes of the revolutionary upheavals. Readers concerned with my reinterpretation of the Central American transitions in light of globalization will want to pay special attention to this chapter and to each of the individual country sections. Chapter three documents the breakdown of the pre-globalization model of accumulation, and its replacement by a new transnational model. The region's emerging profile in the global division of labor is based on maquiladora production and other non-traditional exports; tourism; and the export of Central American labor to the North American labor market. Chapter four is an open-ended exploration into diverse social and institutional changes as the region integrates into global society. These include the transnationalization of the Central American state and civil society, financial reform, the new dominance of finance capital, privatization, depeasantization, a new capital–labor relation, transnational migrations, and the experience of Central American women in the new model.

Chapter five identifies the social contradictions of the emerging transnational model in Central America, and argues that these contradictions are *internal* to the system of global capitalism. By way of conclusions, it points to the implications for such looming issues as: the prospects for popular transformation in Central America and elsewhere under the new conditions of global capitalism; the changing nature of social movements and revolutions in the new global order; and the shifting relationship between development and space/geography. This last issue is of particular concern. I explore the current "impasse" in development theory and new directions in the sociology of development. But a full exploration of such issues is beyond the scope of this study. This concluding chapter raises theoretical questions that remain matters for ongoing social science research. This leads me to observe, as a caveat, that there are natural limits to any study. Inevitably the breadth of analysis I am attempting to undertake means that it is not possible to address each topic raised in the book in all its relevant aspects and complexity. This is especially so for chapters three and four, in which the subsections are not intended to give exhaustive treatment to specific topics in the way that a scholar with expertise in a particular area might in a specialized study. My hope is that these sections, and the book more generally, will inspire and point the way forward for further research on each topic.

Finally, I should state that my interest in Central America is not purely academic. A good chunk of my young adulthood was dedicated to active participation in the effort to bring about revolutionary change in the region. All observers of the social world are also protagonists in it. Proper conceptualization of the social world is required for effective intervention in the world. Social science is an enterprise undertaken in explanation of the social world and, as such, a guide to social action. How we perceive the world, including the possibilities that inhere to our social action as well as the limits to that action, will shape in large measure our social protagonism. I don't believe there is such a thing as neutral social science. Our observations are always theory and value-laden. "Theory is always *for* someone and *for* some purpose," as Robert Cox points out. "We need to know the context in which theory is produced and used; and we need to know if the aim of the user is to maintain the existing social order or to change it."[9] The job of the critical social scientist is to provide a perspective on the social universe, grounded in underlying reality, that allows us to properly conceive the structure, character, and historic tendencies at work in a given social reality. But it is also, in this way, to adumbrate the real possibilities for change in historic social structure in favor of subordinate majorities and the future that is latent within them.

1

The Dialectics of Globalization
and Development

The latter part of the twentieth century, and the beginning of the twenty-first, formed a period of momentous change worldwide. It was also a period in which the *pace* of historic change—indeed *time* itself—seemed to accelerate. Fernand Braudel saw historic time as constituted of different tempos. Change is very slow in the first, geographic time. Continental plates move and mountain chains rise and fall. Change is quicker in the second, social time. In this, Braudel's *longue durée*, social structures change fundamentally. The third is individual time, marked by the changes that we experience through the individual events and specific conjunctures of our lifetimes. Historic tempos seemed to overlap as we entered the new century. Changes began that are part of an epochal shift, of a complete reorganization of social structures worldwide. Those generations that live in the transition period between one epoch and another experience, at the phenomeno-logical level perhaps, the sensation of an overlap in individual and social time. The structures we were familiar with and the concepts that we used to understand our world changed dramatically. At the beginning of the twenty-first century, profound change is underway in every corner of the world, and no community can avoid being swept up in the great historic transformations. The changes and the speeding up of the tempo of change itself are in my view best captured by the concept of *globalization*.

Globalization as a historic process rather than an event represents *not* a new social system but a qualitatively new stage in the evolution of the system of world capitalism. It involves agency as much as structure even though it is *not* a project conceived, planned, and implemented at the level of intentionality. As a process at the structural level it elicits the response of social forces in manifold ways that feed back into the process. The contours of globalization are thus continually shaped and reshaped through the dialectical interplay of structure and agency, just as the process of globalization is itself the outcome of the particular way in which structure and agency interacted in earlier periods. For instance, capitalists plan their activities, social classes and groups engage in struggle, state managers adopt policies, and so forth, all in reflexive response to perception of structural processes. These activities, struggles, and policies in turn shape the direction of change in social structure.

The Problematic of Globalization and Development

Globalization as Epochal Shift and Systemic Change

Globalization represents an *epochal shift*. The periodization of capitalism is an analytical tool that allows us to grasp changes in the system over time. This epochal shift involves changes of *systemic* importance, by which I mean fundamental worldwide changes in social structure that modify and even transform the way in which the system in which we live functions. We are at the threshold of a new epoch, the fourth in modern world history. The first was ushered in with the birth of capitalism out of its feudal cocoon in Europe and its initial outward expansion. This was the epoch of mercantilism and primitive accumulation; what Karl Marx referred to as the "rosy dawn of the era of capitalist production." The second, competitive, or classical, capitalism, was marked by the industrial revolution, the rise of the bourgeoisie, and the forging of the nation-state. This epoch spanned what Eric Hobsbawm in his seminal historical works calls the ages of revolution, capital, and empire.[1] The third was the rise of corporate ("monopoly") capitalism, the consolidation of a single world market and the nation-state system into which world capitalism became organized. We can say the first epoch ran from the symbolic dates of 1492 through to 1789; the second to the late nineteenth century; and the third into the early 1970s.

The turbulent decades of the late twentieth century were, in the words of political scientist John Ruggie, an "epochal threshold."[2] The 1970s were a time of great economic turbulence and most agree that it was in this decade that a profound restructuring of world capitalism began. Behind this turbulence was the transition from the nation-state phase of world capitalism and its distinct institutional, organizational, political, and regulatory structures to a new, still emerging transnational phase. A single nation-state or geographically conceived headquarters for world capitalism had become untenable as the process of transnational market, financial, and productive integration proceeded. A new epoch, that of globalization, was upon us. This emerging transnational phase of capitalism is qualitatively new. This is not merely a *quantitative* process involving the deepening of global interconnections and of our awareness of such interconnections, as social scientists have argued.[3] As in all epochal shifts, quantitative change gives way to *qualitative* change.

There is certainly no consensus among social scientists about exactly what globalization is, if it should be explained by changes in the capitalist system, or if in fact the phenomenon actually exists. My definition is as follows: the core of globalization, theoretically conceived, is the near culmination of a centuries-long process of the spread of capitalist production around the world and its displacement of all pre-capitalist relations ("modernization")—what Istvan Meszaros calls "the end of capital's historical ascendancy."[4] The very constitution of human societies has always involved interconnections. But capitalism was the first *form* of society to

spread globally and to incorporate all societies into a single social formation, giving rise to the "modern world-system."[5] Capitalism has always been
an expansionary system in a double sense. Commodification constantly
deepens (its intensive expansion), and commodification has constantly
extended outward around the world (its extensive expansion). The final
stage of capitalism's extensive enlargement began with the wave of coloni-
zations in the late nineteenth and early twentieth centuries and concluded
with the (re)incorporation of the former Soviet bloc and Third World
revolutionary states in the early 1990s.

The spread of capitalist production relations as a result of the breakup
of the old colonial system and its distinct colonial modes of labor control
and property relations, the dramatic rise in direct multinational corporate
investment, an ongoing transfer of labor-intensive phases of international
production to the South, the incursion of market relations into the Third
World countryside, and so on, accelerated in the late 1960s and on with
new technological changes. It has allowed for a much more fluid movement
of capital and its penetration into diverse regions. Intrinsic to this penetration is the capital–labor relation (i.e., tautologically, the capitalist production relation). As capitalist production relations penetrated pre-capitalist
reserves in dramatic fashion, they broke up pre-capitalist communities and
commodified economic activity. This resulted in rapid class restructuring,
including the accelerated proletarianization of peasant communities and
the creation of new rural and urban working classes. Hence, capitalism
began a dramatic new expansion in the late twentieth century. But this
expansion was intensive rather than extensive. Because globalization does
not involve the earlier geographic expansions, such as new territorial
conquests, this enlargement of capitalism is not as visible. Capitalist production relations are replacing what remains of all pre-capitalist relations
around the globe. The era of the primitive accumulation of capital is
coming to an end. The logic of exchange value, as production for the
purpose of accumulating capital through market exchange and the exploitation of wage labor, is ever-more pervasive in human affairs. But exchange
value is deepening rather than enlarging its domain. It is invading and
commodifying all those public and private spheres that previously remained
outside of its reach. New proletarian masses worldwide are brought into
direct capitalist relations in the moment of globalization.

World-system theory has long noted that economic relations are embedded in larger social structures, that nation-states are part of a larger unit
(the capitalist world-system) and that national development is conditioned
by—indeed, some world-system theory suggests it is determined by—the
larger world-system. My theoretical propositions on globalization, however,
differ from world-system theory on several crucial counts, discussed here
and in subsequent sections. World-system theory applies Max Weber's
definition of capitalism as a market or exchange relation over Marx's
definition of capitalism as a production relation. Accordingly, the "modern world-system" (circa 1500 to date) has always been "capitalist" since
production was undertaken to sell on the market for a profit. Those

following Marx's definition of capitalism argue that a broader capitalist world economy "articulated" for much of the modern period diverse modes of production under the hegemony of the capitalist mode.[6] This distinction is not mere semantics, and is relevant to the discussion of globalization. The former position implies that globalization can only be a *quantitative* intensification of a 500-year-old process, whereas the latter allows for quantitative change to give way to *qualitative* change, with important implications for macrosocial analysis. The world-system approach, by definitional *fiat*, cannot conceive of globalization in the way posited here, but must be content with emphasizing that it is a quantitative intensification of connections and systemic exchanges. But if my proposition regarding the integration of the entire superstructure of world society is a conception of the current epoch that differs from that found in world-system analysis, which posits a world-system of separate political and cultural superstructures linked by a geographic division of labor, it also differs from many Marxist analyses, which see the nation-state as immanent to capitalist development.[7]

In my view, the two distinctive features of globalization are the rise of transnational capital and the supersession of the nation-state as the axis of world development. The well-known changes in technology, particularly the communications and information revolution, but also revolutions in transportation, automation, robotization, and so on, and those facilitated in marketing and management, have made it possible for capital to achieve global mobility and out of this mobility capital has become transnational. This is the basis for economic globalization. New patterns of accumulation based on the "third wave" technology—communications, informatics, computerization, etc.—both require and make possible economies of scale that are truly global, and require a more generalized commodification of the world economy. New global economic and social space has been accompanied by new forms of configuring political space beyond the nation-state. Each epoch in modern world history has seen a successive expansion of world capitalism over the preceding epoch that has deepened webs of relations and progressively broken down local, national, and regional autonomies. Each wave has also seen the establishment of sets of institutions that made this expansion possible and organized long-term cycles of capitalist development. From the seventeenth-century treaties of Westphalia, which enshrined the nation-state system, into the 1960s, capitalism unfolded through a system of nation-states that generated concomitant national structures, institutions, and agents. Globalization has increasingly eroded these national boundaries, and made it structurally impossible for individual nations to sustain independent, or even autonomous, economies, polities, and social structures. A key feature of the current epoch is the supersession of the nation-state as the organizing principle of capitalism, and with it, of the inter-state system as the framework of capitalist development. The intensive and extensive expansion of capitalism tends to make uniform the conditions of social life in the zones of capitalism. Globalization, in the process of creating a single, and increasingly undifferentiated, field for world capitalism, integrates the various polities, cultures, and institutions of national societies into an emergent transnational or global society. This theme runs throughout the present study.

In sum, economic globalization brings with it the material basis for the emergence of a single global society, marked by the transnationalization of civil society and political processes, the global integration of social life, and a global culture. We thus have economic, political, cultural, and other dimensions of globalization. How do we order these dimensions? Is there a determinacy? The conception of globalization I advance here posits a material over an ideational determinacy and assigns structural determinacy to the global economy. I now turn to an analysis of the global economy as the material basis of the whole process.

From a World Economy to a Global Economy

With its newfound global mobility, capital has been reorganizing production worldwide in accordance with the whole gamut of political and "factor cost" considerations. In this process, national productive apparatuses become fragmented and integrated externally into new globalized circuits of accumulation. We can distinguish between a *world economy* and a *global economy*. In the earlier epochs each country developed national circuits of accumulation that were linked to each other through commodity exchange and capital flows in an integrated international market. In the world economy, different modes of production were "articulated" within a broader social formation, or a world-system.[8] In the emerging global economy, the globalization of the production process breaks down and functionally integrates these national circuits into *global* circuits of accumulation. The distinction between a world economy and a global economy is the *globalization of the production process itself*, or the rise of globalized circuits of production and accumulation, as expressed in figures 1.1 and 1.2.[9] This process takes place together with the centralization of command and control of the global economy in transnational capital. Globalization, therefore, is unifying the world into a single mode of production and a single global system and bringing about the organic integration of different countries and regions into a global economy.

This distinction between a world economy and a global economy is crucial. Economic globalization has been well researched. Although no one doubts that it is taking place, as discussed previously, debate has raged over the extent to which the phenomenon represents something qualitatively new or if it simply represents a quantitative extension of historical patterns. One influential school in recent studies of the world economy has argued that economic globalization is overstated, or even illusory, and claims that the current period is merely a quantitative intensification of historical tendencies, not a qualitatively new epoch.[10] But this argument does not distinguish between the extension of trade and financial flows across national borders, which in my conception represents *internationalization*,

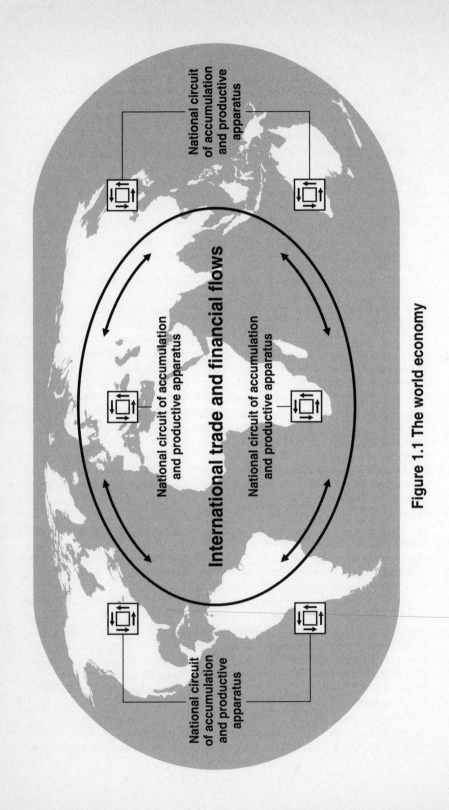

National circuit of accumulation and productive apparatus

National circuit of accumulation and productive apparatus

International trade and financial flows

National circuit of accumulation and productive apparatus

National circuit of accumulation and productive apparatus

National circuit of accumulation and productive apparatus

National circuit of accumulation and productive apparatus

Figure 1.1 The world economy

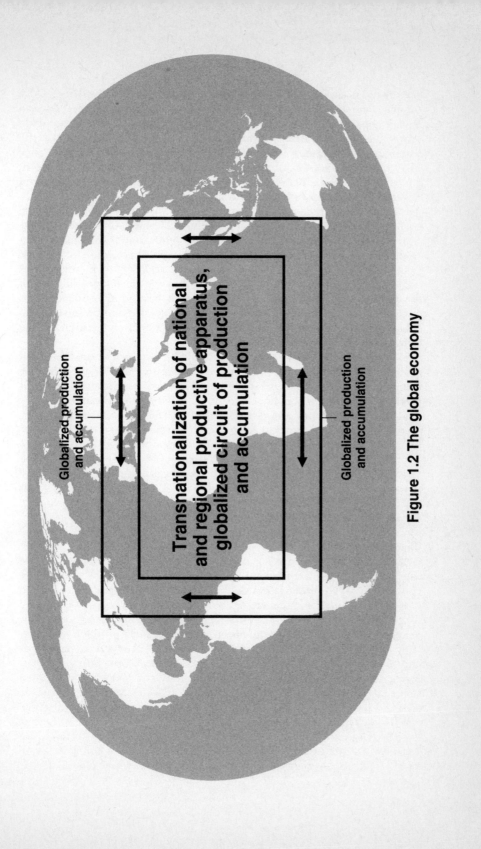

Figure 1.2 The global economy

and the globalization of the production process itself, which represents *transnationalization*.[11] These accounts point to the high degree of world trade integration in the period prior to World War I (indeed, the world economy was at that time at least as integrated economically as it is at the beginning of the twenty-first century). But they fail to note what is qualitatively new. The pre-1913 integration was through "arms-length" *trade* in goods and services between nationally based production systems and through cross-border financial flows in the form of portfolio capital. In that period national capitalist classes organized national production and service chains and produced commodities within their own borders which they then traded for commodities produced in other countries. This is what Peter Dicken, in his authoritative study on the global economy, *Global Shift*, calls "shallow integration."[12] It is in contrast to the "deep integration" taking place under globalization. This involves the transnationalization of the *production* of goods and services. The globalization of production has entailed the fragmentation and decentralization of complex production chains and the worldwide dispersal and functional integration of the different segments in these chains.

Here we can use Marx's scheme for capitalist production, or the circuit of capital, to illustrate the point. This circuit is represented by the following formula, M-C-P-C'-M', in which M is money, C is commodities, P is production, C' is new commodities, and M' is the greater amount of money than was present when the circuit began, representing accumulation. In the earlier period of "shallow integration," the first part of this circuit, M-C-P-C', took place in national economies. Commodities were sold on the international market, and profits returned home, where the cycle was repeated. Under globalization, P is increasingly globally decentralized, and so too is the entire first part of the circuit, M-C-P. Globally produced goods and services are marketed worldwide. Profits are dispersed worldwide through the global financial system that has emerged since the 1980s, which is qualitatively different from the international financial system of the earlier period.

Global capitalism is not a collection of "national" economies but the supersession through transnational integration of "national" economies, understood as autonomous entities related through external exchanges to other such entities. Fundamentally, there has been a progressive dismantling of autonomous or "autocentric" national production systems and their reactivation as constituent elements of an integral world production system. Until recently, according to Dicken, "in terms of production, plan, firm and industry were essentially national phenomena." But during the past few decades, "trade flows have become far more complex . . . transformed into a highly complex, kaleidoscopic structure involving the *fragmentation* of many production processes and their *geographic relocation* on a global scale in ways which slice through national boundaries."[13]

This reorganization of world production has taken place through the phenomenal spread since the late 1970s of diverse new economic arrangements, such as outsourcing, subcontracting, transnational intercorporate alliances, licensing agreements, local representation, and so on, alongside the proliferation of foreign direct investment, mergers and acquisitions, and other forms of transnational capitalist integration. These arrangements result in vast transnational production chains and complex webs of vertical and horizontal integration across the globe. The transnational corporations (TNCs) that drive the global economy are, according to Dicken, "also locked into *external* networks of relationships with a myriad of other firms: transnational and domestic, large and small, public and private." It is through such interconnections that small local firms and economic agents in one country may be directly linked to a global production network, even when such firms or agents serve only a very restricted geographic area. Such interrelationships between economic agents and firms of different sizes and types "increasingly span national boundaries to create a set of *geographically nested relationships from local to global scales* . . . There is, in fact, a bewildering variety of interorganizational *collaborative* relationships. These are frequently multilateral rather than bilateral, polygamous rather than monogamous."[14]

What Dicken's study underscores is the increasing interpenetration on multiple levels of capital in all parts of the world, organized around transnational capital and the giant TNCs. It is increasingly difficult to separate local circuits of production and distribution from the globalized circuits that dictate the terms and patterns of accumulation worldwide, even when surface appearance gives the (misleading) impression that local capitals retain their autonomy. There are, of course, still local and national capitals, and there will be for a long time to come. But they must "de-localize" and link to hegemonic transnational capital if they are to survive. Territorially restricted capital cannot compete with its transnationally mobile counterpart. As the global circuit of capital subsumes through numerous mechanisms and arrangements these local circuits, local capitalists who manage these circuits become swept up into the process of transnational class formation.

Global production and service chains, or what sociologists have alternatively referred to as global commodity chains,[15] then, is a key concept in the study of globalization and we will see in subsequent chapters its centrality to understanding the transformation of the Central American political economy. These chains link sequences of economic activities in which each stage adds some value or plays some role in the production and distribution of goods and services worldwide. Transnational capital, as organized into the giant TNCs, coordinates these vast chains, incorporating numerous agents and social groups into complex global networks.

With the rise of transnational production chains and circuits of accumulation, transnationally oriented capitalists in each country moved their sites from national markets to global markets. The structural properties of these chains or networks are *global* in character, in that accumulation is embedded in *global* markets, involves *global* enterprise organization and sets of *global* capital–labor relations, especially deregulated and casualized labor pools worldwide, as I discuss shortly.[16] Competition dictates that firms must establish global as opposed to national or regional markets. Transnationally oriented capitalists promote a switch from "inward-oriented development," or accumulation around national markets such as the Import-Substitution Industrialization (ISI) models that predominated in many Third World regions in the middle part of the twentieth century, to "outward-oriented development" involving export-promotion strategies and a deeper integration of national economies into the global economy. This switch involves the emergence of new economic activities and structures of production in each country and region integrating into the global economy. These new activities generally imply local participation in globalized circuits of accumulation, or in global production and service chains, such as, for instance, maquiladora assembly operations, transnational banking services, tourism and leisure, and so forth. This will be discussed in more detail later with the particular example of Central America.

The diverse new economic arrangements in the global economy have been associated with the transition from the Fordist regime of accumulation prevailing for much of the twentieth century, associated with a large number of easily organizable workers in centralized production locations and fixed, standardized production processes, to new post-Fordist *flexible* regimes.[17] The global economy is made possible at a strictly technical level by flexible accumulation models, which involve two distinct dimensions: new technologies, and organizational innovations. Many new "globalizing" or "third wave" technologies are based on the revolution in information technology, or the convergence of computerization and telecommunications and the emergence of the internet, and include new transportation technologies such as containerization, intermodal transport, and refrigeration, robotization and other forms of automation, CAD/CAM (computer-aided design, computer-aided manufacturing), and so on. Novel organizational forms include, among others, new management techniques, vertical dis-integration, "just-in-time" and small-batch production, subcontracting and outsourcing, and formal and informal transnational business alliances. These changes make possible new subdivisions and specializations in production. Different phases of production become broken down into component phases which are detachable and can be dispersed around the world.

Despite the importance of technology and organizational innovation, globalization is not driven by a technological determinism, as technology is not causal to social change but a dependent variable. What has caused the dynamic of economic globalization is the drive, built into capitalism itself by competition and class struggle, to maximize profits by reducing labor and other factor costs. The study of globalization is fundamentally *historical*, in that events or social conditions can be conceived in terms of the previous social processes and conditions that gave rise to them. The world capitalist crisis that began in the 1970s followed a lengthy period of worldwide class struggle, from the 1890s to the 1970s. This crisis ushered in a new period of restructuring and led to the search for new modes of accumulation and to globalization as an accumulation strategy. Globalization refers not to a static condition or to a complete project, but to a process characterized by relatively novel articulations of social power which were not available in earlier historic periods. The total mobility achieved by capital has allowed it to search out around the world the most favorable conditions for different phases of globalized production, including the cheapest labor, the most favorable institutional environments (for example, low taxes) and regulatory conditions (for example, lax environmental and labor laws), stable social environments, and so on.

I wish to emphasize here that at the core of flexible accumulation is a new capital–labor relation. The restructuring of the labor process associated with post-Fordist flexible accumulation—what some have called the global casualization or informalization of labor—involves alternative systems of labor control and diverse contingent categories of labor. Globalization has brought about a worldwide change in power relations between capital and labor, a new global division of labor, the rise of the newly poor and newly rich, and worldwide social polarization. The newfound relative power of global capital over global labor is becoming fixed in a new global capital–labor relation. We will see later the centrality of flexible production, transnational capital, and the new capital–labor relation to the globalization of Central America. It is worth reiterating that the segmentation and decentralization of production processes across the globe takes place simultaneous to the concentration of ownership and control of global resources and the means of production, and global centralization of management of global production, in the hands of transnational corporate capital. *Transnational capital* has become the hegemonic fraction of capital on a world scale.

The implications of economic globalization are vast and can only be alluded to here in brief. Economic changes always involve social, political, cultural, and ideological change as well. New technologies and organizational innovations have resulted in a new wave of what David Harvey calls "time-space compression," or the shrinkage of space and the reduction of time in social relations. The increasing dissolution of the factor of space in production and the separation of the logic of production from that of geography is without historical precedent. The entire process tends to generate pressures not just for the standardization of production and labor conditions around the world but also for the standardization of social, political, and cultural practices. The new flexible accumulation and total mobility of capital breaks down spatial and time barriers around the globe, integrating the world into the so-called "global village."

To recapitulate and summarize, the emergence of globally mobile transnational capital from the 1970s on has allowed for the decentralization and functional integration around the world of vast chains of production and distribution, the instantaneous movement of values (or flows of wealth), and the unprecedented concentration and centralization of worldwide economic management, control, and decision-making power in transnational capital and its agents. In the emerging global capitalist configuration, transnational or global space is coming to supplant national space. Nations are no longer linked externally to a broader system but internally to a singular global social formation. There is no longer anything external to the system, not in the sense that it is now a "closed" system but in that there are no longer any countries or regions that remain outside of world capitalism or still to be incorporated through original accumulation and in that there is no longer autonomous accumulation outside the sphere of global capital. The internal social nexus is a global one. Here we may note the sociological principle that organic social relations are always institutionalized, which makes them "fixed" and makes their reproduction possible. As the organic and internal linkage between peoples becomes truly global, the whole set of nation-state institutions is becoming superseded by transnational institutions. In sum, the whole worldwide social structure is changing profoundly and fundamentally. A truly *transnational social structure* is emerging and should be a principal focus for a renewed research agenda in transnational studies.

Beyond Nation-State Paradigms: Towards a New Transnational Studies

Studying development and social change in the new epoch requires that one adopt a transnational or global perspective. And this means moving beyond a focus on the social world emphasizing country-level analysis or an international system comprised of discrete nation-states as interacting units of comparative analysis. Globalization has posed serious difficulties for theories of all sorts, trapped as they are within the straightjacket of what I have termed in an earlier study a nation-state framework of analysis.[18] Macrosocial inquiry has run up against certain cognitive and explanatory limitations in the face of globalization since nation-state conceptualizations are incapable of explaining phenomena that are transnational in character. I suggest that globalization has placed existing paradigms of macrosocial inquiry, including development studies and international relations, at an impasse and that the way out of this impasse is to break with nation-state centered analysis.

Paradigms consist of particular ontological assumptions and particular epistemological principles and embody as well a set of theoretical principles. Most importantly, they provide a definition of the appropriate domain of inquiry to which these principles are to be applied. Despite their divergent theoretical principles, the distinct nation-state paradigms share as the domain of their inquiry the nation-state and the inter-state system. As a consequence, these paradigms are unable to account for the mounting anomalies brought about by globalization. Nation-state paradigms describe how motion occurs given a set of historical structures. But their limitations become clear when one attempts to ontologically comprehend fundamental transformation in the historical structures upon which the analysis of motion is predicated. The nation-state is not trans-historic. Good social analysis requires that we study not only the laws of motion of a *given* set of structures, but also the transformation of those structures—in both the synchronic and the diachronic dimensions. The nation-state system is the historically specific correspondence between production, social classes, and territoriality. The material basis for the nation-state is presently being superseded by globalization. Thus, a truly transnational studies requires a return to a theoretical conceptualization of the state, not as a "thing" but as a specific social relation within larger social structures that may take different, historically determined, institutional forms. Viewing the inter-state system as an immutable structure in which social change and development occur has resulted in a *nation-state reification*.

The essence of this reification is the twin conflation of the nation-state with the state and with society. The problem is manifest in the way the terms "state" and "nation" are used almost interchangeably in nation-state paradigms. The imputation of a trans-historic character to the nation-state is erroneous in that it assigns a universal character to a relatively fixed set of historic structures whose foundations were laid in the sixteenth century. Yet the presupposition of an immutable nation-state structure and inter-state system still constitutes the basis of research in international relations and remains one of the central theoretical tenets of sociology's world-system analysis and of development sociology in general.

The second conflation contained in the nation-state reification is the conflation of the nation-state with society. Following Giddens' assumption that society and the nation-state tend to be coterminous,[19] many approaches to globalization and transnationalism pose a research agenda that implicitly and often explicitly rests on interactions among nation-states as societies and propose that the task of transnational studies is to examine such exchanges between national societies. The problem with this construct is the proposition that social relations across the formal juridical boundaries of nation-states are somehow "extra-societal." "Society" as social structure cannot be limited to the specific historic form of the nation-state. The nation-state is a historically bound phenomenon, emerging in the last 500 years or so, in conjunction with the European transition from feudalism to capitalism, the consolidation of national markets and productive structures, and concomitant states and polities. The emergence of territorially based *national* economies regulated by the (nation) state led to peoples' derivation of subjective identities from their sense of geographic space, with a certain congruence also between subjective identity and the material coordinates of life in the pre-globalization period. The phenomenology of the nation-state period of world history led in turn to the "nation" as a Sorelian myth, or what Benedict Anderson has pointedly characterized as an "imagined community."[20] But nation-states cannot be understood as isolated social systems under the assumption of a transhistoric symmetry between nation-states and social structure that rules out by ontological assumption the study of social structure which is truly *supra* or *trans*-national in character. Transnational studies must move beyond the notion that nation-states are the organizing principle of modern society since globalization involves the emergence of truly supranational social structure. The "inter-societal systems" approach proposed by Giddens[21] does not resolve the national–global antinomy. This approach views the nation-state as the basic unit of analysis, assumes that a nation-state "society" is a totality, and posits relations between nation-states as an object of study external to the study of nation-state societies. For Giddens globalization is the "universalization of the nation-state" through a deepening of the modernization process.[22]

The global economy is eroding the actual material basis for the nation-state. Territoriality and production are no longer bound together. Yet many social scientists are still trapped in outdated notions of international relations as a phenomenon whose principal dynamic is interaction between nation-states. The terms developed are highly revealing and underscore a problem of commensurability: *inter*-national, or *inter*-state, meaning between nations or national states; comparative *national* development; and so on. This nation-state reification plagues paradigms in development studies, and comparative sociology more generally, in international relations and in other fields of macrosocial inquiry, as I have argued at length elsewhere. What is problematized is how globalization *modifies* the dynamics of the nation-state system (in international relations), or the international state system (in world-system theory), *rather than how globalization transforms and transcends the nation-state system itself.* As the global economy removes the territorial and national basis to capital, globalization tends to redefine the historic relationship Marxists have posited between class power and state power. Conflict between capitals in a global setting continues in such forms as fierce oligopolistic competition over world markets, but this competition corresponds ever-less to nation-state competition and rivalries, given such factors as the interpenetration of formerly "national" capitals and the transnationalization of capital and of classes. It cannot be assumed that the contradictions of capitalism necessarily manifest themselves under globalization as contradictions between nation-states representing the interests of competing national capitals.[23]

With the onset of globalization, there has been increasing recognition of the obsolescence of the nation-state as a practical unit of the global political economy, and concomitant recognition of the need for new perspectives and for paradigmatic reorientation. These concerns led in the 1980s and 1990s to attempts to develop new approaches, including calls in development studies and in international relations for a new global focus.[24] But research continued to posit the nation-state as the basis for analysis. The literature in development and international studies exploring globalization dynamics suggested that, with few exceptions, the focus was still on the nation-state and the inter-state system. The sociology of development focused on globalization processes as a new context for comparative *national* development and international studies research took a similar tack, both posing in essence the following question: How is globalization modifying the context in which relations between nations—or *inter*national relations—unfold? In both areas, globalization was seen as some new stage in *inter* or *cross*-national relations as the interaction among nation-states. The challenge was seen as one of how to modify existing frameworks or paradigms. But the same underlying ontological and epistemological assumptions bound up with the concepts of nation-states and the inter-state system were accorded continuity.

Mindsets—in this case, nation-state centered mindsets—are exceedingly difficult to break, even when confronted with problems of logical inconsistency and empirical validity. The various efforts to grapple with globalization "are prepared to admit the emergence of a world economic system but are unwilling to admit the possibility of the ultimate disintegration of nation-states and national cultures," observes Malcolm Waters. "Indeed, they often resort to a theoretical dualism in which contradictory causal effects are allowed to reside in separate parts of the theory." Given the tenacity of this theoretical dualism, one might justify Waters' extraordinarily harsh criticism of these logical inconsistencies as intellectually "schizoid."[25]

What is required is an "epistemological break." "Prevailing modes of analysis simply lack the requisite vocabulary" to address transnational realities, notes Ruggie, "and what we cannot describe, we cannot explain."[26] This problem of language—continued reliance on nation-state terms, and along with them, the concepts they denote and the particular nation-state centered framing and interpretation of empirical data they imply—is indicative of an underlying problem of incommensurability. In the view of Kuhn and of Althusser, the relations among rival or successive paradigms are always liable to be that of disjuncture and incommensurability, in which the central concepts and procedures of one paradigm or problematic are unstable in the language of the other.[27] The different "nation-state" paradigms have a language that is unsuitable for grasping transnational or global dynamics and require a certain epistemological break. So long as social structure was commensurate with the *historically specific* form it took through the system of nation-states, then we had a type of incommensurability advanced by Feyerabend.[28] The different theoretical perspectives, or paradigms, could enter into dialogue with the aim of appreciating each other's views even though they were not strictly comparable, since they involved sharply contrasting and often diametrically opposed interpretations of data (and also normative structure). For instance, what was called the "new comparative international political economy" of the 1980s and 1990s suggested just such a dialogue take place within development studies, while a new "international political economy" called for the same thing in international studies, proposing as the goal a theoretical synthesis around these efforts. However, the fundamental epistemological assumption that undergirded these and related endeavors was precisely the nation-state framework of social analysis, around which the three paradigm sets I have identified here—modernization/liberalism; dependency and world-system/realism; and Marxism—all converged. Globalization requires therefore an epistemological break—that is, a break with the underlying assumption driving currently competing theories.

What is at issue is the relation between our knowledge of the world and social structure. Social structure is becoming transnationalized; an epistemological shift is required in concurrence with this ontological change. Transnational studies requires that social science methods and the episte- mological assumptions that underpin them revert back to those of classical political economy and sociology, which set out to theorize a set of relation- ships that were not self-evident in contemporary practices in order to highlight both structures and the historic movement latent in existing conditions. In the case of transnational studies, this means distinguishing in social analysis between appearance (national phenomena derived from nation-state analysis) and essence (transnational phenomena). Facts and theory are interpenetrating, and therefore nation-state theories will guide, and circumscribe, our interpretation of data. Utilizing the nation-state framework for social analysis can be highly misleading and illusory, leading us to believe that we are observing phenomena that is nation-state in character when in fact it is transnational. An essential task of a new transnational studies is to decipher the transnational essence in social phenomena which appear as national.[29] Our view of reality is mediated by our finite cognitive abilities, which are structured by evolving theories and concepts and their units of analysis. A shift in the unit of analysis from the nation-state to the global system facilitates a switch to a more powerful set of "cognitive lenses" and yields, in my view, quite dramatic results. Several examples will suffice.

National in Appearance; Transnational in Essence

The old units of economic analysis, such as national trade deficits and current accounts balances, acquire an entirely different meaning once we observe that the vast majority of world trade is currently conducted as "intra- firm trade," that is, as trade among different branches of a few hundred oligopolistic transnational corporations that are themselves constituted on the basis of the interpenetration of numerous former national capitals. With intra-firm trade, what *appears* as trade between "nations" is actually move- ments between different branches and units of global corporations that have no single national headquarters. Gilpin has estimated that such intra- firm trade accounted for some 60 percent of what are called "US imports,"[30] and the World Bank that intra-firm trade within the largest 350 transnational corporations contributed about 40 percent of global trade.[31] Seen through the lenses of the nation-state system, the "US trade deficit" is characterized as a situation in which the United States imports more goods from other countries than it exports to other countries. But this is a meaningless construct. In reality the trade deficit has nothing to do with nation-state exchanges, but is a consequence of the operation of fully mobile transna- tional capital, moving between the ever-more porous borders of nation- states across the globe, and through the institutional form of a competitive oligopolist cluster of global corporations. To be sure, trade and current account deficits are not irrelevant (and indeed, I will discuss them with respect to Central America in subsequent chapters). They are still important indicators, but must be seen in a different light. They are not indicators of national economies competing with each other over trade and markets, nor are they proxy indicators for political competition, state rivalries, class conflicts, and so on, conceived along nation-state lines. Instead, they are factors which upset macroeconomic indicators in individual national territories and therefore impede the cross-border operations of transnational capital, with consequent implications for socioeconomic and political conditions in distinct geographic areas. A correct understanding of intra-firm trade and fully mobile transnational capital demonstrates how inappropriate and misleading the old nation-state framework of analysis can be.

A second example is relations between the United States and Japan, which according to nation-state centered analysis have been characterized by the dynamics of rival world economic powers. Here, we have a situation of *uneven globalization*, or the uneven pace of transnationalization among different countries and regions, which produces dynamics that are easily misunderstood. In the 1980s and 1990s Japan was accused of dumping its automobiles on the US market, to which it has full access, and of undercutting US auto industry interests, and, at the same time, of blocking US access to the Japanese market. Analysts saw this as national rivalry characterized by mounting tensions over trade competition and the protection of distinct "national" capitals and "national" markets. But in fact quite another dynamic—a globalization dynamic—was at work: the globalization of the auto industry.

By the 1990s there were joint ventures between Chrysler Motors and Mitsubishi and between General Motors (GM) and Suzuki, among others. Ford Motors had purchased a controlling interest in Mazda and major stocks in Nissan, GM held 35 percent of Isuzu and Toyota stocks, and 50 percent of Daewoo stocks (from South Korea), in turn owned in majority by several Japanese firms. In tandem, these same firms in Japan transnationalized their auto production, ending the paternal corporate alliance with Japanese workers, a pre-globalization arrangement, in which manufacturing jobs were kept within Japan.

Since the automobile complex was at the core of accumulation activities of world capitalism in the twentieth century, these changes are highly instructive. By the 1990s it was impossible to speak of "US" and "Japanese" auto companies—much less, to attribute the evolution of US–Japanese relations to automobile industry rivalry. More accurately, there were global automobile corporations with diverse branches and operations spanning many countries. The auto industry by the 1990s had become, in the words of one researcher, a "transnational spider's web ... stretch[ing] across the globe,"[32] in which "US," "European," and "Japanese" auto firms had become so interpenetrated that national distinctions had lost meaning. In order to explain US–Japanese relations it is necessary to cut through surface appearance and get to the transnational essence of the phenomenon. In the late 1980s, at the height of "Japanese bashing" among US politicians and trade unions over the auto issue, the ratio of US exports of cars to Europe relative to imports was 1:9, whereas for Japan it was about 1:6.[33] In other words, the United States maintained a more unfavorable trade relation in cars with Europe than with Japan. Applying a nation-state centric framework of analysis, there should have been even greater US–European than US–Japanese trade tensions. But outdated nation-state centric analysis obscured the transnational essence of the phenomenon. The transatlantic interpenetration of capital that took place from the 1960s onward included the interpenetration of US and European auto firms and also saw the establishment on both sides of the Atlantic of operations by these transnationalized firms. A similar process between US and Japanese based firms, however, did not mature until the 1980s and early 1990s, and once it did, trade tensions lessened in the auto industry even though Japanese autos continued to be a major component in the ongoing trade deficit between the United States and Japan.

So how then, moving beyond nation-state centric analysis, do we assess the widespread public perception in the 1990s of US–Japanese "trade wars" and rivalry? For one, the phenomenology of the nation-state and nationalism as an ideology ironically serve functions for transnational elites. A 1993 United Nations Conference Trade and Development (UNCTAD) study reported that transnational auto companies adopted a strategy of attempting to accentuate the insider–outsider distinction in the US among the government and the public as a public relations strategy aimed at maximizing market shares by influencing a host country's public's sense of "who is us."[34] In other words, a transnational auto company in the United States will engage in "Japan-bashing" and generate public perceptions of unfair Japanese practices as tactics of manipulation in its marketing strategy. Framing a phenomenon whose essence is transnational as a nation-state phenomenon can make good sense for the profit-seeking strategies of transnational corporations. But more importantly, the talk of "trade wars" and so forth accompany, as ideological discourse, the liberalization pressures exercised in the global economy by transnational forces. This is really the transnational core of the phenomenon. In the mid-1990s, US and Europe state managers publicly pressured Japan to open up to transnational investment its communications system, its financial markets and institutions, and even its shipping and commercial air transport systems. In October 1997, Japanese port and shipping interests, under a public threat from US authorities, threw open Japanese ports to international shipping. These and related events were once again pointed to as proof of fierce rivalry between three antagonistic blocs (see below). However, it more precisely showed how states, controlled by transnational fractions, modify economic and social structures around the world to deepen the globalization process. This became clear in Asia, more broadly, in the wake of the crisis of the late 1990s, which was used by transnational elites to modify that region's social and economic structures in a manner conducive to furthering globalization. The outcome of the Asian crisis was not a protectionist retrenchment or the enhancement of the powers of national or regional-based elites but rather deeper externalization of the region and more thorough integration into globalized circuits of accumulation, and along with this, the strengthening of transnationalized fractions among the

Asian elite. In fact, each shock in the unfolding world economic crisis, from Mexico to Asia, from Russia to Brazil, tended to result in the accelerated transnational integration in affected countries of local capitalists into the ranks of a transnational capitalist class.

In a final example, on the basis of the logic of a competitive nation-state system, much international relations, world-system, and Marxist literature has searched for signs of a "new hegemon" as a continuation of the historic succession of "hegemons," from the United Provinces to the United Kingdom and the United States. Among the predictions are the emergence of a Japanese or Chinese-centered Asian hegemony, a Pacific Basin hegemonic bloc incorporating the United States and Japan (the "Nichibie economy"); a split in the centers of world capitalism into three rival blocs and their respective peripheral and semi-peripheral spheres (North America and its Western Hemispheric sphere, Western Europe and its Eastern European and African spheres, and Japan and its Asian sphere), and so on.[35] These different neo-mercantilist scenarios of a new "hegemon" or "hegemonic bloc" among regional rivals are all predicated on important phenomena in the global economy. The problem lies in how to interpret the empirical data, and the pitfall of looking for a new hegemon based on the outdated notion of a competitive nation-state system as the backdrop to international relations.

The "three competing blocs" prognosis correctly notes that each bloc has developed its own trade, investment, and currency patterns and made reference in this regard to widely circulated *World Investment* reports in the first half of the 1990s by the United Nations Centre on Transnational Corporations.[36] These reports concluded that investment patterns by Transnational Corporations were driving the evolution of the world economy, and that three "clusters" based in the United States, Japan, and the European community each had a "pole" around which were a handful of "developing" countries. But what the "three competing blocs" prognosis failed to note was that each "cluster" was thoroughly interpenetrated by the other two. The United Nations reports, in fact, stressed that the three regional structures formed an integrated global "triad." This was based on the high level of interpenetration of capital among the world's top TNCs, such that countries in the South tended to become integrated vertically into one of three regional poles, while the triad members themselves exhibited horizontal integration. In effect, regional accumulation patterns do not signify conflicts between regions or core country "blocs" but, rather, certain spatial distinctions complementary to increasingly integrated transnational capital which is managed by a thoroughly transnationalized and now-hegemonic elite, an agency that does not exhibit a particular national identity. In my view, the cycle of nation-state hegemons has come to an end. We are not going to witness, for instance, the rise of a hegemonic "East Asian regime." Instead, in the twenty-first century we will witness a transnational configuration establish its hegemony. It is important to stress that globalization does *not* imply an absence of global conflict, but rather a shift from inter-state to more explicit social and class conflict.

Towards a New Conceptualization of Development

Development sociology was purported to have reached an "impasse" in the 1980s, from which it has yet to find the way forward, but the social processes that we refer to as "development" have certainly not ground to a halt.[37] The increasing subordination of the logic of geography to that of production, the heightened separation of class power from nation-state power, the rising disjuncture between the fortunes of social groups and of nation-states, and other processes bound up with globalization, demand that we reconceive development. The propositions that follow raise questions that are open-ended. My objective here is to suggest possible solutions, and then, throughout the book, to explore what light study of the changing fortunes of one particular region under global capitalism, Central America, throws on the issues.

Reconceiving development as a transnational or global phenomenon does not as a matter of course mean that space or geography has become irrelevant. It is in the nature of global capitalism to create uneven spaces, if only because of the mapping of functions onto space within the system. It is not space that becomes irrelevant under globalization. Instead, the social configuration of space can no longer be conceived—if indeed, it ever could be—in the nation-state terms that development theories posit but rather in processes of uneven development denoted primarily by social group rather than territorial differentiation. Development becomes less a national or territorial process than a dynamic of the dialectics of conflict and cooperation among social classes and groups within transnationalized social structures. Geography still remains important, but how is open to question. The well-known empirical evidence of the growing gap between countries and between North and South can be misleading to the extent that it obscures the parallel widening of the gap between the rich and the poor within countries and the processes of uneven accumulation that unfold in accordance with a social and not a national logic. The problem of measurement is also relevant here, since basic measurements and indicators are all based on nation-state data and by *fiat* structure interpretation into a nation-state framework that may be highly misleading and illusory, leading us to believe we are observing phenomena that are nation-state in character when in fact they are transnational.[38]

There are two factors to highlight insofar as we are concerned with reconceptualizing development. First, in the age of globalization, wealth can just as easily be moved as it can be generated. By simply pressing "enter" on a computer keyboard, billions of dollars can be relocated within seconds. Therefore, exactly *where* wealth is produced becomes less important in the issue of development. Second, even when we focus on material production rather than on money and finances, there is an increasing *impermanence* of fixed production activity, as a result of diverse changes in recent decades bound up with flexible accumulation, ranging from the decrease in turnover time and production runs, to the enhanced mobility of production sites. I want, therefore, to draw attention to the impermanence of production conditions, the increasing dissolution of space barriers, and the separation and subordination of the logic of geography to that of production. As the world has become a single field within which capitalism operates, the relative advantage that transnational capital finds in particular spatial locations is by nature contingent on impermanent conditions. This compels us to reconsider the geography and politics of the nation-state, and with it, the concept of development.

Much recent research into globalization and development has posed the underlying issue as: How does national development become affected by globalization? Rather, it should be: How might development be reconceived as a transnational rather than a national phenomenon? Nation-state paradigms posit development as a national phenomenon, but the decentralized and globally fragmented nature of complex production processes under globalization means that the actual productive activity that takes place in a specific nation is not a "national" activity, and should not be seen as such. It may appear that one can assess outcomes by an analysis of national development strategies as if they were determinative, or through established models of comparative national development. But such outcomes are increasingly a consequence of fully mobile transnational capital, locating and relocating accumulation processes in different global zones of a single, open global economy, in accordance with the most congenial conditions in each local zone and diverse practical and conjunctural considerations. The dramatic mobility of the factors of production in the current period and the hegemony of globalized money capital, which has become the regulator of the international circuit of accumulation, strongly suggests that such local conditions and considerations that determine where transnational capital will locate and what it will do where it alights are ephemeral, and have as much—if not more—to do with short-term and entirely unpredictable social and political factors as with long-term developmental processes. This was evidenced in the ease and rapidity with which $25–30 billion in money capital fled Mexico and the subsequent near-collapse of the Mexican economy following the 1994 New Year Zapatista uprising and other local political shocks, throwing a model of "success" in the global economy into a model of dismal failure overnight. And when transnational finance capital pulled out en masse from Mexico following the peso crisis, it did not "go home" to the United States or any other one country, but dispersed throughout North American, European, and Asian markets in search of new opportunities. Comprehending phenomena such as this requires moving beyond nation-state frameworks of analysis.

The abundant research into the global restructuring of labor and of production suggests that the type of "polarized accumulation" that observers have long noted in the case of South Africa and Brazil[39] is becoming a worldwide phenomenon under globalization. In this model, an affluent "developed" population, including a privileged sector among segmented labor markets linked to Fordist-oriented production and consumption and new patterns of flexible accumulation, exists alongside a superexploited secondary segment and a mass of supernumeraries constituting an "underdeveloped" population *within the same national borders*. This implies developed and underdeveloped *populations* with no nationally defined geographic identity. It seems increasingly appropriate to reconceive development not as *national* development, but in terms of developed, underdeveloped, and intermediate population groups occupying contradictory or unstable locations in a transnational environment, and how accumulation processes which are no longer coextensive with specific national territories determine levels of social development among this global population increasingly stratified along transnational class and social lines.

Frobel and his colleagues argued in their influential 1980 study that an emergent New International Division of Labor (NIDL) involved the concentration of capital, technological innovation, knowledge-intensive production and management in the core, and a shift in the labor-intensive phases of global production to the periphery.[40] The core here is conceived of as the developed nations of the world capitalist system and the periphery as the underdeveloped nations. However, subsequent evidence suggested that this NIDL was giving way gradually to spatially diffuse and decentralized circuits of production utilizing globalized labor markets. The services that were purported to be a new core monopoly in the NIDL, for instance, were themselves becoming transnationalized.[41] New labor-intensive sweatshops have been located in "global cities" inside core countries, where (Third World) populations work under similar wage and labor conditions as their counterparts in the periphery, while core areas also become sites of offshore labor-intensive production, in a process of the "thirdworldization" of the core.[42] This reflects a more general tendency of "peripheralization" of labor in advanced capitalist countries, and involves diverse new hierarchies and modes of labor control (varied contingent and casualized labor arrangements) which have themselves become globalized.[43] The increasing mobility of factors of production (labor included, despite state restrictions) under globalization has led transnational capital, in its search for cheap labor along with other factor cost considerations, to combine strategies of relocation to the periphery *and* the use of immigrant, ethnic, and female labor pools in highly segmented labor markets in the core. These labor pools become an established labor market reality and lend themselves to the further disjuncture between geography and the locations of clusters of developed and underdeveloped social groups, independent of corporate planning per se.

The plummeting of wages and living conditions among broad majorities in core countries, "downward levelling" and the global "race to the bottom" have been well documented.[44] Witness, for example, seas of poverty and islands of wealth, and the breakdown of social infrastructure, in any Northern city that is increasingly approximate to any Third World metropolis. But this social bifurcation under globalization is a general worldwide phenomenon, perhaps a structural feature of the global system. On the one hand there are "subnational" development processes. Different regions within a single country develop at entirely different levels and rhythms in the pattern suggested by earlier theories of internal colonialism or center–periphery relations within a single country. A few well-known examples are: Mexico's industrializing and relatively developed North and its severely underdeveloped and marginalized South; the advanced enclaves in northern Italy surrounded by poor and marginalized regions; the underdevelopment of the US Southwest, and so on. In this scenario, a region within one country may approximate that of another country in terms of socioeconomic conditions and levels of development more than it may approximate other regions within the same country. On the other hand, these subnational processes, even as they make clear the inadequacies of a nation-state notion of development, still suggest a territorial or geographic notion and are therefore misleading. Polarization in the labor process under flexible accumulation involves a social bifurcation in which each high-skills job created is accompanied by several low-skills jobs such that wealth and poverty, and more broadly, different levels of social development, adhere from the very sites of social productive activity; that is, from *social*, not geographic, space.

Some nation-state centric theorists acknowledge that production and distribution have become globally fragmented and decentralized, but they argue, in a modification of the NIDL thesis, that core states retain high value-added segments of the complex global commodity chains, which are characterized by a high degree of monopolization, while low value-added segments are transferred to the periphery and are characterized by a high degree of competition. In this way core–periphery relations are reproduced.[45] But in fact transnational capital began in the 1990s to relocate highly monopolized and high-value segments of global commodity chains to the South. One example is the shift in software program development and engineering design from the United States and Western Europe to India and elsewhere in the Third World. In the mid-1990s, Texas Instruments, IBM, Morola, Hewlett-Packard, and other TNCs began to relocate and/or subcontract software development to the Indian city of Bangalore, dubbed "Silicon Valley East." In 1995, these TNCs accounted for a third of the 300 software firms operating in Bangalore, as the conversion of the city into a world production center for software spawned the growth of Indian software firms and of joint ventures. In this way, Indian capitalists became integrated into emergent transnational circuits and into the process of transnational class formation. As predicted, a "First World" affluent *population* of Indian computer programmers, engineers, administrators, and so on, sprang up in Bangalore, which integrated into the global consumer lifestyle characteristic of the high-income sector of global society. "Bangalore has almost self-consciously built an image for itself as the city for young, affluent professionals," one observer noted. "It's become the first city in India where pubs are accepted places for the white-collar set simply to hang out." Touring the plush offices where some 10,000 highly skilled technicians worked in the industry, "you could easily be in California."[46]

To explain the movement of values between different "nodes" in globalized production, clearly we need to move beyond nation-state centric approaches and apply a theory of value to transformations in world spatial and institutional structures (the nation-state being the central spatial and institutional structure in the hitherto history of world capitalism). The notion of net social gain or loss used by development economists has little meaning if measured, as it traditionally is, in national terms, or even in geographic terms. The distribution of social costs and gains must be conceived in transnational social terms, not in terms of the nation-state vis-à-vis the world economy, but transnationally as social groups vis-à-vis other social groups in a global society. Globalization fragments locally and integrates select strands of the population globally. The centralization and concentration of economic power is accompanied by a disintegration of the cohesive structures of nations and their civil societies. Thus the effect of local economic expansion is often the advancement of some (delocalized) groups and deepening poverty for others. We shall see throughout this study that as Central America has integrated into the global economy and society around a new set of transnational accumulation activities there have been winners and losers and a more complex stratification of groups as defined by their relation to the global economy, along with a general social polarization at the local level mirroring the worldwide polarization process under globalization. The nation-state cannot be the unit for measuring development in Central America or elsewhere. The global economy itself emerges as the only unit of development, if one must conceive this process in terms other than social.

The law of combined and uneven development postulates that the unevenness or inequality between regions together with their combination in a single international division of labor underlies capital accumulation.[47] The spatial distribution of unequal development between North and South (or center and periphery) as a particular territorial feature of the world-system was determined in large part by the role of states as instruments of territorially bound classes (this is an essential argument, for example, of Immanuel Wallerstein) and by the distinct socioeconomic and historical conditions that capitalism confronted in its genesis and worldwide spread. The reality of capital as a totality of competing individual capitals, and their concrete existence as a class relation within specific spatial confines determined geographically as nation-states, worked against a trans, or supranational, unifying trend. Yet the liberation of capital from such spatial barriers brought about by new technologies, the worldwide reorganization of production, and the lifting of nation-state constraints to the operation of the global market taking place under globalization imply that the locus of class and group relations in the current period is not the nation-state.

As globalization erodes the linkages between territoriality, production, classes, and state power, the tendency for self-reproduction in the international division of labor is increasingly counterbalanced and undermined by diverse economic, political, and social globalizing dynamics. We can expect sustained class polarization and also continued uneven accumulation between regions or areas characterized by hierarchies and divisions of labor in which some zones are selected for global production activities, others assigned "feeder" roles (for example, labor or raw materials reserves), and still others marginalized entirely from the global economy (the so-called "fourth world"). But there is no theoretical reason to posit any necessary affinity between continued uneven development and the nation-state as the particular territorial expression of uneven development. The fallacy of orthodox world-system theory on this point is to conflate the historicity (historically specific) of the nation-state system as the particular historic form which the birth of the world-system took with a feature immanent to the system itself.

The persistence, and in fact *growth*, of the North–South divide cannot be dismissed, at the level of aggregate data and even at that of the most cursory observations by world travelers who move between the North and the South. This divide therefore remains important for its theoretical and practical political implications. On the one hand, Fernández Kelly has noted that theories of development in their sequential stages have underplayed the impact of development upon segments of the population differentiated by class, by gender, and by ethnicity.[48] Certain forms of conceptualizing the North–South divide obscure our view of social hierarchies and inequalities across nations and regions. On the other hand, at issue is whether the divide is something innate to world capitalism or a particular spatial configuration of uneven capitalist development during a particular historic phase of world capitalism, and whether tendencies towards the self-reproduction of this configuration are increasingly offset by countertendencies emanating from the nature and dynamic of global capital accumulation, such as the search by mobile transnational capital to seek varied investment all over the world. I concur with Cox's claim that "it is [increasingly] difficult to give the terms *core* and *periphery* generalizable concrete points of reference ... Although the functional characteristics of core and periphery remain analytically valid, their association with specific geographical positions must be considered to be a matter of perhaps transitory circumstances, not of immutable destiny."[49] The process underway clearly involves not the supersession but the *erosion* of a great dichotomous center–periphery divide in the world economy.

Development and underdevelopment should be reconceived in terms of global social groups and not nations, in which core–periphery designates social position rather than geographic location. To continue to posit a center–periphery divide along geographic nation-state lines, we would have to: 1) provide a coherent theoretical explanation for capital's need to concentrate spatially and geographically; 2) explain why the "imagined community" of a nation, given the increasing separation of classes and territoriality, of class power and nation-state power, and the rising disjuncture between the fortunes of social groups and of nation-states, might want to concentrate these activities; 3) argue that capital accumulation still corresponds to national capitals, a proposition that has ever less empirical validity.

In sum, in its transnational stage, the national–international axis upon which the world capitalist system has been based has mutated into a qualitatively new global axis in which world zones (for example, center, semi-periphery, periphery) and nation-states are no longer the central locus of social change. However, the supersession of the nation-state system will be drawn out over a lengthy period and checkered by all kinds of social conflicts played out along national lines and as clashes between nation-states. Social science should be less concerned with static snapshots of the momentary than with the dialectic of historic *movement*, with capturing the central *dynamics* and *tendencies* in historic processes. The central dynamic of our epoch is globalization, and the central tendency is the *ascendance* of transnational capital, which brings with it the transnationalization of classes in general. In the long historic view, the nation-state system and all the frames of reference therein are descendant. However, capitalist globalization is a process, not so much consummated as in motion, and is unfolding in a multilayered world-system. Determinacy on the structural side is shifting to new transnational space that is eroding, subsuming, and superseding national space as the locus of social life, even though this social life is still "filtered through" nation-state institutions. This situation underscores the *highly contradictory* nature of transnational relations as well as the *indeterminacy* of emergent transnational social structure.

In this regard, a new transnational studies should take a dialectical approach that combines structure and agency in such a way that allows room for human agency, and for historic contingency, in the past, the current, and the future configuration of world capitalism. Just as the particular and historically specific nation-state *form* that the world capitalist system took in the period now being superseded was not inevitable, the particular transnational structures that emerge in the period we are now entering will be impermanent and will be shaped by the dialectical interplay of structure and agency. These ascendant structures should no more be reified than should the descendant nation-state. History might be open-ended, but the past shapes the present and the future. Decaying structures (in this case, the nation-state system) condition and mediate emergent structures. Transnational structures are emerging from the womb of a nation-state system which itself is unevenly developed and exhibits different levels of paces of transnationalization between countries and regions. Behavioral responses to globalizing processes are uneven, and are being shaped in part by the particular character of nation-state development and the variegated and distinct sets of social contradictions therein, including extant ethnic conflict, the relative strengths of competing dominant and subordinate groups, the uneven development of transnational vis-à-vis national class fractions, and so on. A new transnational studies should strive to avoid any teleological notions of an inevitable unfolding of a particular set of transnational structures—a pitfall that would be tantamount to reifying a unified global system as the inverse to the reification of the nation-state. In the same vein as the nation-state was (is) a transitional institutional form in the unfinished evolutionary development of the world capitalist system, emergent transnational structures should be seen as similar *transitional* forms in the evolution of an open-ended system. How the contradictions of global capitalism are (or are not) resolved and the particular forms that transnational social structure take will be conditioned by struggles among the diverse social forces brought into play by the globalization process. The synthesis in the dialectic between nation-state and global capitalism is highly contested.

Contours of Global Capitalist Society

The global economy may exercise a structural determinacy in the process of globalization. But production does not take place in a vacuum. It is embedded in larger social structures, including relations of social power, politics, state practices, and culture. These larger social structures become transformed with economic globalization and are the focus of part two of this chapter. I examine transnational class formation, the transnationalization of the state, transnational hegemony, the conformation of a global social structure of accumulation, global cultural practices, and a conception of local–global linkages. These diverse dimensions of globalization are "operationalized" for the concrete case of Central America in subsequent chapters, where we will see the great utility of the concepts introduced here for understanding social change and just how implicated Central America is in these transnational processes.

Global Class Formation: From National to Transnational Classes[50]

Parallel to the burgeoning research on economic globalization, studies in more recent years have focused on the process of transnational class formation. Kees van der Pijl's excellent theoretical work stands out here.[51] He has analyzed the fractionation of capital along functional lines in the post-World War II period in advanced capitalist countries; the internationalization of these fractions and their projects as a consequence of the transnational expansion of capital; and the consequent development of an internationally class-conscious bourgeoisie and of a "comprehensive concept of [bourgeoisie class] control" at the international level. Relatedly, the "Italian School" in international relations has attempted to theorize a global social formation that is increasingly outside the logic of the nation-state.[52] Robert Cox discusses "an emergent global class structure," and Stephen Gill has identified a "developing transnational capitalist class fraction." From an entirely different direction, Leslie Sklair's "theory of the global system" involves an idea of the transnational capitalist class that brings together the executives of transnational corporations, "globalizing bureaucrats, politicians, and professionals," and "consumerist elites" in the media and the commercial sector.[53] What all these accounts share, with the exception of Sklair's, is a nation-state centered concept of class. They postulate *national* bourgeoisies that converge externally with other national classes at the level of the international system through the internationalization of capital and, concomitantly, of civil society. World ruling class formation is seen as a product of the international collusion of these national bourgeoisies and the resultant international coalitions. The old view of internationalization as national blocs of capital in competition is merely modified to accommodate collusion in the new globalized age. But globalization compels us to modify some of the essential premises of class analysis, particularly the notion that classes are by definition attached to nation-states.

Class formation is an ongoing historical process that proceeded through the institutional and organizational logic of the nation-state system in earlier epochs of capitalism. Dominant and subordinate classes struggled against each other over the social surplus through nation-state institutions and fought to utilize national states to capture shares of this surplus. As a result, to evoke Karl Polanyi's classical analysis, a "double movement" took place late in the nineteenth century,[54] made possible because capital, facing territorial, institutional, and other limits bound up with the nation-state system, faced a series of constraints that forced it to reach a historic compromise with working and popular classes. These classes could place redistributive demands on national states and set some constraints on the power of capital because national states enjoyed a varying but significant degree of autonomy to intervene in the phase of distribution, capturing and redirecting surpluses (these possibilities also contributed to the split in the world socialist movement and the rise of social democracy). Subordinate classes mediated their relation to capital through the nation-state. Capitalist classes developed within the protective cocoon of nation-states and developed interests in opposition to rival national capitals. These states expressed the coalitions of classes and groups that were incorporated into the historic blocs of nation-states. The outcome of world class struggles in this period were Keynesian or "New Deal" states and Fordist production in the cores of the world economy, and diverse multiclass developmentalist states and populist projects in the periphery.

There was nothing transhistoric, or predetermined, about this process of class formation worldwide. It is now being superseded by globalization. What is occurring is a process of transnational class formation, in which the mediating role of national states has been modified. A global class structure is becoming superimposed on national class structures. As national productive structures become transnationally integrated, world classes whose organic development took place through the nation-state are experiencing supranational integration with "national" classes of other countries. As classes are restructured by the globalization process, transformations include the rapid proletarianization of vast sectors of formerly pre-capitalist classes, particularly national peasantries and urban artisans, and also of sectors of small and medium-sized manufacturers and other middle classes that were tied to the domestic market and the demand it generated.

New urban and rural working classes linked to transnational production processes appear. One of the many consequences of the contraction of domestic markets involved in globalization is a reduced demand for labor simultaneous to a dramatic increase in newly proletarianized groups from the ranks of dissolving pre-capitalist classes (or the dissolution of employment in the former private capitalist sector and state bureaucracies). Combined with post-Fordist production techniques that dramatically alter the role of human labor and the organic composition of capital on an ongoing basis, the result is the rise of millions of supernumeraries, or superfluous labor with no role to play in the *formal* local structures of globalized production. This is one of several structural factors behind the vertiginous expansion of the informal sector, in both core and peripheral regions, and we will see this later with regard to Central America. However, it should be recalled that the informal economy is functionally integrated into the formal economy, and the two are complementary.[55] These vast pools of supernumeraries have become alienated from the means of production but not incorporated as wage labor into the capitalist production process, and are of no *direct* use to capital. But indirectly they hold down wages and disburse intersubjective groups that might otherwise pose a direct political challenge to the status quo.

Globalization, by redefining the phase of distribution in the accumulation of capital in relation to nation-states, also redefines the relations between social classes and groups within and among nations. The liberation of transnational capital from the constraints and commitments placed on it by the social forces in the nation-state phase of capitalism has dramatically altered the balance of forces among classes and social groups in each nation of the world and at a global level towards a transnational capitalist class and its agents. The declining ability of the nation-state to intervene in the process of capital accumulation and to determine economic policies reflects the newfound power that transnational capital has acquired over popular classes. On the surface this newfound power is expressed as the structural power of transnational capital over the direct power of national states. In its essence, the relative power of exploiting classes over the exploited classes has been enhanced many times over, at least in this momentary historic juncture.

This power is becoming fixed in the new global capital–labor relation discussed earlier, in the global casualization or informalization of labor, or diverse contingent categories, involving alternative systems of labor control associated with post-Fordist flexible accumulation. Central to this new capital–labor relation is the concept of a restructuring crisis. The crisis that followed the long post-war boom in the 1970s ushered in a radical shift in the methods and sites of global capitalist accumulation, resulting, in Hoogvelt's analysis, in a transformation in the mechanisms of surplus value extraction.[56] Capital began to abandon earlier reciprocities with labor from the 1970s on precisely because the process of globalization has allowed it to break free of nation-state constraints. In this new capital–labor relation, labor is increasingly only a naked commodity, no longer embedded in relations of reciprocity rooted in the social and political communities that have historically been institutionalized in nation-states. Each laborer is expected to become a seller "freed" from political or social constraints, an "entrepreneur" who is the owner of him/herself as a commodity.

New systems of labor control include subcontracting and contract labor, outsourcing, part-time and temp work, informal work, home-work, and the revival of patriarchal, "sweatshop," and other oppressive production relations. Well-known trends associated with the restructuring of the labor–capital relation taking place under globalization include "downward leveling", deunionization, "ad hoc" and "just-in-time" labor supply, the superexploitation of immigrant communities as a counterpart to capital export, the lengthening of the working day, the rise of a new global "underclass" of supernumeraries or "redundants" subject to new forms of social control and even to genocide, and new gendered and racialized hierarchies among labor. These new labor patterns have been facilitated by globalization in dual ways: first, capital has exercised its power over labor through new patterns of flexible accumulation made possible by enabling "third wave" technologies, the elimination of spatial barriers to accumulation, and the control over space these changes bring; second, globalization itself has involved the culmination of the primitive accumulation of capital worldwide, a process in which millions have been wrenched from the means of production, proletarianized, and thrown into a global labor market that transnational capital has been able to shape. Global class formation has involved the accelerated division of the world into a global bourgeoisie and a global proletariat. These trends point to the rise of a global proletariat stratified less along national than along social lines in a transnational environment, insofar as this new generalized capital–labor relation reflects the emerging uniformity in the conditions of production worldwide.

The Rise of a Transnational Bourgeoisie and National/Transnational Class Fractionation[57]

With the consolidation of national corporations and markets in the late nineteenth and early twentieth centuries, local and regional capitalists crystallized into national capitalist classes in core countries. These became powerful ruling classes that restructured society and ushered in a new era of corporate capitalism. We are in the earlier stages of the same process now replicated at the global level. Under globalization, national bourgeoisies are metamorphosizing into local (national) contingents of an emergent transnational bourgeoisie. To the extent that local productive apparatuses are integrated into globalized circuits of production through the process of transnationalization, the logic of local and global accumulation tend to converge and the earlier rivalries between capitalists no longer take the form of national rivalries. Competition between capitals continues. But given the separation of accumulation from determined territories and the transnational integration of capitalists, competition is now between oligopolist clusters in a transnational environment.

As the agent of the global economy, transnational capital has become the hegemonic fraction of capital on a world scale. Here *fraction* denotes segments within classes determined by their relation to social production and the class as a whole. The new transnational bourgeoisie or capitalist class is that segment of the world bourgeoisie that represents transnational capital. It is comprised of the owners of the leading worldwide means of production as embodied principally in the transnational corporations and private financial institutions. This class is *trans*national because it is tied to globalized circuits of production, marketing, and finances unbound from particular national territories and identities, and because its interests lie in global over local or national accumulation. Its members therefore exhibit a congruence of objective interests, if not always subjective identities, that set it apart from specific nation-states. Transnational capital controls the "commanding heights" of the global economy. It is that fraction of capital that imposes the general direction and character on production worldwide and conditions the social, political, and cultural character of capitalist society worldwide. What distinguishes the transnational capitalist class from national or local capitalist fractions is that it is involved in globalized production and manages global circuits of accumulation that give it an objective class existence and identity spatially and politically in the global system above any local territories and polities. This transnational capitalist class is the new ruling class worldwide and it is represented by a class-conscious transnational elite. At the level of agency, the transnational capitalist class is class-conscious, has become conscious of its transnationality,[58] and has been pursuing a class project of capitalist globalization, as reflected in its global decision-making and the rise of a transnational state apparatus under the auspices of this fraction, as discussed below. At the apex of the global economy is a transnational managerial elite, based in the centers of world capitalism, which controls the levers of global policy-making and which responds to transnational capital.

The rise of transnational capital draws into the vortex of the global economy national capitalist classes. Globalization creates new forms of transnational class alliances across borders and new forms of class cleavages globally and within countries, regions, cities, and local communities, in ways quite distinct from the old national class structures and international class conflicts and alliances. The diverse mechanisms that promote the transnationalization of capitalist groups include the spread of TNCs, the expansion of direct foreign investment, cross-national mergers, strategic alliances, the interpenetration of capital, interlocking directorates, worldwide subcontracting and outsourcing, the extension of free enterprise zones, and other economic forms associated with the global economy. Such new forms of organizing globalized production are important because they contribute to the development of worldwide networks that link local capitalists to one another, generate an identity of objective interests and of subjective outlook among these capitalists around a process of global (as opposed to local) accumulation. They therefore function as integrative mechanisms in the formation of the transnational capitalist class and act to shift the locus of class formation from national to emergent transnational space. We will see how this process has unfolded in Central America.

It is in the Third World where transnational class formation is weakest and where "national" bourgeoisies may still control states and organize influential political projects. However, even here transnational class formation is well underway. Foreign Direct Investment (FDI) has increased sharply to developing countries. The average annual flows increased more than three-fold between the early 1980s and the earlier 1990s for the world as a whole, while for developing countries it increased fivefold.[59] National capitals in the South have themselves increasingly transnationalized by their own FDI and by integrating into global circuits of accumulation. In 1960, only one percent of FDI came from developing countries. By 1985, this figure had increased to around 3 percent, and by 1995 it stood at about 8 percent.[60] Southern-based TNCs had invested $51 billion abroad by that year, while, as I have stated, developing countries absorbed an increasing proportion of FDI in the 1990s.[61] The top fifty TNCs of the Third World augmented their foreign assets by 280 percent between 1993 and 1995, while those of the top 100 corporations based in the core countries increased by only 30 percent.[62] The bourgeoisie of countries such as Singapore, South Korea, Taiwan, Brazil, Chile, and Mexico are becoming important "national" contingents of the transnational capitalist class. In 1996 for the first time two third-world companies, Daewoo Corporation of South Korea and Petroleos de Venezuela, joined the ranks of the top 100 transnational corporations. South Korean and Taiwanese-based companies not only moved into cheaper wage zones in Southeast Asia and Central America but also began "South to North" relocations. In the first six years of the 1990s, fourteen Korean companies invested a total of $2.6 billion in the United Kingdom alone.[63] By the mid-1990s Mexico had twenty-four billionaires who became world-class investors and major shareholders in leading TNCs, among them Del Monte Corporation, Apple, and Microsoft, investing abroad in media, cement and glass production, and so on.[64] These transnationalized fractions of local dominant groups in the South are New Right "technocratic" elites in Latin America, Africa, and Asia (where they are sometimes termed a "modernizing bourgeoisie"), who have overseen sweeping processes of social and economic restructuring and integration into the global economy and society.

Class fractionation is occurring along a new national/transnational axis with the rise of transnational corporate and political elites.[65] The accelerated concentration of capital and economic power around the transnational capitalist class has profound effects on arrangements between existing social groups, class constellations, and political systems in every country of the world-system. Political and economic power tends to gravitate towards new groups linked to transnational capital and the global economy, either directly or through location in reorganized local state apparatuses. The penetration of the global economy and the emergence of transnational fractions among dominant groups sparks new polarization between transnational and national fractions and groups on numerous levels. The contradictory logics of national and global accumulation are at work in this process. The interests of one group lie in national accumulation, including the whole set of traditional national regulatory and protectionist mechanisms, and the other in an expanding global economy based on worldwide market liberalization. These two fractions have been vying for control of local state apparatuses since the 1970s. Transnational fractions ascended politically in countries around the world, clashing in their bid for hegemony with nationally based class fractions. In the 1970s and the 1980s incipient transnationalized fractions set out to eclipse national fractions in the core capitalist countries of the North and to capture the "commanding heights" of state policymaking. From the 1980s into the 1990s, these fractions became ascendant in the South and began to vie for, and in many countries, to capture, national state apparatuses.

The struggle between descendant national fractions of dominant groups and ascendant transnational fractions was often the backdrop to surface political dynamics and ideological processes in the late twentieth century. These clashes were played out in numerous sites, from electoral contests, to disputes for leadership among national business associations, to sometimes bloody infighting among ruling parties. To give one example, this was behind the bloody Mexican power struggles of the 1990s within the ruling Institutional Revolutionary Party (PRI). The "dinosaurs" in the power struggle represented the old bourgeoisie and state bureaucrats whose interests lay in Mexico's corporatist Import-Substitution Industrialization version of national capitalism. The new "technocrats" were the transnational fraction of the Mexican bourgeoisie that captured the party following fierce intra-party struggles in the mid-1980s, and then captured the state, with the election in 1988 of Carlos Salinas de Gortari. Transnationalized fractions pursuing the globalization project took power and have been thoroughly transforming the vast majority of countries in the world, including Sweden, New Zealand, India, Brazil, Mexico, Chile, South Africa, and so on. In every region of the world, states, economies, and political processes are becoming transnationalized and integrated under the guidance of this new elite. In the process, very often what appears in world politics as clashes among nation-states are actually clashes between national and transnational fractions in a globalized setting. This is another instance of national in appearance and transnational in essence.

National states, once captured by these transnational groups, internalize the authority structures of global capitalism; the global is incarnated in local social structures and processes. The disciplinary power of global capitalism shifts actual policymaking power within national states to the global capitalist bloc, which is represented by local groups tied to the global economy. In countries where states have been captured by popular classes or by national fractions of local dominant groups, such as Haiti, Nicaragua, South Africa, Venezuela, and elsewhere from the 1970s into the twenty-first century, the transnational elite has been able to use the structural power of the global economy to instill discipline and undermine policies contrary to globalization. Gradually, transnational blocs became hegemonic within the vast majority of countries in the world and began to transform their countries. They utilized national state apparatuses to advance globalization. They set out to implement restructuring and integrate into the global economy, establishing in the process formal and informal liaison mechanisms between the national state structures and transnational state apparatuses.

If one set of conflicts was between fractions of dominant groups, a second was among subordinate groups and classes as globalization altered their traditional patterns of social mobilization, political identity, and livelihood. Popular class organizations and grassroots social movements became sites of intense struggle as globalization created new cleavages and eroded earlier loyalties and identities, particularly those constructed on corporatist models of subordinate class incorporation characteristic of national capitalism in Latin America and other peripheral zones. But the principal social contradiction in global capitalism is still between dominant and subordinate classes. Global elites have pursued their transnational agenda amidst sharp social struggles and multiple forms of resistance from subordinate groups and also from dominant groups not brought into the emerging global capitalist bloc. Changing class structure, mass social dislocations, the plummeting of living conditions, growing inequalities, and the rise in absolute and relative poverty levels have been met by a myriad forms of organization and resistance by popular sectors around the world.

Transnationalization of the State[66]

The transition from the nation-state to the new transnational phase of world capitalism also involves the reorganization of the state in each nation and the rise of truly supranational economic and political institutions that begin to acquire the characteristics of a transnational state—what I will henceforth refer to in this book as a TNS. The notion that the continued internationalization of capital and the growth of an international civil society has involved the internationalization of the state as well has been recognized by a number of traditions in the social sciences.[67] The interdisciplinary literature on globalization is full of discussion about the decreasing power and significance of the nation-state and the increasing significance of supra or transnational institutions. However, these diverse accounts assume phenomena associated with a TNS to be international extensions of the nation-state system. The conception is one of *inter*national institutions created by nation-states individually or collectively as mechanisms to regulate the flow of goods and capital across their borders and to mediate inter-state relations. This nation-state centrism entraps proponents in a global–national dualism.

Nation-states are geographical and juridical units and sometimes cultural units, and the term is interchangeable as used in this study with country or nation. States are power relations embodied in particular sets of political institutions. The conflation of these two related but analytically distinct concepts is grounded in a Weberian conception of the state, in which the economic and the political (in Weberian terms, "markets and states") are externally related, separate, and even oppositional spheres, each with its own independent logic, and nation-states interact externally with markets.[68] In these recurrent dualisms, economic globalization is increasingly recognized but is analyzed as if it were independent of the institutions that structure these social relations, in particular, states and the nation-state. Separate logics are posited for a globalizing economy and a nation-state based political system. I have argued elsewhere that the way out of these antinomies is to move beyond Weber and return to a historical materialist conception of the state. In the Marxist conception, the state is the institutionalization of class relations around a particular configuration of social production. States as coercive systems of authority are class relations and social practices congealed and operationalized through institutions. In Marx's view, the state gives a political form to economic institutions and production relations.[69] Consequently, the economic globalization of capital cannot be a phenomenon isolated from the transformation of states and of class relations. The state is the congealment of particular and historically determined constellations of class forces and relations, and states are always embodied in sets of political institutions. Hence states are: a) a moment of class and social power relations; and b) a set of political institutions (an "apparatus"). National states arose as particular embodiments of the constellations of social groups and classes that developed within the system of nation-states in the earlier epochs of capitalism. But these relations have now "outgrown" the nation-state. The institutional structures of nation-states may persist in the epoch of globalization, but globalization requires that we modify our conception of these structures. There is no reason to assume that the rise of a transnational state means that nation-states need disappear. A TNS apparatus is emerging under globalization *from within* the system of nation-states.

What then is a transnational state? It is a particular constellation of class forces and relations bound up with capitalist globalization and the rise of a transnational capitalist class, embodied in a diverse set of political institutions. The TNS comprises those institutions and practices in global society that maintain, defend, and advance the emergent hegemony of a global bourgeoisie and its project of constructing a new global capitalist historical bloc. This TNS apparatus is an emerging network that comprises transformed and externally integrated national states, *together with* the supranational economic and political forums and it is one that has not yet acquired any centralized institutional form. The rise of a TNS entails the reorganization of the state in each nation (*national states*) and it involves simultaneously the rise of truly supranational economic and political institutions. These two processes—the transformation of nation-states and the rise of supranational institutions—are not separate or mutually exclusive. In fact, they are twin dimensions of the process of the transnationalization of the state.

The TNS apparatus is multilayered and multicentered, functionally linking together institutions that exhibit distinct gradations of "state-ness" and have different histories and trajectories. The supranational organizations are both economic and political, formal and informal. The economic forums include the International Monetary Fund (IMF), the World Bank (WB), the World Trade Organization (WTO), the regional banks, and so on. Supranational political forums include the Group of Seven (G-7) and the more recently formed Group of 22, as well as more formal forums such as the United Nations (UN), the European Union (EU), and so on. They also include regional groupings such as the Association of South East Asian Nations (ASEAN), and the juridical, administrative, and regulatory structures established through regional agreements such as the North American Free Trade Agreement (NAFTA) and the Asia-Pacific Economic Cooperation (APEC) forum.

These supranational planning institutes are gradually supplanting national institutions in policy development and the global management and administration of the global economy. They are representative of new forms of state power in the context of an emergent TNS, in which state apparatuses and functions (coercive and administrative mechanisms, etc.) do not necessarily correspond to nation-states. The function of the nation-state is shifting from the formulation of national policies to the administration of policies formulated by a transnational elite operating through supranational institutions. However, it is essential to avoid the national–global duality: national states are not external to the TNS but are becoming incorporated into it as component parts. The supranational organizations function in consonance with transformed national states. They are staffed by transnational functionaries who find their counterparts in transnational functionaries who staff transformed national states. These *transnational state cadre* act as midwives of capitalist globalization. The International Financial Institutes (IFIs)—truly supranational planning institutes of the global economy—coordinate (impose) the process in each country and region of adjustment and integration into emergent global structures. We will see in detail in subsequent chapters just how a TNS and TNS apparatuses have functioned in Central America as midwives of globalization in the region.

The TNS is attempting to fulfill the functions for world capitalism that in earlier periods were fulfilled by what world-system and international relations scholars refer to as a "hegemon," or a dominant capitalist power that has the resources and the structural position which allows it to organize world capitalism as a whole and impose the rules, regulatory environment, etc., that allows the system to function. We are witnessing the decline of US supremacy and the early stages of the creation of a transnational hegemony through supranational structures that are not yet capable of providing the economic regulation and political conditions for the reproduction of global capitalism. Just as the national state played this role in the earlier period, the TNS seeks to create and maintain the preconditions for the valorization and accumulation of capital in the global economy, which is not simply the sum of national economies and national class structures, and requires a centralized authority to represent the whole of competing capitals, the major combinations of which are no longer "national" capitals. The nature of state practices in the emergent global system resides in the exercise of transnational economic and political authority through the TNS apparatus to reproduce the class relations embedded in the global valorization and accumulation of capital.

But if I have argued that the state is a class relation, then how is the newfound relative power of global capital over global labor related to this analysis of the transnationalization of the state? Out of the emerging transnational institutionality the new class relations of global capitalism and the social practices specific to it are becoming congealed and institutionalized. For instance, when the IMF or the WB condition financing on enactment of new labor codes to make workers more "flexible," or on the rollback of a state-sponsored "social wage" through austerity programs, they are producing this new class relation. Similarly, the types of practices of national states that became generalized in the late twentieth century—deregulation, fiscal conservatism, monetarism, tax regressivity, austerity, etc.—produce this relation, resulting in an increase in state services to, and subsidization of, capital, and underscoring the increased role of the state in facilitating private capital accumulation. With this comes a shift in income and in power from labor to capital. These outcomes generate the broader social and political conditions under which the new capital–labor relation is forged.

But now we need to specify further the relationship of national states to the TNS. Capital acquires its newfound power vis-à-vis (*as expressed within*) national states, which may act as transmission belts and filtering devices. But national states are also transformed into proactive instruments for advancing the agenda of global capitalism. This assertion that transnational social forces impose their structural power over nations and the simultaneous assertion that states, captured by transnational fractions, are proactive agents of the globalization process, only appears as contradictory if one abandons dialectics for the Weberian dualist construct of states and markets and the national–global dualism. Governments undertake restructuring and serve the needs of transnational capital not simply because they are "powerless" in the face of globalization, but because a particular historical constellation of social forces now exists that presents an organic social base for this global restructuring of capitalism. Hence it is not that nation-states become irrelevant or powerless vis-à-vis transnational capital and its global institutions. Rather, power as the ability to issue commands and have them obeyed, or more precisely, the ability to shape social structures, shifts from social groups and classes with interests in national accumulation to those whose interests lie in new global circuits of accumulation.

Transnational elites set about to penetrate and restructure national states, directly, through diverse political-diplomatic and other ties between national states and TNS apparatuses and functionaries, and indirectly, through the impositions of transnational capital via its institutional agents (IMF, World Bank, etc.) and the structural power that global capital exercises over nation-states, particularly small peripheral ones. Transnational nuclei, or pools, are cultivated and liaise with the transnational elite as "in-country" counterparts through a shared outlook and interest in new economic activities and through diverse external political, cultural, and ideological ties. These nuclei act as "transmission belts" of the transnational agenda by capturing key state apparatuses and ministries, by the hegemony they are expected to achieve in civil society, and by the power they wield through their preponderance in the local economy and the material and ideological resources accrued through external linkages. In this process, the "externalization" of national states and civil societies ensues. The more peripheral their status, the deeper or more rapid their externalization and the less their autonomy—although this is a question of degree, as the autonomy of all national states is eventually broken down and subordinated to the logic of the global system.

Far from the "end of the nation-state," we are witness to its transformation into "neo-liberal national states." As component elements of a TNS, neo-liberal states perform three essential services: they 1) adopt fiscal and monetary policies which assure macroeconomic stability; 2) provide the basic infrastructure necessary for global economic activity (air and sea ports, communications networks, educational systems, etc.), and; 3) provide social order, that is, stability, which requires sustaining instruments of direct coercion and ideological apparatuses. When the transnational elite speaks of "governance" it is referring to these functions and the capacity to fulfill them. This was made explicit in the WB's World Development Report for 1997, *The State in a Changing World*, which points out that the aegis of the national state is central to globalization. In the World Bank's words, "globalization begins at home."[70] But the functions of the neo-liberal state are contradictory. Although they do not disappear, national states experience dramatic fracturing and restructuring. As globalization proceeds, internal social cohesion declines along with national economic integration. The neo-liberal state retains essential powers to facilitate globalization but it loses the ability to harmonize conflicting social interests within a country, to realize the historic function of sustaining the internal unity of a nationally conceived social formation, and to achieve legitimacy. Unable to resolve the contradictory problems of legitimacy and capital accumulation, local states opt simply for abandoning whole sectors of national populations. In many instances, they no longer even try to attain legitimacy among the marginalized and supernumeraries, who are isolated and contained in new ways, or subject to repressive social control measures (such as the mass incarceration of African-Americans in the United States).[71] The dramatic intensification of legitimacy crises is a contradiction internal to the system of global capitalism.

The continued division of the world into nation-states constitutes a fundamental condition for the power of transnational capital because nation-states can only exercise jurisdiction/sovereignty within national borders, but transnational capital operates beyond national borders, and is thus not regulated or responsible to any single political authority.[72] This point is crucial: the continued existence of the nation-state system is a central condition for the power of transnational capital. For instance, transnational corporations during the early 1990s were able to utilize the institutions of different nation-states in order to continuously dismantle regulatory structures and other state restrictions on the operation of transnational capital in a process of "mutual deregulation." In this process, core or "hard" national states, as components of a larger TNS apparatus, play key roles in global restructuring. Transnational fractions among dominant groups are able to use these core states to mold transnational structures. This helps us to understand the preponderant role of the US national state in the integration of Central America into the global economy and society.

Thus we do not see the complete withdrawal of the state. Rather, the role of the neo-liberal state is to serve *global* (over local) capital accumulation. The state under capitalism has always fallen short of Adam Smith's liberalism. The "free" market, historically speaking, is an illusion. The "visible hand" of the market has always been the state. States intervene in the market both to generate the general conditions for accumulation to take place and to provide specific assistance for concrete accumulation processes. Nicos Poulantzas' thesis that the state organizes capitalists and fragments and disorganizes workers seems to hold true here regarding the TNS and the neo-liberal states.[73] As in the past, when states forced bourgeoisies to modernize whether they wished to or not, the TNS and local neo-liberal states, despite the withdrawal of the latter from many areas, have organized and led dominant groups into capitalist modernization under globalization. The "free" market in global society means freedom of accumulation vis-à-vis institutional constraints and the social forces that have imposed these constraints. In this sense, the neo-liberal state intervenes in order to support capital over diverse social forces that may constrain its freedom of accumulation. We will see in subsequent chapters how the nation-state system remains highly functional to the process of capitalist globalization. The state played a leading role in the enormous transformations in Central America. As in all major transformations of capitalism, state intervention in Central America has been necessary, nay *central*, to the development of a new model of accumulation. This transformation was not, as is often depicted in the literature, a crude imposition of international organizations representing the core powers. It was a process facilitated by the TNS that included national state apparatuses in Central America and the active involvement of local dominant groups.

Transnational Hegemony and a Global Social Structure of Accumulation

Towards a New Global Capitalist Historic Bloc

The revival of the ideas of Antonio Gramsci in recent years has brought some of the central notions of Gramscian thought into the mainstream of social theory and practice. Such Gramscian concepts as hegemony and historical blocs have opened up new directions in research in areas such as political sociology, international relations, cultural studies, history, and development, and are of tremendous utility, in my view, in comprehending emergent transnational phenomena. Gramsci's historic formulation that "International relations [the character of the international system] flow from social relations"[74] has been developed by the neo-Gramscian or "Italian School" in international relations, for instance, into the edict that changes in social structure lead to modifications in state–society relations and in transnational social relations conceived as distinct from the histori-cally specific form of national exchanges. Globalization pressures modify all national social structures and institutions in such a way that they become transnationalized.[75] Crucial here is Gramsci's concept of hegemony as consensual domination; his focus on civil society as the locus of hegemony; and on the "extended state" comprised of political society plus civil society, as the axis of social structure.

The particular local social structures of accumulation that developed during the nation-state phase of world capitalism often took the form of corporatist, welfare, and developmentalist projects, all predicated on a redistributive logic and on incorporation of labor and other popular classes into national historical blocs. As modes of accumulation corresponding to national capitalism eroded under the thrust of globalization, these social structures of accumulation, and the class alliances and arrangements between dominant and subordinate groups that they embodied, began to break down. As capital became liberated from the nation-state and assumed tremendous new power relative to labor with the onset of globalization, states shifted from reproducing Keynesian social structures of accumulation to servicing the general needs of the new patterns of global accumulation and the transnational capitalist class, which meant an end to redistributive projects. In the United States and other core countries this spelled the end of the Fordist era. In the second world, it spelled the rise of transnationali-zed fractions among aspiring elites who began to liaise with the global bourgeoisie and articulate a project for full (re)integration into world capitalism. In the Third World, the nationalist bourgeoisie, petty-bourgeois, and revolutionary regimes became displaced by transnationalized fractions of local elites as multiclass developmentalist projects unravelled.

This newfound power helped transnational capital in its efforts to mold highly favorable global social structures of accumulation. As social structure becomes transformed and transnationalized in each region of the world, a new global social structure of accumulation is becoming superimposed on, and is transforming, existing national social structures. A social structure of accumulation refers to a set of mutually reinforcing social, economic, and political institutions and cultural and ideological norms which fuse together and facilitate a successful pattern of capital accumulation over a specific historic period.[76] The new global social structure of accumulation has mutually reinforcing economic, political, and cultural norms. The transnational capitalist class is in the process of constructing a new global capitalist historic bloc; a new hegemonic bloc consisting of various economic and political forces that have become the dominant sector of the ruling class throughout the world, among the countries of the North as well as of the South. The politics and policies of this ruling bloc are conditioned by the new global structure of accumulation and production. This historic bloc is composed of the transnational corporations and financial institutions, the elites that manage the supranational agencies, major forces in the dominant political parties, media conglomerates, and technocratic elites and state managers in both North and South. The world politics of this new global ruling class is not driven, as they were for national ruling classes, by the flux of shifting rivalries and alliances played out through the inter-state system.

How, then, do we conceive of hegemony in the emerging global order? For realists, world-system analysts, and Marxists, hegemony is inextricably tied up with state power, and state power is conceived in terms of the nation-state. The logic of a competing nation-state system as the basis for analyzing world dynamics leads analysts to search for hegemony in some type of nation-state configuration in the new global order. I want to argue that we are witness to an emerging transnational hegemony as expressed in the emergence of a new historic bloc, global in scope and based on the hegemony of transnational capital. But this proposition has been contravened by those who claim that the dominant role of the United States in world affairs is proof of a nation-state based world order under US hegemony. I suggest that interpreting the US state as playing a leadership role on behalf of a transnational hegemony is a more satisfactory explanation than that of advancing "US" interests, as we will see when applying the concepts of hegemony and world order to the study of Central America. The United States has played a key role in the globalization of Central America. This role is more properly understood as US sponsorship of the region's restructuring and integration into global capitalism on behalf of a transnational project, not a project of "US" hegemony in rivalry with other core powers for influence in the Isthmus.

Central America's political and social structure has always been closely linked with a major world power, first Spain, then briefly Great Britain, and then the United States, and its integration into the world economy has been highly conditioned by such relations. In the post-World War II period, Central America was largely a dependent "protectorate" of the United States, linked almost exclusively to the US market. Although core capitals had already begun the period of internationalization and interpenetration, this was still the period of multinational rather than transnational capital. The United States played the key international role in the formulation of Central America's economic policies and international articulation. But the successive Spanish, British, and US "eras" in Central America are being replaced now by an era of transnational hegemony over the region, concomitant to the emergence of a transnational hegemony at the level of the global system. It was in this context that the US role in Central America in the late twentieth and early twenty-first centuries must be understood. US–Central American relations in the current epoch are *not* a continuation of the historic "hegemony" that the United States has exercised. The region's reinsertion into the global economy and new transnational class alignments and international political relations therein have transpired under the tutelage of the United States, conceived not as the "hegemonic power" but, in the Gramscian sense, as the dominant world power playing a leadership role on behalf of an emergent hegemonic transnational configuration. Central America's relations with the world "pass through" its relations with the United States. As such, an important focus in the study of Central America's insertion into the emergent global order is an examination of Central American–US relations and US intervention in Central America.[77]

The Transnational Elite Agenda[78]

As the transnational ruling bloc emerged in the 1980s and 1990s it carried out a "revolution from above," involving modifications in global social and economic structures through the agency of TNS apparatuses, aimed at promoting the most propitious conditions around the world for the unfettered operation of the new global capitalist production system. This global restructuring, the so-called "Washington consensus,"[79] or what has come to be know as neo-liberalism, is a doctrine of laissez-faire capitalism legitimated by the assumptions of neo-classical economics and modernization theory; by the doctrine of comparative advantage; and by the globalist rhetoric of free trade, growth, efficiency, and prosperity. Global neo-liberalism has involved twin dimensions, rigorously pursued by global elites with the backing of a powerful and well-organized lobby of transnational corporations. One is worldwide market liberalization and the construction of a new legal and regulatory superstructure for the global economy. The other is the internal restructuring and global integration of each national economy. The combination of the two is intended to create a "liberal world order," an open global economy and a global policy regime that breaks down all national barriers to the free movement of transnational capital *between* borders and the free operation of capital *within* borders.

Worldwide market liberalization accelerated dramatically with the Uruguay Round of the General Agreement on Tariffs and Trade (GATT) negotiations in the 1980s, which established a sweeping new set of world trade rules to regulate the new global economy based on: 1) freedom of investment and capital movements; 2) the liberalization of services, including banks; 3) intellectual property rights; and 4) a free movement of goods. Transnational elites also promoted regional integration processes, including the North American Free Trade Agreement (NAFTA), the European Union (EU), and the Asia Pacific Economic Conference (APEC), among others. Between 1948 and 1994, 109 regional trading arrangements were negotiated worldwide. The World Trade Organization (WTO), created in 1995 following the Uruguay Round, is perhaps the most potent symbol of the liberalized global economy. With its independent jurisdiction and unprecedented powers to enforce the GATT provisions, it is the first supranational institution with a coercive capacity not embedded in any particular nation-state but rather directly in transnational functionaries and the transnational corporate elite.

Alongside this world market liberalization, economic restructuring programs have swept the majority of countries in the world. These programs, designed in the 1970s and 1980s by the international financial agencies and the think-tanks of the emerging transnational elites and accompanied by a new neo-liberal development discourse,[80] sought to achieve within each country the macroeconomic equilibrium and liberalization required by transnationally mobile capital and to integrate each nation and region into globalized circuits of accumulation. The model attempted to harmonize a wide range of fiscal, monetary, industrial, labor, and commercial policies among multiple nations, as a requirement for fully mobile transnational capital to function simultaneously, and often instantaneously, over numerous national borders. The program called for the elimination of state intervention in the economy and the regulation of individual nation-states over the activities of capital in their territories. Between 1978 and 1992 more than seventy countries undertook 566 stabilization and structural adjustment programs imposed by the IMF and the World Bank.[81] These programs become the major mechanism of adjusting local economies to the global economy. What took place through these programs was a massive restructuring of the productive apparatus in these countries, and the reintegration into global capitalism of vast zones of the former Third and Second Worlds, under the tutelage of the emergent TNS.[82]

In the neo-liberal model, stabilization, or the package of fiscal, monetary, exchange, and related measures, is the first phase and is intended to achieve macroeconomic stability, an essential requisite for fully mobile transnational capital to function simultaneously across numerous national borders. Stabilization is followed by a second stage, "structural adjustment": a) liberalization of trade and finances, which opens the economy to the world market; b) deregulation, which removes the state from economic decision-making; c) privatization of formerly public spheres that could hamper capital accumulation if criteria of public interest over private profit were left operative. Grounded in the assumptions of neo-classical economics, the neo-liberal model is justified by the need to generate a trade surplus to accommodate debt service payments and reduce trade deficits, the alleged "inefficiency" of the public sector, the need to control inflation, to close budget deficits, and restore fiscal solvency and macroeconomic equilibrium. Trade liberalization and a reallocation of resources to the external sector are intended to increase exports and by definition result in a process of rearticulation and integration into the global economy. This opening to the world market is accompanied by the privatization of "inefficient" public sectors and internal liberalization, such as deregulation of financial systems and labor laws, in order to attract investment and allocate resources "efficiently." Fiscal solvency is to be achieved through austerity programs involving expenditure reductions and revenue increases, which usually entail cuts in social programs, regressive taxes on consumption, the elimination of subsidies, public-sector layoffs, and a rise in interest rates.

Notwithstanding the ideological claims of its promoters, the neo-liberal model is driven more pragmatically by the breakdown of the earlier Keynesian-redistributive nation-state based accumulation strategies in the face of transnationalization and the need for a renovated policy regime capable of facilitating the new global model. Indeed, in the larger context, disequilibrium itself is a consequence of the breakdown of earlier national accumulation structures. The neo-liberal program is rational vis-à-vis the *logic* of global capital accumulation.[83] The model generates the overall conditions for the profitable ("efficient") renewal of capital accumulation. Internal conditions of profitability are determined by compatibility of the local with the global environment. Adjustment creates the policy environment and the market signals for a shift in resources to external sectors. Economic reactivation in each adjusted country is achieved through the introduction or expansion of activities linked to the global economy and the integration of "national" accumulation circuits into globalized circuits. However, from the viewpoint of a broader *social logic* the model is irrational. With few exceptions, neo-liberal adjustment results in a decline in popular consumption and social conditions, a rise in poverty, immizeration, and insecurity, "food riots," heightened inequalities, social polarization, and resultant political conflict.[84]

By synchronizing each national economic environment to an integrated global economic environment, neo-liberalism is the policy "grease" of global capitalism. It keeps the gears of the system in synch with one another. Greased by neo-liberalism, global capitalism tears down all non-market structures that have in the past placed limits on, or acted as a protective layer against, the accumulation of capital. Non-market spheres of human activity—public spheres managed by states and private spheres linked to community and family—are being broken up, commodified, and transferred to capital. By prying open and making accessible to transnational capital every layer of the social fabric, neo-liberalism disembeds the global economy from global society, and the state cedes to the market as the sole organizing power in the economic and social sphere. Nonetheless, the economic and the political merge here in a broader project of hegemony. Restructuring gives an immanent class bias to agents of the external sector. These agents tend to fuse with political managers of the neo-liberal state and to coalesce gradually, in a process checkered by contradictions and conflict, into a transnationalized fraction of the elite.

This local elite is expected to become hegemonic and to construct new national "historic blocs" that tie local social order to transnational order. The mechanics of this process can be quite complex and require "concrete analysis of concrete situations," as I undertake for Central America in subsequent chapters.

By the early 1990s, global elites had achieved what appeared as a veritable Gramscian consensus around the neo-liberal project. It was indeed a *consensus* in that: it represented a congruence of interests among dominant groups in the global system; these interests were being advanced through institutions that commanded power (the world's national states and the TNS apparatus); and this consensus had achieved ideological hegemony by setting the parameters for, and the limits to, debate among subordinate groups around the world on options and alternative projects. In this sense, the "Washington consensus" reflected the emergence of a new global capitalist hegemonic bloc under the leadership of a transnational elite. However, cracks in the consensus had become apparent by the close of the century in the face of the deep social contradictions generated by the model. Having achieved initial adjustment around the world, neo-liberalism may prove to be a transitory feature of global capitalism, an issue I will consider in the concluding chapter.

But the transnational agenda also had an explicitly political component. If the economic component was to make the world available to capital, the political component was to "make the world safe for capital." As I have analyzed at considerable length in earlier research, developing the social control systems and political institutions most propitious for achieving a stable world environment revolved around the promotion of "democracy," or what is more accurately called *polyarchy*.[85] This refers to a system in which a small group actually rules, and participation in decision-making by the majority is confined to choosing among competing elites in tightly controlled electoral processes. This type of "low-intensity democracy" does not involve power (*cratos*) of the people (*demos*), much less an end to class domination or to the *substantive inequality* that has grown exponentially under the global economy. Transitions to polyarchy should be seen in light of the changing nature of transnational social control under globalization.

The crisis of elite rule that had developed throughout the Third World in the 1970s and 1980s, in the context of globalization, was resolved through transitions to polyarchies. What transpired in these contested transitions was an effort by transnational dominant groups to reconstitute hegemony through a change in the mode of political domination, from the coercive systems of social control exercised by authoritarian and dictatorial regimes to the more consensually based systems of the new polyarchies. At stake was what type of social order—the emergent global capitalist order or some popular alternative—would emerge in the wake of authoritarianism. Masses pushed for a deeper popular democratization while emergent transnationalized elites, who had behind them the structural power of the global economy and the inordinate political and ideological influence that this brings, and who often counted on direct US political and military intervention, were able to gain hegemony over democratization movements and steer the breakup of authoritarianism into polyarchic outcomes. This was very evident, as we shall see, in the transitions in Central America.

Polyarchy has been promoted by the transnational elite as the political counterpart to neo-liberalism. Interaction and economic integration on a world scale are obstructed by authoritarian or dictatorial political arrangements, which are unable to manage the expansion of social intercourse associated with the global economy. Authoritarian systems have tended to unravel as globalizing pressures break up embedded forms of coercive political authority, dislocate traditional communities and social patterns, and stir masses of people to demand the democratization of social life. The demands, grievances, and aspirations of the popular classes tend to become neutralized less through direct repression than through ideological mechanisms, political co-optation and disorganization, and the limits imposed by the global economy. While mediating inter-class relations, polyarchy is also a more propitious institutional arrangement for the resolution of conflicts among dominant groups. With its mechanisms for intra-elite compromise and accommodation and for hegemonic incorporation of popular majorities, polyarchy is better equipped in the new global environment to legitimize the political authority of dominant groups and to achieve enough of a minimally stable political environment, under the conflict-ridden and fluid conditions of emergent global society, for global capitalism to operate.

The universal imposition of economic or "market discipline" as the principal worldwide means of social control has tended to substitute extra-economic or political discipline exercised by states as sites of direct social control. Transitions to polyarchy are in this sense adjustments of political structure to the economic changes brought about by capitalist globalization. The emergence of global networks of accumulation require stable rules for economic competition that new capitalist and professional sectors are eager to construct while excluding the rest of the population from meaningful participation in economic and political life.

Transitions from authoritarianism to polyarchy in Latin America and elsewhere afforded transnational elites the opportunity to reorganize state institutions and create a more favorable institutional framework for a deepening of neo-liberal adjustment.[86] The transnational elite demonstrated a remarkable ability to utilize the structural power of transnational capital over individual countries as a sledgehammer against popular grassroots movements for fundamental change in social structures. Indeed, it is the structural power of global capitalism to impose discipline through the market that (usually) makes unnecessary the all-pervasive coercive forms of political authority exercised by authoritarian regimes. The shift from authoritarianism to polyarchy as the dominant form of political authority in much of the world represents a shift from coercive to consensual forms of social control at the transnational level, or in the Gramscian sense, the shift to global hegemony.

Conceptualizing Global-Regional-Local Change

Global capitalism is a concrete totality, but the world economy is not a general abstraction. On the one hand, it is the laws of capitalist development that drive the overall system and that also constitute the unifying basis and the common linkage of all the different constituent elements of the system, such as "national" and regional economies and social formations. On the other hand, the world economy becomes manifest in specific regions and their interrelations. When we study one region, such as Central America, we are studying a piece of a larger system. The larger system cannot be understood without looking at its "pieces" and how they fit together. Neither can any "piece" be understood outside of how it fits into the larger, and encompassing, system. National and regional studies (such as Central America) constitute concrete and specific mappings (spatial-political) of the ways in which general tendencies of capitalism manifest themselves and are not discrete studies that are radically different as objects of investigation from other parts of the system.

The transition from the nation-state to the transnational phase of capitalism involves changes that take place in each individual country and region *reciprocal* to, and in dialectical interplay with, changes of systemic importance at the level of the global system. A critical focus of a renewed transnational studies should be exploration into the dynamic of change at the local, national, and regional levels in tandem with movement at the level of the global whole. The concern should be about how movement and change in the global whole are manifest in particular countries or regions, but with the focus on the dialectical reciprocity of the two levels, that is, on the dialectic between historically determined structures and new transnational structures. Such an approach requires a supersession of the nation-state mode of analysis. But what changes by superseding this mode of analysis is not the object of inquiry per se (for example, Central America) but our understanding of the nature and meaning of those changes taking place within particular countries and regions. Transnational processes and globalizing dynamics are "filtered through" particular nation-states and regions. They unfold in the context of what Holm and Sorensen have called *uneven globalization*.[87]

Uneven globalization implies that the essential economic process has lagged in certain regions (for example, a good portion of Africa). But the pressures emanating from the substructural process are felt around the world, including as they are "filtered through" policies, such as those of the United States or of TNS apparatuses, and these superstructural changes are at work in every region. Most world industrial production, for instance, has not shifted to Africa and has largely shifted selectively to Latin American, Asian, and Eastern European zones. But the *general* process of macroeconomic restructuring associated with globalization and a changing global division of labor has affected virtually every country and region of the world (witness the application of Structural Adjustment Programs—SAPs—in almost every country of Africa). The sets of policies developed by the centers of world power in response to globalizing pressures, such as promoting neo-liberalism and polyarchy, are applied throughout the world. More generally, globalization is characterized by related, contingent, and unequal transformations. To invoke globalization as an explanation for historic changes and contemporary dynamics does not mean that the *particular* events or changes identified with the process are happening all over the world, much less in the same way. It does mean that the events or changes that take place are understood as a consequence of globalized power relations and social structures.

This study of development and social change in Central America departs from an analysis of the larger global system. The locus of analysis is the mediation of distinct social forces in the dialectic of transformations taking place at the level of the global system and transformations in particular nations and regions. It is not possible to understand anything about global society without studying a concrete region and its particular circumstances; a part of a totality, in its relation to that totality. All knowledge is historically situated and, as Immanuel Wallerstein insists, requires a synthesis of nomothetic and ideographic accounts. The general is always (and only) manifested in the specific; the universal in the particular. We do not want to hypostatize ideal-types; all historical studies would be unnecessary if theory and history actually corresponded as such. Universal (worldwide, general) processes manifest themselves in the concrete local forms and these must be the starting point for understanding general historical and social processes.

Transnational Processes and Transitions to Global Capitalism

A Globalization Model of Third World Transitions

Transition as Rearticulation and Integration into Global Economy and Society

The term "transition" became the vogue in the 1980s and 1990s, referring to two different but related processes around the world.[88] One was the shift from dictatorial and authoritarian regimes in the Third World to "democratic," or polyarchic regimes. Academic literature on "democratic transitions" and new "democratization" theories proliferated. The other process was the transition in the former Soviet bloc and some Third World revolutionary countries from non-capitalist to capitalist systems and their integration into global capitalism. These two processes, encapsulated in the popularized cliché "market democracy," were actually component dimensions subsumed in a more encompassing process, which has affected every country and region of the world, of rearticulation and/or integration into the emergent global system. This structural process is the macro-historical-structural backdrop to conjunctural events around the world over the past thirty years. Integration into global society is the causal structural dynamic that underlies the events we have witnessed in nations and regions all around the world over the past few decades. The breakup of national economic, political, and social structures is reciprocal to the gradual breakup, starting in the 1970s, of a pre-globalization nation-state based world order. New economic, political, and social structures emerge as each nation and region becomes integrated into emergent transnational structures and processes.

The term *transition* therefore, as it is used in this study, refers to the manifold changes that take place in different countries and regions as they become swept up in globalizing processes. By "transitions" in the Third World, I mean a prolonged period of change in the social structure of particular nations and regions, reciprocal to and in dialectical interplay with changes at the level of the global system. Each country and region enters global society on the basis of specific national histories and structures, and therefore the worldwide transition has taken a myriad of different forms and specific dimensions in each region. Neo-liberalism, as a policy model for establishing the conditions that allow for transnational capital mobility and globalized circuits of production and distribution, is a general component of transitions to global capitalism. But it has taken different forms in different countries and regions. In the former Soviet bloc, the transition has involved political regime change, from authoritarian communist party rule to (tenuous) polyarchic regimes, and also the very rapid imposition of a capitalist economy over the former planned economies. In many First World countries, the transition has entailed the switch from a manufacturing to a service base, dismantling of social welfare states, a restructuring of classes and labor markets, and so on, as Keynesian social structures of accumulation and the class alliances they involved that corresponded to the nation-state stage of world capitalism unravelled and gave way to a new post-Fordist structure. What concerns us here is an analysis of the Central American transitions as regional-specific processes of integration into the emergent global economy and society.

While it is therefore legitimate to discuss transitions to polyarchy ("democracy") or transitions to capitalism ("a market economy"), it is important to clarify from the outset that by transition I do not refer to conventional notions of "transitions to democracy" in the Third World or of regime change conceived as changes in sets of state managers and political systems that are separate from historic movement in social structure. Dominant "democratization" paradigms such as those put forward by O'Donnell et al., or by Diamond et al., disaggregate social totalities in a way that obscures rather than elucidates historic movement.[89] These paradigms advance a narrow institutional definition of democracy that rests theoretically on structural-functionalism, in which different spheres of the social totality are separated and assigned a functional autonomy, such that movement may occur in distinct spheres independent of the totality and political change is analyzed as the evolution of functionally independent institutions. By assigning a functional autonomy to the political sphere they obscure our understanding of political regime change as a subset of broader patterns of structural change over time, for example, change in Central America from the 1960s to the twenty-first century.[90] Characterizing the notion of "transitions to democracy" in Central America and elsewhere in the Third World is also problematic because it assumes the countries in question are actually in the process of becoming democratic societies, something which I do not see occurring in Central America or in much of the Third World (or the former Second and the First World as well). Authentic democratization based on power (*cratos*) of the people (*demos*) has not taken place, and movement is away from, rather than towards, any meaningful democratic content to social change.

Transition, therefore, to recapitulate, refers to a change from one set of social arrangements to another. In this sense, we can speak of a transition as change in social structure and we can develop modes of classification and comparison of such social change. Transitions from authoritarianism to polyarchy are transitions in the particular mode of social control and in the form of the exercise of political domination. Similarly, in those countries that were either pre-capitalist (for example, under a predominantly feudal/tributary mode of production) or those that were non-capitalist or post-capitalist (for example, the former Soviet bloc countries), we can refer to transitions to capitalism as change in the economic organization of society, along with concomitant change in productive structures and also property and class relations. The concept of transition as used here subsumes particular changes in social structure under overall change in a social formation.

Central America from the 1960s into the 1990s underwent a transition in the predominant mode of social control from authoritarianism to polyarchy. But it did not undergo a transition to capitalism. The region has been integrated into the capitalist world economy since the sixteenth century, and capitalism has been the predominant mode of production since at least the nineteenth century. However, capitalism did dramatically expand in the thirty-year period, largely displacing pre-capitalist production relations, as the region became rearticulated to larger world structures as globalization advanced and in consonance with the emergence of the global economy.

From an International to a Global Division of Labor and Regional Profiles in the Global Economy

Epochal changes in the system of world capitalism have had transformative effects on the world as a whole and on each region integrated into or rearticulated to the system. The birth of capitalism in Europe and its initial mercantile expansion reoriented nearly every society in the world towards newly formed webs of interconnection, including new world trading patterns, the demand for novel products, changes in the labor and productive activities of most peoples and civilizations and an international division of labor. Mercantilism also involved the unprecedented deployment of coercion on a world scale to destroy whole civilizations, impose colonial authority, reorient production, and organize labor supplies. The transition from mercantilism to classical competitive capitalism brought with it a new wave of core expansion and colonization that similarly transformed the international division of labor, productive structures, classes, and polities around the world, and also generalized the nation-state as the modern political and institutional form. As competitive capitalism gave way to corporate, or monopoly capitalism, each country and region again experienced dramatic economic, social, political and related changes. In this way, world society has been continuously constituted and reconstituted by the spread of a social system at the world level, and gradations in this spread offer clues to patterns of change over time and place (this is the theoretical insight of world-system theory).

Global capitalism is now having a similar transformative effect on every country and region of the world. The current epochal shift from a world to a global economy and from a nation-state based to a transnational world order has dramatic implications for local, national, and regional processes. Changes in the economic structure provide the material basis for changes in the complex of superstructural practices and institutions, including the political, class structure, and so forth. The fundamental focus in analyzing transitions to global capitalism around the world is change in a particular country or region's productive base and in its place within the global economy. Economic analysis provides the basis and starting point for the broader analysis of change in the entire social order.

Globalization induces a reorganization of productive structures in each nation reciprocal to the reorganization of global production, a process through which each national economy becomes subordinated to the global economy, and new economic activities linked to globalization come to dominate. The center–periphery division of labor created by modern colonialism reflected a particular spatial configuration in the law of uneven development which is becoming transformed by globalization. The process deepens diversity as much among population groups *within* countries as among countries and regions. The shift from the predominant worldwide model of Keynesian or Fordist accumulation to post-Fordist flexible accumulation models tends to accentuate the division of labor within specific countries into "core" and "peripheral" labor pools, while the space, or geography, between these groups dissipates. At the same time, however, new patterns of flexible accumulation accelerate diversity and uneven development among countries and regions in accordance with the matrix of factor cost considerations and the configuration of diverse social forces, historic factors, and contingent variables. Unequal exchanges—material, political, cultural—implied in a social division of labor on a world scale are not captured so much in the concept of an *international* division of labor as in a *global* division of labor which implies differential participation in global production according to social standing and not necessarily geographic location. Social order is increasingly organized globally, and with it inequality—the regenerative consequences of capitalist social relations—is organized globally, involving new forms of poverty and wealth and labor hierarchies that cut across national boundaries.

Saskia Sassen has suggested that the international mobility of capital creates new specific forms of articulation among different geographic areas and transformations in the role played by these areas in the world economy, for example, zones of export processing, offshore banking, global cities as nodes of worldwide management and control.[91] Here I wish to accomplish two things; first, to apply this proposition to Central America to explore the region's changing articulation to the global system in light of the transnationalization of capital; second, to expand Sassen's focus to concrete social forces in historic struggles and how the outcome of these struggles becomes central to the types of rearticulation that regions and populations will acquire and what modified profiles they will display in the global system. The particular *form* of rearticulation that emerges through transnational processes has varied from region to region. As national and regional productive apparatuses are fragmented, restructured, and integrated into the emergent global productive apparatus, each country and region acquires a new profile as components of a globally integrated economy. The webs and structures of globalized production exhibit numerous segments and mixes of geographically scattered activities with varied value-added contributions, and levels of benefit for local communities. They generate novel and fluid spatial agglomerations of economic activity. The form of this profile is determined by sets of historic factors and by certain configurations of social forces, as well as by contingent variables, such as the natural and human resources with which each region is endowed, and so on.

This "economic regionalism," in which different regions acquire profiles in a changing global division of labor, is best seen as a fluid rather than a fixed structure and as a transitionary parentheses between decaying national productive systems and the further fragmentation and spatial reorganization of emerging global production systems. Different regional contributions to the global division of labor tend to form part of global commodity chains, or globally dispersed and decentralized production processes. Specialization in the world economy, rather than specialization of economic activities within a national framework, notes McMichael, began to emerge from the 1970s and on as the criterion of development.[92] The basis of "economic regionalism" is the fragmentation of functional integration of constituent elements of globalized production processes. "The technical division of labor associated with the hierarchies of the global production system now overlays the social division," notes McMichael. "Instead of countries specializing in an export sector (manufacturing or agriculture), production sites in countries specialize in a constituent part of a production process spread across several countries. The global decentralization and fragmentation of production processes indicates a shift from the production of national products to the transnational production of world products.[93]

What concerns us here is the particular profile that Central America is acquiring under a new global division of labor and the type of social, political, cultural and related institutional changes in the region that are bound up with the transformation of its productive base and rearticulation to the global economy. In Latin America, more generally, the pre-globalization model of society was replaced in the late twentieth and early twenty-first centuries with a new transnational model. In broad strokes, the national model involved: national development projects, particularly along the lines of ISI and the expansion of domestic markets, which was a variant of Fordism; the salience of national classes tied to these markets (national bourgeoisie and subordinate groups); national political projects (often populism under authoritarian arrangements), and so forth. In the transnational model of society ISI has been replaced by a full neo-liberal opening to the global economy and what has been termed in international development discourse Export-Led Development (ELD) that favor new circuits of production and distribution linked to the global economy, and often organized along the lines of flexible accumulation. Transnational classes have gained ascendance over national classes. Authoritarian systems have been replaced by polyarchic political systems. A culture of hyperindividualism and consumerism has eclipsed nationalist and developmental ideologies. We shall see that Central America does conform to this Latin America-wide pattern of transition to global capitalism, but with its own particular circumstances, variations, and subprocesses.

A Model of Transnational Processes

We have seen in this chapter that the changes involved in this transition to global capitalism are multifarious. The analytical instrument I develop for understanding these changes are *transnational processes*. By transnational processes I mean the diverse structural, institutional, and organizational changes associated with each country and region's incorporation into emergent global society. This includes the economic and concomitant social, political, and cultural changes associated with the transition to global capitalism, as discussed in this chapter.[94] A *typology of transnational processes* is an analytical construct that facilitates analysis of these changes. Presented as an ideal-type, transnational processes include the following four aspects, *inter alia*, which taken together constitute a globalization model of Third World transitions:

a) subordination and integration of formerly national and regional economies into the global economy, including the introduction of new economic activities. Different countries and regions assume new specialized profiles in the global division of labor;

b) a complete class restructuring, in which domestic classes tend to become globalized, pre-globalization classes such as peasantries and artisans tend to disappear, and new classes and class fractions linked to the global economy emerge and become dominant. This is part of what I refer to more broadly as *transnational class formation,* a process unfolding in both North and South;

c) the transnational project of neo-liberalism and polyarchy takes hold as the hegemonic project under the guidance of transnationalized fractions of the elite;

d) local political systems and civil societies become transnationalized, and states become integrated externally into supranational institutions and forums that gradually assume more and more functions that corresponded to the nation-state in the pre-globalization period. National states remain important, but they become transmission belts and local executers of the transnational elite project.

The next three chapters explore how these processes have unfolded in Central America.

2

The Politics of Globalization and the Transitions in Central America

The Central American conflict captured world attention from the 1970s to the 1990s—its causes and outcome, and its broader implications—but faded from view after pacification. How do we account for the regional conflict? The more proximate causes, as the literature on the subject notes, were: the dramatic growth in poverty and inequality associated with the particular model of capitalist development that took place; a rigid authoritarian political structure that blocked more consensual forms of social change; and the particular behavioral response of different collective agents, such as the revolutionary movements, the United States, and so on. I will discuss these proximate causes in this chapter and show how globalization exercised a structural determinacy over them. This chapter situates Central America as a site of transnational processes. It starts as an overview of the Central American transition, and then presents case studies in transitions to global capitalism for each of the five republics. Each country study has its own unique focus or dimensions that are emphasized, as I have tried to capture what I believe to be the most important subprocesses and dynamics that characterized each case of globalization. But, while attentive to historic particularities, these studies also place the transitions in comparative perspective and highlight several key themes that emerge from each case and underscore a certain underlying uniformity throughout the region in the process of globalization and social change. These key themes include: 1) the social, political, and military crises that followed the region-wide breakdown of the old model of accumulation; 2) the rise of transnational fractions and how they became organized; 3) contestation over the state in each republic and their eventual capture by transnationally oriented groups; 4) neo-liberal restructuring and the introduction of new economic activities representing the region-wide emergence of the new transnational model of development; and 5) the preponderant role of the United States and other institutions of the TNS.

Central America as a Site of Transnational Processes

Central America's Integration into the Global Economy and Society

The economies, states, polities, class structure, and external relations of the five Central American republics—Costa Rica, Guatemala, El Salvador, Honduras, and Nicaragua—were fundamentally transformed from the 1960s into the early twenty-first century. This thirty-year transition in the region can be characterized as Central America's ongoing, gradual, highly conflictive, and highly contradictory, rearticulation to the world economy and global society.

Central America was first *created*, and then integrated into the world capitalist system through colonial conquest in the early sixteenth century, as part of the system's genesis and the period of primitive accumulation of capital (mercantilism). In this process, the region's pre-colonial social fabric was thoroughly transformed and a colonial structure established and sustained until well into the nineteenth century, despite formal independence early in 1821. In the latter part of the nineteenth century, Central America deepened its insertion into world capitalism with the introduction of coffee and other export products that linked the country firmly to the world market at a time of its rapid expansion and extension, and had profound transformative effects on class and socioeconomic structure and on the internal political system. This second fundamental internal transformation, the establishment of what Torres Rivas has termed "agro-export societies,"[1] coincided with a new phase in world capitalism, characterized by a second wave of core colonial expansion, the export of capital, and the supplanting of classical competitive capitalism by monopoly capitalism. The region's insertion was further deepened and transformed in the twentieth century, and particularly in the post-World War II period, with the expansion of agro-exports and Import-Substitution Industrialization (ISI), through the Central American Common Market (CACM). Since the 1970s, what has transpired is a transition to a qualitatively different mode of insertion corresponding to globalization.

Between the 1970s and the 1990s, the typology of transnational processes discussed in chapter one has taken hold as the region has become integrated into the emergent global economy and society. This integration has involved the following:

Economy: maquiladora production (particularly of garments), tourism and hospitality, non-traditional agricultural exports, and the export of Central American labor and remittances from Central Americans working abroad, have risen dramatically in prominence as the four new dynamic economic activities linking the region to the global economy and have begun to overshadow the region's traditional agro-export model, which corresponded to the pre-globalization period. Neo-liberal restructuring has advanced in every country in the region. The ISI model of populist development has been replaced by the neo-liberal model of free-market capitalism, including sweeping liberalization and privatization.

Class Restructuring: The Central American peasantry, artisan class, national industrial and other pre-globalization classes have tended to gradually disintegrate, and three principal globalization groups have come to the fore: transnationalized fractions of the bourgeoisie, technocrats, and professionals tied to the new economic activities; new urban and rural working classes; and a new class of supernumeraries, or superfluous labor pools. A huge portion of the latter have migrated to the United States, where it constitutes a denationalized immigrant labor pool.

Polities and Social Forces: At the level of the dominant project, the old authoritarian regimes have crumbled through transitions to polyarchy, and leftist movements that in the 1980s posed an anti-systemic alternative to integration in the emergent global order have been defeated or transformed. In each Central American country, a transnationalized "technocratic" or New Right fraction gained hegemony within the dominant classes and pushed the transnational agenda of neo-liberalism and the consolidation of polyarchies through diverse institutions, including political parties, states, and the organs of civil society. At the level of subordinate group projects, the model of revolutionary change through capturing states and attempting to effect a transformation of the social structure failed. At the same time, the incursion of global capitalism into the social fabric combined with the collective experience of the revolutionary upheaval has generated an awakening in civil society and new bottom-up social movements.

State and Political System: Each Central American state has been reduced and transformed. The International Financial Institutes (IFIs) and diverse United Nations and Organization of American States (OAS) units and other transnational actors have come increasingly to assume functions of states through the design and imposition of economic policies, management of peace accords, sponsorship of institution-building, and so on. The five Central American states have moved gradually towards supranational integration. This integration is political, taking place through new formal and informal forums, such as the *Sistema de Integracion Centroamericana,* the Central American Parliament, and includes the negotiation of a new free trade zone based on collective integration into the North America Free Trade Agreement (NAFTA), and beyond it, the global economy.

Chapters three and four will document and explore this new transnational model of society. First, I analyze in this chapter the social forces in struggle during the 1960s–1990s transition and their determination in the outcome of that transition.

Social Structures and Social Forces in Central America:
An Overview of the Transitions

Seen in analytical abstraction, the typology of transnational processes presented above is predicated on the notion of a shift from one set of structures to another. The first set corresponds to the nation-state phase of world capitalism, and the second to the still-emerging transnational stage, in which transnational processes take hold and begin to exercise a structural determinacy in the regional social formation. In the dialectical approach, the new germinates out of the contradictions manifest within the old. Social structures are constructed and constantly reconstructed through the struggles of diverse social forces. Social structures are not only subject to change but in fact generate within themselves the forces that bring about that change. Relations of domination and subordination produce conflicts of objective interests over prevailing social arrangements; out of the unravelling and resolution (or non-resolution) of these conflicts comes social change. This is an ongoing and open-ended historical process.

Sets of structures usually become stabilized during periods of equilibrium, or stalemate, among contending social forces, and then unravel as internal contradictions mature and give way to new upheavals. From the 1960s and on the post-WWII social structure in Central America could not be reproduced and began to unravel.[2] As Carlos Vilas notes, this was a period of very rapid—and *successful*—capitalist development in the Isthmus. The massive dislocations brought about by capitalist development and the new sets of social contradictions, rather than the lack of changes and development, spawned the social crisis, the political, and later the military conflict that engulfed the region.[3] As foreign capital poured into Central America in the 1960s and 1970s, as part of the US-promoted Central American Common Market, it integrated the region into the emergent global economy, displacing the peasantry and local artisans, and creating new capitalist fractions opposed to the type of "crony capitalism" that traditional autocrats such as the Somozas in Nicaragua or the strongmen and military rulers in the other republics tended to practice. All this laid the structural basis for the social upheavals of the 1970s–1990s.

Each expansion in the world economy has produced a rearticulation of Central America to it, including the transformation of social forces and the restructuring of economies, states, and power blocs. The picture I present here divides the underlying historic movement in the region in recent decades, which is the gradual introduction of globalizing dynamics and transnational processes, into a three-part periodization for the purpose of analytical conception. It then transposes over that periodization an analysis of three distinct blocs of social forces in dispute over the social structure in Central America. The three overlapping periods are: 1) the "reign of the oligarchies" (1945–1970s). This period, reciprocal to the nation-state phase of world capitalism, stabilized during the dramatic post-WWII expansion of the world economy under US domination that followed the 1930s crisis of world capitalism; 2) the period of revolutionary ascendance and revolutionary challenge to oligarchic dictatorships (1970s–1980s). This period represented the response of social forces in the region to oligarchic dictatorship within the structural backdrop of worldwide stagnation and instability that began in the 1970s. In turn, this period of global uncertainty reflected the dislocations and restructuring associated with the breakup of a world order based on nation-state capitalism; and 3) the period of the emergence, ascendance, and hegemony of the transnational project for Central America (1980s–early twenty-first century). This period is still open-ended. It is reciprocal to the incipient consolidation and hegemony of the new global capitalism.

Three broad social forces representing three distinct projects for the region were in dispute during the 1960s–1990s upheavals and transition. The landed oligarchies and dominant groups tied to the traditional agro-export model sought to sustain and reproduce the old model of capital accumulation, and the particular set of social privileges and relations of domination based on authoritarian political systems. Oligarchic domination was the organic expression of the actual socioeconomic structure. It was the outcome of an intense period of class and social struggle in the region between the two World Wars, and particularly the 1930s crisis of world capitalism. These struggles ranged from Sandino's 1926–33 movement in Nicaragua, to the failed 1932 uprising and subsequent *matanza* (massacre) in El Salvador, to the CIA-orchestrated overthrow of Jacobo Arbenz in 1954 marking the end of the reformist period in Guatemala. The dominant groups granted an unusual amount of autonomy to civilian-military dictatorships to contain the contradictions generated by the socioeconomic structure itself, including the threat from below *and* their own disorganization and internal divisions. As the "autumn of the oligarchs" approached, the popular sectors and the mass revolutionary movements sought radical reformism, such as mass redistribution of land, as well as more far-reaching revolutionary and socialist-oriented alternatives for the region, that would have deeply undermined the class structure, upset relations of domination, and redistributed power and resources in favor of popular majorities.

As the regional conflict unfolded in the 1970s and 1980s, on the surface it appeared as a bipolar contest between the old oligarchies and the popular revolutionary movements. But, in fact, globalizing dynamics had begun to have a transformative effect on local social forces. A New Right gradually cohered in the 1980s, in fits and bouts, into local transnationalized fractions of dominant elites and acquired its own political protagonism. Jeffrey Paige, in his study *Coffee and Power: Revolution and the Rise of Democracy in Central America*, argues that the Central American agro-industrial fraction broke with the agrarian fraction in the 1980s crisis.[4] I am pushing this line of analysis further. A fraction tied to new economic activities and the global economy broke with the old agro-export oligarchy that included agrarian and agro-industrial economic groups. Just as class relations changed from the heyday of the coffee economy of the first half of the twentieth century to the more diversified agro-export economy of the post-WWII period, these class relations have changed again under the current economic reorganization of the globalization period.

The project of the new dominant groups was to advance the agenda of the transnational elite. This transnational fraction was not a group that came into being from outside of the traditional oligarchy but from within, from the same family networks.[5] Often this fraction and the new economic groups represented, literally, a new generation, sometimes referred to as the "young Turks," trained in business administration and economics in the United States, who were aware that it would not be viable for them to simply take over the economic enterprises and continue the same economic activities or political practices of their parents. Put differently, they were becoming cognizant of the structural differences between the sources of wealth and elite power of the previous generation and those that a new historic conjuncture presented to them.

These groups' prospects for accumulating further wealth and privilege were less linked to restoring the traditional agro-exports and industries under pre-1980s social relations as they were to converting the region into a new export platform. They sought to submit backward oligarchic property relations to a capitalist modernization through a program of neo-liberal restructuring and to a new "competitive" insertion into the global economy. The New Right project sought to modernize the state and society without any fundamental deconcentration of property and wealth, and without any class redistribution of political and economic power. It also promoted, together with the United States, transitions from authoritarian to polyarchic political systems. The immediate aim was to preempt the movements for a more far-reaching popular democratization through immediate polyarchic reform, such as the replacement of military by civilian personnel and "demonstration elections." But beyond this conjunctural consideration, any renewal of capital accumulation in the region would require a political system with the promise of achieving more lasting social stability through consensual modes of social control rather than the old oligarchic dictatorships. Developing viable polyarchic political systems involved demilitarization, peace negotiations, the institutionalization of procedurally correct electoral processes, states with a functional separation of powers, and so on.

The persistence of an oligarchic political structure combined with rapid capitalist development spurred on by the region's incipient integration into the emergent global economy in the 1960s and 1970s had sparked the revolutionary upheavals by the late 1970s. There was a disjuncture between the political superstructure molded from the conditions of the preceding period and the economic changes that were taking place. The political system was hostile to capitalist modernization. It had to change. And it did change. The revolutionary movements succeeded in breaking the hegemony of the landed oligarchy and rich industrialists and financial groups that had come into existence within the CACM. However, due to a complex confluence of factors, these social forces were unable to impose and stabilize their project of a radical redistributive and socialist-oriented reconstruction of the region. One of these factors was massive US political and military intervention. A second was the contradictions and weaknesses internal to the revolutionary project itself, in the context of a changing world order. At the structural level, the emergence of the global economy and the growing power of transnational capital and the world market to impose discipline on anti-systemic movements made inviable the revolutionary project. A third was the changing composition of the dominant classes, their socioeconomic articulation, and their political-ideological project.

These three factors cannot be separated; they are internally related and should be seen as different dimensions of a process whose structural determinacy was the emergence of the global economy and the influence of globalizing pressures on the complex set of regional agents and social, economic, and political structures. This study is limited largely to structural analysis. However, the notion of determinacy here is not one of functionalist teleology. Collective behavioral responses to changing structures in themselves shape, modify, and feed back into structural change. It was the threat of revolution from the popular classes that made inviable the reproduction of the old structures and that led to US intervention. US policymakers changed the objective of interventionism, from the mid-1980s and on, from a military defeat of revolutionary forces through counterinsurgency and counterrevolution to a more thorough political and economic restructuring of the region and its social forces via the linkage of Central America to emergent global structures. This included a shift in policy to "democracy promotion" as a means to neutralize through *incorporation* the threat posed by anti-systemic forces in the broader effort to construct a new historic bloc in the region.

In turn, from the mid-1980s and on, changes in the US strategy and new opportunities as well as constraints opened by globalization and a changing world order for the distinct social forces in dispute accelerated the articulation of alternative political-ideological discourse and projects among sectors of the dominant groups that would gradually cohere into a New Right elite. The emergence of the neo-liberal New Right in the 1980s in each of the Central American countries was thus, in part, a result of the revolutionary upsurge, which altered the dominant power blocs in each country. It was also, in part, a result of the changes in the world order with the emergence of the global economy and a transnational elite as both a political and economic protagonist. The insurgent New Right groups would wage battles in every country against the old economic groups. They would establish a host of new business associations, elite think-tanks, and political parties. They vied for, and achieved, hegemony over the elite as a whole in the 1980s. They turned to political mobilization and went on in the 1990s to struggle for, and win, state power and to implement the program of global capitalism in the region.

This outcome was historically contingent and *not* predetermined. There *could* have been a very different path of historical development in Central America, if for instance the revolutionary forces had seized state power in El Salvador and Guatemala. An accumulation of region-wide counter-hegemonic forces could have expanded into the Caribbean, including Granada, which had a revolution in 1979, Cuba, Jamaica, Guyana, and so on. The global economy would have come down hard on the entire region (as it, along with US intervention, did anyway) and would probably have prevented a revolutionary transformation. But a different (for example, deeper and more radical) transformation of socioeconomic structures and class forces at a region-wide level throughout the Greater Caribbean Basin could have established a different foundation upon which the region would have been integrated into the global economy and society.

The recomposition of the social order involved a new social structure. Political regime change in each country (except Costa Rica) was only one aspect of a broader transition in the nature of political authority and the mode of social control in the region. What took place structurally from the 1960s to the 1990s was the breakup of authoritarian systems on the heels of the mass socioeconomic disruptions and political mobilization caused by the massive entry of foreign capital through the CACM, new economic activities, and social class protagonists, which signalled the beginnings of globalization in the Isthmus. The outcome of the social upheaval was the partial displacement of the old oligarchy, the conditional defeat of the broad popular sectors in Central America, and the conditional victory of the new dominant groups.

My analysis runs contrary to conventional wisdom, according to which the old oligarchies had disappeared by the end of the 1980s but neither the popular forces nor their adversaries, the new dominant groups and the US, could prevail. According to this view, a stalemate had been reached. This stalemate created the conditions for a historic compromise between contending social forces; a "modus vivendi." Peace settlements and processes of democratization and demilitarization would allow for competition through elections and peaceful mobilization. This conventional interpretation fails to note that the gross social and economic inequalities which in the first place gave rise to the conflict were *exacerbated* from the 1970s to the 1990s. The dominant groups did not give up their power and privilege. A redistribution of property and wealth was not on the agenda of the peace negotiations. Not only did the peace accords not threaten the established social and economic structures; they paved the way for the full implementation of the project of global capitalism in Central America. The structure of property and socioeconomic inequality has not been significantly altered. The lives of the vast majority of Central Americans have got worse, not better. The larger system of world capitalism that sustains the regional order is more firmly embedded and hegemonic in Central America than before the upheaval. The popular majority was conditionally defeated in what it set out to do—fundamentally alter the social order in its favor.

This outcome—the conditional defeat of the popular sectors and the conditional victory of the new dominant groups—was formalized in the internationally sponsored peace negotiations of the late 1980s and early 1990s, followed by diverse *concertación* (convergence/consensus-seeking) and "reconciliation" forums which transferred social contradictions from the military to the political terrain, and hammered out fragile and temporary pacts. This political outcome paved the way for the transnational model to take hold. The transnational nuclei of the local elite, to reiterate, achieved hegemony over the elite as a whole in the 1980s, assumed state power in the 1990s, and set out to implement the program of global capitalism in the region. The region's next rearticulation to world capitalism—corresponding to the fourth epoch, that of globalization—is constituted on that program.

The struggle of social forces in Central America is being played out in the early twenty-first century as a battle for hegemony between newly transnationalized dominant groups and popular sectors that have been transformed as well by capitalist globalization and are in a process of recomposition. The transnational elite and its local nuclei in the region are striving to construct a new hegemonic historic bloc, the regional expression of the emergent global capitalist historic bloc. Popular sectors are striving to articulate new projects of transformation and congeal a counter-hegemonic challenge from below in civil society. The social contradictions that gave rise to the upheaval have not been resolved in this new period; if anything, they have intensified. What has changed is the constellation of social forces and the entire structural context and therefore the social and political terrain in which these contradictions manifest themselves and in which social forces struggle.

The remainder of this chapter provides a more detailed reconstruction of the 1960s–1990s transitions in each Central American country. Chapters three and four then explore, in historical perspective, the new transnational economic and social model.

Divergence and Convergence in Paths to Globalization: Country Case Studies

Nicaragua: From Revolution to Counterrevolution[6]

Nicaragua is a highly instructive case: in the process of globalization, the country experienced both types of "transitions" considered in mainstream literature—regime changes and "democratization" and also movement away from and then back to a capitalist system integrated into world capitalism. Regime change in Nicaragua involved shifts from an authoritarian to a revolutionary regime, and then from a revolutionary to a polyarchic regime. The breakup of the authoritarian political system with the demise of the Somoza dictatorship in 1979 was followed by a failed attempt to construct a revolutionary democracy by the Sandinista regime (1979–90), and by another regime change in 1990, to the Violeta Chamorro government, which represented an attempt to install a stable polyarchy. Transnational processes were the underlying causal dynamic in what appeared on the surface as dramatic disjunctures between authoritarian, revolutionary, and polyarchic periods.

As in El Salvador, the United States played such a preponderant role in Nicaragua that US intervention is a pivotal element in the analysis. US support for the Somoza family dictatorship for nearly five decades, from 1935 to 1979, reflected the pre-globalization "elective affinity" between authoritarianism and US domination in the Western Hemisphere. But authoritarianism could not manage the social dislocations and reorganization generated by capitalist penetration and the insertion of Nicaragua into the nascent global economy from the 1960s and on, engendering pressures for its breakup. The US state had attempted to facilitate a transition from authoritarianism to polyarchy (from Somoza to the anti-Somoza elite) in 1978–79, but this effort failed owing to a host of country-specific reasons and historic timing. Most notable was the historic underdevelopment and political weakness of the Nicaraguan bourgeoisie as a class, and therefore the absence of a "third force" between dictatorship and revolution—the specific insurrectional strategy designed by the Sandinistas based on an accurate reading of national and international conditions—as well as the lack of an established and well-oiled US "democracy promotion" apparatus that could complement traditional diplomacy in US policy.[7]

The Sandinista revolutionary forces constructed a viable counter-hegemony to the dictatorship and seized state power in the 1979 revolution. But the structural constraints of globalization, combined with US policy, made a viable basis for consolidating and sustaining a social revolution out of the initial political opening impossible, independent of behavioral factors such as Sandinista state conduct. The project collapsed owing to a host of internal and external, subjective and objective factors, which included a model of revolutionary popular/participatory democracy that was flawed due to the subordination of civil society to the state and Sandinista "vanguardist" abuses of power. But *irrespective* of the shortcomings of the Sandinista model of revolutionary democracy, the project was not viable due to global structural factors. This structural power of transnational capital, conjoined with the vastly superior direct power of the US state, was applied through a massive destabilization campaign and complex interventionist strategies designed to disaggregate Nicaragua's external linkages and undermine its internal cohesion, to make unworkable a popular alternative to polyarchy and free-market capitalism.[8] We see in this process the link between the structural and the behavioral. The structural power of transnational capital was expressed precisely in the ability of the US state as the behavioral agent of hegemonic transnational capital to isolate Nicaragua from international markets and credits and to transform in diverse ways the behavior of domestic Nicaraguan actors.

The links are complex and multifarious between the structural pressures bound up with globalization and changes in internal Nicaraguan economic, social, political and other variables from the 1960s to the 1990s. Apart from behavioral factors (for example, concrete policy decisions taken by the

Sandinistas), the global structural context Nicaragua faced in the 1980s pushed the revolutionary government into class alliances with modernizing capitalist fractions that had emerged in the 1960s and 1970s.[9] These fractions, distinguishable from Somocista crony capitalists, remained linked to the world capitalist market during the Sandinistas' rule, increasingly replaced the state as the principal intermediary between Nicaragua and those markets, and developed ties to emergent US-led transnational fractions. They acted as points of access for US-transnational penetration, including a structural capacity to impose policies on the Sandinista state, such as private agri-business and industrial subsidies, which undermined the classes that constituted the revolution's social base and reoriented internal power away from those classes and towards an elite in the process of reconstitution.[10] The United States launched a massive counterrevolutionary campaign that devastated an already war-torn and exhausted population. The spearhead of this campaign was the US organization, training, supply, command, and logistical support for a counterrevolutionary military force that grew to over 20,000 troops by the second half of the 1980s. The "contra" war resulted in the death of nearly 31,000, the injury of twice as many, and economic damages in excess of $12 billion. This was on top of 50,000 people killed in the last five years of the struggle against Somoza, 100,000 wounded, and $4.1 billion in damages—all this in a country with barely 3.5 million people and with an annual GNP of some $2 billion. Proportionally equivalent figures for the United States would be approximately five million casualties and economic losses of $25 trillion.[11] This was a war of attrition aimed at destroying the revolution by bringing about its collapse from within. The war lasted throughout the 1980s, but in the second half of that decade and on the US objective changed from a military overthrow of the Sandinistas by an externally based counterrevolution seeking an authoritarian restoration, to new forms of political intervention under the rubric of "democracy promotion" in support of an internal "moderate" opposition.

This opposition, organized and trained through large-scale US political aid programs, operated through peaceful (non-coercive) means in civil society to undermine Sandinista hegemony, culminating in the 1990 electoral defeat of the Sandinistas and restoration of the elite through a nascent polyarchic political system.[12] After the elections, a coalition led by an embryonic transnationalized nucleus (known at the time as *Grupo de Las Palmas*) took over the state, particularly such key ministries as Finances, the Economy and Development, the Central Bank, and Foreign Affairs, and the highly centralized executive itself, through the powerful Ministry of the Presidency, headed by Antonio Lacayo, son-in-law of the new president, Violeta Chamorro. Some members of this nucleus were Finance Minister Emilio Pereira, Deputy Foreign Minister José Pallais, and several Central Bank Presidents, all technocrats trained at Harvard or other elite "global universities" and with transnational ties developed during posts held prior to 1990 in such institutions as the World Bank and the Inter-American Development Bank (IDB). They represented the Nicaraguan 1990s variant of the Chilean "Chicago Boys," quietly advancing the neo-liberal agenda behind the noisy and much more visible conjunctural political squabbling of a fractious political elite.[13] The reinsertion of Nicaragua into the global economy and a far-reaching neo-liberal restructuring ensued.

The global economy from the 1960s to the mid-1990s squeezed domestic market producers in general, and in particular, the Nicaraguan peasantry, which became semi-proletarianized in the post-WWII period. The Sandinista agrarian reform prolonged the life of this class and other domestic economic agents. But the reconstitution and preservation of a peasantry was not viable structurally. To give one example, it required state subsidizing of peasant production for export and of internal consumption (the attempt at national autonomy) to align internal prices with world market prices (the global structural factor beyond national control). Price supports and other subsidies in turn fed macroeconomic disequilibrium, which further undermined the viability of a revolutionary project trying to survive in an integrated global economy and society. To give another example, the need for labor in the agro-export sector, whose continued existence was dictated by extra-national forces (reflecting the well-known tension between agro-export production and agrarian reform), largely in the hands of a rural bourgeoisie, limited the scope and pace of agrarian reform and strengthened the Sandinista alliance with objectively counterrevolutionary forces.[14] The push and pull of rural class transformation became linked with a US-led armed counterrevolution (the "contras") whose social base became the peasantry. Peasant resistance to Somoza and the Sandinistas responded to the incursion of socioeconomic forces that undermined their status yet also made impossible a new equilibrium for the peasantry as a class.[15] The neo-liberal program in place in the 1990s, including the restoration and modernization of agri-business and credit and price structures that closely tied the domestic economy to the world market, constituted the consummation of globalizing pressures in the Nicaraguan countryside. It was doing away, possibly for good, with a peasantry.[16]

The global capitalist economy exercised macro-structural causality in this highly complex scenario spanning several decades. The US state acted as the point of external linkage with the transnational pool from 1990. Globalization pressures reached a "critical mass" with the transfer of state power from the Sandinistas to Chamorro, and opened the way for the crystallization of the transnational agenda in the country. Following the formal change of government, US intervention entered a new stage, that of advancing the transnational agenda under Nicaragua's unique conditions of an unravelling revolution, an uncertain regime change, and war-torn economic and social structures. The agenda was advanced through the IFIs and other transnational state agencies, through the judicious use of US economic and political aid allocations, and through bilateral diplomacy and other forms of core power statecraft.[17] The goals became: 1) to dismantle what remained of the revolution, including the partial transformation of property relations in favor of the popular classes that had taken place, the revolution's juridical structure, and its military apparatus; 2) to reconstitute a propertied class and a political elite under the leadership of New Right "technocrats" tied to the global capitalist order and attuned to the transnational agenda; 3) to construct a neo-liberal state; 4) to deepen the process, begun in the 1980s, of penetrating Nicaraguan civil society and constructing a counter-hegemony to that won by the Sandinistas therein, and; 5) to oversee the reinsertion of Nicaragua into the global economy and tie internal social order to transnational order.

Nicaragua experienced changing transnational political alignments and articulations during the transition. Under Somoza, Nicaragua's foreign policy was a subservient and dependent appendage of US Cold War considerations in Latin America and reflected a pre-globalization external dependency that was almost strictly bilateral with the United States. The Sandinistas pursued a worldwide foreign policy aimed at establishing diplomatic networks in support of their attempt to weaken dependency on the United States and diversify economic relations and strategic alliances with a variety of international forces. The Chamorro and the Alemán governments (the latter assumed office in 1997), was largely "economistic," seeking to link the Nicaraguan state to multilateral agencies, identify new markets and sources of bilateral aid and reestablish those markets and credit sources lost under the Sandinistas, attract foreign investment, and secure preferential debt and trade treatment, in pursuit of the overall project of reinsertion into the global economy under the neo-liberal model.[18] Nicaragua signed more than 200 international agreements between 1990 and 1995, the vast majority intended to delineate the terms for the operation of transnational corporations in Nicaragua and the mechanisms of international economic and concomitant political arbitration under emerging conditions of integration and globalization.[19] In this way, the Nicaraguan state functioned through its foreign relations to make compatible the country's internal juridical superstructure with emergent transnational political superstructures that regulate the global economy.

Post-revolutionary relations with the United States were less ones of complete bilateral dependence and integration than a close US tutelage in the process of reinsertion into the global system. Such tutelage began in earnest in 1991. After a year-long study, the newly opened Agency for International Development (AID) mission in Nicaragua (the AID had withdrawn from the country altogether in 1981) stated in a report laying out overall US policy for 1991 to 1996, the year in which the next elections were scheduled: "The strategy presented in this document is an extremely ambitious one. It is difficult to overemphasize the degree of change in the Nicaraguan economy and Nicaraguan society which it envisions."[20] The *Strategy Statement*, a remarkable blueprint for the construction of a neo-liberal republic, laid out a comprehensive program for restructuring every aspect of Nicaraguan society on the basis of the economic power the United States and the IFIs would be able to wield over the shattered country. The strategy involved what Angel Saldomando termed "counter-reform" in every institutional and policy arena.[21] Such massive economic and institutional restructuring would logically lead to change in the correlation of internal political and social forces and thus provide a solid material basis for the more gradual cultural and ideological dimensions of "slow-motion counterrevolution."

Slow-Motion Counterrevolution

The Sandinistas surrendered the formal executive apparatus. But this transition unfolded within a juridical framework developed under the revolution, whose social, economic, political, and ideological structures were still in place. The Sandinista National Liberation Front (FSLN) in 1990 was still the largest and best organized party in the country. The popular classes remained politicized and mobilized in the old mass organizations, and even more so, in new social movements that flourished after the 1990 elections. The vote for the Nicaraguan Opposition Union (UNO) did not represent internal consensus on a neo-liberal program. And neither old and new fractions of the Nicaraguan elite nor the United States could count, in 1990, on a repressive military apparatus to impose their agenda, since the Sandinista People's Army (EPS) remained largely intact following the change in government. The difficulties in the neo-liberal project became evident in the months following Chamorro's April 1990 inauguration. The new government announced sweeping neo-liberal measures, including massive public-sector layoffs, privatizations, rate increases in transportation, utilities and other services, a sharp reduction in social spending, and the elimination of subsidies on basic consumption. The measures triggered two consecutive national strikes, in May and in July, both of which paralyzed the country and demonstrated the popular classes' willingness and ability to mount resistance. The new government was forced to compromise. The program would have to be implemented gradually, through a strategy of "slow-motion counterrevolution." Nicaragua entered a period of endemic social conflict, in which cycles of standoff, negotiation, and compromise alternated with peaceful and violent strikes, demonstrations, and clashes in the countryside and the cities. Chronic instability and social conflict provided the backdrop to ongoing realignments of the country's political forces and a "creeping" implementation of the neo-liberal program.

Following the elections, Washington approved a two-year $541 million assistance package, including approximately $25 million in political aid channeled through the AID and the National Endowment for Democracy.[22] The AID program in Nicaragua became the largest in the world, and the Embassy became the most heavily staffed in Central America. Personnel increased from 78 accredited diplomats in 1989 to over 300 by mid-1990.[23] Penetration of the Nicaraguan state following the vote was immediate. The AID sent advisors and funds: to the National Assembly "to improve its internal operations in resolving conflict and forging consensus on national policy" and to implement "constitutional reforms"; to the Electoral Commission, "to prepare for and monitor the 1996 national elections"; to judicial institutions and to the Comptroller General, "to install financial controls in government institutions"; and to municipal governments, to help in "implementing overall [US] strategy."[24]

The ideological dimensions of slow-motion counterrevolution involved two objectives. One was rooting out any vestige of Sandinista influence and incorporating into a new historic bloc the Nicaraguan masses, whose consciousness and "daily practices" had been transformed in ten years of revolution. As Nicaraguan sociologist Oscar René Vargas noted, revival of a latent fatalism and submissiveness of the popular classes would have to rely heavily on cultural and ideological mechanisms.[25] The other objective, which proved even more difficult and elusive, was inculcating a polyarchic political culture (a "civic culture") among the elite as an important component of reconfiguring a domestic bourgeoisie. The Sandinista revolution had further disfigured a bourgeoisie that as a class had remained truncated as a result of Nicaragua's particular history, external dependency, and decades of dictatorship and US intervention. Political aid played an important role in these endeavors.

The development of a polyarchic political culture among the elite and the legitimization of a neo-liberal social order among the population was the crucial counterpart to eroding the revolution's value system. The manipulation of religious values, patriarchal and traditional cultural patterns, and economic insecurities were central to this political-ideological endeavor. One example was the penetration and restructuring of the educational system as a key institution of ideological reproduction. The AID allocated $12.5 million to replace textbooks used in public schools that were developed under the Sandinista government. The old texts were ordered burned by the new Minister of Education, Humberto Belli. The new "depoliticized" textbooks began with the "Ten Commandments of God's Law," referred to divorce as a "disgrace" and to abortion as "murder," and stressed the importance of "order in the family," as well as "obedience to parents and legitimate authorities." Catholicism was defined in the geography textbook as the world's dominant religion, "based on the preaching of Our Lord Jesus Christ." The world history text asserted that all US interventions were carried out to bring "peace and stability" to countries around the world. The AID's director in Nicaragua, Janet Ballantyne, stated that the textbooks would help "reestablish the civics and morals lacking in the last eleven years."[26] Parallel to the penetration of the Nicaraguan state, US officials continued funding political aid programs to assist anti-Sandinista groups that had begun in the mid-1980s and also introduced new ones. The purpose of these post-electoral programs was not the same as the pre-electoral programs, which sought to develop anti-Sandinista constituencies in civil society that could contribute to the effort to displace the Sandinista government from state power. Rather, the objective was to contribute to a depoliticization of the population, to eclipse the more militant grassroots social movements, and to incorporate key sectors into an emergent historic bloc under the hegemony of a reconstituted private sector.[27]

While US political aid poured into the country along with economic aid, military aid to the EPS was ruled out by US officials. The preservation of a popular army born out of revolution deprived the Nicaraguan propertied classes of a repressive instrument. "The military and the police are currently dominated by Sandinista supporters," stated the AID *Strategy Statement.* "Loyalty of these institutions and its members to the current government is questionable and their actions in response to public disturbances over the last year have raised doubts about whether they respond to the dictates of the party or the mandate of the government." It concluded: "These institutions must be 'professionalized' so they can perform their proper function in society as guarantors of security and justice."[28] The US government applied enormous pressure following the elections, including diplomatic threats and the temporary suspension of US aid disbursements on several occasions, to purge the EPS leadership and to "de-Sandinistize" both the army and the police, as part of broader pressures to push forward slow-motion counterrevolution.[29] By the mid-1990s, these pressures had registered some success. A combination of defunding, restructuring, and the recruitment of new police officers from the ranks of the former contras and right-wing political activists had gone a long way in turning the police into a typical Latin American repressive force, routinely breaking up strikes, disbursing popular protests, and so forth. More importantly, the EPS leadership itself came to develop a corporate identity of its own once it was no longer tied to a revolutionary state. It came to view the army's institutional integrity as dependent on achieving legitimacy in the eyes of the local and the transnational elite, and this meant demonstrating its ability to repress protests by popular sectors when such protest transgressed legal or institutional channels (and even when they did not transgress these channels). During the 1990s the EPS began more and more to violently dislodge peasants who had taken over land in the countryside, to attack striking workers who occupied factories or government offices, and to break up often-peaceful street demonstrations.

Meanwhile, US economic aid, with a more long-term focus, went to bolster the debilitated private sector, for balance-of-payments assistance, and to pay debt arrears to the World Bank and the IMF. The AID made disbursal of all assistance dependent on stringent conditions with regard to the Chamorro government's social and economic policies. The AID's *Strategy Statement* stipulated across-the-board conditionality. The largest portion of US aid never even entered the country since it went to pay arrears to private foreign lenders and international agencies, which reestablished the country's credit standing and opened the way for new lending from the World Bank and the IMF. World Bank and IMF representatives, together with AID officials, designed a comprehensive neo-liberal structural adjustment program and made all credits, disbursements, and debt restructuring contingent on compliance with this program.[30] After 1992, bilateral US aid was phased out and largely replaced with funding from the IFIs.[31] US aid was a transitional mechanism for Nicaragua's insertion into global financial structures. The Nicaraguan government signed its first Contingency Agreement with the IMF in 1991, and then signed a comprehensive three-year Enhanced Structural Adjustment Facility (ESAF) with the Fund in 1994, followed by a second ESAF in 1998.

This foreign aid inserted Nicaragua inexorably into the global economy. By 1992, Nicaragua's foreign debt stood at nearly $11 billion, one of the highest per-capita debts in the world. Of a total of $1.2 billion in foreign bi- and multilateral aid allocated for the country in 1991, over $500 million—or 43 percent—went for debt servicing. Another 26 percent went for imports, mostly of consumer goods. Figures for 1992 and 1993 showed an almost identical pattern. Nicaragua paid out $495 million in 1992 *in interest alone* on its debt, and another $508 million in 1993 in debt servicing (principle and interest). In comparison, export earnings stood at $217 million in 1991. Debt restructuring brought servicing down to $330 million by 1996, but the figure shot up again to $730 million in 1997 as new obligations fell due.[32] Debt servicing was clearly a powerful mechanism in compelling a thorough restructuring of Nicaragua's productive structure in accordance with a changing world market and an evolving global division of labor. This point is crucial: the need to earn foreign exchange to pay back the debt requires that nations restructure their economies towards the production of exports ("tradables") in accordance with the changing structure of demand on the world market. Over an extended period, debt contraction and subsequent reservicing strengthens those sectors with external linkages and redistributes quotas of economic and political power towards new groups linked to transnational capital.

The global economic straightjacket imposed on Nicaragua was accomplishing what direct repression might have accomplished under authoritarian arrangements in an earlier period, or elsewhere, such as in the counter-reform program in Chile following the 1973 coup d'état. For instance, the AID's "agricultural reform" did not propose the forcible return of lands to their prior owners. Rather, it called for privatization of the economy, the promotion of agro-exports, and property ownership determined by free market forces. This purely "economic" criteria, applied under the banner of "efficiency" and fiscal and monetary policies to achieve macroeconomic stability, acted as non-coercive mechanisms that alienated peasant smallholders, undermined the peasantry as a class, reconcentrated land, and fomented a new, modernized capitalist agri-business sector. Macroeconomic stability mandated "realistic" interest rates, a drastic reduction in bank credit to smallholders, and the elimination of government price guarantees for the peasant sector. At the same time, the government was explicitly prohibited by the 1994 ESAF agreement signed with the IMF to replenish state bank funds, yet new international credits went to capitalizing new private banks. While state banks catered almost exclusively to peasant producers, the private banks lent almost exclusively to agri-business.[33]

Deprived of credit and other state services, and therefore the means to compete in the market, peasants were forced to sell their land. The promotion of large-scale export agriculture over food production for

internal consumption also undermined the peasantry, since peasant producers accounted for nearly 100 percent of domestic food production,
while export crop production was mostly in the hands of large landholders
and agri-business. The credit structure and fiscal and monetary policies
designed by the AID and the IFIs benefited a reorganized domestic
propertied class that set about to reinsert Nicaragua into global markets. In
1993, for instance, 28,000 small farmers received no credit whatsoever,
while just nine newly consolidated capitalist agri-business and export groups
monopolized over 30 percent of all credits.[34] In late 1994, the *Banco
Nacional de Desarrollo* (the principal state bank catering to peasant production), prohibited from recapitalizing by agreement with the IMF, was forced
to shut down twenty-two of its branches around the country and to raise
interest rates to market levels determined by the large-scale capitalist sector,
effectively denying credit to 50,000 peasant families. "It is more profitable
to lend $20,000 to just one producer than to lend $1000 to twenty small
farmers," stated one Bank official, explaining the logic of "efficiency"
imposed by the IMF.[35] This same credit and related adjustment policies
also undermined urban workers and smallholders. US and IFI financing,
for instance, was made conditional on the speedy privatization of some 400
state enterprises, representing 40 percent of the GNP. Militant labor
struggles to have public enterprises turned over to workers' collectives led
to the creation of a new trade union-owned "Area of Workers' Property,"
comprising some 25 percent of privatized firms. But the same mechanism
of credit allocation began to undermine the viability of these worker-run
enterprises. Privatization thus became synonymous with a reconcentration
of property.

Trade liberalization was also a powerful instrument of internal social
recomposition and economic reorganization, complementary to the effects
of the debt and of other adjustment policies. In 1991, public consumption
dropped 35 percent and private consumption rose 33 percent, indicating a
converse relation between the drop in government spending on social
services for the popular sectors and an increase in private consumption
among the tiny upper and middle classes. As a result of the sudden opening
of the market to imports, Nicaragua experienced an import boom that
forced thousands of small-scale industrial and agricultural producers into
bankruptcy. The majority of new imports were not inputs for production
but consumer goods, especially luxury items, benefiting a new high-income
sector, as well as large-scale importers who began to use newly accumulated
capital to purchase properties and establish financial concerns, thus contributing to the process of a reconcentration of wealth and a restoration,
under new conditions, of pre-revolutionary property relations.[36]

Commercial reactivation through non-productive imports was a calculated element in US strategy, conducted through a Commodity Import
Program (CIP) whose stated purpose was to strengthen the private sector.[37]
The CIP was tied to a program to create ten private banks, for which
purpose the AID spent $60 million in 1991 and 1992 alone in capitalization
funds and in commodity imports by large-scale private importers financed

by these private financial institutions. The importers and the members of the new banks' boards of directors often overlapped, fomenting the development of powerful new economic groups.[38] In this way, private banks rather than the Nicaraguan state channeled external resources, including balance of payments support that flowed in to the private banks from the AID and the IMF.[39] A private banking system was to act as a direct link between emergent Nicaraguan entrepreneurs and transnational finance capital. The AID *Strategy Statement* stated that a key purpose of these banks would be to mobilize internal resources for the activities of domestic and foreign investors. Another purpose was to transfer the money supply, credits, credit policy-setting, and the financial levers of the economy from the state to the private sector, thereby giving a powerful boost to the reconstitution of a hegemonic propertied class linked to transnational capital and with the capacity and resources to foment a new economic model for Nicaragua.

The consequences of these financial, credit, commercial and related adjustment policies are an example of how, in the era of the global economy, transnational capital comes to penetrate, disrupt, and incorporate into its structures sectors previously outside of (or enjoying a certain autonomy vis-à-vis) the global economy. Land reconcentration meant immizeration for the expanding ranks of the newly dispossessed peasantry. Simultaneously, in the first year of the adjustment program alone, nearly 20 percent of the country's salaried workers lost their jobs as a result of mass dismissals of civil servants *and* of workers in productive public enterprises. Some 60 percent of the Economically Active Population (EAP) was under or unemployed by 1991.[40] Yet, in the larger scheme of things, the alienation of smallholders, property reconcentration, and the contraction of public sector employment helped facilitate conditions for the new economic model for Nicaragua envisioned by transnational capital and its local representatives.

New Economic Activities and Class Relations

In this model, Nicaragua's reinsertion into the global economy was to be based on a modernized agro-export sector emphasizing Non-Traditional Agricultural Exports, or NTAEs, on tourism, and on maquiladora assembling activities in urban-based duty-free export zones, as part of Central America's position as the southern rump of the emergent North American free trade zone, as will be discussed in the next chapter. Between 1990 and 1997 the government passed a series of laws and incentive programs to facilitate this new economic activity, among them, an export promotion law, a foreign investment law, a law authorizing the establishment of offshore export processing zones, and various tax exemptions and rebates for non-traditional export products. Government and private sector representatives also set up a number of bodies for this purpose, such as the public–private Center for Exports and Investments (CEI), while private capitalists established the Association of Non-Traditional Producers and

Exporters of Nicaragua (APENN), set up to promote the new economic model and to lobby for liberalization.[41] In 1990, the government set up in the outskirts of Managua the first of what was to be a series of tax-free *zonas francas* for transnational companies. By 1993, some one dozen companies were operating mostly textile plants, paying wages of $30 a month to mostly female workers under state regulations prohibiting unionization. Export-oriented agri-business and maquiladora assemblage required abundant cheap labor drawn from a huge pool of propertyless laborers and the unemployed, alongside a reserve army of the unemployed keeping wages down. The neo-liberal program was creating just such a labor force through privatization, mass public-sector layoffs, the reconcentration of rural and urban property holdings, and so forth.

All this was part of the far-reaching process of class restructuring, including atomization of the formerly well-organized working class, prole-tarianization of the peasantry, and the development of a New Right elite comprised of a modernized private sector and administrative technocrats. US aid was used to finance several elite universities and technical institutes, including a new program in the Central American Institute of Business Administration to "train consultants" and place them in different govern-ment ministries as "technical and economic advisors."[42] The transnational agenda could not be realized without national actors strong enough to act as mediators and attuned to the transnational strategy. Direct US support for a reorganized private sector through the CIP, the private banks, the privatization process, and so forth, had the precise intent of building up these national actors. The goal was to foment a "modernizing" elite with the capacity to: 1) influence state policies; 2) influence civil society through predominance in the economy; 3) serve as local links to transnational capital; and 4) develop its own economic power and give it the ability to promote and manage capital accumulation within the new economic model. US programs intended to build ties to local elites and challenge popular sectors. These programs sought to penetrate the state and civil society, to form a network of institutions in civil society as structures parallel to the state and able to instrumentalize the state, and to develop a nexus of state–civil society linkages displaying an interpenetration of interests and personnel between the government and "private" spheres. These linkages were developed through close coordination among, and institutional inter-penetration between, the government (managing the state) and a private-sector elite hegemonic in civil society. Although the appointment of numerous US advisors in key economic, social, and policy-planning minis-tries was a requirement of US aid disbursals in the first years after the elections,[43] a more important activity funded by the United States was the creation of a core of New Right technocrats thoroughly trained and ideologically seeped in the worldview and logic of the transnational elite—people who, in the long-term transnational elite strategy, would eventually go on to assume the reins of the Nicaraguan state and establish internal hegemonic order linked to transnational hegemony.

Political realignment, transnational class formation, and neo-liberal restructuring continued throughout the 1990s under the Alemán (1996–2000) and Bolanos (2000–) governments. At the risk of simplifying highly complex phenomena, in the post-electoral period the Nicaraguan elite divided roughly into two groups grounded in the productive reorganization of different fractions of capital. The first was attuned to the transnational agenda of polyarchy and neo-liberalism, with a more long-term vision of capitalist modernization based on the new economic model mentioned above. This group was clustered in the executive inner circle, in key ministries such as Finance and the Central Bank, and in the new universities, think-tanks, and financial concerns set up with US and multi-lateral assistance. It was tied economically to the liberalized commercial, banking and other service sector activities, the NTAEs and incipient maquiladora operations.[44] The second was grounded in the old agro-export oligarchy and declining domestic market activities, imbued in the traditional politics of partisan corruption and patronage, and inclined to restore a Somocista-style authoritarian order. The struggle between and within these two groups often took the form of highly visible political infighting and clashes over personal interests. In part, this is a result of Nicaragua's particular political culture, and it indicates the complex and often contradictory relation between structural processes (globalization) and the behavioral response of specific agents (the Nicaraguan elite). But it also reflected a more fundamental conflict over class formation and fractional interests therein, intermeshed with the penetration and germination of the transnational project for Nicaragua.

A careful study of the Nicaraguan economy and social structure from the 1970s into the twenty-first century reveals that the hegemonic groups were those linked most directly to the external sector, in particular, finances, new commercial activities, reconstituted agri-business, management of transnational capital, and ties to international agencies. Yet the coalescing of a transnational kernel in Nicaragua was a highly contradictory and incomplete process. The New Right could not achieve a politically coherent formula and new economic groups were unable to find stable political representation or to construct a secure power bloc. Moreover, as we will see for other countries as well, the transnational kernel was itself not immune from personal ambition, factional disputes, elite feuds over the spoils of state, and a historically ingrained political culture of authoritarianism and clientalism. These practices in fact characterized its political behavior and impeded its ability to advance the transnational agenda. This scenario did not lend itself to simplified interpretations, and confused observers who analyzed conjunctural phenomena or focused on behavioral factors alone—an issue to which I will return in the other country case studies and elsewhere in the book.

This scenario is furthermore complicated by the crisis and transformation of the Left. The electoral defeat plunged the Sandinista party, its social base and legitimacy already seriously eroded, into a sharp internal crisis over programs, ideological orientation, and strategy. While the Sandinista grassroots engaged in sustained resistance in the early 1990s to the counterrevolutionary program, a new Sandinista elite was also making its appearance among those who had acquired substantial properties during the 1990 regime change. This pillage and personal appropriation by Sandinista leaders and bureaucrats of state property was known in Nicaragua as the *piñata*. New Sandinista landlords and businessmen and women began to develop an affinity of class interests and to merge with the bourgeoisie, especially with transnational fractions clustered in the commercial and financial sectors.[45] As the 1990s progressed, infighting in the FSLN increasingly had less to do with political differences than with power struggles and opportunism among Sandinista leaders, for whom defending the FSLN's institutional clout and organizational resources constituted their own source of power, authority, privilege, and material comfort. This new Sandinista elite gradually moved from leading the popular classes in their resistance to the counterrevolutionary program to utilizing the party's (dwindling) authority to *contain* these classes and control their mobilization. The masses became a manipulable bargaining chip. They were to be mobilized to protest when the Sandinista elite, in its efforts to force a recomposition of the dominant groups so as to win additional quotas of power and influence, needed to apply pressure on the government and the non-Sandinista elite, and to be demobilized, contained, and pacified when such protest actually threatened the new elite order and the Sandinista elite's place in it. This elite continued to legitimate itself with a revolutionary discourse that no longer corresponded to any political program or conduct other than that of furthering its own group interests and securing a place among the dominant bloc in the new order.

The transnational elite, less interested in an anti-Sandinista ideological crusade once the revolutionary order had been reverted than with the prospects of *incorporating* elements of the Sandinista leadership into a new dominant bloc, did not view the rise of a Sandinista elite as an obstacle to the transnational agenda, and in fact encouraged it.[46] The dynamics of recomposition within the dominant bloc and changing modalities of managing subordinate groups explain what came to be known as Sandinista–Chamorro "co-government" (1990–95), in reference to the close cooperation that developed between the FSLN and the Chamorro government. In fact, the new Sandinista economic groups developed close business and personal ties with transnationally oriented capitalist groups associated with the Chamorro government.[47] These dynamics also underlaid a pact reached in 1999 between the FSLN and the Liberal Alliance leadership. While on the surface the Sandinista and the Alemán camps remained bitter enemies, the two political forces began to negotiate a sharing of power soon after the 1996 election, culminating in the 1999 "pact" by which they agreed to divide up governmental power. It appeared by the turn of the century that a two-party Sandinista–Liberal political system would become entrenched. The pact was the conjunctural outcome of the effort by new elite groups to achieve the "governability" necessary for the country to proceed with a more orderly integration into global capitalism. The FSLN had become the key prop to the transnational elite order in Nicaragua.[48] In sum, what took place in Nicaragua, more than in any other Central American country, was a *circulation of elites*, made possible (or unblocked), ironically, by the revolution.

Looking backward from the early twenty-first century, the transnational elite project registered important successes in Nicaragua but has also run up against numerous complications. Whereas, as we shall see, the project had fallen into place, despite difficulties, in El Salvador, Honduras, and Costa Rica by the turn of the century, in Nicaragua, along with Guatemala, there was a more significant gap between goals and outcome, or intent and ability. In these cases, the deep social and political contradictions in emergent global society, including its dark underside of social apartheid and "poverty amidst plenty" and the elusive goal of "governability," became quite apparent. For Nicaragua and for elsewhere in global society the crises of elite rule that became manifest in the 1960s to 1970s were not resolved with the triumph of global capitalism. Exuberant over the success of the 1980s campaign against the Sandinistas, US officials originally expected the transnational elite agenda to fall smoothly into place in the 1990s. The AID *Strategy Statement* stated:

> Over the course of the [1991–96] period, we anticipate a major transformation of the Nicaraguan economy and society. By the end of this period, the economy will be dominated by the private sector, traditional exports will be growing rapidly, and a variety of non-traditional agricultural exports will be well-established. By 1996, enclave manufacturing will have moved beyond an initial concentration in textiles into a wide variety of manufacturing operations. The United States will once again become Nicaragua's principal trading partner . . . Civic education efforts and the spread of a wide range of ideas through the media will have helped achieve general acceptance of democratic ideas, attitudes and values.[49]

But reality proved to be less rosy than US forecasts. Social inequalities and consumption differentials, the concentration of wealth and income, and widespread impoverishment, a result of unbridled free-market forces released under the neo-liberal program, advanced at an alarming rate in the 1990s. Relative poverty for much of the population under the Sandinistas became absolute poverty under the new government. For instance, real wages dropped 50 percent in the first year of the new government, 69 percent of the population lived in poverty in 1992, and per capita food consumption fell by 31 percent between 1990 and 1992.[50] The health, educational, and other social gains achieved in the 1980s, although they deteriorated late in that decade as a result of the war, suffered a dramatic reversal with the change of government and the application of the neo-liberal program.[51] Cholera, malaria measles, and other diseases that had been eradicated or nearly eradicated reappeared in the early 1990s and reached epidemic proportions. The infant mortality rate rose from under 50 per 1,000 births in the 1980s to 71 per 1,000 in 1991, and to 83 per 1,000 in 1992.[52] The crime rate more than doubled between 1985 and

1995, including a striking increase in rapes, a sign of the deterioration of the social fabric.[53] Widespread rural immizeration and the government's policies of squeezing the peasantry fueled renewed military conflict in the countryside. Although the old Sandinista–contra antagonisms played a part, the new rural conflict, including land invasions, spontaneous violent clashes, and even organized warfare in some areas, reflected the emergence of class polarization and class-based conflict in the countryside. Adding fuel to the fire was opulence amidst mass poverty that did not exist in the Sandinista period, generating a sociological relative deprivation and further heightening social conflict.

"Investors will be looking for clear indications that political turmoil will be contained and for evidence of progress toward the establishment of a free-market economy," the 1990 AID *Strategy Statement* warned. The government "will need to demonstrate that it has developed a working legal and regulatory structure such that it can guarantee contracts, establish property rights, resolve disputes, and enforce laws which govern business and investment. It must also be able to demonstrate that law enforcement entities have the capability to maintain order in accordance with government directives and policy."[54] But by the turn of the century only the first of the three functions of the neo-liberal state, achieving macroeconomic stability, had been met. Endemic corruption had become a major concern for the transnational elite, threatening to make impossible implementation of the transnational agenda in the country.[55] Nicaragua, seen from the logic of the transnational project, was caught in a vicious circle. Structural adjustment was to have provided the macroeconomic stability for private capital to enter and operate freely. Private foreign investment was to bring about growth and development. Growth and development was to bring about social peace and political stability. But the twin legacies of a decade of revolution and a historically fractious elite made social stability and the consolidation of polyarchy highly problematic. The popular classes would not allow an anti-popular project to stabilize, and the elite was unable to reach consensus in its own affairs, and thus the economy continued to sink. Transnational capital, literally with "the world to exploit," would hardly choose Nicaragua to invest in, given chronic instability, less docility among the popular classes than in other countries in the region, and the inability of the dominant groups to achieve hegemony.[56] The possibility of consolidating a polyarchic political system and elite social order and renewing externally oriented capital accumulation seemed bleak at the turn of the century. The popular classes resisted being drawn into a renewed elite hegemony. They became increasingly restive, putting aside political allegiances as the entire country became polarized into an impoverished mass and an affluent minority. These difficulties in Nicaragua and in the rest of Central America underscore the contradictions internal to global capitalism and the transnational elite's project of "market democracy."

El Salvador: Transition Under Direct US Tutelage

We can summarize El Salvador's transition as follows: A massive popular movement burgeoned in the 1970s and combined with a guerrilla movement that snowballed by the early 1980s into a full civil war between the government's armed forces, death squads, and right-wing supporters, on the one hand, and the guerrilla army and its mass base of civilian supporters, on the other. While the revolutionary forces, organized in the Farabundo Marti National Liberation Front (FMLN), came to threaten state power, the US-led mobilization of counterinsurgency staved off a triumph similar to that which had taken place in Nicaragua. However, behind the very visible battle between the revolutionary armed movement and the US-supported dominant groups was a more significant process: the reorganization of the Salvadoran state and economy in conjunction with movement at the level of the global economy; a reconfiguration of the dominant groups; and the emergence of a lucid New Right fraction within the ruling party itself, the Nationalist Revolutionary Alliance (ARENA). The insurgency, *combined with changes in the dominant project itself*, shattered the old oligarchy and its project. The program of limited political and economic reform of the Christian Democratic government that governed in the 1980s, in the years prior to the rise to power of the ARENA, under the sponsorship of the US state was a conjunctural strategy and a component part of the counterinsurgency campaign.

The dominant groups, squeezed between the revolutionary forces and limited reform, began to reorganize and acquired a political expression in the ARENA. Beyond conjunctural reforms were structural changes and novel opportunities opened up by the global economy in the 1980s. Trade liberalization and economic development programs sponsored by the AID and the IFIs stimulated dynamic new external sector activities such as banking and international commerce, non-traditional exports, and the first maquiladora plants. These changes began to have a transformative effect on the dominant groups' prospects and outlook. A transnationalized fraction cohered with the help of political clearing houses and economic associations tied to the transnational elite, such as the AID-funded Salvadoran Foundation for Social and Economic Development (FUSADES). Representatives of this emergent fraction gained control over the ARENA party, and then of the state, with the election of Alfredo Cristiani in 1988. This fraction was able to gain hegemony over the elite and over the transition as a whole, and implement sweeping neo-liberal transformation from 1988 and on.

For much of the 1980s the FMLN threatened the Salvadoran state. The revolutionary forces, considerably stronger than their counterparts in Guatemala, often held the military initiative. They achieved at several moments in the 1980s a military parity and came close to disputing state power. They established control over significant portions of the country's territory, where they forced the state to withdraw, developed an organic social base, and exercised a "dual power" in the zones under their territorial control. In distinction to Guatemala, the United States took a more direct and open role in the transition in El Salvador: it was the threat of an insurrectionary triumph of the Left, as well as of a complete economic collapse, that led to massive US intervention starting in 1980–81. As the war unfolded (eventually taking at least 75,000 lives), the country was brought under US tutelage in a manner unprecedented in Central American history, except perhaps for the US occupation of Nicaragua in earlier decades of the twentieth century. The United States mobilized political and economic resources with the aim of a far-reaching restructuring of Salvadoran society. The military strategy of *low-intensity warfare*, developed in the wake of the US defeat in Indochina, involved a counterinsurgency war by Salvadoran proxy under the guidance of US military advisors, rather than the direct introduction of US troops.[57] The strategy sought to defeat the insurgency by winning the political support of the population rather than militarily destroying the guerrillas. It involved a more complete and synchronized application of military programs, with political, economic, and social programs, including a broad reform program. It relied not just on a Salvadoran military trained, supplied, and advised by US special forces, but also, and more importantly, on a reorganized state and economic and political restructuring. As discussed earlier, the task of destroying the old oligarchic political and economic structures fell to the revolutionary movements in Central America. These agents therefore created the overall conditions for the transition to the transnational model. But the same must also be said of the region-wide counterinsurgency. The dialectic of revolution and counterrevolution became the agency of change and transformation. In the first instance the counterinsurgencies were reactive movements in response to the proactive challenge of revolution. In the second, they became powerful instruments of dominant groups locally and transnationally for the thorough social, political, and economic restructuring of the region.

US intervention in El Salvador was in this sense a modernizing force. Accounts that characterized the intervention as an effort to sustain the old oligarchic structures, or simply dismissed the reforms as cosmetic dimensions of counterinsurgency, missed the point. US strategy was aimed as much at transforming the landed oligarchy and its praetorian state as it was at defeating the popular uprising. US intervention sought to remove the obstacles that the local state and the elite placed on the country's transformation and rearticulation to world capitalism. The revolutionary movement combined with the counterinsurgency reforms led to a rapid and more extensive recomposition of the dominant group and the power bloc, compared to Guatemala, where the old oligarchy retained much of its power and cohesion in the 1990s. The counterinsurgent reforms, including land reform, the nationalization of the financial system and of coffee and sugar export marketing, weakened the landed oligarchy and paved the way for the rise of New Right fractions that could modernize the country and reintegrate it into the global system. But this massive US penetration of the Salvadoran state and society would not have been possible were it not for the revolutionary forces: US tutelage would never have been accepted by the dominant groups had the revolutionary movement not threatened their very survival, forcing them to rely on US intervention and to accept, however grudgingly, the terms and conditions that accompanied that intervention.[58]

Between 1981 and 1992, the United States provided an imposing $6 billion in economic, military, and covert aid for El Salvador and mobilized at least another $1 billion from the IFIs. This compares to the approximately $150 million in US aid provided in the sixteen years from 1963 to 1979.[59] US intervention thoroughly penetrated and transformed Salvadoran society—apart from those areas under FMLN control—from government ministries, to social service institutions, the private sector, the mass media, and civil society organizations.[60] If the immediate goal was to prevent an economic collapse and to contain the insurgency, the broader objective was to integrate the country into the global economy and society on the basis of an entirely new composition of social forces. This included "modernizing" the outlook of the country's economic and political elite, promoting neo-liberal reform, establishing the hegemony of the private sector, and cultivating distinct agents that could take the reins of the transnational project in the country.

Of the total US aid package, some 30 percent was in the form of direct military assistance and was crucial in preventing an insurgent victory.[61] Military aid went to increase the size of the government forces by nearly 600 percent, to training and advice, the provision of modern weaponry, including land, air, and sea-based weapons systems, the organization of mobile units, and a restructuring of the systems of command, control, communications, and intelligence. This military intervention aimed to crush the Left and popular forces in tandem with restructuring driven by economic and political dimensions of the intervention. As Breny Cuenca points out, a majority of the US economic aid was disbursed in the form of highly conditional Economic Support Funds (ESF), a program designed to expedite an imperious US political influence in receiver countries.[62] Funds of this type are deposited directly into the receiver state's current accounts and allow US personnel to influence the entire structure of state allocations in social services, the operations of distinct ministries, military spending, investment and infrastructure, and so on. ESF funds for El Salvador were earmarked specifically for use by private sector groups and they therefore played a key role in the development of new economic agents and the redistribution of economic and political influence among dominant groups in the process of recomposition. Foodstuff donations from the Public Law 480 Program constituted another major portion of the US program. The P.L. 480 program gives the United States an inordinate influence over agricultural policy in the receiver country. But perhaps more importantly, the donations are marketed as subsidized imports and therefore undercut domestic market production, benefit commercial groups linked to the world market, and bolster the external sector over domestic market agents, with important transformative effects on the social structure.[63] Still a third area of US funding was social services, which, as a condition for the disbursement of funds, were to be administered by the private sector. As social services became privatized new economic groups came to accrue additional influence through control over the institutions of social reproduction. "As this process unfolds, new groups within the private sector tend to form or become consolidated," notes Cuenca. "These groups must strengthen their commercial ties to the United States and obtain good access, in the first place, to AID officials, and in the second place, to officials from governmental agencies (for example, Central Bank, the Treasury, Ministry of Planning) that determine eligibility for diverse import-export activities. ESF funds therefore act as an instrument for reforming the private sector and for selecting groups that become engaged in international market relations."[64]

A key component of the intervention strategy was to achieve the hegemony of capital in Salvadoran society. The goal was to build up the private sector in civil society, redefine the relationship between the state and capital, and transfer key functions and resources from the government to private capital. It was to this end that the United States encouraged the creation by wealthy Salvadoran business people of the FUSADES, in 1983. The FUSADES obtained in that year a $185,000 contract from the AID to promote the Caribbean Basin Initiative (CBI), and then received over the next ten years at least another $150 million and became the main outlet for AID monies for civil society.[65] The FUSADES played a critical role in bringing together a New Right nucleus that would go on to assume state power in 1989 and become the internal agent for the country's reinsertion into the global system. Between 1983 and 1988 the FUSADES established an array of organizations, among them the Investment and Export Promotion (PRIDEX) association, the Business Foundation for Educational Development (FEDAPE), and the Agricultural Diversification Program (DIVAGRO). It also set up a string of "municipal foundations" at the local level. These associations in turn undertook a broad range of projects to support the reorganization of the private sector, the expansion of new economic activities, the development of neo-liberal social and economic policies, and to liaise with the state. In its political work, a core of New Right technocrats clustered in the FUSADES, and its associated organizations provided a clearing house for building elite consensus around the transnational project of polyarchy and neo-liberalism. The FUSADES thus became an institutional headquarters for the development of a transnational fraction and its project, and for its bid to establish hegemony within the private sector, civil society, and the state. The FUSADES helped this fraction develop a policy formulation and political action capacity and facilitated a policy dialogue with the state. The web of private-sector social and economic organizations set up by FUSADES extended deeply into civil society. An "enlightened" transnationalized elite developed through networks that crisscrossed political and civil society within El Salvador and transnationally.[66]

All this took place as the country underwent a transition to polyarchy that involved regime change and a far-reaching reorganization of the political system. US intervention *converged* with the activities and the emergent projects of distinct Salvadoran agents, particularly with those of reformist middle class sectors and of the New Right. In October 1979, as the dominant power bloc began to unravel, junior officers in the army overthrew the military regime of General Carlos Humberto Romero and installed a junta of reformist officers and center-left civilians, thereby momentarily preventing a total polarization and defusing a revolutionary insurrection. Months earlier, in the wake of the Sandinista triumph in Nicaragua, the United States had announced its intention to withdraw support for the military dictatorships that had ruled virtually uninterrupted since the 1931 coup d'état by General Maximiliano Hernández Martínez, and to support a transition to polyarchy. US officials stepped up military and economic aid for the junta and set out to strengthen the centrist forces in the coalition supporting the junta, particularly the malleable Christian Democratic Party (PDC), and to marginalize the Left, which was forced to withdraw in early 1980. The PDC, a party of reformist middle class and professional sectors with José Napoleón Duarte at its helm, became the chosen internal political vehicle for the program of reform and counterinsurgency.[67]

Between 1980 and 1984, Washington pieced together a counterrevolutionary coalition comprised of the armed forces and police, factions of the PDC and other centrist elements, and private-sector groups, under overall US sponsorship. Washington organized during the 1980s a sequence of electoral exercises that established a new polyarchic institutionality and a constitutional order. Given the state of war, the military siege of the popular sectors, the exclusion of the Left, and massive human rights violations, the transition to polyarchy appeared to be more facade than substance in the 1980s. "Demonstration elections" in the context of low-intensity warfare and the civilian governments that emerged from them were intended less to democratize the country than to provide the international legitimacy and a favorable internal political environment for the US intervention program.[68] However, these electoral exercises helped disaggregate the old dominant bloc and played an important part in the political recomposition of the dominant classes.

The Duarte government administered economic and social reforms in the first part of the 1980s. Neo-liberal restructuring was deferred in the face of the threat of a Leftist triumph and an immediate economic collapse. US superintendents allowed the Salvadoran government to run huge budget and trade deficits and did not push it to privatize state properties and productive resources. The reforms involved regulating market forces and a state-sponsored redistribution of property and resources—measures that under "normal" circumstances are anathema to neo-liberal restructuring. But in the case of El Salvador they were promoted as necessary; first, to rescue the social order itself; and second, to lay the groundwork for the transnational project. In Guatemala, the dominant groups refused to even broach the issue of land reform and transnational elites certainly did not push the matter. In El Salvador, in contrast, the United States pushed a land reform program in the face of sharp resistance from the oligarchy, as an urgent measure to preempt the revolutionary forces and restructure the country. The landless population had increased from 12 percent of the rural population in 1961 to about 30 percent in 1971 and then over 40 percent by 1975, while peonage and share-cropping under seignorial relations prevailed in the countryside.[69] The US-financed reform program, modelled by the AID on programs introduced in South Vietnam in the 1960s and adopted by the Salvadoran government in 1980, established three phases. The first, implemented in the early 1980s, provided for the expropriation with compensation of all estates over 1235 acres and their transformation into cooperatives. Phase II, the redistribution of holdings over 618 acres, was never implemented, while Phase III, a "Land to the Tiller" program, provided for legal title through state financing of lands worked by peasant tenants. The first phase diluted the power of the landed oligarchy and also contributed to rural pacification and the creation of a social base for the counterinsurgency project.[70] More specifically, the first phase, along with the other reform measures, helped to shift internal economic power from landed groups to those engaged in finances, international commerce, and other services.

The agrarian reform undercut the landed oligarchy *and also* paved the way for a more modernized market in land. The newly created cooperative sector enjoyed US support in the first half of the 1980s. The government and the AID provided agricultural credits, rural infrastructural projects, and health and educational services, for the reformed sector, in areas newly populated by the regime with political supporters, and in territories wrested from FMLN control. In the late 1980s the AID began to promote the individual parcelization of land earlier distributed to cooperatives, as well as to finance phase III of the agrarian reform. The result of the sequential stages in the agrarian reform was: 1) politically, the partial displacement of the old landed oligarchy and the pacification of those areas of the countryside out of direct FMLN control; 2) economically, the basis for the creation of a market in land and a more complete transition in the countryside from oligarchic-seignorial to capitalist agriculture. These were not "latent" but "manifest" functions of the reform. A reading of AID documents from the time makes clear that a market in land and a transition to full capitalist agriculture ("modernizing agriculture") were key objectives. Similarly, the nationalization of coffee and sugar marketing and of the banking system limited the investment options of the oligarchy. It gave the state some control over the mechanisms for the reproduction of capital and contributed to the shift in resources to new economic activities, including import-export trade, modernized capitalist agricultural sectors, and maquiladora textile production.[71]

The reforms were implemented in conjunction with other US social and economic policy initiatives. From 1984 and on the AID began to promote the new transnational model of accumulation. It encouraged the expansion of non-traditional agricultural exports through the National Center for Exports (CENTREX), an autonomous institute attached to the Central

Bank, and funded the Agricultural Diversification (DIVAGRO) and the Investment and Export Promotion (PRIDEX) programs of the FUSADES think-tank. AID monies were also made available for private agri-business interests involved in non-traditionals. In 1988, the AID made P.L. 480 donations conditional on the government's enactment of an Export Promotion Law, which stipulated, among other things, tax benefits and related incentives for maquiladora production.[72] As part of the AID's Industrial Stabilization and Recovery Program, described by the AID as its "lead vehicle for facilitating non-traditional exports and investments," some $50 million was provided to the FUSADES to distribute throughout the vast private-sector network the Foundation had organized.[73] Between 1979 and 1988, the export of traditional goods declined by some 50 percent, while non-traditional exports increased by 35 percent.[74]

The impact of the agrarian and other reforms on the oligarchy has been the subject of debate and should not be overstated.[75] Lungo and others point out, for instance, that the reformed sector encompassed no more than 25 percent of the country's agricultural lands, that only 50–60 percent of the cooperatives received technical assistance and other services, and that Phase II was never implemented.[76] But the agrarian and other reforms need to be placed in the larger context of recomposition of the dominant power bloc and of structural transformation. Lungo argues that the reforms did not substantially fracture the oligarchy. But he reaches this conclusion without distinguishing between fractions and distinct projects among the dominant classes, such that continuity in the domination of the bourgeoisie as a class becomes in his analysis synonymous with continuity in the power of the old oligarchy.[77] For structural reasons independent of the reforms, the dominant classes could not go on accumulating in the old ways and nor could they go on ruling in the old ways. The reform program also triggered political response among distinct agents, particularly old and new fractions among the dominant groups, that were important to the outcome. They hastened the downfall of the reactionary political coalition in the state. Here the political implications of the reforms were more important than the actual economic changes they brought about in determining their significance for class recomposition and the transition in El Salvador. Moreover, the war itself was a key catalyst of change within the elite, damaging landed interests in favor of finance capital, commerce, and export processing. Military conflict and the FMLN presence in the eastern half of the country, for instance, led landowners to abandon their properties, many of whom shifted their energies and capital into other activities. Stanley reports that by 1984, 46.6 percent of coffee lands had been abandoned and coffee production fell by half from 1980 through 1990.[78] The general direction of transformation of the elite wrought by the war was guided by the reform process and by the active promotion of the transnational model as an alternative.

From Agrarian Reform to Neo-Liberalism

By the second half of the 1980s the social and economic reforms had achieved their limited purpose from the vantage point of region-wide pacification. The reprieve given the country from structural adjustment to carry out reforms that accelerated the demise of the oligarchy had come to an end and the moment arrived to unfurl the neo-liberal program. The AID began from 1985 and on to withdraw its support for the earlier reforms and to push privatizations, lifting of state price controls, fiscal austerity, raising tariffs, and so on.[79] In the late 1980s and early 1990s the financial system and international marketing were reprivatized.[80] The period of social, economic, and political reform was thus an interlude, a bridge between the collapse of the old oligarchic order and the construction of the new neo-liberal order. The internal social forces that could—indeed, did—protagonize the transnational project were now emerging. The emerging consensus on neo-liberalism was not shared by the Duarte government, which was bent on deepening the social and economic reform program in the framework of ISI-CACM as part of its own Christian Democratic project. The Duarte government became an obstacle to the transnational project. As tensions over a devaluation and other neo-liberal adjustments mounted between the AID and Duarte, the United States strengthened its ties to emergent New Right forces organized in the FUSADES and other associations and began to search for a political alternative just at a time when the dominant classes were becoming politically organized.[81]

The old oligarchy, often referred to as the "fourteen families," had held sway for over a century but since 1932, in the wake of a military coup d'état and the *matanza*, it had not ruled directly.[82] The problem of social order had been resolved, for the time being, with the imposition of a military dictatorship. From 1932 on, the oligarchy abandoned the political scene and concentrated on its economic activities, entrusting direct control of the state to the military. The military exercised a coercive domination over society and thereby assured the social and political conditions for capitalist development in exchange for corporate privilege and for spoils of state acquired through systematic and organized corruption, in what Stanley terms the "protection racket state" and what Enrique Baloyra has character-ized as "reactionary despotism."[83] In the post-WWII period the oligarchy was represented politically, first by the Revolutionary Party of Democratic Unification (PRUD), and later by the National Conciliation Party (PCN), which governed for much of the 1960s and 1970s as the instrument of the military. But this arrangement did not, in Lungo's words, resolve the "recurrent crisis of hegemony" of the dominant classes. "Intimately tied to this issue [is] the lack of a political party, in the strictest sense, of the bourgeoisie."[84]

As the power bloc unravelled from 1979 in the face of the popular uprising, the dominant classes began to search for a political expression, just at a time when these classes were beginning a process of internal fractionation and transformation. What took place in the 1980s among the dominant classes was a period of sharp and rapid recomposition, including political organization. "[The] historic blindness of the bourgeoisie had one fundamental cause: its failure to exercise direct power, to develop its own class-based parties, and to nurture its own organic intelligentsia," argues Lungo. "This pattern brought on a paralysis from which the Salvadoran bourgeoisie did not begin to recover until 1982, a point at which the revolutionary upsurge had brought bourgeois power to the verge of collapse." The dominant classes now confronted "a challenge to the very essence of the system, not merely to the form of government. This served as an incentive for them to unite in a process of reconstitution as a political class with its own organic expression, a development that would crystallize by the end of the 1980s."[85] The ARENA would become the party of a reconstituted and newly mobilized Salvadoran bourgeoisie.

However, Lungo's analysis needs qualification. Transnationalized groups emerged from within the very womb of the old oligarchy and of political reaction. ARENA was founded in 1981 by a shadowy group of right-wing military officers, paramilitary operatives, and conservative members of the oligarchy. The key mover in its formation was Major Roberto D'Aubuisson, a former military intelligence officer and death-squad organizer. Between 1983 and 1988, however, partly as a result of the determination of incipient New Right sectors to mobilize politically, two competing factions emerged inside ARENA and disputed control over the party. One faction was closely tied to the old landed oligarchy and military cliques, and the other to emergent financial, industrial, and commercial interests that began to develop an alternative discourse of political moderation, economic modernization, and right-wing populism. If the ARENA thus emerged as the party of the economically dominant classes that began to mobilize politically, these classes, far from unified, were experiencing a deepening process of fractionation, expressed in the struggles inside ARENA. This explains the sharp factional infighting throughout the 1980s and early 1990s in ARENA, a party that housed multiple class fractions, and the shift in ARENA from a proto-fascist party of reaction in the early 1980s to a neo-liberal party of Salvadoran capital in the late 1980s.

Between 1985 and 1988 the two party factions vied for influence. The creation of an advisory council in 1985 of prominent business leaders to influence the decisions of the party's executive committee marked an important change in the party's formal structure and signalled the rise of the New Right in the party. During this time the FUSADES became an incubator of organic intellectuals for a neo-liberal project that ARENA began to champion and for private-sector leaders who began to provide political and financial support for the party. In fact, the FUSADES Board of Directors read like a virtual who's who of the technocratic fraction of the ARENA leadership and the FUSADES technocrats would take over key ministries and state agencies in the Cristiani, and later the Calderón Sol, governments.[86] With their confidence growing and their project cohering, the New Right groups launched a business strike in 1987 against Duarte under the banner of the ARENA opposition—demanding not a return to the old oligarchic arrangements but a neo-liberal program. In that same year the National Association of Private Enterprise (ANEP) suspended discussions with the government over economic policy and instead threw its support behind ARENA. In 1988 the transnational fraction gained control of the party with the nomination of Alfredo Cristiani as its presidential candidate, and then of the state with Cristiani's inauguration in 1989. Although infighting between the two fractions continued into the 1990s, the transnational kernel was able to establish its hegemony within ARENA and within the country's elite as a whole from 1988 and on.

Contingency and the uncertain play of social forces were important in this outcome. The ARENA had not been contemplated in the post-1980 US counterinsurgency scheme and did not enjoy Washington's support. The US government feared a restoration of "reactionary despotism" and was disconcerted by the rise of ARENA. Washington, in fact, intervened extensively in the 1984 elections to assist Duarte in defeating ARENA candidate Roberto D'Aubuisson.[87] But US policy adapted to developments as they unfolded and adjusted them to the larger program for the country. It is unlikely that newly organized sectors of the bourgeoisie would have chosen a proto-fascist movement through which to become politically mobilized had that movement not presented itself as an established reality and as a social force, an alliance with which became necessary for the defeat of the revolutionary forces, the development of an alternative to the PDC middle class reform program, and the generation of a social and political base upon which to make a bid for the hegemony of a new project.

In 1988, in anticipation of ARENA's electoral victory, the FUSADES drafted an Economic and Social Program.[88] For this purpose, the AID and the FUSADES contracted twenty-five international advisors, among them Arnold Harberger of the University of Chicago, one of the original "Chicago Boys," the team of free-market economists who had worked out in the 1970s the ideological and programmatic bases of neo-liberalism. FUSADES economist Mirna Lievano de Marqués, who coordinated the program, became Cristiani's Minister of Planning. The Foundation's Program was adopted wholesale in 1989 by the incoming ARENA government as its official economic program. What followed was sweeping neo-liberal reform, including trade liberalization, devaluation of the currency, privatizations, the lifting of subsidies, the promotion of non-traditional exports, and the expansion of free trade zones and maquiladora activities.[89] The ARENA government also reached a quick agreement with the IMF in 1990, which opened the floodgate for post-war reconstruction financing from the IFIs. Over one billion dollars flowed in from multilateral sources between 1990 and 1992 and replaced bilateral US aid, signalling the transition from US to transnational tutelage.[90] Between 1989 and 1992, non-traditional agricultural exports rose by an annual average of 25 percent and maquiladora textile production by 50 percent.[91]

Cristiani was succeeded after the 1994 presidential elections by a second ARENA president, Armando Calderón Sol. Calderón Sol was a compromise candidate linked to both groups in the ARENA, who had won the nomination in the face of the inability of the New Right candidate, Roberto Murray Meza, a millionaire industrialist and FUSADES founder who had administered AID funds under Cristiani, to win sufficient support. However, by the 1990s the New Right had established itself firmly in state and party institutions, and with foreign funders and agents, and could exercise enough influence over Calderón Sol to ensure that he would be responsive to the transnational program. Under the guidance of his new Minister of Finance, Enrique Hinds, a World Bank official prior to being recruited by the new administration, Calderón Sol deepened the neo-liberal reform program first drafted by Cristiani. His program included sweeping privatizations, further fiscal austerity, tax reform, and a lowering of tariffs. In early 1995, Calderón Sol relaxed regulations imposed earlier stipulating that maquilas had to be located in one of the free trade zones in order to receive tax benefits. The new regulations allowed maquila plants to receive most of the benefits irrespective of where they were located. The goal in Calderón Sol's words, was to "incorporate ourselves into the world production chain," to "turn all of El Salvador into one big free zone" and to convert the country into "the Hong Kong of Central America."[92]

The globalization process affects the interests of national fractions, particularly those among the dominant groups, embedded in pre-globalization structures of accumulation, such as agro-export oligarchies, and nationally based industrialists and merchants linked to local markets. The contradictions between multiple fractions and sectors acquire political expression in electoral and other arenas, such as in the internal party struggles in ARENA. The complexity of local political scenarios defies simplistic explanation and can give misleading impressions when viewed in too narrow conjunctural terms. As in Nicaragua, local rivalries, vendettas, corruption, and other idiosyncratic factors particular to El Salvador overlapped with local political dynamics and social conflicts with such structural factors as the opposing interests of class fractions. Some of the intra-party disputes in ARENA, for instance, were over which elite cliques would benefit from the spoils of the privatization of state holdings and had little to do with ideology and fractional interests per se.[93] But behind these conjunctural dynamics were the more fundamental issues.

By the late 1990s the internal struggles in ARENA had spilled out into the open. Party leaders from the military and landowning groups in the eastern and western agricultural regions charged that commercial and financial "country club technocrats" had taken over the party and betrayed its principles. The disputes took a violent turn by 1996—including death threats against Cristiani and company, car bombs ignited near the residences and business establishments of "technocrat" party leaders, assaults, and kidnappings—similar to the violent intra-party struggles that wracked the Institutional Revolutionary Party (PRI) in Mexico in the mid-1990s. As in Mexico, these battle lines were clearly between the "dinosaurs" tied to the old economic and political model and the "modernizers" whose fate was bound up with free market integration into the global economy. Major desertions from ARENA took place in March 1997 legislative elections and the party suffered a 35 percent drop in votes compared to the 1994 elections. Revealingly, the principal beneficiary of the desertions was the moribund National Conciliation Party (PCN), the old political vehicle of the military and the oligarchy. The PCN, benefiting from the defection of agricultural interests from ARENA, staged a remarkable comeback, winning eleven out of eighty-four seats in the National Assembly.[94] In 1997 Cristiani took over leadership of the ARENA bench in the National Assembly. The following year the transnational fraction was able, once again, to impose its candidate, Francisco Flores, a technocrat from the Ministry of Planning, to head the party's presidential ticket in the 1999 elections.[95] Although Flores won the 1999 elections and continued to implement the transnational project (he in fact deepened and extended the adjustment process and formally dollarized the economy), it was not clear in the early twenty-first century if ARENA could hold together or whether it would remain the sole party of the Salvadoran bourgeoisie.[96]

Meanwhile, a decade and a half of war and restructuring, as in Guatemala, had thoroughly transformed the social structure in ways conducive to globalization. Commenting on the post-war social fabric, one somber report noted: "A small elite continues to dominate economic and political life, although power within that elite has shifted from landed to commercial interests; a middle class sector of white collar management and technical employees has grown in numbers but as yet has no independent political vehicle to espouse its interests; urban workers, and particularly unionized workers, have lost influence as a result of privatization of state enterprises and the rise of maquiladora industry; and the mass of peasants, in whose name the armed struggle was waged, are in a more desperate condition than before the civil war began."[97] *Descampesinación* through the displacement from the land and urban migration of the rural population and the proletarianization of former peons affected up to a third of the rural population. The cities contained at least 30 percent of the working population by 1990 and a burgeoning informal sector.[98] A mass of alienated Salvadorans became available as an immizerated labor force while a new outward-looking strata of urban nouveau riches and high-consumption middle classes offered a social base for the new transnational bloc. Between 1977, when the terminal crisis of the old order began, and the late 1990s, the Salvadoran working class, once the best organized and most militant in Central America, had become disaggregated and atomized. A 1996 World Bank survey of what managers in Salvadoran enterprises thought on "obstacles related to contracting inflexibility, labor management relations, labor regulations, and union activity" ranked El Salvador the most congenial country in Latin America for business. It reported that unionized workers had dropped to 14 percent of the work force, that strike activity had plummeted since 1990, and that "firings appear to be easy; the process took about three days."[99]

The transition in El Salvador begot the appropriate conditions for global capitalism in the country. But first the war had to be brought to an end.

The military stalemate made it impossible for the emergent transnational bloc to stabilize the new social order. The war was an obstacle to El Salvador's participation in the global economy. The erosion of the alliance between the military and the economically dominant classes, the decision by the latter to politically organize themselves and to govern directly, provided the New Right, once it rose to hegemony, with the political autonomy necessary to negotiate with the FMLN. This "sacrifice" of the military made it possible for the Cristiani government to sign the January 1992 Chapultepec peace accords despite the fierce resistance of the old guard in ARENA and sectors of the armed forces. In this sense the peace process was as much a mechanism for concluding the process of transforming the Salvadoran state and the class structure as it was for ending the military conflict and accommodating the FMLN in the new order. The corporatist military structures were dismantled through the peace process, which represented a triumph of the New Right over the old oligarchy.

Stanley's fascinating study on the military "protection racket state," typical of much scholarship and political analysis of the Salvadoran peace process, is flawed on this account. In his "state-centered" Weberian analysis, the state is less an expression of underlying social structure than an independent institution whose activity is driven by competition among its cadre and by external demands. Seen from the lens of this state–society dualism, the problematic is less the social order than the institutional order. Change in the relationship between civilian/"social elites" and military/"state elites" through negotiated institutional reform is seen as having paved the way for the resolution of the Salvadoran conflict. The problem is reduced from transforming the social order to reforming the institutional order. This type of state reification appraises demilitarization and civilianization of states in Central America as the victorious outcome of the mass struggles in the period under investigation here. This is the essential conclusion of the mainstream democratization literature of the 1980s and 1990s. Moreover, the transnational elite shares this analysis and its normative conclusions, as do some sectors among the Central America Left that argue for an alliance with "progressive capitalists" (the transnational fraction) and for a pacification of popular struggles against the social order in the name of preserving the new institutional order. Shutting down the racket as reform of the institutional order represents the resolution of the problematic—which is the extent of change, and no more, that the transnational elite set out to achieve in the region.

But it is precisely as the Central American states became purged of "protection rackets" in the 1990s that the social structural—rather than institutional—causes of the conflict came sharply into focus. For these reasons it is necessary to critique the underlying normative structure that flows from the institutional and agency-driven analysis advanced by Stanley and others. Stanley concludes that structural transformation of the Salvadoran socioeconomic system is unlikely in the post-war period given the power of global economic forces over the country. The severe limits on change in the social order contributes to the maintenance of peace since the dominant groups in El Salvador would not have much reason to violently oppose an FMLN government should it come to power and hence they would not seek the restoration of a coercive military state. Such a state is less necessary in the era of globalization since the global economy exercises strictly economic coercion (market discipline) over popular majorities. The reorganization of the institutional order in Central America does contribute functionally to the maintenance of "peace" in terms of the absence of overt military conflict. The logically consistent conclusion we can draw from this analysis is that: 1) a collective mobilization from below which threatens the dominant groups and the social order itself is a threat to "peace"; 2) the limits that global capitalism places on the popular classes' ability to change the social order or to put an end to elite domination becomes a guarantor of "peace"; 3) backed by the veto power of global capitalism over the transformation of the social order, the new institutional order will survive because it will be able to contain this threat from below; and 4) the conditions under which the popular classes could threaten the social order become those which could undermine the peace.

This type of "problem-solving" institutional analysis and its normative undercurrents is in contrast to a critical approach that embeds analysis of institutional change in analysis of structural change, and which focuses on the prospects for social change that exposes the factors which make possible change in the institutional order (the mode of domination) without concomitant changes in the social order. After presenting data indicating the different economic activities that separated the old oligarchy from new bourgeois groups that emerged from the 1970s and on and analyzing the "gradual divergence [in the late 1970s] between the interests of the traditional oligarchy and of the modern sectors of the bourgeoisie," Enrique Baloyra notes: "There seems to be agreement that the latter could not dominate the former, but that, somehow, they managed to control the military government. It is one thing to prevent government interference, that is, to resist government initiatives, however, and quite another to force the government to do something. Apparently, the Salvadoran private sector had sufficient *influence* to do the former but not enough *power* to do the latter."[100] But the point to stress here is that by the mid-1980s and on this situation had changed. The new bourgeois fractions *could* "force the government to do something," precisely by organizing politically and assuming direct state power, as analyzed above. This state power is ulti-mately an expression of a determinant constellation of social and class forces in civil society. Once these forces became reaccommodated—and as the military no longer represented the interests of the fraction that had now become hegemonic within the elite—the state changed. When the oligarchy lost its hegemony, its representative in the state lost power. It was the rise of a global economy with the structural power to veto a popular transformation of the internal socioeconomic system that made it possible to dispense with the coercive protection racket state. Globalization was determinant in the institutional reorganization that redefined relations between the military and the dominant classes (between coercion and consent). These types of class struggle between popular majorities and the dominant classes in El Salvador, and between fractions, are the social mechanisms linking globalization processes to national political dynamics and state transformation. Here we see how domestic political structures become part of the evolving fabric of transnational class relations and political-economic processes.

The Chapultepec accord laid the basis for an accelerated integration of El Salvador into global capitalism. The National Reconstruction Plan became an instrument for consolidating the neo-liberal project.[101] This Plan was drafted by government bureaucrats with the assistance of the AID following the Chapultepec accord. The program emphasized the reconstruction of infrastructure and relief programs that could facilitate private-sector activity, foreign investment, and a speedy rearticulation of the country to world markets. Analytically speaking, the conversion of the reconstruction program into an instrument of the new dominant bloc was only possible because this bloc had imposed a conditional defeat on the popular revolutionary bloc, as formalized in the accords. The accords preserved the class rule of the Salvadoran elite and left the government, the state's institutionality, the economic system, and the social order intact. They were limited to mandating institutional changes that allowed the FMLN to transfer its struggle from the military to the internal political arena and that eliminated, in Stanley's words, "the military's ability to operate a protection racket," allowing therefore for a rationalization and modernization of the system of domination. What was negotiated were the terms under which the FMLN became integrated into the *existing* social order.

It is doubtful the FMLN could have achieved anything more at the particular historical conjuncture in which the old forms of struggle were becoming ineffective and new forms had not yet come of age. The FMLN demonstrated throughout the 1980s and early 1990s spectacular political-military success and in this sense the revolutionary movement was not a failure. But military stalemate and a negotiated settlement did *not* demonstrate that no-one won the war or that the outcome was, as some have claimed, a "negotiated revolution."[102] The conflict did *not* end "either in a revolutionary reconstitution of society at large, or in the common ruin of the contending classes," to evoke the famous phrase of Marx and Engels. The ARENA's rise represented the incomplete victory of a class fraction and its project. Victory is gauged by outcomes. If the transnational bloc could only consolidate its project through a negotiated peace, the FMLN by the late 1980s had lost the possibility of implementing *its* project. Political-military power in revolutionary struggle is not an end but a means to bring about the transformation of the social order. The success of popular struggle must be measured by the extent that it results in structural transformation, in an improvement in the cultural and material conditions of life for popular majorities, and in the empowerment of majorities to shape social structures and cultural processes in their interests. The FMLN's political-military success was a "national" phenomenon that became increasingly impotent in the face of globalization. Paradoxically, the success of the revolutionary forces does *not* show that popular change is possible under globalization. It demonstrates, to the contrary, how constraints imposed by the global system severely limit the effectiveness of popular struggles and local power. National Liberation movements have run their course; "national" liberation is not possible. Indeed, apart from the handful of remaining anti-colonial struggles, "national" liberation is no longer a particularly meaningful concept in the age of globalization. This assessment does not imply an end to the struggle of popular majorities in Central America but only the end of one round in an ongoing historical process. The next round will have to involve a transnational struggle protagonizing regional and transnational social movements that search for viable formulas of social and economic democratization, political empowerment, and the construction of a counter-hegemony under the new conditions of global capitalism.

Guatemala: The Paradoxes of the "Counterinsurgency State"[103]

To summarize Guatemala's transition: The traditional agro-export oligarchy was the most deeply entrenched in Guatemala and in control of the state—which was administered directly by the military for much of the 1980s—and a transnationalized fraction was the weakest, with the possible exception of Nicaragua. As in El Salvador, the US-supported Christian Democratic project that came to government in the 1980s as part of broader counterinsurgency efforts was intended to defuse the popular movement with reforms and at the head of very visible transitions to (largely dysfunctional) polyarchy. The Christian Democrats established transitional political and institutional arrangements but were not the bearers of the transnational elite project. With the introduction and expansion of new economic activities in the late 1980s, including a powerful new financial sector tied to international banking, maquiladora textile production, NTAEs, and new commercial activities, a transnationalized fraction of the elite assumed its own profile and clashed with the old state-protected oligarchy over fiscal, tax, liberalization, and related policies. This tiny fraction articulated in the early 1990s a coherent program for economic and political modernization attuned to the transnational elite agenda, as epitomized in the policy proposals that flowed out of a number of AID-funded associations, among them the Association for Research and Social Studies (ASIES) and the Entrepreneurial Chamber (CAEM). Representatives of this transnationalized fraction assumed the reins of the state with the electoral triumph in 1994 of the National Advancement Party (PAN), whose leadership came primarily from professionals, administrators, and technocrats schooled in neo-liberal economics and a modernizing outlook. Unlike El Salvador, where the insurgency actually came to dispute state power and constitute a dual power, the Guatemalan revolutionary movement did not threaten the state. But the movement could continue to wage an indefinite insurgency that would make it impossible to ever pacify the countryside and establish the stability that transnational capital required for the country and the region as a whole. The New Year's Eve 1996 peace accords established the basis for the hegemony of the transnational elite project for Guatemala. In 1997, the PAN government adopted a structural adjustment plan drafted by the ASIES, a number of whose leaders joined the PAN economic cabinet, and committed itself to deepening and consolidating a long-term program of neo-liberal transformation that had been implemented in bits and pieces since the Christian Democratic presidency of Vinicio Cerezo (1986–91).

The relative strength of the oligarchy and underdevelopment of the transnationalized fraction were rooted in the particular development of the Guatemalan state and social forces and accounts in part for the tardiness of the transnational project. The agro-export oligarchy developed out of the core group of political and economic elites of the colonial period, in what was then the General Captaincy, or headquarters, of the regional colony. The Guatemalan economy was the strongest in the region and the oligarchy became the most powerful. Yet the popular classes mounted a major challenge to this oligarchy early in the post-WWII years. The uprising against *caudillismo* and *continuismo* that shook every republic in the 1930s and 1940s culminated in Guatemala in the installation of a democratic and reformist regime in 1944. Unlike Costa Rica, where the capitalist class supported the 1948 "revolution" that reformed and modernized the country, the dominant economic groups in Guatemala fiercely resisted the reform project. A coalition of the CIA and reactionary Guatemalan forces enjoying limited Latino middle-class support overthrew the reformist government of Jacobo Arbenz in 1954.

The coup was followed by the construction of what a number of scholars have called a "counterinsurgency state" that militarized state institutions and political and social life much earlier, and much more thoroughly, than, by comparison, was the case in El Salvador.[104] The result was a more thorough cohesion of the dominant classes in the face of the threat from below, given the collective memory of land reform, redistributive programs, and state-sanctioned social mobilization. The 1944–54 "Guatemalan Spring" and its aftermath bequeathed conditions less favorable to the development of new fractions among the dominant groups that could articulate an alternative hegemonic project linking internal change to global change. In comparative perspective, the old oligarchy was crushed in Nicaragua in 1979, displaced in Costa Rica in 1948, and transformed in Honduras by US intervention and regional dynamics. In El Salvador, US and transnational actors promoted tax, land, and other reforms as a component of the counterinsurgency program—in the process, weakening the old oligarchy and strengthening a transnational fraction—in response to the power of the revolutionary movement. In Guatemala, oligarchic hegemony became entrenched within the dominant classes long before economic crisis, mass popular mobilization, and ruling class fractionation began to shake the oligarchic structures in the Isthmus. The all-pervasiveness of the counterinsurgency state and its near-total coercive domination over much of civil and political society "was a legacy of the revolution [of 1944–54] and the violent rejection of it by the dominant classes," argues Guatemala scholar Susanne Jonas. "These experiences gave a striking internal cohesion to the Guatemalan ruling coalition—much greater . . . than its counterpart in El Salvador. This reflected a determination never again to permit a land reform or a mobilization of the popular classes or the Indian population . . . Yet this very strength of the ruling classes in imposing their will on the popular classes was also a weakness, in that it prevented them from formulating a project with any broad legitimacy in Guatemalan society."[105]

However, these conclusions must be placed in perspective. The unity of the dominant groups in Guatemala should not be overstated. The ruling classes faced a deep structural crisis by the late 1970s and early 1980s and a renewed threat from subordinate classes that had reorganized and were again contesting political power. If one legacy of the 1954 counterrevolution was the relative strength of the traditional oligarchy vis-à-vis other dominant fractions and subaltern groups, another was its relative inability to organize itself politically or construct a functional political society. Instead, the Guatemalan ruling class turned over to the military—to what in Althusserian terminology could be called an *overdetermined* counterinsurgency state—the task of organizing a response to the renewed popular mobilization of the late 1970s and early 1980s. Paradoxically it was this overdetermined counterinsurgency state operating with an autonomy from civilian elites and in the absence, in the early and mid 1980s, of a visible reformist and "modernizing" technocratic group, that first articulated a project of internal change that would eventually open the way for the transnational elite project. The military ended up doing for the dominant classes what they were unable to do for themselves. The military's all-out counterinsurgency (what it termed "total war") acted as a perverse midwife to the transnational elite project in Guatemala. In El Salvador, by comparison, the dominant groups, although divided and in a state of flux and transformation, were organized enough to assume the reins of the state, socioeconomic restructuring, and a transition to polyarchy, in the years following the 1979 coup d'état that first displaced the old oligarchy and its direct military allies. In Guatemala the dominant groups were too incoherent to take the reins of this project when it was first launched in 1982.

Thus when the popular classes launched a new round of mobilization and struggle in the late 1970s and early 1980s, including a sustained insurrection by the highland Mayan Indian majority and an expanding guerrilla insurgency organized by the Guatemalan National Revolutionary Unity (URNG), the military remained in direct control of the state with the approval of the traditional dominant groups. In any event, these groups and their "proximate policymakers" were fused with the military in political society through such political outlets as the Democratic Institutional Party (PID), the Authentic Nationalist Federation (CAN), and the National Liberation Movement (MLN). The unprecedented counterinsurgency program launched by the military regime in 1982 was one of the most brutal in modern history, a totalitarian project in the veritable sense of the term, surpassing the terror unleashed by the Pinochét regime in Chile or the 1991–94 military regime in Haiti.[106] Coercive domination came to pervade every aspect of social relations. Up to 150,000 civilians were killed or "disappeared," over one million people were displaced internally and some 200,000 sent into exile, and over 440 villages entirely destroyed in scorched earth campaigns and indiscriminate terror.[107]

This repression was not an anomaly to the transnational project but a necessary first step in the development of that project. The popular upsurge from below threatened the New Right alternative as much as it threatened the traditional oligarchy. But the counterinsurgency also resulted in the transformation of the socioeconomic structure and in the composition of social forces in the country, particularly among the Indian communities in the rural areas, in such a way as to facilitate the penetration of global capitalism and create the internal conditions for Guatemala's reinsertion into the global economy. The scorched earth counterinsurgency had the effect, whether intentional or as an unanticipated outcome, of destroying the peasant economy and peasant forms of organization, bringing the Indian population, which constituted the majority of labor for the country's agro-export sector, under the sway of capitalist economic laws. In hothouse fashion, the counterinsurgency involved a rapid transformation of rural social structure and production relations. This extra-economic coercion broke up autonomous Indian peasant communities at a pace and to an extent that the strictly economic coercion involved in the process of capitalist development could never have achieved.[108] The counterinsurgency was an instrument of primitive accumulation. It was "the most violent form of proletarianization—through military means."[109]

The crisis of the agro-export model was expressed in stagnant world prices and demand but also in increasing difficulties in the particular system of labor supply on which it rested. In Guatemala there is a major structure of ethnic inequality and oppression overlaid with class dynamics. Since the Spanish conquest and settlement, Indian labor has been the Guatemala elite's "comparative advantage." The system for extracting low-cost labor from the Indians has determined the social structure at any historic moment.[110] The colonial and post-colonial hacienda system evolved from diverse forms of forced labor (not until 1945 was the last forced labor law official revoked). The new transnational model—a shift to sowing blue jeans and picking exotic fruits and vegetables for the world's rich—required not only a continuation but an increase in cheap and controllable Indian labor, but under new conditions. But it had become increasingly difficult to organize this labor through the traditional system of seasonal migration and having a small number of permanent agricultural workers. Rearticulation to the world market through a renewal of accumulation required a more steady labor supply and also a more fully capitalist labor supply system.

Both the peasant sector and the traditional agro-export sector declined in the 1980s and 1990s as the *latifundia-minifundia* system of land tenure broke up and gave way to a capitalist wage labor system, reflecting the crisis of the old agro-export model and the internal social structure that sustained that model. Jeffrey Paige has argued that the prelude to the 1980s counterinsurgency was an effort to resolve a crisis in the agro-export economy that revolved around conflict between military agribusinessmen and a migrant semiproletariat Indian population.[111] Smith argues that the counterinsurgency was an attempt to destroy what remained of economic autonomy among the Indian communities, such as regional market networks, and thus complete the process of proletarianization in order to make this peasant population available for the agro-export production sites. She shows how "(1) it [the counterinsurgency] removed Indian peasants from one large 'underdeveloped' zone slated by Guatemalan businessmen (many of them members of the military) for forest clearance, cattle ranching, and the extraction of minerals; (2) it forcibly nucleated dispersed farming populations so that they could not farm, forcing them to seek wage work in order to survive; and (3) it helped reduce peasant self-sufficiency throughout the highlands." The military regime, from 1982 and on, emphasized in its counterinsurgency program the attainment of "national integration" and "incorporation" of "different ethnic groups" into "national development projects,"[112] which meant integration into a renewed process of capitalist development.

Whatever the case, it is clear that the crisis of the oligarchic export model was both of social reproduction and resistance among its Indian labor base, and of the model's inability to link to globalization. This crisis generated a counterinsurgent upheaval that resolved both "problems" for the transnational project: that of the old oligarchic-feudal structures and that of the popular masses. The model involved the gradual destruction of the *minifundia*, or tiny below-subsistence peasant holdings among the highland Mayan Indian population that constituted the bulk of rural labor for the agro-export sector. The *minifundia* and the autonomous Indian highland communities provided for social reproduction (thus internalizing to labor the cost of reproduction) and for seasonal subsistence, but also obliged the labor force to migrate annually to the plantations to supplement their income. The *minifundia* structure built into the agro-export model involved from the onset a coercive system of labor control, aggravated in the Guatemalan case by the intersection of class exploitation with ethnic domination of the Mayan Indians in a pervasive system of *de facto* apartheid. But the expansion in the post-WWII period, and especially in the 1960s and 1970s, of the agro-export sector, involving progressive seizure of land from Indian communities, new waves of land concentration, and the increasing semi- and complete proletarianization of the Indians, intensified the system of coerced labor. Combined with the subdivision of *minifundia* plots, and massive land grabs by military officers and landlords through counterinsurgency, the *minifundia* system began to crumble, heightening the crisis of survival among the Indian population. This was the structural underpinning of the Indian uprising of the early 1980s. The spiral of coercion and resistance, culminating in the uprising and guerrilla movement, and in the bloody counterinsurgency, was the social response to the crisis and exhaustion of the old model.

The manifest function of the counterinsurgency was suppression of the revolutionary challenge and the Indian insurrection. But its latent function was the application of state terrorism to modify socioeconomic structures (the two are linked, since the loss of economic autonomy dramatically curtailed the Indians' capacity to mount resistance and develop indepen-dent political action.) State terrorism became the instrument of capitalist globalization in Guatemala, conforming "national" structures to emerging global structures. The proletarianization of the Indian peasantry marked the more complete penetration of capitalism into the Guatemalan country-side. Carol Smith noted in 1990, "Peasant means for maintaining autono-mous forms of employment—in food production, artisan production, and trade—is dramatically less than what it had been in the late 1970s. Large numbers of people, probably the majority, must now seek wage employ-ment either in the cities or on plantations ... Because of the scarcity of work (and the desperateness of their situation), most highland Indians are willing to accept whatever wage they can get ... Guatemala is now in a much better position to turn toward intensified industrial production of assembly, based on cheap labor, because it has created so much more 'free' cheap labor than it had before."[113] In turn, these changes formed part of the larger process of transnational class formation discussed earlier, whereby pre-capitalist classes have tended to disappear. The crisis of the agro-export model, the penetration of capitalism into the Indian highlands and the proletarianization of the peasantry paved the way for the new transnational model.

These effects of counterinsurgency dovetailed with the neo-liberal open-ing to the global economy, which accelerated the disintegration of the old agro-export model. For instance, the increase in food imports from the United States under neo-liberal measures taken in the 1980s flooded local urban and rural markets with foreign beans, rice, and corn and undercut domestic food production largely in the hands of small producers.[114] US "food aid" programs went hand in hand with programs funded by the AID and promoted by the local New Right business associations aimed at converting peasant food production into the production by small and medium producers of NTAEs. Cultivation of these products, in turn, required seeds, fertilizers, and other agro-industrial and industrial inputs, resulting in an extension of market relations in the countryside, the rise of a market in land, and the development of a class of medium-sized capitalist farmers linked to exporters and transnational corporations (see next chapter). One can observe the following cycle: increased food imports undercut the viability of domestic food production, shifting agriculture towards the NTAEs and accelerating the turn to capitalist farming and market integration, which for its part facilitates the transfer of resources and power towards the external sector linked to the global economy and feeds the process of transformation of the class structure in the countryside. This cycle is fundamentally a *transnational* process.

"In the past years, these [the highland Indian] communities have had to abandon their productive activities due to political violence," noted one AID-commissioned report, "thus increasing the supply of skilled labor."[115] The report, prepared by the Guatemalan Non-Traditional Exporters' Association (GEXPORT), is highly revealing because it suggests that at the level of agency the new capitalist groups were quite aware of the structural changes brought about by counterinsurgency and of the new economic opportunities opening up as a result of the changes. With the guerrilla insurgency largely contained and the installation of a civilian regime, a number of Guatemalan capitalists who had transferred their capital abroad in the face of the crisis in the early 1980s began to repatriate and coalesce into a number of interlocking financial groups that formed a new private financial sector.[116] Much of this capital was put to speculative activity, but it was also invested in maquiladora production, in consort with transnational companies, in NTAEs, and in new commercial activities (see next chapter).

In the early 1990s, GEXPORT and other New Right associations and investor groups began to organize, in consort with such transnationals as Liz Claiborne, Van Heusen, and Gitano, subcontracting networks in the Indian highlands. In this arrangement, local Guatemalan contractors hired Indian women, and sometimes whole families, to produce garments in small rural shops or even out of their houses in their home villages. In this way, labor costs amounted to 25 percent less than in the centralized maquiladora plants in Guatemala City. A "putting out" system, in effect, became incorporated into the lower rungs of complex global commodity chains which brought together Guatemalan and East Asian subcontractors, transnational corporate contractors, and proletarianized Indian labor and their communities, which were integrated directly into globalized production on the heels of the destruction of their pre-globalization economic structure and community autonomy.[117] Similarly, many of those communities restructured by the violence became subject to AID programs to promote NTAEs such as strawberries, snow peas, and broccoli.[118] Unlike food production for local consumption, these crops require capital and technology inputs such as chemical fertilizers, insecticides, fungicides, and a steady supply of seeds, obtained through loans from the IFIs channeled through local networks. In this way, Indian communities were drawn into national and international capitalist markets, a process which also spawned new class distinctions and polarization.

The "total war" launched by the military regime, including its political dimensions (a transition to polyarchy) confused observers in that it appeared on the surface as a process conducive to the retrenchment of the military and the traditional oligarchy. But the political, economic, and social changes generated by the "total war" were laying the basis for the emergence of the transnational project in the country. When placed in the context of regional and global dynamics, the "total war" was the acutely perverted form in which this project was incubated. The military had already, by the late 1970s, become divided between the old guard and a modernizing, technocratic sector. This latter sector would become the initial agent of the transnational project, beginning in 1982 with the US-supported coup d'état that brought to power General Efrain Ríos Montt as the head of this technocratic sector. The Ríos Montt regime promulgated a National Security and Development Plan that included the launching of an all-out counterinsurgency but also a revival of political parties, elections, and a return to civilian government as the declared means of legitimizing the Guatemalan state nationally and internationally.[119] While Ríos Montt was himself overthrown in 1983, his replacement, General Oscar Mejía Victores, oversaw the return to polyarchy in the 1985 elections that brought Vinicio Cerezo and the Christian Democrats to power. The new Minister of Defense, General Héctor Gramajo, became a leading figure inside the Guatemalan state, promoting consensus on the need to modernize the system of political domination.[120] The military-civilian think-tank organized through his office, the Center for Strategic Studies of National Stability, became a forum for bringing together members of the modernizing sector in the army with representatives of an incipient technocratic New Right among the civilian elite and the private sector.

The transition to polyarchy was not merely a ploy of the counterinsurgency program. Continued insurgency and counterinsurgency made renewed accumulation impossible. Instability provoked a massive flight of foreign capital from Guatemala and a similar massive transfer by Guatemalan capitalists of private investment funds out of the country, largely to bank accounts abroad, in order to "wait out" the war.[121] A change in the mode of social control and the system of domination was the precondition for a recovery and reorganization of a process of capital accumulation. Polyarchy was a means to the end of stability, but stability was the precondition for restructuring and not an end in itself. The military's state-oriented capitalist development strategy clashed with the elite's plans for private-sector capitalist development anchored in a civil society under its hegemonic sway. Demilitarization became necessary because an uncontrolled military was increasingly counterproductive, not to the more immediate objective of defeating the popular challenge, but to the more long-term objectives of thoroughly restructuring the Guatemalan state and cultivating a transnational fraction among the elite. Both these processes—class development and state restructuring—proceeded through the transition to polyarchy.

Transnationally Oriented Groups Organize

For the historic reasons alluded to above, the dominant groups in Guatemala displayed a disjuncture between the levels of their political and economic organization. Having turned over a great deal of autonomy to the military since 1954 in the state's social control functions, these groups were poorly organized politically but well organized economically, bolstered in their internal cohesion by the unifying element of memory of the 1944–54 period and fear of a repetition. The powerful Chamber of

Agricultural, Commercial, Industrial and Financial Organizations (CACIF) brought together all fractions of the oligarchy and the bourgeoisie—for the most part tied to corporative state economic structures—and operated as a nearly monolithic lobby over the military states (and civilian bureaucracies) in promoting policies favorable to business and blocking reforms. The strength and coherence of this economic lobby explains, in part, the difficulties later encountered in the implementation of the transnational project, especially in neo-liberal economic measures such as tax reform that affected oligarchic, and more generally, capitalist interests.

The project of global capitalism in Guatemala could not advance without the development of a transnationalized fraction as its internal protagonist. But as transnationally oriented groups began to coalesce they became economically organized more quickly, and well before they achieved a coherent political organization. The development of a transnational fraction can be divided into three stages. In the first, the late 1970s until the transition to polyarchy, the New Right cohered and began to organize economically. In the second, under the Cerezo government, this emergent fraction began to liaise with the state and engage in extensive policy development. In the third, 1990 and on, it began to acquire its own political protagonism. This process unfolded in close cooperation with transnational actors, especially the AID. The transition to polyarchy provided the Guatemalan state with the international legitimacy needed by the AID to dramatically expand its programs in the country. AID assistance for Guatemala went from $97 million between 1980 and 1984 to $847 million between 1985 and 1990, which was double the total of all US assistance to Guatemala in the preceding forty years.[122] Much of this was provided as direct assistance to the private sector, beginning in 1986, under an AID program, the Private Enterprise Development (PED). The PED included seven components: "policy dialogue"; "promotion of investment and exports"; "management training"; "financial and credit assistance"; "privatization"; "assistance for micro and small businesses"; and "tourism development."[123] Helping the private sector to organize entailed funding through the PED the creation and the activities of a vast array of private-sector organizations that would become protagonists, in diverse ways, in economic and political restructuring.

Two of the most important of these organizations were the Entrepreneurial Chamber (CAEM) and Free Market Chamber (CLE), which acted as clearing houses for the development of new economic groups and for a string of specialized associations.[124] The CAEM was formed in late 1981 in order to negotiate the terms of Guatemala's participation in the Caribbean Basin Initiative (CBI), a US-sponsored program designed to transform the region's participation in the world market in the context of global restructuring, and particularly, to promote non-traditional exports and liberalize the regional economy (see next chapter). The CAEM and the CLE acted as an incubator for a modernizing neo-liberal discourse, bringing together business people tied to non-traditional exports, New Right technocrats, and ideologues. In turn, the CAEM and the CLE established a spate of think-tanks and policy-planning institutes, among them: the Foundation for Integral Development (FUNDAP); the Guatemala Development Foundation (FUNDESA); the National Economic Research Center (CIEN); and the aforementioned GEXPORT. This latter association was organized into distinct commissions, each one concerned with promoting a specific non-traditional export, such as maquila-produced garments and new agricultural products.[125] The AID did not suspend relations with the old guard, organized largely in the CACIF. Rather, it sought to gradually undercut the influence of the oligarchy by building up these new associations and promoting the development of a transnational fraction that could wrest leadership from the CACIF. The once monolithic CACIF, the domain of the traditional oligarchy, eventually became wracked with internal divisions, while the rising technocrats spoke of the aging oligarchy as "outmoded" and "reactionary." "A growing band of private Guatemalan entrepreneurs are quietly changing many aspects of life for their countrymen," proclaimed one GEXPORT official. "They look at coffee barons and other traditionals as Neanderthal types."[126]

The emerging New Right groupings began to explore the development of the transnational project in Guatemala and to gain an instrumental hold over the state in policy development. The CAEM and the CLE, for instance, placed numerous representatives on government commissions set up to draft programs and policies for long-term socioeconomic restructuring, such as the State Tourist Institute, the National Wage Commission, and the National Export Council.[127] The AID also funded the creation of the National Council for the Promotion of Exports (CONAPEX) as a joint government–private sector forum. Reflecting the fusion of this emerging New Right private-sector bloc with the state, the CONAPEX, founded in 1986, was comprised of five economic cabinet ministers and five private-sector representatives appointed by CAEM. The AID also funded studies undertaken by the slew of new modernizing capitalist associations, organized training programs for the interlocking leadership of these associations, and supported them in their negotiations with the government over policy reform.[128] AID assistance was "directed principally to improving the ability of the private sector to develop and negotiate its own agenda with the government in vital affairs related to improving the conditions for investment, employment, and exports."[129] Through these processes the oligopolist model of power in a polyarchic system under the hegemony of capital, as political scientist Thomas Dye and sociologist G. William Domhoff, among others, have cogently analyzed for the United States, began to take hold in Guatemala, as in the other Central American countries.[130] In this model, policies in the interests of the hegemonic fraction of capital are devised in civil society, particularly among business associations and policy-planning institutes, and then filtered upward to the state through such mechanisms of private-sector representation in the government.

In sum, throughout the 1980s and 1990s, the cluster of technocratic New Right associations gained influence over the organizations of the traditional elite, interlocked with the state and with transnational actors, and became the local agent of globalization.[131] At the behest of this emerging private-sector bloc, the government approved a series of liberalization and deregulation measures, among them the creation of free trade zones for maquila production, tax breaks and other incentives for new export products, the lifting of capital controls, exoneration from import restrictions and the lowering of tariffs, the establishment of a government Export Fund with $20 million loaned by the World Bank, and so on.[132] Nonetheless, the neo-liberal program was only partially and sporadically implemented in Guatemala in the 1980s and 1990s. Efforts by the transnational elite to promote several reformist redistributive measures and neo-liberal modernization, such as fiscal and banking reform, and particularly tax reform, met with the strong protest and stiff resistance of the Guatemalan business elite. This resistance from the old guard was vociferous, most visibly from the CACIF, but also came from some quarters within the New Right (many of whose members also remained active in CACIF), even though they identified more broadly with the transnational project.[133] The transnational fraction did not achieve the amount of influence over state policy as it did, for instance, in El Salvador and Costa Rica. The Guatemalan state and its policies continued to be influenced by rival fractions of capital and competing elites and the old guard, epitomized in CACIF, retained a significant, if diminishing, influence. Because the old oligarchy was stronger in Guatemala than elsewhere, it had more success in blocking reform, something which generated friction between it and the transnational elite and complicated the transition in Guatemala. But by the middle of the 1990s it began to exercise considerable pressure on the local elite and to impose a conditionality.

It became clear that if the transnational project were to make more systematic headway its local agents would have to organize politically. The neo-liberal New Right reached the point by the 1990s where it had reduced the influence of the traditional oligarchy and military sectors enough for it to stand on its own. It set about to achieve hegemony over the business elite as a whole, and to secure control over a (transformed) state and leadership in civil society. Even though it was less successful in this endeavor than its counterparts were elsewhere, it was able to take advantage of the transition to polyarchy to launch its own political protagonism, and to partially eclipse and replace the old political right. Groups such as the MLN and the PID, once important political clearing houses of the dominant groups, as epitomized by MLN leader Mario Alarcón Sandoval, the godfather of the oligarchy and the death squads, began to fade into increasing political insignificance. In 1990, some of the most powerful of the new economic groups formed the "Pyramid Group" as a forum to liaise with several "modernizing" political parties: the Union of the National Center (UCN), the Solidarity Action Movement (MAS), and the PAN. With support from the Pyramid Group, the MAS's Jorge Serrano won the 1990 vote, set up a coalition government with the PAN, and appointed a number of representatives of the New Right modernizers.

The Serrano government announced a sweeping structural adjustment program in 1991, drawn up by the ASIES, but the government's collapse in 1993 in the wake of Serrano's failed attempt to dissolve Congress and suspend the constitution (what was referred to as his "self-coup" or the *Serranazo*) and his subsequent flight from the country, put a further hold on the neo-liberal program.[134] The interim government of Ramiro de León Carpio revived Serrano's 1991 program but his administration followed a "holding pattern" and was unable to push the program forward either. But the New Right continued its internal organizing and was able to assume a more direct representation in the state with the election of PAN leader Alvaro Arzú, a businessman drawn from its own ranks, in the 1995 elections.[135] The first priority of the Arzú government was to accelerate the peace negotiations between the Guatemalan state and the URNG that began under the previous two civilian regimes.[136] A peace accord was essential for the transnational elite to push forward its agenda. The accords signed on December 29, 1996 set the entire stage for restructuring the Guatemalan state and society into the twenty-first century, including relations among dominant groups and fractions. It was a prerequisite not just for stability but for the larger project of constructing a neo-liberal order as part and parcel of the transition.

The Peace Accords: Success or Failure?

The peace plan called for a comprehensive accord on human rights, the further expansion and institutionalization of the polyarchic system already in place through incorporation of the guerrillas that were to be demobilized, and related measures, and a formal constitutional subordination of the armed forces to a civilian state. It also defined Guatemala as a "multiethnic, multicultural, and multilingual" country and contained many specific provisions for indigenous rights and protections. As well, it included social, economic, and agrarian dimensions which called for growth, equity, and sustainable development. But the plan was explicit in endorsing absolute property rights and the prevailing distribution of property, and implicit in ruling out any structural transformations of the socioeconomic order and in endorsing a neo-liberal framework on these issues.[137] In fact, the social, economic, and agrarian dimensions of the plan were negotiated and drafted with the active participation of the IFIs, so that structural adjustment became embedded within it.[138] In 1997, the IFIs and donor countries promised $1.9 billion in post-war reconstruction funds for 1997–2000 and made disbursements conditional on implementation of the accords, what Boyce termed "peace conditionality."[139]

Resistance of the Guatemalan elite to a number of reforms mandated by the accords, and the pressures placed by transnational elites on the oligarchy to comply, created the image of the transnational project as "progressive" and obscured the essential polarizing and pauperizing consequences of neo-liberalism. By promoting global capitalism in Guatemala the transnational elite was objectively anti-oligarchic, but this should not obscure its overarching project of constructing a neo-liberal order in Guatemala. For instance, transnational elites clashed repeatedly with Guatemalan oligarchs over the issue of reforming the tax system. At 8 percent of GDP, Guatemala had the lowest tax ratio in the hemisphere. The accords called for this ratio to increase to 12 percent by the year 2000, which in any event would have still been below the average for developing countries (14 percent) and below any other Latin American country.[140] A progressive tax reform could have redistributed income downward and financed social spending. But the accords did not endorse the principle of progressive taxation, and the concrete reforms designed by the IFIs proposed indirect taxes levied largely on consumption, in a regressive tax system in which 80 percent of taxes already came from indirect levies and only 20 percent from direct taxes on income and wealth.[141] The tax reform was seen by the IFIs as an essential macroeconomic instrument for resuming transnational capital accumulation in Guatemala and proceeding with a more sweeping adjustment. The poor and popular classes were being asked to finance through austerity an accord whose purpose, seen from the view of the transnational elite, was to stabilize the country so that a neo-liberal order could be constructed.

By way of further example, the "land reform" called for in the peace accords took the approach of "agrarian modernization," stipulating the creation of a land registry and the sale of available private lands. It respected the existing distribution of land, and contained no mechanisms for redistribution or for internal financing for the purchase of land on this open market by the poor and the landless. It was not intended to benefit the dispossessed rural majority, much less achieve social justice. It was a measure pushed since the 1980s, well before the peace process, by the IFIs for the purpose of further facilitating the transition begun several decades earlier to a more fully capitalist agriculture, including a market in land and labor, in the countryside.[142] In this sense, it was similar to the types of land policies associated with the Green Revolution and with 1960s land reform programs promoted by the capitalist powers in the Third World. These programs were aimed at extending and intensifying capitalist agriculture, including the introduction of the types of agri-business schemes contemplated for Guatemala. In doing so, they resulted in an increased concentration of land, a rise in inequalities, and the proletarianization and further impoverishment of the rural population.[143] In Guatemala, this process also resulted in the 1990s in increased differentiation in the countryside, as richer farmers were able to buy out poorer farmers, part of the process of class formation *within* indigenous communities.[144]

So how are the Guatemalan peace accords to be assessed? To the extent that they helped put an end to the reign of brutal human rights violations, opened up even partial and limited political space through polyarchy, and at least legitimized, if not realized, such demands as indigenous rights, the accords were of historic importance. Yet they also helped to legitimate the emergent neo-liberal order by precluding fundamental change in the socioeconomic system and delegitimating opponents of this system (for example, dispossessed campesinos invading land and those who support them) as "extremists who reject peace." The contribution of the accords to democratization and development should be gauged not by what was agreed to on paper but by the extent to which proposed changes were actually implemented and to which these changes actually affected the lived experience of democratization and development among the poor majority. Just as the proposed land and tax reforms were perfectly compatible with an exclusionary neo-liberal order that preserved and even regenerated the larger structures of power and domination, indigenous cultural issues addressed in the accords were disassociated by the transnational elite from socioeconomic changes and autonomous political power for the indigenous.

"The negotiation process was a great step forward for Guatemalan democracy," argues Susanne Jonas, expressing the conventional interpretation of the Central American peace processes. "The accords constituted a truly negotiated settlement, much like El Salvador's of 1992. Rather than being imposed by victors upon vanquished, they represented a splitting of differences between radically opposed forces, with major concessions from both sides."[145] But it is difficult to see what concessions the poor majority of Guatemalans won from the new dominant groups or from the system of global capitalism that the latter sought to advance. As Spence, et al., noted in their 1998 report on the accords, "there is a growing belief among the citizenry at large that the accords have little relevance to their lives.[146] A year later, in May 1999, over 80 percent of the population abstained from participating in a referendum on constitutional reforms called for in the accords. I do not disagree with the conjunctural reasons that Jonas advances for this abstention and for the defeat of the referendum, including the intense campaign against reform launched by reactionary forces.[147] But the larger meaning of the abstention is to be found, in my view, in the alienation of the Guatemalan majority from a political process that they had come to see as not in their control and as reproducing their subordination.

Achieving even the limited objectives of the accords proved elusive. A spate of land invasions that began even before the accords were signed and that intensified throughout the late 1990s were met by forcible evictions, large displays of police power, injuries and death. The accords required the government to increase health and educational spending by 50 percent by 2000. The requirement was not met, but even if it had been, it would have amounted to an increase of a mere $4 per person for the year 2000 budget, given that such spending was already the lowest in Latin America, with health standing at 0.9 percent and education at 1.6 percent of GNP in 1996.[148] While poverty and inequality intensified in every country of the Isthmus in the 1980s and 1990s, social and economic indicators were even more alarming for Guatemala than in the other republics. Nearly 40 percent of the population was illiterate, and the average adult had only 3.2 years of schooling. Malnutrition affected one in three children. About 50 percent lacked access to electricity, and 64 percent to running water.

Under and unemployment affected nearly 40 percent of the population, and a full 65 percent of the labor forces was relegated to the informal sector.[149] The poverty rate rose from 70 percent of the population in 1980 to 87 percent in 1991, while the percentage of Guatemalans unable to afford the "minimum diet" climbed from 52 percent to 72 percent.[150] By 1998, when it became clear that the government would be unable to meet its commitments, it quietly negotiated with the IFIs a modification of the targets of the peace process regarding tax reform, agrarian policy, justice, rural development, public security, and constitutional reforms affecting the military and the indigenous, further exonerating the Guatemalan state from working towards any type of structural transformation that could achieve a modicum of social justice.[151] "Peace conditionality" for the IFIs did not mean making international assistance conditional on social justice or popular sector interests but on the macroeconomic performance and fiscal solvency necessary for the country to integrate into global capitalism.

Jonas attributes to me the view that the peace processes in Central America are "doomed to failure."[152] This is not, in fact, my view. I have argued that notions of "success" and "failure" in historical processes are not particularly meaningful unless they are assessed relative to the interests and the objectives of distinct social forces in struggle. The Central American peace and reconciliation accords were remarkably successful in resolving obstacles to the "normalization" of the region's integration into global capitalism. Jonas recognizes as much, explicitly, when she states: "There is no question that globalization and neo-liberalism have dramatically increased Guatemalan poverty, both nationally and locally, during the peace process years as well as the decades of war. Furthermore, independent of the resistance of both oligarchical and indigenous/popular sectors to being incorporated, the world-economy is coming to Guatemala."[153] Regional peace negotiations were a transnational political process that formalized the outcome of the 1960s to the 1990s upheaval, accurately reflecting shifts in the historic balance of forces that emerged in the late twentieth century under capitalist globalization.

Linking this to the issue of tensions between Guatemalan and the transnational elites, by way of conclusion, such tensions should be seen as symptomatic of the asymmetric relations between "Southern" and "Northern" contingents of transnational classes. The process of transnational class formation proceeds among classes whose historic development has taken place through nation-states and their institutions and is not one of equals. The mutation of the international class alliance of national bourgeoisies of the post-WWII period into a transnationalized bourgeoisie in the globalization era is one fraught with tensions and conflict. The ruling classes originating from the cores of world capitalism exhibit a structural dominance in the process as the consequence of asymmetries that historically characterized the world-system. Such asymmetries have meant that organic intellectuals operating at the world-systemic level have tended to come from the centers of world capitalism (although they are increasingly located within the TNS apparatus). The role of the "organic

intellectual" among the dominant classes in Central America has historically been played by the United States. As representatives of the dominant
outside power, US policymakers have been able to take a long-term and
more "detached" perspective on the requirements of preserving the
regional social order and shaping the direction of change—a role that has
shifted more fully to a transnational elite—while local ruling classes have
tended to concentrate more on their immediate interests and short-term
considerations. Thus US state managers or transnational elites have promoted reformist measures to undercut revolutionary change, or to facilitate
the modernization of capital accumulation, that affect the immediate
interests of dominant groups, or certainly of powerful sectors among those
groups. This explains, but only in part, strong tensions between the
Guatemalan and the transnational elite.

It should be recalled that relations between the United States and other
core powers, and now the transnational elite, and indigenous elites such
as those in Central America have historically been, and remain, checkered
with tension, conflict, and contradictions, even though affinities of interest
are organic. The logic of globalization as the underlying structural process
under discussion here does not neatly determine the behavior of agents.
Rather, it interacts in a highly complex manner with other factors, including local conditions and histories, learning processes, identity formation,
and so on. Explaining the conduct of agents requires a skillful combination of structural and behavioral levels of analysis. Actors often operate
on the basis of multiple logics that imply conflicting rationalities. For
instance, the well-documented problem of widespread corruption among
the new technocratic state elites throughout Latin America is a logical
consequence of opportunities for illicit enrichment that have been made
available by the neo-liberal model itself, which focuses on the privatization
and deregulation of the public sector and a greatly reduced role for the
state, including its internal surveillance functions.[154] Corruption is a
rational response to the conditions generated by the transnational project,
even though it conflicts with the objectives of that project. In this regard,
New Right governments that have swept to power throughout Central
America have become deeply mired in corruption. That a ruling group
comes to constitute a transnational fraction linked to the emergent global
system does not mean that these groups are honest, clean, and democratic
in their governing conduct; they are willing to engage in extra-constitu-
tional and criminal activity, prone to violence, and so on. Rather, constituting a transnational fraction means that their material interests and
identity lie with integration into the emergent structures of global capitalism and with the rationalization and modernization of both accumulation
and domination.

Honduras: A Divergent Route to Globalization

The Honduran transition converges in some respects with those of its neighbors and diverges sharply in other. As throughout the region, the dialectics of popular class struggle, counterrevolution, and US intervention drove political transformation and capitalist modernization. We see a similar sequence of events as in El Salvador. *First*: militarization and US intervention starting in 1979 as Honduras became swept up into the regional conflict. Honduras, however, did not experience a revolutionary movement that threatened a general breakdown in the social order. The crisis that descended on the country in the late 1970s and early 1980s became displaced through the recomposition of social forces and changes in the political system of domination. Militarization was undertaken to support counterinsurgency in El Salvador and to service the campaign of low-intensity warfare in Nicaragua, and only secondarily to suppress popular sectors within the country's own borders. The dominant groups remained firmly in control during the transition despite a strong popular movement that swelled in the 1970s and 1980s. *Second*: an incomplete transition to polyarchy in the early 1980s along with US sponsorship of economic development and restructuring programs. *Third*: the recomposition of social forces and the rise of transnationally oriented groups among the local elite able to navigate the waters of the transition. The transnational fraction began to cohere in the 1980s in consonance with—indeed, under the canopy of—the virtual US occupation of the country and its conversion into a rearguard for regional counterrevolution, amidst sharp struggles between old and new economic groups and an extreme fragmentation of private capital. But this New Right did not acquire a clearly delineated political expression and was more inchoate than in neighboring countries. A key turning point in the Honduran transition came in 1989, when Rafaél Callejas, backed by powerful new business sectors, won the presidency as the National Party candidate. *Fourth*: subsequent demilitarization, sweeping neo-liberal restructuring, and integration into the global economy in the 1990s as the regional conflict wound down. Successive Liberal and National Party governments in the 1990s continued, and deepened, the process begun under Callejas of neo-liberalism and globalization.

The Honduran case illustrates the importance of particular national histories in the trajectory of integration into global capitalism. In Honduras, both the subordinate and the dominant classes were historically the least developed in Central America, and the state and economy the most backward. The "absent Honduran oligarchy" thesis of Torres Rivas and other scholars goes a long way in explaining the country's unique history within the region as well as its particular transition under globalization.[155] According to this thesis, Honduras' lack of the rich volcanic soils of its neighbors, its geographical isolation, and a chronic labor shortage ever since the relatively small Indian population was decimated in the aftermath of Spanish conquest, stymied the rise of an agro-export oligarchy or of a national bourgeoisie tied to world markets. Whereas the introduction of coffee in the other Central American republics in the nineteenth century spawned the rise of a powerful coffee oligarchy and liberal revolutions (see next chapter), in Honduras there was no comparable process of internal accumulation that could develop the social structure. The political and economic elite directly tied through its own productive activity to the world economy that emerged in the other Central American countries and led national development, never cohered in Honduras. Moreover, what little coffee production did develop was largely in smallholder hands, unlike El Salvador and Guatemala, where the crop was controlled by powerful coffee oligarchies. It was not until the 1950s and 1960s that the country began to diversify its exports to include coffee, cotton, cattle, and sugar, and to become more broadly incorporated into the world economy. The weakness of Honduran social forces and the state allowed for the vulgar domination of the country by foreign companies, making Honduras the quintessential "Banana Republic." Introduced in the late nineteenth century, bananas, along with silver mining on a more limited scale, finally linked the country more fully to the world economy early in the next century. But production was almost exclusively the monopoly of foreign (US) companies, led by Standard Fruit and United Fruit. The banana companies organized the sector as a classical enclave, even importing much of its labor force from the nearby Caribbean.[156] It is useful to elaborate, retracing this background and the trajectory of globalization in Honduras.

The chaotic disequilibrium among internal social forces for much of the nineteenth and twentieth centuries led to the extreme instability and precariousness of the Honduran state and polity. No less than 117 different presidents took office between 1824 and 1933, usually by force of arms or other non-constitutional intrigues, under the competing pressures of a small landed oligarchy, mid-sized ranchers, bureaucratic elites, and mass peasant and worker mobilizations. Given the limited possibilities for enrichment through economic activity, the upper classes gravitated towards politics and engaged in ferocious struggles for power and the spoils of office. Government by caudillo became an institutional fixture of the political system from independence until the rise of the military to power in 1956.[157] In the absence of a dynamic agro-export sector, a peasant-based land tenure system did not represent an impediment to elite development. The Honduran peasantry was less disrupted by proletarianization and became a more enduring social force. Peasant movements were often launched in combination with militant working class struggles among banana plantation, silver mine, port, and railroad workers. The popular classes were able to influence the country's polity and provide a somewhat heterogeneous base for the state, expressed in the more populist orientation of political regimes in the twentieth century in Honduras than in neighboring countries and contributing to a strong corporatist tradition. The incorporation of subordinate groups through a corporatism that helped temper the struggles of popular classes and bought time for the dominant groups to regroup is a further factor that helps explain why the crisis of capitalist development in Honduras, when it hit at the end of the 1970s, did not snowball as it did elsewhere into a revolutionary challenge to the social order.

The inability of the civilian elite to manage the tensions of capitalist development of the post-WWII period underlay the military coup d'état of 1956. The coup signalled the transformation of the military from a corrupt constabulary in the pay of the oligarchy and the banana companies to a politicized and institutionally autonomous corporate body mediating class and intra-elite conflict. But the character of military rule in Honduras was distinct to that of Guatemala, El Salvador, and Nicaragua. In those countries, local bourgeoisies and landed oligarchs ceded autonomy to military guardians of the social order as military authoritarianism became the political superstructure for capitalist development of the post-World War II period. In Honduras, however, for reasons analyzed above, the relationship between the military and dominant and subordinate classes was distinct. A 1972 coup d'état that followed a brief interlude of civilian government was led by young reformist officers who had displaced their more conservative seniors in the aftermath of Honduras' defeat in the 1969 Soccer War with El Salvador. The younger officers favored a nationalist and developmentalist outlook and the regime that came to power, led by Oswaldo López Arellano, was more akin to the progressive military orders of Peru and Panama than to the reactionary military regimes in Central America. The regime undertook a series of reforms that had been resisted by the economic elite and the political parties—what Dunkerley has called "progressive Bonapartism."[158] Under a leftist popular discourse, and with the support of North Coast entrepreneurs (who would constitute a decade later the nucleus of the New Right), the Arellano regime between 1972 and 1975 redistributed land to peasants, established a minimum wage and progressive labor laws, and promoted industrialization. These reforms, the outcome of a tension-ridden convergence of popular pressures from below among a radicalized peasantry, the interests of the state, business groups, and international actors, "unblocked" capitalist development in the 1970s and helped pave the way for the next stage of economic transformation under globalization.

By the late 1970s, however, military reformism had run its course. The military had become discredited through corruption and incipient economic stagnation. The regime was unable to manage the combined pressure of resurgent dominant groups and spreading popular mobilizations that were transgressing the limits of corporatism from above. Structurally, the space for the type of populism embodied in the military reformist project was narrowing. This was the moment of transition from the post-WWII period of capitalist development to that of globalization. The world economy had stagnated and accumulation through the ISI model of industrialization, domestic market expansion, and the extension of traditional agro-exports, was reaching its limits. Although the process of recomposition was late in Honduras relative to the rest of the region, the social forces, both dominant and subordinate, that would protagonize the transition had begun to emerge in the 1970s. This included a strong popular movement that for the historic reasons discussed above did not acquire an armed revolutionary character and was able to exercise more influence on the state through corporatism and reformist mobilizations than its counterparts elsewhere. It included as well new groups among the dominant classes seeking modernization. In 1978 the military announced plans for a return to civilian rule, a process that would absorb and redirect the struggle of the popular classes as well as of dominant groups seeking a renewed political expression.

The US Occupation

It was on the basis of this institutional transition at a moment of crisis and redefinition that the United States stepped in, following the 1979 Sandinista triumph in Nicaragua, as part of a much larger project for Honduras, and for the region, that would unfold throughout the 1980s. The dual program called for a combination of political reform and militarization as Honduras gained new strategic importance as the hub of regional counter-insurgency.[159] As in El Salvador, Honduras came under massive US influence in the 1980s, receiving $1.6 billion in economic and military aid between 1980 and 1992, and accommodating a US diplomatic corps that swelled to 1,300.[160] The US strategy was based on converting Honduras into a platform and rearguard for region-wide counterinsurgency and counter-revolution, given that it bordered on all three countries facing revolutions. The strategy involved three dimensions: 1) the development of a functioning polyarchic system; 2) a dramatic expansion and modernization of the military, including the further militarization of the Honduran state and society (even though this objective was in contradiction with the first); and 3) economic restructuring and capitalist modernization. The strategy brought together a tenuous and conflictive alliance of local conservative political elites, much of the private sector, and the military, with the United States. The strategy also drew in important new groups in the process of modernization, for whom the overall project provided conditions for their emergence, and later on, for its bid to achieve hegemony with the dominant groups and a more direct control over the state. This three-pronged strategy had a transformative effect on the Honduran state and society, securing the control and participation of the Honduran military in the regional counterinsurgency program, acting as a lever over the Honduran government, and shifting economic and political influence towards new groups in society.

The transition to polyarchy involved the election in 1980 of a Constituent Assembly, charged with drafting a new constitution (approved in 1982), followed in 1981 by a well-publicized election, organized under heavy US tutelage, as much a "demonstration election" to legitimate the overall intervention program as the first step in institutionalizing political competition and electoral processes. The view, so prevalent in much of the foreign literature on Honduras, that the country was a mere "puppet" of

US intervention (a view which reduces the agency of Central Americans to their responses to history made elsewhere), obscures a more complex reality: a convergence of interests among Honduran and international forces over a project of transformation from above, the direction of which was open to dispute throughout the 1980s. In particular, there developed an alliance and convergence of interests among the dominant groups and US-transnational forces *against* the popular sectors and their advancing struggle in Central America, and in favor of the transformation of the system of domination. The mobilization of popular forces had been growing in the late 1970s as the economy deteriorated and socioeconomic conditions worsened. Nearly uninterrupted military rule since 1963 had discredited the armed forces as well as the National Party that supported military rule. The return to civilian government in 1980 achieved a broad consensus, although it did not last long, among internal social forces, including popular sectors, professional and middle classes, and groups among the elite, as a political alternative to the looming national and regional crisis. The 1981 election was won by the Liberal Party candidate, Rafaél Suazo Córdova, and was followed by regular elections in 1985, 1989, 1993, and 1997. The resumption of electoral processes helped to forestall popular mobilization in the face of deteriorating social conditions. New internal actors, among them recently organized peasant and worker associations, became incorporated into the political arena through these electoral exercises. The move to polyarchy sparked sharp divisions in the two traditional parties, the Liberal and Nationalist, which had been inactive for much of the twenty-two-year military interlude, as old and new political groups sought to gain leverage.

The US program also involved the penetration of Honduras' densely organized civil society. Millions of dollars in AID funding went to grassroots sectors in an attempt to achieve their subordinate incorporation into the project rather than their coercive exclusion. "The US Agency for International Development . . . has attained a central position in the Honduran society and economy," noted Norsworthy, writing in 1993. "At first glance, no sector of the society seems untouched. Everyone and every organization appears to be on the AID dole. Political parties, judges, military/civic-action teams, business associations and businessmen themselves, journalists, unions, development groups, charitable organizations, churches, cattlemen, and, of course, government ministries and ministers depend on regular AID handouts."[161] Here the objective was to establish political, social, economic, and cultural organizations that could compete with more militant popular organizations, fragment resistance, win support from within civil society for the emergent transnational project, and foster petty entrepreneurialism among refugees, uprooted peasants, displaced workers and others swelling the informal sector. "Largely because of the country's strategic role in US foreign policy in the 1980s, there was a rapid rise in nongovernmental organizations (NGOs) involved in development, refugee relief, business promotion, and social service operations," notes Norsworthy. "Between 1980 and 1990, the number of NGOs in Honduras tripled

... Nowhere in Central America was the US-linked boom of NGOs so pronounced as in Honduras during the 1980s."[162]

Although the military formally withdrew from power following the 1981 election, the strategy was based on bolstering the Honduran armed forces so that they could ensure enough internal stability for Honduras to assume the role of a regional staging ground for counterrevolution. Militarization involved an unprecedented buildup of the armed forces, which doubled in size between 1978 and 1984, and the creation of an advanced airforce with regional offensive capability, as US military aid increased more than twenty-fold (in 1982, Honduras received $31.3 million in military aid, slightly more than it had received for the whole period from 1946 to 1981), and military spending came to consume up to 30 percent of the national budget.[163] It also involved the creation of new counterinsurgency, intelligence, and clandestine units (the latter, know as Battalion 3–16, functioned as an official state death squad), the construction of dozens of new installations, capable of supporting the expanded role for the military and of accommodating the large-scale deployment of US military forces, and the militarization of numerous civilian branches, including immigration, customs, the national telecommunications system, and the merchant marines.

Under overall US direction, the Honduran military had three distinct missions: 1) provide a coercive canopy for the stabilization of the Honduran state and impose enough control over the elite so as to suppress its own centrifugal tendencies[164]; 2) suppress a very nascent revolutionary movement and prevent a burgeoning popular movement from acquiring a revolutionary dimension; and 3) provide support for regional counterrevolution. The 1982 constitution actually strengthened military autonomy. It conferred to the military independent control over "national security" matters, transferred from the civilian president to the head of the armed forces the title of commander-in-chief, and mandated the creation of a National Defense and Security Council (CSN) comprised of six military officers and four civilians, to oversee all aspects of internal and foreign policy. The CSN became the nerve center of the Honduran state. State power became subordinate to the military, and via this circuitous route, the Honduran state became subordinate to the US-transnational project.

The construction of a national security state in Honduras converged with a US military occupation of the country. By the mid-1980s the United States had installed in Honduran territory several dozen of *its own* military and airforce bases, intelligence centers, and regional command posts, and a training center for Salvadoran soldiers run by US commandos, until it was closed down in 1985. In Honduras during the 1980s, several hundred thousand US troops took part in joint military exercises with their Honduran counterparts—an integral military and psychological component of the regional counterrevolutionary campaign, intended to project US military power and also as a cover for the massive transfer of war materials to the Nicaraguan contras and other counterinsurgent forces. Honduras also became the rearguard for 20,000 Nicaraguan contra troops, whose supply lines involved a vast network stretching from US and Honduran military bases to the contra camps along the border with Nicaragua. Both Honduran and US forces utilized the Honduran military infrastructure as a platform for advice and training, logical and intelligence support, and also direct participation, in contra military operations.

If participation in the regional counterrevolution was one side to militarization, the other was to contain the popular movement inside Honduras, and more specifically, to prevent it through preemptive repression from developing into a revolutionary armed movement. The threat from below to the social order was both real and potential. The popular sectors had intensified their organization and mobilization in the 1970s, forming new trade union and campesino federations, grassroots associations, Christian base communities, and student groups. In the early 1980s new human rights groups, ethnic and Amerindian organizations, women's forums, and popular coalitions emerged as political actors. If this movement had not by the early 1980s reached the levels of visible mobilization and confrontation as in neighboring countries, it was nevertheless developing a capacity to contest the authority of dominant groups and was the strongest in the region relative to the dominant groups it confronted. Moreover, several political-military organizations had been formed in the late 1970s and in 1981 guerrilla fronts became operative. It was the deepening economic crisis from 1979 and on that threatened to spread discontent and provide the material basis for a popular challenge. Income per capita declined by nearly 12 percent between 1980 and 1984.[165] Honduras was visited in the 1980s by counterinsurgency and state terrorist methods never before used in the country, such as "anti-terrorist" laws, disappearances, and state-organized death squads, as the population fell victim to the same mass violation of human rights as in neighboring countries.

In El Salvador clear lines of demarcation emerged during the 1980s between competing projects that disputed the direction of society and control of the state. In Nicaragua revolutionary forces achieved state power and hegemony in civil society. And in Guatemala new dominant groups had come together early in the decade, even if their struggle to impose their project was far from complete. But in Honduras neither dominant groups nor the reformist or revolutionary forces could muster the ability to put forward a coherent project. Aspiring transnational groups faced well-organized national capitalist sectors that put up stiff resistance to an external opening. The Honduran Council of Private Enterprise (COHEP) was formed in 1966 and brought together sectorally organized economic groups, from landed capital to merchants, bankers, and industrialists. But this private-sector umbrella group was controlled during the 1980s by national capitalists tied to the older national circuits of accumulation and state-sponsored development strategies.[166] New entrepreneurial groups seeking to develop through a commercial opening, maquiladora production and other non-traditional exports did not find support in COHEP. Instead, these aspiring transnationally oriented groups established new corporate organizations and business associations.

The old economic groups in Honduras maintained considerable influence in the 1980s. They managed to resist the sets of fiscal, tax, exchange-rate and other policies pushed by the AID and the IMF that favored a shift in accumulation from the internal market to the external sector. On the other hand, transnational agents such as AID officials who prodded the country to open up to the global economy found support among New Right groups, whose further development they encouraged and even openly assisted. These transnational agents thus became involved in—and transnationalized—the process of internal class formation. In Honduras the fragmentation of capitalist groups was considerable, as was the struggle between these groups, resulting in a stalemate that was not broken until the end of the decade.

Key business figures and technocrats sustained efforts throughout the 1980s to organize transnationally oriented groups.[167] With AID financing and assistance, they established an array of private-sector associations and elite think-tanks. In a pattern seen throughout the region, these associations sought to form "new business leaders," promote the reorganization of the private sector, spread their influence within the state and in civil society, foster new economic activities (especially non-traditional exports), and to develop neo-liberal social and economic policies.[168] Among the nearly two dozen groups created with the assistance of AID was the Foundation for Investment and Export Development (FIDE), perhaps the most important, which played a role similar to that of FUSADES in El Salvador, although on a smaller and less effective scale. Others included: the National Council to Promote Exports and Investment (CONAFEXI); the Federation of Agro-Export Producers (FEPROEXAH); the National Association of Honduran Exporters (ANEXHON); the National Association of Industrialists (ANDI); the Associated Managers and Entrepreneurs of Honduras (GEMAH); the National Development Foundation of Honduras (FUNDAHEH); and the Honduran American Chamber of Commerce (HAMCHAM).[169]

The development of new Honduran capitalist groups took place within the framework of the transition. Transnational processes became enmeshed with internal class formation and tied it to the larger process of regional (and worldwide) transnational class formation. The civilian state remained weak, all but lacking in autonomy, and mired in corruption and clientelism in the face of militarization. The US program largely bypassed this weak state. Resources were channeled instead directly to the private sector. Between 1980 and 1990, Honduras received some $1.6 billion in economic and military aid. Over half of the economic aid, or $711 million, was in the form of Economic Support Funds (ESF) for balance of payments support, utilized in a manner similar to that described in the previous section for El Salvador, and with much the same effect.[170] In turn, half of the local currency created by ESF payments went directly to the private sector, entirely bypassing the government.[171] US officials exercised influence over distinct ministries, state allocations, and macroeconomic policies, including agricultural policy, through this ESF aid, another $355 million in development assistance, and $173 million in "food aid" under P.L. 480. The aid program bolstered private-sector hegemony, as we have already seen in El Salvador and in the other countries, including the attendant shift in resources from the domestic market to the external sector, and in influence from domestic market agents to new commercial and financial groups linked to the global economy.[172] Also as in neighboring countries, the creation and funding of dozens of private-sector organizations dedicated to administering health, education, and other social programs helped to transfer social reproduction from the state to the private sector.

As the 1980s progressed, the transnationally oriented groups moved their sights from corporate to direct political mobilization. The acute factionalization of the Liberal and National (conservative) parties that dominated the political system, owing to the particular circumstances in which the Honduran polity developed, made them malleable to influence by organized cliques and power groups (corrientes). The Liberals had historically developed a social base among the country's small and mid-sized domestic market producers, the commercial sector and professional and middle-class strata, whereas the Nationalists were closely tied to landed interests, the Church, and the armed forces. Unlike Guatemala and El Salvador, in Honduras there was no viable centrist group that could play a prominent role in the transition. The Honduran Christian Democratic Party (PDCH) formed in 1968 and only granted legal status in 1981, never became a significant political force, nor did the social democratic Party of Innovation and Unity (PINU). Although the Left gained influence from the 1960s into the 1990s through mass movements it was unable to make headway in the formal political arena. The left-of-center parties garnered less than 3.5 percent of the national vote, for instance, in the 1989 elections. The two party Liberal–National system thus became the political vehicle for the transnational agenda in Honduras. Embryonic transnational groups gravitated to both parties during the transition. As we shall see, this was also the precise pattern in Costa Rica, where both the National Liberation and the Social Christian Parties became agents of globalization, and it sets these countries apart from El Salvador and Guatemala, where New Right groups became politically active through entirely new parties formed in opposition to the older ones.

Although Suazo Córdova, the first Liberal government president (1981–85), represented the old conservative populist coalition within the party, early on his administration's policies came under the influence of US and IMF officials, the "Facusse group," and the Association for Honduran Progress (APROH). The second Liberal president (1985–89), Azcona Hoyo, was the candidate of a modernizing cluster based among industrialists from the north-coast agro-industrial, manufacturing, and financial region centered around San Pedro Sula. This wing of the party had formed the Liberal Alliance of the People (ALIPO) as an internal faction. During the 1980s as well new business sectors and technocrats waged an internal modernizing movement within the National Party. By the later part of the decade the National Party had been captured by a new generation of urban businessmen from the country's industrial city of San Pedro Sula and neighboring Puerto Cortés, El Progreso, and Trujillo, where most of the maquiladora plants would be located, and young "technocrats" in the capital city of Tegucigalpa, which housed the state bureaucracy and also much of the country's service sector. These sectors had formed their own party faction, the Rafaél Callejas Nationalist Movement (MONARCA), as a vehicle to gain control over the party, modernize and reorient it away from its rural and oligarchic origins and in a "New Right" direction, and to build an electoral machine for Callejas' presidential candidacy. MONARCA developed close ties with the ARENA party in El Salvador and other New Right forces in Central America. In 1989 Callejas himself was elected vice-president and representative for Latin America of the International Democratic Union (IDU), a worldwide grouping of New Right parties, after being nominated for the position by Margaret Thatcher.[173]

Following a decade-long struggle over the leadership of COHEP, which had resisted AID and IMF pressures for adjustment and an external opening-up for much of the 1980s, the transnational fraction was able to achieve hegemony over the private-sector grouping in early 1988. In that year the Callejas group managed to place their representative, Richard Zablah, a maquiladora businessman, in the presidency of COHEP and to win the umbrella organization over to a program of reform. With that, the AID resumed its funding for the COHEP, suspended early in the decade.[174] Shortly afterwards, COHEP sponsored an international conference in Honduras on "bases for a new model of economic development," featuring the Chilean economist and key "Chicago Boy" Arnold Harberger, and then, following the conference, declared its support for the Callejas presidential campaign.[175] Writing in 1985, Crosby had noted: "Who or what represents the private sector? It is quite apparent that the COHEP no longer represents it. Instead of a common front, there now exist multiple fronts. These multiple fronts represent interests in conflict, to the extent that the export-oriented groups favor policies that would apparently end up sacrificing the interests of the import-substitution groups."[176] By 1988 the new groups had managed to reunify the private sector around their program, but it would be another two years before they could implement it with the full support of the state.

The Transnational Project Takes Hold

The turning point in the transnational project came in 1989, when Callejas won the presidency with 52 percent of the vote. The transnational fraction now had direct control of the state. Under Callejas it developed policies for a sweeping neo-liberal reform and integration into the global economy. Callejas, an agricultural economist, banker, and investor from one of the wealthiest families in the country, had served as director of many state enterprises, and drew his cabinet from private-sector figures and foreign-educated economists closely tied to the AID programs. Callejas also enjoyed the backing of the United States in the 1989 vote. His electoral team received US funds passed through the National Endowment for Democracy (NED) to the Center for Economic, Political, and Social Studies in Honduras, a policy-planning forum of New Right groups that actually drafted the National Party's policy platform.[177] Following the elections, Callejas and his advisors were able to unify the rival factions within the National Party and establish its hegemony. Similar to ARENA in El Salvador, the National Party had gone from being the party of landed elites and the military to a party of Honduran capital and the clearing house for the New Right.

In sum, the New Right did not develop in the 1980s or even in the 1990s into a unified or hegemonic force within the elite and the country's political system. Instead, clusters came together, penetrated, and largely captured both parties by the 1990s, but without the same type of political coherence that the New Right acquired in, for example, El Salvador, or even Guatemala. Perhaps because these groups did not confront an obstinate landed oligarchy they did not experience the centripetal political effects of such a confrontation. Indeed, two leading representatives of the transnationally oriented bourgeoisie, Callejas and Carlos Flores Facussé, who represented the same ALIPO New Right faction of the Liberal Party that had backed Azcona Hoyo in the 1985 vote, were rivals running on opposing party tickets in the 1989 elections. Flores lost to Callejas in those elections, and Callejas was then replaced in the 1993 vote by a more left-leaning Liberal candidate (see below). But Flores went on to win the Liberal Party nomination again, and then the presidency, in the 1997 election. In office, Flores continued the neo-liberal program, with little to distinguish his government from that of the Nationalists.

The neo-liberal program in Honduras was only a secondary US-transnational concern so long as the regional war continued. Conditionality attached to US aid involved the drafting by the AID itself, in consultation with the IMF and the World Bank, of no less than three economic programs, one for each of the Honduran administrations elected in the 1980s: Suazo Córdova in 1981, Azcona Hoyo in 1985, and Rafaél Callejas in 1989.[178] The Honduran government passed a number of legal reforms, among them, an Export Promotion Law in 1983 and the Temporary Import Law in 1984, to promote non-traditional exports and assembly manufacturing, respectively, and the Law of Agricultural Modernization in 1992, which accelerated the transition to capitalist agriculture.[179] Despite pressure placed on the Honduran government to adopt a structural adjustment package, Honduras' strategic role in the regional counterrevolution allowed the government to postpone much of the planned reform. As in the rest of the Isthmus, the war made economic stability and restructuring impossible. Between 1979 and 1982 alone, Honduran capitalists transferred some $600 million in private investments abroad, mostly to bank accounts in Miami (by the time the decade drew to an end at least $1.5 billion had left).[180] Private investment fell by 69 percent between 1980 and 1984, and by another 65 percent between 1984 and 1987.[181] Capital flight was estimated at $100 million each year that the conflict dragged on.[182] Honduran participation in the regional conflict kept transnational capital away in the

1980s, and the free port facilities set up at Puerto Castilla stood empty for much of the decade. The renewal of accumulation in Honduras would require political stability. Regional peace and demilitarization became a mantra of the New Right.

The full turn to neo-liberalism and the new model of accumulation only came once the Sandinistas had been removed from power in 1990. In March 1990, within weeks of his inauguration, Callejas launched his *paquetazo*, or economic reform package, negotiated earlier with the IMF, the AID, the World Bank, and the Inter-American Development Bank. These institutions disbursed several billion dollars to support the Structural Adjustment Program (SAP) over the next few years. The paquetazo included a 50 percent devaluation of the national currency, the Lempira, tax hikes on consumption, austerity measures, the elimination of price controls, a sharp tariff reduction (and abolition in some cases), new export incentives, and a privatization program.[183] Along with the neo-liberal program came the arrival of transnational capital, in what was locally referred to as the "Asian invasion," the near overnight entry of the maquiladoras, along with a commercial opening-up and new service activities. The first offshore center had been established by the government in Puerto Cortés in 1976, but the free zone was not filled until the early 1990s, when the government opened another five such state-sponsored free zones. In addition, private-sector consortiums, including the Continental Group and the Canahuati family, opened at least five of their own export processing zones in the San Pedro Sula area under the same conditions of tax and duty exemptions as the government zones. In this way, the booming maquiladora sector became an important site of transnational class formation within the Honduran elite. Between 1990 and 1996, the number of maquiladora factories rose from twenty-six to nearly 200, and included use by firms from Korea, Hong Kong, Taiwan, and the United States, exporting name-brand apparel such as OshKosh B'Gosh, Warners, Best Form, the Gap, and Sara Lee (see next chapter). The number of workers jumped from 9,000 to over 75,000 (75 percent of them women) and the value of clothing exported to the United States from $112 million to $1.2 billion. In 1996, the maquiladora industry became the third most important generator of foreign exchange, after bananas and coffee.[184]

The SAP signed by Callejas with the IMF in 1990 was the first in a sequence, followed by a second SAP adopted by his successor, Carlos Roberto Reina (1994–98), and a third implemented by President Carlos Flores, who took office in 1999.[185] Under Reina, the government promulgated the Great National Transformation Project, a program drafted by the Facusse Group with the support of the IFIs. The "Great Project" called for a further and far-reaching insertion into the global economy over the following decade through the promotion of non-traditional exports and tourism, the creation of a Super Free Trade Zone in major stretches of the country, and vast infrastructural and energy projects that would make every corner of the country accessible to transnational investors. "The primary objectives are designed to satisfy the needs of the international community

and not the needs of the domestic market," affirmed Roger Marin, the
Reina government official in charge of the project, in a remarkably candid
statement. "The Great Project should not be thought of as a domestic
project linked to such needs as basic grains. The new strategic focus of the
country's development is to satisfy the needs of the international community."[186] Callejas' and subsequent governments extended the program
of incentives for non-traditional exports begun in the 1980s, including
concessions for producing new fruits and vegetables, for maquiladora
production, particularly electronics and apparel assembly, and for the
development of tourism, among other non-traditional external sector activities. With AID funding, the Ministry of the Economy set up an Investment
Promotion Office. The AID financed private-sector organizations as well,
such as the FIDE and the CONAFEXI, that worked closely with the state to
promote new export activities.[187]

The veto power of the global economy over local economic policymaking
worked to ensure the neo-liberal course throughout the 1990s. Carlos
Roberto Reina, who headed an insurgent progressive, social democratic-
oriented faction within the Liberal Party, won the 1993 elections on a
populist platform of opposition to the neo-liberal program, with the
backing of national fractions among the elite threatened by the opening to
the global economy, and broad popular sectors whose resistance to neo-
liberal austerity mounted in the early 1990s. In his first year in office, Reina
attempted to negotiate with IMF and AID officials greater flexibility in
implementing the Enhanced Structural Adjustment Facility (ESAF) signed
by his predecessor. But under the threat of a suspension of new bi- and
multi-lateral credits and the denial of much-needed debt relief, the government recommitted Honduras to the terms of the original ESAF, and then
in 1997 signed a new agreement for a dramatic deepening of the adjustment process. Reina's own social base rapidly deteriorated and his government faced a spiral of popular protest and loss of legitimacy in the
mid-1990s.[188]

The gradual demilitarization of state and society that took place in the
1990s in Honduras and elsewhere was not a sign of rupture between a
period of conflict and one of pacification, as so much of the literature
proposes.[189] The military became anachronistic in the 1990s in Central
America once the revolutionary forces were contained, peace had been
imposed, and the structural coercion of the globalization process had taken
hold. Demilitarization occurred in the 1990s because the military and its
far-reaching influence became both unnecessary and unproductive for the
transnational agenda, *and* because a new fraction among the bourgeoisie
and the bureaucratic elite was vying for hegemony over the internal
political system and felt constrained by an omnipresent military. A new
bourgeoisie was coming into existence and trying to impose a coherent
direction on society on the basis of larger worldwide transformations and
the possibilities they opened up. In each country of the region, with the
exception of Costa Rica, where a national bourgeoisie had never relin-
quished its direct rule, local states were reclaimed by rising transnational

fractions from civilian-military regimes that had exercised largely uninterrupted direct rule since the 1930s crises. In chapter one I noted that
historically, newly strengthened dominant groups can quickly constrict state
autonomy as they make more intensive use of the state in times of major
capitalist restructuring, and suggested that this is what has happened in
general worldwide since the onset in the 1970s of world economic crisis.
What becomes clear here is that just such a process took place at the local
level in Central America as well, and that this was linked to the larger
global process.

Another picture that emerges from these different country studies is the
creation for transnational capital of a pool of available labor in the region,
disembedded from pre or non-capitalist relations of reciprocity, to work in
the maquiladoras, the new agricultural centers, and service sectors, along
with taking part in the older economic activities. We have seen that a key
dynamic underlying the cycle of revolution, counterrevolution, and transformation in the region was the struggle of popular classes in the face of
alienation and proletarianization wrought by capitalist development. In this
cycle, direct political-military mechanisms of labor supply have increasingly
been replaced by the structural (market) mechanisms brought into play
through political conflict and attendant social and economic restructuring.
These operative mechanisms have acted in tandem with the uprooting
brought about by the military conflict itself. They include, among others,
the creation of markets in land, the privatization of credit (including the
market determination of interest rates and an end to state-sponsored credit
programs), US food aid programs, and commercial openings to the world
market. In turn, depeasantization has worked to undermine peasant movements as a popular oppositional force. These processes were all at work in
Honduras from the 1970s into the twenty-first century.

The agrarian reform program had already been largely gutted by the
late 1970s and in the 1980s it ground to a halt. Then in 1992 the government formally terminated the program and replaced it with an Agricultural Modernization Law, which effectively accelerated the transition in
the countryside to full capitalist agriculture and the emergence of a market in land. Drafted by the AID and the World Bank, the law eliminated
all state intervention in agriculture (including any further state expropri-
ations), strengthened property guarantees, called for the acceleration of
land titling and the conversion of all titled land into marketable property
(including the "right" to use property as collateral against loans), the
conversion of cooperative lands into individual tradeable shareholdings,
stipulated the privatization of state support infrastructure, such as grain
storage facilities, and the privatization of the National Agriculture Development Bank (BANDESA), and promoted new foreign and domestic
investment in export agriculture.[190] In effect, the BANDESA was privatized
following the passage of the law. The newly privatized bank ended subsidized credits for peasant producers, adjusted interest rates to the market,
and shifted its loan portfolio from peasants to largeholders.[191]

Nonetheless, pressure for land acquisition continued into the 1980s and

1990s, with 100,000 peasants organizing land invasions in the Northwestern agricultural heartland in 1987 alone, the largest of its kind in the history of the country. While the Honduran peasant movement remained a major social and political force, it was becoming gradually eclipsed in the 1980s and 1990s by ongoing proletarianization and the rise of a new working class among maquiladora and service workers. Meanwhile, poverty and crime spread and socioeconomic conditions deteriorated for the majority in the 1980s and 1990s, along with a simultaneous boom in conspicuous consumption among new middle and upper classes and elites who provided a social base for the transnational project—the now-characteristic social polarization under globalization. But the Honduran popular movement continued to burgeon in the 1990s, with the formation of dozens of new women's groups, community associations, peasant and worker organizations, and so on. Many of these groups came together in 1989 into the Platform of Struggle, the only organization in the country to actively promote an alternative to neo-liberalism and free market integration into the global economy. For the historic reasons discussed above, however, these Honduran popular classes did not acquire an explicitly political expression and did not operate through the political party system. This might be considered a factor in their favor, insofar as the battle for civil society in Central America has often involved the establishment of hegemony by dominant groups through political party structures.

Costa Rica: From "Exceptionalism" to Globalization

In Costa Rica, a very different path of twentieth-century development did not deter the outcome in the 1980s and 1990s of integration into the global economy under terms similar to the region as a whole and with the characteristic changes in internal social forces. The hegemony of the landed oligarchy was broken in the 1948 civil war and replaced by an alliance of emergent industrial, commercial, and financial capitalists. This united and relatively modernized dominant class was able to incorporate the peasantry and working classes into a stable hegemonic bloc and establish a functioning polyarchic political system. Under the model of ISI industrialization and agro-export expansion, with an important redistributive component and significant levels of social welfare spending, Costa Rica experienced levels of development well beyond its neighbors. This particular model of dependent capitalist development had become exhausted by the late 1970s and came to a crisis in 1981, when the government fell behind on its debt payments and temporarily suspended interest payments. The financial crisis gave impetus to a gradual restructuring throughout the 1980s and 1990s and reinsertion into the emergent global economy of the entire Costa Rican productive apparatus. Under close AID and IFI tutelage, successive governments oversaw liberalization, austerity, deregulation, the privatization of public production and service facilities, and the development of a dynamic Export-Led Development (ELD) model that began to replace the old ISI model. The thorough socioeconomic restructuring generated new entrepreneurial groups favoring the ELD model within both parties of the elite, the social-democratic National Liberation Party (PLN) and the Christian-Democratic Social Christian Unity Party (PUSC), as transnational nuclei emerged within their ranks and gained control of their parties.

The high level of Costa Rica's development and the stability of its polyarchic system in the post-WWII period has given rise to a myth of "exceptionalism," according to which the country is a democratic paradise rooted in its distinct colonial and post-colonial history. The dominant yeoman or "rural democracy" thesis notes that Costa Rica, lacking valuable mineral resources and a significant Indian population that could be put to work, did not develop the systems of coercive labor control that in other Central American colonies led to hierarchical, violent, and authoritarian social relations and political structures. The territory, with the weakest link among the colonies to the Spanish metropolis and with no major export products that tied it firmly to the mercantile system, was settled slowly, never became burdened with a latifundia structure, and remained the poorest province in Central America. As a result, Costa Rican economy and society was built on a small, ethnically homogenous "white" population engaged in self-sufficient farming; a "yeoman society" free from major class and ethnic cleavages, social stratification, and an oppressive landed oligarchy.[192]

This thesis offers important insights into Costa Rica's historic trajectory, in particular, the importance of labor shortages to subsequent development. But the version of a classless society of subsistence farmers living in a rural democracy is little more than myth. The historical evidence indicates significant wealth and status disparities in colonial Costa Rica, and outside of the Central Mesa, the land tenure system was similar to that of other Central American countries. As Stone has shown, the elite can trace its ancestry to the original conquistadores and the nucleus of early Spanish settlers that followed in their wake, who utilized their access to Indian labor and tributes to institutionalize their dominance even after the Indian population had all but disappeared.[193] And although Costa Rica might have had a less violent and hierarchical social order, it was not a polyarchy during the colonial and post-colonial period. The political system was based up until the mid-twentieth century on the near complete control of an oligarchy mired in violent factionalism among rival groups, and was characterized by dictators, coup d'états, militarism and civil wars, and the disenfranchisement of the majority.[194] Costa Rica's early history, Wilson concludes, "is different from those of other countries in the region, but more in a sense of scale than of type."[195]

What the absence of a large exploitable Indian/*mestizo* labor force does help explain is the distinctive manner in which the oligarchy evolved and the types of structured relations it developed with subordinate classes. The oligarchy's source of wealth extraction was less the direct mobilization of coerced labor than control over trade, finances, and political-religious administrative command. With the introduction of coffee in the early nineteenth century the landed oligarchy rapidly consolidated its power and dominance over national life. However, labor shortages made the operation of large estates uneconomical. Smallholders accounted for a large portion of cultivation despite the rise of a coffee-planting aristocracy. Instead the large coffee growers controlled processing, financing, marketing, and exporting. The oligarchy was thus as much commercial and financial as landed, in distinction to elsewhere, which provided a historic basis for a more unified ruling class in the post-WWII period of capitalist expansion and for a political system that relied less on sheer coercion than on ideological hegemony.

If this history bequeathed more favorable conditions than elsewhere, it was the 1930s crisis, culminating in the 1948 civil war, that actually launched Costa Rica down a different path of development.[196] The world economic crisis of the 1930s brought social mobilization from popular classes and dominant groups throughout Latin America, as discussed in the next chapter, and gave rise to diverse multiclass populist projects around a new economic model of domestic market expansion and ISI development. The popular and reformist movements were crushed in other Central American countries and the landed oligarchy retained its dominance. But in Costa Rica social mobilization from above and below created an alliance of popular classes with reformist elements among the dominant groups, led by Rafaél Angel Calderón, who in the post-war period saw a redistributive program as necessary to address the economic crisis of the Depression and WWII. Calderón was himself a prominent oligarch, but his reform program, his alliance with communists and workers, and the corruption of his administration after he was elected president in 1940 antagonized the coffee oligarchy, much of the business elite, and urban professional and middle strata.

José "Pepe" Figueres, himself a coffee grower and businessman, managed to put together an unstable coalition of the oligarchy with sectors in favor of reform to overthrow the Calderón regime in the brief six-week civil war in 1948. This "revolution" was based on an anti-communist populism, anti-oligarchic reform, and social democratic developmentalism. Figueres took reformism away from the radical direction in which it appeared to be moving. The repression of the Left and its powerful unions emasculated organized labor and converted reform into a process controlled from above, "safe" for the oligarchy and new dominant groups. Figueres and his supporters quickly decapitated the popular classes with a wave of repression against communists, trade unionists, and their supporters. But he also neutralized the threat of an oligarchic backlash by abolishing the army (which was replaced by loyal forces that became the Rural Guard and the Civil Guard). He nationalized the banking system and imposed a tax on the agro-export oligarchy. The 1948 "revolution" did not initiate but culminated in the movement to displace the landed oligarchy and modernize the country. It paved the way for the rise of a new industrial and commercial bourgeoisie that became the core of a new constellation of social forces that hegemonically incorporated peasants and workers along with new middle classes and state managers.

The nationalized banking system and taxes on the oligarchy allowed for a portion of the surplus generated by coffee to be captured by the state and redistributed into social programs, industrialization, and infrastructure. The post-1948 regime, in fact, undermined the independent political development of the popular classes. But the coffee aristocracy was not undermined as much as subordinated to a larger project of ISI moderniza-tion and development under the hegemony of new bourgeois groups. This, in my view, is the key demarcation from its neighbors that launched Costa Rica down a distinct path.[197] The outcome of the 1930s–1940s crisis elsewhere was the subordination of emergent reformist bourgeois and middle class forces to the oligarchy, which presided over a new round of post-WWII capitalist expansion. While these reformist bourgeois and mid-dle class forces came to the fore in Costa Rica in the wake of 1948, they remained subordinate to the oligarchies in neighboring countries, despite periodic reversals such as those in Guatemala from 1945 to 1954, until the 1980s regional upheaval definitively shattered the old oligarchic structures. Rapid growth in Costa Rica, the expansion of social services, and rising living standards established a material basis for a more solid hegemonic system than elsewhere. Before 1948, the Costa Rican GDP and per capita income were roughly on a par with those of its neighbors. Prolonged growth and the dramatic improvement in social indicators only came in the 1950s–1970s.[198] The Costa Rican state acquired a capacity to absorb class conflict and maintain social peace. The state actively intervened in civil society, limiting the autonomy available to popular sectors, and achieved a level of legitimacy unsurpassed in Central America. But this in turn rested on the material changes and opportunities opened up by the particular unfolding of social forces in the twentieth century.

Costa Rican polyarchy was well institutionalized, based on the hegemonic incorporation of subordinate groups through a two-party political system which proved capable of managing intra-elite tensions and accommodating subordinate groups. The social democratic PLN and the more conservative PUSC (which was formed in 1983 out of the "Unity" opposition bloc) have rotated in power, routinely accounting for 95 percent of the vote between them, with the PLN winning seven of fourteen elections between 1948 and 2002.[199] The PLN, the party of the modernized urban bourgeoisie, became the agent of the ISI project in the post-WWII period, developing a base among state employees, small and medium-sized agricultural producers, and urban working and informal sectors, under a moderate social demo-cratic program of redistribution and expansion of social services and an ideology of developmentalism. The PUSC tended to represent landed interests and more conservative sectors of the business community as well as diverse groups dissatisfied with the PLN.

Despite Costa Rica's development success, the model of accumulation had become exhausted by the late 1970s, as discussed in the next chapter, and entered into a terminal crisis with the world recession that began in

1978. Between 1977 and 1982, the external debt rose to $4 billion, un and underemployment increased from 11 percent to 24 percent, inflation topped 90 percent, and real disposable income plummeted by more than 40 percent, as GDP contracted by 3.6 percent in 1981 and by another 6 percent in 1982.[200] The crisis became the initial catalyst for restructuring. Costa Rica was one of the first countries in Latin America to undertake structural adjustment and became a showcase for neo-liberal reform. The early 1980s saw a massive restructuring of Costa Rican economy and society in a transition from the old economic model based on ISI and traditional agro-exports to another model of accumulation based on integration into the global economy through new economic activities.

At the onset of the crisis the ruling groups in Costa Rica were highly divided over how to confront it. Initially, there was tremendous resistance among dominant groups and much conflict among them over the dismantling of state institutions and the prevailing model of accumulation. The elite feared that the economic crisis would generate social and political instability, threaten the social order, and draw the country into the regional maelstrom. Indeed, strikes, boycotts, and labor conflicts spread rapidly in the early 1980s, the Left extended its influence, and several guerrilla cells even appeared. This fear gave great political leverage to US officials and transnational functionaries, which in turn was used to strengthen groups inside Costa Rica favorable to the transnational project. The process was in many respects more far-reaching and dramatic than elsewhere. The global elite linked up with transnational clusters among the business and political elite in Costa Rica, who became internal agents of globalization, nested in both of the dominant political parties and throughout the state apparatus. This transnational fraction was perhaps stronger and more coherent than in any other Central American country, with the possible exception of El Salvador.

Costa Rica paved the way for the transnational agenda in Central America. What set Costa Rica apart in the eyes of so many commentators vis-à-vis the regional conflict was that it was "democratic" and did not require a transition to polyarchy. But these commentators often failed to appreciate that Costa Rica did become swept up in the regional upheaval. It was the breakdown of the regional economic model, of which Costa Rica was an integral part, that threw the country into economic crisis and major political and social quandaries. The same transnational processes that swept through the region as a whole also engulfed Costa Rica, even though the transition there did not involve regime change, and the country was not visited by major military conflict within its borders, or threatened by a breakdown of the social order.

Costa Rica's geo-political position as a bulwark against revolution in Central America and as a political and military rearguard for the Nicaraguan counterrevolution assigned it a key role in the regional conflict. This role begot San José an enormous amount of international assistance, which allowed the country to undertake massive adjustment while avoiding major dislocations or social upheavals threatening its own stability. Between 1982, when the crisis first hit, and 1990, the AID provided $1.3 billion (compared to just $220 million in US aid in 1946–81), supplemented by nearly $1 billion in loans from the IFIs.[201] By 1983 Costa Rica stood only second to Israel in terms of per-capita US aid.[202] The majority of US funds—some 75 percent—were in the form of ESF for balance of payments support. Smaller amounts were provided as P.L. 480 food assistance, as Development Assistance, and for Peace Corps and scholarship programs.

US aid was a political counterpart to the campaign to destabilize Nicaragua, intended to stabilize Costa Rica as a paragon of capitalist and polyarchic development in contrast to revolutionary Nicaragua. In 1981, Costa Rica received less than 6 percent of US aid to Central America, whereas this proportion rose to 28.4 percent in 1982 and to 35 percent in 1983.[203] The country became a second rearguard, after Honduras, for the Nicaraguan contras and an anti-Sandinista political platform. Washington provided over $30 million in military aid between 1982 and 1987. By the late 1980s the country's security apparatus was four times larger than a decade earlier and, in Dunkerley's words, "in logistical terms, quite capable of staging a coup."[204] This military aid provided the Costa Rican state with a capacity to contain popular opposition and helped construct a support infrastructure for the Nicaraguan contras' "southern front," including a logistical and intelligence apparatus.[205] By the time US funding began to dwindle in the early 1990s the Sandinistas had been removed from power and Costa Rican society had been dramatically reorganized and drawn into the globalization process.

The Ascent of Transnationally Oriented Groups and a "Parallel State"

Transnationally oriented groups were able to maneuver within both parties of the elite and, amidst fierce intra-party struggles, to capture the leadership of both parties during the 1980s, given the tradition of strong factionalism within the party system and institutional arrangements that make centralized control difficult. Ironically, it was not the more conservative PUSC that oversaw the initial transition in the 1980s. The PLN governments of Luis Alberto Monge (1982–86) and Oscar Arias (1986–90) launched restructuring starting with a series of austerity measures introduced by Monge shortly after he took office. During Monge's presidency the PLN became wracked by infighting as two factions fought for control over the party's policy apparatus and influence within the state: the previously dominant social democratic groups and their supporters among the bourgeoisie still tied to the old model, and newly ascendant transnationally oriented factions backed by new bourgeois groups. Both factions had agreed to the short-term austerity measures promulgated by Monge, but the latter group called for an entirely new economic model based on the country's opening to the global economy and the introduction of a new set of accumulation activities, non-traditional exports. The key struggle between these two factions took place between 1982 and 1984. In late 1983, the neo-liberal technocrats released a PLN document calling for a wholesale dismantling of ISI and a new economic model. Then in early 1984, amidst sharp infighting, a cabinet shuffle dramatically changed the composition of the government, placing the New Right technocrats in important positions. These technocrats were led by the new Central Bank president, Eduardo Lizano, a governor of the IMF, the World Bank, and the IDB, who would serve as a key "point man" for the transnational agenda, and by others closely identified with the AID and the IFIs. The appearance of this new technocratic cabinet heralded the rise to hegemony of the New Right within the PLN and the government.[206] The PUSC also became engulfed in party factionalism in the 1980s, and was thoroughly captured by the transnational fraction in that decade, culminating in the electoral triumphs on the PUSC ticket of Rafaél Calderón (son of the 1940s reformist leader) in 1990 and of Miguel Angel Rodríguez in 1998, both leading figures from the New Right business community.

Restructuring was sustained throughout the 1980s and then deepened in the 1990s under both PLN and PUSC governments. In 1985, the government signed the first Structural Adjustment Loan with the World Bank, known as SAL1, which was followed in 1989 by SAL2, and in 1995 by SAL3, involving the typical panoply of austerity and restructuring measures stipulated in coordination with AID and IMF programs.[207] Between 1980 and 1990 the government also signed seven agreements with the IMF and annual Economic Policy and Recovery Agreements with the AID.[208] But restructuring in Costa Rica did not proceed in "shock" fashion, as elsewhere. Rather, it pushed forward gradually but implacably, in the face of mounting social conflicts and intra-elite clashes.[209] The main instruments of assault on the old model included: 1) the liberalization of capital markets; 2) the privatization of public-sector institutions and enterprises; 3) an austerity program and progressive dismantling of the welfare state; 4) broad incentives to promote non-traditional exports; and 5) elimination of government support for domestic market producers, especially the peasant farm sector. But the central objective underlying the whole strategy was to bolster the private sector: to expand its economic control, achieve its hegemony in civil society, and maximize its influence over state policymaking.

This objective was pursued through the creation of a vast private institutional apparatus that became the instrument for organizing the transition from within the country and to which functions of state agencies could be passed in the process. It was in Costa Rica that the notion of a "parallel state" fomented by local transnationally oriented elites and international financial agencies first originated. In the predicable pattern seen throughout the Isthmus, the transnational elite in consort with the ascendant New Right established numerous private-sector associations and non-governmental organizations to promote and organize neo-liberal transformation from within civil society and the state. And just as in El Salvador and Honduras, US funds bypassed the Costa Rican state and went to bolster the private sector and to promote and fund new economic activities. In Costa Rica the assault on the state would not be frontal but through a "war of attrition," given the strength of the old model and the entrenchment of established state institutions, including several dozen autonomous institutes administering social services, finances and credits, utilities, and public works, among other activities, and the Costa Rican Development Corporation (CODESA), a powerful state holding company and development bank.[210] The privatization of CODESA began in 1984 when the AID founded and funded a private holding company, the Transitional Investment Trust (Fiduciara de Inversiones Transitorias, FINTRA), with a $175 million grant. FINTRA purchased CODESA's companies, one by one, and administered them until private investors could be found to buy them, a process that was concluded by 1997.[211]

Among the medley of private-sector business and political associations and think-tanks established with AID funding, the most important was the Coalition for Initiatives in Development (CINDE). Created in 1983, it brought together the diverse Chambers of Agriculture, of Industry, of Commerce, and Exporters, associations of export trading companies, drawback (maquiladora) manufacturers, private bankers, branches of transnationals, and public accounting firms. Among its activities were export promotion (for which the CINDE duplicated the government's Center for the Promotion of Exports, CENPRO), investment promotion, lobbying the Costa Rican government, media campaigns, policy studies, and organizing conferences and seminars, for which it received grants from the AID, between 1983 and 1994, totalling over $70 million.[212] Between 1984 and 1989, the CINDE's budget, which came 100 percent from the AID, was more than seven times that of CENPRO.[213] The AID funded the CINDE to set up the Export Promotion Program (PIE) and the Private Council on Agriculture and Industry (CAAP) to promote non-traditional agricultural exports, a task formally in the remit of the Ministry of Agriculture. Between 1986 and 1990, the AID provided CAAP with $35 million. In 1988 alone the CAAP budget was $10.3 million, while by comparison the budget for the entire Ministry of Agriculture for that year was only $7.7 million.[214] The AID provided another $118 million for the creation of the Regional Agricultural School for Humid Tropics (EARTH), which competed with public universities, as well as with the Center for Agricultural Research and Education, a Central America-wide school that conducts technical and research support and training for the traditional agricultural sector.[215] Yet another AID project was funding the creation of the Association of Costa Rican Development Organizations (ACORDE), an umbrella organization that in turn fomented and funded NGOs in civil society.

If this host of private-sector organizations constituted an infrastructure for the dismantling of the old accumulation model and the development of a new one, it also served as an overlapping and multitiered clearing house for the cultivation of a cohesive transnational fraction among the dominant groups. Hundreds of representatives from the country's political and economic elite passed through these associations or participated in their programs, receiving in the process training, political socialization, and often subsequent placement in the state bureaucracy or in political office.[216]

Top leaders of both political parties were hired by one of the parallel institutions and/or by the AID as consultants for these organizations. In this way the network of parallel institutions cemented an alliance between the New Right and the AID and became the axis for the transnational project in the country. The directors of the associations read like a who's who of the transnational fraction in Costa Rica, and included Thelmo Vargas, Fernando Naranjo, Guido Fernández, Frederico Vargas, Ernesto Rorhmoser, Eduardo Lizano, Juan Rafaél Lizano, Jorge Manuel Dengo, Carlos Manuel Castillo, and Richard Beck, all of whom served on different occasions as cabinet ministers or as heads of state-autonomous institutes.[217] Moreover, as Sojo documents, this new "political class"—the politicized strata of the transnationally oriented groups—became interlocked with, and came to politically articulate the interests of, the new economic groups based in banking, commerce, and other services that flourished with the opening to the global economy and became deeply integrated into transnational corporate networks.[218] Having been incubated and coalesced through the quasi-state apparatus, the transnational fraction waged a prolonged assault on the defenders of the old model still in the state and in the political parties. It managed to remove, as the outcome of one political clash after another within the different administrations of the 1980s and 1990s, those resisting the transnational project, and to place representatives from its own ranks in their stead.

The private-sector associations worked with considerable success to establish elite consensus around the transnational model. This effort included a reorganization of the corporate organization of capital. For instance, non-traditional exporters pulled out of the once-powerful National Chamber of Agriculture and Animal Husbandry (CNAA), which united medium and large landholders, agro-industrialists, and merchants and defended the interests of traditional agro-exporters and domestic food producers. They also pulled out of the Costa Rican Chamber of Industries (CIC), which represented the ISI industrial sector producing for the domestic and Central American market. The non-traditional exporters then joined forces with private bankers and others to form, with AID assistance, the Costa Rican Chamber of Exporters (CADEXCO) and the Foundation for Exports (FUNDEX).[219] Yet despite the splintering of the private sector into rival associations of those still tied to the domestic market and/or enjoying state protection and those integrated into new liberalized global markets, the transition to the new model involved less a displacement of national capitalists and other large producers for the domestic market, than pressures and incentives to encourage them to shift into export activities, including a judicial use of credit from the newly created private banking system.[220]

The de-nationalization of the state banking system and the creation of private financial markets were crucial for the implementation of the transnational agenda. The process was implemented in stages, starting with the Currency Law (Ley de la Moneda) introduced by President Monge as a condition the AID had stipulated for the release of economic support funds, and passed in August 1984 by a coalition of PLN and PUSC legislators and private-sector groups.[221] The law deregulated the banking system, allowing for the establishment of private financial institutions. It was followed by reforms in 1988 and 1995, and then by the sale of the four state-owned banks themselves, starting in 1997.[222] Already by 1991, private banks had captured more than 50 percent of all credit to the private-sector investment market.[223] The legal changes allowed private banks to benefit from international lines of credit from the AID and other lenders and donors. Without private banks able to receive funds from abroad, the AID would have had to deposit credits directly into the state banking system. Over 40 percent of the assets held by private banks in the 1980s came from AID credit lines, which were then funneled as subsidized loans to private business, in particular to those capitalists engaged in non-traditional export activities.[224]

As has been seen in the case of Nicaragua as well, private banking became a key mechanism in economic restructuring and in capitalist class formation. Controlling the financial circuit became a means of promoting new class groups and their relative weight vis-à-vis other groups. Capitalized by the US aid program, newly created private banks made possible a redistribution of financial resources towards the transnational fraction of the local capitalist class and the new financial, commercial, and production activities it became engaged in. For instance, in 1985, following the passage of the Currency Law, one billion colones of fresh external funds entered the Central Bank for national distribution as credit. Of these, 900 million went to the private banks and only 100 million to the state banking system. The private banking sector funds were used to provide credit for non-traditional production and export operations in agriculture and industry.[225] Hence de-nationalization of the banking system resulted in a reorientation of credit from small and medium-sized peasant farmers and domestic market producers to new exporting groups.

In conjunction with private banking, the government established a new government ministry, at the behest and funding of the AID, the Ministry of Exports, to promote non-traditional exports. The Ministry served as the liaison point within the state with the CINDE in developing and implementing policies and laws to promote new export-oriented economic activities, including maquiladora production, NTAEs, and tourism. The Ministry, in conjunction with CINDE and AID advisors, drafted and pushed through a slew of export promotion bills in the 1980s, including legislation authorizing the establishment of free trade zones and maquiladora industries, and numerous incentive programs for non-traditional exporters and other economic agents tied to the external sector.[226] The ELD model took off in the 1980s. Dozens of transnational firms took advantage to set up assembly operations, largely of garments, but also electronics, mechanical parts, and prosthetics. Exports of garments to the US market rose from $62 million in 1985 to $377 million in 1993 (see next chapter). Non-traditional exports, including maquiladora production, cut flowers, ornamental plants, fruits and other NTAEs, and seafoods, rose from $90 million in 1983 to $781 million in 1992.[227] The number of tourist arrivals nearly doubled, to more than 600,000, between 1983 and 1992, as transnational corporations descended on the country to construct luxury hotels and "megaprojects."[228]

State, Class, and Transnational Processes

The Costa Rican case provides critical insight into the relationship between the state and capital as it has evolved under globalization in Central America and elsewhere. What is most interesting in Costa Rica is the clarity with which we can observe the role of transnational state practices in: 1) promoting global over national accumulation circuits through a transformation of national productive apparatuses; 2) bolstering the local agents of these global circuits and simultaneously undermining agents tied to local circuits. To take the case of state incentives and subsidies for the private sector discussed above, these programs promoted new economic activities but they also aggravated the fiscal deficit. In 1991 one single incentive plan, the Tax Rebate Certificate (CAT) program, accounted for a full 62 percent of the fiscal deficit.[229] Yet the fiscal deficit was a key rationale for budget cutbacks and for a shift in resources from the internal to the external sector. This appears on the surface as circular reasoning: the deficit must be decreased = income must be increased through exports = state spending to promote exports must increase = this state spending increases the deficit = the deficit must be decreased. Yet there is nothing contradictory when we take several paces back from the short-term nitty-gritty of adjustment and bring into focus the "big picture" of globalization.

The persistence of the fiscal deficit in the 1980s and the 1990s was grease for the transnational agenda. It sustained pressures for cutbacks in state spending on social welfare and on support programs for domestic market producers. Debt rescheduling and new loans from the IFIs were tied to drastic cuts in state spending in these areas and in the layoff of thousands of public-sector employees. Public social services became privatized and commodified. But state credits to domestic market producers, especially to smallholders producing food for national consumption, became the principal target of budget cuts. The PLN administrations of the 1980s launched a "New Agriculture" program to reorganize agricultural production. The program promoted the diversification of agricultural exports through the spread of NTAEs (see next chapter) and the elimination of supports for the domestic food-producing sector, which was largely in the hands of peasant producers. The National Production Council, a government grain-trading board that provided price supports for basic grain production, was de-funded as an explicit AID condition.[230] The curtailment of credits to peasant farmers throughout Central America facilitated the spread of capitalist agriculture and the more complete integration of the agricultural sector into the global economy, especially through the conversion from food crops to NTAE crops. The result was an accelerated proletarianization of the peasantry, the concentration of land, credit, and other resources in new exporters, who were generally large landholders and/or agri-business firms, an increase in transnational corporate control of Costa Rican agriculture and agro-industry, amidst an escalation of rural conflict.[231] "The policy of attracting investment and promoting new exports has rested heavily on broad fiscal subsidies," notes Sojo. But "it is the state, not the market, that has shored up the rate of profit enough to make new exports to the global market an attractive option for producers and investors ... This explains why the multilateral financial organizations and the AID have been 'flexible' with regard to persistent fiscal imbalances, and it helps us to understand why, when they propose steps to control public spending, what is targeted is a reduction in public employment and the public wage as well as the budgets for social programs."[232]

The AID and the IFIs exerted an extraordinary amount of pressure on the Costa Rican state through conditionality, a point stressed by many observers. Cross-conditionality between IFIs was in fact systematic and reprisals for noncompliance were swift. The Costa Rican government signed annually an Economic Policy and Recovery Agreement with the AID in the 1980s and early 1990s stipulating a series of covenants that detailed government policy reforms, institutional changes, and macroeconomic targets as conditions for the disbursement of funds. In these Agreements, the AID mandated a total of 357 covenants stipulating specific policy reforms.[233] Despite this tremendous external pressure, the standard explanation that the transnational agenda has been unilaterally imposed on Central America from without is unsatisfactory, I have argued throughout this chapter, as it ignores the dynamics of transnational class formation at work within the social structure in Central America. Social forces from within Central America were protagonists in their own right. Sectors among the dominant groups came to identify their own interests and development with a reinsertion into the world capitalist system through a new model of accumulation that would integrate the region more fully into the global economy. The institutions of an emergent transnational state liaised with these sectors in a convergence of interests marked by swings of conflict and cooperation. As discussed in the case study on Guatemala, these sectors often pursued their own more "parochial" interests even as they overall identified with the transnational agenda.

Local groups, as was clear in Costa Rica, also had to maintain the legitimacy of the state and their own hegemony. This required a certain responsiveness to subordinate sectors, including compromise, concessions, and accommodation, pressures not experienced by the transnational elite. Moreover, in Costa Rica the national bloc led by nationally based capitalists, planters, and state elites was very strong and put up ferocious resistance to transnationalization, with support from trade unions, civil servants, and peasant producers. Popular classes were never passive and concessions to them were not a "gift" from the dominant classes. Instead, according to Sergio Soto, the particular "culture of social struggle" that emerged entailed "a set of formal and informal mechanisms to mediate class relations and institutionalize the class struggle."[234]

But these observations do not negate the internal basis for the transnational agenda, as seen clearly in Costa Rica. With the crisis of the ISI model and the breakdown of the protected CACM in the late 1970s, groups within the business community and representatives from both the PLN and the PUSC had been searching for a change to a new economic model that could provide renewed opportunities for profitable investment and class development. In this endeavor they turned to the IFIs for support. And the IFIs did in fact apply a very stringent conditionality that helped force the hand of the Costa Rican state. But conditionality also afforded local transnational groups with a device for legitimating the neo-liberal program. Transnational functionaries provided the global framework for national restructuring, concrete guidance, material resources, and political support. Wilson notes that private-sector groups represented in both parties sought the de-nationalization of the banking system in the early 1980s—a key demand of the AID—because they were interested in participating in a deregulated bank market and in developing private outlets that could capture and channel financial resources into new accumulation activities. He observes:

> One high-ranking neo-liberal PLN technocrat candidly recalled that 'some people in the administration, myself included, tried to use the multilaterals to fight within the PLN, to use USAID, to use the World Bank. Sometimes we would try to sell them some ideas so that they would not be presented as my ideas, or so-and-so's ideas, but would appear like the World Bank or USAID was pushing an idea. Sometimes we were able to go through the back door to get our [neo-liberal] ideas accepted.'[235]

In fact, Central Bank president Eduardo Lizano and other prominent members from both parties approached US ambassador Curtin Winsor to propose that the AID condition its assistance on a liberalization of the banking system and a privatization of CODESA holdings.[236]

Transnationally oriented elites in Costa Rica were also essential protagonists in the transformation of the Costa Rican state from a developmental to a neo-liberal state. The Commission for the Reform of the Costa Rican State, formed by state bureaucrats, intellectuals, and entrepreneurs drawn from the PLN and the PUSC, declared in 1990: "The restructuring of private markets brought with it the need to revise the nature and dynamic of the state in a conjunctural situation of fiscal crisis . . . the idea was to develop a state that could corral support for private enterprise so that the latter could develop its ability to compete successfully abroad."[237]

It must be recalled, therefore, that privatization, liberalization, deregulation, and the other changes associated with the transnationalization of the state did not mean in Costa Rica—or elsewhere in global society—that the state was dismantled. The transnationalization of the state entails a *reorientation of state services to private capital*, and within private capital, *a reorientation of services from national to transnational fractions*. Sojo observes in his twin studies on the restructuring of the Costa Rican state and society in the

1980s and early 1990s, *The Utopia of a Minimal State* and *The Visible Hand of the Market,* that state spending was *not* considerably reduced in the 1980s. Rather, there was a "functional transformation of the Costa Rican state" in which resources were reoriented from social service and public-sector activities to support for private capital accumulation. State spending on social services and for public enterprises experienced a decrease in relation to GDP, whereas state subsidies for private capital, and particularly for new capitalist groups engaged in export production, experienced an increase, without a significant net change in state spending as a percentage of GDP.[238]

In Costa Rica, as Sojo shows, the state represented capitalist interests in advance of capitalist sectors, who reacted to opportunities opened up by globalization and presented to them by the Costa Rican and transnational state. Costa Rican capitalists often functioned "more as executors than as designers and planners" of the new strategy of accumulation. "The promotion of the market is a transnational public policy. The undeniable identity behind the mechanisms of the 'free market' at the start of the twenty-first century becomes clear: the visible hand of the market is the state."[239] To Sojo's analysis we must add that the neo-liberal national state in the age of globalization becomes a local component of the transnational state, as argued in chapter one. This transnational state promotes the conditions for the accumulation of capital. It provides this service, however, not for just any capital but for transnational capital. In this way it represents the interests of the agents engaged in global circuits of accumulation, often against the interests of those capitalist fractions and other economic agents based in national circuits of accumulation.

In his notable study on Central America, *Power in the Isthmus,* James Dunkerley observes with regard to Costa Rican state managers in the post-WWII period that they "never sought the development of a state capitalism so much as a national capitalist circuit in which foreign capital would be fully represented and supported where it could operate more efficiently."[240] But the inverse of Dunkerley's observation seems to be more accurate in light of the globalization of Central America: transnational state managers seek to create global capitalist circuits of accumulation in which "national" capital can be fully represented. It is clear, as well, that transnational state practices in Central America were perfectly consistent with more general patterns worldwide under global capitalism: local states are captured by transnational fractions who utilize the state to integrate their countries into the global economy by generating the conditions—including programmatic and ideological conditions—and providing the services necessary for the development of globalized production processes.

But this process generates new social contradictions. As the state in Costa Rica lost its capacity to capture and redistribute surpluses in the 1980s and 1990s the polarizing effects of the global market were unleashed internally. Between 1980 and 1990, real wages dropped by 17 percent.[241] Public investment in real terms declined by almost 40 percent between 1982 and 1996.[242] Between 1981 and 1990, the state's per capita spending on education dropped by 21 percent.[243] More alarming, the national health budget declined from a high of 11.4 percent of GNP in 1979 to 5.7 percent in 1989, while real per-capita health expenditures dropped 56 percent. Health clinics were closed, food distribution centers and community health programs cut, and the installation of sanitation, sewage treatment, and potable water curtailed. As a result, the number of children treated for malnutrition in the 1980s doubled and many infectious diseases reappeared.[244] The privatization of social services induced a bifurcation of services into high-quality provision for the better off and a deterioration of services for a majority.

Nonetheless, the government was able during the 1980s and 1990s to negotiate adjustment while protecting, relative to other countries, the health and educational systems and other social services. The result has been a more gradual deterioration of popular living standards, but a deterioration nonetheless. At the close of the twenty-first century Costa Rica exhibited some of the general trends in the region: polarization, insecurity, spreading corruption, crimewaves, and rising government repression. The countryside has been visited by a sharp increase in rural landlessness and unrest as the smallholder economy was broken up by the spread of capitalist agriculture and the introduction of new agro-export crops (see next chapter). The cities have seen the characteristic rise under globalization of a new urban poor of casualized and informalized labor, and the marginalized.

The hegemonic system was strong enough in Costa Rica for the country to weather the crisis of the 1980s. The whole political spectrum became consolidated around a neo-liberal "bipartisan" bloc that achieved a measure of hegemony despite growing polarization and social conflict. With the convergence around the transnational program in the 1990s, the transformation of the PLN from a social democratic into a neo-liberal party (even though the party's legitimating discourse continued to be social democracy), and a more solid ruling class consensus than elsewhere, the two dominant parties became increasingly indistinguishable in the 1990s. Emasculated through political repression after the 1948 "revolution," the Left never became a significant political force in the post-WWII period and, after an increase in its influence following the economic crisis of the early 1980s, nearly disappeared from the political map in the 1990s. The polyarchic system remained intact as the dominant groups restructured the economy, dismantled social services and entitlements, and oversaw a sharp rise in inequalities. Although popular protest became a fixture of the country's political life, Costa Rica did not experience a revolutionary movement or breakdown in the social order during its transition. There was no institutional discontinuity, even though the Costa Rica of the early twenty-first century was a radically different country to the Costa Rica of the 1970s.

3

The New Transnational Model in
Central America:
I: Incorporation into the Global Economy

Change in the Central American economy and society under globalization has been referred to in international development discourse as modernization. Modernization theories of the 1950s and 1960s popularized the notion of "modernization" to denote the process conceived as replication of the Western experience of development. Development implied the spread and consolidation of capitalist economy and society into the underdeveloped regions (the unproblematized assumption was that capitalism would generate development). Development would come about by the action of two modernizing agents: the developed capitalist countries that would facilitate the process through aid, policy formulation (imposition), and investment; and local enlightened elites who would organize the modernization process from within each country. Dependency, world-system, and other critical theories of underdevelopment in the 1960s and 1970s exposed the system-maintenance bias of modernization theory in favor of the rich countries and local elites. The problematic posed by these theories was the formation of the nation-state and the possibility of a greater or lesser degree of autonomy achieved by these units vis-à-vis the world economy. International asymmetries in wealth and power were sustained, and the structures of underdevelopment generated and reproduced, through the very process of world accumulation that modernization theory purported would achieve development.

The transition from a world to a global economy entails modernization in each region that becomes incorporated into emergent transnational structures. But by modernization I refer to the regenerative process of adjusting local structures to changing world structures. To the extent that modernization connotes the spread and consolidation of capitalism then the agents of this process are "modernizing" groups whose development is coterminous with the development of capitalism at particular historic conjunctures. Modernizing groups as agents of capitalist development reorganize local accumulation processes so that they synchronize with world accumulation processes to which they are articulated. These groups act as modernizers not because any functional determination requires that they do. Their class and group interests are advanced through a viable articulation being the basis for local power and privilege. As part of modernization local economic practices must be calibrated to prevailing world standards. For example, the process of introducing computers into office work and state record-keeping once computerization has become generalized worldwide can be said to constitute the "modernization" of office work and record-keeping. Modernization in the current epoch entails the adoption of new communications, transportation, management, and other technologies that make possible the integration of local into global circuits of production and exchange. Modernization also includes institutional adjustments in the state apparatus and in local polities, modifications in the legal system, and changes in cultural norms in calibration with economic change. In its technical dimension, modernization is a cumulative process that entails the progressive application of rational, scientific, and technological knowledge to the processes of social production and organization. But its essence is social, not technical: *of decisive importance is the social character of the process.* It is usually a top-down process linked to class projects. And it involves essential social control dimensions insofar as modernization results in a renewal of control by dominant groups over the labor process and the social product.

The "modernizers" as agents of capitalist development have shifted historically as Central America has gone through a series of rearticulations to world capitalism. The effective linking of the region to the world market took place in the latter part of the nineteenth century through the introduction of coffee cultivation. The Liberals that dominated nineteenth-century Central America were the "modernizing" groups in their moment who led the region into a new relationship with the world economy based on coffee and restructured domestic institutions. Each rearticulation since then has involved a restructuring of domestic institutions and of social classes and groups. The industrial and commercial elite and middle classes associated with the expansion of agro-exports and industrialization after World War II comprised the "modernizing sector" in that period. Post-war modernization referred to the introduction of new economic activities as leading sectors of the economy, new forms of social and economic organization in these sectors, and also to institutional adjustments in the state apparatus that facilitated the expansion of the agro-export model.

Transnational fractions of the local elite have become in international development discourse the "modernizers" in Central America under globalization. They are agents of a new rearticulation and of a more advanced application of the criteria of capitalist rationality to Central American economy and society in the current epoch. This rearticulation involves integration into world structures that are themselves fundamentally being altered by the globalization of production and the transnationalization of superstructural processes and institutions. The gradual disembedding of groups, structures, and institutions from the nation-state context in which they have been traditionally studied modifies the focus of critical underdevelopment theories. In contradistinction to modernization theory, these theories focused on the dialectical convergence of internal and external factors as the axis of development and change. But globalization increasingly blurs the boundaries between the internal and the external and shifts the focus to a transnational synthesis of the two. The concluding chapter evaluates the potential for the new model of accumulation to bring about development to Central America.

Central America in the World Economy Prior to Globalization

The Crisis of Central America's Post-WWII Social Structure of Accumulation

Each epoch of world capitalism has produced a rearticulation of Central America to it, including the transformation of social forces and the restructuring of economies, classes, states, and power blocs. Each expansion period has been shorter than the previous, indicating the increased rate of change worldwide under capitalism. The first cycle, a colonial mercantile insertion, lasted until its collapse in the mid-nineteenth century. The second, based on coffee and bananas, ran from the 1870s until it entered into crisis in the 1930s. The third, based on a new set of agro-export products and ISI industrialization, became established after WWII and entered into crisis by the late 1970s. In the 1980s Central America began to acquire a new profile in the global division of labor (GDL), the region's fourth cycle of capitalist expansion and articulation to the world economy. This fourth cycle was based on a new set of activities. Before turning to the current rearticulation, let us review the previous one.

Capitalist development in Central America following WWII to the 1970s included an expansion of the agro-export sector, particularly the large-scale introduction and/or extension of beef, cotton, and sugar alongside traditional coffee and banana production, and dependent industrialization in the framework of the CACM and the ISI model,[1] as shown in tables 3.1 and

Table 3.1. Expansion of Agro-Exports,* 1950–79 (as value-added, 1970 prices, millions $)

	1950	1960	1970	1979
Costa Rica	62	69	135	165
El Salvador	94	133	220	306
Guatemala	94	152	206	345
Honduras	59	56	106	135
Nicaragua	24	41	100	153
Regional total	333	451	767	1104

* Coffee, bananas, cotton, and sugar.

Source: Bulmer-Thomas, *The Political Economy of Central America Since 1920*, 1987, Table A-5, pp. 316–7.

Table 3.2.   Growth of Manufacturing, 1950–79 (as value-added, 1970 prices, millions $)

	1950	1960	1970	1979
Costa Rica	34	74	173	333
El Salvador	66	113	246	365
Guatemala	98	154	321	556
Honduras	29	72	103	163
Nicaragua	26	52	149	165
Regional total	253	465	992	1582

Source: Bulmer-Thomas, *The Political Economy of Central America Since 1920*, 1987, Table A-8, pp. 322–3.

3.2. This expansion was linked, in turn, to the dramatic period of post-WWII world economic growth, including increased demand in core country markets for raw materials to feed industrial expansion and rising consumer demand. We can associate these regional changes with the third epoch, that of corporate capitalism. New middle classes emerged through the transformation of handicrafts and secondary trade, the expansion of services, the formalization of merchant activity, and state-sponsored education. Pressures for industrialization came internally from these new modernizing sectors. Pressures came externally from the drive at the cores of world capitalism to capture local consumer markets and to expand Third World markets for their capital goods, technology, and loans, reflective of the changes in the international division of labor that emerged with the post-war boom in world capitalism. The dominant power bloc was again reorganized to accommodate the newly created industrial, commercial, and financial elites and new capitalist planters spawned by industrialization, along with a bureaucratic elite, and the diversification and expansion of agro-exports that took place after World War II, as part of the region's rearticulation at a moment of dramatic growth in the world economy.

Capitalist development affected all social groups. The new hegemonic bloc was led by the landed oligarchy, except in Costa Rica, where this class's hegemony had been broken in 1948 (see chapter two), in alliance with emergent national industrial, commercial, and financial capitalists and middle class strata. Subordinate classes included a semi-proletarianized peasantry, integrated part-time or seasonally into the formal wage sector, and a peasantry producing for subsistence and the internal market, both under semi-capitalist relations, along with a growing urban proletariat and "lumpen-proletariat."[2] Capitalist development affected all social groups. This Central American ISI populist model was a truncated version of the Latin American and general Third World model. ISI strategies elsewhere formed part of broad-ranging populist movements protagonized by autonomous national classes in a more precarious alliance with international capital. In Central America, the agro-export oligarchy dominated the project, unlike South America, Asia, and elsewhere, where this oligarchy was displaced by new elites.[3] Social forces and political structures (power relations) shape inasmuch as they are shaped by material conditions. Given the political weakness of the elite and the inchoate response of the subordinate classes to the 1930s crisis, authoritarian civilian-military regimes (with the exception of Costa Rica) remained in place. This political model met the need for internal social control and imposed discipline among different elite fractions engaged in a multitude of clashes in a rapidly changing milieu.

Central American authoritarianism in contrast to South American populism is explained in part by the nature of the political system imposed by the region's dominant groups in the 1930s in response to the crisis of the liberal oligarchic state. However, these dictatorial political structures stunted the development of the dominant classes and eventually retarded capitalist development. The highly skewed class structure and the lack of cohesion among popular and working classes resulting from this situation helps explain, in turn, the inability of the popular classes to mount a concerted class project that could have resulted in a more redistributive populist developmental direction as an outcome of the 1930s crisis. As a result, the project in Central America stood out for the very narrow autonomy exhibited by local states and dominant groups, the extremely firm insertion of the CACM into US-sponsored accumulation processes in the Greater Caribbean Basin, and the lack of popular and working class insertion into the project. The emphasis, unlike elsewhere, was on private rather than public investment. The project in Central America was thus not particularly conducive to either state or working class development, a factor which helped shape the political and social conditions under which globalization would later proceed and the particular profile the region would acquire in the GDL.

The breakdown of the third articulation is reflected in the drastic economic crisis that started in 1979, as discussed for each country in chapter two, and as indicated in table 3.3. While all of Latin America experienced the "lost decade" of the 1980s, Central America was particularly hard-hit, suffering twice the decline in real income as Latin America as a whole.[4] Between 1980 and 1983, unemployment soared as GDP per capita and wages dropped precipitously in every country. Real consumption dropped 26 percent in Costa Rica, 39 percent in El Salvador, 9 percent in Guatemala, 19 percent in Honduras, and 39 percent in Nicaragua.[5]

The immediate causes of this crisis owed to such factors as the world economic shocks of 1979, recession in core countries, and mounting debt burden and rising interest rates as the 1970s wave of international borrowing came to an end. But the underlying structural cause was the exhaustion of the accumulation model based on expanded agro-exports and ISI development. The saturation of world markets for these agro-exports due to changing market demand, the failure of Third World producers to organize effectively to control global surpluses, and the substitution of

Table 3.3.   Central American Growth and Stagnation, 1970–90 (average annual percentage change)

	GDP (average annual percentage change)			GDP per capita (cumulative)	
	1970–80	1980–85	1985–90	1970–80	1980–88
Costa Rica	5.5	0.2	4.3	31.2	−6.6
El Salvador	3.1	−2.0	1.8	9.0	−15.1
Guatemala	5.7	−1.1	0.0	31.4	−19.5
Honduras	5.5	0.6	4.0	22.0	−10.8
Nicaragua	0.3	0.6	−4.2	−23.3	−28.6
Regional total	4.0	−0.3	1.2	14.6	−16.2

Source: CEPAL, *Annual Report*, various years.

tropical food products by First World alternatives (not unlike the experience in the nineteenth century with synthetic dye substitutes, which almost overnight wiped out Central America's indigo and cochineal-based economy), signalled the limits to the model, as reflected in rising foreign exchange crises and a secular decline in the terms of trade for these products (see table 3.4). In addition, the particular type of industrialization severely restricted internal market demand and therefore sustained growth, given the limited employment opportunities and the lack of a redistributive dynamic immanent to the model. Industrial growth under the model depended on rising imports of capital goods, technology, and related producer goods. Growth is eventually arrested by fiscal and foreign exchange crises, which leads to cycles of foreign borrowing in order to sustain production and a rising debt burden (see tables 3.5 and 3.6).

As for much of the developing world, the debt crisis became the proximate imperative for neo-liberal restructuring and deeper integration

Table 3.4.   Price Indices of Central American Traditional Exports

	1980	1982	1985	1987
Bananas	100.0	99.9	101.4	100.5
Beef	100.0	86.6	78.0	86.4
Coffee	100.0	90.6	94.4	72.8
Cotton	100.0	77.4	63.9	79.8
Sugar (world market)	100.0	29.3	14.1	23.6
US import	100.0	66.3	67.8	72.7

Source: IMF International Financial Statistics, as cited in Conroy, *et al.*, *A Cautionary Tale*, Boulder 1996, p. 18.

Table 3.5. Central American Total External Debt, 1970–90 (millions $)

	1970	1975	1980	1985	1990
Costa Rica	246	684	2744	4401	3772
El Salvador	183	412	911	1854	2132
Guatemala	120	243	1166	2653	2777
Honduras	109	379	1470	2728	3525
Nicaragua	155	611	2176	5728	10623
Central America	813	2330	8467	17365	22829

Source: World Bank, various years, *World Tables.*

into the global economy. Changes in the organization of world capitalism, including the globalization of production, new consumption patterns, and shifts in profitability worldwide towards new activities, especially finances, compelled capitalist modernization and opened up concrete possibilities for a new articulation.[6] The prevailing oligarchic political structures, however, performed the contradictory functions, on the one hand of containing popular sectors and middle strata and maintaining internal social order, and on the other, of constraining full capitalist development. The persistence of these structures meant a sharp disjuncture between oligarchic power and politics, and the material and social change brought about by capitalist development. The political system had to be made compatible with the economic changes. The old militarized oligarchic political structures had to be destroyed. And they were.

In the dialectical approach, the new germinates out of the contradictions manifest within the old. Social structures are constructed and constantly reconstructed through the struggles of diverse social forces. As I observed earlier, sets of structures usually become stabilized during periods of equilibrium, or stalemate, among contending social forces, and then

Table 3.6. Central America's Debt Burden (as percentage of value of exports of goods)

	1980–81	1988–89
Costa Rica	32.4	45.0
El Salvador	7.9	44.8
Guatemala	6.3	42.6
Honduras	21.6	48.5
Nicaragua	38.0	73.3
Central American average	21.2	50.8

Source: Inter-American Development Bank, *Economic and Social Progress in Latin America*, 1990.

unravel as internal contradictions mature and give way to new upheavals. From the 1960s and on the post-WWII social structure in Central America could not be reproduced and began to unravel. The breakdown of the ISI/ agro-export model was felt with particular severity in Central America because the antiquated system of political authority was unable to provide a flexible response to structural changes. The exhaustion of the model of accumulation built on the third reinsertion, together with the political crisis of oligarchic power, led to the regional conflagration of the 1980s.

Each of Central America's three articulations to world capitalism became undone as the prevailing models of accumulation became exhausted and as social contradictions made impossible their reproduction. The dissolution of the colonial insertion came through incessant civil wars. The next insertion had become exhausted by the early decades of the twentieth century. The crises and upheavals of the 1930s and 1940s paved the way for the third insertion, which in turn became undone in the 1970s and 1980s. But exhaustion alone is not sufficient for the breakdown of a prevailing articulation to world capitalism and for a rearticulation to occur. What replaces a particular model is not predetermined. This is a matter of empirical and historical investigation into configurations of social forces, historical conjuncture, and structural context, as explored in earlier chapters with regard to Central America, and as summarized in table 3.7.

The task of destroying the oligarchic structures fell to popular and revolutionary movements that in the process sought a more radical social transformation from the bottom up, a possibility opened up by the very tenacity of these structures and the inability of bourgeoisie and middle classes to modernize society. The dialectic of revolution and counterrevolution nudged these "modernizing" classes into their own anti-oligarchical and counterrevolutionary project only when the world conditions presented by globalization made a process of modernization both possible and necessary. As Elizabeth Dore and John Weeks argue, the revolutionary movements mustered the social forces to definitively destroy the old order in Central America and remove the obstacles to capitalist development.[7]

But there is a distinction between objective structures and projects of collective agency. The popular and revolutionary movements were the unwitting midwives of capitalist development in the age of globalization. Social change is a contradictory and conflictual process. Outcomes are often the unintended consequence of the collective intentions of multiple social forces in struggle. This raises theoretical issues which beckon exploration, among them, how structures become imposed through those very social forces that attempt their destruction. Perhaps the necessary can only assert itself in the possible. The popular and revolutionary movements fought to smash feudalism in order to transform and transcend capitalism. The global economy, as the world historic juncture, not only "allowed" the revolutionary movements to destroy feudal structures as impediments to capitalist globalization but also and simultaneously brought forth the social forces that would protagonize successful counterrevolution and a new cycle of capitalist development, as incarnated in the transnational model of

Table 3.7. Central America: Four Waves of Capitalist Expansion and Integration into World Economy (an approximation)

Time frame	Stage in world capitalism	Main economic activities	Key dominant groups	Key subordinate groups	State form
1520s–mid-1800s	mercantile	– labor and foodstuffs for neighboring colonies – indigo – cochineal	– colonial elites – creole landowners – ecclesiastical authorities	– Indian communities – mestizo peasants	– colonial state/ Conservative proto-states
1870s–1930s	classical/competitive	– coffee and bananas	– coffee oligarchy – merchant elite	– Indian communities – mestizo peasants	– 'Liberal oligarchic states'
1940s–1970s	corporate/monopoly	– beef, sugar, and cotton	– coffee oligarchy – capitalist planters – financial, industrial, and commercial elite	– semi-proletarianized peasants – urban workers – lumpen-proletariat	– civilian-military regimes/ caudillismo
1980s–	global capitalism	– maquiladora manufacturing – NTAEs – Tourism/ transnational services – export of Central American labor/ remittances	– local transnational bureaucratic elites – transnational fractions of bourgeoisie	– new and old working classes – peasants – supernumeraries – emigrant labor – informal service sector-labor	– polyarchic regimes (revolutionary interregnum in Nicaragua)

accumulation. Counterrevolution *meant* not a conservative restoration but political, social, economic, and cultural modernization as the preconditions for a new round of capitalist development. The political structures resulting from the collapse of the liberal oligarchic states were not flexible and could not respond to the requirements of capitalist modernization. Globalization has ushered in a new era of capitalist political as well as economic rationality. The revolutionary movements as collective agency could not push the regional structures beyond the boundaries set by the larger global structure, which both called forth and set the limits to change.

Capitalist development in the 1980s and on was predicated on another rearticulation to the world capitalist system. The political outcome of the social upheaval of the 1980s, as discussed in chapter two—the displacement of the old oligarchy, the conditional defeat of the broad popular sectors, and the conditional victory of the new dominant groups—paved the way for the transnational model to take hold. As has been seen on a country by country basis, transnational nuclei among local elites vied for, and achieved, hegemony over the elite as a whole in the 1980s and 1990s, and utilized state power to implement the program of global capitalism in the region. The region's next rearticulation to world capitalism—corresponding to the fourth epoch, that of globalization—is constituted on that program. This program could not be implemented until pacification was achieved. The conflict made the region unavailable to transnational capital. The process of capitalist modernization that ran from the 1930s into the 1970s could only continue after the political obstacles were removed by the revolutionary upheaval. The social contradictions that have driven Central American development since the nineteenth century have been modified once again but not resolved. But the contradictions which present themselves this time around are internal to (global) capitalism rather than between capitalism and atavistic elements. The underlying dynamic of capitalist modernization is now bound up with that of capitalist globalization.

Central America's Emerging Profile in the Global Economy

The Fourth Period of Central American Rearticulation and Expansion

In the new model, technocrats from transnational state institutions set out to persuade Central American state officials and private-sector leaders to embark on a new round of export expansion. This new rearticulation is based on what is called "Export-Led Development" (ELD) in current international development discourse, and involves a transition to a transnational model of accumulation, based on the introduction of novel activities tied to the global economy and the new globalized circuits of accumulation. "Underway in the region is an economic transformation that has the potential to be as profound as the political transition of the 1980s," stated a major AID policy document on the region in 1991.[8] Neo-liberal restructuring and the program of free-market capitalism, including sweeping liberalization and privatization, have created the overall environment for the new model. A series of cumulative changes is producing a new profile for the region in the GDL rather than an abrupt abandonment of the agro-export society. The new model involves elements of both continuity and discontinuity, the culmination of one period of social change and the beginning of another.

The shift to the new model can be traced to the world economic shocks of 1979. These shocks dramatically affected macroeconomic performance in the region, undermined financial and exchange rate stability and triggered a cyclic downswing unprecedented since the 1930s. The crisis revealed the impending exhaustion of the prevailing model. Between 1980 and 1983 all the Isthmanian countries entered into negotiation with the IFIs, particularly with the IMF, and embarked on adjustment programs. Precursors to full-blown neo-liberalism, these programs were at first limited and not subject to conditionality. But as the decade progressed adjustment increasingly involved conditionality and it became clear that major economic restructuring was in the works. The IMF, the World Bank, IDB, the AID, and other institutions of a transnational state began to press the dominant groups in Central America to turn towards "outward-looking" strategies. Using the region's escalating external debt and balance of payments crisis as leverage, they emphasized liberalization and non-traditional export-promotion, including export tax exemptions, credits, and the use of Free Trade Zones. Increased aid tied to restructuring was supplemented with trade measures under the CBI. The CBI was part of a broader offensive by the US and transnational elite to sweep away the barriers to the free movement of capital around the world. Formally launched in 1984, it gave the Central American countries (except Nicaragua) duty-free access to the US market.[9]

Non-traditional exports became a centerpiece of ELD strategies throughout Latin America during the 1980s and 1990s. Bulmer-Thomas and his colleagues have referred to these strategies as the "New Economic Model [NEM] in Latin America."[10] The NEM, what I am referring to here, with broader connotations, as the transnational model, entailed essentially the package of neo-liberal structural adjustment measures, among them trade liberalization, fiscal austerity, privatization, and labor market deregulation and flexibility, as the mechanism for a shift from "inward-looking development" to "export led growth." External debt pressures and fiscal crises "led to a shift in the development paradigm in the mid-1980s,"[11] in which resources would be shifted from the internal to the external sector and non-traditional exports promoted as the basis for a new insertion into the world market. "Gradually, the Central American countries have come to realize that the old economic model—a hybrid based on agricultural exports and regional import substitution within the framework of the Central American Common Market—was not sustainable," stated the AID in reference to the new model in the Isthmus. "Though traditional exports from the region continue to stagnate because of low world prices, the rapid growth of non-traditional exports is increasingly providing the foreign exchange needed to meet resource requirements. Non-traditional exports rose from $423 million in 1983 to $1.3 billion in 1990, and have the potential to rise to $4 billion by 1996 if outward-oriented economic policies continue to be implemented. This will reflect a fundamental economic transformation."[12]

In Central America, the watershed in the turn to the new model was the 1984 Kissinger Commission Report, a virtual blueprint for neo-liberalism and the transnational model in the Isthmus. In its political/military dimension the report called for transitions to polyarchy and for the defeat of the Nicaraguan revolution and the leftist insurgencies in El Salvador and Guatemala. But the military crisis did not stop the Commission from developing a long-term vision of neo-liberal reconstruction. In its economic dimension it called for the integration of the region into the global economy. Concrete measures included a roll-back of local state intervention in the economy, a greater opening up to transnational corporate investment, the elimination of price controls and dismantling of ISI industries, export promotion, particularly of non-traditionals, and the establishment of free trade zones. The Kissinger Commission Report reflected the consensus reached by the transnational elite on the requirement of reestablishing hegemonic order in Central America, including a new role for the region in the global economy.[13] Here we get another glimpse of the interface between agency and structural change. The intervention of agency at the level of the global system in the form of transnational functionaries from the US state and the IFIs liaised with agency at the local level in the form of ascendant transnational fractions.

The model of ELD leads to, and is driven by, the extension of capitalism in the region. The transnational model of development has shifted the entire productive structure more fully towards the world market. What has taken place is a process of "export substitution." Through integration into the global economy the region is becoming rearticulated on the basis of a more complete transition to capitalism. In this new stage primitive accumulation in Central America is coming to an end.

Each new rearticulation has resulted in the expansion of the region's accumulation model and the introduction of new economic activities. Old accumulation activities usually continue but decline in *relative* importance to new, more dynamic sectors, and the vitality of the old activities becomes conditioned on the dynamic of these new sectors. Thus the introduction of coffee and bananas in the latter half of the nineteenth century determined the social and economic development of the region. But coffee and bananas did not disappear. Their importance decreased *relative* to dynamic new sectors of accumulation (the absolute value of coffee output actually rose considerably), and these new sectors exercised a transformative effect on the social fabric. Similarly, in the transnational model, the older agro-export products have not disappeared but declined in relative importance, while dynamic new sectors stimulate fundamental social, economic, cultural, and political change.

The new rearticulation, in Central America and throughout the developing world, reversed what McMichael refers to as the "development project" of nationally managed economic growth and social development. The debt crisis of the 1970s and subsequent neo-liberal project institutionalized the new definition of development as participation in the world market and the transition from managed national economic growth to managed global economic growth. The "solution" to the debt crisis and stagnation was not just increased exports but export diversification. Such new export profiles, in Central America as elsewhere, became the path of integration into the globalized economy then emerging. New export portfolios have included: 1) participating in component phases of globalized industrial production. This may entail component processes, component capital and intermediate goods, and component consumer goods,[14] and includes maquiladora production; 2) the production of new products in response to new demands on the world market and shifts in world consumption patterns. For example, income polarization associated with post-Fordist flexible accumulation entails the creation of new high-consumption world market segments, and these segments may demand new products, such as NTAEs (for example, exotic fruits and flowers); 3) the supply of new raw materials as part of the far-reaching changeover that has taken place in the world production base; and 4) new services to facilitate the global accumulation process, including but not limited to financial services (for example, travel and leisure may also fit in here). With the exhaustion of the previous model, the shift to the ELD model in Central America has been driven by a convergence of social forces in struggle and of technical possibilities in organizing transnational production, as later sections in this chapter make clear.

The "non-traditional" exports such as maquila production, tourism, and new agricultural and agro-industrial products are based on utilizing the region's "comparative advantage" in cheap labor as the basis for rearticulation to the world economy. The strategy has been to attract transnational capital investment for world market exports. A "competitive" reinsertion into global markets has been achieved through a new set of exports, the demand for which has itself been created through the globalization of production, the restructuring of the world economy, and a new structure of world income. It is to these new activities that I now turn.

From ISI to the Maquiladoras

The maquiladora phenomenon is often seen as the quintessence of the global economy and has become one of the most widely studied aspects of globalization. Export Processing Zones (EPZs) are a type of Free Trade Zone, sometimes called *zona francas*, established as enclaves outside the customs territory of a particular country whose chief attraction for transnational capital is the supply of abundant, cheap labor from the host country. Products are stored, processed, and manufactured free from the payment of import duties on equipment, machinery, and raw materials and with the intention of exporting most or all of the output to the world market. Firms in these EPZs, known as maquiladoras, or assembly plants, are provided with a generous package of incentives, generally including tax holidays, freedom from foreign exchange regulations, and most notoriously, even guarantees against unionization of the labor force.[15] EPZs have spread rapidly as production has become transnationalized, from just a handful in the 1970s to 200 or so in the mid-1990s employing roughly four million workers in some fifty countries. About 90 percent of the EPZs were located in Latin America and East Asia, with the strongest concentration in the Greater Caribbean Basin.[16]

In their landmark 1977 study, *The New International Division of Labor*, Frobel and his colleagues argued that the spread of maquiladoras was leading to a "new international division of labor" as core capital relocated low-wage phases of manufacturing to cheap labor zones in the Third World. TNCs established new export platforms, the EPZs, installing maquiladora, or what they called "world market factories." "The development of the world economy has increasingly created conditions (forcing the development of the new international division of labor) in which the survival of more and more companies can only be assured through the relocation of production to new industrial sites," they claimed, "where labour-power is cheap to buy, abundant, and well-disciplined: in short, through the transnational reorganization of production."[17]

The study was the first to draw attention to the now-notorious sweatshop conditions of superexploitation, labor repression, the degradation of women, child labor, Taylorist control, and dehumanization at the maquiladora factories, as the counterpart to "runaway factories" and rising structural unemployment in the traditional core. "What this process means for those it directly affects is, first and foremost, unemployment and the devaluation of skills for workers in the traditional industrial countries, and the subjection of the populations of the developing countries to inhuman working conditions, with no hope for improvement in the foreseeable future. Furthermore, the inevitable development in this process means that in the years to come working people will be threatened even more drastically than in the past with the degradation and rigid discipline which reduces them to the status of mere appendages of the machine."[18] In fact, in the same year that *The New International Division of Labor* was published in English, in 1980, the export of manufactured goods from the Third World for the first time surpassed that of raw materials.[19]

Although NIDL theory has been superseded by more recent theorizing on the global economy, and the 1977 study is now outdated, it remains a classic statement on the maquiladora phenomenon:

Free production zones are industrial areas which are separated off from the rest of the country, located at places where labour is cheap and designated as sites for world market oriented industry . . . Production in world market factories is highly vertically integrated into the transnational operations of the individual companies and involves non-complex production operations; the manufacturing of parts, assembling of parts, or final assembly . . . textiles and garments are one example. The employment structure in free production zones and world market factories is extremely unbalanced. Given a virtually unlimited supply of unemployed labour, world market factories at the free production zones, or other sites, select one specific type of worker, chiefly women from the younger age groups. The criteria used for the selection of workers are quite unambiguous: the labour which is employed is that which demands the least remuneration, provides the maximum amount of energy (i.e. fresh labour which can be expected to work at a high intensity) and which is predominantly unskilled or semiskilled.[20]

This description is still valid for much maquiladora production in Central America, especially garment production, which under the model of ELD has largely replaced the earlier ISI pattern of industrialization. The turn toward globalization has involved two types of export-oriented industrialization: the internationalization of national industries established under ISI, and the installation of maquiladora enclaves.[21] Recent industrial growth in Central America has been largely of the latter variant. Economic considerations by transnational capital and political considerations by the US state combined with shifts in the global economy resulted in the massive entrance to Central America of garment assembly starting in the mid-1980s. Although EPZ manufacturing around the world ranges from toys to sporting goods, optical instruments, and footwear, the vast majority of world maquiladora production is in textiles/garments and electronics, while a single industry tends to dominate EPZ activity in most countries where it becomes established. In Central America, maquiladora production is almost exclusively of garments, outside of Costa Rica, where electronics and pharmaceutical/medical equipment also represent a significant share.[22]

Following the general tendency in the restructuring of capitalist production, the garment industry has undergone an increasing decentralization, segmentation, and subdivision of tasks in the production process. This includes the automation of some of these tasks and the transfer to low-wage zones around the globe of those tasks that are difficult to mechanize and which remain labor-intensive (sewing operations in particular are very labor-intensive). The garment industry has three major phases: fibers production in which the general tendency is towards the production of technologically advanced synthetics; textile production which remains highly labor-intensive; and a final retail phase. This complex Global Commodity Chain (GCC), to evoke the concept developed by Gereffi and Korzeniewicz, is "buyer driven," dominated by huge transnational retail outlets, such as Sears Roebuck, J.C. Penney, the GAP, and so on.[23] "Producer driven" GCCs are those in which TNCs play the central role in coordinating production chains, including forward and backward linkages, and this "is most characteristic of capital and technology-intensive commodities, such as automobiles, aircraft, semi-conductors, and electrical machinery." In turn, "buyer driven" GCCs are those in which "large retailers, brand-name merchandisers, and trading companies play the central role in shaping decentralized production networks . . . typical in relatively labor-intensive consumer goods such as garments, footwear, toys, and housewares."[24]

As the global economy emerged in the 1960s and 1970s, US textile-apparel producers shifted the labor-intensive middle phase to the East Asian low-wage zone, and also developed subcontracting ("outsourcing") networks, whereby East Asian, particularly Taiwanese and South Korean, capital organized local production in consort with transnational capital. By the 1980s and 1990s, this process had resulted in the integration into transnational accumulation circuits of East Asian capitalists themselves, who began to shift production to new low-wage zones, particularly mainland China, Southeast Asia, and Central America and the Caribbean, in the face of rising wage levels and other factor cost considerations in their home countries. The social dislocations generated by capitalist development in Central America as globalization proceeded from the 1960s and on, together with the disruptions caused by the political-military conflagration, had generated a huge pool of available—and potentially revolutionary—labor in Central America by the 1980s and 1990s. Moreover, the region was ideally situated geographically for access to the US market. This is the economic backdrop to the appearance of the garment industry in Central America. The political backdrop was the US CBI program, which allowed factories operating in the region duty-free access to the US market and provided further incentives for the massive influx of foreign capital from East Asia to Central America. The more conjunctural strategic objective of the CBI on the part of US policymakers was the expectation that CBI-induced development would help subdue revolutionary movements in the region.[25]

I wish to highlight here the determinacy, in the last instance, of *social forces* in historic developmental outcomes in general, and in the particular case under study, how social forces in struggle in an emergent transnational environment shape the profile of particular countries and regions in the global economy. The conditional defeat of the popular classes in Central America and their exhaustion, as discussed in chapter two, made the region a relatively attractive site as a global investment zone for the new economic activities associated with its modified profile in the GDL, just as constraints were emerging in the earlier-established zones, such as Southeast Asia, due to rising wage levels, worker militancy, labor shortages, and state pressures for greater technology transfers. There was a complex convergence of US geo-political interests with the evolving class interests of East Asian capitalists in the process of integration into transnationalized circuits and with the changing composition of social forces in Central America.

From a structural perspective, the CBI was part and parcel of economic globalization, and illustrated how the US state functions to facilitate the conditions for the globalization of production and to promote the interests of the transnational elite. The AID, for instance, funded and guided Central American states and local business foundations and think-tanks in the establishment of free trade zones and the development of policies and programs conducive to maquiladora production. In this way, local elites operating in the state and in civil society became integrated into these emergent transnationalized circuits in Central America, which spurred on the development of transnational fractions among the elite. A nation-state centric analysis of this situation, which would have "East Asian" capital competing with "US" and other national capitals, conceals the transnational essence of this phenomenon: in the complex global commodity chain, "US," "East Asian," and local "Central American" actors are all component agents of *transnational* circuits of capital accumulation. They are experiencing a process of transnational class formation on the basis of an objective identity of interests and organic integration, and as part of what Sassen refers to as the formation of a "global marketplace" of sites for globalized production and services.[26]

The Maquiladora Industry in Central America

Table 3.8 shows the dramatic appearance of garment-assembly enclaves in Central America from the mid-1980s to the mid-1990s. Between 1984 and 1991 every Central American country enacted laws creating EPZs and offering incentives ranging from tax holidays, import duty exemptions, guarantees for profit repatriations, and exemptions from labor laws.[27] Interestingly, legislation in all five countries contains provisions allowing maquiladora plants to locate anywhere in national territory (outside of the confines of the EPZs), so that in effect the entire Isthmus has been constituted as a single mega-export processing zone. Given the US economic embargo of Nicaragua and the country's relative marginalization from the world market during the Sandinista period, this enclave lagged behind in that country. But in 1991 the Nicaraguan government became the last in the region to approve an EPZ law and reopened the Las Mercedes *zona*

Table 3.8.   Garment Assembly Industry in Central America (as measured in imports to US in millions $)

	1983	1986	1990	1993	1996
Costa Rica	64	142	384	653	706
Guatemala	4	20	192	552	809
El Salvador	6	11	54	251	721
Honduras	20	32	113	510	1241
Nicaragua	–	–	–	3 (1992)	232 (1998)

Source: US Department of Commerce.[28]

Table 3.9. Maquiladora Employment (as percentage of manufacturing employment)

	% of Manufacturing Employment		% of Manufactured Exports
	1990	1996	1996
Costa Rica	16	24	40
Honduras	11	36*	N/A
Nicaragua	45	33	60
El Salvador	N/A	28	45
Guatemala	N/A	38	30

* Figures for 1995

Source: Jenkins, *et al.*, "Export Processing Zones in Central America," 1998, pp. 27–30.

franca outside of Managua. By 1992, over a dozen transnational firms had set up assembly plants for export, mostly to the US market.

By mid-1995, conservative estimates placed the number of workers employed in the maquiladora industry at 235,000 for the five republics, including 50,000 in Costa Rica, 50,000 in El Salvador, 80,000 in Guatemala, 48,000 in Honduras, and 7,000 in Nicaragua.[29] Whether measured as the percentage of total manufacturing employment or as the percentage of total manufactured goods exports, the export-oriented maquiladora industry is coming to replace the inward-oriented ISI sector that corresponded to the previous model of accumulation, as indicated in table 3.9. The importance of the maquiladora sector to the new model of accumulation is also evident in the growth of net export earnings it generates (the amount of foreign exchange actually earned by the host country), as shown in table 3.10. Maquiladora export earnings for the region as a whole amounted to about $1 billion in 1996 out of total regional receipts of some $7.7 billion,

Table 3.10. Export Earnings from Maquiladora Production (in millions $, and as percentage of total export earnings)

	Net Earnings		As Percentage of Total Earnings
	1990	1996	1996
Costa Rica	107	265	10
Honduras*	30	291	25
Nicaragua	0	53	8
El Salvador	22	214	20
Guatemala	39	184	9

* Figures for 1995

Source: Jenkins, *et al.*, pp. 27–30.

Table 3.11. National Origin of Capital in the Central American Maquiladora Industry (as percentage of 791 plants in EPZs, mid-1990s)

	Origin of Capital				
	Local	US	Korean	Other Asian	Other*
Costa Rica	21	60	2	2	16
El Salvador	65	11	8	6	10
Guatemala	43	9	44	2	2
Honduras	32	36	21	10	1
Nicaragua	16	32	16	32**	5

* Largely Central American and European
** Largely Taiwanese

Source: International Labor Organization.[33]

or about 13 percent of the total.[30] Seen from another angle, maquiladora products replaced traditional agro-exports as the chief product imported from Central America by the United States, which is still the region's principal trading partner. In the late 1990s, 51 percent of US imports from Central America consisted of maquiladora products, largely clothing, while agricultural products represented only 37 percent.[31] Moreover, at the behest of apparel manufacturers, the US government enacted legislation in 2000 establishing CBI parity with the NAFTA, which lifted quotas and tariffs on clothing made in the CBI countries. US retailers and apparel producers expected the measure to generate a 500 percent growth in Central American garments production in the ensuing years (the NAFTA led to a similar 500 percent growth in clothing production in the five years after it went into effect).[32]

In sum, the maquiladoras account for a significant and rapidly growing share of the region's industrial output, employment, and foreign exchange earnings.

A highly noteworthy aspect of the maquiladora industry in Central America, as indicated in table 3.11, is the large percentage of local entrepreneurial participation, as measured by the national origin of capital invested in the 791 maquiladora plants operating in the region. In Costa Rica, 21 percent of maquila plants in the EPZs are owned by local investors; in El Salvador, 65 percent; in Guatemala, 43 percent; in Honduras, 32 percent; and in Nicaragua, 16 percent. Local capitalist developers have also been heavily involved in constructing and administering EPZs and industrial parks in all five republics, and especially in Honduras and Nicaragua.

This high proportion of local participation points to the emergence of a new Central American entrepreneurial class more thoroughly integrated into transnational production circuits than the old oligarchy, whose external linkage was strictly market-based.[34] It suggests as well less a comprador relation, in which local bourgeoisie are mere managers and administrators of transnational firms, than a relation between capitalists able to operate at the local or regional levels and those able to operate at the global level, and merits a brief theoretical digression. Capitalists at the local and regional levels such as maquiladora entrepreneurs in Central America, it would seem, come to participate in the global economy as subordinate partners dependent on global capitalists operating through the oligopolist TNC structures. But this does not justify nation-state centric conclusions because, among other reasons, in the "core" there are capitalists that operate only locally and in the "periphery" there are capitalists that operate regionally and globally. More fruitful approaches, although they cannot be pursued here, might involve exploring the relationship between transnational capitalists in more competitive and in more monopolistic sectors of the global economy, just as political economists earlier identified the relations between capitalists in functionally integrated competitive and monopoly sectors within national accumulation processes.[35] Capitalists in the competitive sectors, whether in the "First" or the "Third" world, increase the rate of exploitation or the transfer of value from labor to capital in the phases of accumulation they control in order to compensate for the transfer of value from their sector to capitalists in more monopolistic sectors in other phases. Clearly, what is required is to move beyond nation-state centrism and to apply a theory of value to transformations in world spatial and institutional structures, and to draw out the concomitant implications for transnational class relations.

The maquiladora sector in Central America exhibits the new forms of transnational collaboration between capitalists discussed in chapter one, especially subcontracting and outsourcing, as well as joint ventures, technical cooperation, licensing agreements, and local supply of TNC operations. Unlike TNC subsidiary production, which predominated in the pre-globalization period, these new forms bring local investors directly into TNC-organized global production chains and foment a more organic integration of Central American capitalists into the transnational capitalist class.[36] These novel relations that develop among transnational capitalists (even those operating only locally are transnational because they are incorporated into globalized circuits) are not "core–periphery" relations as seen through the lens of nation-state centrism. Hopkins and Wallerstein note that "core" and "peripheral" nodes within global commodity chains are competitive and monopolistic, respectively, and then go on to correlate core nodes in GCCs to core (nation) states in the world-system and "peripheral" nodes to peripheral (nation) states.[37] But what we see as the apparel industry globalizes is the existence of competitive and monopoly phases of fragmented and decentralized production *within* nation-states. Apparel production in the United States, for instance, involves a more monopolistic sector constituted by the large chain retail outlets that control overall production and pricing. What apparently occurs is a disproportionate appropriation of value from productive capital by commercial and finance capital. And the competitive sector is constituted by the garment-production phase, involving competitive clusters of sweatshops in New York, Los Angeles, the southeastern states, and elsewhere, alongside monopolistic sector retailers who control production through market control, financial, pricing, subcontracting and other mechanisms.[38] We also see similar wage and labor conditions in some of these US sweatshops as in the Central American sweatshops.

"Contractors, who are near the beginning of the fashion-oriented chain, retain a periphery-like status even though they may be located in the United States," observes Taplin. "Like their overseas counterparts, domestic contractors capitalize upon large pools of low-wage labor, extracting value via wage-deepening tactics ... production is fragmented *between* firms domestically, *between* firms globally, and *within* firms domestically."[39] On the other hand, profit margins in the garment maquilas in Central America are remarkably high—a 40 percent return on investment in some cases.[40] Clearly, greater value added, or values transferred among nodes in GCCs, does not necessarily denote "core" and "peripheral" nation-state relations. "Peripheral" nodes operate in the United States and "core" nodes in Central America and nation-state centric conclusions are not justified. To be internationally competitive, according to GCC theory, means precisely to decentralize distinct nodes across the globe in accordance with the whole matrix of factor cost considerations. As Taplin appropriately observes, "Because different production links in the commodity chain occur *within* the United States, a core country, it suggests that countries are not the most appropriate unit of analysis in talking about globalized production in apparel. Furthermore, industry sectoral differences demonstrate the saliency of local rather than national production systems as parallel commodity chains are integrated into global production networks."[41]

A focus on the maquiladora industry in one country of the region, Guatemala, as a case study that reveals some general patterns in Central America as well as certain country-specific features of the sector, also sheds empirical light on these larger issues of transnational class and state formation. The establishment of the maquila sector in Guatemala was the result of a concerted and coordinated effort by the AID, the World Bank, the Guatemalan state, transnational capitalists and their "home states," together with transnationally oriented Guatemalan business elites. These had later become organized into private-sector associations, such as the Chamber of Business and GEXPORT, dedicated to promoting non-traditional exports and neo-liberal modernization (see previous chapter). Shortly after its founding in 1982, GEXPORT set up a special commission, the Apparel Manufacturers Export Commission (VESTEX) to promote maquila operations in Guatemala. In 1984, the Guatemalan government, working closely with the AID and Guatemalan private-sector associations, approved legislation to attract export-assembly investment. At the time the law was passed, there were only six factories assembling apparel for export employing barely 2,000 workers. By 1992 maquila production had become the fastest-growing sector of the Guatemalan economy, with more than 250 plants employing over 50,000 workers and exporting nearly $350 million in garments to the world market.[42]

In the structure of maquila production in Guatemala as part of a GCC, US-based TNCs, led by such brand names as Liz Claiborne, Sears, Bugle Boy, Levi's, and Phillips-Van Heusen, contracted nearly all of the garment production to transnational textile firms as suppliers to the brand-name retailers. These suppliers in turn contracted out to South Korean, Guatemalan, US, German, Israeli, and a spattering of firms from other countries of origin. While this general pattern is typical for the region, Guatemalan production was dominated in the early 1990s by investment capital originating in South Korea, which accounted for nearly half of all output, while Guatemalan investors accounted for over 40 percent (see table 3.11), and joint ventures between transnational and local investors, typical of maquila operations elsewhere in the region, were less significant.[43] South Korean investors included medium-sized Korean firms but also several TNCs, among them, Samsung, Sam Phoong, and Lucky Goldstar. It appears that South Korean investors picked Guatemala largely under the guidance of the South Korean government, which had developed close diplomatic relations with Guatemala military regimes in the 1970s and targeted the country to be the nucleus for Caribbean-wide operations.

As part of the Korean government's drive to transnationalize the Korean economy, the Korean state, in much the same way as it organized and directed Korean capital inside the country in the 1960s and the 1970s, organized Korean capital's transnationalization in the 1980s and early 1990s. This included a search for new apparel export platforms. Once Guatemala was chosen as the major Western Hemisphere site in the wake of the CBI and the opportunities it presented, the Korean state provided a packet of services, including information bureaus, loans, subsidies, and tax breaks at the departure end in South Korea. It also provided a host of services at the arrival end in Guatemala, such as liaison with the Guatemalan state, investor insurance, market studies, and the establishment of Korean–Guatemalan air flights for the massive transfer of apparel plants to Guatemala and Guatemala-to-US garment shipping arrangements. As researcher Kurt Petersen reports, the opening of a Korean factory in Guatemala marked the closing of one in Korea, a process in which "entire factories transfer their contents to Guatemalan warehouses and begin anew."[44] "As the life source of Korean factories, the Korean embassy staff [in Guatemala] are advocates, spokespersons, mediators, and consultants for individual Korean factories."[45] The embassy micromanaged the external and sometimes internal affairs of Korean investors, including assistance in settling labor disputes and legal aid. Korean ambassador to Guatemala Key-Sung Cho played the archetypical role of a "chief executive officer" for Korean transnationals in Guatemala.

In this way, the Korean state was replicating at the transnational level, now in the service of global capitalism, the same role it played at the national level in the development of Korean capitalism. This was not a particularly "Asian" capitalist strategy and conforms to the expected relationship between capital and the capitalist state. The AID played a nearly identical role throughout the Greater Caribbean Basin in generating the conditions for capital investment, but the AID promoted less "US" capital than transnational capital in general. More specifically, in Guatemala AID officials solicited and served as guides to representatives from US-based TNCs interested in contracting work or investing directly in the maquila industry, and the AID even contracted a former embassy official to work full-time with GEXPORT to encourage collaboration between Guatemalan and US entrepreneurs.[46] While pursuing the logics of their own institutional strategies, US and Korean officials in Guatemala were thus on-the-ground activists of the transnational project in Central America. And both the US and the Korean national states conducted this activity in coordination with the Guatemalan national state. In either case, national state apparatuses acted objectively to facilitate the transnationalization of capital. When the Korean state acts to transnationalize Korean capital, and when these activities are complementary to and coordinated with those of the US and the Guatemalan state, it is engaging objectively in transnational state practices aimed at fomenting a globalized accumulation of capital.

In analytical abstraction, the IFIs, the AID, the Korean, and the Guatemalan states should be seen as components of an emergent TNS apparatus which played the role, taken as a whole, that we would expect of the capitalist state: organizing the conditions for capital accumulation (promoting neo-liberal reform, providing investment incentives, and so on), and overseeing the larger social, political, and cultural conditions under which this accumulation takes place (promoting peace processes and polyarchy, and so on). Ambassador Cho, AID officials, and Guatemalan state officials were in effect transnational state managers. For their part, Guatemalan, US and South Korean investors, as agents diretly involved in capital formation in the garments industry, are constituent members of an emerging transnational capitalist class whose activities were facilitated by transnational state managers. Indeed, members of this class begin to see subordinate classes—which are themselves transnationalizing—in the same light regardless of geographic location. "The Guatemalan *campesino* is very much like the Korean peasant," explained one Korean maquila factory manager. "They are docile. They work hard. And, they even have short names like our peasants."[47]

Guatemala led the way in the region's maquila sector, and became a staging point for the spread of operations into the "Northern triangle" (Guatemala, El Salvador, and Honduras). The arrival of the industry demonstrated how the transformation of the regional social structures through conflict generated by capitalist development created the general conditions for the region's globalization, especially the creation of a reserve army of uprooted labor available to transnational capital. Guatemala offered transnational capital the same conditions as in the rest of the region: a cheap and relatively pacified labor force close to the US market and local governments that had created the appropriate macroeconomic and legal environment through neo-liberal reform. But these conditions were particularly fortuitous at the time the maquilas took off in the late 1980s. Labor costs in Guatemala in 1991 were the lowest in Central America and the Caribbean (and thirty times lower than US wages).[48] The aftermath of the "total war" had established the internal conditions for maquila operations, as epitomized by the establishment of maquilas in Indian villages. While the vast majority of maquila investment was in Guatemala City, several TNCs chose to locate operations in rural Mayan Indian communities that, as discussed in the previous chapter, had become thoroughly restructured by the counterinsurgency and integrated into capitalist production relations. These communities threw up ready pools of laborers compelled by hunger to embrace maquila production as coercive labor control gave way to more purely market control through the destruction of local autonomy. In one case, Phillips-Van Heusen, the world's largest manufacturer of men's shirts, set up joint subsidiary operations with a local Guatemalan firm for production in the Indian village of San Pedro, Sacatepequez, where labor costs were 25 percent cheaper than in Guatemala City.[49] Elsewhere in the Indian highlands transnational firms established a "putting out" system among Indian women. Liz Claiborne, for instance, recruited Indian women to knit sweaters on a piece rate basis deep in the highlands of Quiche, a region in northwest Guatemala that in the mid-1980s was the scene of major military conflict.[50] Here we see empirically how national social structure becomes transformed by globalization and integrated into transnational social structure.

Working Conditions, Labor Struggles, Gender and Other Dimensions

Perhaps the most phenomenal growth of the maquiladoras took place in Honduras, which had just one EPZ in Puerto Cortes in 1990, but within a few years had constructed five government-sponsored zones and five privately run industrial parks. Such well-known US-based TNCs as Sara Lee, OshKosh B'Gosh, and Warners set up shop, along with Korean investors who arrived en masse from Sunny Industries, the Dong Bank Corporation, and the Hanil Group, among others, and Hong Kong, Taiwanese, and Singaporan investors.[51] Employment rose from 9,000 in 1990 to 20,000 in 1991 and 48,000 in 1995, as the country went from a "banana republic" to a sweatshop republic. El Salvador also experienced an amazing growth in the industry. Maquila exports to the United States increased by 3,800 percent between 1985 and 1994, from $10 million to $398 million, while the number of workers shot up from 3,500 to 50,000.[52] Costa Rica's maquiladora sector took off in 1986, after the government began the "industrial reconversion program" it negotiated with the IFIs, aimed at reorienting the country's industry from the domestic market to exports.[53] In the 1980s the sector almost exclusively produced apparel, but by the 1990s investors were assembling electronics, medical equipment, and other products requiring greater capital investment.[54] Whether Costa Rica would become the one Central American country to move down the "Asian path" of greater value-added and backward linkages was not clear by the turn of the century, an issue that will be examined in the concluding chapter.

Workers in the Guatemalan maquilas, which resemble the typical working conditions in the sector throughout the Isthmus, labored typically in twelve to fifteen-hour shifts during the 1990s on primitive shop floors in sweatshop conditions, earning between two and four dollars per day.[55] Most of the factories were set up makeshift in old warehouses that are poorly ventilated, poorly lit, and present dangerous fire hazards. Workers were generally locked in during working hours and labored in prison-like conditions, suffering numerous health traumas as a result of exposure to harmful chemical fumes and dust, overwork, and the near-total lack of safety conditions. Fainting and collapsing due to exhaustion and dehydration were commonplace. In 1992, less than half the factories had worker cafeterias and few had any health facilities. Bathrooms were unsanitary and in disrepair, and workers required permission for bathroom breaks, provoking exasperation and indignation. Workers also suffered rampant abuses from supervisors, including routine sexual and physical assault, verbal abuse, and threats. The piece rate system in place in most maquilas assured breakneck work for minimum and sub-minimum wages. Child labor was rampant,[56] and the illegal dismissal of pregnant women was a regular practice. The lack of job security was compounded by an extreme anti-union atmosphere backed up by the Guatemalan state, which promoted a union-free industry and worker docility as one of the key attractions for transnational investors.

These working conditions were replicated throughout the region.[57] In a visit to the maquiladoras in Nicaragua's Las Mercedes zona franca, this author observed rows of buildings that looked like vast warehouses. At 7:00 a.m. what appears to be an army of workers, the vast majority of them women, stream into the red chain-link gates that cordon off the zona franca, just a few minutes from the international airport, in the northeastern corner of Managua. The atmosphere inside the plants is frighteningly regimented, as well as overcrowded, hot, stuffy, and poorly ventilated. There are separate areas for each of the assembly stages. Rows and rows of sewing machines dominate floor space, where hundreds of workers (almost all women) sit for ten to fifteen-hour shifts, with one fifteen-minute break in the morning and another half-hour lunch break in the afternoon as their only rest time. On one side of the shop floor, workers use electrical blades to cut thick stacks of fabric, while in another area, industrial washing machines spew steam and noxious fumes into the air, while sweating workers, both men and women, load and unload bundles of clothing.

In recent years, international labor and anti-sweatshop campaigns have brought attention to these sweatshop conditions in the Central American maquiladoras and to ongoing worker struggles. Wages in the maquiladoras remained largely stagnant in the 1990s, while the real minimum wage outside the sector declined. That maquila wages did not decline (neither did they rise) may be explained, in part, by the absorption of labor available around some EPZs (this was clearly the case in Honduras).[58] Moreover, wages within the sector were above the national minimum in some countries, although not all.[59] But this did not mean that they amounted to a *living wage*, as called for by the international anti-sweatshop campaign. The average wage in the Nicaraguan maquiladoras, for example, was about $60 a month in 1999, whereas the calculated monthly salary to meet the minimum basic needs of a family was $125. Moreover, charges levied by the anti-sweatshop movement of *absolute* exploitation of Central American maquiladora workers appear to be authentic. According to figures compiled by the National Labor Committee, a US-based international workers' rights organization, following a May 2000 visit to the Las Mercedes zona franca in Nicaragua, workers at the Chentex plant received just 18 cents for every pair of Kohl's "Sonoma" shorts that retailed for $24 in the United States (just 7/10th of 1 percent of the retail price). They received just 28 cents for each $34 pair of Gloria Vanderbilt jeans they sewed (8/10th of 1 percent of the retail price), 22 cents for each pair of $19.99 Arizona jeans for J.C. Penney (just 1 percent of the retail price), and so forth. Average wages at Chentex, including bonuses and overtime rates, were some 48 cents an hour.[60] In its promotional material to attract investors, FIDE, the chief business association representing new capitalist groups in Honduras (see chapter two), advertises the "fully loaded labor cost per hour" (that is, including all benefits and extras) at 63 cents.[61]

Maquiladora work is quintessentially organized along the lines of flexible accumulation, under the new capital–labor relation discussed in chapter one. Work in the EPZ is extremely unstable and turnover is high. Workers are generally not hired permanently but on the basis of temporary renewable contracts, which in any event do not stipulate guarantees against dismissals, and are not officially protected inside the zona francas as by national labor laws. Moreover, this type of work is seasonal, dependent on fluctuating demand that regularly draws in and then expels "just-in-time" labor. Many firms fire workers at the end of peak seasons, as demand slackens off, or when stocks are reduced. In El Salvador's San Bartolo EPZ, one common practice is to fire workers at the end of the year and hire them again a few weeks later in order to avoid a "thirteenth month" bonus payment (or *aguinaldo* in Spanish) and other year-end benefits, which have a long tradition in Latin America.[62]

The maquiladora sector is largely nonunionized. The second half of the 1990s saw an upsurge in workers' struggles throughout the region's maquiladora sector, leading to a number of agreements signed in the region by Labor Ministries conceding workers the right to form unions, and "codes of ethics" and other statements by TNCs promising to respect international labor standards. However, these were for the most part more public relations maneuvers than signs of real change in government or company policies. The mass firing of workers attempting organizational drives, the selective firing of identified leaders, and other forms of repression, were routine occurrences through the region in the 1990s as government and employers mounted a concerted effort to wipe out the labor movement and clear the way for the expected expansion of the sector. By 2000 there were still no functioning unions in El Salvador and Guatemala, while the handful of officially recognized unions in Nicaragua and Honduras were under attack. The case of Nicaragua was typical, where a union formed at the Chentex plant in 1998, after many years of clandestine worker organization, was the first ever to be recognized by the Ministry of Labor (which had earlier enacted a decree prohibiting unions in the zona francas) and by the plant employer, a Taiwanese subcontractor for Kohl's, J.C. Penney, K-Mart, and Wal-Mart. Following recognition of the Chentex union, five more formed over the next year, but each was destroyed between 1999 and 2000 through company repression, ranging from selective and mass firings, lock-outs, refusal to negotiate despite prior promises, the use of public police and private security forces to evict protesting workers, and so forth.[63] In Costa Rica, the government and Costa Rican employers promoted *solidarismo* organizations within the maquiladora plants as non-threatening alternatives to independent worker organizations. These employee–management associations do not engage in collective bargaining or confrontation over actual wages and working conditions, promoting instead mutual assistance and savings schemes in the manner of a credit union. "The absence of powerful trade unions . . . and the existence of the *solidarista* associations make Costa Rica an ideal place to establish maquiladoras," explained one maquila plant executive in San José.[64] An International Labour Organization (ILO) delegation to Costa Rica in the early 1990s reported that threats, dismissals and other forms of repression were routinely used against workers who attempted to organize genuine unions.[65]

The vast majority of workers in EPZ plants around the world are young women aged 16–25 years. This is especially so with regard to unskilled and labor-intensive work in garments and electronics. The disproportionate, often almost exclusive, employment of women in the EPZs, who face superexploitation and often blatant abuse, is a constant theme in the literature on the subject, and will be examined in the next chapter. Some 80 percent of maquiladora workers in the Central American EPZs are women.[66] In 1990 a business group in El Salvador, epitomizing the convergence of female degradation, labor exploitation, and dehumanization that have made the maquiladoras infamous, placed an advertisement in *Bobbin*, the trade magazine of the US spinning industry, vaunting "Rosa Martínez." "You can hire her for 57 cents an hour," stated the caption below a picture of a young Salvadoran woman at work behind a sewing machine. "Rosa is more than just colorful. She and her co-workers are known for their industriousness, reliability, and quick learning."[67] A study on maquila workers in Guatemala City found that at least four-fifths were women between the ages of fourteen and twenty-four who suffered extreme gender discrimination on top of the conditions faced by their male counterparts. They were routinely harassed sexually and dismissed for pregnancy. "My ideal worker is young, unmarried, healthy, thin and delicate, lives close, and does not have previous experience," explained one personnel manager. "If they have experience they come with many vices. They do not like to follow orders. We like to teach them ourselves. Old people are also not good because they are sick often and do not look good anymore." Another manager complained, "Nothing disturbs our production more than women getting pregnant. These women are irresponsible. They do not seem to be able to control themselves."[68]

As we shall see throughout this and the next chapter, the new transnational model of accumulation profoundly alters as it transnationalizes the local social structure. The maquiladora sector has acted as a magnet drawing in labor far beyond the immediate peripheries of the EPZs, heightening the flow of rural-to-urban migration and bringing changes to local communities. "Once young people leave the peasant world, they usually do not want to return, and even become magnets that attract other relatives and friends," notes one team of Honduran researchers. "The migration of males is provoking a scarcity of field hands that is in turn causing an increase in the pay rate for day laborers" in the agricultural sector, while the flow of young women into the maquiladoras has placed upward pressure on the salaries of domestic workers in the cities. "For men as well as women, working in a factory is both more lucrative and more prestigious than working in the fields or in the kitchen."[69] Moreover, young men and women incorporated into maquiladora work, especially those entering the money economy for the first time, develop new outlooks and rising expectations, and are often drawn into global capitalist culture. "The integration of young people into the factories has generated new businesses that profit off of their wages," noted el Cid and her colleagues. "For example, catalog companies have expanded their markets to include factory communities. Monthly catalogs circulate, offering clothing, perfumes, cosmetics and adornments. This is producing changes in the standards of beauty for both men and women . . . At the same time, 'needs' are being created that didn't exist before. Both men and women worry about keeping up with the latest fashion . . . Gradual indebtedness is a new economic reality, more among young women, because they spend a good part of their salaries on clothing and adornments."[70]

Non-Traditional Agricultural Exports

While traditional agro-exports continue to predominate in Central America's agricultural production for export, they are diminishing in overall importance relative to NTAEs, such as fruits, flowers, ornamental plants, winter vegetables, and spices.[71] Maquila production and NTAEs combined accounted by 1993 for more than half of all export earnings in Costa Rica (57.3 percent), El Salvador (61.3 percent), and Guatemala (57.7 percent), while the figures for Honduras and Nicaragua were 37.8 percent and 43.5 percent respectively.[72] The term non-traditional can refer to a product that has not been produced in a particular country before, such as snow peas in Guatemala. Or it can refer to a product previously produced for domestic consumption and now exported, such as mangoes and other tropical fruits. Or it can refer to a traditional product produced to meet the needs of a new market, such as the export of Central American bananas to Eastern Europe.[73] As used here, NTAE refers to the first and/or the second meaning, and has involved the export since the 1980s from Central America for the first time of a wide range of vegetables, such as broccoli, cauliflower, string beans, and squash, fruits such as melons, strawberries, papaya, and pineapples, and also a number of spices, tubers, cut flowers, and ornamental plants.

Some of these products, and others NTAEs exported from elsewhere in Latin America—fruits such as kiwis, passionfruit, and carambola (star fruit), and vegetables such as cassava, arugula, chicory, and baby vegetables—were once relatively unknown or exotic items in the North, and certainly too pricy for mass consumption. Other products such as winter vegetables were at one time produced only in temperate zones and were seasonally marketed. The new ability to outsource this production through global food commodity chains makes them available year round and presents seasonal market opportunities in temperate zones for tropical countries. The reduction in costs that has been achieved by the globalized "flexible" production of these items has made them more available and commonplace among consuming strata, particularly in the North.[74] But the phenomenon also reflects the process of post-Fordist income polarization and new class consumption patterns from the 1970s and on. This has involved a shift in production from standardized to more specialized products catering to segmented markets, entailing the rise of "niche" markets among a high-income and high-consumption sector of professional and middle strata worldwide, increasingly fed by the "global supermarket" and consuming gourmet coffees, exotic fruits, and other specialty food products.

The globalization of food production and the new global food regime is thus the larger backdrop to Central America's experience with NTAEs.[75] The rise of "global supermarkets" and the global reorganization of food production and distribution has involved the transformation of national and regional agricultural systems all around the world. National agricultural systems have been incorporated into global agricultural commodity chains. In the 1970s the United States had pursued a "green power" strategy as part of the "green revolution," an aspect of which was to promote an international division of agricultural labor in which highly mechanized crops such as grains were concentrated in the labor-scarce and high-wage zones of the North and labor-intensive crops such as fruits, vegetables, and sugar, in cheap labor zones in the South.[76] While this international pattern still holds, it has increasingly been superseded in subsequent decades by a global food regime characterized by the rise of truly global agri-business in which agricultural production worldwide has been reorganized along "flexible accumulation" lines.

Agri-business firms, just as their manufacturing counterparts in the maquiladoras, use global sourcing strategies. The food trade, as Philip McMichael notes, is one of the fastest-growing industries in the world, especially in processed foods and in fresh and processed fruits and vegetables, in which companies stretch across the globe organizing producers on plantations and farms to deliver products for sale in higher-value markets around the world.[77] This globalization of markets for high-value foods such as off-season fresh fruits and vegetables has become the centerpiece of growth strategies for agri-business. TNCs such as Dole, Chiquita, and Del Monte have branched out from their traditional concentration in bananas and pineapples. These TNCs often subcontract local peasants or capitalist firms in developing regions to produce specialty horticultural crops and off-season fruits and vegetables. They also process foods such as fruit juices, canned fruits and frozen vegetables, boxed beef, chicken pieces, and so on, often in export processing zones, for shipment to expanding consumer markets around the world.

The extension of transnational agri-business, the conversion of local production from food and traditional export crops to new crops, and growth in worldwide trade of exotic fruits and vegetables are made technically possible by new transportation, refrigeration, and other innovations. "Cool chains," for instance, maintain chilled temperatures for moving fresh fruits and vegetables from Third World farms to urban and First World supermarkets. These technologies have resulted in a "time-space compression." The constantly falling prices in transportation and communications make it economically viable to locate production in low-cost zones. Perishables are produced anywhere in the world to be marketed elsewhere with little regard for distances between production and consumption and the time between these two. By creating and operating in markets across the globe, agri-business is able to make use of time-space compression in ways which result in the incorporation, transformation, and subordination of local agricultural systems. As globalized agri-business commodifies production it has concentrated upon a relatively narrow range of food crops, especially grains and durable foods. But a wide variety of new agricultural commodities has also been promoted for world market production as a central component of the outward-oriented development strategies associated with integration into the global economy. The operation of food markets across time and space means that global prices have a direct and often immediate bearing on local prices, thereby undermining the possibility of nationally contained agricultural systems.

NTAEs in the form of fresh fruits and vegetables is the particular path that the globalization of food production worldwide has taken in Central America. The new global food regime has given rise to what Harriet Friedmann has called "new agricultural countries" (NACs), analogous to "newly industrializing countries" (NICs) insofar as agro-industrialization for urban and export markets, in consort with transnational agri-business, becomes a cornerstone of local accumulation strategies.[78] With the arrival of the NTAE industry in the Isthmus the Central American countries may in certain respects be considering emerging NACs. If the rise of a global food regime is one part of the backdrop to the spread of NTAEs in Central America, the other is the role of the transnational elite in promoting

Table 3.12. Central American NTAEs to the World (millions of $)

	1980	1985	1989	1994
Costa Rica	43	48	138	400
El Salvador	13	16	11	90
Guatemala	73	75	106	350
Honduras	42	60	53	70
Nicaragua	7	12	6	50
Central America	178	211	314	960

Source: Conroy, *et al.*, p. 21, Table 1.6, for 1980–89 data; Brockett, p. 56, Figure 3.5, for 1994 data.

NTAEs as part of the much broader strategy for Central America of structural adjustment and rearticulation to the world economy. The spread of NTAEs in Central America and elsewhere has been promoted by local states with financing and guidance (and often imposition through aid conditionality) from the AID and the IFIs, especially the World Bank, and under the provisions of the CBI and other incentive programs.[79] The CBI, intended to foster the rearticulation of the Caribbean Basin region to the global system through the establishment of new export industries, included duty-free entry of certain exports to the US market, tax breaks, guarantees, and other benefits for transnational capital investing in these industries.[80] The AID set up a special office, the Support Project for Non-Traditional Agricultural Exports (PROEXAG) to promote NTAEs in the region.[81] AID funds throughout the 1980s and 1990s, although provided as official government-to-government aid, were allocated specifically to fund NTAE production and were consistently channeled through the network of private business associations established in the region, the "parallel state" that emerged in the 1980s.[82] Costa Rica and Guatemala were among the first countries in the Caribbean Basin, along with the Dominican Republic, to adopt NTAE strategies.[83] NTAEs took off by the middle of the 1980s, especially in these two countries, as table 3.12 shows. Costa Rica, in particular, was touted by the AID as an example of the benefits that the NTAE strategy, and more generally, AID-sponsored reform, could bring to Latin America.[84]

NTAEs and Capitalist Agriculture in Central America

The study of NTAEs offers a good window on to the spread of capitalist agriculture under globalization and the effects of incorporation into global markets and production chains. As we have seen, the arrival of NTAEs has occasioned a new round of commercial agricultural expansion in the Isthmus; the industry entails new production conditions that have a transformative impact on land tenure, resource allocation, employment, class structure, gender relations, the environment, and so forth. NTAE production takes place more fully under capitalist relations than earlier domestic and export crops and it entails a much deeper market integration. First, NTAEs require more systematic and much higher levels of financing than traditional crops. This draws producers more fully into the financial system, which itself is in the process of transformation and globalization. Second, NTAE production is highly dependent on an assortment of industrial inputs, from imported seeds and pesticides, to chemical fertilizers and farm equipment. Third, NTAE production involves more sophisticated techniques and technical know-how in planting, maintenance, harvesting, and handling than traditional crops. Technological knowledge is increasingly considered a fourth factor of production, after land, labor, and capital, and its centrality to NTAEs creates dependencies on market-based technical assistance. It is difficult to get around the need for such assistance since the global market imposes new quality and esthetic demands that imply a more rigorous production process. Finally, NTAEs require insertion into a complex global marketing structure. Ultimately, global market control becomes the key to profitability in the NTAE industry, as we shall see. Global market relations thus penetrate the Central American countryside through the spread of NTAEs. Peasants are drawn into webs of market relations and subsumed under a capitalist production regime that helps to further undermine what remains of pre-capitalist agriculture.[85]

Although generalizations should be drawn with caution, given the variegated nature of NTAE production (see below) and plenty of experiences which fall outside of evident patterns, overall the effects of the industry over time have included heightened land concentration, greater domination over agriculture of local and foreign agri-business through the control of credits and other resources, and a further proletarianization of peasants, who become "casualized" farm labor. Social differentiation and incipient new forms of class polarization in the countryside have generally ensued in the wake of the introduction of NTAEs. The modern capitalist structure that emerges is in contrast to the old oligarchic rural structure. As in the case of the maquiladora industry, NTAE activity has drawn in not a landed oligarchy but dynamic new entrepreneurial sectors, often urban-based, linked to the global economy through finances and webs of relationships with transnational corporations.[86] Indeed, these fractions among the local bourgeoisie dominate the NTAE sector. The transnational strategy of promoting NTAEs is mutually reinforcing with the political objective of shoring up transnational groups in the region as internal agents of the neo-liberal program and capitalist globalization.

The NTAE industry is transnationally organized in a vertical and horizontal chain that begins with suppliers of inputs and moves through farming, packing, shipping, wholesaling, and retailing. There are three phases in the vertical chain.[87] The first, "pre-farmgate," involves those activities necessary for production in the field to take place, and includes the manufacture, shipping, and marketing of inputs such as fertilizers, pesticides, farm tools and equipment, and seeds, as well as the organization of land tenure arrangements, and the provision of credit. The second phase, "inside-farmgate," involves the actual labor of plowing, planting, weeding, and harvesting, and also includes a host of technical assistance activities. The third phase, "post-farmgate," entails packing, freezing, trucking and shipping, advertising, wholesaling, and final retailing. In turn, each one of these vertical phases incorporates a horizontal structure of different agents and firms that participate in the particular phase. In the pre-farmgate phase, for instance, financial concerns, landlords, and transnational suppliers provide land, credits, and inputs for production, while in the post-farmgate phase brokers are heavily involved as cross-border agents arranging purchase, shipping, and marketing. Let us look first at the structure of production within the chain, and particularly, at the point of production (inside-farmgate) and the distinct agents involved, and then at the larger transnational structures into which the chain is inserted. Here the focus is on how transnational capital exercises overall control of the entire production chain, and how the chain exercises a transformative effect on Central America in the context of the more general processes associated with globalization, including effects on the class structure.

NTAE production in Central America exhibits two patterns, what have been called the "satellite production" system and "estate-plantation farming."[88] In the first, packers/exporters purchase crops from many individual farmers and market them through TNC-controlled commodity chains. These packers/exporters are often themselves TNCs or their local representatives, or are contractors or national groups who in turn operate within TNC marketing and other structures, as discussed in more detail below. The pattern of transnational control over purchase, marketing, and processing originates in practices set up by the banana companies in the post-WWII period. Following the watershed 1954 banana strike in Honduras and mass peasant mobilization for agrarian reform there, for instance, the companies learned to look favorably on producer cooperatives as a new accumulation strategy, whereby they would transfer production to smallholders and concentrate on purchase, processing, and international marketing, retaining profits while eliminating risks and labor problems. This is the principal direction in which transnational agri-business moved in the 1980s and early 1990s, as flexible accumulation structures made it possible for TNCs more generally to minimize risk in fixed investment. When a crisis arises, the company can simply pick up and move on. Satellite production arrangements involve two variants: packers/exporters purchase crops on the open market, or they contract local producers, often supplying inputs, credits, and so forth. But they almost never provide a price guarantee and rarely provide a guarantee that crops will actually be purchased, which will depend on market conditions (particularly demand) at the time of delivery, the quality of output, and other factors. The rejection of harvests has been a constant problem for small producers. The open market arrangement provides the fewest risks for firms but also makes efficient, planned utilization of packing capacity difficult and can hinder quality control and optimal timing, whereas contract arrangements provide greater external control over the production process.

The "contract farming" arrangement implied in the satellite production system has been a keen object of research among development specialists in recent years.[89] These arrangements are part of the larger phenomenon of subcontracting and outsourcing associated with new decentralized modes of flexible accumulation. One advantage of the satellite production system for transnational firms is that they can take maximum advantage of peasant production conditions, in particular, the exploitation of unpaid family labor.[90] Many NTAEs are short cycle labor-intensive crops that require ongoing care throughout the period of cultivation (especially vegetables), lending themselves to production regimes based on extended family labor. In this way the cost of labor is born by the small producer. Local producers are left with risks of hurricanes, floods, disease, political crisis, and market fluctuations, and when family labor is not the norm they must themselves organize labor supply, including the control of labor conflicts. United Brands/Chiquita has made extensive use of the satellite contract system in Honduras's melon-producing region of Choluteca, among others, while the satellite contractor form is also most prevalent in the Guatemalan highlands, where indigenous farmers plant broccoli, snow peas, and other winter vegetables. In El Salvador, larger growers of melon who are also packers have developed the satellite system in which they sub-contract small growers in the Ahuachapan region.[91]

The second pattern, estate-plantation farming, has been called the "new plantation system" in Central America. In this arrangement, local or transnational agri-business firms directly organize production on large estates, generally hiring a small corps of permanent workers, among them, technicians, agronomists, administrators, and foremen, and large numbers of casualized part-time and seasonal workers. This is the system generally employed, for instance, by Standard Fruit (Dole) for pineapple production in Honduras, by national and transnational producers of melons in Guatemala, and by pineapple producers in Costa Rica. In the mid-1990s, some exporters began to shift more directly to controlled estate farming, as many small producers were proletarianized after being driven out of the NTAE sector and became employees of large-scale operations.[92]

Regardless of the particular arrangements, diverse agents involved in the NTAE industry are swept up into the transnational production chain and subordinated in various ways and degrees, to the overall control of transnational capital, in particular the giant agri-business firms that dominate the world food regime. As global production becomes reorganized along flexible accumulation lines, the transnational fruit companies may outsource production to various countries, shift production quotas from site to site as production and marketing conditions vary, and subcontract numerous local agents. In this way, the structure of the world food regime increasingly resembles what has been variously called in the globalization literature a "coordinator enterprise," a "vertically disaggregated network organization," a "flexible business network," "global webs," and so on. In these transnational structures, TNCs control complex production or commodity chains, just as we have seen in the case of garments, capturing the lion's share of value added and profits through overall coordination and management of geographically dispersed activities and control of information, marketing, and financial transactions. Value passes "upward" in the chain of NTAEs, while risks and attendant losses are passed "downward." At the end of the line in the chain are small peasant farmers and casualized agricultural workers, who ultimately bear the brunt of fluctuating prices, natural disasters, and so on.

For example, as Conroy and his colleagues have documented for El Salvador, melons are grown through a two-tiered system. Small growers sell their output to large growers who are also packers/exporters and who are usually tied to transnational fruit companies and suppliers. Large growers are able to pay themselves higher prices for their own output than what they pay for the melons they purchase from small producers. They are able to prioritize the purchase and export of their own output and regulate the amount of fruit they buy from small producers, assuring a buffer against fluctuating demand and prices, as set by brokers and retailers in US markets. Friedmann, in his study on melon production in Western El Salvador, found that for 1990–91 small producers earned $3.98 per box of fruit, whereas large firms reported $9.46 per box. "The explanation for this difference is in the structure of production/marketing that prevails in the country, in which the large producers are also the exporters," he notes. "Their price reflects production and export yields."[93]

Small producers, after having entered into debt to invest in their melon crops, often find that they are unable to sell their output to the packers/exporters and have to sell on the local market or even discard their perishable produce due to the lack of a market.[94] "In essence, the small farmer who grows melons for export to the United States is a farm worker paid to work on his own fields, who additionally must personally assume 100 percent of the risks of crop failure, lessened quality, or market vagaries," note Conroy and his colleagues. "The clear winners from the globalization of the melon commodity chain are international shippers and brokers, or the giant fruit companies in the case of integrated enterprises."[95] National agri-business firms are the principal exporters of melons from El Salvador, among them, Frutas S.A. de C.V., Exfrusa, Melopac, Fruvex, Exsalva, El Salvador Fresh, and CAPECA. Here we see the transnational fraction of the Salvadoran bourgeoisie concentrated in this activity. "In studying the promotion of NTAEs in El Salvador, one observes that a principal objective has been the selection, preparation, and consolidation of a relatively small but very dynamic group of Salvadoran entrepreneurs well connected abroad," notes Friedmann. These groups "are the principal national protagonists of the NTAE industry and form the link between internal promotion and production and external demand."[96]

The bulk of value-added and the lion's share of profits in the NTAE industry lie in the pre- and post-farmgate phases. In their study on the distribution of value-added in the melon commodity chain, Conroy *et al.*, found the following for El Salvador in 1991: US shipping and retailing captured 76.6 percent of revenues; international shippers, 9.1 percent; imported inputs, 5.1 percent; US brokers, 2.6 percent; packer/exporter profit was 2.5 percent; miscellaneous in-country services, 3.5 percent; and finally, farmers' profits accounted for only 0.6 percent of revenues from the commodity chain. In that year, a pound of Salvadoran melon retailed in the United States for 65 cents but about half a penny actually went to the farmer as income.[97]

What is taking place here, as part and parcel of the transformation of Central American agriculture into capitalist agriculture, is that industrial activity, in the form of industrial inputs such as synthetic fertilizers, pesticides, industrially produced seeds, and so on, comes to subordinate agricultural activity, and to appropriate surplus produced in agriculture. In this process, industrial, financial, and service activity comes to account for a steadily rising proportion of value added as the agricultural product increasingly becomes, conceptually, an input in what is more appropriately seen as industrialized production and financial/service sector activity.[98] Value flows from the point of agricultural production to the points of control over marketing and financing. Embedded in the incorporation of Central American agriculture into the global supermarket are the class relations of the exploitation of Central American agricultural labor, in the form of peasant producers and agricultural workers, by transnational capital. Let us look more closely at these class relations.

NTAEs, Class Relations, and Social Transformation

In 1991, an estimated 60 percent of NTAE producers were small farmers. Medium producers and larger individual farmers, national commercial/corporate operations, and foreign companies, made up the remainder.[99] However, the relative contribution of these groups to the total value exported was highly skewed: foreign companies accounted for 25 percent; medium and large national companies for about 40 percent; and small farmers for only 35 percent. Even when production is in peasant hands, local transnational groups gain control through financing and related servicing of NTAE activity, such as the supply of inputs, which are also largely controlled by TNCs and of local agents who are often distributors of local contractors for the TNCs. As noted earlier, the production of NTAEs requires a large amount of inputs in the form of fertilizers and pesticides, equipment, and seeds, which in turn means that producers must obtain large amounts of credit. As Fuentes notes for Guatemalan highland production with the introduction of NTAEs, "the use of agricultural credit for production became a common practice in a region in which it was formerly non-existent."[100] A successful NTAE harvest can register high profit margins. But they are also a capital-intensive crop, involving high costs of production and high risk. A producer of snow peas, for example, risks about $4000 a hectare in costs versus only $250 to $375 for corn or $750 for mechanized coffee production.[101] And the market for NTAEs is extremely volatile. NTAE product prices fluctuate dramatically from season to season in accordance with unstable demand and shifting supply. Peasants who shift from food and other traditional crops to NTAEs are quickly driven into debt. One bad crop or a precipitous drop in prices due to erratic world market conditions can wipe out small producers. Peasants, squeezed between suppliers of inputs and buyers of their produce, are often unable to sustain production, even after a season or two of success, and having become caught up in a web of market relations, face the threat of bankruptcy and the loss of their land. The stage is set for depeasantization.

The introduction of NTAEs often drives up land prices as outside investors, either nationals or transnational companies, rent or buy land in the local market. As a result, rents become out of reach of small producers and sharecroppers, or production costs and attendant difficulties rise for peasants with few resources. Similarly, technical information is a key input in NTAEs. Under the neo-liberal program it is no longer a state service provided for peasants but increasingly a commodity bought and sold in a capitalist agriculture market. Here, large local producers and TNCs (although the distinction is rarely clear, as local producers are often associated with TNCs through numerous arrangements) are at a distinct advantage, while peasants enter into relations of technical dependency. Moreover, the giant fruit companies themselves often supply technical assistance and professional consultants to producers under contract. Small producers also face an array of difficulties in competing with larger producers and agri-business. They simply cannot exercise enough control over the gamut of factors and phases involved in production to remain competitive. Among the advantages of large producers are ample subsidies provided to them through internationally financed incentive programs, despite free market rhetoric, and inherent market biases in favor of those with greater economic weight and bargaining position. During the 1980s and 1990s transnational corporate producers of NTAEs in Central America enjoyed substantial local state subsidies not available to small producers.

The conversion of land producing food for domestic consumption to land for NTAEs has the same familiar result of a rise in food imports as did the introduction of earlier generations of agro-exports. NTAEs tend not to displace traditional agro-exports but to displace basic grain production for the domestic market, under the rationale that grains don't earn foreign exchange and that the region has a "comparative advantage" in NTAEs. Brockett has shown how NTAE expansion in the 1980s and 1990s resulted in a decrease in the ratio of food to export crop production. But this situation has been aggravated by the trade opening under neo-liberal adjustment that has resulted in a flood of basic grain imports, which almost doubled from 1980 to 1990 in Central America parallel to the introduction of NTAEs.[102] Revealingly, basic grain production dropped most in the 1980s precisely in those regions where NTAEs were introduced.[103] In Costa Rica, which has the most developed NTAE sector, food imports from the US went from 1,000 tons in 1974–75 to 235,000 tons in 1987–88.[104] As discussed in chapter two, the US P. L. 480 Program was originally intended to increase US agricultural commodity exports and gain influence abroad under the rhetoric of "food aid." By flooding local markets with cheap grains this program undercut peasant production and accelerated the commodification of agriculture in recipient countries.[105] It became in the 1980s and 1990s a powerful instrument over the Isthmus (and many other Third World countries) in imposing structural adjustment programs and promoting capitalist agriculture. The rise in food imports combined with the need to import much of the inputs, such as fertilizers, pesticides, and seeds, makes it very questionable to what extent NTAEs actually increase available foreign exchange earnings rather than result in a deepening cycle of debt.

In addition, the neo-liberal program involved the elimination of diverse state supports for the peasant sector and the privatization of former state services for agriculture.[106] Moreover, because they receive little or no pre-market processing (apart from packaging), especially the more profitable fresh produce, NTAEs tend not to stimulate significant forward or backward linkages or agro-industrialization. Rising land values in NTAE production areas were accompanied in the 1980s and 1990s by declining profitability of traditional activities, which combined to displace peasant producers. Although the IFIs sold the idea of NTAEs with the claim that this activity was suitable for small farmers, the World Bank admitted in the early 1990s that "smallholders unable to move into the new [NTAE] activities might have to sell their land and become landless workers."[107] The evidence indicates that over time the introduction of NTAEs has led to further depeasantization, the increasing concentration of land, and greater rural class differentiation, social inequalities, and polarization, as the Central American countryside becomes more deeply involved in the global economy.

The familiar pattern in NTAEs has been an initial participation of many growers, as AID and other transnational agents and local governments promote a switch from traditional to new crops, followed by gradual concentration. In the typical sequence, peasant farmers experience a short boom during the first one or two crops, followed by a bust cycle. Some success stories conceal a general pattern of rural household deterioration in the wake of the introduction of NTAEs. One AID evaluation of the impact of NTAEs on the Guatemalan NTAE cooperative in the highland community of Chimaltenango, once it had passed from the boom to the post-boom phase, frankly admitted that "real incomes have fallen for all households between 1985 and 1991," and that even though income differential between those cooperative members and non-members remained positive, it was "sharply lower in 1991 compared to 1985." Moreover, in 1989 cooperative members began to sell off their land, and in 1991 reported that land had become too expensive to buy.[108] Similarly, Carletto, Janvry, and Sadoulet found, in their longitudinal study on cooperative producers of snow peas in the highlands, that initial success in the first few years was eroded by pest problems, rising pressure over scarce land, and soil degradation, which increased capital costs and risks, leaving "only the better endowed households" in a position to sustain profitable production.[109]

One study of melon production in Guatemala's Fragua Valley by the Guatemalan research institute AVANCSO revealed the various mechanisms by which small and medium producers organized individually and in cooperatives are at the whims of the TNCs, their local agents, and brokers. One is an arbitrary lowering of purchase price by packers in accordance with world market prices, so as to ensure a steady profit margin by passing on the cost of price fluctuations to producers. Another is the raising and lowering of rejection rates and arbitrarily redefining quality standards in accordance with how much fruit the companies will be able to market profitably each harvest. "The producers argued that the US market was adverse during the latest harvest and the company [BASICO, a local exporter affiliated with Chiquita Brands] decided in response to make selection more strict as a mechanism to avoid purchasing more fruit than it could sell ... This was a policy of transferring market risks from the company to producers."[110] Following this particular dispute, in 1991, Chiquita transferred production elsewhere (including to Hermosillo, Mexico, and to Honduras, through its subsidiary there, PATSA) and decided to dig up and take with it the irrigation tubes it had laid in the 1980s, the cost of which it had long since recovered by charging producers for water use.[111]

Changes in the production process always have a transformative impact on extra-economic factors, such as gender relations and the family. NTAE production, as with the maquiladoras, transforms and transnationalizes subordinate groups—relations among them and between them and the dominant groups. In the case of gender relations, women's increasing employment in industrial export processing is the most conspicuous and well-researched feature of the gender dimensions of the labor force restructuring associated with globalization. For a variety of factors that will be discussed in the next chapter, women have been incorporated into the formal labor force and this has involved in particular the differential incorporation of women and men into the expanding non-traditional sectors. Sociologist Laura Raynolds has studied the increase of women's participation in NTAE production in Latin America, and found that women often play a predominant role in the industry but remain gender-segregated within it and are generally paid less than men. In her case study on the Dominican Republic, she found that supervisory and professional jobs were reserved almost exclusively for men, who also ran machinery and packed containers, whereas women were concentrated in sorting fruits and vegetables, washing and labelling, and other assorted activities requiring (according to managers) a supposed "natural" female dexterity. In the fields, men tended to prepare land, plant, and apply chemical inputs, while women predominated in cultivating and harvesting. Raynolds found that women's overall earnings were typically below men's because of their limited access to better-paid supervisory and technical jobs and their concentration in seasonal activity.[112]

There is a lacuna of similar studies for Central America but scattered evidence suggests a similar pattern and that the NTAE industry in the Isthmus has entailed a gendering of agricultural labor. One study by the AID of NTAEs in Guatemala, Honduras, and Costa Rica revealed that women make up more than half of the labor force in those countries in harvesting, processing, and packaging.[113] Guatemalan researcher Claudia Fuentes found, in another study detailing NTAE production in the Guatemalan highlands, the population of which is principally indigenous, that women have predominated as hired laborers, although they are consistently paid less than their male counterparts (a number of other studies have found this as well).[114] She also found that, as family labor has become reorganized to produce NTAEs among small land holders, women and daughters have assumed a major portion of the labor involved, even as they continue to be responsible for traditional household chores within the gendered division of labor in the family. However, men predominate in selling output to local intermediaries (known as "coyotes"). In this way preexisting patriarchal structures, in which men take charge of the family's external relations, tend to reinforce male economic control over income earned through NTAEs.[115] Glover and Kusterer found a similar pattern.[116] In her survey of women engaged in NTAE production in the highland department of Sacatepequez, Fuentes reported that 53.3 percent were wage workers, the vast majority contracted by two large agro-exporting firms that dominate the industry in the region (the remainder worked on family farms). Of the wage workers, approximately two-thirds were casual workers and the rest enjoyed permanent employment. Nearly 40 percent were less than thirty years old (26 percent were ten to seventeen years of age), 51.4 percent were single, and over half had no children.[117] Here we see a pattern similar to female employment in the maquiladoras, whereby young single women tend to be recruited by firms.

Just as there are local losers in the NTAE industry there are also winners. Local benefits include new employment and income opportunities, access to new consumer goods, social and productive infrastructure, and so on.[118] But these benefits are highly unevenly distributed. The NTAE industry has benefited a class of medium-level producers, many of whom have bought out their poorer neighbors thereby changing the class structure. This process is notable, for instance, in the central highlands of Guatemala and has contributed to a more general process of class formation among the indigenous population, as mentioned in chapter two.[119] Fruit and vegetable brokers in US and European ports also play a prominent role in the NTAE industry, generally as well-remunerated agents of the transnational fruit and retail companies. Shippers, often themselves subsidiaries of TNCs or contractors for them, are big winners, as are suppliers of inputs and in-country buyers, who may be local packers and exporters (themselves often large producers), local holding or financial companies, or, as is often the case, local agents of TNCs. Local packers/exporters have set up companies throughout Central America and in practice tend to become junior partners of the transnational fruit companies. They purchase produce from local producers and sell to the TNCs, acting as intermediaries that link local groups to transnational capital.[120]

As the NTAE industry progresses, TNCs have come to exercise ever-greater control, working their way "backward" from marketing to production. The industry is dominated by three giant fruit companies. Chiquita, formerly United Brands (and before then, United Fruit Company), runs numerous subsidiaries in the region, from its Chiquita Tropical Products Company in Costa Rica, to PATSA in Honduras, and BASICO and BANACORP in Guatemala. Castle and Cook (which absorbed Standard Fruit in 1968) runs its own set of subsidiaries, as does Del Monte, which merged with and became an affiliate of R. J. Reynolds in 1979. Del Monte has established, among others, its COAGRO subsidiary in Guatemala and its PINDECO in Costa Rica. Other TNCs with a significant share of the Central American NTAE industry include Chesnut Hill Farms, Hanover Brands, Coca-Cola, PolyPack, and Seaboard Corporation.[121]

In Costa Rica, Del Monte exported 95 percent of that country's pineapple production in the early 1990s, while Dole accounted for 96 percent of pineapple exports from Honduras. In the least concentrated commodity in Costa Rica, cassava, the three largest firms out of thirty-three controlled one third of exports. In papaya, Del Monte exported 94 percent of Costa Rican production, as well as a substantial quantity of mangoes and strawberries. TNCs control approximately 80 percent of Costa Rican fern exports, 50 percent of cut flower production, and 40 percent of macadamia nut exports.[122] In Costa Rica's Guanacaste province, heavily targeted in the 1980s and early 1990s for NTAE production and held up as a showcase of NTAE success, local and transnational investors quickly acquired control over the industry. Corporations such as Laechner and Saenz—a holding company that owns Costa Rican dealerships of Xerox, IBM, Apple, Chevrolet, and Isuzu—and the fruit transnational, United Brands/Chiquita, began developing extensive plantations of melons, mangoes, miniature papayas, guanabana, irrigated cacao, and other non-traditional products.[123]

Of an estimated twelve thousand hectares of melon production in Central America in 1991, about four thousand were either satellites or estates of the big four transnational fruit companies. ALCOSA, a local Guatemalan subsidiary of Hanover Brands, is the largest exporter of frozen vegetables in that country. Conroy and his colleagues also found that in Costa Rica six grower/packers dominate NTAE production; in El Salvador, four or five; and in Nicaragua only three or four.[124] However, there is no reason to assume that particular production arrangements, such as the mid-1990s pattern of an increase in TNC plantations, will become dominant. These arrangements will most likely vary into the foreseeable future. *Flexibility* is the very essence of flexible accumulation: the production and appropriation of value in a global setting can and does mean constantly shifting patterns of organizing production.

It is interesting to observe the local social groups most involved in the NTAE industry. Local influence over the industry is exercised largely through finances. Under the neo-liberal program state banks providing low-cost credit to peasant producers have been closed or restructured along market lines (see next chapter). Most credit for NTAEs comes from private banks, from TNCs that provide commercial credits for their contractors (or simply use their own capital for direct investment), and increasingly, from investment houses in urban areas, known as *financieras*. These financieras function like investment funds, where urban professionals and middle strata, along with capitalists, invest their money in shares.[125] Urban import-export groups, such as those that own foreign automobile or computer dealerships, have entered NTAE production by organizing these financieras, which replace state credits that were established in the pre-globalization period of ISI and state-led development. It is worth noting that under globalization the relationship between financial investors and material production has been redefined. Tendencies associated with financial globalization such as the global mobility of money, new forms of financial commodification (derivatives, etc.), the hegemony that money capital has achieved over investment capital in recent decades, and so on, have facilitated the appropriation by money irrespective of geography of value produced through material production. Globally mobile money can snatch up material surpluses with much greater ease, and value acquired in this way becomes totally mobile.[126]

The montage of a NTAE industry in Central America is contributing to the creation of a more diverse and integrated regional agricultural labor market, involving new pools of seasonal contract labor drawn from communities uprooted due to the whole gamut of processes discussed here and in earlier chapters, including the alienating dynamics of the NTAE industry itself.[127] In the current period of globalization, however, outward migration resulting from the commercial reorganization of agriculture is as much transnational as it is from the countryside to cities within each country. Migration to the United States and other countries is a process involving the creation of an integrated North American labor market, as will be discussed later in this chapter. As AVANCSO notes, "The [Fragua] Valley region has expelled [uprooted] a large population, a great part of which has migrated to the United States, to the capital city, or to the Atlantic Coast. Many have come in this way to depend on remittances or family assistance [from those who have migrated]."[128]

Historically, the introduction of new export crops has driven peasants off their land and resulted in waves of rural strife and the social reorganization of the countryside.[129] NTAEs are still in the early stages and are part of a larger project of transformation and integration into emergent global structures. Recent depeasantization, the capitalist transformation of agriculture, and the integration of local agriculture into the global agricultural regime has entailed little direct coercion. In earlier rounds of commercial agricultural expansion, such as with the spread of coffee, and later cattle and cotton, peasants were forcibly, and often violently, expelled from the land by oligarchs backed by state power. In contrast, peasant alienation and proletarianization is being effected in the current epoch strictly through the economic coercion of the market. The structural power of the global economy is exercised through NTAE global commodity chains as a market discipline resulting in an intensified subordination of agricultural producers to transnational capital. Where these processes might lead is not clear and this is an issue examined in the concluding chapter.

Tourism and Hospitality

The transnational model is exemplified by the growth of the international tourism and hospitality industry in Central America in the 1990s. Tourism and hospitality, along with import-export commercial activity and finances that have flourished with trade and financial liberalization, constitutes the dynamic core of transnational service sector activity in the Isthmus. It has become a key activity inserting the region into the global economy. Tourism in the social science literature is not limited to leisure travel and may include international travel for reasons of business, government activity, professional work, and so on. English provides the conventional sociological definition that I follow here: "A Tourist is any person visiting, for at least 24 hours, a country other than that in which he or she usually resides, for any reason other than following an occupation remunerated from within the country visited. The purpose of this visit can thus be classified under one of the following headings: leisure (recreation, holidays, health, study, religion and sports); or business, family, mission, meetings."[130] The more accurate phrase that captures the phenomenon explored in this section is therefore *tourism, hospitality, and travel*, although for the sake of simplicity I will here generally use the term "tourism."

The dramatic rise in tourist flows worldwide since the 1960s is a phenomenon of the global economy *par excellence*, a product both of the technical economic changes involved in capitalist globalization and as well, perhaps principally, its social implications.[131] Technological developments in air transport, particularly the jet plane and cheaper and more efficient air transport systems, communications networks, computerized travel coordination, and so on, have advanced time-space compression to the point that the whole world has been brought into the purview of tourism and has made technically possible the explosion of this global service industry. New information and media technologies have globalized images and the possibilities of projecting them for tourist marketing purposes. The transnationalization of services, including banking, accommodation, transportation, along with the standardization of these services, provides any destination in the world with access to global markets for tourists and for the industrial and service inputs that tourism requires. With the rise of a standardized international cuisine, meals one is accustomed to eating at home can now be found replicated almost anywhere in the world. So can the same hotel chains and other global amenities for world travelers.

Table 3.13.   Growth in International Tourist Arrivals since 1962

Year	Arrivals	Average Annual Growth Rate (%)
1962	81,329,000	–
1972	181,851,000	8.4
1982	286,780,000	4.7
1992	481,463,000	5.3
2000	660,000,000*	4.0
2010	940,000,000*	3.6

* estimates

Source: WTO, as reported in Husbands and Harrison, 1996.[134]

Tourism thus became in the late twentieth century a central economic activity in the global economy, reportedly the largest industry in the world, having surpassed the oil business in the 1980s. One estimate placed the total economic value of the industry at $3.6 trillion in 1996, or 10.6 percent of gross global product, and calculated that tourism sustained more than one in ten jobs around the world, providing work for 255 million people.[132] Global tourist flows grew phenomenally from the 1960s into the twenty-first century, as shown in table 3.13. Tourism plays a major role in the economies of 125 of the world's 170 countries.[133] It has become the fastest-growing economic activity, and even the mainstay, of many Third World nations.

The tourist industry is organized as a complex and multitiered global service commodity chain connecting activities and groups from the most local and isolated tourist sites to TNC headquarters in global cities. The chain links together travel agencies and tour operators, often based in rich countries, with transnational airline, cruise line, car rental, credit card, public relations, and advertising firms, along with the global media. It also brings in state and private tourism bureaus in both sending and host countries and a host of "inbound" agents, including tour operators, ground transporters, guides, accommodation and meeting facilities, national and private parks and other recreational sites, cultural and craft centers, and so on. The neo-liberal program of removing national barriers to the free movement of capital has facilitated the increasing transnationalization of local tourist and travel activity and heightened overall TNC control (deregulation, for instance, has thrown open national airspaces to the transnational airline companies). These TNCs operate at all levels of the industry, which exhibits considerable vertical and horizontal integration and increasing concentration. The largest global hotel chains, for instance—Holiday Inns, Sheraton, Hilton International, Inter-Continental, Club Méditerranée, Hyatt International, Marriott, and so on—are as well multi-service and financial corporations, often participating in car rental, tour operation, air travel and other activities, and are themselves interpenetrated with global banking, telecommunications, food and beverage, and shipping TNCs.

The take-off of the global tourist industry is not a spontaneous phenomenon or the result of uncontrolled demand. A powerful and well-organized lobby of industry representatives and transnational state institutions, increasingly reliant on information technology and global marketing techniques, has been aggressively promoting tourism since the 1960s. It has unfolded "under the impetus of a powerful tourist promotion mechanism, supported at the highest international level: the World Tourism Organization, the International Monetary Fund, the United Nations, the World Bank, UNESCO, etc.," notes Lanfant. "An intensive propaganda campaign was directed at the less developed countries, which were enjoined to place the tourist sector high on the list of priorities for their economies, to open their frontiers to tourists, to welcome foreign capital for investment in the tourist domain, and to concede tax advantages and guarantees to it."[135] The industry has engaged in systematic corporate and transnational state planning aimed at producing the conditions, including induced demand, for this activity worldwide. "The tourism industry is a structure of economic institutions which strive for increasing control over space on a global scale, providing flexibility to adjust to seasonal and other variations in such increasingly valuable resources as climate, environmental conditions, and labor costs," observes Jozsef Borocz. "The tourism industry is unique . . . in the sense that the product which it markets is the very geographical, spatial, climatic, and cultural diversity of the global economy itself."[136]

But the rise of a global tourist industry is above all a phenomenon of the social consequences of global capitalism, a major dimension of the relationship between the rich and the poor in global society. Tourism is a labor-intensive industry, attractive to cheap, relatively unskilled labor as chambermaids, waiters, drivers, and so on, and made possible by the expansion of labor pools of the unemployed and marginalized worldwide. Under the new "global social apartheid," the structure of global production, distribution, and consumption increasingly reflects a skewed income pattern, whereby since the early 1970s the income of 20 percent of the world population has risen simultaneous to a decline in income among the remaining 80 percent. The expansion of the middle classes worldwide, and the integration of these middle classes into the global economy as consuming strata, has provided a tremendous impetus to global tourism. Worldwide growth should be seen as a result of the tendency towards social polarization inherent in global capitalism, and the new opportunities for accumulation that *this particular* structure of world income and demand generates. Tourism as it is practiced in global society takes for granted this division between the rich and the poor and the "right" of the wealthy to be pampered and waited on by the poor, whether their travel activities are for leisure or business. The viability of tourism is thus tied to the reproduction of global inequalities.

North–South tourist flows are still largely unidirectional, from North to South, while the flow of much of the income generated by world tourism is from South to North, but this pattern began to change in the late twentieth century. The rise of a global tourist industry has involved the opening up of vast tracts of the Third World to international travelers. While all regions

of the world experienced growth in international tourism arrivals in the
1980s and 1990s, there was a redistribution of arrivals among regions, with
the share of arrivals to developing countries increasing relative to developed countries, and with some regions exhibiting marked increases over
others. Although Europe and the United States still account for the
majority of tourist activity, the relative participation of developing countries
in the industry has been increasing since the 1980s. In the mid-1970s, 8
percent of all tourists were those traveling from the developed countries to
Third World countries. This figure had jumped to 17 percent by the mid-
1980s, and to 20 percent by the mid-1990s.

The once-established "pleasure periphery" that surrounded wealthy
industrialized zones in the form of nearby tourist locations, such as the
Mediterranean for Northern Europe, the Caribbean and Mexico for the
United States, Southeast Asia for Japan, and so on, has given way to more
globalized forms of tourism and the opening up of more "exotic" and
"risky" environments. Increasingly, high and even middle-income strata
from the developed countries have sought out these new "exotic" destinations in the Third World for their tourist travels. "Europeans and North
Americans now swarm across the planet as one after another destination
becomes fashionable in Africa or Asia," notes Malcolm Waters. If the old
mass tourism characterized by pre-packaged holidays to the pleasure
periphery was associated with standardized Fordist accumulation, what
Mowforth and Munt term the "new tourism" is situated within the transition
to post-Fordist flexible modes of accumulation. Global tourism now involves
"niche" or segmented markets catering to different income and "lifestyle"
groups worldwide, including new middle and professional strata from the
service and information sectors. These groups, disposing of increased
leisure time, more flexible lifestyles, and seeking to accumulate "cultural
capital," search out, in Waters' words, "the last morsels of authentic and
exotic culture or of pristine environment." New middle-class tourist niches
have been filled by "new age travelers," "ecotourists," "trekkers," "adventure
tourists," "small-group tourism," and other forms of "alternative tourism."[137]
Moreover, the evidence suggests an increasing segmentation of, and participation in, the world tourist market in ways much more complex than a
simple North–South divide.[138] Most international tourists are still from the
rich countries, but there has also been a steady if less conspicuous increase
in global tourism among the rising middle classes of the Third World, as
well as the rise of domestic tourist industries in all countries of the world
catering to new and established high-consumption groups.

Tourism and Hospitality in Central America

It is in this context that Central America opened up to global tourism in
the 1990s. The region's pacification and integration into the global economy made it an increasingly viable destination. As the Central American
conflict unwound and the local and transnational elites turned their
attention more fully to economic reconstruction, they proposed the expan-

Table 3.14. Subregional Growth in International Tourism Arrivals per World Region, 1988 and 1992

World Subregion	Arrivals		Average Annual Growth Rate (%)
	1988	1992	
Southern Africa	1,379,000	2,583,000	17.0
Central America	1,426,000	2,400,000	13.9
Micronesia (Oceania)	847,000	1,402,000	13.4
Southeast Asia	14,662,000	21,498,000	10.0
Central/East Europe	37,663,000	49,118,000	6.9

Source: WTO, as reported in Husbands and Harrison, 1996.[141]

sion of tourism as a chief activity that could provide new opportunities for economic growth and insertion into global markets.[139] "Ecotourism" in particular made the region a new "hot spot." The strategy called for carving out a special niche within the global tourist market for the region by promoting its impressive pre-Colombian archeological sites and present-day indigenous cultures and ecological preserves, along with the more routine attractions of tropical beaches, forests, and rivers. By the early 1990s the IFIs and other international agencies were providing diverse support for the establishment of the tourist industry, ranging from loans, to technical support and training programs, feasibility studies, and so on.[140] Central America became one of the fastest-growing subregions in the world for tourist arrivals, surpassed between 1988 and 1992 only by Southern Africa, as table 3.14 shows.

Table 3.15 gives an idea of the dramatic growth of the tourist, hospitality, and travel industry in Central America. By 1995, regional tourism receipts had surpassed the $1 billion mark and accounted for approximately 22 percent of foreign exchange earnings in that year.[142] Between 1990 and 1997, approximately 15.6 million international travelers arrived in Central

Table 3.15. Income from Tourism in Central America (millions $)

	1970	1980	1992	1993	1994	1995	1998	1999
Costa Rica	22	87	431	577	626	661	713	730
El Salvador	9	7	49	41	29	39	67	125
Guatemala	12	183	243	228	258	310	325	280
Honduras	4	27	32	60	72	80	120	173
Nicaragua	13	22	21	30	40	50	78	90
Total	60	326	776	936	1025	1140	1303	1398

Source: For 1970–95, *Ecocentral*, June 13, 1996; for 1998–99, *World Almanac and Book of Facts*, Primedia Reference Inc., Mahwak, NJ, 1999 and 2000 edition.

America, generating some $7.5 billion in foreign exchange earnings for this eight-year period, and employing some 232,000 salaried workers.[143] Tourism displaced bananas in 1994 as Costa Rica's principal source of foreign exchange receipts and became in that year the second most important source in Guatemala, after coffee. Between 1990 and 1997, tourism became the third most important source in Nicaragua, up from eighth in 1989, and the third most important source in Honduras as well.[144]

As noted earlier, tourism is not limited to leisure travel, which may be the less important of the different travel categories subsumed under the definition. The more profound connection between tourism and globalization has often been missed by tourism researchers, and has to do with the tremendous increase in cross-border social intercourse and worldwide travel that the process of economic globalization itself generates, apart from leisure. As Central America came out of the war-ravaged 1980s, reconstruction gave rise to a tremendous surge in the tourism, hospitality, and travel industry as a necessary infrastructure for economic reactivation, and this would have been the case even if leisure tourism had not been promoted. The region became inundated with foreign investors and business people, participants at peace conferences, professionals arriving to network, officials from the IFIs, United Nations and other agencies, development workers, bureaucrats from non-governmental organizations, and so on. These conditions of reactivation and integration into the newly globalized economy created a huge demand for expansion of the industry. In Central America, leisure tourism is in fact a major category and of principal concern to policymakers and private capital, but is not the only factor accounting for the phenomenal growth of the industry. Guatemala may be representative of the tourist breakdown. In 1996, 44 percent of visitors came for holidays, 20 percent were business visitors, 19 percent came to visit friends and relatives, 7 percent to learn Spanish, 4 percent to attend professional congresses and conventions, and the remainder belonged to miscellaneous categories.[145]

As with other new transnational accumulation activities, the Central American states have actively promoted tourism in collaboration with the local private sector and transnational capitalists. State measures have included immigration policies, infrastructure development, deregulation (such as the adoption of region-wide "open skies" policies), broad incentives for investors, international public relations campaigns, negotiating international credits for tourist projects, and so on. Each republic has established either a ministry of tourism or an official government tourist institute. Costa Rica became the first to appoint a minister of tourism in 1990, followed in 1994 by Nicaragua, and then by the other republics.[146] In their May 1996 presidential summit meeting, the five Central American presidents drafted a comprehensive "plan of action" to coordinate tourism promotion and convert it into an economic mainstay of the regional economy.[147] Recognizing that international tourism requires peace and security, the five governments launched an international public relations campaign following the summit to convert the region's image from one of

Table 3.16. Distribution of Tourist Arrivals in Central America, by Country, 1990–97

Country	Number of Total Arrivals (in thousands)	% of Total Arrivals	% of Regional Earnings
Costa Rica	5,358	34.4	57.3
Guatemala	4,308	27.6	27.5
Honduras	2,097	13.4	7.7
El Salvador	2,063	13.2	4.1
Nicaragua	1,774	11.4	3.4
Total	15,600	100	100

Source: Calculated on the basis of Barrera Perez, 1998.[150]

a zone of war and conflict to one of beaches, archeological ruins, lush tropical preserves, and hospitable meeting facilities.

As a regional pacesetter, Costa Rica provides a good illustration of tourism within the globalization process. In the 1980s, the government began to invest seriously in tourism as part of its export diversification policies. The government offered tax, import, exchange, credit, and other incentives for large national and foreign investors, complemented by a $15 million publicity campaign to attract foreign tourists. The industry soon overtook agro-exports as the major foreign exchange earner. The country boasted of seventy-nine "ecolodges" and many more smaller preserves, hostels, and attractions catering to "ecotourists."[148] But the government's policies also included a campaign to attract foreign investment in luxury resort projects, most notably, the Pacific coast Papagayo megaresort project, undertaken by Mexican, Costa Rican, and other international investors and billed as the Cancun of Central America. By the late 1990s, beach resorts lined Costa Rica's coasts, many of them owned by transnational firms. In contrast to large investors, small-scale entrepreneurs were not eligible for state incentives, with the result that a two-tiered industry structure emerged, with small-scale tourist operations catering to less affluent visitors and passing on most profit to national and transnational tour operators and other service providers through the latter's control over international air travel, hotel chains, and other "commanding heights" of the tourism infrastructure.

As indicated in table 3.16, between 1990 and 1997, Costa Rica captured the largest share of visitors, and income, followed by Guatemala, and then Honduras, El Salvador, and Nicaragua, in that order. But tourism has expanded in all five republics. According to the World Tourism Organization, Nicaragua showed the highest growth in tourist arrivals between the 1986 to 1996 ten-year period, with an average annual rate of 21 percent, followed by Costa Rica, with a rate of 11.6 percent, El Salvador, at 7.8

percent, Guatemala, at 6.1 percent, and Honduras, at 5.1 percent. These are some of the highest growth rates for tourism anywhere in the world.[149]

All five countries were engaged in major tourist expansion projects in the 1990s. For instance, thirty-eight new tourist projects were underway in Nicaragua in 1997 alone, most of them in hotel and resort construction. Indeed, the World Tourism Organization predicted (probably with over-optimism) that by the year 2010 tourism would generate over two billion dollars in Nicaragua and become the principal foreign exchange earner.[151] Guatemala underwent a boom in hotel construction as the industry took off following the signing of the peace accords in December 1996. The Hyatt Regency opened its first hotel in Central America in Guatemala late that year, followed by Inter-Continental, Radisson, Choice Hotel International, Quinta Real, and Holiday Inn, among others, along with a $7 million International Meeting and Convention Center built by Camino Real.[152] Guatemala teamed up with El Salvador, Honduras, Mexico, and Belize to develop the "Ruta Maya" (Mayan Route), an international tourist circuit of ecological and archeological attractions centered around the ancient Mayan city of Tikal, in Guatemala's northern Peten jungle. Honduras, too, was investing in the development of the Cobán archeological site and in the Caribbean coastline. Although El Salvador trailed behind, the number of visitors jumped by 50 percent in the early 1990s and the government expected that its Pacific beaches, considered to provide some of the best surfing in the Americas, would be a major selling point for the industry's expansion.[153]

There is a rich literature on the relation between tourism and development focusing on the economic and the sociocultural effects of the tourist industry on host countries. The international financial and development agencies have long argued that as an industry "without chimneys" and requiring relatively low initial capital investment, tourism is an attractive option for developing countries and have been promoting it as a development strategy in recent decades. But tourism has also been criticized for making a more marginal economic contribution than raw data on tourist receipts would suggest and for its high social, cultural, and environmental costs. As many studies have shown, the capacity for tourism to contribute to development is linked to the twin issues of its multiplier effect and of "leakages." Underdevelopment theory has pointed out that the more industrialized and diversified a country or region is to begin with, the more it will be able to supply within its borders the diverse inputs into the tourist sectors, thereby generating multiplier effects on the economy as a whole, including expanding employment opportunities outside of the tourist sector itself. Low levels of prior development, by contrast, minimize the multiplier effects and generate "leakages" whereby tourist dollars will tend to go towards imports to sustain the tourist industry and satisfy tourist demand and to other factor payments abroad, such as profit remittances and fees.[154]

A general appraisal of tourism in Central America is difficult because this sector is under-researched. There are no major studies from a social scientific perspective as there are for other regions, such as the Caribbean, the Mediterranean, or North African countries, and data is largely dispersed and incomplete. However, it is highly unlikely, given the region's limited industrialization, the sectoral disarticulation that characterizes its economy, and the central role of transnational capital, that the emerging tourist industry generates the types of multiplier effects which could make it a centerpiece of an integral development process in the region. The major portion of tourist earnings is captured by transnational capital without entering the host country to begin with, going to the TNCs that control air travel and the tour operators and travel agents that organize and coordinate the global tourist traffic.

It would be a mistake, however, to characterize these arrangements, in Central America or elsewhere in the Third World, along the old dependency theory lines of metropolitan capital dominating local economies with the support of comprador groups. The problem of "leakages," for instance, takes on a distinct meaning once we move beyond the nation-state centrism of traditional underdevelopment theory. The wealth generated in the global economy is not "leaked" back to the metropolitan country but appropriated by transnational capital, which may circulate it anywhere around the world. The majority of international hotel services in the Third World, for instance, are now linked to the TNC hotel chains: 75 percent in the Middle East, 72 percent in Africa, 60 percent in Asia, and 47 percent in Latin America. But the TNC hotel chains rarely engage in direct ownership and management. Rather, most arrangements involve local investors who sign some combination of management contracts or leasing, franchise, or technical service agreement. These are precisely the same mechanisms applied by a TNC chain to exercise control over local groups when it sets up a hotel in any First World country. The local groups occupy the same structural location within the chain: they are subject to the same TNC control and must levy a tribute to the TNCs irrespective of whether they are located in the First or the Third World.[155]

Tourism and other new global accumulation activities reorganize and transnationalize social structure in ways that redefine the relationships between different groups spanning both "host" and "sender" countries. New productive activities and social relations may bring gains to some groups caught up in changing structures and disadvantages to others. Even for the least developed countries discussed in England's notable study on tourism and North–South relations, money spent by tourists for goods and services supplied in these recipient countries remained to remunerate local labor, landowners, and capitalists, suggesting that tourism may generate substantial benefits for some local groups. The notion popularized in the underdevelopment literature of tourism as a form of colonialism is valid insofar as it refers to the colonization—for the purpose of providing services and making profits—of some social groups in global society by others, but not some nations by others. Global tourism reflects the domination of the rich over the poor in global society. But it is increasingly inaccurate to characterize this in nation-state centric terms as the domination of an imperialist core over the periphery.[156] Tourism as a service activity that integrates Central America further into the global economy has significant social, class, and political ramifications. The escalation of tourism and travel amenities in the Isthmus occurs simultaneous to heightened impoverishment of popular majorities. Yet, as with the maquiladoras and NTAEs, tourism reshapes local social structure in ways that generate local winners and losers as it contributes to the overall process of social stratification among groups as defined by their relationship to the global economy and society. The tourist industry in each region is part of the larger structures of a globalized economy whose salient social contradiction, I have argued, is polarization between groups within a transnational environment.

The globalization of the tourist industry draws in local contingents around the world in diverse ways. There is much evidence to suggest that a good portion of the transnational tourist industry in Central America involves substantial participation by local capitalist groups. In Guatemala four of five new luxury hotels built by transnational firms in the mid-1990s were franchised out to local investors, many of them new entrants into the industry.[157] Much hotel and resort construction in Nicaragua in the 1990s was in the hands of local entrepreneurs who invited the participation of transnational capital.[158] In addition, "outbound" tour operators, often located in the developed countries, subcontract with "inbound" operators in host countries to handle a wide array of services. Such subcontracting arrangements are becoming more diverse and widespread as the "new tourism" spreads and the industry becomes more "flexible" and decentralized. These instances foment the formation of transnational groups at the local level. Affinities of interests develop that transcend national boundaries. The tourist industry in Central America has generated benefits for established local investors and new entrepreneurial groups as well as for professionals, middle strata, and some enterprising poor people, who have set up throughout Central America Spanish language schools, interpreting, translation, and personalized consulting firms, guest houses, cultural centers, commercial outlets for local arts and crafts and other cultural products, local tour packages, and so on, to cater to the legions of leisure tourists, business callers, and related international visitors. These groups are not lackeys of imperial capital but agents of new economic opportunities opened up by the integration of Central America into the global economy and the elevated cross-border flow of human beings it brings.

As tourism spreads around the world it opens up new regions to commercial exploitation and draws local communities into expanding market relations. In Central America it is incorporating hitherto isolated or at least more autonomous communities into the global market and bringing far more of the items these communities produce into that market. This marketization of the physical and human environment ranges from the commodification of peasant and indigenous lands in Costa Rica, Guatemala, and Honduras into "ecotourist" or archeological sites, to the mass production of "tourist art" that commodifies and commercializes art, crafts and other cultural products, and the proletarianization of local producers who become workers in new hotels, restaurants, resorts, consulting firms, and tour companies. Tourism foments land speculation, with its predictable consequences, among them the commodification of peasant and community lands and a rise in land values. These effects are acute because most tourist sites are developed not in established zones of agro-export production but in areas previously marginalized economically, such as agricultural frontiers and less accessible or populated backwaters that served as outlets for displaced rural populations. For example, in order to promote tourism along Honduras' North Atlantic coastal area, a major regional attraction due to its lush beaches, tropical coral reefs, and inland Mayan ruins, the government in 1999 lifted constitutional provisions that prohibited the sale to foreigners of land along the country's borders and coasts. The changes opened the way for developers and speculators to grab lands along the coast and was followed by government repression of militant protests by indigenous and Afro-Caribbean groups threatened with a loss of their lands.[159]

"Sustainable Development" and "Ecotourism"

"Ecotourism" became a buzzword in the 1990s, describing the most rapidly expanding sector of world tourism. The industry has advertised Central America's biodiversity in order to market the region as a major global site for "ecotourism." Costa Rica, with its famed biodiversity, during the 1980s went from a low-key destination for tourists seeking natural preserves and quiet beaches to the foremost ecotourist destination in the Americas. The other Central American countries followed suit and jumped on the bandwagon in the 1990s. Ecotourism is billed as a component of "sustainable development," a highly contested concept that has been the focal point of political and ideological struggles in the globalization process (see chapter five). It is sold as a means to protect and preserve the environment while at the same time empowering poor communities. By the 1990s, environmental organizations had joined the tourist industry and international financial and development agencies in heralding ecotourism as the panacea that would conserve fragile ecosystems, benefit rural communities, instill environmental awareness, and promote development. This "green" tourism came about as a convergence of pressures from the global environmental movement with growing public concern over degradation of traditional vacation spots, and mounting criticism in the Third World of conventional international tourism—captured by the "four S's" slogan of sun, sea, sand, and sex—as a scourge of uneven development, environmental pollution, and invasion by culturally insensitive and economically disruptive foreigners.

The World Bank and the other IFIs embraced "sustainable development" at the 1992 Earth Summit in Rio de Janeiro and subsequently began to fund "ecotourism" ventures. The AID, for instance, had established 105 projects in the mid-1990s, totaling more than $2 billion in funding with an "ecotourism" focus, including a region-wide "Paseo Pantera" (Panther Walk) project to establish national ecotourism councils in Central American countries.[160] Transnational state functionaries situated this newfound emphasis on ecotourism as part of the larger strategy of debt repayment, market liberalization, export-led development and integration into the global economy. They emphasized the central role of the private sector in developing ecotourism projects, the privatization of public tourist facilities, and policies to attract transnational investment capital into local ecotourism. These functionaries and industry representatives claimed that by making the environment a commodity the self-interest of the tourist industry would assure that its "assets" did not decline and would prompt a sustainable approach to environmental resources. They also claimed that it would save land and culture by offering income-earning opportunities to local communities who would otherwise engage in depredation of local resources through misuse or expansion of the agricultural frontier into virgin areas. But this claim ignores the fact that depredation of the environment and the expansion of the agricultural frontier is the result of capitalist development itself, which converts nature into an exchange value, displaces local communities, and shifts resources from them to new capitalist enterprises that tend to deploy environmentally destructive production systems and externalize the costs.

The Ecotourism Society has defined ecotourism as: "Responsible travel to natural areas that conserves the environment and improves the well-being of local people."[161] There is no reason why in the abstract tourism and protection of the environment cannot operate in tandem. Historic sites and buildings, such as Mayan ruins in Guatemala and Honduras and colonial districts in Nicaraguan cities, have been rehabilitated as tourist attractions, and increased public awareness of environmental issues has come about as a result of ecotourism and the broader concept of sustainable development. However, as a growing number of studies have cautioned, ecotourism at its best offers a set of principles and practices that may potentially promote both ecological aims and development. But this new form of tourism has provided a convenient "green" cover for practices that result in further degradation both of fragile ecosystems and of the conditions of poor and marginalized human communities.[162]

Much "green" tourism is in reality little more than a crude marketing ploy, what Honey has more euphemistically termed "ecotourism Lite." For instance, hotels and tour operators sell as "ecotourism" token measures which may be pleasing to "new age travelers" seeking to reconcile their pursuit of pleasure and cultural capital with concern over the environment. These measures may include a brief walk through a rainforest, not changing hotel guests' sheets and towels every day, using recycled-paper menus in restaurants or biodegradable soap in bathrooms, placing recycling bins in lobbies, and so on. Tourism in Central America has been billed as "ecotourism" simply because it is related to nature and distinct from the "four S's" of conventional tourism, from excursions in Nicaragua into forests or lakes, to a glass-bottom boat ride over coral reefs off Honduras' Caribbean coast, white-water rafting in Costa Rica, and a visit to archeological ruins in the Guatemalan countryside, irrespective of the social or environmental impact of this activity and the broader principles of ecotourism. And despite the official objective of promoting community development and empowerment, and with a few notable exceptions, local communities in Central America have not generally benefited from the tourist industry. Instead, whether eco or conventional tourism, the pattern seems to be a rise in social stratification as market relations spread, opening up new opportunities for some and displacing and marginalizing others.

The cases of Tortuguero, on Costa Rica's north Caribbean coast, and of Monteverde, in the mountainous forests to the northwest of San José, are instructive. As tourist arrivals in Tortuguero rose sharply, the percentage of the tiny local population of some 500 people that made a living from tourism rose from less than twenty in 1986 to seventy in 1991 and an apparent prosperity has been brought to the area. However, as Honey notes in her firsthand study, "there is a growing economic gap between those few local owners or tourism businesses and those who are either salaried employees or are totally outside the tourism sector."[163] Similarly, Costa Rica's Monteverde reserve, home to some of the country's rapidly vanishing rainforest, was hit by a flood of visitors in the 1990s. The area was previously an autonomous farming community while the Monteverde reserve was run by Quakers as a low-key research center and nature preserve. With the tourist boom, visitors grew in number from 450 in 1975, to 8,000 in 1985 and then more than 50,000 annually in the late 1990s—an increasing number of them arriving on prepaid package tours. In 1989, the famed "golden toad," which was found only in the reserve, was declared extinct, believed to be victim to the disruption of the reserve's ecosystem by human visitation.[164] As in Tortuguero, the introduction of a mass tourist industry profoundly reshaped the local social structure and increased inequalities. The industry has drawn an influx of people from surrounding areas. "You have people with capital who can afford to build the hotels and people who come in and work as chambermaids and cooks," observed the former co-director of the Monteverde Institute. "It benefits the whole community but it's creating differences in wealth as well."[165] The price of land shot up and local dairy farmers were forced to sell their farms. Some converted their farms into pensions and hostels, although a number of these smaller operators defaulted on their bank loans and ended up losing their businesses as well.

The creation of reserves in Central America often means the removal, sometimes forcible, of people from their lands, followed by the turning over of these reserves to private capitalists to be developed and converted into profit-making ventures. With the take-off of the tourist industry in the 1980s in Costa Rica, for example, the number of private reserves created by wealthy foreigners rose sharply, numbering several hundred by the end of the 1990s and equal to an estimated 2 to 5 percent of the country's territory.[166] Land prices have shot up in the areas surrounding these reserves with the frequent result that small landowners have been forced to sell. "In the name of ecotourism, our poor peasants are giving away their land for pennies," warned one Costa Rican legislator and environmentalist.[167] But if squatting and land invasions were key mechanisms that the government tolerated, and even supported, in the post-WWII period as part of its social democratic agrarian reform program (see chapter two), as traditional farmlands were converted to tourist reserves the Costa Rican state pledged to quickly remove any would-be squatters from those lands. Stonich and her colleagues found similar results in their study on the costs and benefits of eco and other forms of tourist development on Honduras' Caribbean coast. They found increased social differentiation, reduced access for local people to land and other resources, escalating prices and land speculation, and a deterioration of the local ecosystem.[168] The same results have also been found in numerous studies on the Mayan communities in Guatemala and Mexico, who take no part, beyond low-cost labor, in the development of a tourist circuit whose principal local contribution seems to be the degradation of indigenous villages that it brings. In June 1996, 300 Mayan peasant families were evicted from land they claimed belonged to the state—police burned down their homes and arrested several of them—to make way for a tourist complex planned by Spanish investors.[169]

Gender relations form part of the larger social relations and practices embodied in tourism. Although the "sex tourism" that has received much attention in some Asian countries has not yet been reported in Central America,[170] the way that the tourist industry has developed in Central America (and in global society) involves the commercialization of sexual images (and of power) and of the image of women. As Kinnaird and her colleagues remind us, tourism practices as power relations are gendered in their construction, presentation, and consumption.[171] Men and women have different access to the employment opportunities opened up by tourism, which are often gender-specific and are based on existing and new sexual divisions of labor. Recent studies have shown that women are generally confined to less stable, unskilled, and low-paid work, such as kitchen staff, chambermaids, and cleaners, a finding entirely consistent with the patterns exhibited in the maquiladora industry and in the NTAE sector.[172] But, as will be discussed in the next chapter, the gender implications of globalization are multidimensional and open to ambiguities. Employment in the tourist industry, in the maquiladoras, and in the NTAE sector can offer women entering the formal labor force greater autonomy vis-à-vis patriarchal households and can have a transformative effect on gender relations in larger communities.

A tourist industry could not be established in Central America so long as the regional conflict continued. The Central American states and business elites have raised repeated concerns that lingering social unrest and political instability could sabotage their efforts to sustain the industry. Here there is a contradiction (examined more fully in chapter five) between the strictly technical and economic possibilities of the transnational model, which certainly allows for a substantial accumulation of capital through tourism, and the social consequences of that model, in that rising poverty and inequalities inherent in the model generate the ongoing social unrest and political tensions that could undermine the industry. Tourism is to a considerable extent marketed on the basis of image and the management of fantasy pitched to the psychological and cultural proclivities of the potential tourist market. But the differences in culture and standards of living between "host" and "guest" highlight inequalities and generate a heightened sense of relative deprivation. Middle-class tourists are interested in arms-length representation, aestheticized poverty, and contrived authenticity that filters out the real world of human rights violations, violent inequalities, deeply rooted racism, and intense class and political conflict in Central America. "Tourists ... visit only those societies which have already reached certain 'acceptable' standards in their physical infrastructure, in public health and in personal safety," notes Harrison. "[T]ourists do not intentionally go to the world's trouble spots and, if unrest does occur, the tourism industry is the first to suffer. In short, although they visit the exotic poor, tourists do so in relative comfort and in the expectation of continued security. Like other international investors, they avoid regions that contain the poorest of the poor."[173] Under these conditions tourism invites heightened social control systems that only aggravate the underlying problems. Guatemala was the first country to deploy a special tourist police corps to the country's major sites to protect visitors from local crime and insulate them from the mass of indigent people.[174]

Much has been written on the local cultural degradation that often accompanies international tourism, including the spread of prostitution, the black market, and drugs as byproducts of conventional tourism.[175] While this may hold for Central America, of particular concern here is how tourism becomes a key conduit for the diffusion of "global culture." Whatever else, tourism, with its demonstration effects, ostentatious consumption, and association with mass advertising, diffuses the global culture of consumerism and individualism and contributes to cultural homogenization processes, in the regions of tourist origin and destination. Indeed, tourism extends the consumer culture in a literal way by redefining human cultures and practices and the physical environment as commodities. Tourism, it should be recalled, need not be a *capitalist* activity. The "social tourism" that predominated in the former Soviet-bloc countries, for instance, was not a commodified activity.[176] It is not tourism per se that converts cultures, peoples, and the environment into commodities, but *capitalist* tourism.

The Export of Labor and Remittances

Central American labor has become a major new "export" linking the region to the global economy, and the remittances that emigrant workers send home have become a vital source of foreign exchange in the transnational model, along with maquiladora production, NTAEs, and tourism and hospitality. The progressive alienation of the Central American peasantry, artisans, and other sectors in the post-WWII period of capitalist expansion, together with the upheavals of the regional conflict, produced a huge pool of surplus labor available to transnational capital for a new round of accumulation under globalization. But this pool appeared in the age of renewed global labor flows, when labor has become a commodity that is itself "marketed" worldwide. Central American labor has become available not only for the regional labor market but for the *global* labor market, exported as far away as Australia and New Zealand. Transnational migration and the expanded employment of Central Americans in the United States, Canada, and elsewhere, has led to an enormous increase in remittances from Latino ethnic labor abroad to extended kinship networks in Central America. This is a complex phenomenon which should be situated within the integration of Central America into the North American political economy as the principal institutional and territorial form in which the region's integration into global structures is taking place. Remittances have become the mainstay of survival for dense kinship networks, and the money sent to the region enters both the formal and informal local economies, as do their bearers, as consumers and as small-scale producers.

As table 3.17 shows, remittances have become the single most important source of foreign exchange entering the Salvadoran economy, amounting to $1.2 billion in 1995. For Guatemala, the figure was $408 million. Thus the remittance itself is a complex transnational economic practice, not a curious anomaly but a constitutive feature of the globalization of Central America and part of transnational processes that are fundamentally transforming the region. Discussion of transnational migrations in Central America is divided between this and the next chapter. In this section, I review the rise of a truly global capitalist labor market, the phenomenon of remittances as part of the workings of this market, and the role remittances play in Central America. In the next chapter I explore the changing patterns of Central American migration and its relation to the restructuring of the North American labor market in the context of globalization processes in the Greater Caribbean Basin.

With the participation of most countries of the world in transnational migration processes, either as exporters or importers of labor, or as both, the flow of remittances has become vital to the global economy. Just as capital does not stay put in the place it accumulates, neither do wages stay put. Remittances redistribute income worldwide in a literal or geographic sense but not in the actual sense of *redistribution*, meaning a transfer of some added portion of the surplus from capital to labor, since it constitutes not additional earnings but the separation of the site where wages are earned from the site of wage-generated consumption. International remittances increased astonishingly, from $2 billion in 1970 to $70 billion in 1995.[177] These remittances have become vital to dozens of Third World countries, and for an increasing number of countries they are the most important source of foreign exchange income, among them, Egypt, the Philippines, Albania, Jamaica, Bangladesh, El Salvador, and possibly Mex-

Table 3.17. Officially Recorded Central American Emigrant Remittances, 1980–2001 (millions $)

	1980	1988	1989	1990	1991	1992	1993	1994	1995	1996	1997	1998	1999	2001**
Costa Rica*	–	–	–	–	–	–	–	–	–	–	–	–	–	–
El Salvador	11	194	228	358	467	687	789	967	1061	1086	1199	1338	1374	1972
Guatemala	0	43	69	107	139	187	205	263	358	375	408	457	466	584
Honduras	0	0	0	0	n/a	n/a	60	85	120	128	160	220	320	460
Nicaragua	0	0	0	0	n/a	10	25	30	75	95	150	200	300	610
Regional total	11	237	297	465	606	884	1079	1345	1614	1684	1917	2215	2460	3626

* Costa Rican data collection agencies did not report remittances
** Source for 2001 is preliminary and from Inter-American Development Bank, Multilateral Investment Fund, 2002 Annual Report. Its method of calculation may vary from the World Bank's.

Source: World Bank, Global Development Finance, Country Tables, 2000 and 2002 reports.

ico.[178] Studies show that remittances are used primarily not for investment but for consumption, including food, clothing, consumer goods, housing, social services such as health and education, and social purposes (such as weddings), while a smaller portion goes to local, often family-level and informal sector, productive and service activities.[179] Remittances have a multiplier effect, augmenting local demand and employment and therefore generating demand for goods from the global factory and allowing the unemployed and marginalized to participate, in however limited a way, in global consumption. Money remittances thus circulate back into the global economy, including into the country or region from which the wage originated. By contributing to economic stabilization and easing, however slightly, political tensions, remittances may help maintain social stability. In sum, remittances make an important contribution to transnational social integration and constitute a significant factor in the reproduction of the global system.

Remittances and the Transnationalization of Labor Markets and Social Reproduction in Central America

Transnational migrations and remittances have been one of the least studied aspects of globalization in Central America, perhaps because of their novelty and complexity as well as the difficulties in researching the phenomena. The amount of official remittances from Central American workers abroad increased an astonishing 279 percent between 1980 and 1989, as at least three million Central Americans, or 15 percent of the Isthmanian population, emigrated.[180] Central American workers abroad send between 5 and 15 percent of their annual wages back as remittances.[181] But it is exceedingly difficult to estimate remittance flows, and data (such as those presented in table 3.17) based on officially recorded remittances fail to capture transfers that take place through informal channels. Studies in a number of countries indicate that only about half of all remittances may travel through official channels.[182] Officially recorded remittances for Nicaragua, for instance, amounted to only $150 million in 1997. But other estimates placed the amount of remittances sent into Nicaragua through formal *and* informal channels at about $800 million in 1998, which was well in excess of annual export income.[183] Similarly, official remittances for Guatemala were $408 million in 1997 but other estimates placed them at approaching $1 billion.[184] Moreover, monetary remittances do not include other forms of "in-kind" remittances, such as shoes, clothing, household appliances and other goods sent by emigrant kin that form an essential part of the survival strategy of Central American families.

The phenomenon of remittances highlights the emergence of a single integrated (but segmented) labor market incorporating the entire North American subcontinent, as a regional component of the global labor market. In this scenario, Central American labor in the United States and other foreign countries becomes a transnationalized economic activity "bonding" together national and regional economies (in this case, the "US" and the

Table 3.18.   GNP, Export Earnings, and Remittances (in millions $)

	El Salvador		Guatemala		Nicaragua	
	1980	1997	1980	1997	1980	1997
GNP	3538	7663	7802	10411	2070	2137
Exports	1215	2708	1730	3175	495	866
Remittances	74	1199	108	408	11	150

Source: CEPAL, *Economic Survey of Latin America and the Caribbean*, various years; IDB, *Economic and Social Progress in Latin America*, 1998–99, World Bank.

"Central American" economies) and integrating them into the global economy. Central American workers meet the labor demands in the deskilled and service sectors in the United States and other labor importing countries (as discussed in the next chapter) and the remittances they send back to the region simultaneously help offset macroeconomic imbalances, and in some cases, avert economic collapse. The data, in fact, strongly suggests that the influx of foreign currency into national accounts through remittances made an important contribution to closing the balance of payments gap in Central America in the latter decades of the twentieth century.[185] By the 1990s remittances had become a critical stabilizing factor in the Central American economy; it is not likely that macroeconomic stability could have been achieved, or maintained, without them. Tables 3.18 and 3.19 place the economic weight of remittances in relative perspective.

Table 3.20 shows that remittances surpassed US aid to the region between 1978 and 1994, the bulk of which went to direct balance of payments support.

Remittances make a weighty contribution to the survival of poor families in Central America and provide a vital source of small-scale capital for micro-enterprises in the informal sector. One study in El Salvador found that in 1997 some 15 percent of all households—and over 40 percent of all households living under the poverty line—received remittances from family members abroad and that they represented an annual income of $348 per family member.[186] Another found that remittances made up an astonishing 47 percent of the total income of Salvadoran families who received them.[187]

Table 3.19.   Remittances as Percentage of GNP and Export Earnings

	Remittances	
	As % GNP	As % Export Earnings
El Salvador	15.6	44.3
Guatemala	3.9	12.9
Nicaragua	7.0	17.3

Table 3.20.   Remittances and US Aid, 1978–94 (in billions $)

Country	Remittances	US Aid
El Salvador	4.5	3.3
Nicaragua	1.1	0.9
Guatemala	0.8	1.1
Total	6.4	5.4

Source: Orozco, *et al.*, p. 55.

In Guatemala, a study on the impact of remittances on the poor in the capital city highlighted the compensatory effect of remittances on the erosion of incomes due to structural adjustment policies.[188] Studies on Nicaragua have been inconclusive, in part because the impact of remittances was more difficult to gauge because virtually the entire remittance flow passed through informal channels until the legalization of exchange houses and dollar accounts in the early 1990s. A 1995 World Bank study estimated that remittances represented only about 5 percent of family income in the country, although a United Nations report several years earlier estimated that remittances constituted up to 30 percent of income for poor families.[189]

It is not surprising that Central American governments have sought to incorporate migration and remittances into their own political strategies. Soon after assuming office in 1989, for instance, the ARENA government in El Salvador promoted the legalization of *casas de cambio* (exchange houses), which encouraged remittances by giving Salvadorans a way to legally change dollars at near the black market rate. These new houses had the double effect of channeling dollars into the formal financial system where they could be used to finance imports.[190] The Nicaraguan and Guatemalan governments took similar steps in the early 1990s. Throughout the decade the Isthmanian governments also collectively lobbied US authorities on behalf of Central American immigrants and protested deportations and repressive immigration legislation.[191]

In sum, remittances expand and integrate regional markets, allowing millions of Central American families (and also Mexican and Caribbean groups in the particular case of the North American market) to survive by purchasing goods either imported from the world market or produced locally or by transnational capital. This is an arrangement, most likely an emergent structural feature of the global system, whereby the site of labor power and its reproduction have been transnationally dispersed. Remittances contribute to reducing the social costs of adjustment, especially for the poorest sectors, allowing for family survival at a time of crisis and adjustment. They are "safety nets" that replace governments and fixed employment in the provision of economic security. Emigration and remittances also serve the political objectives of pacification. Emigration to the

United States in the 1980s and early 1990s helped dissipate social tensions and undermine labor and political opposition to prevailing regimes and institutions, thereby shoring up the political conditions for an environment congenial to transnational capital.

Conclusions

A new cycle of capitalist expansion and modernization appears to be underway in Central America on the basis of a new set of economic activities as the region has become rearticulated to the world economy in the aftermath of the political-military upheaval of the 1980s. This concluding section aggregates the data presented in earlier sections on the growing importance of these activities in order to provide a more complete empirical picture of this rearticulation. A comparative analysis of the data on new or "non-traditional" economic activity is extremely difficult, given the limitations to such data previously discussed, such as differences between countries and between data collectors about what is considered traditional and non-traditional, and the fact that tourist earnings and remittances are not exports per se even though they are external sector activities and key measures of the growing integration of the region into the global economy. Yet no matter how this rearticulation is measured, the historical tendency underway is clear: a new set of economic activities covered under the broad concept of non-traditional exports is on the ascendancy and already by the 1990s represented a major transformation of the Central American political economy. The following tables and the accompanying discussion should not be taken as definitive measurements. They should be viewed with caution as giving estimates and approximations that provide some loose empirical indications of the historical transition to the region's fourth rearticulation to world capitalism.

Table 3.21a is based on Brockett's calculations and shows the sharp decline in the relative importance of Central America's five traditional

Table 3.21a.   Traditional Five Exports* as Percentage of Total Exports, 1962–94 (Brockett's estimates)

	C.R.	E.S.	Guate.	Hond.	Nic.
1962	82	77	82	66	69
1980	60	69	56	63	67
1986	61	70	58	67	74
1994	40	37	43	43	41

* Coffee, bananas, sugar, cotton, and beef.

Source: Brockett, p. 62, Table 3.2.

Table 3.21b.   Coffee As Percentage of Total Export Receipts, 1980–2000

	1980	1985	1990	1995	2000
Costa Rica	26	23	18	25	5
El Salvador	36	56	46	38	22
Guatemala	32	40	28	28	21
Honduras	26	26	26	26	24
Nicaragua	38	32	22	24	27

Source: ECLAC, Statistical Yearbook, 2000.

exports (coffee, bananas, cotton, sugar, and beef) from the 1980s on.[192] The five traditional export products as a percentage of total exports dropped dramatically in each republic over the period to 1994 (table 3.21b shows the figures for coffee since the 1980s). As a measure of the magnitude of traditional compared to total exports, the data in table 3.21a does not include tourist receipts or emigrant remittances.

Table 3.22, elaborated on the basis of Willmore's estimates,[193] is a somewhat different measurement of the very rapid growth in the relative weight of non-traditional exports within Central America's export portfolio. It compares the change in traditional exports and non-traditional exports between 1986 and 1994. As the table indicates, non-traditionals increased from a region-wide average of 27 percent of the value of traditional exports in 1986 to 42 percent in 1990 and 52 percent in 1994. However, these figures do not include foreign exchange receipts from non-traditional production and service activities that are not exports per se, such as maquiladora earnings, tourism receipts, and worker remittances.

Table 3.23 shows another side of the picture of Central America's rearticulation to global markets. It combines distinct indicators in order to illustrate the relative weight of non-traditional production and services—exports proper *and* other external sector activity—in the generation of foreign exchange earnings. Of the four new economic sectors discussed in this chapter, three are not exports per se but external sector, or outwardly oriented, activities that link the regional economy to the global economy. Sources of foreign exchange in Central America are central to internal social reproduction and link local circuits of accumulation and distribution to transnational circuits in the same way that exports proper do. The real measure of linkage to the world economy is in fact activity that is globally marketed and that earns hard currency which makes possible international economic intercourse. The first column in the table indicates what was documented throughout the present chapter: the dramatic increase in *absolute* terms of the value of the four economic activities associated with the transnational model. But more importantly, the weight of these economic activities as foreign exchange earners linking Central America to the global economy increased *relative* to the value of total exports as a generator of foreign exchange, as is shown in the second and third columns. To use

Table 3.22.   Traditional and Non-Traditional Exports*, in millions \$, 1986–1994 (Willmore's estimates)

	1986		
	Trad. Exports	Non Trad.	Non Trad. as % of Trad.
Costa Rica	711	374	34
El Salvador	594	161	21
Guatemala	731	313	30
Honduras	694	198	22
Nicaragua	201	57	28
Regional total	2931	1103	27

	1990			1994		
	Trad. Exp	Non. Trad.	as % Exp.	Trad.	Non. Trad.	as % Exp.
C.R	685	764	53	1018	1234	55
E.S.	298	283	49	321	497	61
Guat.	666	545	45	711	840	54
Hond.	659	172	21	537	306	36
Nic.	240	91	38	209	143	41
Regional total	2548	1855	42	2796	3020	52

* Traditional exports include coffee, bananas, sugar, cotton, beef, and seafood, plus cardamom and petroleum in Guatemala and wood in Honduras. Non-traditionals include all other exports but exclude earnings for maquiladoras, tourism, and remittances.

Source: Calculated from Willmore's estimates from various sources, p. 66, Table A.

the example of Guatemala, the value of the four new activities of the transnational model represented 23.5 percent of the value of total exports in 1990 and 54.6 percent in 1996.

Finally, table 3.24 shows that the rate of growth of exports in the 1990s was considerably above that of GDP growth in the region, and is a measure of the *increasing external orientation and integration* of the Central American economies. It is interesting to note that the rate of growth of exports was roughly equal to that of GDP growth in the 1970s. The crisis of the 1980s shows the disruption of external linkages reflective of the breakdown of the pre-globalization model of accumulation. In the 1990s, exports growth does more than rebound; it overtakes GDP growth dramatically in every country except Honduras, and is nearly double the rate of growth in the region as a whole.

Table 3.23. Central America's Rearticulation to Global Markets

	Value of Non-Traditional Foreign Exchange Earning Activities* (in millions $)		Exports of Goods and Services (in millions $)		Non-Trad. Foreign Exchange Earnings as % of Total Export Earnings	
	1990	1996	1990	1996	1990	1996
C.R.	597	1415	1963	3370	30.4	41.9
E.S.	411	1500	973	1768	42.2	84.8
Guat.	368	1224	1568	2242	23.5	54.6
Hond.	140	869	1033	1192	3.6	72.9
Nic.	70	228	392	726	17.9	31.4

* NTAEs, maquiladora and tourist earnings, and remittances.

Source: Non-traditional foreign exchange earnings are author's estimates based on earlier tables and reference materials, this chapter. Total export earnings from IDB, *Economic and Social Progress in Latin America*, 1998–99, Table B-5, "Export of Goods and Services."

This increasing outward-orientation has been facilitated by complex sets of international agreements that have opened up the region to transnational capital, including a renewal of the process of regional economic integration. However, the integration process that took place under the previous model of accumulation and resulted in the formation of the

Table 3.24. "Export Substitution" and Export-Led Growth in Central America, 1970–2000.

	GDP Average Annual Growth Rate (%)			Exports Average Annual Growth Rate (%)			Trade in Goods (as % GDP)	
	1970–80	1980–90	1990–97	1970–80	1980–90	1990–97	1990	2000
Costa Rica	5.6	2.2	3.5	6.6	5.4	8.6	60.2	77.2
El Salvador	n/a	−1.5	5.2	n/a	−4.8	13.8	38.4	59.2
Guatemala	5.7	1.1	3.9	5.7	−1.4	6.9	36.8	39.1
Honduras	5.3	2.3	3.3	4.3	0.3	2.0	57.9	70.9
Nicaragua	0.0	−1.1	2.4	1.4	−4.7	10.8	95.9	100.9
Regional total	4.1	0.8	3.7	4.5	−1.0	8.4	57.8	69

Source: IDB, *Economic and Social Progress in Latin America*, 1998–99, Tables A-1 and B-5, trade in goods data (right-hand column) is from World Bank, *World Development Indicators*, 2002, Table 6.1.

CACM was a form of "inward" integration, intended to create a regional market for Central American and multinational (largely US) capital to take advantage of economies of scale. The type of integration proceeding under globalization is "outward," aimed at creating a single field for global capitalism in the Isthmus.[194] Regional integration in this scheme is a stepping stone for global integration (for example, into a free trade zone of the Americas) rather than a strategy to build up the region's internal productive forces. New activities integrated into the global economy do not constitute "enclave economies" per se but phases in global production and service chains. This is a new form of socioeconomic organization, in which whole chunks of Central America's economic structure and geography become integrated into a transnational productive configuration, just as "global cities" become delinked from their hinterland within core "national" economies and integrated into de-territorialized global economic networks.[195] Given this reality it was no wonder that the Central American governments began to negotiate a monetary union in 2001 in step with the increasing dollarization of financial systems in each of the countries.[196]

In sum, the most dynamic economic sectors in Central America now appear to be those linked directly to globalized circuits of production and distribution and whose introduction has been facilitated under the neo-liberal model. These sectors appear to be at the cusp of a renewed cycle of capitalist expansion and modernization, in which the region is being drawn more fully into the world economy. But this transformation of the region's political economy has been accompanied by major change in the social structure. New working-class contingents and popular forces as well as new capitalist groups and middle strata have become central historical agents. The next chapter explores diverse social, political, and cultural phenomena and subprocesses as elements of the great social transformation underway as the Isthmus becomes globalized.

4

The New Transnational Model in Central America: II: Incorporation into Global Society

Rearticulation to the world economy through the introduction of a new economic model is the material foundation upon which Central America is becoming integrated into the global economy and society. But the globalization of the Isthmus involves change in all aspects of society. This chapter is an open-ended exploration into some of the varied dimensions of the transnational model in Central America. Each topic is not a finished piece of research but a limited and tentative look at the transformations underway at every level of Central American society, indicative of social change around the world more generally under globalization. Here readers will find that my overviews raise the key issues involved in each theme, point the way forward for more in-depth research on these diverse issues in Central America, and provide a framework of ideas for exploring globalization and social change in other regions of the world as well.

Restructuring the State and Civil Society

The Rise of Transnational Fractions and "Technopols" in Central America

The transnational fractions of the capitalist class and the state bureaucracies that have risen to power in Central America and elsewhere in the South are not the comprador class of the dependency theorists, who were seen as well-paid junior partners of imperialist capital. They are local contingents of a transnational capitalist class and other strata whose economic interests and social advancement reside less in the development of national capitalism than in the global capitalist system that they participate in and defend. A new technocratic elite has emerged from among these transnationally oriented groups. These transnational technocrats became strategically placed in new private-sector associations, in political parties, educational institutions, and local states in designing and implementing the transnational agenda in Central America. The analysis of technocratic elites is a part of the established literature in development and political economy. They are identified as bureaucratic groups with a cosmopolitan outlook and international professional standards who apply capitalist rationality to state policies. But the *transnational* technocratic elite is a new breed, thrown up by the political and economic dynamics of globalization and transition, that has risen to prominence in countries and regions around the world. Technocrats apply a capitalist rationality in place of rentier state activities, patronage networks, clientelism, corporatist structures, "crony capitalism," and like forms of economic organization. The transnational technocratic elite, in turn, applies the rationality of the global economy over the logic of nation-state capitalism.

Jorge Dominguez and his colleagues have coined a new term for the foremost individuals among this new technocratic elite: *technopols*.[1] As the term implies (techno=technocrats, pols=politicians), technopols combine "the introspection of the thinker with the sociability of the politician."[2] Beyond mere technocrats, they are political organizers and leaders who are able to build legitimacy within local political systems for the program of integration into global capitalism. Dominguez *et al.* describe former Brazilian president F. Enrique Cardoso, Christian Democratic leader and former finance minister of Chile Alejandro Foxley, former Argentine finance minister Domingo Cavallo, and former Mexican finance minister Pedro Aspe (along with the less accomplished Evelyn Matthei of Chile), as technopol successes reflective of a more general phenomenon. According to Dominguez, technopols are: "(1) political leaders at or near the top of their country's government or political life (including opposition political parties) who (2) go beyond their specialized expertise to draw on various different streams of knowledge and who (3) vigorously participate in the nation's political life (4) for the purpose of affecting politics well beyond the economic realm and who may, at times, be associated with an effort to 'remake' their country's politics, economics, and society."[3] What most impresses Dominguez and his colleagues is the ability of technopols to build consensus in promoting the program of neo-liberalism, through adept navigation of the often conflictive and unpredictable waters of polyarchic systems, and their skill in adapting the global to specific national contexts. They are portrayed as the heroes and heroines of democracy and economic progress, promoting free markets and polyarchy in Latin America and elsewhere.

Putting aside these normative considerations, and extrapolating from Dominguez *et al.*, the concept of technopols captures the idea of the leading politicized individuals drawn from the ranks of transnational fractions. Often schooled at Harvard and other world-class universities in neo-classical economics, technopols are connected to each other and to transnational economists and policymakers in other countries through a common ideology, curriculum, and program. They develop into transnational "epistemic communities," pools of organic intellectuals of global capitalism spread throughout countries around the world.[4] Elite policy-planning institutes, often based in the United States or Europe, such as the

Washington-based Institute for International Economics, serve as transnational clearing houses for these networks.[5]

Technopols are charismatic organic intellectuals who impose the capitalist rationality of the global economy. They conceive, design, and implement the transnational project in particular local conditions and histories. Technopol clusters work within key state apparatuses in each country. From within the national state apparatus they link up directly with transnational functionaries in TNS apparatuses, such as the IMF and the World Bank. One high-level US National Security Council official in the Clinton administration explained, US policymakers "sought to associate the United States with the technopols' projects . . . we consciously placed US prestige—and at critical moments, international financial resources—behind [neo-liberal economic and political] transformation."[6] These clusters are local versions of the "Chicago boys," what Javier Corrales calls the "Cavallo-boys" in regard to Argentina, or what we may term the "Salinas-boys" in Mexico under President Carlos Salinas. They are "cosmopolitan team builders," organizing policy-oriented teams that "colonize" key ministries and government departments upon coming to power, "technically skilled and politically savvy leaders who [hold] key positions during critical periods of change."[7] These clusters constitute crucial intermediaries between the transnational elite and local dominant groups, linked "outward" to the transnational elite and the TNS and "inward" to the local state and society. They are proactive agents of globalization and play a key role in transnational class formation.

The concept of technopols can be applied to Central America to indicate the foremost representatives of new transnationally oriented economic and political groups. Technopols in each republic, as the politicized strata and local organizers of transnationally oriented groups, played a major role in devising the local strategies, political programs, technical plans, and ideologies, for integration into the new global order. They put together "blocs" within the state, among the dominant groups, and in society, to push the transnational project of capitalist globalization. And given the profundity of the transitions in Central America, the technopols were indeed "associated with an effort to 'remake' their country's politics, economics, and society."

Transnational technocrats establish institutional bases from which to develop programs and assemble teams. In Central America, these bases were largely constituted by new private-sector associations and elite foundations created during the transitions, often with AID and other international funding. These associations became key vehicles for organizing, politicizing, and bringing to power transnational fractions. Every Central American republic established, in coordination with the AID and the IFIs, technocratic New Right business associations that actively engaged in policy development and liaised with local states in the promotion of neo-liberal restructuring and of the new activities associated with the transnational model. These associations provided leadership to increasingly coherent transnational fractions among local private sectors, helped these fractions to shape state policies, and furnished a platform for advancing the globalization of Central America. The rise of transnational fractions was symbolized by the administrations of Cristiani in El Salvador, Calderón in Costa Rica, Lacayo/Chamorro in Nicaragua, Callejas in Honduras, and Arzú in Guatemala (see chapter two). Through these administrations the transnational technocrats—the "Cristiani-boys" in El Salvador, the "Callejas-boys" in Honduras, the "Calderón-boys" in Costa Rica, and so on—conquered enough of the local state apparatus to push forward their programs. In some cases, the technocratic elite has "led" local capitalists into a transnational reorientation of outlook and activities, as we saw earlier in the cases of Costa Rica and Guatemala. In other cases, they constructed networks which they then strived to attach to potential winning political parties and candidates, creatively utilizing polyarchy in this game of transforming emerging economic power into political rule. Such processes were clear, for instance, in El Salvador and Costa Rica, where new capitalist groups captured and reoriented the ARENA and the PLN, respectively, and then "rode" these parties into power, or in Honduras, where these groups penetrated and transformed the two principal parties in a similar manner.

From the "Developmental State" to the "Neo-Liberal State" and the New Hegemony of Capital

The profound transformation of the Central American political economy also implies the reconfiguration of Central American states, civil societies, and class relations. Changes in the state–capital relation have occurred in tandem with the restoration of capital's hegemony in society. Throughout the transitions the weight of capital and the private sector in the dominant blocs in each country steadily increased, parallel to the rise to dominance within each private sector of transnationally oriented capitalists. Private capital also became more autonomous from the state and reasserted its dominance over the state, reverting the tendency in state–capital relations towards state dominance in the earlier period of capitalist development. This process is explained in part by the more consensual forms of domination associated with the transition from authoritarian systems to polyarchy, in which the site of social control and ideological production shifts more fully to the "private" sphere of civil society. It is also explained, in part, by the effects that economic restructuring, including the transfer of resources from the public to the private sphere, and within the private sphere, from the domestic to the external sector, has had on state–class relations.

The transnational model of accumulation has entailed a change from the "developmentalist state" corresponding to the earlier national model to the "neo-liberal state" serving the new model. The neo-liberal states in Central America serve global over local accumulation and have functioned to adjust national structures to emergent global structures. In this process, each individual state was penetrated by two new social forces, one from "within" and the other from "without." From "within," transnationalized fractions vied for, and gained control over local states (the "colonialization" mentioned above), particularly over key ministries tying each country to the global economy and society, such as ministries of foreign affairs, finances, economic development, and Central Banks. From "without," diverse transnational actors representing an emergent TNS apparatus penetrated local states, liaised with transnationalized fractions therein, and helped design and guide local polities. These transnational actors include the AID and other bilateral agencies and representatives from the IFIs, and multilateral political entities such as UN and Organization of American States (OAS) units. "Consultative Groups" were set up in the 1990s in each country, generally representatives of the G-7 and the largest donors of the Organization of Economic Cooperation and Development (OECD) countries, as well as IFI representatives, to devise overall economic guidelines and strategies, monitor progress, and link national state economic policymaking to transnational state policymaking. In this process, Central Banks and other key branches often gain an autonomy which shields them from the pressures of the government apparatus, such as social ministries and legislatures, and from the larger political system.[8] These branches of the neo-liberal state apparatus become gateways between the local and the global, arteries through which transnational macroeconomic policies flow bi-directionally in and out of the globalized country. The site of macroeconomic policymaking and enforcement, conceptually, is removed from the country and linked to a transnational policy arena. Thus a policy apparatus is carved out within the national state that is insulated from mass pressure, on the one hand, and from elite groups and their rivalries, on the other. In this way, "chunks" of national states break off and become functional parts of a TNS. These ministries and branches become de-nationalized; transnational entities linked organizationally to nation-state institutions. They do not become representatives of some other nation-state (for example, of US imperialism), as nation-state theories suggest, but of transnational capital and the transnational elite.

The transnationalization of the state in Central America is thus central to understanding the restructuring of classes and the reconfiguration of civil society. These have been reciprocal processes. The state had to be restructured along neo-liberal lines in order for it to implement the policies of adjustment and integration into the global economy, and in turn these policies favored the development of transnational fractions at the expense of the old national fractions of the elite. It was through these reciprocal processes that the private sector became reconstituted and capital's hegemony was restored.

New capitalist fractions participating in globalized circuits of accumulation no longer need to go "through" states in order to articulate with global capitalist networks, and in fact may be hampered if they do. Global production processes, with the heightened movement and turnover time of capital and the articulation of diverse phases through global computerized communications systems, as sociologist Kathleen Schwartzman, among others, has noted, "hollow out" the state by limiting the role of national governments, and alter the relationship that the state has with fractions of capital on the one hand and with working classes on the other.[9] The state "sheds" much of itself with the end of populist and developmentalist projects and the expiation of popular class representatives from the dominant blocs. The integration of national and regional economies into the global economy has increasingly convinced business groups (and some political elites) that they no longer need a central state as an intermediary between themselves and sources of investment and accumulation in the global economy.

This does not mean that the dominant groups have no need of the state. Neo-liberal states perform three essential functions for global capital accumulation: 1) they adopt fiscal and monetary policies which assure macroeconomic stability within each country; 2) they provide the basic social and physical infrastructure necessary for global economic activity (air and sea ports, communications networks, educational systems, etc.), and; 3) they provide social order, that is, stability, which requires sustaining instruments of direct coercion and ideological apparatuses. As Guatemalan scholars Jorge Escoto and Manfredo Marroquin note with regard to the rise of neo-liberal states in Central America: "The functional and institutional 'realignment' of the state . . . should be conceived as a mechanism that has allowed the state to provide the appropriate response to the changes sought within, and for, the private sector and the free market which is the core of the current strategy. The strategy is no longer to strengthen the benefactor state but rather to strengthen the state's ability to provide services and infrastructure to (private sector) productive activity."[10] States have always intervened in the market, both to generate the general conditions for accumulation to take place and to provide specific assistance for concrete accumulation processes. The neo-liberal state continues to perform these services, but the "concrete accumulation process" for which it does it are the new transnational circuits of accumulation.

The neo-liberal national states in Central America thus play a central role in globalization but a redefinition of the relationship of the state to the dominant groups is part of this process. There has been a great reduction of state autonomy granted to the military regimes and a much more direct "instrumentalization" of the state in function of restructuring. This is not surprising, as state autonomy tends to vary historically and decrease in times of major restructuring, as theories of state autonomy suggest.[11] The representatives of capital had first begun to organize into corporate associations in the 1930s as new planter, industrial, and commercial groups emerged. By the 1960s many had coalesced into powerful umbrella organizations representing the private sector as a whole. Torres Rivas notes that private business groups, or "intermediary organizations related to the propertied class," were established as earlier patrimonial forms of public–private linkage eroded in the face of capitalist modernization. "Though not a vertical integration of private interests, this state 'corporatist' tendency represented an unquestioned amount of influence."[12] Through globalization, however, propertied groups have come to exhibit less of a corporatist relationship to the state than an instrumental one. But those forces "instrumentalizing" the state are *transnational* agents. Local Central American states have become more explicit instruments of the new export, commercial, and financial groups tied to the global economy together with transnational functionaries.

In the 1980s and 1990s the AID and other transnational actors undertook broad programs to bolster and restructure the private sector in each Central American country. These programs sought to reorient capitalist groups around new economic activities linked to the global economy and to cultivate modernizing fractions. In 1981, the AID launched its Private Enterprise Initiative, part of a broad shift in US aid strategy from a "predominantly public sector, or government-to-government, focus to one that emphasizes market forces and active private indigenous productive sectors." An analysis of the AID's Initiative is highly instructive, as it reveals the thinking of the transnational elite with regard to the restructuring of state–capital relations worldwide and spells out a sweeping program to reassert the hegemony of private capital around the world.[13] AID programs undertaken through the Initiative involved three components: 1) policy reform, including the gamut of neo-liberal restructuring policies, with a special emphasis on the privatization of state enterprises and public services; 2) assistance for the private sector, including funding the establishment of private-sector associations attuned to the transnational agenda. This entailed the creation of a policy development and political action capacity on the part of the private sector; and 3) a shift from the state to the private sector as the agent managing US and international development assistance (and therefore, a shift from the state to the private sector as the redistributive agent).[14] The Initiative was given particular prominence in Latin America, and within Latin America, Central America was singled out for attention as part of the larger strategy of counterrevolution, restructuring, and globalization.[15] The emphasis within AID and other programs was to prepare a New Right private sector to become "proximate" undertakers of Central America's transformation and rearticulation to the global economy and society.

But restoring capitalist hegemony did not mean restoring the domination of the old oligarchies or economic groups. The process therefore involved sharp conflict among dominant groups. Many of the constituent guilds belonging to the old private-sector associations were tied to the pre-globalization model of accumulation. These traditional associations were wracked by conflict from the 1970s as restructuring and global integration redefined the relative weight of different sectors. The struggles over specific fiscal, budgetary, tax, and other policies favoring either the old or the new model converted the state into a battlefield between capitalist fractions and other economic agents. The landed oligarchies and older industrial and commercial elites strongly resisted in all countries the changeover to new sets of policies favoring export-led development and global integration. Plans such as the CBI "do not offer equal benefits for the private sector in Central America," noted Benjamin Crosby. "Part of the effect of US policy has been to encourage conflict between the private and public sectors, and on occasions among distinct segments of the private sector . . . the AID has rarely worked through the 'traditional' private-sector organizations. Instead, it has lent organizational and financial support for the creation of a new set of organizations that could serve new functions."[16] As a result, in all countries, these traditional groups were eclipsed by new ones: in Guatemala, the CACIF by the CAEM and other chambers; in El Salvador, the ANEP by the FUSADES and its associated organizations; in Honduras, the COHEP by the FIDE and related associations; in Costa Rica, the CNAA and the CIC by the CINDE and its numerous associated groups; and in Nicaragua, the COSEP by the APENN, the Commission for the Promotion of Non-Traditional Exports (CPXNT), and other groups.

Capitalist groups in Central America as local contingents of a transnational capitalist class have abandoned their particular national namesakes in favor of a regional, and increasingly a transnational, identity. In the early 1990s, the private-sector groups in each Central American country (and Panama) joined together to form the Federation of Private Sector Entities of Central America and Panama. The purpose of the federation, known by its acronym FEDEPRICAP, was to develop a single Central American private-sector platform on economic policies and political issues and coordinate initiatives regarding the region and its relation to the global system. In 1998, the federation drafted a comprehensive position paper endorsing liberalization and calling for the dismantling of remaining regional barriers to integration into the global economy.[17] This convergence of national bourgeoisies is very significant because historically, as Torres Rivas observes, "conflicts between propertied groups of the five participating countries [in the Central American Common Market] were 'horizontal,' that is, national confrontations,"[18] which often exploded into major international conflict, such as the 1969 "Soccer War" between Honduras and El Salvador. While political conflicts may well continue *between* the five republics, the globalization of Central America is clearly having a unifying effect on the capitalist classes in the region.

The regional integration of Central American capitalists parallels the gradual supranational integration of the five Central American states. This integration is political and has progressed through new formal and informal forums, such as the *Sistema de Integracion Centroamericana* (SICA), the Central American Parliament (PARLACEN), and regular presidential summits and region-wide ministerial meetings. It is also economic, and includes the negotiation of a new free trade zone based on collective integration into the NAFTA, and beyond it, the global economy. Although the extent of this process should not be overstated, there has been a progressive convergence, if not formal integration, of distinct national institutions. It is not clear how far this process of supranational integration would actually go, but the process has been attuned to the need to provide a region-wide institutional framework for consolidating the transnational project.

Transnationalization of Civil Society in Central America

There has been an immense new interest in "civil society" since the 1980s, epitomized in the oft-cited works of political scientist Robert Putnam, among others.[19] The notion of civil society, which is of course an abstraction, refers to different "non-state actors" that include formal representative organizations (such as political parties, trade unions, and professional associations), formal functional organizations (schools, universities, and the mass media), and more informal political and social networks (ranging from local volunteer groups to social movements [NGOs are included here]). But there are competing conceptions of civil society. Gramsci's critical formulation has gained in influence in recent decades against the classical liberal or pluralist approaches. In Gramsci's formulation, the spread of capitalist production relations separates social life into two distinct spheres: the "public" sphere that becomes the domain of the state and the "private" sphere that becomes civil society. This corresponds to the formal (apparent) separation under capitalism of the "political" and the "economic." The much-heralded "rise of civil society" in recent decades is not surprising, given the intensification of capitalist relations around the world under globalization.

Civil society is not a homogenous and unitary actor, opposed to another homogenous and unitary actor, the state. It is the site of both dominant and subordinate groups. It includes diverse economic agents originating in the market, including capital, which strives to achieve its hegemony there, and conservative political and social forces as well, such as the Catholic Church, just as much as it includes the popular classes and their social movements, trade unions, peasant associations, and grassroots community groups. In distinction to the direct domination exercised by the state, civil society is the site where the cultural and ideological hegemony of dominant groups, or the counter-hegemony of subordinate groups, is constructed. It is a site of permanent contestation, wracked by conflicts among diverse opposing social forces within it and struggles over competing hegemonies. But Gramsci's distinction between civil society and the state is purely methodological; the state and civil society are fused or intertwined. The counterposition of civil society to the state that the classical liberal conception posits is a false dichotomy. Gramsci's concept of the extended state clarifies the intricate interpenetration of state and society and overcomes dualist notions of the two. In Gramsci's famous dictum, the extended state is "political society + civil society, hegemony protected by the armor of coercion."[20] The rise of civil society, once the capitalist mode of production has become consolidated, is at the core of the historic process. Under capitalism, state power ultimately rests on a given correlation of social forces in civil society.

This view of civil society as an arena for exercising domination runs counter to conventional (particularly pluralist) thinking on the matter, which holds that civil society is a buffer between state domination and groups in society, and that class and group domination is diluted as civil society develops. Much recent scholarship has tended to endorse this conventional view. "Conservative and progressive analysts and activists alike," note Alvarez and her colleagues, "tend to sing the praises of civil society's democratizing potential on a local, national, regional, and global scale."[21] Notions of a harmonious civil society reflect the underlying consensus theory and pluralist assumptions contained in their scholarship.[22] There are in fact two overlapping accounts of civil society in this literature, both grounded in the classical liberal conception. The predominant neo-liberal formulation equates the expansion of civil society with the spread of the market. The expansion of civil society as the realm of the "private," of "autonomy" and of "freedom," is synonymous with the freeing of the market from the state and of capital from social constraint. The projection of civil society as "a virtuous pole against the state" becomes an ideological construct that legitimates a global capitalist program of dismantling state-led development projects and proceeding with the privatization and deregulation of the state. The pluralist formulation projects an image of civil society as some unified social force representing subordinate groups while the state is the bastion of the powerful. It then equates the upsurge of civil society perforce with democratization and the empowerment of citizens and social movements. The pluralist formulation is apparently more appealing than the neo-liberal. But it is silent on numerous forms of oppression and inequality in civil society. It also ignores the presence of capital and its private organization in civil society, and the numerous mechanisms through which dominant groups operating in civil society develop manifold links to the state as part of an organic structure of domination (the flipside is the lack of popular class access to the state).

The emergence of a global economy provides the material basis for a global civil society. For many analysts of globalization, the civil societies of each country are becoming transnationalized through integration into associational networks that span numerous countries. This process includes of course transnational class formation, and also the spread of transnational social movements, the rise of International Nongovernmental Organizations (INGOs), other novel forms of cross-border social organization, and issues of hegemony and counter-hegemony exercised in the "private" sphere of an expanding global civil society. Liberal-pluralist accounts, transposing their assumptions about national civil society to the transnational sphere, argue that global civil society opens up a new "cosmopolitan democracy" of world citizens that will hold states responsive to grassroots needs. According to Martin Shaw, we are witness to "the beginning of the development of what we may call global civil society, in which members of global society are starting to try to make the state system responsible—in the way in which national societies have, in the past, generated pressures to ensure the accountability of national states."[23] But increasing linkage among civil societies does not necessarily prove emancipatory for popular majorities and emergent global civil society does not generate an automatic globalization-from-below representing popular aspirations. The official

development discourse of "fostering and strengthening civil society" trans-
lates in practice into the penetration of civil society downward, from the
global capitalist system to the most local community and municipal level.
Social relations at the local grassroots level become integrated into the
larger social relations of the global political economy through this transnationalization of civil society. Transnational capital is the driving force in the
global economy and the prime agent in the creation of a global civil society.
Global civil society reproduces the conflicts and contradictions of national
civil societies from which it emerges, while generating new contradictions
that reflect struggles and power dynamics at the level of the global system.[24]

Civil society in Central America has been swept up into this process of
transnationalization. One direction in which this has proceeded is region-
wide integration of the organs of each national civil society. PARLACEN,
created in 1991 as a consultative forum for representatives from the
region's political parties, is one example. Another is the creation of
FEDEPRICAP out of an amalgamation of national business associations.
There are numerous other region-wide organizations that link together
national associations. These range, to mention but a few, from the Association of Peasant Organizations for Cooperation and Development (ASO-
CODE), to the Commission for the Defense of Human Rights in Central
America (CODEHUCA), the Broad Women's Movement of Central America (MAdeM), and the Civil Initiative for Central American Integration
(ICIC).[25] This emerging regional civil society network has in turn been
integrating into global civil society through an increase in ties with organizations of other countries and regions. These ties range from professional
exchanges, participation by Central Americans in INGOs and diverse
collective undertakings. These diverse forms of transnationalization involve
both popular and dominant groups, whose struggles are transposed from
national and regional terrain to the global system.

Precisely because of the lack of a more inclusive, populist developmentalist project from the 1930s into the 1970s, as occurred elsewhere in Latin
America, organs of civil society were late to develop in Central America.
What occurred through the transitions from the 1960s into the 1990s
was the expansion and reconstruction of civil society as new economic
agents and social actors, among them, uprooted peasants, new rural and
urban working classes, transnational capitalists, the urban informal sector
and the marginalized, became mobilized and engaged in diverse forms
of organization. In this process civil society became extremely polarized,
with a radicalization of the grassroots approximating more than elsewhere a situation of "civil society against the state"; the former became a
bastion of the popular classes and the latter an exclusive preserve of the
elite. Although popular forces became well organized in civil society in
the 1970s and 1980s they were not integrated into the state (Nicaragua
under the Sandinistas and Costa Rica under its corporatist polyarchic
system were exceptions). Reciprocally, the dominant groups remained
weak and underdeveloped, exhibiting a more "vertical" corporatist integration into the state than a "horizontal" integration into civil society. These

dominant groups had to beat back the revolutionary challenge by relying principally on the state. They did so in the 1980s by linking up with transnational forces and mounting counterinsurgency and counterrevolutionary campaigns.

By the 1990s, with political society having been reorganized and secured by the dominant groups, transnational elites in and out of the region turned to penetrating and conquering civil society. The challenge was to undercut the autonomy of popular sectors by incorporating them "upwards" into the state and at the same time to strengthen dominant groups in civil society as a counterweight to the popular sectors. This process involved a massive penetration of Central American civil society in the 1980s and 1990s by the transnational elite, through diverse programs, including creating and funding new organizations in civil society that could compete with popular groups, bolstering the more conservative groups that already existed, establishing NGO networks (as discussed below), and so on. As grassroots organizations, progressive NGOs, and popular social movements spread in the 1980s and 1990s they also received support from external sources.

"Democracy promotion" programs, often organized by the US government, stand out here. I have shown in several earlier studies how these programs entailed the creation of a network of civic groups in each intervened country, ranging from business and professional associations to trade unions, media outlets, think-tanks, women's, youth and student organizations, community centers, peasant leagues, and so on, sympathetic to the transnational agenda.[26] These political intervention programs conducted under the rubric of "democracy promotion" resulted in the creation of a society-wide network of political, social, cultural, business, and civic organizations. With few exceptions, the leaders of these organizations, whose directorates are generally interlocking, were drawn from the local elite—specifically, transnational fractions among the elite—as the counterpart in civil society to elite power in political society. Their efforts were aimed at competing with, or eclipsing, existing broad-based popular organizations (which received no US support) and neutralizing efforts by popular sectors to build their own organizations in civil society. Dozens of organizations in civil society in Central America were either created from scratch through US "democracy promotion" programs or supported by these programs.[27]

Through this process civil society in Central America became a transnational battlefield. Segments of civil society linked to the global economy and transnational capital have expanded dramatically. The restoration of capital's hegemony discussed in the previous section rests on its increased organization and influence in civil society and on new forms of control over the state this influence has allowed it to exercise, expressed in part in the rise of powerful new private-sector associations and the change in the relationship between the public and the private spheres. The social role of the new economic groups associated with globalization has heightened dramatically, and their easy access to the state increases their social influence. But popular sectors have also become powerful contenders in civil society. Popular social movements and sectoral organizations in the region have become increasingly transnationalized, linking up across borders within the region and, more generally, in the global system at large, a theme to which I will return in the concluding chapter.[28] This contest for civil society is a transnational one in which the agency of contenders is less "national" than transnational.

In sum, and to recapitulate, in the 1980s, mass organizations challenged elite hegemony in civil society as the revolutionary movements fought for control of the state. The contest over the state was resolved in the 1990s in favor of the new dominant groups. This gave way after the end of the wars to an expanded battle for hegemony in civil society. This battle should be conceptualized as the particular local expression of the clash of social forces in global civil society. The pertinent question as regards analyses of globalization in Central America is if the agents of *transnational* capital have been able to establish their ideological hegemony in civil society to complement their domination in political society (the state). Domination in the state and ideological hegemony in civil society is the formula for a hegemonic project, as distinct from a project of domination in itself. Global capitalism has become the dominant social order in Central America. It is my contention, however, that transnational capital has *not* achieved its *hegemony* over the region. Civil society in Central America will remain for the foreseeable future a raging battlefield.

The NGO Phenomenon in Central America

"Civil society" has increasingly come to be identified with the welter of NGOs that have proliferated worldwide. The United Nations Development Program (UNDP) estimated that over 50,000 NGOs had sprung up in developing countries with external assistance by the late 1980s.[29] NGOs represent a particularly clear case of the transnationalization of civil society, since they are generally foreign-funded or linked with foreign counterparts or are themselves transnational organizations with local chapters, referred to as international NGOs (INGOs). By 1995, the United Nations reported the existence of nearly 29,000 of these INGOs, up from just a few hundred after WWII.[30] It is not possible here to fully visit the debate on NGOs and new modalities of international "aid," which are rightfully subjects of another study.[31] Here I am concerned with the relevance of these issues to social change in Central America.

As with civil society, the predominant view sees the rise of NGOs as a positive contribution to democracy and development worldwide. The crisis of the old development models, the decay of socialism, the communications revolution, and global economic growth, according to these accounts, have led to the rise of an educated middle class with a declining interest in the welfare state and a new concern for civic engagement.[32] "We are in the midst of a global 'associational revolution' that may prove to be as significant to the latter twentieth century as the rise of the national state was to the latter nineteenth," according to Lester Salamon.[33]

Yet the spread of NGOs is in fact linked to the shrinkage of the state and the transfer of former state functions to private groups as much at it is due to heightened levels of popular organization and mobilization from below. "The principal reason for the recent boom in NGOs is that Western governments finance them," notes *The Economist*. It adds, "This is not a matter of charity, but of privatization: many 'non-governmental' groups are becoming contractors for governments."[34] In this regard, the spread of NGOs is itself part of the transnational agenda. NGOs often work in close collusion with governments, with considerable organizational overlap, exchange of personnel, and financial links, making it difficult at times to distinguish the dividing line between the "private" and the "public." Even when they represent popular sectors or progressive causes, most NGO funding comes from governments, IFIs, and corporations, the latter either directly or through foundations or other conduits (in 1997 NGOs raised $5.5 billion from corporate donors, although indirect funding could be much higher). Notes *The Economist*, "Any distinction between the corporate and the NGO worlds is long gone."[35]

The rise of NGOs, according to Hulme and Edwards, is the deliberate result of donor consensus on what they term the "New Policy Agenda."[36] Ankei Hoogvelt similarly traces the new importance of NGOs in development issues to the "new aid agenda" that emerged in the 1980s and 1990s.[37] "Development aid" has always been an instrument of core powers to open up new markets, secure access to resources, and integrate post-colonial regions into the capitalist world economy. If this is still very broadly its purpose, the modalities of "development aid" have changed under globalization. The new aid agenda has unified what were previously disparate criteria among donor countries, according to Hoogvelt, and revolves around a shift from the state to NGOs as aid recipients and administrators of development programs. This "redirection of 'aid' away from national governments and towards civil society is a 'reverse agenda' "[38] that entails the rhetoric of "good government," "grassroots participation," "empowerment of local communities," "fostering of civil society," and "promoting democracy." This rhetoric, what Hoogvelt terms the "political conditionality" of the new aid agenda, stands out in that "*perforce* of its own conceptualization of good governance and an enabling environment, it wilfully and openly *does* meddle in the internal affairs of state, targeting a plurality of actors, be they non-governmental organizations, micro-businesses, local communities and grassroots organizations."

If the ideology of the earlier aid agenda was developmentalism, the ideology of this new agenda is "communitarianism" (a variant of classical individualism) in which local communities are to be responsible for their own development, no longer conceived as a national project organized by the state. Such an ideology serves the political goal of the IFIs and the transnational elite of directing popular aspirations into local "self-help" projects administered by NGOs and thus keeping the popular classes from placing demands on the neo-liberal state. The concept of development advanced by the NGO network is primarily a technical problem to be solved with a combination of technical skills (the NGOs) and financial resources (the IFIs). "Development programs" such as those typically administered by NGOs, whether of conservative or progressive persuasion in Central America, as we will see shortly, have become part of the project of capitalist modernization.

The AID's Private Enterprise Initiative explicitly called for the creation of NGOs as new conduits for international resources. "Changing priorities from support for government to support for the private sector are reflected as well in a shift of resource transfers," the AID noted in 1989. "Although most assistance is still directed through governments, in the Latin American region in 1985, almost half was run through non-governmental groups, half of these for-profit organizations. Further, AID no longer funds projects to assist parastatal development."[39] Thus the traditional government-to-government aid approach was to be replaced not only with the new government-to-private sector programs discussed earlier but also with government-to-NGO programs. The IFIs and other OECD governments undertook a similar shift. According to a senior World Bank official, the IFIs "are beginning to see NGOs as important vehicles for dissemination and constituency-building for a variety of macroeconomic efforts including structural-adjustment programs."[40] The Bank began to advocate the idea of "participatory development" and became involved in a major effort to bring NGOs into its projects, setting up in 1996 a "Civil Society Fund" with $100 million allocated that year to support NGOs.[41] International assistance to NGOs increased from $1 billion in 1970 to $7.2 billion in 1992,[42] representing a change from only 1.5 percent of total NGO income worldwide in 1970 to a full 30 percent by 1992. International support for NGOs, whether from specific states, the IFIs, or Northern NGOs, by definition drives the transnationalization of civil society. But more than this, in practice it transnationalizes the particular relations of power and domination exercised within local civil societies and also often gives the power to set agendas to those who control global resources.

The spread of NGOs in official development discourse is synonymous with the "empowerment" of civil society. But this discourse conflates NGOs and social movements. NGOs are not social movements but *alternatives* to them. They do not invariably defend popular sectors and may well represent dominant groups in civil society. Critical analyses have underscored how even when their stated mission is to be oppositional and critical, in practice NGOs tend to depoliticize society. They are less mobilizers than service providers that replace mass struggles and social movements with professional bodies that seek international funds to hold workshops, conduct training courses and conferences, and to *advocate* rather than to organize. In the more cynical of these critical accounts, although it may well be the more accurate, the NGOs, by administering the activities of popular sectors, dilute the latter's self-organization and militancy and thus become a structure of social control at the grassroots. Most NGO activities are limited to local projects and remove from the focus of popular social change the larger system to which these projects are subordinated. Even when NGOs are rooted in popular sectors and advance an alternative ideology and discourse they are severely constrained in their action by economic and political structures. Indeed, the real power of popular classes lies in their capacity to challenge *from without* these structures, whereas the NGOs channel the protagonism of these classes into those structures. They do not, for instance, encourage strikes, demonstrations, or civil disobedience, and they eschew organizing along class lines. Although they may criticize specific state policies, rarely do they offer a critique of capitalism. Specific policy demands may be of benefit to popular constituencies but they do not address underlying structural problems. NGO activity becomes reduced, at best, to negotiating better terms of incorporation into the existing—or the emergent transnational—order.

Political scientist James Petras lambasts "post-Marxists" or former activists of the Left who staff the legions of NGOs and in his view defend the neoliberal program in the name of "pragmatism." "The post-Marxists try to justify their organizational vehicles (NGOs) for upward mobility by arguing that they operate outside of the state and in 'civil society' when in fact they are funded by foreign governments to work with domestic governments," argues Petras. They "complement the activity of the neo-liberals by severing the link between local struggles and organization and national/international political movements. The emphasis on 'local activity' serves the neo-liberal regimes just right, as it allows its foreign and domestic backers to dominate macro socioeconomic policy and to channel most of the state's resources on behalf of export capitalists and financial interests."[43] Petras' account may be too much of a generalization, insomuch as it does not allow for the heterogeneity of NGOs or for the notion that the NGO network is itself contested terrain. And the prominent role of former leftists in the NGO network reflects as much the crisis of the Left as it does the initiative of transnational elites.

I suggest that the redirection in "aid" away from governments and towards NGOs is part of the broader shift discussed earlier, from domination within the state to hegemony in civil society. Without winning hegemony in civil society the transnational project cannot be stabilized. NGOs, as distinct from social movements per se, are becoming part of the new global capitalist historic bloc under construction, anchored in the hegemony of the transnational elite in global civil society. Such a hegemony *cannot* be based among dominant groups. It must achieve the consensual incorporation of subordinate groups around the world—women, workers, peasants, the indigenous, the poor. The transnational elite has recognized this potential of NGOs to defuse the demands and redirect grievances of popular sectors. "Unless this [people's participation in governance] is done, and done in time, the irresistible tide of people's rising aspirations will inevitably clash with inflexible systems, leading to anarchy and chaos," warned the UNDP.

"A rapid democratic transition and a strengthening of the institutions of civil society are the only appropriate responses. Among the many specific steps that must accompany such a transition, the two main ones are to decentralize more authority to local governments and to give much greater freedom to people's organizations and non-governmental organizations—instruments of people's participation."[44] Indeed, as Petras observes, "where the NGOs become firmly established the radical social movements have retreated . . . There is a direct relation between the growth of movements challenging the neo-liberal model and the effort to subvert them by creating alternative forms of social action through the NGOs."[45]

That individual NGOs may strive to play a counter-hegemonic role does not alter this assessment because the NGO phenomenon cannot be appraised at this individual level. I suggest that the global NGO network functions as a *structure* which mediates relations between the popular classes and states in the new transnational order. Dominant groups have operated through transnational networks that bring together the apparatus of a transnational state (IFIs, the UN agencies, the OECD countries, etc.) with national and international NGOs. This global network forms a multitiered structure that links together local, national, and transnational space. Popular and grassroots organizations at the local level become joined to the highest level of the global system through a number of intermediary links. The top tier of this pyramidal structure is the transnational state apparatus, which has organized a shift of resources from states to NGOs in civil society. The intermediary tier is comprised of national states and INGOs. The bottom tier is the individual NGOs that interact "in the field" with social movements and popular sectors.

In theory this network may be interactive. Yet the evidence from Central America, the Middle East, Africa, and elsewhere, suggests that transnational elites have been able to filter down their agenda through NGO networks with much more ease than popular classes can percolate their demands upward through this network.[46] These NGOs are becoming an important link in the chain managing the contradictions between an immizerated majority and dominant groups in the global order. Resources and programs are channeled downward as sites of grassroots social control are constructed. The NGO network in this formulation became a vehicle for penetrating civil society from the global system downward to the local grassroots. What seemed to be emerging at the turn of the century was a TNS-NGO structure that connected an expanding transnational civil society with the apparatus of an emergent TNS. Here, the same linkages that developed historically between political and civil society in nation-states are reproduced in new forms in the global system as linkages between the TNS apparatus with global civil society. The promotion of NGOs is a condition of "the dynamics of market expansion and the political imperatives associated with it," concludes Fowler. Aid to NGOs "supports and protects a globalization of the market" by creating an "international system of social welfare" in a way that parallels at the global level "the contribution of state welfare to historical processes of capital reproduction experienced by countries of the North."[47]

NGOs and the Popular Classes in Central America

During the 1980s and 1990s, diverse programs promoted by the TNS in Central America, especially the US state, created a vast network of organizations in civil society and NGOs that competed with popular social movements and advanced an alternative to their agenda of radical social change. After the wars, the NGO phenomenon reflected new forms of political intervention on the part of transnational forces involving a deeper penetration of civil society. Some 4,000 NGOs in Central America received an estimated $350 million annually from diverse sources during the 1990s.[48] This expansion of NGOs was linked directly to the efforts of transnational forces to manage the effects of social upheaval. NGOs were utilized, and often created, to deliver "humanitarian" aid and provide services as part of counterinsurgency and counterrevolutionary campaigns. Many of the NGOs involved cooperated with governments and military institutions. In particular, dozens of NGOs that set up operations in Central America were linked to more immediate US foreign policy goals in the 1980s, and in the 1990s these and other NGOs became involved in the broader project of globalization.[49]

Some former critics of US foreign policy embraced the incorporation of NGOs into international aid programs in Central America in the 1990s as a progressive departure from earlier practices. Haugaard, for instance, praises US AID programs in Central America in the 1990s for "[paying] greater attention to consulting with local partners." US officials "cast their net more broadly to consult with and fund progressive as well as conservative NGOs and individuals," and provided funding for peace processes, anti-poverty and "democracy promotion" programs.[50] The several billion dollars in reconstruction funds that flowed into Central America following pacification (see chapter two) did include programs to "promote democracy," implement peace accords, demobilize and integrate former combatants into civilian life, and so on. These programs helped to manage the aftermath of the revolutionary upheaval and to restore order. This apparently progressive change in the modality of development aid did not alter in any way the essential structures of global capitalism in the region and, it is my contention, were essential to *consolidate* the transnational order, which could not be imposed through the old methods of political exclusion and coercion. The following is a brief look at some of the internationally supported NGO programs during the transition.

In El Salvador, of some $50 million made available to NGOs in reconstruction aid by the international donor community in the wake of the 1992 peace accords, $17 million was assigned to the FEDISAL, a Salesian-run NGO whose board of directors was drawn from the elite. In contrast, NGOs identified with the FMLN were assigned a mere $300,000 (with perhaps $1.5 million more channeled through intermediaries).[51] Sociologist Adam Flint, in his field research on social movements and NGOs in El Salvador in the 1990s, found that "social movement leaders were under pressure [following pacification] to reinvent themselves and their organizations to conform to the demands of funders, and to the new technical and professional demands of a competitive NGO sector." As social movements became "NGO-ized," these movements "got bogged down in literally thousands of loosely coordinated projects, while few resources remained for the political task of transforming the priorities of the state." He continues, "There is a strong current of ideas emerging from US AID-funded NGOs (that is by no means limited to them) that has established the nostrum that the big problem with the Salvadoran NGO sector is that it is too politicized. Their proposed solution is for NGOs and movements to get out of politics and focus on technical questions and productive projects. The idea is that NGOs and movements should devote their energies to entrepreneurial reengineering and the search for insertion points in the world capitalist system following the 'rules of the game'."[52]

In Guatemala, the AID funded the umbrella Association of Development and Service Entities of Guatemala (ASINDES). "Most NGO activity in Guatemala is characterized by its paternalistic, welfare nature, in contrast to a style that could be more supportive of community organizing and popular education," notes Barry. "Neo-liberal economic strategies emphasizing the free market along with private initiatives that gained prominence in the late 1980s have combined to create new space for NGO operations. For the most part, however, the business sector rather than the popular sector has taken the lead in exploring new possibilities for NGOs in areas such as education and micro-enterprises."[53] Norsworthy documents the penetration of Honduras' dense civil society in the 1980s and 1990s by international, especially US, aid programs. "Largely because of the country's strategic role in US foreign policy in the 1980s, there was a rapid rise of nongovernmental organizations involved in development, refugee relief, business promotion, and social services ... Between the 1980s and 1990, the number of NGOs in Honduras tripled."[54]

In Nicaragua, the United States undertook a massive program in support of local NGOs and civic associations as the anti-Sandinista strategy shifted from military counterrevolution to political intervention, spending up to $40 million in an effort to build up anti-Sandinista forces in civil society between 1987 and the 1990 elections.[55] "Almost immediately following the election, several hundred NGOs appeared in Nicaragua," notes Macdonald. "Many of these resulted from the need for middle-class professionals who had previously worked in the state and lost their jobs because of cutbacks under the Chamorro regime to find new employment."[56] Petras' thesis is certainly supported by the Nicaraguan case, where dozens of NGOs set up by former Sandinista leaders provided little leadership for popular sectors in the 1990s, instead providing critical support to the Chamorro and Alemán regimes in the name of promoting "national reconciliation" and "stability," even as the popular sectors mounted widespread resistance to structural adjustment programs.

In Costa Rica, notes Macdonald, the strong state corporatist tradition in the post-WWII period resulted in "the absence of an independent civil society [which] allowed the US AID to place an indelible stamp on the character of the NGO scene . . . Through support of NGOs in Costa Rica, the United States hoped to ease social tensions, diminish the reliance of lower-class groups on the state and promote market-oriented production systems."[57] During the 1980s and 1990s the CINDE, a private-sector association created with AID support, in turn passed funds on for the establishment of numerous other NGOs. In 1987, the CINDE and the AID officially established the ACORDE as a funding and coordinating organization for NGOs. "The AID mission selected the members of ACORDE's board of directors," notes Silvia Lara in her country study, "all of whom were members of the country's business and professional elite."[58] The provision of funds by the AID and other international donors to Central American elite foundations and business associations for subsequent distribution to local NGOs was an important mechanism for establishing elite influence in civil society throughout the region and is an example of the multitiered TNS-NGO structure identified above.

Apart from the more explicitly political NGO activity, what development strategies did the 4,000-plus NGOs in Central America pursue? In her excellent study on NGOs, Macdonald identifies three main NGO strategies in the Isthmus (apart from purely humanitarian assistance): 1) "structural adjustment strategies"; 2) "micro-level basic needs strategies" and; 3) "redistributive economic transformation."[59] The first often involves NGO support for peasants and other producers to participate in non-traditional export production through provision of credit, technical assistance, training, and marketing support. Sectors thus displaced in the transition from the earlier model of development are here helped to integrate into the transnational model. This might be done through the paternalist approaches of mainstream NGOs or the approaches of progressive NGOs that stress "conscientization" or "political empowerment." But the intent of facilitating the insertion of subordinate groups into the new economic model remains the same. It is essentially a strategy of market integration. The second often constitutes "ad hoc responses to the pressing needs of the community since the majority of NGOs do not have an explicit and conscious strategy for macroeconomic development. This may take the form of subsistence production or provision of basic social services or infrastructural support (such as the construction of schools or health centers or potable water systems)."[60] Here, local development programs become privatized and NGOs substitute for the withdrawal of the neo-liberal state from social services. The third strategy is one that views "the micro-level approach as an inadequate response to the problems of underdevelopment, and insist[s] on the need for macroeconomic transformation . . . which orients the productive structures of the nation toward the basic needs of the poor majority and away from external dependence."[61]

This third strategy may, in theory, contribute to a counter-hegemonic alternative project. "What is the fundamental difference that distinguishes an NGO with a popular orientation from an NGO linked to the neo-conservative strategy?" asks a statement signed by members of the Regional Committee of Development Organizations (*Concertación Regional de Organismos de Desarrollo*). "Both implement small projects; they both link themselves with the most vulnerable social groups ... In reality, what distinguishes [them] ... lies in how they view the problem of power. In the first case, the activity of the NGO is oriented at provoking change in order to avoid modifications in the structure of power. In the second case, the NGOs try to promote changes in order to achieve transformations in the relation of social forces in a manner which favors the majority." Yet in practice many NGOs in Central America that proclaim the need for an alternative exhibit a productivist ideology and carry out programs oriented towards enhancing the ability of poor communities and marginalized groups to participate more effectively in the new economic model. "Although the aim and origin [of the neo-conservative and popular NGOs] may be totally distinct," asserts the director of one "progressive center" in Costa Rica, Oscar Jara, "isn't it serving to achieve the same objective: depoliticization, the isolation of small groups, the disenchantment with popular struggle?"[62]

As Macdonald notes in her case study on the Costa Rican Center for Development Training (CECADE), although it is described as a "progressive center" committed to the third strategy, it was dedicated in the 1980s to organizing "income generating" (market integration) strategies among peasants in northern Costa Rica, entailing technical and financial assistance for cocoa production (a NTAE) and other micro-enterprises such as pig-raising. There is "thus some evidence to support the view of critics of productive projects that such projects inevitably lead to emphasis on technocratic concerns and detract from more purely political and partici-patory work," Macdonald concludes, even though she sees the contribution of NGOs such as CECADE as positive.[63] By 1991, some of the more militant peasant unions in Costa Rica had become increasingly hostile towards the "progressive centers." "We think that the NGOs played an important role at the beginning," argued Carlos Hernandez, the leader of one of these unions, *Tierra Nuestra*. "At one point they helped in the process of organiz-ation of some groups. But the centers have gradually became [*sic*] an end in themselves and lost their original purpose, which was to help the popular organizations by channeling funds from the international NGOs. Their original sin was that they were born outside of the popular movement—from small groups of the left—not as a result of the suggestions of the popular movement."[64]

Structural Adjustment in Central America: Commodification, Financial Liberalization, and Proletarianization

One key mechanism in the spread of capitalist production relations through globalization is the wave of privatizations around the world. Akin to what Marx called "the alienation of the state," this process can be seen, theoretically, as one form of primitive accumulation that results in the commodification of formerly public spheres managed by states, such as utilities, transportation systems, education, health, and other social services. Privatization has been legitimated as necessary to reduce government spending and balance budgets, to free up resources for debt repayment, and because the private sector is "more efficient." The average number of privatizations in the Third World expanded ten-fold in the 1980s.[65] These privatizations, as Philip McMichael notes, accomplished two radical changes: 1) they reduced the state's ability to engage in economic planning and implementation, thereby privileging private-sector control; and 2) they extended the transnationalization of the ownership of assets in the Third World.[66]

Privatization has taken on different patterns and forms depending on particular local histories and conditions, ranging from how states and public sectors have evolved, to the relative size and composition of pre or non-capitalist spheres prior to globalization, political conditions, and the balance of social forces. The wave of privatizations in Central America from the 1980s into the twenty-first century has included national phone companies, electrical, water, gas and other public utilities, airports and seaports, sugar refineries, public banks, pensions, insurance services, tourist centers, and parastatal production enterprises. *Government itself* has been privatized to the extent that numerous state functions have been transferred to the private sector and converted from a social (public) to a market (private) logic. Health, education, and other services have become *for profit*, meaning that these activities are reorganized not in order to meet human needs but in order to make money.

Privatization results in a pure market-determined distribution. Given the highly skewed structure of income distribution, the process tends to aggravate inequalities and social polarization. It has predictably sparked sharp conflicts. In Nicaragua, the struggle of public university students against budget cuts became an annual affair in the 1990s at budget time each spring, resulting in pitched and often bloody street battles in which students and their supporters faced off against government security forces, paralyzing the capital and other cities for several weeks each year. In El Salvador, health workers repeatedly closed down the national health system in prolonged strikes, often escalating into violent confrontations with authorities, to protest privatization of services. In Costa Rica, the introduction by the government in early 2000 of legislation to privatize state electrical and telephone utilities triggered a week of violent nationwide protests, resulting in bloodshed and mass arrests—highly unusual for Costa Rica. The riots only ended when the government withdrew the legislation, at least temporarily, after concluding that the bloody media images would scare off international tourists and investors.

These incidents suggest that capitalist penetration and commodification contain within them the elements for continued political conflict and social instability in the Isthmus. Rising inequalities and new insecurities generate tensions that undermine the social peace necessary to sustain the transnational model. I shall explore these contradictions in the final chapter. In this section I examine several aspects of the process of privatization and commodification, including reform of the financial system, neo-liberal social policies, depeasantization, and informalization.

Financial Liberalization and the New Financial Elite

The deregulation and transformation of the global financial system is considered by many to be at the very heart of the globalization process. The dramatic developments in the world financial system have been widely discussed (and hotly debated) in recent literature on the global political economy. They include financial deregulation, the rise of hyper-mobile transnational finance capital as the hegemonic fraction of capital on a world scale, the apparent decoupling of financial from productive activity, and the frenzied global speculative bustle of "casino capitalism." These developments are often linked to technological changes and the possibilities opened up by informatics. But they clearly have more structural roots, in particular the Kondratieff cycles, in that the end of long swings (for example, of the post-WWII boom) is characterized by an abundance of capital savings and accumulated surplus values expressed in the hegemony of money capital and financial speculation.[67]

The existence of national financial regulation regimes and public banking sectors in many countries was problematic on several counts as transnational finance capital rose to prominence in the 1980s. State banking sectors served as the intermediaries between states and private capital accumulation, and flows of transnational capital often had to pass through, or at least conform to regulations imposed by, national banking systems. The risk was that these state banking systems would be unlikely to service emerging global accumulation circuits, financial as well as commercial and productive. These sectors, capturing savings and controlling the flow of financial resources, were susceptible to pressures from diverse local producers and consumers, such as peasants, artisans, and small and medium-sized manufacturing and commercial entrepreneurs oriented towards domestic markets and national accumulation processes.

Thus one of the first sectors targeted for reform was national banking systems. Financial deregulation became a core component of structural adjustment in Central America and elsewhere and a standard condition around the world for loans from the IFIs. In 1989, the World Bank dedicated its annual *World Development Report* to the theme of financial reform, calling for deregulation and liberalization around the world.[68] According to the neo-liberal doctrine, government controls on interest rates limit the growth of financial intermediation in economic development; lifting these controls will result in greater savings that can be channeled into investment. Moreover, interest rates set by the market will ensure that financial resources are channeled to the most "efficient" (profitable) investors, which in practice in Central America and other developing countries has meant restricting credit for peasant and small producers and expunging any alternative social logic from the financial system.

Given the history of state regulation of credit and capital flows and bank nationalization in pre-globalization development models, the banking system remained, in the words of the IMF Managing Director Michel Camdessus, the "Achilles heel of the global economy," since a sound banking system is essential for the rapid movement of finance capital through transnational circuits.[69] In much of Latin America, the neo-liberal states set about to privatize state banking systems or to facilitate the creation and expansion of private banking networks, often in conjunction with the IFIs. The goal was to create private banking systems that, shielded from public accountability, could bypass states in servicing transnational capital and their local contingents. Along with the privatization of banking systems, the neo-liberal program involved the creation of autonomous monetary authorities, free from both popular pressures and government bureaucracies. National banking systems linked to transnational finance capital were to become vehicles for channeling financial resources to economic sectors, both national and foreign, linked to global production circuits, including import-export trade, maquila manufacturing, and other export-oriented activities.[70]

As we have seen in chapter two, financial liberalization and the transformation of the banking system took on distinct forms in different Central American countries, but were an essential component of the region-wide globalization process. In Central America we have not generally seen the large-scale transnational financial speculation and the growth of "speculative bubbles" so characteristic of other "emerging markets," such as Mexico, Brazil, Thailand, South Korea, Russia, and so on. This is in part because of the region's greater marginality from the financial heights of accumulation in the global economy and its particular profile in the global division of labor as a source of new primary goods and cheap labor. The region does not offer a major outlet for the mass of globally mobile finance capital in currency and real estate speculation, or a significant market in equities, bonds, international securities and other tradable financial instruments. But this may simply be a matter of scale and timing. The Isthmus may well be behind other regions in Latin America and Asia, but it exhibits all the symptoms of the rise to hegemony of global finance capital, including a new transnationally integrated financial elite that has ascended in each republic, the spectacular growth of a dynamic new private banking industry, the creation of stock markets, and increasing speculative activity by these new financial agents, especially in real estate, in foreign currency trading, and in financial instruments tied to government and private debt. More important, however, the ascent of financial elites is tied to the importance that private banking assumed during the transitions as the mechanism for administering transnational credits and financing the changeover from the previous to the new model of accumulation. The AID, in its key strategy statement for Central America for the 1990s, called for banking reform in order to achieve a "greater reliance on market forces in allocating resources" and to "strengthen the ability of the financial sector to mobilize domestic resources and channel them efficiently to the most productive sectors of the economy," identified as the export sector and in particular non-traditional exports.[71]

The financial system in Central America originated to service the coffee trade in the latter half of the nineteenth century and has experienced transformation with each new rearticulation to the world economy. Reform of the incipient system established monetary stability in the 1920s, but this was followed by the turmoil of the Great Depression, which led to the creation of Central Banks in every republic in the 1930s and 1940s. By 1950 a financial regulatory regime was in place that would last until its dismantlement through adjustment programs in the latter two decades of the twentieth century.[72] The financial system benefited the most powerful economic groups and was plagued by favoritism and corruption. But these state financial systems nevertheless played a key role in promoting the post-WWII accumulation model, their role legitimated by the Keynesian notion, shared at that time by international institutions, that control of financial flows was of strategic importance to development. The banking system fomented agro-export expansion, regional integration around ISI industrialization, and the domestic market (especially food) production of peasants and smallholders. The state-directed banking system set interest and exchange rates, channeled credit to priority sectors, and even established amounts to be loaned to different productive activities. The banking system was nationalized in Costa Rica in 1948, in Nicaragua in 1979, and in El Salvador in 1980. State financial regulation and public banking sectors weakened the traditional oligarchies, strengthened the new industrialists, planters, and merchants of the post-WWII developmentalist era, and to some extent democratized access to credit.[73] But the financial liberalization of the 1980s and 1990s would diminish the influence of the economic agents that prospered in the previous development model and in turn promote the new economic groups of the transnational model.

The regional economic collapse of the early 1980s and the subsequent promotion by the AID and the IFIs of an alternative model gave impetus to new financial groups in Guatemala, Honduras, and Costa Rica (Nicaragua and El Salvador faced distinct circumstances of revolution and insurgency),

know as the "financieros," or financial houses. These groups made spectacular profits in the 1980s in speculation, especially in unofficial (and
often illegal) foreign exchange markets, and in informal financial markets.[74] Their call for financial liberalization was echoed by the AID and the
IFIs throughout the 1980s. By the earlier 1990s, the New Right technopols
had taken power in every republic. Moreover, presidents Cristiani of El
Salvador and Callejas of Honduras, as well as Antonio Lacayo of Nicaragua,
son-in-law of president Violeta Chamorro, and the Chamorro family itself,
were closely tied to banking interests (see below three). The World Bank,
along with the IDB, played the key role in promoting financial liberalization
in the 1990s.[75] The process was sweeping. It began in each country between
1991 and 1993 and concluded by 1995 (with the exception of Costa Rica,
where reforms had begun in 1984 (see chapter three)), entailing similar
measures and institutional reforms in every republic.[76] Banking reform
included the passage of laws giving Central Banks and bank superintendents independence from governments and prohibiting the Central Banks
from financing central government deficits. Other legal reforms replaced
direct control over banks with a more laissez-faire relaxed regulation
("prudent norms"); lifted capital and foreign exchange controls; stipulated
the privatization of state banks; ended state-subsidized credit programs;
deregulated interest rates;[77] legalized dollar accounts; established stock
exchanges in each republic; and created several private banks that could
bypass Central Banks entirely in receiving international credits for internal
redistribution to private-sector groups.

The de-nationalization of the state banking system and the creation of
private financial markets was crucial in Costa Rica and Nicaragua for the
implementation of the transnational agenda. In Costa Rica, the state banks
were not privatized outright, given strong political opposition and legal
obstacles. Instead, the creation of a "parallel state" involved ongoing legal
reforms and gradual privatization alongside the capitalization by the AID
and other IFIs of a new private banking sector which gradually replaced
the state system in the allocation of financial resources.[78] This process
began in 1984 and concluded in 1995. A similar process unfolded in
Nicaragua, where the institutional and political legacy of the Sandinista
revolution made outright privatization of these banks difficult. The reform
strategy was to gradually supplant state credit policies and savings capacity
through decapitalization and the creation of a parallel set of private
commercial banks, a process which began in 1991 and continued into the
twenty-first century.[79] In El Salvador, the banking system, nationalized in
1980, was re-privatized outright between 1991 and 1994 under the ARENA
administrations. In both Guatemala and Honduras, structural adjustment
and public-sector reform led to the spectacular growth of the private
banking industries. By 1995 there were thirty private commercial banks in
Guatemala, fourteen of which were established after 1990. In Honduras, of
the twenty private banks, six began operations after 1990. In Costa Rica,
most of the twenty-four private banks in existence in 1995 had been created

since 1980. In Nicaragua, all eleven private banks were established after 1990. And in El Salvador, six of the twelve private banks were founded after 1991.[80]

The Central American stock markets were still in their infancy in the early twenty-first century. The Costa Rican exchange was established in 1977, the Guatemalan in 1987 (although second indexes were founded in both countries in the 1990s), the Salvadoran in 1992, the Nicaraguan in 1992, and the Honduran in 1993. Reflecting their disproportionate economic weight and also the late entry of the latter three countries, the Costa Rican and Guatemalan exchanges accounted for some 80 percent of the $22 billion in transactions registered in 1995. In his study on financial reform, Trevor Evans notes that the new commercial banks were the principal participants in these stock markets, and that these markets were in the process in the mid-1990s of regional integration.[81] The stock markets in the Isthmus have not been systematically studied. But their establishment can be expected to allow for a more fluid integration of the region into the global economy and facilitate the melding of "national" and "foreign" property holdings into simply *transnational* ownership of the region's capitalist assets.

Reflecting the general approach adopted by all the republics, the Guatemalan government in the early 1990s pursued a strategy of fiscal solvency based on attracting short-term financial investors. The government issued new bonds with high interest rates to generate an inflow of foreign capital flows and also sought to attract capital into short-term transactions in financial instruments on the stock market (such transactions represented over 80 percent of all exchanges in 1994).[82] The policy did result in an inflow of foreign exchange, in part the repatriation of Guatemalan capital that had left the country with the onset of the crisis in the late 1970s. Subsequent government payment on bond issues accrued to new financial groups who pressured for complete deregulation (achieved in 1995) and who began to acquire increasing influence with the elite. By 1992, debt servicing on the domestic debt surpassed the external debt as a proportion of government expenditures.[83] Combined with expanded consumption taxes (know as the IVA), which fell disproportionately on the poor and working classes and a lowering of corporate taxes, fiscal reform in Guatemala had the effect of redistributing wealth upwards, and within the elite, towards the financial sector. Yet Guatemala in the early 1990s also caught up on foreign debt payments, which had been in arrears, and moved towards fiscal solvency (although progress was upset for other reasons).[84] This is the pattern found generally in neo-liberal restructuring, whereby behind the improvement in macroeconomic indicators lie income polarization and a redistribution of wealth towards new class groups.

The region's other governments also hoped that high private bank interest rates, the stock exchanges, and the lifting of capital controls, would attract a mass of foreign money capital into the Isthmus. Evans reports that short-term capital inflows were substantial in El Salvador, Costa Rica, and Guatemala, surpassing in the latter two countries $500 million per year in the early 1990s.[85] This influx of transnational finance capital is a similar story as elsewhere. It does not represent fixed productive investment; it has alighted in the region in search of quick profits and may be withdrawn just as quickly as it arrived.[86] The lifting of interest, exchange-rate, and capital controls by Central American states and their determination by global market forces eliminated these states' ability to utilize the financial system for any planning that might have offset world market forces. Combined with the reforms designed to attract mobile (and volatile) money capital into local banks, bond, and equity markets, it becomes evident that the integration of a reformed Central American financial system into the global financial system provided a powerful new avenue through which the global economy exercised its structural power over the region.

In every republic the new financial elite had a hand in the reorientation of state policies towards restructuring and globalization. Financial reform provides one illustration of how transnationally oriented groups in the Isthmus were able to take advantage of new opportunities opened up by the global economy and to utilize local states in pursuing these opportunities. In three countries the presidents and their inner circles were themselves direct representatives of the new banking groups. In the case of El Salvador, Cristiani was able to use executive power to gain advantage for himself and his inner cohorts in the privatization of the state banking system in the early 1990s. Cristiani himself, along with his wife, became the principal owners of Banco Cuscatlán, the second largest in the country. In Honduras, the liberalization of interest rates promoted by Callejas provided a bonanza for the banks, including the Banco Mercantil, of which Callejas was a principal shareholder. In Nicaragua in 1990, the well-known banker, Haroldo Montealegre, became economic advisor to the incoming Chamorro government and drafted the "Program for Stabilization and Structural Adjustment for Nicaragua, 1990–93," which provided the blueprint for financial reform and the establishment of private banks. Following the adoption of the plan, Montealegre resigned from his post to establish the Banco Mercantil, the first of the new private entities. Antonio Lacayo, the son-in-law of President Chamorro and the Minister of the Presidency (a post from which he served as *de facto* prime minister), was closely associated with the largest private bank in the country, the Banco de America Central. Lacayo's father was chair of the bank's board of directors, and Lacayo himself acquired interests in three of the new banks established after 1990.[87]

Throughout the Isthmus the new industry exhibited an oligopolist structure, interlocked with commercial houses and controlled by leading capitalist families. In Nicaragua, the two principal capitalist groups, BANIC and BANAMERICA, were disarticulated following the 1979 revolution but were able to transfer much of their capital to offshore accounts in the Caribbean and Miami. In the 1990s they achieved a fairly rapid and far-reaching reconstitution through the new private banking system, according to a study on "new business groups" conducted by Nicaraguan researcher José Luis Velázquez.[88] Research into the principal economic groups in Honduras shows that six families grouped around the Banco Atlántida, the biggest private bank, controlled 56 percent of the country's private capital, agglomerated into interpenetrated industrial, agricultural, and service concerns.[89] It should be recalled that Banco Atlántida is the banking group for the power transnational fraction of the Honduran capitalist class based in the Atlantic coast city of San Pedro Sula, heavily involved in maquiladora production and other transnational commercial and service activities (see chapter two). Costa Rican sociologist Carlos Sojo has researched the financial system and changes in the composition of the dominant bloc in Costa Rica, demonstrating that structural adjustment has weakened the primary and secondary sectors of the economy to the benefit of new commercial and financial sectors. This has facilitated a shift within the capitalist class in power and influence towards commercial, service, and financial groups. "Practically every powerful economic group has its own bank" around which it is organized, he notes.[90] The rise of new financial groups in El Salvador with the ascent to power of President Cristiani in 1989 is notorious. Several studies have shown how some fractions within the old dominant groups displaced in the 1980s by agrarian reform and bank nationalization shifted their capital into new commercial and financial activities in the 1990s. "In the process, some groups who previously were of secondary importance [within the capitalist class], such as Cristiani himself, have been able to increase their standing," notes Evans in summarizing these studies, "while other families from the old dominant groups who left the country during the war were unable to transfer their capital to the dynamic new urban economic sectors and have been relatively marginalized."[91]

The rearticulation of Central America to the world economy through globalization has been a process increasingly mediated by the financial sector. Deeper integration into the global economy results in the disruption of traditional established communities, in the contraction of domestic demand, and a heightened concentration of wealth and productive resources in groups tied to the external sector and to global accumulation circuits. In turn, the sources of profitability in Central America, as elsewhere, have shifted from productive to commercial and financial activities as outlets for new investment. The high real interest rates made possible by financial deregulation have helped shift the distribution of profits from productive (and commercial) enterprises to banks.[92] There has been a relative growth of employment in the commercial and financial sectors (see table 4.1). Private bank capital has been the principal beneficiary of financial liberalization, although it has allowed new commercial sectors to flourish as well, while access to credit has been restricted for industrial and traditional agricultural producers, and above all peasants and smallholders, as discussed below. Financial liberalization thus contributed to social polarization. The reforms became a powerful instrument for reorienting the Central American economy and class structure, shifting power relations among different social and economic groups, and integrating the region into global structures. Financial services appear to have displaced tra-

Table 4.1.   Distribution of Commercial Bank Credit by Economic Activity
(percentage of total)

	Agriculture and Ranching	Industry	Commerce	Services	Other
Costa Rica					
1990	19	44	17	7	13
1993	12	25	26	17	20
1995	8	24	27	19	22
Guatemala					
1990	16	29	29	9	17
1993	10	15	36	11	28
1996	10	9	37	8	36
Honduras					
1990	18	23	36	9	14
1993	13	19	41	9	18
1996	10	20	46	7	17
Nicaragua					
1990	24	32	44	0	0
1993	34	27	40	0	0
1996	17	29	41	0	13
El Salvador					
1989	12	11	63	2	12
1993	16	25	34	5	20
1996	9	21	41	5	24

Source: Consejo Monetario Centroamericano, *Boletin Estadistico 1996*, San José,
1997. As compiled from Evans, *Liberalizacion Financiera*, Annex 3.1–3.5,
pp. 116–20.

ditional agro-export and industrial production as the core of accumulation,
reflective of the hegemony of finance capital globally. "It is noteworthy that
in countries such as El Salvador and Nicaragua," observes Evans, "the young
men and women of the most dynamic ruling class families are to be found
not in production but rather, having returned from doctoral studies in the
United States, they are now directing the new private banks."[93]
   The "terciarization" of the Central American economy indicates the rise
worldwide of the service sector around which economic activity is organized. Financial liberalization has combined with the elimination of trade
barriers to spark an import boom in the region, financed in part by the
banks. The commercial sector was one of the few able to pay the high
interest rates associated with financial deregulation. Table 4.1 indicates the
change in the distribution of credit by sector; the relative decline for

agriculture, ranching, and industry, and the favorable position of the commercial sector.

Neo-Liberal Social Policies: The Privatization of Social Reproduction

The privatization of social services in Central America and around the world represents a structural change towards the *privatization of social reproduction* immanent to the extension of commodity relations into public, family, and community spheres which previously remained outside of the logic of exchange value. The conversion of these services into *for profit* and often privately run activities is accompanied by a shift from the ideology of the old Keynesian New Deal and developmentalist social structures of accumulation, which were legitimated precisely by the state's role in social reproduction, to ideologies of individualism and communitarianism that legitimate the withdrawal of the state and capital from reciprocal commitments to labor and society. Social services, and the very possibility of social reproduction, move from being a right of workers and citizens to a privilege based on one's ability to pay in accordance with a distribution of income determined by unmediated market forces.

But the actual mechanics of privatizing social reproduction rarely involve an outright withdrawal of the state. More typically—and this has been the predominant model in Central America—what takes place is a *delegation* of state/public functions to private capital. Privatization in this model may not involve the actual sale by the state or the acquisition by private capital of social service systems, such as the public education, health, or sanitation systems. Rather, through a variety of institutional mechanisms, public responsibilities are transferred to private entities. This delegation, as Pablo Gentili explains, takes two forms. One is the "delegation of financing" and the other is that of "supply."[94] In the first, the more common variant, individuals and families no longer receive services for free, and may choose to pay fees either to public institutions, which are defunded and generally deteriorate dramatically in the restructuring process, or to private institutes, which tend to proliferate. In the second, the state transfers the administration of social services to the private sector and pays private entities to provide the particular service. Privatization of social services in the Isthmus has involved a combination of these two variants. There has been a wholesale privatization of some facilities and the proliferation of new private facilities alongside defunded public ones. Combined with income polarization, the process has led to an increasing bifurcation of social services into high-quality provision for the better-off and a deterioration of services for a majority. The living standards of popular classes whose social reproduction is dependent on a social wage (the public sector) have deteriorated, while privileged middle and upper classes become exclusive consumers of social services channeled through private networks. The rise of a bifurcated society in Central America—"one rich, one poor"—is a general trend worldwide and mirrors the same bipolarization of global society.

In Costa Rica, which once boasted one of the most advanced public health and educational systems in the developing world, private facilities began to proliferate in the 1980s and 1990s. "The compensatory emphasis in social policy since the early 1980s has had palpable, detrimental effects on earlier efforts to universalize access to health and educational services," observes Lara, noting the rise of contagious diseases such as measles and meningitis, the increase in cases of hepatitis and diarrhea, and outbreaks of malaria and other diseases associated with the decline in the potable water and sewerage systems and preventative health services.[95] In Nicaragua, the cutback and privatization of social services was felt with particular severity because these services had been a centerpiece of the Sandinista revolution. The health, educational, and other social gains achieved in the 1980s suffered a dramatic reversal in the 1990s under the application of neo-liberal social policies. With the defunding of public health programs, cholera, malaria, measles, and other diseases that had been eradicated or nearly eradicated reappeared and reached epidemic proportions. The infant mortality rate, brought down to 50 per 1,000 births in the 1980s, had risen to 83 per 1,000 by 1992.[96] Reconstruction in El Salvador after the war reinforced the pattern of bifurcated services, as evidenced in the chronic budgetary crises of the public health system and steady decline in services alongside the proliferation of luxury private hospitals and clinics providing world-class standards of service.[97] While such private facilities multiply, in public hospitals throughout the region catering to the poor, patients are often required to bring their own sheets and food due to a lack of resources. Social indicators in Guatemala, although the worst in Central America and already appalling before the transition, had begun to rise in the 1960s and 1970s only to decline once again in the 1980s and 1990s in the face of repeated budget cutbacks. In one telling incident in 1992, hospital workers at Guatemala City's notorious municipal hospital, where patients often die due to unsanitary conditions, walked off the job because the facility had run out of medicines and supplies and because running water and electrical power had been suspended. "This is not a strike. There is no budget," explained the banner they erected.[98]

In the 1990s the World Bank became the main source of international health funding, surpassing both the World Health Organization and UNICEF.[99] The Bank called for a reduction in public health expenditures, implementing user fees, scaling back the involvement of the public sector, privatizing services, and emphasizing the responsibility of the individual for health. The Bank and other IFIs also promoted an expanded role for transnational corporations in healthcare throughout the world. This has taken place through the spread of transnational corporate "health management organizations" (HMOs, also known as managed care organizations).[100] These policies were rationalized with the characteristically simplistic—and ideological—argument that "long-term growth and economic progress benefits health in the long run"; in turn a free market in health, as in every other area of social life, provides the best condition for economic growth.[101] The Bank's claim that public health sectors are "inefficient" was entirely beside the point, since adjustment was intended not to improve the efficiency of the public sector but to limit its role. Besides, arguments such as these in favor of converting services into profit-making activities run by the private sector ignore that access to private services is in the first place determined by income distribution, already highly unequal and aggravated by the adjustment process.

Austerity programs and adjustment policies led to escalating poverty rates in the 1990s in many developing regions. In Latin America, the number of people living in poverty went from 118 million in 1980, or about a third of the region's total population, to 196 million in 1990, representing nearly half of the population.[102] Alarmed over the social unrest resulting from neo-liberal reforms—the infamous "IMF riots"[103]—the IFIs began to encourage governments implementing structural adjustment to launch externally funded social programs to give a "human face" to the reforms. The first such program was created in Bolivia in 1986 with a World Bank loan. By the 1990s "social compensation" funds had become a central feature of IFI reform policy.[104] Each program in Latin America came to include an adjunct "social fund," such as Mexico's well-known Pronasol (or Solidaridad), the Solidarity and Social Investment Fund in Chile, and so on, usually financed jointly by local governments and the IFIs, putatively intended to "target" the poor. The key institutional mechanism of what came to be called in development discourse the "new social policy" was the privatization of social services which were earlier universalized and administered by states, and their decentralized administration as charities through new NGOs acting in partnership with local governments and supranational organizations, as discussed earlier. Here, social policies that formerly corresponded to the national state became de-nationalized and transnationalized.

But the poverty to be managed by these programs was considered in the conception of the "new social policy" to be a pathology, not a consequence of the economic system itself. "Hence it isolates poverty from the process of capital accumulation and economic development," according to Carlos Vilas. "Social policy is reduced to a limited series of measures intended to compensate the initial negative effects of structural adjustment among certain sectors of the population."[105] These programs have not been able to ameliorate the spread of poverty and deprivation. They operate within the logic of the neo-liberal model, largely as temporary relief to those marginalized by the model, without modifying the structural causes of that marginalization. The challenge is how to *manage* the social fall-out of restructuring and depoliticize the problem of inequality. The aim of these programs was to contain the discontent generated by adjustment programs through the incorporation of grassroots sectors from the "bottom up" into self-help and charitable programs in synchronization with state and trans-national activity that operates from the "top down."

Social Investment Funds (FIS) were created in El Salvador, Nicaragua, and Honduras in 1990 and in Guatemala in 1993.[106] By the middle of the decade these Central American FIS were handling several hundred million dollars provided by the World Bank, the United Nations Children's Fund, the IDB, the AID, and other bilateral donors and international charities. They consisted largely of public-works employment programs providing people with short-term employment in building classrooms, latrines, health clinics and other small-scale infrastructure projects around the country. Those displaced by structural adjustment were thus brought temporarily into the market as contract laborers and as consumers. Each Fund operated independently of government ministries, and was controlled centrally by an Administrative Council appointed by the office of the president and accountable directly to the executive and to the IFIs that provided financing. Private-sector contractors, often in partnership with local NGOs, were paid by the FIS to actually undertake the infrastructural and construction projects. These Funds were therefore a further privatization of public services: state ministries were removed from activities formerly under their jurisdiction and private capital was provided with funds and labor by transnational state institutions and their local offices. (The FIS were allegedly more "efficient" than governments in that there was no government bureaucracy as an intermediary between funds and projects, although the actual bureaucratic intermediation was simply transferred out of the country to the transnational state apparatus.) Although the "new social policy" utilized the rhetoric of "empowering" local communities, decision-making was centralized in the hands of FIS officials attached to presidential offices and outside consultants representing the IFIs, while grassroots constituencies in fact exercised little or no control over projects.[107]

Neo-Liberal Education and the "Human Capital" Thesis

Meanwhile, educational systems in Central America have been transformed through the neo-liberal program under the auspices of the IFIs and other transnational actors. In its ideological expression, this transformation of the educational system responded to one of several new concepts that became popularized in globalization and development discourse in the 1990s, among them, "human capital." At a 1993 conference sponsored by the UNDP and the IDB in Washington, the IFIs concluded that economic reform should be accompanied by long-range investments to improve "human capital" in Latin America, that is, the skills, knowledge, and technical training of the region's labor force.[108] Here, a brief theoretical excursion is useful. "Human capital" theory views labor as a commodity whose "value" (and therefore earnings) may be increased through "investment" in improving skills, knowledge, and technical training. The assumption is that poverty is a result of a deficiency in human capital and that inequality can be explained by the unequal distribution of such capital.[109] Behind this is the (flawed) assumption of neo-classical economics that the market may result in *equality* so long as those entering it bring with them the same set of individual skills and capabilities. Applied to neo-liberal development claims, the supposition is that an increase in the educational, technical, and cultural skills of a given population is central to its development prospects.

The belief that poverty and underdevelopment is to be explained not by structural factors but by the individual and collective attributes of those experiencing this condition is not new. Earlier modernization and related political culture theories in the 1950s–1970s, having removed power relations from the analysis of underdevelopment, advanced the proposition that the attributes of the poor, in particular their cultural and behavior patterns, explain poverty and underdevelopment, and that development would result from a modification of such attributes. This "blame the victim" reasoning found its First World counterpart in the "culture of poverty" thesis in the Western academy that expunged from the analysis (or considered of secondary importance) racism and the larger social forces of power, inequality, and marginalization, in attempting to explain the poverty of oppressed groups in the core, such as African-Americans. One version of the thesis, dual labor market theory as elaborated by its more conservative adherents, economists Peter Doeringer and Michael Piore, concluded that African-Americans constituted a poorly rewarded and marginalized sector of the labor force because of their own cultural underdevelopment. The solution would be to raise their cultural level and modify their personal behavior patterns in order to close the gap in the dual labor market.[110] (A more radical interpretation of segmented labor markets advanced by David Gordon and his colleagues demonstrated that such markets are structurally grounded in a process of capital accumulation that differentiates distinct population segments and structures systematic inequalities, and that behavioral responses are derivative and often entirely rational within the logic of this structure.[111])

Intrinsic to the "culture of poverty" thesis was the "human capital" claim that the IFIs and other representatives of the transnational elite revived, updated to the conditions of the global economy, and incorporated into recent development theory. The proposition contained in the "human capital" argument that became popularized in official discourse was that each country could maximize its possibility of attracting investment by offering transnational capital a productive labor force through raising the human capital of its population. This development strategy reflected the "competitive state" thesis in globalization literature,[112] according to which each country must become "competitive" in the global market by competing with every other national population in the effort to attract transnational capital as the putative motor of development. Those most rewarded will be populations who can best sell themselves to transnational capital (more precisely, those states that can best sell their populations). As agents of development, neo-liberal state managers are expected to become the "pimps" of global capitalism, making their labor forces attractive to transnational corporations and therefore "marketable" in the global economy. David Mulford, Undersecretary of the Treasury in the first Bush administration, explained: "The countries that do not make themselves more attractive will not get investors' attention. This is like a girl trying to get a boyfriend. She has to go out, have her hair done up, wear makeup . . ."[113] How else could one explain a 1990 advertisement in *Bobbin,* the trade magazine of the textile industry—which showed a photo of a Salvadoran woman working at a sewing loom with the caption "You can hire her for 57 cents an hour. Rosa is more than just colorful. She and her co-workers are known for their industriousness, reliability, and quick learning"[114]—other than as an impulse to prostitute local populations embedded in the very structure and logic of global capitalism and its institutions?

The "competitive state" thesis is an ideological construct that serves the interests of transnational capital. Each country's effort to create the most propitious conditions in its own territory for global profit-making places downward pressure worldwide on wages and general working conditions and for a lifting of social restrictions on capital—what Brecher and Costello call the worldwide "race to the bottom."[115] The thesis, however, is legitimated by the assumptions of the "human capital" argument: the more human capital a country disposes of the better it is able to attract higher value-added activities in the global economy. In fact, there is no necessary correlation between educational levels and wages and living standards outside of particular historical contexts, nor is there any reason to assume that the presence of more skilled labor will lead capital to develop more skills-intensive jobs. But does the privatization of social services not contradict the call for increasing human capital? Neo-liberal states are expected to develop policies to raise the general educational level of the population and at the same time to cut back on social spending and privatize education. It is in the surface discourse but not the actual content of transnational elite policy that the proposition appears contradictory. The diverse activities of transnational capital do require trained personnel; population clusters with the right mix of skills in different localities and regions within the global division of labor. This is not at all incompatible with cutbacks and the privatization of education. In fact, the neo-liberal transformation of educational systems is conducive to the need of transnational capital for a global labor pool exhibiting a highly stratified mix of skills and training. The strategy seeks to shape each educational system in distinct countries and regions so that its "output" will conform more closely to the market's need for labor.

In the late 1980s and early 1990s, the transnational elite set out to forge an international consensus around educational reform as a social policy concomitant to global economic restructuring. Two positions emerged in the international development community on educational policy. The World Bank and the regional banks argued for "prioritizing primary education" and "private initiatives" in Third World educational systems, while the United Nations Educational, Science, and Cultural Organization (UNESCO, the UN agency that specialized in providing technical support to national education systems), promoted the development of integrated educational systems in lieu of the contribution that multiple educational and skills levels makes to development.[116] In the 1980s, spending on education in Latin America had fallen from $164 per student annually to $118.[117] By the end of that decade, the World Bank was able to sideline the UNESCO in the debate, taking over not only the financial aspects of education at a world level, but also its technical, conceptual, and orientation aspects, integrating them into official development policy. The following year, in 1990, the Bank began to draft educational policy reforms for debtor countries and to fund these reforms as part of its lending activity. The absolute priority accorded to primary education became a consensus in the international development community in the 1990s. By 1997, over 450 World Bank educational advisors were staffed in educational ministries around the world.[118]

Hence the new educational strategy of the transnational elite in Central America and elsewhere, articulated in World Bank and IDB policy statements and in an array of funding and technical programs, was to prioritize primary education within public school systems and to simultaneously privatize education, including the introduction of school fees.[119] The Bank did not recommend increasing public spending on public education; rather, it proposed diverting money that used to go toward financing high schools and universities in order to expand access to primary schooling. Critics saw such a strategy as "locking" the educational system in those regions set aside as reserves of cheap labor for the global economy, such as Central America and Africa, into the function of providing essential literacy and numeracy skills and no more.[120] Universities are not necessary for the supply of cheap labor for the global economy, but the transnational model does require primary education because it guarantees a cheap yet minimally skilled labor force.

The social nature of work has also helped determine the structures and content of education. Performing the types of work that correspond to Central America's participation in the global economy, such as maquiladora assembly, agricultural labor, or tourism and other service provisions, does not require a highly educated work force. Very little of this work requires advanced education; in fact, much of it can be performed with nothing more than primary education. This particular set of economic activities requires a large group within the labor force composed of docile workers with minimal literacy and numeracy skills. And it *also* calls for smaller groups of skilled technicians and managers. What is the appropriate "mix" of educational levels required for this type of economic model? What educational "output" would conform most closely with the needs of the labor market in Central America? Primary public education may provide the first category of worker, an abundance of workers with minimal literacy and numeracy skills, while high-tuition private universities, the second category, skilled technicians and managers.

The neo-liberal transformation of the educational system in Central America in the 1990s involved the defunding of public universities; their transformation into money-making institutions promoting technical and business-oriented careers while traditional disciplines in the social sciences and humanities were increasingly marginalized; the introduction of tuition in formerly free public schools; budget cuts and the privatization of secondary education; and a dramatic expansion of private schools, particularly private universities. This *elitization* of higher education has led to a dual system: well-funded private universities service the better-off sectors, while underfunded public universities in a state of disrepair service the poor. Private institutions have attracted a growing number of students and begun to dominate national university systems. In Nicaragua, sixteen private universities opened between 1990 and 1997, where tuition payments averaged $200 per month, nearly five times more than the minimum wage. These institutions had a combined enrollment of 30,000 students by the end of the decade, compared to the 50,000 who attended public and state-subsidized institutions.[121] The World Bank, in one of its first programs in Nicaragua following the electoral defeat of the Sandinistas, provided $38 million for an educational reform program that began the complete transformation of the educational system under the supervision of Minister of Education Humberto Belli, an important ideologue of the transnational fraction in Nicaragua.[122] In El Salvador, at least thirty-five new private universities were established in the 1980s and early 1990s, while the public University of El Salvador suffered severe budget cutbacks and a deterioration of services.[123] Among the slew of elite private universities that sprang up during this period were the Autonomous University of Central America (UACA), the Higher Institute of Business Administration (ISAE), the Higher School of Business Administration (ESAE), and the Technical Institute of Business Administration (ITAE).[124]

Neo-liberal restructuring of the educational system in Central America has aligned these systems more closely to the market's need for labor. The broader implications of this type of educational reform can be garnered from Harry Braverman's famous study *Labor and Monopoly Capital*, which called attention to the separation of conception and execution in the labor process under capitalism.[125] "Increasing technological productivity and the ongoing cheapening of labor power constitutes a worldwide process," notes Mexican sociologist Pablo Gonzalez Casanova, "one that is closely tied to the divide between those who conceive of the tasks of work and those who carry them out."[126] The dissolution of the natural unity of the two proceeds in hothouse fashion under the new labor conditions of flexible accumulation associated with globalization. This has given rise to two types of education: education for those who conceptualize and education for those who carry out the tasks of work. But there are also political implications. Since the early twentieth century public universities in Central America have been platforms for political challenges to the status quo, contributing intellectuals and leaders for popular movements. These hotbeds of dissent have performed the role of national "think-tanks" for alternative development and social change projects. Defunding and transforming public higher education, including phasing out liberal arts subjects such as sociology and philosophy, contributed to depoliticizing the population.

Even at the remaining public universities, new technocratic rectors were appointed to turn them into money-making institutions offering careers predominantly in business administration, accounting, and law.[127]

The privatization of social reproduction has generated new contradictions whose management has become a concern for agents of the transnational project. Even by the World Bank's *own* logic, its health and educational policies are irrational. For instance, forcing poor households to pay for health services takes money away from other basic needs, such as food, and is likely to have an adverse effect on household health. And expanding primary education requires higher education to train additional teachers for primary school. Social policy in the capitalist system performs the two functions of supporting capital accumulation by reproducing the labor force and of legitimating the social order by providing vital services not otherwise dispensed by private capital. Public services such as education, health care, housing, and worker training in Keynesian models of accumulation relieved private capital of the need to invest in social reproduction and were considered an element of investment rather than an expense. But in the neo-liberal ideology the market is expected to provide social services under conditions of economic growth so long as it is unrestrained by states. Social policy moves from being a government investment to an expense and the concept of social development gives way to that of social compensation. But it is not clear how the new social structure of accumulation will meet the two traditional functions of social policy of providing for accumulation and legitimation.[128]

Rural Transformation, Depeasantization, and Urbanization

The disappearance of pre-capitalist classes is accelerating in Central America and signals a broader worldwide process brought into sharp relief under globalization. Are we in the twilight of the primitive accumulation of capital on a global scale? The immense variety of agrarian social forms certainly defies empirical generalization. But running through the study of these forms as a constant theme is the world historic process of capitalist expansion and transformation of agrarian societies, although how this process manifests itself in different times and places is tremendously varied. Referring to the dissolution of "natural" economies, Karl Marx noted that "the expropriation of the agricultural producer, of the peasant, from the soil is the basis for the whole process. The history of expropriation, in different countries, assumes different aspects, and runs through its various phases in different orders of succession and different periods."[129] But the more complete displacement of peasant and smallholder production by capitalist agriculture is a relatively recent development in the history of capitalism. During the period of the growth and consolidation of capitalism, pre-capitalist relations of production predominated in agriculture, whether it was unfree labor in Eastern Europe, the Caribbean and Atlantic seaboard, peasant tenancy in Western Europe and North America, or various forms of peasantry and peon or semi-serfdom relations in Latin America and Asia. It was not generally until the twentieth century, and especially the post-WWII period, that capitalism came to transform rural relations in the world capitalist system into distinctively capitalist relations. For Hobsbawm, "the most dramatic and far-reaching social change of the second half of the [20th] century . . . is the death of the peasantry."[130]

This transformation sparked raging debates in the social sciences on the future of the peasantry and capitalism. Would the spread of capitalism inexorably do away with the peasantry? The "disappearance" thesis maintained that peasants are bound sooner or later to be transformed into wage workers or capitalist farmers. The "permanence" thesis, in turn, argued that peasant economies for various reasons do not abide by the laws of capitalism and exhibit a logic of their own that results in the survival of the peasantry and in the conditions of the peasantry's reproduction in the countryside.[131] While it is not possible here to revisit these debates, globalization certainly poses new challenges for the topic. A good many studies, as Farshad Araghi observes in his work on *global depeasantization*, fail "to understand local social phenomena [the peasantry within a country] as simultaneously global processes . . . nation-centered analysis prevails in peasant studies."[132]

Araghi divides depeasantization in the post-WWII period into two phases. He shows that in the first, from 1945 to 1973, there was a *relative* rather than an absolute decline in Third World peasant sectors, due to diverse "nation-state oriented programs" such as agrarian reform and state subsidies in the developmentalist period that offset in part the effects of world market forces. The world food regime organized by the United States in this period, in particular the expansion of agro-exports alongside food aid programs that served as an outlet for US grain surpluses and as an instrument of political leverage, acted to undermine peasant food production and push peasants into diverse market arrangements. In the second phase, from 1973 and on, the pace of depeasantization accelerated as a result of globalization. The peasantry has fallen victim to deregulation and structural reform programs associated with the dismantling of the old inward-oriented models and the pursuit of export-led growth policies, including the deeper spread of commercial agriculture (especially the industrialized agri-business variant), drastic cuts in farm subsidies and price supports, the deregulation of land markets, currency devaluations, and so forth. Araghi's empirical research suggests that the world-historic trend supports the disappearance thesis, although he cautions that depeasantization is neither a unilinear process, nor has it taken the historically particular form of increasing class differentiation in the countryside within every nation-state.[133]

In Central America, the proletarianization of the peasantry has been historically linked to the growth of the world economy and the region's ever deeper articulation to it. Recent data on rural class structure in Central America is meager. The restructuring of rural class relations, especially the twin processes of proletarianization and social differentiation, cannot be adequately explored here and remains a topic for future study. It is clear, nonetheless, that the process of world market penetration and commodification of the Central American countryside has accelerated dramatically through the current rearticulation. The agricultural sector, as we saw in previous chapters, is being thoroughly transformed through the extension of capitalist agriculture, including markets in land, the elimination of state credits for producers, the introduction of NTAEs, the conversion of previously marginal lands into tourist facilities, and so forth.

The steady march of peasant expropriation and the concentration of land through successive waves of commercialization has been a constant theme in the study of the region's history, political economy, and social upheavals. William Durham, among others, has demonstrated the links between expanding production of crops for the world market and the concentration of land, rural proletarianization, food scarcity, increased poverty and malnutrition, and cyclical political conflict.[134] Already by the mid-1970s, in El Salvador the largest 1.5 percent of holdings had 49.5 percent of the land; in Guatemala 2.6 percent of holdings had 65.5 percent; in Honduras 4.2 percent of holdings had 56 percent; in Nicaragua 1.8 percent of holdings had 46.8 percent; and in Costa Rica 9.1 percent of holdings had 67.2 percent of the land.[135] Charles Brockett, for his part, observes that in earlier periods the expansion of export agriculture, although it linked the region to world capitalism, occurred with less disturbance to pre-capitalist class relations, whereas in recent decades the class structure itself has been increasingly transformed along capitalist lines and sharecropping has generally been replaced by rural wage-laborers.[136] He shows how the export ratio of land (the amount of land devoted to export crops) steadily expanded following WWII into the 1970s. Then, largely as a result of agrarian reform and other domestic market and pro-food policies in Nicaragua and El Salvador in the 1980s (a result in turn of popular struggles in those countries), the overall regional export ratio actually fell. Finally, in the 1990s, the export ratio grew once again.

We should recall that depeasantization may entail numerous distinct transformations, among them, from peasant to rural worker and from peasant to urban worker, supernumerary, or informal sector agent.[137] Depeasantization may also involve the transformation of rural groups such that they no longer have direct access to the production of their means of subsistence without a necessary reconcentration in urban locations (i.e., capital accumulation in the countryside). This appears, for instance, to be the case in some highland communities in Guatemala (see chapter three). In other cases, peasants may be converted into small commodity producers, as, for example, when smallholders in Honduras or Guatemala switch from subsistence agriculture to producing fruits and vegetables for the "global supermarket" under NTAE schemes. Historical experience would suggest that the status of such small commodity producers is transitionary as market integration undermines the ability to sustain independent production and generates further transformation. This is certainly the tendency among many of the small NTAE farmers, as observed in chapter three. The

Table 4.2.   Labor Force Participation by Sector (by percentage)

	1960	1970	1980	1990
Costa Rica				
Agriculture	52	42	31	26
Industry	18	20	23	26
Services	30	38	46	48
El Salvador				
Agriculture	62	56	43	36
Industry	17	14	19	21
Services	21	30	38	41
Guatemala				
Agriculture	67	62	57	49
Industry	13	17	17	19
Services	20	21	26	32
Honduras				
Agriculture	70	65	60	44
Industry	10	14	16	16
Services	20	21	24	33
Nicaragua				
Agriculture	62	51	46	43
Industry	16	16	16	14
Services	22	33	38	43

Source: CEPAL, *Anuario Estadistico de America Latina y el Caribe, 1994*, various years.

reconcentration of the population in urban locations as measured in urbanization data tells only a part of the story, as does data on labor force participation by sector. Aggregate national data does not necessarily reveal rural class transformations; what is required is the nitty-gritty of field study and historiographic research. Moreover, the phenomena of transnational migration and the rise of transnational communities throw into question the entire notion of nation-state based "rural" and "urban" as well as labor force categories.

With these cautionary observations, table 4.2 provides a rough indication of the shift in the regional labor force out of agriculture and largely into the service sector (both formal and informal), while table 4.3 shows the process of rapid urbanization. As indicated, the population living in urban zones surpassed the 50 percent point in the 1990s.

The transnational model in Central America entails an across-the-board weakening of the ability of local states to service traditional clients linked to the earlier accumulation model. Nowhere is this more clear than with regard to the peasantry. The ministries of agriculture in each of the Central

Table 4.3. Deruralization in Central America (urban population as percentage of total population)

	1960	1980	1990	1997
Costa Rica	37	43	47	50
El Salvador	38	41	46	50
Guatemala	32	38	42	45
Honduras	33	36	44	49
Nicaragua	40	53	65	75
Regional average	36	42	49	54

Source: IDB, *Economic and Social Progress in Latin America*, Annual Report, various years.

American republics were downsized during the decade of sharp adjustments in the 1980s, as shown in tables 4.4 and 4.5. Ministry expenditures declined as a proportion of total government expenditures, even when government expenditures declined as proportions of GDP, as in El Salvador. These ministries were charged with promoting rural development, with promoting agrarian reform, and servicing the peasant sector with credit, technical assistance, and other forms of support.

The reform of the financial system discussed above also severely undermined peasant access to credit. In each Central American republic state banks set up in the post-WWII years to provide subsidized credit for small farmers producing largely food crops, such as corn and beans for domestic consumption, were downsized, and even closed down altogether, following lengthy struggles between peasant and other internal market producers and new external sector agents. State support for the peasant sector should not be exaggerated. The public banks were often corrupt and inefficient, and channeled the lion's share of credit to the larger growers that dominated agriculture. But they did nevertheless offer financing based on a social logic that went beyond strictly market criteria and on a developmentalist project that incorporated peasant producers (even if as adjunct

Table 4.4. Percentage Changes in Staff and Expenditures for Agricultural Research and Extension by State Agencies, 1978–88

	Staff (S)	Expenditure (E)	E/S
Costa Rica	+26.4	−51.5	−61.6
El Salvador	−4.4	−63.3	−61.8
Honduras	+301.0	+120.4	−44.8
Guatemala	+79.4	+104.6	+11.1

Source: Conroy, *et al.*, p. 73.

Table 4.5.   Changes in Ministry of Agriculture (MAG) Expenditure
Relative to Total Government Expenditures, 1979–88

	1979 %	1983 %	Percentage Change
MAG/government expenditures			
Costa Rica	3.4	1.2	− 64.7
El Salvador	8.7	4.8	− 44.8
Honduras	12.4	5.0	− 59.7
Guatemala	5.0	4.8	− 04.0

Source: *Ibid.*, p. 74.

suppliers of food) into the larger social structure of accumulation, in distinction to the current model, which expels them.

The most dramatic case in this regard is Nicaragua's National Development Bank (BANADES). Founded in 1913, BANADES was virtually the only source of credit for small rural producers until it was closed by the government in 1998, after having suffered nearly a decade of defunding and downsizing. From more than 80,000 producers financed in 1990, BANADES provided credit to fewer than 7,000 in 1997.[138] The IMF had pressured throughout the decade for the bank to convert its loan program to strictly commercial criteria or to close down altogether. The IMF argued its case based on the fact that the bank had been unable to recover an estimated $50 million in loans annually from 1991 to 1996, and that the resulting losses strained state finances. But the Bank's losses had less to do with its favorable policies for peasant producers than with a series of multimillion-dollar loans made to agri-business concerns who used their political influence to take advantage of concessionary terms. The Bank became mired in such political scandal throughout the 1990s, a situation that provided ammunition for the neo-liberal position.[139] But the closure of the Bank was part of the broader combination of market and political pressures against the peasantry and in favor of a switch from food to export crop production, particulary of NTAEs. Table 4.6 indicates the dramatic drop in public financing for peasant food production in Nicaragua.

The story is similar, if only a bit less striking, in the other republics. At the behest of the IFIs, the Costa Rican government in 1992 eliminated a credit program for small farmers through the National Bank that provided preferential interest rates below the Central Bank's basic rate.[140] The Honduran government announced in 1995, after negotiations with the IDB, that it would sell 40 percent of its shares in the National Bank for Agricultural Development (BANADE) to private investors and begin to apply commercial criteria in the Bank's loan portfolio.[141] Subjecting producers to exchange rates determined by the market and to commercial criteria of creditworthiness means in practice a market bias against peasants and in favor of more powerful economic agents. The private banks have no

Table 4.6.　　Corn and Bean Production Financed by BANADES, in Hectares

1990–91	219,000
1991–92	187,000
1992–93	87,000
1993–94	88,000
1994–95	66,000
1995–96	25,000

Source: Nicaraguan Central Bank, as reported in Evans, *Liberalizacion Financiera*, p. 47.

objective market-based motive to lend to peasants and smallholders. High administrative costs, climatic risks, the precariousness of land ownership among peasant smallholders, the poor quality of roads and communications, are all disincentives for banks to work with the smallholder sector.

Small-scale farmers have faced a sharp deterioration of their living standards and an unravelling of their communities. The exodus from rural to urban zones so central to the process of capitalist expansion, and which is a frequent point of discussion in the literature on development and social change, has continued unabated, although a great portion of migrants leave the region entirely (see next section). As elsewhere in Latin America, the rapid transformation of the Central American countryside and its unsettling integration into global capitalism is sparking a new round of peasant rebellion. The dramatic resurgence of rural popular struggles, epitomized in Latin America by the Zapatista movement in Chiapas, Mexico, the Landless Rural Workers Movement (MST) in Brazil, and the indigenous struggles in Ecuador led by the Confederation of Indigenous Nationalities of Ecuador (CONAIE), is the social response to the disruptions generated by the new round of capitalist intrusion registered throughout the hemisphere with the onset of globalization.[142] As Edelman shows in his detailed case study on peasant resistance to globalization in Costa Rica, the popular movements and political protagonism of a disintegrating peasantry remain a vital element in the region's future.[143] Depeasantization has made available to transnational capital a surplus of wage workers in urban zones (and *also* in rural areas) in Central America and elsewhere. A consequence of capitalist development in the first instance, however uneven and differentiated, the phenomenon in turn exercises a recursive effect on capitalist globalization by generating conditions conducive to the relocation to new low-wage zones of transnationally mobile capital and the reorganization of the political economy in these zones.

Transnational Social Structure

Restructuring the Central American Labor Force: Informalization and the New Capital–Labor Relation

The restructuring of work and labor in the context of the transition from Fordist to flexible accumulation is a constant theme in the literature on globalization.[144] The ability of workers to consume the goods they produce was central to Fordism, whereas post-Fordism delinks economic growth from the expansion of consumer markets. In my view, this delinkage is a central condition for the new capital–labor relation under globalization because it implies that the reproduction of capital is no longer dependent on that of labor. In the larger picture, it suggests that capital is increasingly able to abandon reciprocal obligations to labor in the employment contract with the emergence of a new post-Fordist political regime of accumulation. And under the new social structure of accumulation (in which the political regime is subsumed), states, with their transmutation from developmentalist to neo-liberal, no longer face the earlier structural imperative in their public obligations to poor and working majorities.[145] This is the backdrop to the general erosion of wages and also underpins, at the societal level, the erosion of what is known as the social wage. This holds true for global capitalist society in general, but especially so for the pattern of accumulation in zones such as Central America, whose principal contribution to the global economy would appear to be the provision of cheap labor. The transnational model of development, by removing the domestic market and workers' consumption from the accumulation imperative, contributes to the demise of the populist alliances between popular classes and national ruling classes that characterized the old development model and paves the way for the new class relations of global capitalism.

Labor-market reform is therefore an essential component of neo-liberal restructuring, centered around making labor "flexible," rationalized with the argument that labor costs must be lowered in order to attract investment and increase the competitiveness of firms producing "tradable" (export) goods. The regulation by states of labor markets and work conditions that protected workers was the result of a long historic period of labor struggles in the Fordist era. This regulation is seen in the neo-liberal discourse as a "distortion" of the free market since labor itself is nothing but another commodity. Labor-market "inflexibility" is a "rigidity" associated with Fordism. Permanent labor contracts, the high costs of dismissals, restrictions on hiring temporary workers, high levels of fringe benefits, and even unionization itself, are said to drive up the price of labor and contribute to high levels of unemployment.[146] Deregulation frees up capital to hire and fire at whim and under conditions that allow it to utilize labor "flexibly" so as to minimize the cost and maximize the control of labor. Labor reform often involves legislation designed to reduce the length and permanence of labor contracts and to substitute individual labor contracts for collective contracts, and "casualizes" labor by allowing it to be hired for any amount of time (a day, a week, a month, etc.) or for part-time work with no fixed commitment on the part of employers to provide benefits or security. "Flexible" labor is also associated with deunionized labor.

Diverse new deregulated forms of work—"contract labor," "temp labor," "part-time labor," "casual labor," "home work," "just-in-time labor," and so forth—are subsumed under the twin but not fully synonymous concepts of the *casualization* of labor and the *informalization* of work. Casualization generally refers to the new unregulated work that labor performs for capital under "flexible" conditions. Informalization refers to the transfer of much economic activity from the formal to the informal economy. Within the labor market, the core of formality is regulated work, while the core of informality is deregulated work. The global labor force is increasingly subject to the conditions of deregulation, casualization, and informalization, a process some refer to as "harmonization," meaning a "downward" equalization of work conditions around the world.

This restructuring of work is bound up with several processes germane to capitalist development in its globalization stage. The constant replacement of human labor by technology, or automation, along with the ongoing deskilling and routinization of labor activities and organizational innovations, is a cyclical process germane to capitalism that has intensified dramatically in recent decades through the diverse applications of information technology. This has led some, such as Jeremy Rifkin, to proclaim "the end of work."[147] At the same time, the secular process of primitive accumulation and depeasantization has quickened, throwing hundreds of millions of people into the global labor market. Some of these become subject to exploitation under new casualized forms of work in the factories, farms, and offices of the global economy. Others join the ranks of the structurally unemployed, the "redundants" or "supernumeraries," where they experience exclusion rather than direct exploitation.

The combination of these cyclical and secular processes has resulted in a global labor surplus that reached historically unprecedented levels by the end of the twentieth century, with unemployment affecting up to one third of the economically active population worldwide.[148] The existence of this global labor surplus favors the new capital–labor relation. It has contributed to an explosion of the informal sector, as millions of people pushed out of formal participation in the economy turn to diverse activities in informal economies that have expanded phenomenally under globalization. However, this informal economy is not functionally independent of the formal economy, as Castells and Portes, among others, have shown, but functionally integrated into it.[149] Globalization progressively erases the boundaries between formal and informal activity. The accelerated informalization of the labor market has been accompanied by the increase of labor flexibility in what remains of the formal sector, with more frequent use of contract work and the use of contingent labor over permanent employment and collective contracts. As TNCs outsource specific production and service tasks to local subcontractors, for instance, the labor they continue to employ is subject to casualization while subcontractors draw on labor from the informal economy. Moreover, as the cost of reproduction is expunged from the capitalist sector it is absorbed by the informal sector, which replenishes the pool of labor. The spread of informalization becomes a condition for the new capital–labor relation, a mechanism for the appropriation of surplus in new ways by capital.

The informal sector has been the only avenue of survival for millions of people thrown out of work by the contraction of public-sector employment, the dismantling of national enterprises, revised labor codes and austerity programs, and the uprooting of remaining peasant communities by the incursion of capitalist agriculture. In the 1990s, more than a third of urban jobs in Asia and Latin America and more than half in Africa were estimated to be informal.[150] The ILO estimates that four out of every five jobs generated from 1980 to 1993 in Latin America were in the informal sector, while other estimates put the figure for the 1990s as high as nine out of every ten jobs.[151] Data collection agencies often report those in the informal sector as "employed," despite the highly irregular and unregulated nature of the sector, characterized by low levels of productivity, low earnings, generally well-below-legal minimum wages, and precariousness, usually amounting to underemployment. In Latin America, the mass informalization of the work force is associated with widespread under and unemployment and a stagnation, and in many places compression, of real wages, as indicated in table 4.7, which shows this deterioration of wages for Central America as well. "The increased international competitiveness of a number of Latin American economies is not, as in the East Asian NICs, a function of rising wages," Veltmeyer notes. "The compression of wages has been the major mechanism of internal adjustment throughout the region."[152]

In integrating their countries into the global economy, local elites, and in particular the transnationalized fractions of these elites, base "development" on the virtually exclusive criteria of achieving maximum internal profitability as the condition *sine qua non* for attracting transnational capital. These elites thus see the erosion of labor's income, the withdrawal of public services, and the curtailment of popular class demands as requirements for the region's successful integration into the global economy. In the logic of global capitalism, the cheapening of labor and its social disenfranchisement by the neo-liberal state become conditions for "development," a theme which I take up in the next chapter. Neo-liberal programs, and especially the twin aspects of a liberalization of labor laws and the reduction and even elimination of the social wage, have placed workers and the poor in a new situation of vulnerability. It is not merely that labor bears the social costs of adjustment, but that adjustment facilitates a qualitative transformation of class relations, establishing the conditions for the new capital–labor relation. In Central America and elsewhere in the South where only more recently the social fabric has been drawn more fully into market structures and commodified, reciprocity in social and economic relations still provided a significant support system

Table 4.7. Evolution of Urban Real Minimum Wage in Latin and Central America (select countries)

	1980	1990	1992	1993	1994	1995	1996	1997	1998	1999
Latin America (index: 1995 = 100)										
Argentina	132	28	58	75	103	100	100	99	98	99
Brazil	122	88	90	99	95	100	104	107	111	113
Chile	88	77	88	92	96	100	104	108	114	123
Colombia	108	114	111	108	104	102	n/a	n/a	n/a	n/a
Dominican Republic	110	83	98	94	100	100	101	102	106	112
Ecuador	210	73	63	73	84	100	110	106	98	89
Mexico	324	128	116	115	100	91	90	90	91	88
Paraguay	88	115	100	96	99	100	102	107	106	102
Peru	676	158	107	76	98	100	103	181	201	195
Uruguay	234	161	141	122	109	100	97	95	98	99
Venezuela	185	88	109	95	107	100	95	81	81	82
Central America										
Costa Rica	84	101	95	100	102	100	102	106	109	112
El Salvador	279	97	102	102	100	100	96	92	95	98
Guatemala	409	197	143	124	110	100	99	91	95	99
Honduras	131	112	121	123	105	100	96	102	105	106
Nicaragua*	391	82	101	93	98	100	98	98	105	109

*Figures for Nicaragua are real average wages.

Source: ECLAC, Economic Survey of Latin America and the Caribbean, 1999–2000, tables VI.4 and VI.5.

and social protection for those in vulnerable positions. For this reason the breakdown of community and state reciprocity associated with the new capital–labor relation is felt with particular severity.

However, the neo-liberal transformation of the labor market results not in a uniform process of downward mobility but in new patterns of social stratification. The increasing bipolarization of labor into high-paid, high-skilled "core" and low-paid, low-skilled "peripheral" workers is an important theme in the literature on post-Fordism and globalization. Transnational labor markets are highly heterogeneous, and as national labor markets integrate into a single global labor market this heterogeneity becomes present within most localities. There is a selective and highly variegated integration into transnational structures through such heterogeneous participation in the global labor market. Although the proposition cannot be pursued here, I suggest that labor markets are determinant within the social, rather than territorial, conception of development I advanced in chapter one. Forms of participation for individuals and groups in the global economy are more important than geographic location or nationality. It is the nature of participation in global production through transnationalized labor markets, not through membership in nation-states, that determines the social development of groups.

Transformation of the Central American Labor Market

How are these tendencies manifest in Central America? The crisis of the 1980s, including the deterioration of wages, the repression of the trade union movement, and informalization, was a powerful catalyst for the restructuring of the Central American labor market. There has been a disintegration of the cohesion of internal (national) labor market structures, which are becoming transnationalized and de-territorialized in step with the new model of accumulation. Costa Rican sociologist Juan Pérez Sáinz has conducted extensive research into the transformation of the Central American labor market under globalization. He identifies four tendencies: the deregulation of formal employment; the appearance of a new proletarianization among those who have become wage workers on the region's new agro-export plantations, maquiladora factories, tourist facilities, and so on; rising exclusion or marginalization, as expressed in increased levels of underemployment and emigration; and the spread of self-employment, generally in the informal economy.[153] Let us explore these tendencies, placing Sáinz's work in the broader context of the general patterns of globalization and the new model of accumulation in the Isthmus.

Deregulation of the labor market has meant the disintegration of a uniform framework for the employment of labor regulated by the state, which corresponded to the previous model of accumulation (and was a feature of Fordism more generally) and its replacement by diverse new categories of employment within a much more heterogeneous labor market. Increasingly, Central American workers are not socially integrated into any cohesive national or regional society via their triangular relationship with capital and with the state. Instead, select strands of the working population have become integrated into distinct transnational networks, while others suffer the negative effects of social disintegration, such as instability, pauperization, and informality. The Central American governments, often as part of negotiations with the IFIs, have revised labor codes and deregulated formal employment to varying degrees in each republic, while further reform was on the agenda in the early twenty-first century in every country. Reform is a more limited process than elsewhere, however, since regulation of the labor market was never part of a full Fordist system, in the societal sense, due to the low level of capitalist development and poorly developed labor markets. There were fewer rigidities in the labor market that needed to be swept away through neo-liberal adjustment. While the old authoritarian regimes rarely complied with labor laws, the new polyarchies ratified in the 1990s the right to trade union organization and collective bargaining, in part as a result of pressures generated by a transnational alliance of Central American federations and the US (American Federation of Labor–Congress of Industrial Organizations, AFL–CIO).

But the withdrawal of the state, casualization, and informalization effectively make such labor rights more formal than real.[154]

There has been a relative decline of the "formal" proletariat and the rise of a new casualized proletariat. An increasing segment of the Central American labor force has been integrated into non-traditional production, including the free trade zones, the NTAE sector, the tourist industry, and so on, which have become the most rapid areas of job creation. Work here has been casualized and the new capital–labor relation predominates. But casualization and informalization are also spreading to all sectors of the economy. The traditional agro-export sector has gone from patronal/ seignorial relations to casualized capitalist labor relations. Abell provides an example from Guatemala:

> A trend begun on the coastal sugar plantations in the 1980s, which is gaining more and more acceptance on the coffee estates of the highlands, is to use seasonal or sometimes daily contract laborers instead of permanent employees. For the owners, efficiencies—i.e., cost-savings—from not having to provide year-round wages and benefits far outweigh the uncertainties associated with having to hire and supervise temporary workers. There is also a secondary financial benefit that comes from releasing hundreds of families into the labor market. Their presence in the contract labor force helps to put further downward pressure on an already distressed labor market, allowing the owner to pay wages far below the legal minimum.[155]

There has been an explosion of the informal urban economy as a consequence of a number of factors bound up, ultimately, with capitalist globalization. The spread of capitalism into the countryside has further alienated what remains of the peasantry and sent a portion migrating to urban centers, where it swells the ranks of the expanding informal proletariat. The regional conflict contributed to this process as well. At least one million people were internally displaced (190,000 in Guatemala, 400,000 in El Salvador, and 350,000 in Nicaragua) and many of these flooded into urban zones.[156] The ranks of the new "informal" proletariat have swelled with the dismissal of hundreds of thousands of workers through the contraction of public sectors, privatization, and the dismantling of national industry, processes that generate un and underemployment. This has included the demobilization of tens of thousands of soldiers in Nicaragua, El Salvador, and to a lesser extent, Guatemala, very few of whom have been absorbed by the formal sector. Moreover, the introduction of flexible accumulation patterns, such as outsourcing, contract and contingent labor, places most workers ambiguously between the formal and the informal economies. In moving from public sector and formal employment to the informal sector, these workers become deprived of both legal protection/ secure employment and the social wages they enjoyed as workers in the formal economy. The new informal employment is extremely precarious. In fact, such precariousness of work relations (the hallmark of casualization) seems to be a characteristic that spans heterogeneous experiences in the emerging global labor market.

But, to reiterate, this informal economy is not a "marginal" sector, in the sense that it is linked functionally and organically to the formal economy. The two are not a dualist but a single structure in which each sector is internally related to the other. Flexible accumulation rests on a large informal sector and decentralized networks of production and services that cut across formal and informal activity. Castells, Portes, and their colleagues show that its members participate simultaneously in capitalist production and in the subsistence economy.[157] The informal sector plays a key role in the renovation of circuits of accumulation. Many are "employed" in the informal urban economy in street vending, small-scale home production of everything from tortillas to furniture, construction, petty repair shops, and various types of personal services, and frequently engage in multiple activities in order to survive. As the informal sector brings together the labor process and the family process it facilitates the transfer of social reproduction responsibility from the state and capital to families. Here, the informal economy is often "the poor producing for the poor," a barter economy in the interstices of the capitalist sector, functional to it because it contributes to social reproduction and maintains a reserve labor pool available for capital to tap when needed, such as for seasonal work or for labor in the maquiladoras, placing downward pressure on wages, and in general exhibiting the functions expected of a reserve army of labor, but under new conditions of flexible production. Subcontracting firms may hire workers in the informal economy or may in turn subcontract with household shops or self-employed workers.

Many of the new informal proletariat live in extreme poverty. These are the "new poor," frequently self-employed, or working with several family members. This structure comes to resemble one of millions of chickens trying to peck out a living in the coop of transnational capital. Nonetheless, informality is not coterminous with poverty, even if it is for the majority. Informal workers are employed by what Portes has described as an "informal petty bourgeoisie" that may hire several workers outside of the family. These are small-scale entrepreneurs who hire on a noncontractual basis; they function as "intermediaries between the modern sector and the mass of unskilled and unprotected labor at the bottom of the class structure."[158] In addition, globalization opens up new opportunities for some groups who may achieve a viable insertion into transnational circuits under conditions more favorable than the new poor face. Women, young workers, ethnic minorities, and the unskilled are more likely to fill less-skilled informal jobs, while better trained or experienced workers and former professionals with more social capital are more likely to become successfully inserted. Insertion into these circuits is itself heterogeneous. More often than not it involves a precarious new informality.

The case of the Palo Alto community in Honduras, located in the rural hinterland of San Pedro Sula, is instructive in what Sáinz terms "neo-

Table 4.8. Under- and Unemployment in Central America (as percentage of EAP, 1980 and 1990)

Country/Year	Unemployed	Underemployed	Combined
Guatemala			
1980	3.2	43.0	46.2
1990	2.0	63.0	65.0
El Salvador			
1980	16.1	55.0	66.1
1990	10.0	50.8	60.8
Honduras			
1980	15.2	64.0	79.2
1990	5.0	36.0	41.0
Nicaragua			
1980	11.2	49.0	60.2
1990	10.0	46.5	56.5
Costa Rica			
1980	6.0	26.0	31.0
1990	4.0	18.0	22.0

Source: PREALA, 1996.[161]

informality," or the conversion of formal into informal work. A US-Honduran firm had initially set up a maquiladora factory in the area producing baseballs for export. But as workers began to organize a trade union the proprietors decided to dissolve the firm and pursue an alternative strategy for labor control. In the new arrangement, they subcontracted hundreds of women from the countryside to sew the hides on the baseballs out of their own homes, combined with the automation of other phases within the factory. This putting-out system allowed the firm to fragment production and corral an informal labor force. We see as well in this example the gendered nature of these new labor relations. The women subcontracted were not young and single but older women with children; hence their productive and reproductive work became fused into a singular process controlled by transnational capital.[159]

Underemployment and informalization have been, in Sáinz's view, the major mechanisms of labor market adjustment to the crisis and the new conditions of globalization. Combined un and underemployment during the crisis years is indicated in table 4.8. It may be that underemployment (or insufficient employment), rather than unemployment, will become a fixed feature of the labor market in the current epoch, characterized by flexible labor, stagnant wages, and informality. Another mechanism of adjustment is emigration, "a manifestation of the logic of exclusion,"[160] as it represents a response to the restriction of employment opportunities and

Table 4.9.   Socio-Demographic Characteristics of the Central American
Urban Informal Economy, 1991

	Guatemala City	San Salvador	Tegucigalpa	Managua	San José
% women	41.7	53.4	50.7	46.8	32.5
% 20 years or less	8.4	9.8	13.1	15.4	9.7
% 60 years or more	12.8	11.5	6.0	6.9	10.1
% self-employed	51.1	50.8	62.7	57.1	67.3
% commerce	39.6	48.9	46.3	44.4	35.9
% working more than 45 hours weekly	59.4	61.6	54.2	19.0*	54.3

* % working more than 50 hours weekly

Source: Sáinz, 1996.[164]

prospects for survival under the neo-liberal order. High levels of emigration
(see next section) drive down the rate of formal unemployment. The social
reproduction of the excluded population that remains behind becomes
dependent on the remittance sent by those who emigrate, as we saw in
chapter three, which may offset or disguise the full extent of un and
underemployment.

It is very difficult to measure and compare informality and underemployment given the problem of how to define these categories and other
methodological difficulties. Using household survey data from the principal
metropolitan areas in the five republics, Sáinz places the percentage of the
urban labor force absorbed by the informal economy in the late 1980s and
early 1990s at 53 percent in Guatemala (1989), 55.3 percent in El Salvador
(1990), 48.9 percent in Honduras (1989), 63.8 percent in Nicaragua
(1993), and 34.4 percent in Costa Rica (1991).[162] Table 4.9 provides a
socio-demographic profile of this urban informal economy. The high
concentration of women in the informal economy stands out as one
indicator of the unequal participation of men and women in the labor
market. The data also confirms the strong tendency for self-employment
and tertiary activity, primarily petty commerce. The length of the working
week in the informal economy is also noteworthy because, as Sáinz observes,
it underscores the precariousness of informal work. "Informality is characterized by long working days in which the physical exhaustion of the labor
force becomes the mechanism that compensates for low productivity and
for earnings that are below formal sector levels."[163]

Micro-Enterprises: Redefining the Marginalized as Entrepreneurs

If the growth of the informal sector was in part the natural outcome of the
process of restructuring and globalization, it also spread through AID and
IFI programs and policies to promote what has come to be known in the

new development discourse as "micro-enterprises," or petty businesses.[165] The promotion of micro-enterprises through government and IFI programs such as small-scale credit, technical training, and the provision of market information, has been extolled as a progressive attempt to democratize the economy by distributing more equitably the assistance usually only provided to large-scale capitalists and TNCs, and to address the problem of poverty and marginality among the millions of people who labor in the informal sector. Such a strategy was made popular by Hernando de Soto's 1986 book, *El Otro Sendero: La Revolución Informal* (The Other Path: The Informal Revolution), which achieved something of a cult status among neo-liberal ideologues and policymakers.[166] De Soto argued that legal and administrative barriers placed on poor people by government regulation of their informal economic activity impede their "entrepreneurial energies" and that market deregulation could allow them to overcome poverty and marginalization. Behind the promotion of micro-enterprises is the assumption of modernization theory that development depends primarily on integration into the market and cultivation of the capitalist habits of saving and rational investment.

Some micro-enterprises in Central America have become "successful" small firms within the very precarious parameters of informality. As new structures of flexible accumulation take hold, for instance, local and transnational firms shed ancillary operations through subcontracting and outsourcing, which allow micro-enterprises to provide highly localized and small-scale services, and this can constitute a niche for new groups. But such "success" is the experience of a minority; the spread of these tiny "enterprises" in Central America is largely identified with the growth of self-employment as subsistence activity. As tens of thousands of people employed in the public sector were dismissed in the 1990s through privatization and other adjustment policies they were encouraged through diverse programs to establish their own micro-enterprises and become "entrepreneurs" as a way of binding to the market sectors of the population recently disrupted from stable socioeconomic arrangements by restructuring. Sáinz found in his research that a minority of micro-enterprises have been able to report income above the average salaries for formal work. Here, "distinct logics" were at work within the heterogeneity of informality in Central America. One of these logics is expanded reproduction, in which micro-enterprises and small firms have been able to reinvest in the shadow of large-scale capital. Nonetheless, among micro-enterprises and small firms in major metropolitan areas, subsistence activity ranged from a low of 42 percent in San José to a high of almost 70 percent in Tegucigalpa. "The logic of simple reproduction, that is, of subsistence, predominates in the informal economy and belies the notion of a general entrepreneurial potential in the world of informality."[167]

But the flexible organization of production in the transnational model also provides new opportunities and allows certain strata to integrate into the global economy as developed (or at least as better-off) social clusters. Hence the heterogeneity of transnationalized labor markets spans the formal and informal sectors. The segmentation of labor markets in the Isthmus is similar to that taking place throughout global society. Most new employment opportunities entail unskilled labor-intensive activities, such as new agricultural and maquila work or petty commerce and self-employment in the informal economy. But there is also the creation of skilled employment, such as tourist workers who must be bilingual or administer facilities, or those who are successful at setting up a small firm in the informal sector. These jobs may bring to the worker or professional the consumption and technological-cultural benefits that global society has to offer.

The story of the Sarchi community in the western region of Costa Rica's Central Valley is illustrative. Liberalization policies in the 1980s threatened the existence of the artisans of this community, who in earlier times produced woodwork items for domestic consumption. But the community successfully reoriented its activities towards marketing hand-made woodwork adornments among foreign visitors as the tourist industry burgeoned. In this way, some 130 local artisans gradually coalesced into an agglomeration feeding the tourist market and inserting itself successfully into the global economy. Nonetheless, as the 1990s progressed the community faced intense competition from neighboring towns attempting to carve out a similar niche within the tourist industry and also from larger firms, as well as the threat of a proposed new highway that would reroute the tourist flow away from Sarchi. This experience demonstrates the precariousness of informal employment even under successful conditions of market insertion, and captures the ambiguity between marginalization and participation in the new "neo-informality."[168]

Promoting micro-enterprises is a way of establishing functional and organizational links between the formal and informal sectors. Guatemalan researchers Escoto and Marroquín, who studied AID programs for micro-enterprises in that country, found that the aim of AID programs was to articulate them vertically to the expanding export production (agro-exports, NTAEs, maquiladoras, etc.) of large-scale enterprises and TNCs, through the provision of localized services. "In the end, the AID was seeking the 'formalization' of micro-enterprises, not as an end in itself, but as a means for the firms in the formal sector to take advantage of the potential services [micro-enterprises] could offer them."[169] Similarly, Sáinz found a process of "progressive territorial agglomeration" of small enterprises. This is linked to the reorganization of production along the lines of flexible accumulation, involving subcontracting and other productive forms that have created space for small and micro-enterprises linked vertically to larger capitalist firms. The lower down one moves in these vertical structures the more likely it is that informal employment, or self- (or family-based) employment predominate.

In any event, programs in Central America to promote micro-enterprises have been very limited, reaching only a few thousand small firms and under restrictive conditions. "In terms of resolving in an integral manner the problems of unemployment and misery, the effects of these programs have been negligible," observe Sáinz and Cordero.[170] They are often administered through select NGOs and become part of a broader struggle over hegemony in civil society. If the exercise does not actually alleviate poverty and marginalization, it does become a mechanism for imbuing the popular classes, especially the excluded, with a market ideology, and for exercising some influence over a sector prone to social unrest. "Micro businesspeople" come under not only the material domination of large business but also under its ideological sway. The logic is one of how to "make the market work" for the poor rather than how to overcome the impoverishing effects of the market itself. The existing structures, with their extant distribution of property and social resources, are legitimated by an ideology of individual rewards and individual responsibilities. The micro-enterprise program and its attendant ideology is oriented toward incorporating into a new historic neo-liberal bloc a sector which is in reality marginalized, exploited, and potentially revolutionary. The transnational model of accumulation and the concomitant social, legal, and political changes, fragment the popular classes and therefore blunt and thwart their collective political protagonism. These intersubjectivities were *brought together* in earlier waves of capitalist expansion and collectively challenged the social order. New subjectivities thrown up by globalization are absorbed by the informal sector. Under the sway of the logic and ideology of the market, this sector acts to thwart a renewed process of intersubjective aggregation.

Transnational Migration

The link between capitalist development and migration is well established in the literature and there has been a recent plethora of studies relating this phenomenon to globalization.[171] What is the importance of transnational migration to the global system? Central to capitalism is securing a politically and economically suitable labor supply, and at the core of all class societies is the control over labor and disposal of the products of labor. But the linkage between securing labor and territoriality is changing under globalization. As labor becomes "free" in every corner of the globe, capital has vast new opportunities for mobilizing labor power where and when required. National labor pools are merging into a single global labor pool that services global capitalism. As we saw in chapter three, the transnational circulation of capital induces the transnational circulation of labor. This circulation of labor becomes incorporated into the process of restructuring the world economy. It is a mechanism for the provision of labor to transnationalized circuits of accumulation and constitutes a structural feature of the global system.

Migration does not stem from a lack of development, we should recall, but from the very dynamics of capitalist development. Lydia Potts has shown that, historically, mass labor migrations are generated by: 1) the expansion of capitalism into new areas; 2) the industrialization of areas already brought into the world capitalist system; 3) intensive new booms in capital accumulation; 4) and when labor imports provide a means of reproducing capital's dominance in specific conjunctures.[172] The confluence of all four of these instances under globalization is resulting in a new wave of worldwide migration. While the need to mix labor with capital at diverse points along global production chains induces population movements, this does not happen automatically and the subprocesses they involve may be identified. Social scientists generally identify "push" factors as those that repel people outward and "pull" factors as those that draw people in, while neo-classical economics emphasizes the forces of supply and demand of labor. At the structural level, the uprooting of communities by the capitalist breakup of "natural" economies creates surplus populations and is a powerful push factor in outmigration, while labor shortages in more economically advantaged areas are a cardinal pull factor attracting displaced peoples. At a behavioral level, individuals and families take the decision to migrate in the wake of socioeconomic disruptions and consequent hardships. Migration and wage remittances become a family survival strategy, made *possible* by the demand for labor abroad and made increasingly *viable* by the conditions of globalization.

However, as Portes and Borocz observe, traditional push-pull and supply-demand theories are inadequate causal explanations in and of themselves as they fail to explain migration in some places and not others where there are similar conditions of social and economic hardship in sender countries and comparative advantage in more advanced regions. In addition, these theories do not specify the mechanisms through which push-pull factors and supply and demand in the international labor market actually induce migration in distinct patterns. They point to the history of prior contact between sending and receiving societies in the context of asymmetric colonial and post-colonial relations, and to the development of transnational migrant networks and institutional interconnections as mechanisms shaping the patterns of migration.[173] "More than movement from one place to another in search of higher wages, labor migration should be conceptualized as a process of progressive network building," argue Portes and Borocz. "Networks constructed by the movements and contact of people across space are at the core of the microstructures which sustain migration over time. More than individualistic calculations of gain, it is the insertion of people into such networks which helps explain differential proclivities to move and the enduring character of migrant flows."[174] Their analysis complements the research of Saskia Sassen, among others, on the relation between the transnational movement of capital and the movement of labor, and how the international migration of labor becomes incorporated into the internationalization of production. She has shown how particular forms of internationalization coalesce with local conditions in the countries that supply emigrant labor. Here, the focus is on specific sets of historic conditions that combine with the more "traditional" variables of poverty and unemployment to induce outmigration, and on the contribution made by cultural, social, and institutional bridges between the regions of origin and of destination of transnationally mobile capital, alongside wage differentials and employment opportunities, in determining the destination of emigrants.[175]

These analyses need to be updated in light of globalization. International migration was the movement from one country to another; transnational migration is the fluid and multidirectional flux of peoples around the world. As we saw in chapter three, migration now takes place from periphery to center, from center to periphery, within the center and within the periphery. Transnational migration further breaks down conventional borders that distinguish the internal from the external, in the social and economic sense, as well as culturally and politically. We can speculate that globalization is generating at the level of the global system (in transnational space) the type of cultural and institutional connections between multiple points that previously became established between specific core and peripheral regions through particular histories of prior contact and core penetration. Global migration flows generate new social hierarchies and forms of inequality which are themselves *trans*national in ways that cannot be characterized by the traditional dichotomies of core and periphery or First and Third worlds.

This is evidenced in the emergence of de-nationalized, *transnational communities*, a concept developed, among others, by sociologist Alejandro Portes.[176] In his analysis, the same social and economic forces unleashed by globalization that allowed capital to move transnationally have also allowed immigrant groups to become *trans*national. In the past, immigrants could not hope to maintain fluid and active ties with the homeland. They became assimilated and set up life anew in a new land. But global communications, transportation networks, and the global economic and financial infrastructure increasingly allow immigrants to maintain active and ongoing exchanges between their home country and their country (or countries) of immigration. Supporting these ties, different immigrant groups have found economic niches in countries of destination, such as marketing indigenous goods from back home, contracting for outsourcing phases of global production chains, setting up enterprises to meet local demand for goods and services among their ethnic kin (which may involve small-scale importing from back home), and so on. These economic activities are themselves a result of flexible global production and commerce which opens up diverse new "niches" around the world. As these mobile immigrant groups institutionalize these networks they come to constitute transnational communities that maintain social, cultural, political, and economic ties in both countries, living between the two, and as intermediaries between communities in different countries. "As the members of these communities travel back and forth, they carry cultural and political currents in both directions," notes Portes. "Their emergence complicates our understanding not only of global trade but also of immigration and national identity." The result of this process, according to Portes, is "the transformation of the original pioneering economic ventures into transnational communities that include an increasing number of people who lead dual lives. Members are at least bilingual, move easily between different cultures, frequently maintain homes in two countries, and pursue economic, political, and cultural interests that require a simultaneous presence in both."[177]

To Portes' analysis we can add that the development of transnational communities contributes in important ways to the transnationalization of social structure. These communities are not rooted in geographic space but in transnational social space, in that the social relations that develop are spatially diffuse and de-territorialized, constituting a structure of reference for positions and social status that shape daily life and identities in ways that transcend national societies. They are collective agents of globalization; socioeconomic and even more so, cultural and political agents.[178] These emergent *global social networks* are transnational structures that erode national ones, blurring the boundaries between the "national" and the "international." Long-standing concepts of immigrant experience are inadequate to capture new realities on the global, national, community, and individual levels. Global migration is no longer a one-way street, with immigrants adapting, as assimilation theory would suggest, to new ways of life in host countries. Immigration affects and is affected by what transpires in communities and countries of origin. Hybrid cultural and political processes develop through the extension and institutionalization of immigrant networks in the new globalized environment.

But here the analysis runs up against an *apparent* contradiction. One of the political ironies of globalization is that capital and goods can move freely across national borders but labor cannot and its movement is subject to heightened state controls. The global labor supply is, in the main, no longer coerced (subject to extra-economic compulsion) due to the ability of the universalized market to exercise strictly economic discipline, but its movement is juridically controlled. This control is a central determinant in the worldwide correlation of forces between global capital and global labor. Here, national borders play a vital function. Nation-states are about the configuration of space, what sociologist Philip McMichael has called "population containment zones."[179] The immigrant is a juridical creation inserted into real social relations. States create "immigrant labor" around the world as distinct categories of labor in relation to capital. The creation of these distinct categories becomes central to the global economy, replacing earlier direct colonial and racial caste controls over labor worldwide.

But why is this juridical category of "immigrant labor" reproduced under globalization? Labor migration and geographic shifts in production are alternative forms of achieving the optimal mix of capital and labor. State controls are often intended not to prevent but to *control* the transnational movement of labor. A *free* flow of labor would exert an equalizing influence on wages across borders while state controls help reproduce such differentials. Eliminating the wage differential between regions would cancel the advantages that capital accrues from disposing of labor pools worldwide subject to different wage levels and would strengthen labor worldwide in relation to capital. As Sassen notes, moreover, the use of immigrant labor allows receiving countries to separate reproduction and maintenance of labor, and therefore to "externalize renewal costs." In other words, the new transnational migration helps capital to dispose with the need to pay for the reproduction of labor power. While the generalization of the labor market emerging from the consolidation of the world capitalist economy creates the conditions for international migrations as a world-level labor-supply system, notes Sassen, "the strengthening of the nation-state creates the conditions for immigrant labor as a distinct category of a nation's labor supply." This component of the labor supply has a distinct role in the labor process characterized by: "(1) the institutional differentiation of the processes of labor-force reproduction and maintenance; and (2) a particular form of powerlessness, associated with formal or attributed foreign status, that meets the requirements of the types of work organization based on direct rather than structural control over the work force."[180] The inter-state system thus acts as a condition for the structural power of globally mobile transnational capital over labor which is transnational in its actual content and character, but is subjected to different institutional arrangements and to the direct control of national states. National boundaries are *not* barriers to transnational migration but are mechanisms functional for the supply of labor on a global scale and for the reproduction of the system. Here we see how the continued existence of the nation-state serves numerous interests of a transnational capitalist class.[181]

US anti-immigrant legislation in the 1990s was revealing because it was *not* intended, rhetoric and commonplace perceptions aside, to keep out immigrant labor. Rather, the objective was to generate the conditions most propitious to the superexploitation of this labor, including absolving employers of any social responsibility that they might otherwise incur should immigrant labor enjoy full legal and social rights. Certain economic activities do not lend themselves to geographic relocation. In US-based garments production, for instance, particularly for seasonal fashions, proximity to the final retail market is vital. And some perishable foodstuffs and numerous services must often be produced close to consumers. It is advantageous for transnational capital to contract out this production inside the United States using immigrant labor pools that enjoy no legal rights and face language barriers and a hostile cultural and ideological environment. This makes them easy to control and they can be dispensed with by the state should the need arise. Several studies have demonstrated how Proposition 187, which was passed in California in 1993 and severely restricted immigrant rights, was backed by employers whose objective was to create the most favorable conditions for the continued utilization of immigrant labor.[182] More than half of the 22,000 registered garment contractors in the United States paid less than the minimum wage, failed to pay overtime, or violated US labor laws.[183] The reappearance of sweatshops in New York, Los Angeles, and other US cities using child, undocumented, and sometimes slave immigrant labor is a reflection of the structural power capital has achieved over an increasingly transnational working class whose ability to exercise its own class power is constrained by the juridical and institutional structures of the nation-state system.

Migration and the Transformation of Central America's Demographic Structure

The foregoing analysis helps place in context the mass migrations of Central Americans to the United States and elsewhere in the closing decades of the twentieth century and the new dynamics of transnational migration in the Isthmus. These decades marked a great transformation in Central America's demographic structure, resulting not from the well-known patterns of rural to urban migration or alterations in the age makeup of the population, but from transnational migration. Until the late 1970s most migration took place within the nations of the region or as intra-regional movements of workers between neighboring countries, from zones of subsistence production to the agro-export plantations and agricultural frontier (much of it seasonal), or to expanding urban centers.[184] The low-end estimates place the number of Central Americans who emigrated to the United States in the 1980s at three million people, or 15 percent of the total Isthmanian population at the time of 20 million, mostly from El Salvador, Nicaragua, and Guatemala (additionally, more than one million people emigrated to other countries within the region and another one million were internally displaced).[185] However, given the status of most as undocumented immigrants and fears of visibility among political refugees, the real figure was probably much higher. US government figures are generally assumed to be *much* lower than the real figure, as they only count those who come in contact with US authorities. The figure for Guatemalan immigrants alone, for instance, estimated at between 1 and 1.2 million in the United States (over 10 percent of the Guatemalan population), is close to the official US government figure for *all* Central Americans in the United States.[186] In fact, Central American countries accounted for four of the top nine countries sending undocumented immigrants to the United States,[187] and by the early 1990s more than 100,000 Central Americans were being deported from the United States each year. A small portion of the emigrants came from the ranks of the traditional Nicaraguan and Salvadoran oligarchies fearful of revolutionary transformations, along with civilian and military personnel of the old regimes, in a situation comparable to the Cuban bourgeoisie who transferred to Miami after 1959. The vast majority were poor people who had become surplus labor.

Central American outmigration does not appear to have subsided in the 1990s and early twenty-first century. The networks formed during the wars are now the social infrastructure for new migrants. If migrants are no longer political refugees, rising levels of informalization, poverty, and unemployment generated by the neo-liberal model constitute new economic inducements to outmigration. Moreover, the process has continued as family members are reunified abroad, as transnational symbolic interchanges intensify, and as transnational social networks become well established and exert a steady pull on migration.[188] Here, the process of "chain migration" is set in motion. Migration flows, once established, as Portes and Borocz observe, tend to continue with relative autonomy as contacts across space, social channels, "family chains," and the new information and interests which they promote, sustain migrations even when the original economic or political inducements have disappeared.[189]

In an earlier study I have focused on the push and pull factors in the dramatic rise in Central American immigration into the United States.[190] Political turmoil, economic crisis, and military conflict in Central America were immediate causes, but the broader context was the uprooting of millions of Central Americans through the post-WWII capitalist expansion. The historic relations of US economic and political domination which converted the region into a semi-protectorate and economic appendage of the US political economy in an earlier moment of the world-system, along with the large-scale penetration of multinational capital originating largely from the United States in the post-WWII period, comprise the "background" to the subsequent pattern of transnational migration. Political turmoil and economic crisis in the 1970s and 1980s along with massive direct US intervention in the region is the "foreground" that triggered the exodus. The main "pull" factor was the reorganization of the US political economy itself under globalization, which has resulted in a transformation of pre-existing segmented labor markets. The expanded opportunities for Central American (along with other Latino) labor in the lower rungs of segmented agricultural, industrial, and particularly service sector labor markets in the United States were a result of transnational capital's search for the most favorable mix of factor costs in the new globalized production. Central American emigrants to the United States have largely moved into the lowest rungs in the service sector, often in the informal sector, including child care, domestic service, hotel and restaurant employment, food processing, cleaning, hairdressing, and so on—what Nigel Harris calls "the sweated trades."[191] New Central American and Mexican agricultural laborers have appeared in the mid-West and the Appalachian region of the United States, and industrial laborers of the same origin have appeared in East and West Coast industries under rigidly segmented labor markets, often displacing African-American and white ethnic laborers. Studies in the early 1990s found that, in addition to concentrations in "traditional" areas such as Los Angeles, Miami, Washington D.C./Virginia, and Houston, Central American immigrants had formed clusters in the formal and informal service sectors in areas where, in the process of downward mobility, they replaced "white ethnics," such as in suburban Long Island, in small towns of Iowa and North Carolina, in Silicon Valley, and in the northern and eastern suburbs of the San Francisco Bay Area.[192]

Transnational processes and related migration patterns in Central America are linked to similar processes throughout the Greater Caribbean Basin. Economic restructuring in the United States involves social dislocations, new gender and racial hierarchies, and other changes deeply tied up with globalization. Latino immigration from the Greater Caribbean Basin is closely related to the issue of minority group formation, the emerging Latino national minority in the United States, and the changing nature of US race relations.[193] Labor-market transformations in the United States and elsewhere contributed to the "new nativism," the worldwide wave of xenophobia and racism against immigrants, or what McMichael calls "the politics of global labor circulation."[194] Shifting political coalitions scapegoated immigrants by promoting ethnic-based solidarities among middle classes, representatives of distinct fractions of capital, and formerly privileged sectors among working classes (such as white ethnic workers in the United States and Europe) threatened by job loss, declining income and other insecurities of economic restructuring.

The long-term tendency seems to be towards a generalization across borders of labor market conditions, characterized by segmented structures under a regime of labor deregulation and racial, ethnic, and gender hierarchies. A number of transnational corporations operating maquilas in Central America also operate maquilas in Los Angeles and New York, by way of example, in which entrepreneurs consider labor conditions to be similar and location is determined by market proximity and other non-labor production considerations. One large-scale South Korean contractor in Guatemala, for instance, operated a sister shop in the garment district in Los Angeles. The Guatemalan factory produced more standardized apparel for general North American marketing while the Los Angeles factory assembles more specialized styles for local market niches. Asked if there were any noticeable differences between the labor force in the two factories, one company official replied that workers in both locations were the same because "almost all the workers in our Los Angeles plant are from Central America. If you walked into our [Los Angeles] plant you would think you were in Guatemala."[195] Estimates for the early 1990s indicated that more than 35 percent of sewing shop workers in Los Angeles were paid less than the US minimum wage, that the majority were not properly compensated for overtime work, and 7 percent of apparel contractors used illegal child labor.[196] Similarly, women represented 81 percent of the labor force in garment production in the United States, and minorities 27 percent.[197] And US apparel wages declined between 1950 and 1987 from 77 percent of average manufacturing wages to 54 percent. The structural similarity, in a cross- or transnational setting, of labor involved in globalized production processes and of labor conditions in these circuits gives us a glimpse into the ways in which transnational processes generate a transnational labor force.

Nicaraguan Immigrant Labor in Costa Rica

If the proposition that labor-market conditions are becoming generalized throughout the Greater Caribbean Basin is true then we should expect to see such conditions, and even minority group formation, beyond US borders. This is in fact just what we find, by way of example, in the case of Nicaraguan immigrant labor in Costa Rica, which is worth exploring in some detail because it is so illustrative of the transnational processes that are the subject of this book. Sociologist Abelardo Morales and his colleagues at the Costa Rican center of the Latin American Social Science Faculty (FLACSO) association have conducted extensive field research into the Nicaraguan immigrant population and ethnic labor market segmentation in that country.[198] They have shown that, as the Costa Rican labor market has become segmented along ethnic Nicaraguan–Costa Rican lines, Nicaraguan immigrants have faced the same segmentation disadvantages, state controls, popular xenophobia and racism, as have Third World immigrant communities in core countries. Just as immigrants anywhere, Nicaraguans were denied labor rights, received sub-minimum wages, and suffered other forms of abuse as a result of their precarious legal status.

Small-scale emigration to Costa Rica has occurred for decades and the border between the two countries has historically been a binational zone. But the massive transfer of Nicaraguans to Costa Rica is a more recent phenomenon bound up with transnational processes. By the late 1990s Nicaraguan immigrants in Costa Rica were estimated at an astonishing 500,000 to 700,000, representing between 12 and 18 percent of the Nicaraguan population, and just as astonishing, equalled an estimated 16 percent of the Costa Rican population and up to 30 percent of the EAP.[199] The immediate cause of this migration on the "push" side was the saturation of both formal and informal employment opportunities in Nicaragua in the 1980s in the face of economic crisis and military conflict. The surplus Nicaraguan population expanded further in the 1990s with the sharp contraction of public employment under neo-liberal adjustment measures and the demobilization of and incorporation into civilian life of some 120,000 Sandinista and contra combatants. On the "pull" side, the transformation of Costa Rica's productive apparatus resulted in a massive shift of Costa Rican workers out of traditional activities in agriculture and resulted in labor shortages. Although Nicaraguans are poorly paid in Costa Rica, wages are four times higher in agriculture in Costa Rica than in Nicaragua, and between two and three times higher in industry and services.[200] This wage differential exerts a substantial pull on surplus Nicaraguan labor. Depeasantization of the Costa Rican countryside left both old and new agro-export activities without a work force, which was replenished by Nicaraguans. As Costa Rican smallholders lost their lands to transnational corporations and Costa Rican capitalists who proceeded to reorient production towards the global economy there was a switch from Costa Rican to Nicaraguan labor precisely at these new or reorganized production sites. "The immigrant work force has become a key factor in the development of a series of new productive activities promoted by the Costa Rican state since the mid-1980s as part of the new export-oriented model."[201]

Beyond agriculture, Nicaraguans are concentrated in unskilled, poorly paid, and precarious jobs, generally manual labor, although they show up in almost every sector of the economy. Traditional agro-exports (especially banana, but also coffee), several NTAE industries (particularly melons), the construction industries, maquiladora factory work, domestic service and other service sector activities have become major "absorption niches" for Nicaraguan laborers. Nicaraguans predominate among security guards, restaurant workers, porters, shoe repair, electronic repair, janitors and cleaners, as hair salon assistants, and so on, in a pattern remarkably similar to immigrant Latino employment in the United States. The massive entry of Nicaraguans into the Costa Rican labor market has coincided with the development of new forms of "flexible" employment associated with the new capital–labor relation, especially temporary, part-time, seasonal, and contract work, and a drop in the general wage level in these categories, so that much work done by Nicaraguans is precarious and provides no benefits or security. The construction industry provides a classical example of ethnic segmentation. Nicaraguan workers comprise up to 70 percent of construction workers during peak periods, but "the social division of work is based on nationality, as Nicaraguans are largely consigned to less skilled labor as peons and assistants, while Costa Ricans occupy the more skilled positions, such as masons, carpenters, electricians, and painters."[202]

Gender segmentation prevails *within* the Nicaraguan labor force, as it does in the broader Costa Rican labor market. While 64 percent of Nicaraguan men are employed in agriculture and industry, only 13 percent work in personal services, whereas 52 percent of Nicaraguan women work in personal services, largely as maids.[203] Here we see the overlap of gender, ethnic, and class hierarchies. While 52 percent of Nicaraguan women were maids only 13 percent of Costa Rican women were domestic workers, down from nearly 40 percent in 1950.[204] In a process that finds parallels in the United States and elsewhere, Costa Rican women have entered the formal labor force in increasing numbers in recent decades and new employment opportunities have been opened up for professional women. This has reduced the supply of Costa Rican domestic workers, while the entrance of women into the formal labor market, especially professional and business women, has increased demand. The gap has been filled by Nicaraguan women who work under informal and unstable conditions. These maids receive only 46 percent of what women working in industry are paid and 33 percent of what female administrative workers earn.[205] Social differentiation among women along class and ethnic lines becomes more apparent as strictly gender barriers to women's social and economic participation have come down (see next section).

The Nicaraguan population in Costa Rica exhibits all the classical sociological signs of a minority group, including systematic subordination within stratification structures on the basis of ethnic identification, the construction of social and cultural barriers that reinforce this subordination, humiliation in the hands of the majority group, social demarcation by characteristics singled out or constructed by the majority group, residential segregation, and an increasing sense of ethnic self-identity and solidarity. Costa Rican researcher Patricia Alvarenga has documented Nicaraguan ethnic formation, the rise of discriminatory discourse and practices, and growing ethnic tensions in the country, "the most novel phenomenon in Costa Rica's social situation in the 1990s," as part and parcel of the transformation of the Costa Rican political economy.[206] The process of creating a Nicaraguan "Otherness" in the 1990s included the construction of a Nicaraguan ethnic identity on the basis of three characteristics used to establish difference: Nicaraguans' distinct accent and colloquialisms;

alleged "violence-prone" behavior patterns among Nicaraguans; and the darker skin tone and more indigenous features of Nicaraguans. Nicaraguan immigrants have in turn incorporated ethnic identity into their own strategies of negotiation and resistance. Regional collective identities (such as Latino or Central American) that may predominate over national identity, observes Alvarenga, are substituted within Costa Rica for Nicaraguan ethnic identity. "State policies, the construction of the Other by 'legitimate' Costa Ricans, and the need to adapt to a new social universe in quite disadvantaged conditions are the basis on which the sentiment of belonging to a Nicaraguan community has developed"[207] and contributed in the late 1990s to mutual aid and intra-group solidarity networks throughout Costa Rica (one wonders if and when resistance in the form of mutual aid may become politicized or develop into an ethnic-based social movement).

Nicaraguan minority group formation in Costa Rica is a process fomented by the state, which has taken a series of measures to create and sustain a juridical category of immigrant workers from Nicaragua and to structure labor market segmentation along these lines. One such measure was the 1995 decision to oblige all Nicaraguans to obtain a "seasonal work card" issued by the government. Each card was valid for only six months at a time, which in effect made it impossible for Nicaraguans to legally obtain stable or long-term employment in better-off jobs. The measure therefore helped to sanction the ethnic segmentation of the labor market, contributed to the casualization of labor, at least in the bottom rungs of the segmented structure, and provided the state with a powerful instrument of control over the Nicaraguan immigrant work force (synchronized with the repressive practices of Costa Rican police and immigration authorities). At the same time, as Alvarenga notes, "there are a significant number of Costa Ricans who also earn their living doing precisely the difficult, unstable, and poorly paid work in which Nicaraguans are employed, and in the context of the country's economic crisis more and more Costa Rican workers have been pushed into the lower rungs of the labor market where Nicaraguans predominate."[208] But because of their greater vulnerability, Nicaraguans are preferred by employers, while the state has intervened in resultant ethnic tensions by encouraging the scapegoating of Nicaraguans through such public proclamations as blaming Nicaraguans for "disloyal competition" in the job market and taking job opportunities away from Costa Ricans. Most troubling, the anti-Nicaraguan sentiment has gained ground among Costa Rican popular sectors as social polarization and the insecurities that adhere to the transnational model have made themselves felt.

The Nicaraguan immigrant work force is becoming a structural feature of the Costa Rican economy, just as immigrant labor in the broader context is becoming a structural feature of the global economy. In the late 1990s, the Costa Rican government loosened northern border restraints to compensate for renewed national labor shortages in the coffee, sugar, and banana industries. The government reached formal agreements with the Nicaraguan government and local businesses to facilitate the temporary transfer of labor. This macrostructure of Nicaraguan migration is sustained by the microstructure of migrant networks. Morales and Castro found that kinship networks are "the principal social capital determining migration."[209] Moreover, a high percentage of emigrant Nicaraguan workers—as high as 91 percent for construction workers—send remittances back home, thus providing a further factor in the formation of structures spanning the two countries that are truly transnational.

The Costa Rica–Nicaragua border region has become what Morales and Castro term "binational transborder space." The border region functions through family networks, local services, and diverse subsistence activities, as a reservoir and replenishment zone for workers whose migration cycles take them to diffuse production sites around the country as they rotate in and out of the Costa Rican labor market. Nicaraguans employed seasonally in agro-export plantations all over Costa Rica or in temporary urban work contracts may rotate back and forth across the border region in between employment. In some cases, transnational corporations and local Costa Rican subcontractors producing for export to the global economy have set up activities in the border region, such as new banana and other NTAE plantations, to take advantage of Nicaraguan migrant labor.[210] In this space, new "demographic realities and the process of sociocultural formation fly in the face of traditional conceptions of the local, such as the notion of the territorial administration of a clearly identified political unit." Instead, "daily practices have given the 'local' a transborder, multidimensional and heterogeneous dimension because the mechanisms of daily subsistence, family networks, and the reproduction of social life in its varied forms take place in spaces that criss-cross the border."[211] The entire border region is "territory in the process of becoming transnationalized, involving the formation of binational micro-regions between Nicaragua and Costa Rica where transborder economic systems have been established with increasingly strong links to the world economy. Nicaraguan labor migration towards these territories is not a variable isolated from this process of territorial transnationalization but rather the most significant social aspect of that process."[212] The establishment of this "transborder space" is not something unique to Costa Rica and Nicaragua but one of several territorial and social forms in which globalized production complexes are materializing. In *Global Shift*, Dicken refers to these types of border regions integrated into global production chains as "transborder clusters." Between what he calls the "macroscale of the global triad and the highly localized agglomerations of economic activities," lies a "mesoscale of economic-geographic organization which crosses, or sometimes aligns with, national borders. In some cases, this scale of organization is actually defined and created by the existence of the political boundary itself. In others it develops in spite of such boundaries and simply extends across them in a functionally organized manner."[213]

In sum, the Costa Rica–Nicaragua case study is fascinating for what it tells us about both the specifics and the generalities, beyond the issue of transnational migration, of transnational processes. Although it is not possible to give further attention to the topic, it is worth quoting Morales and Castro at some length:

> The productive contribution of this immigrant mass has been fundamental in dynamizing certain activities that are of central importance to Costa Rica's economic transformation in the context of globalization. This labor emigration is the most importance social expression of a process of binational interdependence and contributes through the establishment of mutual aid social networks among immigrant communities to the creation of transnational social spaces. The deployment of the immigrant Nicaraguan population throughout Costa Rican territory is a dynamic articulated to deeper structural transformations that are underway in both countries. As a social phenomenon it is caused by factors specific to Nicaragua and to Costa Rica. But these specific realities conceal a series of circuits that criss-cross both [national] social structures and that suggest that the most relevant aspect is not these national structures but the [transnational structure emerging from] relations between the two.[214]

The case of Nicaraguan workers in Costa Rica is the only example within the region of the full development of a segmented market and of ethnic group formation around it. Such intra-regional migrations are becoming more fluid, including bidirectional movements between Honduras and El Salvador, the migration of Salvadorans to Guatemala, and so on, and need to be further studied.[215] The elimination of visa requirements for Central Americans traveling between countries within the region in the early 1990s as part of the regional integration processes (see below) has facilitated this movement. But the process is rooted structurally in the breakdown of autonomous national economic structures and points to the creation of a single Central American labor market as a regional component of the global labor market.

Meanwhile, transnational migration has transformative effects on the Central American social structure. It draws off a portion of the surplus labor in Central America and, as with the remittances, is a social and political escape valve. Opting for migration rather than resistance works against political mobilization. The evidence suggests that what started as Central American migrant networks are evolving into transnational communities that exhibit the traits described by Portes and whose activities help transnationalize the social structure in Central America and in the countries of Central American immigration.[216] By way of anecdote, in many towns in El Salvador, the church of the plaza has been replaced as the main social gathering place by Antel (the local telephone office), as residents gather to telephone family members and contacts in the United States and elsewhere. One Guatemalan community in Houston used faxes to organize a transnational birthday celebration for a family member in their hometown of San Cristóbal Tononicapan.[217]

In their survey and focus group research on sending communities in El Salvador, Lungo and Kandel found that migration modified existing and introduced new sociocultural practices.[218] Migration altered family and communal relations, with the temporary or permanent retirement of family members that migration implies, resulting in changed roles for those who stayed behind. When men migrated women often assumed new roles as heads of households, changing their own and other family members' perceptions of them. When women or both parents migrated, kin from extended families, and even persons who were not relatives, took on the role of head of household. In general, new forms of extended families have come into existence, providing for new dynamics in gender relations, although these do not necessarily break down but may reproduce patriarchal relations in new ways. Interestingly, transnational migrations also contributed to the formation of new social elites at the local level. Most traditional elite families, as a result of the political-military conflict and economic transformation, migrated from smaller rural and urban communities to major industrial centers, which opened up space for new elites. These spaces have often been filled either by returning migrants who bring with them new social and cultural capital, or by families who have been able to accumulate local influence through small-scale remittance wealth or through their integration into transnational community networks.

Transnational migration assures constant and ongoing exposure to other forms of lifestyles associated with globalizing cultural dynamics. Included here is increased and more diversified consumption stemming from the remittance, from returning migrants, and from other forms of symbolic and material exchange linked to the development of migrant networks and transnational communities. "Agriculture has stopped being a productive and cultural reference point" for youth, observe Lungo and Kandel. "Instead, the emphasis is on migration and remittances ... Young adults faced with the loss of agriculture as an economically viable option for one's livelihood are forced to confront identity problems and uncertainty about what they will do with their lives. In addition, the traditional campesino way of life must compete against the attractions portrayed by the media, fashions, urban and transnational lifestyles that are closer to their process of socialization."[219] Remittances and transnational community networks become transmission belts for the penetration of a global consumer culture and cosmology that has little to do with "traditional" national social and cultural practices.

Women and Transnational Processes: Global and Central American Dimensions

There has been a growing consensus that the process of globalization affects men and women differently, and that the process entails contradictory social-gender effects. Gender has played an important role for many researchers of globalization for two reasons. First, much of the debate in the 1970s and 1980s on the New International Division of Labor (NIDL) emphasized the phenomenon of young women working for transnational corporations in export-processing enclaves.[220] Second, the "feminization of poverty" thesis has pointed out that the worldwide rise in poverty in the late twentieth and early twenty-first centuries associated with global economic restructuring and neo-liberalism has affected women disproportionately, and that the "new poor" are disproportionately women (and children). These two respective aspects are relevant to Central America in that women have indeed made up a large part of the labor force engaged in new transnational economic activities, as analyzed in the previous chapter, and in that women have disproportionately borne the brunt of structural adjustment.

Women, Development, and Globalization

The differential effects of capitalist development on men and women were first underscored in the 1970s and 1980s in the Women in Development (WID) literature, which tended to argue that women were not integrated into development processes and had not benefited from them.[221] But the WID literature became outdated on several counts. First, as a number of its critics noted, it assumed that women were "excluded" from development rather than integrated into it in ways that made their social and economic contributions invisible, such as their work in the non-monetized/unpaid sector. Second, much of the literature shared the assumption of modernization theory that integration into the capitalist market would bring about an improvement in the status of women, establishing as its problematic how women could be better integrated into market structures rather than how those structures and the power relations that adhere in them could be transformed.[222] As a result, the themes of Gender and Development (GED) and Women, Environment, and Alternative Development (WED) arose as more critical approaches focusing on gender relations and capitalist development. But more central to the purposes here, the whole issue of gender relations and development is becoming transformed by globalization.

Globalization has major implications for the sexual division of labor, for gender relations, and for the transformation of the family itself. Most researchers agree that the inequality women face must be analyzed on two levels: production and reproduction. Gender asymmetries in the labor market, in particular gender segmentation/segregation, are central to gender inequality in the economy and society, but in turn these asymmetries are grounded in the household division of labor, family relations, and the domestic "private" sphere of reproduction. A central concern of research into the political economy of gender and development has been how these two spheres are articulated and mutually linked to political and cultural subprocesses. Shifting the focus to the systemic-level perspective of world capitalism, the fate of women in the global economy is closely tied to the creation of a world labor market, historically involving two aspects. One was securing pools of labor to be imported and exported around the world. The second was the reproduction of a world labor supply. Both these aspects have dramatic gender dimensions, since women serve the world

Table 4.10. Women as Percentage of Labor Force by Region

	1970	1990
Developed countries	33	42
Sub-Saharan Africa	39	38
Latin America	20	34
Asia	31	39

Source: For world regions, UNDP, *Human Development Report 1995*.

economy both as a supply of labor and as reproducers of labor on a global scale. As Lydia Potts points out:

The object of the measures adopted during both phases [a colonial phase of encouraging reproduction in the Third World and a post-colonial phase of coercive population control] of the world market for labour power and of demographic evolution was to control the ability of women to bear children and thereby to find a level of reproduction high enough on the one hand to guarantee the supply for the capitalist sector, nationally and internationally, of a sufficient number of suitable workers, but also so low and socially selective that social and political development would remain controllable.[223]

These world labor market dynamics help explain the deterioration of the status of women under globalization. The transformations in capitalism that have given rise to a mass superfluous and potentially disruptive population worldwide have turned women from reproducers of labor power required by capital into reproducers of supernumeraries for which capital has no direct use. Female labor is further devalued, and women denigrated, as the function of the domestic (household) economy moves from rearing labor for *incorporation* into capitalist production to rearing supernumeraries. This is one important structural underpinning of the global feminization of poverty and is reciprocal to, and mutually reinforces, racial/ethnic dimensions of inequality. It helps explain the dismantling of Keynesian social welfare programs in a manner that disproportionately affects women and children (and racially oppressed groups). On the other hand, there has been a growing incorporation of women into the formal labor force worldwide as the process of capitalist development has accelerated under globalization (see table 4.10).

This entrance of women into formal labor markets is most pronounced among new economic activities linked to the global economy. "The 1980s might be labeled the decade of labor deregulation. It has also marked a renewed surge of feminization of labor activity," notes Guy Standing in his study, "Global Feminization through Flexible Labor." "The types of work, labor relations, income, and insecurity associated with 'women's work' have been spreading, resulting not only in a notable rise in female labor force participation, but in a fall in men's employment, as well as a transformation—or feminization—of many jobs traditionally held by men."[224] The phenomenon of female employment in Free Trade Zones (FTZs) or world market factories has been most researched, especially in the transnationalized textiles and garments, electronics, and pharmaceuticals industries. Around the world, women's share of industrial employment hovers around 30–40 percent, but in export processing factories it is often as high as 90 percent.[225] Some 80 percent of the worldwide work force in free trade zones is women, the majority 15–25 years of age, who earn wages 20 to 50 percent lower than those of men working in the same zone.[226]

Here, we see a fusion of patriarchal structures and existing gender relations of inequality with new capitalist relations of domination. Historically, capital appropriates pre-capitalist sets of relations—rather than destroying them, as both modernization theorists and Marxists predicted—when they can be functional to accumulation. The social control advantages associated with patriarchal social relations and sex-role differentiation—the extension of the sexual division of labor in the family to the labor market—help explain the preference by transnational capital and by local capitalists tied to transnational networks for women in offshore sectors and globalized economic activities. The following is a typical statement made by a maquiladora manager: "[Because of] their mothering instincts, women are . . . more responsible than men; they are raised to be gentle and obedient, and so they are easier to deal with. They are also more nimble and meticulous and they don't get tired of doing the same thing nine hundred times a day . . . We hire them because we know we'll have fewer problems."[227]

Increased female labor market participation, especially in new economic activities linked to the global economy, is due to a confluence of factors bound up with capitalist globalization, among them, the predictable pattern that accompanies capitalist development in general, the need for families to send an increasing number of family members into the labor market with the decline in real wages and household income, and the predilection of transnational capital to hire "docile" female labor, particularly in maquila production. The drive of transnational capital to keep labor costs low through flexibilization raises the demand for female labor. But if female labor initially is (or is perceived to be) more easy to control, this is the result, we should recall, of gender socialization combined with real relations of patriarchy and gender inequality and pre-existing sexual divisions of labor which, in combination, render female workers (initially) more powerless than their male counterparts.

The restructuring of work and of gender relations under globalization is a singular process and inseparable from the transformation of the labor market and from other subprocesses examined earlier in this and other chapters. Transnational capital takes advantage of the double segmentation of labor markets, both international and sexual. As Standing notes, the "increasing globalization and production and pursuit of flexible forms of labor to maximize competitiveness and profits, and changing job structure in enterprises" favors "feminization of employment" in a dual sense: first, there is an increase in number of women in the labor force; second, there is a deterioration of work conditions (labor standards, income, employment status).[228] Much of the work available to women in the globalized economy is poorly paid, insecure, and demeaning, and in general informal or casualized in nature, including seasonal, temporary, and part-time work, home-based work, and informal economic activities. As a consequence of the continued burden of household responsibilities and child-rearing, women find themselves in a particularly vulnerable position vis-à-vis incorporation as "flexible" labor into the labor market, because such arrangements make it possible for them to simultaneously carry out domestic responsibilities and child-care, and thus to bear a gendered double burden of production and reproduction. At the same time, the general decline in wages and household budgets income associated with globalization pushes women to seek jobs. Lourdes Benería sums up the phenomenon well:

> The reasons for this new preference for women workers, as presented by different studies, are more complex than what is implied by the cheap labor argument and can be summarized as falling into three categories. First, women workers are assumed to facilitate *labor control and labor malleability* for a variety of reasons, such as their willingness to follow orders, their greater discipline, and other characteristics falling under the stereotype of docility. Whether these "gender traits" are real or assumed, they can be one of the reasons for this preference. Second, in some cases, women are hired for reasons having to do with *productivity*, when it is reported that women work better with small objects. This is the old nimble fingers argument which, in some cases, represents the recognition and use of skills that women have acquired through their gender socialization and work experience, as with the case of garment work. Third, women provide an important source of *flexible labor* through their predominance in temporary contracts as well as in part-time and unstable work: this flexibility facilitates the maximum adjustment of labor supply to the requirements of and oscillations in labor demand. The importance of this adjustment is apparent for the peripheral, informalized labor processes, but it also applies to more formal types of work.[229]

With the decline in male employment and real wages brought about by neo-liberal restructuring, women have assumed a growing absolute and also relative importance as wage earners and their contribution to household economies has increased. The reorganization of production on a global scale is thus feminizing the labor force and changing the previous gender demarcation of domestic and wage labor. However, gender inequality is reproduced in the work force at the same time as it continues in the household: the systematic subordination of women in the sphere of reproduction is coupled with the systematic inequality of women in the sphere of production. It is clear that what is taking place under globalization is a transformation of the sexual division of labor. New forms of labor market segmentation between men and women and wage differentials in the formal sector converge with nonremunerated domestic labor and hardships imposed in the sphere of gendered social reproduction and result in a deterioration of the status and social condition of most women. From the maquilas of Mexico, Central America, and the Caribbean, to the new transnational agri-business plantations in Chile and Colombia, and the new industrial complexes in Brazil's northeast, to take the case of Latin America, women disproportionately—and in some cases, often exclusively—engage in deskilled, labor-intensive phases of globalized production.

Many studies have shown how neo-liberalism and structural adjustment programs have a particularly adverse effect on women, especially poor and working-class women.[230] Women are generally responsible for household budgeting and maintenance. Adjustment leaves them to cope with increased prices, shrinking incomes, and dwindling social services. The decline in wages and work conditions associated with the new capital–labor relation at the site of production thus takes place at a time when women increasingly make up the ranks of the work force. At the same time, the costs of reproduction of the labor force are assumed by women without compensation, and these costs rise dramatically to the extent that neo-liberal adjustment removes state and public support for that reproduction, which becomes "privatized" and reverts more exclusively to the household. The state's withdrawal from providing basic services linked to social repro-duction takes place at a time when the need for these services has grown with the rapid increase in urbanization and commodification.

These twin processes—stated in simplified terms, the deterioration of wages and social wages—have had a devastating impact on women and children in Latin America. It is estimated that 70 percent of the poor in Latin America are women.[231] Women in Latin America have a 34 percent probability of belonging to the bottom 20 percent of the income distribu-tion, as compared to a 15 percent probability for men.[232] Table 4.11 supports the observation that as women have entered the formal labor force they encounter a gender-segmented labor market in which they are disproportionately concentrated in low-wage employment and excluded from high-wage employment. This inequality in labor force participation aggravates other gender-based social inequalities. As women enter the labor force they are also disproportionately relegated to the informal economy, as part-time domestics, laundresses, street vendors, industrial homeworkers, and so on. Women in Latin America account for fully 70 percent of all new jobs in the informal sector,[233] and by the 1990s an estimated 130 million women and children were eking out a living in the informal sector.[234]

These general patterns in Latin America and worldwide are evident in Central America as well. Women have entered the formal and informal labor force in the Isthmus in mass numbers in recent decades, with a huge jump in participation from 1990 and on (see table 4.12), along with their increasing prominence in the informal economy.

But as Central American women enter the labor force they do so on unequal terms. As we saw in the previous chapter, women workers predom-inate in the maquila sector. Although less research has been undertaken on female employment in new transnational agri-business sites and chains worldwide, such as the NTAE sector in Central America, studies have

Table 4.11. Workers' Wages by Decile and Gender for Select Countries (as percentage, female)

	Income Decile		
	1	5	10
Argentina			
1980	70.7	30.7	12.7
1989	70.3	36.6	18.8
Bolivia			
1986	67.8	39.5	14.4
1989	71.2	37.1	20.8
Brazil			
1979	64.3	27.9	12.4
1989	61.1	33.4	19.5
Colombia			
1980	43.2	43.5	18.2
1989	47.5	42.0	24.7
Costa Rica			
1981	30.6	23.4	27.8
1989	51.5	23.7	23.5
Guatemala			
1986	34.4	16.2	23.6
1989	34.3	12.0	25.4
Honduras			
1986	78.8	32.4	23.1
1989	50.9	21.9	27.6
Panama			
1979	69.8	32.6	33.3
1989	54.9	33.8	28.6
Uruguay			
1981	72.6	37.0	13.2
1989	73.7	43.1	16.6

Source: Calculated from World Bank data, *Poverty and Income Distribution in Latin America*, 1997, pp. 197–202.

uncovered a similar phenomenon. One study of NTAEs in Guatemala, Honduras, and Costa Rica revealed that women made up more than half of the labor force in harvesting, processing, and packaging.[235] A similar pattern holds for transnational services as well, including tourism.[236] Even when the absolute number of women employed in the maquiladoras and

Table 4.12.   Entrance of Women into the Formal Labor Force (as percentage of women in the EAP in formal labor force)

	1950	1960	1970	1980	1990	1995	2000
Costa Rica	15	16	18	21	22	30	37
El Salvador	16	17	20	25	25	34	46
Guatemala	12	12	13	14	16	26	36
Honduras	12	12	14	16	19	30	40
Nicaragua	14	18	20	22	25	36	47

Source: for 1950–95, James W. Wilkie (ed.), *Statistical Abstracts of Latin America, 1993, 1995, 1999*, for 2000, UNDP, *Human Development Report*, 2002.

other globalized economic activities in Central America is small relative to those women working in traditional and informal sectors, we should recall that the indirect effects of such transnational employment of women can be vast, including multiplier effects through subcontracting chains that can involve many women in home work or family labor, such as we saw for NTAEs, or in numerous ways in the informal economy.

Moreover, discussion of the participation of Central American women in the global economy would have to include female employment in the United States and other countries of emigration, where they work in gender-segmented occupations as nannies, nurses, domestic workers, food servers, cleaners, and so on, even though this is not reflected in strictly nation-state data such as that presented in table 4.12.[237] Transnational migration, whether by men or by women, contributes to the disruption of patriarchal family structures and to the reorganization of male and female economic roles, as does the entrance of women into the formal labor force and the contraction of male employment. Latino labor destined for the lower rungs of the US economy is produced and reproduced in Central America, that is, in Central American families inserted into rapidly changing local economic structures.

At the same time as they become incorporated into the formal economy, Central American women continue their functions in the household economy. Transnational processes are increasingly the "double burden" experienced by Central American women in both production and reproduction.[238] The stresses of the economic crisis and deteriorating socioeconomic conditions have contributed to an escalation of violence against women throughout the region, despite new Family Codes and other forms of legislation passed in all five republics in the 1980s and 1990s, designed to protect women and strengthen their juridical equality, as part of the political modernization process. In Costa Rica, for instance, the cases of battered women increased by over 200 percent from 1983 into the early 1990s.[239] In El Salvador, the World Health Organization reported that 57 percent of all Salvadoran women suffered physical abuse at home.[240]

One 1999 United Nations report on Central America summarized continued and deepening gender inequalities thus:

The situation of [Central American] women is clearly more disadvantaged than that of men. Throughout the region, the HDI [Human Development Index] value declines when the focus is on inequalities women suffer in education, health, and income ... Moreover, women are worse off in the world of work and in political participation. Other evidence of gender inequality is lower rates of female participation in the labor market and higher rates of open unemployment. The regional illiteracy rate is on average 18.3 percent higher for women. Poverty has become feminized and domestic violence against women continues to be a major problem.[241]

A new Central American family structure is emerging, spurred on by transnational processes. This restructuring of the family in Central America is part of a broader process of family transformation under globalization that involves as well the rise of new transnational family structures. These new structures shape and are shaped by, among other factors, transnational migration, new gender identities, and economic and cultural roles beyond the nation-state, such phenomena as "global marriage markets," the development of webs of affective bonds across borders and regions, and a global "care-giving" industry involving new confluences of everyday gender, ethnic, and class hierarchies. The globalization literature has increasingly focused on these more "textured" dimensions of social transformation in the global age.[242] Returning more specifically to the global political economy in Central America, structural adjustment, as in much of the greater Caribbean Basin, by contracting male employment and, increasingly, female economic responsibility, contributes to an increase in female-headed households.[243] In urban zones, women have predominantly become heads of households, and are thus responsible for the household economy and also for linkage to the monetized economy. "Faced with [the economic and social] crisis, Central American families and women are regrouping in a number of different ways," notes Faune. "They are diversifying their maintenance and reproductive strategies. New components of these strategies are: 1) internal and international migration; 2) informal marketing of products prepared in the home that were previously used for barter or self-consumption; and 3) the sale of personal services."[244] These households frequently involve several women; kin and daughters operating as collective heads of households. In the larger picture of the political economy, women have moved from being producers of labor for incorporation into production processes to producers of "supernumeraries," which has dramatically reduced women's social status and aggravated female degradation. These issues are under-theorized and require further exploration in future research.

Formal Equality, Lived Inequality: Class, Gender, and the Dilemmas of the Women's Movement

The deleterious effects of globalization and neo-liberalism on most women underscore the contradiction between the formal gains made by women alongside continued—and deepening—social inequality between men and women. We should recall the United Nations' famous 1980s declaration that women do two-thirds of the world's work, receive one-tenth of the world's income, and possess less than one-hundredth of the world's property. This is the structural basis of inequality between men and women, and it is at odds with the tremendous formal gains that women have made worldwide.

Issues of domestic violence, abortion, and sexual harassment have been placed on the agenda, along with the liberal principle of equality in the political system and equality of opportunity in the market, as a result of the feminist movement worldwide. But the social inequality that women experience based on unequal participation in economic processes and the double burden of production and reproduction has been aggravated. Although there has been significant progress in such areas as securing equal political representation in public offices and other public and private institutions, considering just how excluded women have historically been, the exercise of public and private authority is still largely a male affair.[245] Moreover, dramatic improvements in education, in legal equality, in the percentage of women in leadership positions, in the availability of birth control, and other tangible gains have not resulted in a diminution of social inequality. The expectation that they necessarily would reflects certain modernization assumptions that a sexual equalization of market conditions would be sufficient to eliminate inequality.

The 1980s and 1990s witnessed a flourishing of participation by women in diverse social movements in Latin America along with a burgeoning of women's and feminist organizations. Women have mobilized to address collective problems that women, children, and poor people face, and also to address the special forms of gender oppression and inequality that they suffer as women. In their diverse forms of mobilization, women have effectively articulated the central concerns of daily life—access to housing, health care, employment, freedom from violence against women and against the poor, democracy, and environmental preservation. Women have struggled as workers in trade unions, as mothers and as citizens in human rights movements, as housewives in shantytowns, as leading organizers and spokespeople for indigenous movements, and as guerrillas in armed movements. Reinforced by global communications, internal and international migrations, rising levels of formal education for women, and increased personal autonomy and mobility, feminism has become a powerful social movement in its own right. By the 1990s hundreds of feminist organizations were operating locally, nationally, and transnationally in Latin America, linked into a powerful hemispheric network and to broader global networks.[246]

The women's movement in Latin America, and more generally, world-wide, has experienced a remarkable dynamic. By force of structural circumstance, it has engaged in a synthesis of the particular struggle against women's oppression with the struggle against the deleterious effects of capitalist globalization at each of the three levels of resistance to capitalism that Van der Pijl has identified in his typology.[247] As women have entered the work force en masse in recent decades they have been at the vanguard of popular struggles around the process of production and exploitation (*the first level*), such as in the maquiladoras. But, in step with the essence of gender inequality and subordination, women remain locked into the sphere of reproduction even as their participation in production becomes formal. Hence women are at the forefront of battles over social reproduction that take place in the "private" (household) and "public" (community, workplace, and state) spheres (*the second level*). Safa argues in this regard that the primary area of confrontation for women's social movements in Latin America "has been not with capital but with the state, largely in terms of women's reproductive roles as wives, mothers, and consumers, both of state services and of private consumer goods."[248] And women have also played a major role in struggles against the incursion of capitalism and its disruption of community and autonomy (*the third level*), as epitomized in the mass participation and leadership roles of women in the Zapatista and other revolutionary movements or in the MST of Brazil.

There has been a debate among feminist scholars in Latin America as to whether capitalist globalization has acted to increase opportunities for women and break down some of the structures of gender subordination or to increase the oppression and exploitation of women.[249] Dialectically speaking these assessments are both accurate and not mutually exclusive. On the one hand, the achievement of legal equality and the incorporation of women in the formal labor force and other changes have helped to break up traditional extended patriarchal family structures and the gender relations they embody. More egalitarian conjugal relations have developed where women's economic contribution to the household has increased. On the other hand, the real, lived status of women has continued to deteriorate dramatically as the burden of survival steadily increases.[250] There is without doubt a gap between *de jure* equality and daily life that disguises an almost deleterious deterioration of women's status.

"Feminism confronted a tension between women's individual claims and the needs of their communities," Fernández Kelly notes, in discussing the differences between the mobilization of middle class and poor women. "The uneasy relation between individual and communal demands exposes class differences: for comparatively affluent women in Latin America, the agenda resembles that forged by feminists in advanced industrial countries; for impoverished women in rural and urban environments, an emphasis on equality with men skirts questions about the meaning and consequences of equality in deprived environments."[251] This "emerging dilemma" underscores the dramatic growth under globalization of group and class inequalities and opportunities that cut across the gender divide, and places both poor and better-off women in a contradictory situation. To the extent that gains in formal equality and opportunity improve the condition of women *as women*, gender inequality is increasingly fused with class and group inequality under globalization. This explains, only in part, the mass participation—and indeed leadership role—of women at every level in the struggle of popular classes and in all of Latin America's social movements. And this explains, but also only in part, the paradox of tremendous gains in the Latin American women's movement side by side with the deterioration of the status and social condition of women under globalization.

The *heightened* importance of class under globalization—as a fundamental social relation and as a category of analysis—is denied by diverse "declining importance of class" theses, often associated with Weberian status analysis or postmodern accounts that reduce collective agency to subjective discourse. Critical feminist analyses have not escaped the tendency to downplay the growing causal importance of class within the structure of gender inequality. Safa, for example, argues that the prominence of women in the new social movements "is based primarily on gender rather than on class," since in her assessment "the bulk of poor women who participate in these movements are conscious of both class and gender exploitation but tend to legitimize their concerns over issues such as human rights or the cost of living primarily in terms of their roles as wives and mothers rather than as members of a subordinated class." But this is a strictly subjective conception of the nature of social mobilization which seems to deny the possibility that gender and class, far from being mutually exclusive, become fused in the mobilization of women. Indeed, as Safa notes, it is not "women" who participate in these movements per se, but *poor* women. Moreover, the transformative potential of diverse women's movements goes well beyond women, affecting the entire social structure and polity.[252]

The original Polanyian "double movement" that spawned Keynesian national social structures of accumulation embedded gender inequalities in the negotiated class relations between (male) employers and (male) employees. The family wage that became incorporated into Fordist regimes of Keynesian capitalism institutionalized the sexual division of labor based on the domestic/wage labor dichotomy. Globalization undermines the family wage as it drives down workers' wages and the social wage and at the same time thrusts women into the labor market. Any new double movement against capitalist globalization cannot reinstitutionalize the dichotomy between production and reproduction that was structured into the original double movement earlier this century. To the contrary, the emancipation of women requires not only a protective movement against global capital (perhaps its overthrow) but (barring its overthrow) also that any protective arrangements which force global capitalism into reciprocal and accountable relations with labor be constructed on the basis of the abolition of the gendered dichotomy between production and reproduction that links female subordination in the former and slavery in the latter.

5

The Contradictions of Global Capitalism and the Future of Central America

A New Cycle of Capitalist Development in Central America?

Central America appears to have embarked on a new cycle of capitalist development. Like earlier cycles, this one is export-led, and is leading to a deeper integration into the world economy. But the current era of globalization provides a different context for such accumulation than did the era of nation-state capitalism in earlier cycles. What are the prospects for export-led development in Central America in the new era? This question involves two dimensions: can the transnational model of accumulation sustain a new round of capitalist expansion? and can such a cycle bring development to the region, defined as an improvement in the lives of Central Americans?

Whether the new model will generate renewed expansion for another historic period is not yet clear. Nonetheless, a glance at several basic indicators suggests that such expansion is in fact underway. Growth and investment were reactivated in the 1990s after nearly two decades of crisis and stagnation, even though the recovery was quite limited. Table 5.1 shows annual growth rates in the 1990s, while table 5.2 places these rates in thirty-year perspective.

Moreover, rates of gross domestic investment and capital formation have

Table 5.1. Annual GDP Growth Rates for Central America

	1991	1992	1993	1994	1995	1996	1997	1998	1999
Costa Rica	2.2	7.1	5.8	4.3	2.2	−0.5	3.5	5.5	7.6
El Salvador	2.8	7.3	6.4	6.0	6.2	1.8	4.2	3.2	2.6
Guatemala	3.7	4.9	4.0	4.1	5.0	3.0	4.3	5.0	3.6
Honduras	2.7	5.8	7.1	−1.9	3.7	3.8	5.0	3.0	−2.0
Nicaragua	−0.4	0.8	−0.4	4.0	4.4	5.0	5.5	4.2	6.9
Regional average	2.2	5.2	4.6	3.3	4.3	2.6	4.5	4.2	3.7

Source: CEPAL, *Annual Report*, various years.

Table 5.2. Average Annual GDP Growth Rates for Central America, 1970–99

	1970–80	1981–90	1991–99
Costa Rica	5.5	2.2	4.1
El Salvador	3.1	−0.4	4.4
Guatemala	5.7	0.9	4.2
Honduras	5.5	2.4	3.1
Nicaragua	0.3	−1.5	3.2
Regional average	4.0	0.7	3.8

Source: CEPAL, *Annual Report*, various years.

recovered and in some cases have overtaken average rates in the decade preceding the regional upheaval, as table 5.3 indicates.

Post-bellicose Central America has again become an attractive investment site for transnational capital. After over a decade of capital flight and disinvestment, foreign direct investment into the region increased steadily in the 1990s, in some cases sharply (see table 5.4). The region's restructuring and integration into the global economy has clearly opened up new opportunities for profit-making. Transnational capital is once again pouring into the region, with the predictable catalytic and transformative effect analyzed in earlier chapters, drawing the Isthmus deeper into webs of world market relations and transnational production and service chains.

But all is not well in the Central American political economy, even when seen through the lens of traditional macroeconomic indicators such as those presented above. It is not clear if the model can become stable enough to allow for a new round of capitalist growth.

Table 5.3. Gross Domestic Investment in Central America, 1970–97 (average annual growth rates)

	1970–80	1980–90	1990–97
Costa Rica	9.7	1.3	4.1
El Salvador	n/a	−3.2	5.5
Guatemala	5.0	−2.9	3.4
Honduras	5.8	−0.6	7.8
Nicaragua	0.3	−2.8	9.5
Regional average	5.2*	−1.6	6.1

* Average does not include El Salvador

Source: IDB, *Economic and Social Progress in Latin America*, Annual Report, 1998–99.

Table 5.4.   Foreign Direct Investment in Central America, 1991–99 (in millions $)

	1991	1992	1993	1994	1995	1996	1997	1998	1999	2000	2001
Costa Rica	172	222	243	292	331	422	407	604	615	404	447
El Salvador	25	15	16	n/a	38	n/a	n/a	875	162	178	196
Guatemala	91	94	143	65	75	77	85	673	155	245	440
Honduras	52	48	52	42	369	90	128	99	237	282	186
Nicaragua	42	42	40	40	375	97	173	184	300	265	180
Regional total	382	421	494	–	588	–	–	2435	1469	1374	1449

Source: CEPAL, *Annual Report*, various years.

Can Capitalist Expansion be Sustained?

There is reason to believe that the new round of expansion launched in the 1990s cannot be sustained. Expansion has been dependent on persistent and growing external sector imbalances and on continued high levels of foreign indebtedness, including a steady increase in some countries, as table 5.5 shows. In Nicaragua, debt renegotiation, largely with the country's former Soviet and Eastern European creditors, reduced that country's debt sharply in the early 1990s, although it began to grow again late in that decade. Debt reduction in Nicaragua accounts for the registered drop in the regional debt total and does not suggest a modification or reversal of the tendency for the transnational model to be associated with high, and even growing, levels of external debt.

The transnational elite had apparently "resolved" in the 1990s the Third World debt crisis that exploded in the 1980s. But this "resolution" of the crisis did not mean an actual reduction in the burden of the debt. The debt increased for the Third World every year in the late twentieth century. Nor did it mean a reduction in the tribute paid to transnational capital

Table 5.5.   Central American Foreign Debt (billions $)

	1991	1992	1993	1994	1995	1996	1997	1998	1999	2000	2001
Costa Rica	3.9	4.0	4.0	3.8	3.9	3.4	3.3	3.5	3.8	4.1	4.2
El Salvador	2.2	2.3	2.0	2.1	2.2	2.5	2.7	2.6	2.7	2.8	3.4
Guatemala	2.6	2.5	2.3	2.6	2.9	3.0	3.2	3.5	4.0	3.9	3.9
Honduras	3.4	3.5	3.9	4.0	4.2	4.1	4.1	4.4	4.5	4.7	4.7
Nicaragua	10.3	10.8	12.0	11.7	10.2	7.0	6.0	6.3	6.7	6.7	6.3
Regional total	22.4	23.1	24.2	32.7	23.4	20.0	19.3	20.3	21.7	21.8	22.5

Source: CEPAL, *Preliminary Overview of Latin America and the Caribbean*, 1999.

through amortization. Rather, the crisis was "resolved" because the debt was made *serviceable* through austerity and economic restructuring and then removed as an issue from the political agenda (although it was placed back on the agenda in the early twenty-first century by the anti-globalization movement). As we saw in earlier chapters for Central America, although the pattern holds true for much of the Third World, the debt became a major mechanism of neo-liberal adjustment. The need to pay back the debt—and payback has been enforced by TNS apparatuses utilizing the structural power of the global economy—has induced a shift in resources and productive apparatuses around the world from domestic markets to the external sector. It has therefore been a major mechanism facilitating globalization, and will continue to play this role in Central America for many years to come. Seen from a larger perspective, we may recall from earlier discussion that transnational finance capital has become the hegemonic fraction of capital on a world scale in the era of globalization, and its hegemony involves new methods of surplus value extraction and wealth appropriation within global accumulation circuits.

Transnational functionaries have pointed to a reduction in the ratio of total interest payments to the value of exports, and to a reduction in the ratio of overall debt to exports, considered in the official development community to be key indicators of whether or not the debt is "manageable." For Central America, interest payments dropped in Costa Rica from 10 percent of export earnings in 1991 to 3.1 percent in 1998. In El Salvador, they dropped from 12.6 percent to 6.5 percent during this same period; in Guatemala, from 7.1 percent to 4.2 percent; in Honduras, from 21.1 percent to 7.8 percent; and in Nicaragua, from 106.5 percent to 19.3 percent. Similarly, during this period, the ratio of total debt to exports dropped in Costa Rica from 182 percent to 51 percent; in El Salvador, from 245 percent to 96 percent; in Guatemala from 155 percent to 102 percent; in Honduras, from 339 percent to 178 percent; and in Nicaragua, from an incredible 2,945 percent to 782 percent.[1]

What this data reflects is the heightened external integration of the Central American political economy; a further reorientation of economic activities towards the global economy. It does not, as we have seen, indicate a reduction in overall level of indebtedness, nor an elimination of the debt-dependent nature of the transnational model. With a total Isthmanian population of approximately 30 million in 1999, debt per capita in Central America that year stood at some $700, which represented about an entire year's earnings for most Central Americans.[2] Interest payments *alone* on this debt in the late 1990s accounted for some 25 percent of government expenditure in Costa Rica, 11 percent in El Salvador, 12 percent in Guatemala, 23 percent in Honduras, and 17 percent in Nicaragua.[3]

But perhaps the two most revealing indicators of what appears to be a structural limitation to sustaining a new round of capitalist expansion are the chronic and growing deficits in the trade balance (see table 5.6) and in the current account balance (see table 5.7). During the 1990s the influx of external resources in the form of loans and credits, FDI, remittances,

Table 5.6.   Central American Trade Balance (FOB), 1988–97 (in millions $)

	1988	1990	1992	1994	1996	1997
Costa Rica	− 98	− 443	− 472	− 606	− 413	− 714
El Salvador	− 356	− 666	− 962	− 1153	− 1243	− 1108
Guatemala	− 340	− 217	− 1044	− 997	− 644	− 940
Honduras	− 34	− 12	− 151	− 257	− 133	− 125
Nicaragua	− 483	− 237	− 548	− 418	− 360	− 742
Regional total	− 1311	− 1575	− 3177	− 3431	− 2793	− 3629

Source: IDB, *Economic and Social Progress in Latin America,* Annual Report, 1998–99.

and so on, generally offset the current accounts deficit and left each republic with a positive balance. But there is nothing inherent in the transnational model to suggest that the inflow of such resources will necessarily be sustained. In fact, the series of regional economic crises in the 1990s, from Mexico, Argentina, and Brazil, to Russia and Asia, demonstrated the volatility of growth dependent on mobile transnational finance capital and suggested that even minor political shocks or economic uncertainties may trigger capital flight and a downward spiral.

Radical development theories would characterize the apparent structural problem of external sector disequilibrium in the transnational model as one of foreign dependence and consequent surplus drainage. I suggest this is an accurate interpretation in and of itself but outdated insofar as such structural limitations to accumulation seem to be more generalized in the global economy. As I discuss below, they may better be seen as a structural feature internal to the global capitalist system than as a property of a "dependent" country or to the international relations of dependency between core and peripheral countries.

Table 5.7.   Central American Current Account Balance, 1997–99 (in millions $)

	1997	1998	1999
Costa Rica	− 330	− 495	− 475
El Salvador	97	− 84	− 290
Guatemala	− 634	− 1036	− 870
Honduras	− 183	− 66	− 380
Nicaragua	− 783	− 812	− 995
Regional total	− 1833	− 2493	− 3010

Source: CEPAL, *Preliminary Overview of Latin America and the Caribbean,* 1999.

There are only three possibilities for overcoming such sustained macro-economic imbalances in the external sector within the boundaries of the transnational development model as it has taken hold. One is continued increase in the foreign debt, which would aggravate rather than resolve the apparent structural problem. The second is a continued inflow of FDI and other such transfers that offset the deficits. It is not possible to predict for how long such transfers may be sustained. The third is an expansion of old and new exports to the world market such that exports overtake imports *and* such resource transfers out of the region as debt amortization, TNC profit remittances, and so on.

The Viability of the Transnational Model

The export-led model is justified with the argument that the external sector will act as a catalyst for the expansion of the non-export sector and the achievement in the latter of self-sustained growth. This might have been the experience of a number of South American and East Asian countries in an earlier moment in the world capitalist system. But there is nothing to suggest that the particular transnational model being implemented in Central America will involve enough backward and other indirect linkages to achieve such results. I will argue that the model is not viable because it is unlikely to generate an improvement in the life conditions of the impoverished majority in Central America, and that the criterion for evaluating the model should be the logic of the social interests of this majority. But even if we assess the model on the basis of more conventional nation-state development criteria, as I do in this section, it is not clear how viable the new accumulation activities will be in the mid to long-term.

The maquiladoras, for instance, constitute an enclave with little or no backward and forward linkage to local social and economic structures, which is key to technology diffusion and development. By its nature—production destined for immediate export—maquilas do not develop forward linkage to domestic markets. The amount of value added by local services and inputs, the chief index of backward linkages, is minimal. "When investment takes place in basic assembly-type production, one has to be careful not to exaggerate the positive effects," notes economist Eva Paus. "While such investments do create employment and generate foreign exchange, they normally create very few linkages with the rest of the economy."[4] We may recall that Central America has been a major producer of cotton, but this was exported as a raw material, only to be re-imported as thread and cloth for the old textile plants that developed under ISI industrialization, and more recently, for final assembly in the maquila garment plants. When pressed to name significant backward links with the Guatemalan economy, the best one AID official could do was to point to the hundreds of street vendors that crowd the entrances to maquila plants selling food to workers at lunchtime.[5] After some fifteen years of maquiladora activity in the region, there has been no genuine industrial development, much less any movement towards "newly industrialized country" status, despite the claims of the "ladder" model of development, whereby industrialization is purported to occur through a series of increasingly sophisticated and capital-intensive export-oriented operations, replicating the experience of the Asian Tigers (Costa Rica may be an exception, as discussed below).[6] We don't see in the Central American maquila sector the development of agglomerated structures characteristic of the development of forward and backward, and horizonal and vertical, linkages.

Maquiladora production is usually characterized by superexploitation of (usually female) workers and by conditions of extreme oppression within the free trade zone enclaves. Attracting transnational capital for maquila production is based on the "competitive advantage" of the provision of cheap labor and therefore this activity by its nature does not bring elevated living standards. Competition among countries that propose to supply cheap labor implies a general downward pressure on wages and working conditions for supplier countries—and competition is especially intense in cheap labor-intensive activities such as garments production, even more so with global trade liberalization and the entrance of China into world markets. This can be offset by a contraction of the labor supply or by an increase in the value added or a change in hierarchical participation in the value-added commodity chain, such as occurred in East Asia.[7] But there is nothing in the current pattern in Central America that suggests these countervailing tendencies are at work or that they are even contemplated by local states and economic agents.[8]

The one exception may be Costa Rica, although it was not possible in the early twenty-first century to reach any definitive conclusions. The country's garments and electronics assembly maquiladoras enjoy little backward and forward linkages or diffusion of technology, and in this respect Costa Rica is similar to its neighbors. But in the late 1990s, several high-technology and information technology companies began to locate in the country. Most notable was Intel, which opened a new plant in April 1997 programmed to produce one third of the TNC's microprocessors and employing about 2,000 Costa Rican workers. Similarly, Taiwan's Acer Group, Microsoft, Motorola, DSC Communications, Sawteck, and Lucent Technologies, among others, announced investment plans in the late 1990s.[9] The Costa Rican government's claims that the country was poised to become Latin America's "high-tech capital" were clearly overstated. But it is possible that Costa Rica could emerge as a local economic hub within the global economy. The matter requires further research. Yet in such an arrangement, Costa Rican-based transnational capital may well develop subcontracting arrangements in neighboring Central American republics, similar to such arrangements initiated by Mexican-based transnational capital in the 1990s. Already in the late 1990s some garments production had been transferred from Costa Rica to its neighbors. Here we see the significance of distinct national histories and structures in determining the trajectory of globalization. Costa Rica's political stability, the greater effectiveness of the state and its judicial system in adjudicating and enforcing contracts, and the higher level of skills and living standards of the labor force, are all key factors in the country's attractiveness for more technologically advanced, and more fixed, global production sites, and are conditions that were themselves the outcome of the struggle among class and social forces in the preceding historic epoch.

In distinction to the maquiladora sector, tourism does stimulate greater local economic activity. Unlike maquilas, tourism is often well integrated into local economies. But this does not mean that it will necessarily make a contribution to integrated development. Tourism generally generates low-skill, often menial and low-wage seasonal employment and is dependent on highly elastic and unstable demand over which host countries have very little control. The global tourist industry is highly competitive. Its contribution is unpredictable and subject to market saturation, fluctuations in supply and demand, changes in cultural fads, and so on. Elasticity and instability in tourist receipts make it impossible to assure a return on fixed investment in the industry and pit each Central American country against the others and in competition with other regions as well, such as the Caribbean. A world economic downturn could quickly snuff out international demand.

As I discussed in chapter three, the spread of tourism itself reflects the social polarization between the rich and the poor. The viability of tourism is tied to the reproduction of global inequalities. Tourism takes for granted the division between the rich and the poor, the "right" of the wealthy to be pampered and waited on by the poor. One person's leisure is another person's work, and these relations are not reciprocal. Relations of subservience lie at the heart of the "new tourism," perhaps even more so than the old mass tourism. At least the latter could be isolated, and one could make the distinction between serving and submission. The global tourist and hospitality industry heightens relative deprivation at a time when global communications have etched the reality of poverty amidst plenty into mass consciousness everywhere. Moreover, tourism is extremely vulnerable to external shocks; relative to most traded goods, it is highly vulnerable to political and other disturbances. Under these conditions tourism invites heightened social control systems that may in the end damage the prospects for the industry.

Neither is it clear how much promise NTAEs may hold. First, production is dependent on a high volume of imported inputs, such as fertilizers and pesticides, which eat up the very hard currency the NTAEs generate, as does the need to import foodstuffs as a result of the substitution of local food production by non-traditionals. Second, demand for specialized NTAE products is even more elastic than for staple products, such as coffee and sugar, of the earlier agro-export cycles, and demand has already begun to stagnate. The world market has always put a brake on Central America's economic prospects, from colonial times into the twenty-first century. The region's ability to produce export crops has been greater than the world market's ability to absorb that production, and there is no reason to assume this will be any different with regard to the new round of NTAE expansion.

The critiques made long ago of the doctrine of comparative advantage, among them, the inelasticity of demand for agricultural raw materials and the decline in the terms of trade, remain perfectly valid. In the mid-1970s, by way of example, Guatemala entered the cardamom market and by 1986 was supplying over 60 percent of world demand. Cardamom accounted for nearly half the value of NTAEs. But by 1988 the world market for cardamom had become saturated, as other countries—Costa Rica, Ecuador, and India—became suppliers. Prices plummeted, and by 1988 nearly half of Guatemalan exporters reported no business that year, while peasant farmers were left without any sources of income and with a crop they could not eat. By the early 1990s, the value of cardamom exports had dropped to half of what it was in the early 1980s.[10]

Historically, the introduction of new export crops has driven peasants off their land. Each such wave has been followed by rural strife that subsides as new landless move to cities or agricultural frontiers and/or become absorbed in new economic activities. NTAEs are still in the early stages and we may expect rural conflicts to intensify. However, the agricultural frontier has already been colonized. This in turn is linked to another concern raised by a renewed round of capitalist development in Central America, as evinced in the NTAE industry, that can only be alluded to here: the ecological holocaust already underway in the region. With the extensive use of chemical fertilizers and pesticides involved—even more than for earlier export crops—NTAE production is highly damaging to the region's already fragile environment. Tourism also draws the natural environment more fully into the commodification process ("ecotourism" in the context of capital accumulation converts environmental concerns into "cultural capital" that can be marketed as well). Both the environment and environmental concerns are "harvested" as objects for the accumulation of capital. The "Plan Puebla Panama," a region-wide mega-development project promoted by transnational corporations and the IFIs and inaugurated in 2001, proposed a vast extension of the transportation and communications infrastructure into the remaining ecological preserves in the Isthmus to facilitate the expansion of the transnational corporate presence.[11] Can the fragile environment sustain a new round of capitalist expansion? Could we see a "Sahelization" of vast tracts of Central America?[12]

Global Capitalism and Social Exclusion in Central America

The model of Export-Led Development (ELD) leads to and is driven by the extension of capitalism. It is linked to the rise of transnational capital and a transnational capitalist class. New economic activities associated with the transnational model, including but not limited to the four examined in detail in this study, and the restructuring of Central America's productive apparatus more generally, have hastened the integration of the region into transnational capitalist production and service chains. The ELD model has also thrown up new modernizing agents among the dominant strata tied to these chains and committed to the project of global capitalism. But it would be a mistake to assume that because the old agro-export oligarchy has been displaced from dominance by this emergent transnational fraction that the class barrier to development has been overcome, as the Barrington Moore thesis, applied to Central America in a number of recent studies, might suggest.[13] It is true that interests tied to the agro-export oligarchy were in the past able to block social and economic reform that could have generated a more authentic process of development and autocentric growth. These interests, for instance, conjoined with transnational capital to distort the original CACM project as a regional industrialization plan with a consumer goods bias and a more limited scope.

The transnational model, however, is *not* a break with the earlier export-led models; it is a *deepening* of those models. It constitutes under globalization a more complete externalization of "national" economies. Development studies focusing on the prospects of "national" development have traditionally emphasized the vertical and horizontal linkage among sectors and the national integration of markets and productive structures as central to the development process, but I do not believe the notion of forward and backward linkages within a "national economy" and other such nation-state based processes are the most appropriate way to assess the transnational model. By definition transnational production is characterized by globally decentralized and dispersed production and service chains in which the locus of linkages is itself the global economy and not any national economy. Here the issue is less "outward-looking" versus "inward-looking" projects than the prospects for improving the material and cultural conditions of life in Central America at a time when development is acquiring a new meaning.

The pre-globalization strategy of accumulation in Central America and elsewhere could not bring about sustained development due to its internal contradictions. Nevertheless, by being based in part on domestic market expansion, it involved a significant redistributive impulse. The logic of the model itself presupposed an improvement in general living conditions even if in practice it could not bring this about. This is not to suggest that an appropriate development strategy for the region would be a reversion to the old model, which is not possible and is not a viable strategy for the popular majority. Nonetheless, the new globalization model ties internal accumulation to global circuits of accumulation and to world market demand, based on the region's "comparative advantage" in cheap labor. This has involved the elimination of the domestic market in the considerations of capital accumulation. Rather than being a potential consumer market whose purchasing power needs to be raised, the popular majority in Central America serves the needs of capital accumulation in the transnational model to the extent that it is kept at subsistence levels.

"Since a free market in labor might produce a real wage rate which could undermine the profitability of goods sold in world markets, an adequate supply of labor was assumed by coffee interests to depend on coercion (debt peonage, vagrancy laws, etc.)," Bulmer-Thomas has argued, "and this conclusion was reinforced in the early 1920s when exchange rate flexibility was abandoned in favor of the gold standard."[14] One could expect that a "real" wage rate under the transnational model of accumulation, based on cheap labor as the region's "comparative advantage" in the global economy, would also undermine profitability. However, there is no reason to assume that a free market in labor results in rising wage rates. Indeed, the comparative advantage of cheap labor is predicated on the creation in recent decades of a surplus labor supply through strictly economic compulsion on the heels of the alienation of the mass of Central Americans. In integrating their countries into the global economy, local elites, and in particular the transnationalized fractions of these elites that came to power in the 1980s and 1990s, base "development" on the virtually exclusive criteria of achieving maximum internal profitability as the condition *sine qua non* for attracting transnational capital. In the logic of global capitalism, the cheapening of labor and its social disenfranchisement by the neo-liberal state become conditions for "development." This may be grounded in the increasing erosion of the link between social reproduction and accumulation under global capitalism. Capitalism has less of a need to procure the social reproduction of labor as a requisite for its own reproduction to the extent that transnational capital now targets the world market rather than national markets. Accumulation processes that place these downward pressures on income and on the social wage and depend in no way on the expansion of domestic markets show no impulse to redistributive reform. The dominant development discourse, through neo-liberal ideology, comes to delegitimize the redistributive demands of popular classes and social movements. Poverty and deprivation become conditions favorable for successful "development." Let me elaborate:

This is a historic outcome, in which previous social processes and conditions have led to the current circumstances. Looking back to the post-WWII period, multinational capital faced two options for world expansion, according to Steven Hymer.[15] Capital could pursue a strategy of "extensive" expansion, which would mean raising demand worldwide and creating mass markets for mass production. The other strategy—the one actually chosen—was an "intensive" expansion that relied on utilizing the existing structure of world income polarization to deepen the consumption of certain groups in the world economy, namely high-consumption groups in the First World and smaller pockets of these groups in the Third World. However, this "intensive" expansion strategy was mediated and reshaped in the nation-state phase of world capitalism by the ability of mass social movements and of national states to shape accumulation structures in particular regions. In Latin America, for instance, the ISI model was based on an expansion, however limited, of domestic markets and middle classes. Although rearticulation to world markets through exports was the principal thrust of the development model in this third wave of capitalist expansion in Central America, the accumulation strategy involved an element of redistributive reform based in the domestic market. Thus the particular unfolding of global accumulation from WWII into the 1970s involved both

Table 5.8. "Inward" and "Outward" Oriented Accumulation Compared

CACM/ISI	ELD/TRANSNATIONAL MODEL
domestic market	world market
redistributive reform	no reform
labor protective legislation	flexibilization of labor rollback of protective legislation revised labor codes
social legislation	strict market allocation of resources
social wage	rollback of social wage

intensive and extensive expansion, whereas the transnational model of development, based on ELD, has shifted the entire productive structure more fully towards the world market. Global accumulation remains driven by an intensive expansion that relies on a new market polarization generated by flexible accumulation and the restructuring of work on top of the previous structure of world income. Achieving a "competitive" reinsertion into the world market through a new set of exports is predicated on the region's "comparative advantage" in cheap labor. The new transnational economic activities that form the basis for a reorganization of the region's productive structures are components of globalized production chains that draw from the local economy population pools as cheap labor but do not generate the conditions for the social reproduction of these populations. This type of fully externalized accumulation eliminates the domestic market from the strategy of accumulation and therefore abolishes the purely economic impulse towards redistributive reform, as shown in table 5.8.

How are these issues linked to those of modernization and development? Development in the broadest sense is an integrated social, economic, political, and cultural process embedded in macrostructures and their changes over time. Seen in territorial terms, development is a global phenomenon that affects regions in diverging ways, in which changes specific to a particular region are linked to broader changes in the global system. The process of modernization can be considered the transformation or "updating" of structures in particular countries and regions so that they make possible ongoing rearticulation to, or continued synchronization with, the larger global whole. A region's structures may remain unchanged or stagnant, which obstructs a renewal of integration into global structures, in which case "development" may not occur (at least as it is measured conventionally in such indicators as economic growth). This may characterize Africa, for instance, during the 1980s and early 1990s. They may also change in opposition to the direction of change or the logic of the structures at the global level. Such "domestic" or regional changes have consequences, as seen in revolutionary Nicaragua's attempt to transform internal structures in opposition to the world capitalist system.

However, "development" as the modernization of structures as such does not necessarily involve meaningful improvement in the lives of majorities, and can (indeed, often does) entail a further relative or absolute deterioration of material and cultural life conditions as well as a widening of asymmetries in social power relations. By social power I mean the collective ability of social groups and classes to shape structures and outcomes in their interests. The type of modernization that took place in the post-World War II expansion of capitalism in Central America, and the renewal underway in Central America under the emergent transnational model of society, has not brought development to the poor majority in the region as much as *maldevelopment*, a term first coined by Samir Amin to describe the deleterious effect on popular majorities of the trajectory of Third World development and world accumulation in the post-World War II period.[16]

What may appear as "backward," such as below-subsistence wages or mass unemployment, can actually be the consequences of modernizing adaptation to the functional requirements of the global economy, and may modernize without developing. This is particularly so in the age of globalization, in which a region's "relative advantage" constitutes the most congenial conditions for transnational capital to generate profit. To the extent transformative processes generate a mass of under and unemployed that hold down the general wage level and that provide a ready pool of reserve labor for transnational capital to tap, or similarly, to the extent that these processes result in a bloated informal sector that transfers the responsibility for social reproduction from the state and from private capital to the marginalized groups themselves, then we can say that these processes— under the conditions of the global capitalist economy—are quite "modernizing" even as they result in marginalization and immizeration.

To reiterate and extend the argument, Central America's insertion into the global economy does not require an inclusive social base; socioeconomic exclusion becomes immanent to the model since accumulation does not depend on internal social reproduction. Whether this is a policy question or a structural feature of global capitalism in the Isthmus becomes crucial to an assessment of the prospects for development and the direction of social change. I suggest that the problem is not one of policy options— as public policy, rational choice, and related theories would insinuate—in part because the outcome is an unintended consequence of the purposive behavior on which these theories focus. The problem resides within the global capitalist system. With global economic integration, ELD pits one region and people against another in competition for global markets and capital, generating downward levelling pressures and polarizing processes. The logic of external integration into global capitalism leads each country—particularly those that come under neo-liberal structural adjustment programs—to contract its domestic market and shift resources towards activities that supply the global market. As domestic markets become less important for the consumption of what is produced, the output of each nation and region is exported to the global level. At the aggregate level of the world economy this means an overall system-wide contraction in demand simultaneous to a system-wide expansion of supply. This is the classic overproduction or underconsumption contradiction, the "realization" problem, now manifest in novel ways under global capitalism. The tendency becomes towards a separation of accumulation from social reproduction. Zones of high absorption become the pillars of the system, or the "markets of last resort," in times of economic difficulty, such as the United States in the mid, and especially the late, 1990s, following the 1997 Asian financial crisis. The markets of last resort may help fuel world economic growth even as many regions experience stagnation and crisis. But at the *systemic* level, the reproduction of capital remains dependent on that of labor, as a matter of course, and this represents a contradiction internal to the global capitalist system. What countervailing tendencies may continue to offset the consequences of this contradiction was not clear in the early twenty-first century.

Here I wish to draw out the implications of these macrosociological propositions for Central America. The larger process at the system-wide level is expressed locally in the removal of the domestic market from the accumulation imperative. To the extent that socioeconomic exclusion is a structural feature the new model can be expected to generate social conditions and political tensions—inequality, polarization, impoverish-ment, marginality—conducive to a breakdown of social order and a renewal of the regional crisis. The social contradictions that have driven Central American development since last century have been modified once again but not resolved. The contradictions that present themselves now are internal to (global) capitalism rather than between capitalism and atavistic elements. The underlying dynamic of capitalist modernization is now bound up with that of capitalist globalization. Now, the most fundamental social contradiction in Central America *and* in global society, is this: the model of polarized (flexible) accumulation does not resolve the social contradictions of capitalism, and cannot, and moreover, tends to aggravate them. The problem therefore is the social structure of accumulation under global capitalism.

Maldevelopment for Whom in Central America?

While a pattern of accumulation based on export-led growth is not new in Central America, and has failed earlier this century under favorable and under adverse world economic conditions,[17] there are several key differ-ences between earlier ELD and the current period. In the earlier period, the domestic/natural economy was not fully incorporated and constituted a reserve buffering social sectors from the ravages of world market forces. The successive waves of capitalist incorporation have progressively con-tracted these reserves and they are drying up under globalization. There-fore, social groups in the region are less protected and more vulnerable

Table 5.9.   Population in Poverty (by Percentage), 1980–2000 (select years)

	Costa Rica	El Salvador	Honduras	Guatemala	Nicaragua
1980	25	68	68	63	62
1990	24	71	76	75	75
1999	n/a	80	70	n/a	79
2000	19	n/a	47	53	44
(% living on *less than* $1 day)					

Source: 1980 and 1990 figures from CEPAL, as cited in Vilas, 1995, p. 148; 1999 figures from UNDP, 1999 report, "Estado de la Region", table 6.6, p. 177; 2000 figures from World Bank, World Development Report, 2000–01.

than in the past in the face of global market forces. The market, in Polanyian terms, has become fully disembedded from society in Central America. Central American society is now run as an adjunct to the global market. The unregulated market, with its naked quest for gain, is unleashing its fury on the social bonds and institutions that allowed in the past for individual survival and social reproduction in Central America.[18] Moreover, earlier ELD, taking place in the pre-globalization period, afforded individual countries and regions a greater degree of autonomy vis-à-vis the world economy. The structural power of the global economy has severely reduced local and regional autonomous space for alternative forms of articulation. This is not to say that alternatives are not possible, only that the space for their development has moved more fully from the local and the regional to the transnational.

As Central America globalizes, therefore, poverty and deprivation seem to become a state of affairs built into the evolving structure and may even be conditions favorable to accumulation. This tendency is reinforced by the neo-liberal model, which specifically precludes the types of policies, such as agrarian reform and redistributive measures, that could ameliorate these conditions. Poverty increased (see table 5.9) and inequality intensified in the Isthmus in the late twentieth century.[19] In Costa Rica, the richest 10 percent earned sixteen times more than the poorest 10 percent of its population in 1980; in 1990, the ratio was 31:1.[20] In El Salvador, the richest 20 percent of the population increased its share of income from 43 percent in 1989 to 54.2 percent, just two years later, while the poorest 20 percent's share of income dropped from 5.6 to 3.4 percent.[21] The richest 20 percent of the population in Guatemala earned thirty times more than the poorest 20 percent, the country with the second highest inequality index in Latin America, after Brazil, which has the highest inequality index in the world.[22]

In surveying the state of human development in the region at the turn of the century, the UNDP notes:

The distribution of income and wealth in Central America continues to be alarmingly unequal and it has not improved, not even in Costa Rica ... Traditional export activities, especially agro-exports and the maquila, continue to provide a major source of wealth for their owners but not necessarily for their workers, who receive low salaries throughout the region. The new export activities, the expansion of services, principally financial, tourism, and other modern sector activities, appear to be equally concentrated in the hands of a few.[23]

Social indicators have deteriorated in Central America.[24] In fact, every single republic dropped in its ranking in the UNDP Human Development Index, as shown in table 5.10. This index ranks all countries based on their human development performance (an aggregate of health, educational, and incomes indices), with a ranking of one being the highest. It is significant that this decline occurred in the 1990s, *after* the wars and pacification.

Table 5.11 shows that inequality in Central America in the late 1990s surpassed virtually all other regions in the world, including much of Africa and Asia, and gives an indication of the regressive redistribution of resources in the region in the wake of the defeat of the popular redistributive struggles of the 1980s (indeed, Nicaragua, which experienced a dramatic redistribution of resources downwards towards the poor majority in the 1980s was by the late 1990s one of the most unequal countries in the world).

Chronic malnutrition affects 25 percent of all children in Central America. One third of Central American adults are illiterate. Approximately one half of all housing in the Isthmus is substandard, and nearly one fourth is considered unfit for human dwelling. Some one third of the region's population has no access to health services (the figure is 60 percent for El Salvador and 43 percent for Guatemala) and some one third has no access to sanitation services (a full 69 percent do not have them in Nicaragua and 38 percent do not in Honduras). Nearly two in five Central Americans have no access to safe water.[26] The rise of street children in Central America, rising levels of drug abuse, pandemics of crime and delinquency, the

Table 5.10. Human Development Index, Central American Ranking, 1990–97

	1990	1997
Costa Rica	28	33
El Salvador	72	112
Guatemala	80	116
Honduras	76	117
Nicaragua	60	127

Source: UNDP.[25]

Table 5.11.   Share of Income, Poorest and Richest, Central America in Comparative Perspective

	Poorest 10%	20%	Richest 20%	10%
Costa Rica (1997)	1.7	4.4	51.0	34.6
El Salvador (1998)	1.2	3.3	56.4	39.5
Honduras (1998)	0.6	2.2	59.4	42.7
Nicaragua (1998)	0.7	2.3	63.6	46.0
Guatemala (1998)	1.6	3.8	60.6	46.0
Norway (1995)	4.1	9.7	35.8	21.8
Hungary (1995)	4.1	10.0	34.4	20.5
USA (1997)	1.8	5.2	46.4	30.5
Italy (1995)	3.5	8.7	36.3	21.8
Mexico (1998)	1.3	3.5	57.4	41.7
Canada (1994)	2.8	7.5	39.3	23.8
Brazil (1998)	0.7	2.2	64.1	48.0
Ecuador (1995)	2.2	5.4	49.7	33.8
Jordan (1997)	3.3	7.6	44.4	29.8
Egypt (1995)	4.4	9.8	39.0	25.0
Madagascar (1999)	2.6	6.4	44.8	28.6
Sri Lanka (1995)	3.5	8.0	42.8	29.0
Tanzania (1993)	2.8	6.8	45.5	30.0
Jamaica (2000)	2.7	6.7	46.0	30.3
Uganda (1996)	3.0	7.1	42.8	28.0
China (1998)	2.4	5.9	46.6	30.4
India (1997)	3.5	8.1	46.1	33.5

Source: UNDP, *Human Development Report*, 2002.

escalation of domestic violence and the abuse of women and children, are all signs of the crisis in the social fabric that has accompanied economic insecurity and hardship, intensified inequalities, the deterioration of social conditions, and the erosion of the norms and values of collective survival.

In sum, and to reiterate, it is doubtful that the transnational model will lift a majority of Central Americans out of poverty, or that it will generate greater equalities or social justice, political empowerment of local communities and control by them of their own resources or the terms of their relationship to the global economy. In *this sense*, the new model will likely sustain *maldevelopment*. However, to ask if the new economic activities associated with globalization in Central America will generate development in the region is to pose the question in the wrong way. By reformulating the questions we ask we can change the focus of inquiry in such a way that better explanations may come into view. It would be better to identify how the new dynamic cores of accumulation in Central America reshape and transnationalize local social structure and generate in the process heightened social stratification, producing winners and losers and contributing to the overall process of social stratification among groups as defined by their relationship to the global economy and society. A presentation of aggregate data on poverty, inequality, and deprivation in Central America conceals the unequal distribution among social groups and population clusters of conditions of misery as well as of privilege. It does not tell the story of the emergence of "two Central Americas," one rich, the other poor. Globalization generates development for some and further marginalization for others. This process is not meaningfully measured in nation-state terms but in terms of the development of some groups and the underdevelopment of other groups within the same space. What distinguishes these groups may be differential integration into larger transnationalized social structures rather than national structures. I will return to this issue shortly.

The increasing difficulty in referring to development in nation-state terms, and increasingly in territorial forms, has not gone unnoticed by international agencies. In its 1999 report for Central America, the UNDP observed that inequality was just as pronounced among distinct regions within Central America, such as more marginal and more centrally located provinces, and so on, and among distinct social groups within Central America, as it was between Central America and rich regions of the world:

> Alongside modern enclaves in capitals and principal cities lie vast zones of poverty and low productivity, often in rural hinterlands and along borders. [There are simultaneously] multiple and broad gaps among social groups—between the rich and the poor, between men and women, between the indigenous, Afro-Caribbeans, and the non-indigenous, for example. These gaps in equality have generated extensive poverty and have excluded majorities from access to social services and to the benefits of development . . . The Central American Isthmus is experiencing multiple asymmetries beyond national political borders that disarticulate any notion of an integrated region or of any single regional dynamic in terms of social, political, cultural, and economic processes.[27]

The Future of Popular Struggle in Central America and in Global Society

Global Polarization and the Crisis of Social Reproduction

Under globalization, national states have progressively lost the ability to capture and redirect surpluses through interventionist mechanisms that were viable in the nation-state phase of capitalism. In redefining the phase of distribution in the accumulation of capital in relation to nation-states, globalization undermines the distinct redistributive and other mechanisms that acted in earlier epochs to offset the inherent tendency within capitalism towards polarization. It also fragments national cohesion around

Table 5.12.   Shares of World Income 1965–90

Population	Percentage of Total World Income			
	1965	1970	1980	1990
Poorest 20%	2.3	2.2	1.7	1.4
Second 20%	2.9	2.8	2.2	1.8
Third 20%	4.2	3.9	3.5	2.1
Fourth 20%	21.2	21.3	18.3	11.3
Richest 20%	69.5	70.0	75.4	83.4

Source: Korzeniewicz and Moran.[29]

processes of social reproduction and shifts the site of reproduction from the nation-state to transnational space. The result has been a rapid process of global social polarization and a crisis of social reproduction. In most countries, the average number of people who have been integrated into the global marketplace and are becoming "global consumers" has increased rapidly in recent decades. However, it is also true that the absolute number of the impoverished—of the destitute and near destitute—has been increasing rapidly and that the gap between the rich and the poor in global society has widened since the 1970s (see table 5.12). Broad swathes of humanity have experienced absolute downward mobility. While global per capita income tripled over the period 1960–94, there were over a hundred countries in the 1990s with per capita incomes lower than in the 1980s, and in some cases, lower than in the 1970s and 1960s.[28]

Global society is increasingly characterized by a three-tiered social structure. The first tier is made up of some 30–40 percent of the population in what have traditionally been the core countries and less in peripheral countries, those who hold "tenured" employment in the global economy and are able to maintain, and even expand, their consumption. The second tier, some 30 percent in the core and 20–30 percent in the periphery, form a growing army of "casualized" workers who face chronic insecurity in the conditions of their employment and the absence of any collective insurance against risk previously secured by the welfare state. The third tier, some 30 percent of the population in the traditional core capitalist countries, and some 50 percent or more in peripheral countries, represents those structurally excluded from productive activity and completely unprotected following the dismantling of welfare and developmentalist states, the "superfluous" population of global capitalism.[30] But no emergent ruling class can stabilize a new order without developing diverse mechanisms of legitimation and securing a social base—the construction of what Antonio Gramsci called a historic bloc. Such a bloc involves a combination of the consensual integration through material reward for some, and the coercive exclusion of others that the system is unwilling or unable to co-opt. Within this three-tiered social structure, the transnational elite is seeking to secure a firm social base in the first tier, to draw in the second tier, and to contain the third tier.

In the earlier epoch core and periphery were spatial coordinates. Core affluence and the attenuating effects it had on social polarization were made possible by the core's relation to a spatially defined periphery. As core and periphery come to denote social location rather than geography, affluence in global society is coming to rest on a peripheral social sector that is not necessarily spatially concentrated. Those who have the equivalent of US $5,000 personal income are considered part of the world of "consumers." In the 1990s, for the first time in history, the absolute number of these in the Third World surpassed those in the First World.[31] But the *vast* majority of humanity are not consumers. TNCs and banks, in their global production and marketing strategies, routinely search out in each locale around the world that 15 per cent of the population that are consumers. These consumers are the world's "bankable" sector, in the words of John Reed, Chair of City Corp, who estimates this global market to constitute some 800 million people. "Many of the problems we have on the globe, be it the global environment or health, are problems of the 4.2 billion, not the 800 million," says Reed.[32]

Such global inequalities lead to a new "politics of exclusion" in which the problem of social control becomes paramount. There is a shift from the social welfare state to the social control (police) state, replete with the dramatic expansion of public and private security forces, the mass incarceration of the excluded population (which is disproportionately made up of minorities), new forms of social apartheid maintained through complex social control technologies, repressive anti-immigration legislation, and so on. Global polarization brings with it increasing residential segregation of the rich, protected by armies of private security guards and electronic surveillance, from the cities of Central America to those of the United States, Europe, Asia and elsewhere. These "gated communities," variously referred to as "enclaves," "citadels" and "fortresses," are "part of the trend toward exercising physical and social means of territorial control," the natural products of global inequalities, and have been spreading to all parts of the world.[33] The politics of exclusion also entails, under the deceptive discourse of "local politics" and "community empowerment," a shift in the responsibility for social reproduction from the state and society as a whole to the most marginalized communities themselves.

What does this mean for development in Central America? Even as elites and new professional and middle classes join the ranks of global consumers, the vast majority of Central Americans do not consume. What does the Isthmus offer transnational capitalists? There are not many bankables in absolute numbers, perhaps a few million out of a population of 30 million. But it is a good place to produce things for the global consuming population—fruits and vegetables for the global supermarket, tourist destinations, and so on.

Development in Central America therefore depends on changes at the level of the global system. Barring the rise of a transnational democratic socialism as an alternative to global capitalism, it seems to me that development depends on restoring social reproduction as an imperative in the world accumulation process. A global regulatory structure might provide developmental prospects for Central America and elsewhere. But from whence would come such a Keynesian modification of the existing structure of the global economy? Chronic instability underscores the fragility of the system and the limits of the neo-liberal variant. From the Mexican peso crisis to the Asian collapse, the Russian and Brazilian turmoil, and incessant world market turbulence at the turn of the century, the global economy seems to be in permanent crisis. We should recall that structural change cannot be explained by analyzing extant structures, which are by definition stable. It is agency that accounts for structural change, which is a result of the dialectic of top-down and of bottom-up pressures. A Polanyian "double movement" that provides a measure of social protection and developmental prospects to the poor majority in Central America and in global society can only be the product of mass globalization-from-below pressure. Precisely because national solutions are no longer viable in the age of globalization, such a movement must be transnational. A new round of mass struggle in Central America, linked in turn to extra-regional resistance and capable of throwing a monkey wrench into the gears of the global economy, is the region's most promising option for development. This runs counter to mainstream thinking on the issue, which holds that pacification of the poor majority ("stability") is necessary to convince transnational capital to invest in the region, and that development therefore depends on containing the mobilization of popular majorities. This reasoning has been accepted by a good portion of the Left in Central America.

The Illusion of "Peace and Democracy" in Central America

The political conditions under which the process of social production unfolds are dynamic, contested, and mutually determining. But the political and the economic are not separate spheres, not in theory and not in practice. Ruling classes seek to organize production under optimal conditions of political stability. Under the social conditions historically prevailing in Central America this has been accomplished more efficiently through direct coercive arrangements as expressed in dictatorships and authoritarian states. The very first economic activity of the Spanish conquerors of the Isthmus, Indian slave-hunting, generated capital invested in mines and agriculture that launched the colonial economy and 500 years of violent, uneven, and unstable accumulation. The coffee and later the agro-export production complexes continued to rely on coercive systems of labor control organized by authoritarian states. At times when the social production complex is stable or in momentary equilibrium—that is, when wealth-generating activities present themselves, and when money-making is easy—the domination of ruling groups over the economy requires less direct manipulation of the state or state creation of economic opportunities. These tended to be the conditions that gave rise to "liberal" core states in the history of the capitalist world system, but were not generally the conditions in Central America, with the partial exception of Costa Rica. At certain moments in Central American history, established and aspiring dominant classes felt the need to become governing classes more directly in order to organize and/or reorient production. This gave rise, for instance, to the liberal republics of the new coffee oligarchy in the nineteenth century. It is also the case, as I argued in earlier chapters, with the rise of neo-liberal states of the new transnational capitalist and bureaucratic groups of the 1980s and on.

The theoretical backdrop to these issues is the relations between states, classes, and transnational processes. I have already touched on this theme at various points in the present study and cannot develop it further here. Suffice it to observe that transitions to polyarchy may have temporarily defused the challenge to the state posed by the popular and revolutionary movements in the 1980s. But the main achievement of these regime transitions was to reaccommodate the power relations between different fractions within the dominant groups—away from the old oligarchies and towards the new transnationally oriented groups—and to establish essential political conditions for state modernization and for neo-liberal restructuring. Precisely because they are more deeply embedded in the political economy of civil society itself, transnationally oriented capitalists and bureaucrats found the new polyarchic regimes to be more effective instruments in pursuing their interests.

To the extent that the regimes that carried through the neo-liberal project did exhibit a degree of autonomy in the 1980s and 1990s, the Central American states displayed more of a Poulantzian class-wide rationality, in the sense that the state organized and cohered the interests of a particular class fraction, than a Weberian corporate coherence. These states were battlegrounds for opposing social forces. The autonomy they may have exercised was from popular classes and, as the transitions advanced, from the old oligarchies, but not from the transnationally oriented groups. These groups operated in a synchronized manner in numerous redoubts of state and civil society to achieve restructuring and integration into the global economy and society. The relative level of state autonomy actually diminished considerably during the transitions. But if the problem of intra-elite contradictions was resolved, the more underlying contradiction remains—that between dominant and subordinate groups. It is not clear how the new polyarchic regimes will manage this contradiction in the face of growing crises of social reproduction and of state legitimacy.

One indicator of the crisis of legitimacy is the steadily declining levels of participation in electoral processes, touted as the premier achievements of "democratization." Abstention among registered voters in presidential elections went in El Salvador from about 42 percent in the 1991 vote, up to 44 percent in the 1994 vote, and then to 65 percent in the 1999 vote. In Guatemala, abstention went from just over 30 percent in 1985, to about 50 percent in 1990, and nearly 60 percent in 1995. In Nicaragua, where the revolution had earlier brought nearly the entire population into the political process, abstention climbed from about 12 percent in the 1990 vote to 25 percent in the 1996 vote. In Honduras, it wavered from 25 percent in 1989 up to nearly 40 percent in 1993 and then down to 30 percent in 1997. Even in Costa Rica, where a hegemonic system has achieved a more secure legitimacy for the state, abstention climbed from about 20 percent in the 1990 and the 1994 votes to nearly 30 percent in the 1997 vote.[34]

In their analysis of the regional conflict and its aftermath, transnational elites don't consider that the crisis had its origins in the nature of the socioeconomic and class structure, much less in the larger capitalist system to which the region belongs. A careful study of internal AID documents, for instance, reveals an assessment that the crisis of the agro-export model, and the political-military conflagration, was a matter of conjunctural events, such as the 1970s oil shocks and poor world commodity prices, together with "misguided" policies (state intervention). These events are seen as the causes of the crisis, not the symptoms of a larger structural problem. The fundamental social and economic structures in the region and in the larger world-system are seen not as causal to the crisis but as positive and necessary for democracy and development in the aftermath of pacification.[35] Transnational functionaries see the way forward as "sustainable development" based on two overlapping goals: 1) further opening up in Central America, and linkage to the global economy; and 2) broadening the internal hegemony of a transnational private business sector.

But the agenda of the transnational elite is just that—an *agenda*, not a consummated reality. Its attempted implementation involves permanent conflict and resistance, and implies contingent outcomes that are themselves constantly being reshaped. As I will discuss shortly, although the revolutionary and popular challenge to the social order was averted by the globalization outcome of the 1990s, the crisis of *hegemony*, in the Gramscian sense, was *not* resolved through pacification and transitions to polyarchy. Legitimacy crises develop into organic crises under certain circumstances. It is too risky (and early) to predict if these circumstances will become present in the coming years in Central America. We should recall that it is in times of rapid capitalist development, not stagnation, that conflict and upheaval are most likely. No one single actor or social force, no matter how powerful (for example, the transnational elite) can dictate outcomes. The transnational outcome to the Central American upheaval was the result of a confluence of forces, and the future history of Central America will as well be a result of such confluences. Social change takes place within the bounds of definite historic constraints but the particular social structures which emerge are not predetermined. How social structure evolves is a result of the dynamic and dialectical interplay of agency with structure. How will dominant groups respond to the crisis of social reproduction and of legitimacy? How will popular classes respond?

On the one hand, globalization has acted as a centripetal force for the new transnational capitalist historic bloc and as a centrifugal force for popular classes around the world. Insertion into the global economy has resulted in a destructuring of the traditional working class, which has contributed to a weakening of labor relative to capital and to the change in the correlation of class forces. Working and popular classes are fragmented by restructuring. Intense competition forced on these classes in each nation debilitates collective action. Subprocesses such as transnational migration and the diffusion of the global capitalist culture of consumerism and individualism provide escape valves that relieve pressure on the system. The popular sectors were *brought together* in earlier waves of capitalist expansion as intersubjectivities and mounted collective challenges to the social order. To the extent that the old subjectivities have been fragmented and dispersed, and new subjectivities have yet to cohere, the transnational model blunts the collective political protagonism of the popular classes.

On the other hand, all over the world, as old corporatist structures crack, new social movements and oppositional forces emerge. In the face of the onslaught of the new global capitalist order old and new forms of resistance have spread throughout Central America. Social movements of workers, women, environmentalists, students, peasants, indigenous people, Afro-Americans, community associations of the urban poor, and other sectors have burgeoned and will play a central role in the development of any prospective counter-hegemonic bloc to the current global capitalist order.[36] The restructuring of the labor–capital relation, while it has disarticulated the earlier unionism, has also led to a change in the center of gravity of the working class. This has shifted from strategic sectors of national production and public services to the burgeoning urban informal economy, from the old places of work, factories and offices, to new places, the streets and communities, where labor becomes less distinguishable as a particular organized constituency within social movements. Ironically, globalization is generating the conditions for a new "social unionism," and alliances with other social movements are increasingly the fulcrum of the labor movement.[37] To what extent social movements and oppositional forces can force concessions from global capital and its regional contingents that improve their lot is a relative one, and should not be counterposed to revolutionary transformation.

"Success" in a political endeavor is often defined from the summits of power as the extent to which the ruling structures are imposed and reproduced, to which accommodation and conformity around these structures are achieved among the different components of the privileged strata, and to which social control is maintained at the base. Authentic democratization and development in Central America would require the incorporation of the excluded majorities in the vital decisions that affect their lives. It would mean political outcomes in the interests of these majorities predicated on the construction of a democratic socioeconomic system, and therefore a massive redistribution of political power, in Central America. In turn, political power flows from economic power, and economic power is based on control over society's resources, wealth, and culture. Democratization and development therefore requires a radical redistribution of wealth and power towards the poor majority. They require the type of fundamental structural change that goes against the very essence of the global capitalist project.

Social change is driven by contradictions that make impossible the continuation of an existing set of historic arrangements. I have referred to the basic structural change in the region as a transition to a transnational model of society reciprocal to changes in the global system. The point I wish to emphasize here is that the globalization of Central America *has not resolved the social contradictions that generated the regional upheaval in the first place, and has simultaneously introduced a new set of contradictions.* The very conditions that gave rise to the conflict are still present and, in fact, have been aggravated in recent years. These conditions are the extreme concentration of economic resources, of wealth, and of political power, in the hands of elite minorities, side by side with the pauperization and powerlessness of a dispossessed majority. The lives of the vast majority of Central Americans have got worse, not better. The very conditions which gave rise to the Central American crisis in the first place, therefore, remain for the most part unaltered. Despite the illusion of "peace and democracy," the roots of the regional conflict persist. The most likely scenario for Central America is renewed social conflict as subordinate groups whose composition has also been altered become rearticulated, develop new methods of organization in civil society, and launch a fresh round of popular struggle against the prevailing social order. The transnational model of society in Central America is inherently unstable, and indicates contradictions internal to global capitalism, including the worldwide social polarization between rich and poor, the loss of nation-state autonomy and regulatory power, and the deterioration of the social fabric in civil society accompanied by crises of authority and state legitimacy.

A Long March Through Civil Society?
The Prospects for Counter-Hegemony

Globalization is the *resistible* renewal of capitalism. Globalization is always partial and incomplete, although the aspiration is one of universality and generalization. Any theory of historic change must address the question of how alternative projects arise, how resistance is articulated and how dominant structures are subverted. Theories of capitalist hegemony are incomplete without corresponding theories of counter-hegemony.

Gramsci distinguished between two types of political struggle: a *war of maneuver* (frontal attack) and a *war of position* (struggle of trench warfare, or of attrition). A war of maneuver, associated with the traditional notions of revolution, can potentially succeed when the power that sustains the existing system is situated in a limited number of identifiable sites, like the police, military, etc. But the expansion of the state into new "private" and community realms under capitalism that Gramsci theorized, and the rise of a civil society in which the power of the dominant groups is anchored in ideological and cultural processes, implies that power is no longer limited to a number of sites and is more dispersed and multidimensional. The formal distinction between a war of position and a war of maneuver is clearly methodological, not real (organic), in the sense that social struggles involve both dimensions simultaneously. Which may be the most salient in strategies and practices of struggle is a matter of historical conjuncture and collective agency.

In Central America, the nature of political domination in the post-WWII period called for, and allowed for the potential success of, a war of maneuver. Dictatorship and entrenched political-military regimes and oligarchies were very identifiable sites, and the struggle against these modes of political domination opened the way for a movement to transform the social order itself. But the transitions analyzed in this study entail new modes of political domination and globalization is leading to a more "thorough" (dispersed) exercise of power. Given the ability of transnational capital to utilize its structural power to impose its project even over states that are captured by forces adverse to that project, perhaps the most appropriate strategy for challenging the social order in the age of globalization *starts with* a war of position—Gramsci's "long march" through civil society.

Social conflicts linked to the reorganization of the world economy will lie at the heart of world politics in the twenty-first century. The challenge is how to reconstruct the social power of the popular classes worldwide in a new era in which such power is not mediated and organized through the nation-state. The universal penetration of capitalism through globalization draws all peoples not only into webs of market relations but also into webs of resistance. Kees van der Pijl has identified three moments in the process of the subordination of society and nature to the reproduction of capital: original accumulation; the capitalist production process; and the process of social reproduction—each of which generates its own form of "counter-movement" resistance and struggle.[38] It is to the social forces from below engaged in resistance at all three of these moments that we should turn to in anticipation of any counter-hegemonic impulse which could develop into an effective double movement, in Central America and in global society at large.

The dominant groups in Central America reconstituted and consolidated their control over *political society* but the new round of popular class mobilization in the 1990s pointed to their inability to sustain hegemony in *civil society*. The renewal of protagonism demonstrated by subordinate groups at the grassroots level has been outside of state structures and largely independent of organized Left parties. Grassroots social movements have flourished in civil society at a time when the organized Left operating in political society has been unable to articulate a counter-hegemonic alternative despite its continued vitality. Many leftist parties, even when they sustain an anti-neo-liberal discourse, have in their practice abdicated earlier programs of fundamental structural change in the social order itself.

The FMLN won 45 percent of the vote in 1997 legislative elections in El Salvador, for instance, and the Sandinistas won 39 percent of the vote in presidential elections also held in 1997. But the Sandinistas and the FMLN abandoned earlier programs of fundamental structural change in the social order itself. Their programs in the 1990s were confined to strategies of state intervention in the sphere of circulation to achieve limited internal redistribution, while respecting the prevailing structure of property and wealth and the model of "free-market" integration into the global economy under the region's emergent profile in the GDL.[39]

Popular classes have organized region-wide organizations that brought together diverse sectoral groups in each country's civil society—reflecting the transnationalization of civil society—such as the Central American Agricultural Producers for Cooperation and Development (ASOCODE), the Central American Federation of Community Organizations (FCOC), the Confederation of Cooperatives of the Caribbean and Central America (CCC-CA), and the Central American Workers Network (COCENTRA).[40] These popular platforms set out to devise a grassroots regional integration model in opposition to the transnational model. The failure of the Left to protagonize a process of structural change from political society helped shift the locus of conflict more fully to civil society. Central America seemed to move in the 1990s to a "war of position" between contending social forces in light of subordinate groups' failure to win a "war of maneuver" through revolutionary upheaval and the limits to "power from above." But as crises of legitimacy, perpetual instability, and the impending breakdown of state institutions spread rapidly throughout Latin America in the early twenty-first century conditions seemed to be opening up for a renovated war of maneuver under the novel circumstances of the global economy and society. This raises critical issues best left for future research. However, an effective counter-hegemony, in Central America and in global society, would require, among other things, four conditions I wish to highlight by way of conclusion.

First, a political force and a broader vision of social transformation that can link social movements and diverse oppositional forces.

The resistance of popular classes needs to be unified through a strategy of opposition to the broader structures that generate the particular conditions which each social movement and oppositional force is resisting. Some argue that global economic and technological change have created a more fragmented and heterogeneous social structure that engenders particularist, decentralized, and disconnected forms of collective action. Social movements and oppositional forces are too partial to mount a hegemonic challenge or to contest the systemic logic of transnational capital and its power, which reveals the fundamental contradiction between the global concentration of power and wealth and the diverse but decentralized forms of resistance under global capitalism.[41]

Notwithstanding postmodernists' fragmented "politics of difference" and rejection of "grand narratives," a vision of transformation that departs from the social totality and a renovated Left are central conditions for the development of a counter-hegemonic project. The challenge for popular social movements is how to fuse political with social struggles through the development of political instruments that can extend to political society (the state) the counter-hegemonic space currently being opened up in civil society through mass mobilization. Popular classes have nothing to gain by limiting their struggles to local and isolated "sites" of oppression and forsaking the development of a larger project of transformation, a project which includes a struggle against the state. In this regard, less coordinated mass protest is also the order of the day throughout Central and Latin America. Hunger strikes, sit-ins, land invasions, marches, street-blockings, and mass meetings in both the cities and the countryside are regular occurrences. An important question is to what extent these more inchoate oppositional forces will be mobilized into the existing and new social movements and augment their capacity to force structural change. Such a project must address how oppression *and exploitation,* and the immediate conditions around which popular sectors are struggling, are linked to and derive from a larger totality, that totality being global capitalism. The Left has espoused a commitment to the autonomy of social movements, to social change from the bottom up rather than the top down, to democracy within its organizations, and to non-hierarchical practices over the old verticalism. These commitments need to be demonstrated in the actual practice of a renovated Left and etched into the organizational forms of a counter-hegemonic project.

Second, a viable socioeconomic alternative to global capitalism.

The ubiquitous search for an alternative economic model is probably the major shared and to some extent unifying agenda of Leftist political parties and popular social movements in the South. By the earlier 1990s, the transnational elite had achieved what appeared as a veritable Gramscian consensus around the neo-liberal project. It was indeed a *consensus,* in that: it represented a congruence of interests among the dominant groups in the global system; these interests were being advanced through institutions that command power (the world's states and the TNS apparatus); and this consensus had achieved ideological hegemony by setting the parameters for, and the limits to, debate among subordinate groups around the world on options and alternative projects. In this sense, the "Washington consensus" reflected the emergence of a new global capitalist hegemonic bloc under the leadership of the transnational elite. However, cracks in the consensus had become apparent by the close of the decade.

The world recession of the 1990s and the sequence of crises highlighted the fragility of the world monetary system and caused rising alarm and exposed important contradictions and growing splits in the global capitalist bloc. The more deeply rooted and complex global capitalism becomes the more each shock to the system generates tensions within the ranks of transnational elites, who have become increasingly fragmented in their globalist discourse, in their political vision, and in their ideological coherence. The debates that dominate the summits of power in global society have less to do with narrow economic-corporate interests than with strategic political issues of *class rule.* Foremost is the question of how best to structure the new global economy, achieve world order, and assure the long-term stability and reproduction of the system. These debates did not transgress the essential premises of world market liberalization and the freedom of transnational capital or propose any sort of a global Keynesianism that might involve redistribution or state controls on the prerogatives of capital. But a rising chorus of voices among transnational elites has called for a broader global regulatory apparatus that could stabilize the financial system as well as attenuate some of the sharpest social contradictions of global capitalism in the interests of securing the political stability of the system.[42]

The ability of social movements and oppositional forces to contest the neo-liberal order depends not only on breaking its current hegemony; the struggle to *oppose* the neo-liberal order is inseparable from the struggle to develop a viable alternative and to *impose* that alternative. Without a concrete and viable programmatic alternative, resistance to neo-liberalism runs the risk of becoming trapped in a reformism that does not challenge the logic of the prevailing system—i.e., advancing proposals that fit comfortably within the framework of that system. Precisely because the neo-liberal phase of global capitalism may be coming to a close, resistance must move beyond the critique of neo-liberalism.

The creation of an alternative cannot be willed into existence. It can only emerge out of ongoing political and economic struggles. The problem of the particular neo-liberal model of development is in the end symptomatic of the *systemic* problem of global capitalism. Beyond calling for a mere change in the particular form of accumulation, a counter-hegemonic alternative needs to challenge the logic of the market in its program and ideology. If not, some new ideology and program designed from above by global elites, such as the so-called "Third Way" promulgated in the United States and the United Kingdom in the late 1990s, may well allow the global capitalist bloc to retain the initiative as crises extend and to forestall the possibilities of more fundamental change. An anti-neo-liberal agenda, however important, must develop into an anti-capitalist—that is, *socialist*— alternative.

Third, popular classes need to transnationalize their struggles.

Developing a viable alternative socioeconomic program is not enough in itself. Social forces operating through nationally based social movements need to transpose to transnational space their mobilization and their capacity to place demands on the system. The tremendous structural power that accrues under the global economy to the transnational elite and their local counterparts has altered the terms of struggle between dominant and subordinate groups and requires a shift from national to transnational emancipatory struggles. It is at the transnational level that the causes are to be found of the conditions which popular forces and their movements seek to address. Moreover, these two are linked. The specifics of an alternative are not clear at this time, but clearly it would need to be a new type of redistributive project transposed from the earlier national to the new transnational space, one that challenges the logic of capitalist hegemony, and that develops an ideology, perhaps along the lines that Chase-Dunn has proposed, of a new "egalitarian universalism."[43]

What, then, is the potential power of popular majorities within a transnational setting? To ask this is to ask what the prospects are that social movements and oppositional forces will develop the mechanisms that allow for transposition of local and national organizing strength to transnational space. Central American social movements, popular and oppositional forces, had in fact begun to transnationalize in the 1990s, moving to create alliances, networks, and organizations that transcend national and even regional borders. For instance, cross-border organizing has been extended and systematized in the wake of multinational US-Canadian-Mexican trade union coordination against the NAFTA in 1993 and has drawn together Central American, Mexican, and North American workers. The anti-sweatshop movement and transnational struggles for a "living wage" are other examples.[44] Local and global struggles may be linked through transnational alliances that set specific goals of establishing protective buffers from global capital, such as minimum wages in the maquiladoras, and so on.[45]

Varying degrees of ungovernability and crises of legitimacy characterize country after country in Central America and in many parts of global society, as the dominant groups find it increasingly difficult to maintain governability and assure social reproduction. The crisis and eventual collapse of neo-liberalism may create the conditions favorable to winning state power and promoting an alternative. It is not clear, however, how effective national alternatives can be in transforming social structures, given the ability of transnational capital to utilize its structural power to impose its project even over states that are captured by forces adverse to that project. The real prospect for counter-hegemonic social change in the age of globalization is a globalization-from-below movement that seeks to challenge the power of the global elite by accumulating counter-hegemonic forces beyond national and regional borders; to challenge that power from within an expanding transnational civil society. Such a countermovement to global capitalism did indeed seem to be taking shape with the rise of a global justice movement (what was usually referred to, not entirely accurately, as the anti-globalization movement), as epitomized in the Seattle protest of late 1999 and the Porto Alegre encounters of 2001 and 2002.

Continued change—in Central America and in global society at large—will be shaped by conflict and crisis among the summits of power as the dominant groups find it increasingly difficult to maintain governability and assure social reproduction, and recomposition of civil society at the base, and by the interplay of the two at the local and the global levels. We should recall that capitalist globalization—indeed, the history of capitalism—is an incomplete, highly contested, and conflict-ridden process that certainly opens up new opportunities for emancipatory projects.

Fourth, organic intellectuals subordinate to and in the service of popular majorities and their struggles.

One of the peculiar features of the current epoch has been the separation of many organic intellectuals from the mass struggles against globalization. Many intellectuals who earlier identified with popular and revolutionary movements have ceded—whether through outright opportunism or sincere confusion—a certain intellectual hegemony to global capitalism. For these intellectuals, the structural constraints set by the system have become accepted and the only alternatives put forward as legitimate and "realistic" are those that respect these constraints. We should recall that the extent of social change may be fixed by historic structures but the outer limits of these structures are always established and reestablished by collective human agency. It is only through struggle against established historic structures that the extent to which they can become transformed is revealed. Intellectual labor as a form of social action may constrict just as it may extend the limits of change.

I want to call for the development of a critical globalization studies. At issue here is how organic intellectuals assume their responsibilities in our institutions, such as our universities, and the mass media, as scholars, as journalists, as opinion-makers, as organizers, and as cultural agents. All intellectual labor is "organic." It either legitimates the prevailing social order and provides technical solutions to the problems that arise in its maintenance or it exposes contradictions and reveals how they may be resolved by transcending the existing order. It is the responsibility of intellectuals to apply their training and experience to elucidating the real inner workings of the social order and the contradictions therein.

A critical globalization studies should expose the dominant mythologies of our epoch, such as the notion that "sustainable development" is actually possible under global capitalism, that Latin America and much of the world has been "democratized," and so on. Such a critical studies needs to exercise in its intellectual labor a "preferential option" for the subordinate majorities of emergent global society and for the future latent within them. Our analysis should focus on the issue of human agency, with how our collective action may influence the direction of structural change, and what we can achieve by working together to move beyond the proclaimed limits of the possible.

Final Considerations

Whither the Sociology of Development?
From a Territorial to a Social Conception of Development

Although development sociology might have reached an "impasse" in the 1980s, the social processes that we refer to as "development" have certainly not ground to a halt.[46] Central America's rearticulation involves integration into world structures that are themselves fundamentally being altered by the globalization of production and the transnationalization of superstructural processes and institutions. The gradual disembedding of groups, structures, and institutions from the nation-state context in which they have been traditionally studied modifies the focus of critical underdevelopment theories. These theories have spanned a comparative national approach that seeks to account for variations across countries to world-system analysis that focuses on the systemic imperatives and constraints of world capitalism. Promising new lines of research and "middle range" theories purport to bridge this span, while other theoretical work has attempted to account for the growing anomalies apparent with the onset of globalization. New theoretical work in the late twentieth century included: the New International Division of Labor; the concept of "divergent development"; global commodity chains theory; postmodern theories (with their emphasis on "deconstructing" the development discourse and subjecting the dominant Western paradigms to scathing critiques);[47] feminist theories; and theories of post-Fordism and flexible accumulation, which I have found most useful.[48]

In chapter one I suggested that the way out of the "impasse" in development sociology is to break with nation-state centered analysis. I argued that: 1) globalization has exposed the limitations of extant paradigms that take nation-states as units of analysis for development; 2) the increasing subordination of the logic of geography to that of production and the rising disjuncture between the fortunes of social groups and of nation-states, among other processes bound up with globalization, demand that we reconceive of development; and 3) global social polarization, the fragmentation of national economies, and the select integration of social groups into transnational networks, suggest that processes of uneven accumulation are unfolding in accordance with a social and not a national logic, and that we may rethink development not as a national process, in which what "develops" is a nation, but in terms of developed, underdeveloped, and intermediate population groups occupying contradictory or unstable locations in a transnational environment. Reconceiving development in this way does not render space irrelevant; it implies that the social configuration of space can no longer be conceived in the nation-state terms that development theories posit but rather as processes of uneven development denoted primarily by social group rather than territorial differentiation. Geography still remains important, but how so is open to question. How may we specify the changing relationship between space and development? Is the tendency for the self-reproduction in the global division of labor countered by processes bound up with globalization?

While at the time of writing I am unable to specify in theoretical terms to my satisfaction the relationship between space and development, I am convinced that the way forward involves, first, a new conception of development based not on territory but on social groups, and second, the understanding that space takes on new meaning under globalization. Space is configured in diverse ways, only one of which is the nation-state. As David Harvey has observed, the diminishment of spatial barriers gives transnational capital a newfound power to exploit minute spatial differentiation to good effect. "As spatial barriers diminish so we become much more sensitized to what the world's spaces contain. Flexible accumulation typically exploits a wide range of seemingly contingent geographic circumstances, and reconstitutes them as structured internal elements of its own encompassing logic."[49]

There is a dispersal around the world of specialized activities that are increasingly component processes in world production and whose distribution exhibits only in part a spatial or geographic significance. Critical geographies have drawn our attention to multilayered relations between space, place, and production over time. The drive to relocate to more advantageous spaces (the geographic movement of both capital and labor) periodically revolutionizes the international and territorial division of labor, adding a vital geographic dimension to the permanent flux, disruption, commotion, and redefinition of capitalism as a social system.[50] The geographers' focus on the dimension of space and territory in accumulation and changes in space over time needs to be more fully integrated into the debate on development. As time and space collapse in the current frenzied global reorganization of capitalism, the territorial or geographic dimensions of accumulation become ever less relevant. The impermanence of production sites means that accumulation is not fixed (time-bound) in geographic coordinates. Fragmentation and recombination brings about constantly new social forms. To the extent that accumulation requires political authority and representation, and to the extent that this representation is territorially bound, then we have a countervailing pressure against the tendency for the de-territorialization of development. But the state itself is in the process of becoming transnationalized. We are left with the social dimension, which is the real essence and subject matter of development as a process and as a condition.

Specific spaces or regions in the global economy acquire their own profiles, as I have discussed in this study for Central America. However, empirical evidence suggests that these profiles may just as easily correspond to sub-regions, even to local municipalities, as they do to countries. Spatial "niches" in transnational production specific to regions and sub-regions, as Harvey notes, have been carved out in Silicon Valley, Los Angeles, the "Third Italy," South Wales, and so on. These spaces present specific political, social, economic, and cultural conditions not coterminous with the conditions of nations, including types of labor available and effective patterns of labor control, conducive to certain activities functionally integrated into the global economy. These profiles in the global economy are not fixed but fluid and are "structured internal elements" of the encompassing logic of globalization. Flexible accumulation makes possible a very broad diversity of participation in the global economy, and also the possibility that social groups structure their own distinct spaces in function of their participation. In this process, development becomes detached from territoriality. In Central America, the particular profile in the global economy has acquired region-wide characteristics, but this does not imply that participation in the global economy differentiated by space is by theoretical *fiat* or systemic imperative *national* space.

We need to move beyond neo-Kantian categoricals. Substituting the concept of the global and the local for the familiar binaries of core/periphery, developed/underdeveloped, and so on, may be useful since it is less concordant with spatial boundaries or geographic regions, is capable of encompassing unequal distribution *within* as well as between national and regional entities, and does not imply a fixed hierarchical division within the totality. Unequal exchanges—material, political, cultural—are not captured so much in the concept of the *international* division of labor as the *global* division of labor, which implies differential participation in global production according to social standing and not necessarily geographic location, and that account for sweatshops in East Los Angeles and Northern Honduras, as well as gated communities in Hollywood and Managua. Social order is increasingly organized globally, and not nationally. It follows that inequality—the permanent consequence of capitalist social relations—is similarly organized globally, that there are new forms that poverty and wealth take. I suggest that the reconceptualization proposed here may allow us to research new social cartographies and to identify in these cartographies relational dimensions and agencies.

A global—rather than international—division of labor is characterized by labor hierarchies and developed and underdeveloped populations that cut across national boundaries. The Central American case reminds us that different regions—that is, geographies—do acquire distinct profiles. But these profiles do not consign the different population groups in each region to underdevelopment by virtue of nationality or spatial location. We want to specify the relationship between regional profiles and the distribution of social rewards among a globally stratified population. On the one hand, participation in structures particular to specific regions may be a status in the same sense that gender and ethnicity are statuses that help shape the distribution of social rewards. On the other hand, geographic location (living in an "underdeveloped country") does not necessarily confer this status on individuals and social groups. Globalization fragments locally and integrates select strands of the population globally. The centralization and concentration of economic power is accompanied by a disintegration of the cohesive structures of nations and their civil societies. Thus the effect of local economic expansion is often the advancement of some (delocalized) groups and deepening poverty for others. What accounts for the variation that social groups experience in their participation in a now-globalized collective labor process and in the distribution of social rewards? And what is the significance of space in accounting for this variation? These are questions for future research. However, the answers we develop will have great significance, in my view, for a renewal of the sociology of development.

There is a shift in the historic tendency from the homogenization of regional labor markets (spatially segmented labor markets) to labor-market diversification (in-place labor-market diversification). The world market seems, in McMichael's words, to "standardize consumption but differentiate production."[51] Marketing strategies by TNCs tend to segment consumers according to class-based income brackets, and produce a narrower range of different products for these brackets which are then standardized and marketed globally to these distinct segments. But these segments are dispersed globally. Affinities of consumption and lifestyle cut across national boundaries and unite (or divide) different social groups in a cross or transnational setting. Shifting the focus in the spatial or geographic dimension of development from national "downward" to subnational space (even down to the local level, for example, inner-city versus affluent suburban space within the same city) and "upward" to regional space may help us to specify the relationship of space to a global totality and to development as a social category. A simple loop by car through any of the Central American capitals and principal urban areas reveals the vast gap between social and cultural worlds within the very same city. Glittering malls replete with the latest the global economy has to offer, fast-food chains, beckoning recreational centers, and well-guarded residential neighborhoods that would be the envy of any First World center stick out as lagoons of wealth and privilege surrounded by oceans of poverty and mass misery, often divided only, and literally, by the very best security systems that social-control technology can buy. One slips from "developed" into "underdeveloped" without any geographic significance beyond urban geography. In an absolute sense the poor in Central America are much more poor than the poor of the United States or Europe. But the social dividing line is clearly not a national one.

There is a longstanding debate in development studies as to whether growth constitutes development, or if it is even a necessary condition for development (as opposed to a mere redistributive restructuring). Globalization largely renders this debate impertinent, to the extent that wealth produced in any one region of the world can be moved elsewhere instantaneously, and to the extent that wealth may be captured and consumed by select social groups whose style of life and levels of development may bear no relation to other social groups in their midst. The claim that the rise of rich regions, such as Northern Italy or Silicon Valley, demonstrate the geographic and spatial nature of development, is not convincing because stratification occurs within these regions. For some this represents a process of "regionalization" as geographic areas realign themselves according to the logic of production and markets rather than national borders. Such regions may actually be subnational zones within national borders, such as Northern Italy, Pusan at the southern tip of the Korean Peninsula, or the Shukoten region of Japan, while others straddle national borders, such as the "Growth Triangle" that consists of Singapore, the Malaysian state of Johore and the Riau Islands of Indonesia, or the US-Mexico border region. This may move us beyond nation-state centrism per se, but not beyond a territorial conception of development. As is well-known, high-income groups generate the need for low-income services, construction, and related workers to attend to the consumption of their strata. Often transnational immigrants, as much recent literature has shown, fill this role, but this phenomenon is not by *fiat*. The generation of wealth produces within the same communities the generation of poverty and marginality. The only reasonable conclusion is a *social* conception of development. What may have offset this and given a geographic dimension to development in an earlier historic moment was the intervention of national states in the accumulation process through regulation and redistribution.

An Afterword on Researching Globalization and Social Change

This study has been an exercise in the development of grounded theory, by which I have tried to bridge the gap between theoretically uninformed empirical presentation and empirically uninformed theory, in investigating contemporary processes of social change. In this undertaking novel conceptual tools have been developed and existing ones renovated to help comprehend a rapidly changing reality under globalization. My view was that the ready-made conceptual frameworks of the past could not simply be applied deductively. New concepts needed to be explored and applied to an empirically changing reality as working propositions oriented towards guiding ongoing research. The result was a "good fit" between the conceptual and theoretical propositions developed in chapter one and elsewhere and the documentation of empirical reality and historical development in Central America.

Of course there cannot be, nor should there be, theoretical closure on the themes raised in the present study. Social reality is more complex, more contingent, and more subject to unanticipated consequences than our rational models and analytical constructs are able to predict. This study has been largely concerned with structural analysis. The relational/behavioral level of analysis can capture the complexities of everyday life and historical processes, whereas structural analysis gives us a sense of the underlying causality and historic determination that lie beneath those processes and inform them. And as a matter of course the present study has not attempted to—and cannot—account in its entirety for what took place in Central America in the late twentieth century. As Portes observes, "the attempt to account for a social phenomenon in its entirety leads to circular reasoning because it inexorably reduces the conceptual space between the thing to be explained and its alleged causes."[52]

The present study has advanced a number of theoretical propositions on globalization and social change. Many of these propositions can be subsumed under the concept of *transnational processes*. In chapter one I presented a *typology* of transnational processes, a descriptive categorization of the types of changes predicted in countries and regions experiencing globalization, defined as integration into the emergent structures of the global system. An ideal-type is a construct that allows us to explain interrelationships of relevant key dimensions of the social world. We should recall that it is not reality but a framework with which to observe and assess social processes by determining how they conform and how they deviate. The empirical data, analyses, and historical discussion in the preceding chapters support my central propositions regarding transnational processes. On the other hand, typologies in themselves are not theories. Theories need to suggest both origin and causation (indeed, *causal origins*) of the social phenomena under investigation. But typologies are essential building blocks of theory,[53] and should lead to theory, or help in the enterprise of testing theory.

Beyond a typology, this study has also advanced a *theory of transnational processes*. In Portes' view, a theory needs to meet the following conditions, beyond typologies: a description of specific instances, identification of a problem in need of explanation and of explanatory factors, and links between the theoretical propositions and other predictive statements. I have explained social change by the world historic process of globalization; by the interactive dynamics of globalization with contingency; and with specific national and regional histories, conditions, and conjunctures. The theory of transnational processes is linked to other theoretical constructs, such as transnational classes and class fractions, transnational state apparatuses and practices, national and global circuits of accumulation, and so on, which constitute interactive effects in transnational processes. I have emphasized as well the general in the particular and the particular in the general. I suggest that these same theories will predict very broadly the underlying dynamics of change elsewhere, i.e., the rise of transnational fractions, the integration of national states into transnational state structures, economic restructuring, etc. It is beyond the scope of this study to explore in comparative perspective change under globalization in other regions. I am confident, however, that those researching other regions will find here typologies, theoretical insights, and orienting guidelines for the study and explanation of change elsewhere in the global system. All knowledge is the result of experience in the world and, ultimately, the test of theory is in the practice. To the extent that this study has provided a clearer understanding of the past and of possible futures then it will have achieved one of its major purposes.

Notes

Introduction: Development and Social Change

1. Fred Halliday, "State and Society in International Relations: A Second Agenda," *Millennium: Journal of International Studies*, vol. 16, no. 2, 1987, pp. 215–29.
2. I have developed this idea in William I. Robinson, "Beyond Nation-State Paradigms: Globalization, Sociology, and the Challenge of Transnational Studies," *Sociological Forum*, vol. 13, no. 4, 1998, pp. 561–94.
3. William I. Robinson, *Promoting Polyarchy: Globalization, US Intervention, and Hegemony*, Cambridge 1996.
4. Earlier works in this agenda have theorized on: change in social structure and the state and the intersection of politics and economics under globalization; the reconfiguration of North–South relations and of world order and hegemony; the transnationalization of political systems, civil society, and culture; global class formation; and democratization and new transnational modes of social control. See, *inter alia*, William I. Robinson, *A Faustian Bargain: US Intervention in the Nicaraguan Elections and American Foreign Policy in the Post-Cold War Era*, Boulder 1992; *Promoting Polyarchy*. See also the sources in note 7 below.
5. See, *inter alia*, Alejandro Portes, "Neo-Liberalism and the Sociology of Development: Emerging Trends and Unanticipated Facts," in J. Timmons Roberts and Amy Hite, *From Modernization to Globalization*, Malden, MA 2000, pp. 353–69. Portes argues that moving beyond the sweeping historical statements of globalization theories requires moving down in the units and levels of analysis.
6. Such an approach is concerned, to evoke Anthony Giddens' terminology, with the *structuration* of macro and microsocial processes, although I reject the indeterminacy and implicit methodological individualism in Giddens' formulation. See *The Constitution of Society: Outline of the Theory of Structuration*, Berkeley 1984.
7. See in particular William I. Robinson, "Beyond Nation-State Paradigms"; "Globalisation: Nine Theses of Our Epoch," *Race and Class*, vol. 38, no. 2, 1996, pp. 13–31; "Social Theory and Globalization: The Rise of a Transnational State," *Theory and Society*, vol. 30, no. 2, 2001, pp. 157–200; William I. Robinson and Jerry Harris, "Towards a Global Ruling Class? Globalization and the Transnational Capitalist Class," *Science and Society*, vol. 64, no. 1, 2000, pp. 11–54.
8. See William I. Robinson, "A Case Study of Globalisation Processes in the Third World: A Transnational Agenda in Nicaragua," *Global Society*, vol. 11, no. 1, 1997, pp. 61–92; "Neo-Liberalism, the Global Elite, and the Guatemalan Transition: A Critical Macrosocial Analysis," *Journal of Inter-American and World Affairs*,

vol. 42, no. 4, 2000, pp. 89–107; "(Mal)development in Central America: Globalization and Social Change," *Development and Change*, vol. 29, no. 3, 1998, pp. 467–97; "Transnational Processes, Development Studies, and Changing Social Hierarchies in the World System: A Central American Case Study," *Third World Quarterly*, vol. 22, no. 4, 2001, pp. 529–63; "Globalization as a Macrostructural-Historical Framework of Analysis: The Case of Central America," *New Political Economy*, vol. 7, no. 2, 2002, pp. 221–49.

9. Robert W. Cox, "Critical Political Economy," in Bjorne Hettne (ed.), *International Political Economy: Understanding Global Disorder*, London 1995, p. 31.

1 The Dialectics of Globalization and Development

1. Eric Hobsbawm, *The Age of Revolution*, New York 1962; *The Age of Capital*, London 1977; *The Age of Empire*, New York 1987.
2. John Gerard Ruggie, "Territoriality and Beyond: Problematizing Modernity in International Relations," *International Organization*, vol. 47, no. 2, 1993, pp. 139–74.
3. See, *inter alia*, Roland Robertson, *Globalization: Social Theory and Global Culture*, London 1992; Anthony Giddens, *The Consequences of Modernity*, Cambridge 1990; Malcolm Waters, *Globalization*, London 1995.
4. Istvan Meszaros, "The Uncontrollability of Globalizing Capital," *Monthly Review*, vol. 49, no. 9, 1998, pp. 27–37.
5. Immanuel Wallerstein, *The Modern World System*, New York 1974.
6. This was known as the "modes of production" debate and has a long history. For a summary of the debate, see Aidan Foster-Carter, "The Modes of Production Controversy," *New Left Review*, no. 107, 1978, pp. 47–78.
7. For this Marxist conception, see, e.g., Nicos Poulantzas, *Classes in Contemporary Capitalism*, London 1975.
8. Nation-states mediated the boundaries between a world of different articulated modes of production. This is implicit in the argument of sociologist Immanuel Wallerstein, the best-known exponent of world-system theory, for whom the determinant distinction between core, semi-periphery, and periphery are different forms of labor control. See *The Modern World System*.
9. Works on the global economy are voluminous. On the globalization of production, which is of most concern here, see, *inter alia*, Peter Dicken, *Global Shift*, third edition, London and New York 1998; Jeremy Howells and Michelle Wood, *The Globalisation of Production and Technology*, London 1993; Roger Burbach and William I. Robinson, "The Fin de Siecle Debate: Globalization as Epochal Shift," *Science and Society*, vol. 63, no. 1, 1999, pp. 10–39; United Nations Conference on Trade and Development, various years, in *World Investment Report*, New York.
10. See, e.g., David M. Gordon's outdated but still influential essay, "The Global Economy: New Edifice or Crumbling Foundations?," *New Left Review*, no. 168, 1988, pp. 24–64. See also the widely cited studies by Paul Hirst and Graham Thompson, *Globalization in Question*, Cambridge 1996. Other works of this persuasion include A. Glyn and Bob Sutcliff, "Global But Leaderless? The New Capitalist Order," in Ralph Miliband and Leo Panitch (eds.), *New World Order: The Socialist Register*, London 1992; Ellen Meiksins Wood, "Unhappy Families: Global Capitalism in a World of Nation-States," *Monthly Review*, vol. 51, no. 3, 1999, pp. 1–2; Linda Weiss, *The Myth of the Powerless State*, New York 1998.

11. Internationalization involves the simple extension of economic activities across national boundaries and is essentially a *quantitative* process which leads to a more extensive geographical pattern of economic activity, whereas transnationalization is *qualitatively* different to internationalization processes, involving not merely the geographical extension of economic activity across national boundaries but also the *functional integration* of such internationally dispersed activities.

12. Dicken, *Global Shift*, p. 5.

13. Dicken, *Global Shift*, p. 2.

14. Dicken, *Global Shift*, p. 223.

15. See, e.g., Gary Gereffi and Miguel Korzeniewicz (eds.), *Commodity Chains and Global Capitalism*, Westport 1994.

16. On this point, see *inter alia*, Ankie Hoogvelt, *Globalization and the Postcolonial World*, Baltimore 1997, pp. 109–13.

17. There is a huge body of literature on the crisis of Fordism/Keynesianism, the restructuring of labor, flexible accumulation, and related themes. See *inter alia*, David Harvey, *The Condition of Postmodernity*, Oxford 1989; Robert W. Cox, *Production, Power, and World Order*, New York 1987; Ash Amin (ed.), *Post-Fordism: A Reader*, Oxford 1994; Dicken, *Global Shift*; Scott Lash and John Urry, *The End of Organized Capitalism*, Cambridge 1987; Hoogvelt, *Globalization and the Postcolonial World*; Alain Lipietz, *Mirages and Miracles: The Crisis of Global Fordism*, London 1987; Folker Frobel, Jurgen Heinrichs, and Otto Kreye, *The New International Division of Labor*, London 1980.

18. William I. Robinson, "Beyond Nation-State Paradigms: Globalization, Sociology, and the Challenge of Transnational Studies," *Sociological Forum*, vol. 13, no. 4, 1998, pp. 561–94. The following section draws heavily on this study.

19. Anthony Giddens, *The Nation-State and Violence*, Cambridge 1985.

20. Benedict Anderson, *Imagined Communities*, London 1983.

21. Anthony Giddens, *The Constitution of Society*, Cambridge 1984.

22. See Giddens, *The Consequences of Modernity*. In somewhat contradictory fashion, Giddens also notes (accurately, in my view) that globalization involves the disembedding or "lifting out of social relations from local contexts of interaction and their restructuring across time and space" (p. 21), what I would characterize as the globalization of social structure. This being the case, it is not clear why the capitalist nation-state should remain the primordial fixed *institution* of social life, as Giddens suggests.

23. See, *inter alia*, Robinson, "Beyond Nation-State Paradigms," and Robinson, "Global Capitalism and Nation-State Centric Thinking: What We Don't See When We Do See Nation-States. Response to Arrighi, Mann, Moore, van der Pijl, and Went," *Science and Society*, vol. 65, no. 4, 2001–2002, pp. 500–508.

24. The literature under these categories is quite broad. See, *inter alia*, Douglas A. Kincaid and Alejandro Portes (eds.), *Comparative National Development: Society and Economy in the New Global Order*, Chapel Hill 1994; Fiala, "Varieties of Expression in the New International Comparative Political Economy"; Peter Evans and John D. Stephens, "Studying Development Since the Sixties: The Emergence of A New Comparative Political Economy," *Theory and Society*, vol. 17, no. 5, 1988, pp. 713–45; Hoogvelt, *Globalization and the Postcolonial World*; J. Timmons Roberts and Amy Hite (eds.), *From Modernization to Globalization: Perspectives on Development and Social Change*, Oxford 2000; Craig Murphy and R. Tooze (eds.), *The New International Political Economy*, Boulder 1991; Stephen Gill and David Law, *The Global Political Economy: Perspectives, Problems and Policies*,

Baltimore 1988; Bjorne Hettne (ed.), *International Political Economy: Understanding Global Disorder*, London 1995; Hans-Henrik Holm and Georg Sorensen (eds.), *Whose World Order?: Uneven Globalization and the End of the Cold War*, Boulder 1995. One very notable exception to this list is the work of Leslie Sklair, whose critique of "state-centrism" is similar but not identical to my critique of nation-state centrism, and who has also attempted to reorient development studies along the lines I propose here.

25. Waters, *Globalization*, p. 28.

26. Ruggie, "Territoriality and Beyond," pp. 143-4.

27. Thomas Kuhn, *The Structure of Scientific Revolutions*, Chicago 1962; Louis Althusser, *For Marx*, London 1966.

28. Paul Feyerabend, *Against Method*, London 1975.

29. There is, of course, a problem of measurement, as Sklair discusses at some length in *Sociology of the Global System*, in which our basic measurements and indicators are all based on nation-state data, leading to "state-centered classifications of the global system."

30. Robert Gilpin, *The Political Economy of International Relations*, Princeton 1987, p. 254.

31. World Bank, *Global Economic Prospects and the Developing Countries*, Washington/ New York, p. 33.

32. Dicken, *Global Shift*, p. 291.

33. Dicken, *Global Shift*, p. 272.

34. Lorraine Eden and Maureen Appel Molot, "Insiders and outsiders: defining 'who is us' in the northamerican automobile industry," *Transnational Corporations*, vol. 2, no. 3, 1993, pp. 31-65.

35. See, e.g., Harry Magdoff, "Globalization—To What End?" in Ralph Miliband and Leo Panitch (eds.), *Socialist Register*, London 1992; Alejandro Bendana, *Power Lines: US Domination in the New Global Order*, New York 1996.

36. See, e.g., United Nations Centre on Transnational Corporations, *World Investment Report 1991* and *World Investment Report 1992*, New York.

37. See, *inter alia*, Frans J. Schuurman, *Beyond the Impasse: New Directions in Development Theory*, London and New Jersey 1993; D. Booth, "Marxism and Development Sociology: interpreting the impasse," *World Development*, vol. 13, no. 6, 1985, pp. 683-95; Booth, *Rethinking Social Development: Theory, Research and Practice*, London 1994; Colin Leys, *The Rise and the Fall of Development Theory*, Indianapolis, London, and Nairobi 1996; R. Peet, *Global Capitalism: Theories of Social Development*, London 1991.

38. In the late 1990s, the annual report of the United Nations Development Program (UNDP), *Human Development Report*, began to disaggregate the findings with regard to its "human development" composite index (HDI). In the United States, disaggregating for race, it found that the HDI for whites was slightly above average compared people in Japan, whereas for blacks it was about the same as for people in Trinidad and Tobago, and for Hispanics it was the same as the average for people in Estonia. Disaggregating for gender, white females ranked higher than any other group anywhere, black females ranked well below, at about the same as the Greek average, and black males ranked slightly above the Bulgarian average. See *Human Development Report*, New York, various years. This data indicates the importance of shifting the approach to development from geographic to social group terms.

39. Andre Gunder Frank, *Crisis: In the Third World*, New York 1981.

40. Frobel, *et al.*, *The New International Division of Labor*.

41. See, e.g., Dicken, *Global Shift*; Philip McMichael, *Development and Social Change: A Global Perspective*, Thousand Oaks 1996.

42. See, e.g., Saskia Sassen, *The Global City*, Princeton 1991; McMichael, *Development and Social Change*, esp. pp. 185–6.

43. See, e.g., Cox, *Production, Power, and World Order*, esp. pp. 322–35; S. Crook, J. Pakulski, and M. Waters, *Postmodernization*, London 1992; McMichael, *Development and Social Change*; Harvey, *The Condition of Postmodernity*; Amin, *Post-Fordism: A Reader*; Kathleen Barker and Kathleen Christensen (eds.), *Contingent Work: American Employment Relations in Transition*, Ithica 1998; Lash and Urry, *The End of Organized Capitalism*; Yates, *Longer Hours: Fewer Jobs*; Frobel, *et al.*, *The New International Division of Labor*.

44. See, e.g., David Korten, *When Corporations Rule the World*, West Hartford 1995; Harrison, *Lean and Mean*.

45. This is the case for a portion of the global commodity chains literature. See, e.g., Gereffi and Korzeniewicz, *Commodity Chains and Global Capitalism*.

46. Dilip D'Souza, "Silicon Valley East," *The New Internationalist*, no. 286, 1996, p. 25. On the software industry in India, see also "India and Pakistan: The Elephant and the Pekinese," *The Economist*, March 18, 2000, pp. 25–8.

47. On applied discussion on the law, an extension of Marx's law of uneven accumulation, Ernest Mandel, *Late Capitalism*, London 1975.

48. Maria Patricia Fernández Kelly, *Political Economy and Gender in Latin America: The Emerging Dilemmas*, Baltimore, Johns Hopkins University, Latin American Program Working Papers, no. 207.

49. Cox, *Production, Power, and World Order*, pp. 319–20.

50. The themes discussed in this section draw heavily from William I. Robinson and Jerry Harris, "Towards a Global Ruling Class? Globalization and the Transnational Capitalist Class," *Science and Society*, vol. 64, no. 1, Spring 2000, pp. 11–54.

51. Kees van der Pijl, *The Making of an Atlantic Ruling Class*, London 1984; "The International Level," in Tom Bottomore and Robert J. Brym (eds.), *The Capitalist Class: An International Study*, New York 1989; *Transnational Classes and International Relations*, London 1998.

52. See, esp., Cox, *Production, Power, and World Order*; Stephen Gill, *American Hegemony and the Trilateral Commission*, Cambridge 1990.

53. Sklair, *Sociology of the Global System*.

54. Karl Polanyi, *The Great Transformation*, Boston 1944.

55. See, e.g., Alejandro Portes, Manuel Castells, and Lauren A. Bendon (eds.), *The Informal Economy: Studies in Advanced and Less Developed Countries*, Baltimore 1989.

56. Hoogvelt, *Globalization and the Postcolonial World*.

57. Robinson and Harris, "Toward a Global Ruling Class?" analyzes the rise of a transnational capitalist class. For a detailed empirical study on the same theme from a somewhat different theoretical viewpoint, see Leslie Sklair, *The Making of a Transnational Capitalist Class*, London 2000.

58. This was noted as long ago as 1974 by Richard Barnett and Ronald Mueller, in *Global Reach*, New York 1974. For "from the horse's mouth" accounts of the reflexive thinking of this transnational bourgeoisie, see Walter Wriston, *Twilight of Sovereignty: How the Information Revolution is Transforming the World*, New York 1992. Wriston is former CEO of Citibank.

59. International Labor Organization (ILO), *World Employment Report 1996–97*, Geneva 1997, p. 2.

60. Dicken, *Global Shift*, p. 44.

61. Burbach and Robinson, "The Fin de Siecle Debate: Globalization as Epochal Shift," *Science and Society*, vol. 63, no. 1, 1999, pp. 20–21.

62. ILO, *World Employment Report 1996–97*, p. xvii.

63. Nicholas Hildyard, Colin Hines, and Tim Lang, "Who Competes? Changing Landscapes of Corporate Control," *The Ecologist*, vol. 26, no. 4, 1996, pp. 125–44. Data cited is on p. 135.

64. For these details, see Burbach and Robinson, "Globalization as Epochal Shift."

65. For discussion on this point, see Robinson, *Promoting Polyarchy*; "Globalization: Nine Theses of Our Epoch," *Race and Class*, vol. 3, no. 2, pp. 13–31, 1996; Robinson and Harris, "Toward a Global Ruling Class?".

66. This section draws heavily on my extended discussions elsewhere on a transnational state. See esp. Robinson, "Social Theory and Globalization."

67. For discussion and critique of the diverse literature on supranational institutions, see *ibid.*

68. See, e.g., Max Weber, *Economy and Society*, Guenther Roght and Claus Wittich (eds.), Berkeley 1978 [1922], for Weber's discussions on these issues.

69. Marx and Engels, *The German Ideology*, note: "Since the state is the form in which the individuals of a ruling class assert their common interests, and in which the whole civil society of an epoch is epitomized, it follows that the state mediates in the formation of all common institutions and that the institutions receive a political form" (80). Marx's discussion on so-called primitive accumulation in *Capital*, Book VIII, highlights the role of the state in facilitating the conditions for new economic and social relations. Here I want to highlight the role of the TNS in facilitating the conditions for the new types of relations developing under globalization.

70. World Bank, *The State in a Changing World*, Washington D.C./Baltimore 1997, p. 12.

71. The movement towards the "decentralization" of the national state, such as "devolution" of administrative powers from the central government to local governments in the United States, or the transfer to municipal governments of formerly central state activities in Latin America, should be seen in light of changes in the state under globalization. No longer able to sustain the activities that provide for popular legitimacy, central states attempt to abdicate social welfare responsibilities and the costs of continued social polarization through the decentralization of such functions to local authorities. This is the "double movement" of the state under globalization, "downward" to decentralized local levels and "upwards" to emergent transnational spaces.

72. See, *inter alia*, Stephen Gill and David Law, "Global Hegemony and the Structural Power of Transnational Capital," *International Studies Quarterly*, vol. 33, no. 4, 1989, pp. 475–99.

73. Nicos Poulantzas, *Political Power and Social Classes*, London 1975.

74. Antonio Gramsci, *Selections from the Prison Notebooks* (New York: International Publishers, 1971), p. 176.

75. Perhaps the best-known exponents of the Italian school in international relations are Robert Cox, see, esp. "Social Forces, States, and World Orders: Beyond International Relations Theory," *Millennium: Journal of International Studies*, vol. 10, no. 2, 1981: 126–155; *Production, Power, and World Order*, and Stephen Gill, see esp., Gill, *American Hegemony and the Trilateral Commission*, and Gill (ed.), *Antonio Gramsci, Historical Materialism, and International Relations*, New York 1993.

76. David M. Gordon, Richard Edwards, and Michael Reich, *Social Structures of Accumulation*, Cambridge 1994.

77. There is an enormous body of literature on US policy towards Central America in the late twentieth century, some of which is discussed throughout this study. For a minutely detailed and documented chronicle of US policy as seen from a Washington perspective, see William M. Leogrande, *Our Own Backyard: The United States in Central America, 1977–1992*, Chapel Hill 1998, and see my review in *American Political Science Review*, vol. 94, no. 4, 2000.

78. The issues in this section are discussed more broadly in Robinson, *Promoting Polyarchy*; "Globalisation: Nine Theses of Our Epoch"; and "A Case Study of Globalisation Processes in the Third World: A Transnational Agenda in Nicaragua," *Global Society*, vol. 11, no. 1, 1997, pp. 61–91; "Promoting Capitalist Polyarchy: The Case of Latin America," in Inoguchi, Ikenberry, and Cox (eds.), *Promoting Democracy*, New York 2000.

79. See John Williamson, "Democracy and the 'Washington Consensus'," *World Development*, vol. 21, no. 8, 1993, pp. 1329–36.

80. See, e.g., Albert Fishlow, Carlos F. Diaz-Alejandro, Richard R. Fagen, and Roger D. Hansen, *Rich and Poor Nations in the World Economy*, New York 1978; Robert W. Cox, "Ideologies and the New International Economic Order . . ." *International Organization*, 33 (1979), no. 2, pp. 257–302; Williamson, "Democracy and the 'Washington Consensus'."

81. Susan George, *The Debt Boomerang: How Third World Debt Harms Us All*, Boulder 1992, p. xvi.

82. On this neo-liberal restructuring around the world, see, *inter alia*, Henk Overbeek (ed.), *Restructuring Hegemony in the Global Political Economy: The rise of transnational neo-liberalism in the 1980s*, London 1993.

83. Which is why the works of well-known economists who explain and defend neo-liberalism from a neo-classical theoretical perspective are not merely "wrong" or ideological in the narrow sense. Well-known studies are, *inter alia*: Bela Balussa, *The Newly Industrialized Countries in the World Economy*, New York 1981, and *Comparative Advantage, Trade Policy and Economic Development*, London 1989; A. M. Choski and D. Papageorgiou (eds.), *Economic Liberalization in Developing Countries*, Oxford 1986; A. O. Kruger, *Foreign Trade Regimes and Economic Development: Liberalization Attempts and Consequences*, Cambridge 1978; Jeffrey D. Sachs (ed.), *Developing Country Debt and Economic Performance*, vols. 1 and 2, Chicago 1989; John Williamson (ed.), *Latin American Adjustment: How Much Has Happened?*, Washington D.C. 1990.

84. For accounts of neo-liberal adjustment and these effects in Latin America, see Duncan Green, *Silent Revolution: The Rise of Market Economies in Latin America*, London 1995, and for Africa, see Fantu Cheru, *The Silent Revolution in Africa: Debt, Development, and Democracy*, London 1989. On the social effects of restructuring, see Michel Chossudovsky, *The Globalisation of Poverty: Impacts of IMF and World Bank Reform*, London 1997; Giovanni Cornia, Richard Jelly, and Frances Stewart (eds.), *Adjustment with A Human Face*, Oxford 1987.

85. See, esp., William I. Robinson, "Globalization, the World System, and 'Democracy Promotion' in US Foreign Policy," and *Promoting Polyarchy*.

86. On these issues, see William I. Robinson, "Promoting Capitalist Polyarchy: The Case of Latin America," in Inoguchi, Ikenberry, and Cox (eds.), *Promoting Democracy*, New York 2000.

87. Holm and Sorensen, *Whose World Order? Uneven Globalization*.

88. Such "transitology" became a faddish academic cottage industry. See, e.g., Valerie Bunce, "Should Transitologists be Grounded?," *Slavic Review*, vol. 54, no. 1, 1995, pp. 111–27.

89. See, e.g., Guillermo O'Donnell, Philippe Schmitter, Laurence Whitehead (eds.), *Transitions from Authoritarian Rule*, vols. I–IV, Baltimore 1986; Larry Diamond, Juan J. Linz, and Seymour Martin Lipset, *Democracy in Developing Countries*, vols. I–IV, Boulder 1989.
90. For detailed critique, see Robinson, *Promoting Polyarchy*.
91. Saskia Sassen, *The Global City: New York, London, Tokyo*, Princeton 1991.
92. McMichael, *Development and Social Change*, p. 109.
93. McMichael, *Development and Social Change*, p. 92.
94. My concept of transnational processes is not the same as Leslie Sklair's notion of transnational *practices* (TNPs) but certainly related to it. According to Sklair, transnational practices are the operational categories for the analysis of transnational phenomena, and operate at three levels: the economic, whose agent is transnational capital; the political, whose agent is a transnational capitalist class; and the cultural, involving a "culture-ideology of consumerism." See Sklair, *Sociology of the Global System.*

2 The Politics of Globalization and the Transitions in Central America

1. Edelberto Torres Rivas, *History and Society in Central America*, Austin 1993.
2. Among many works on the Central American post-WWII political economy, see Torres Rivas, *History and Society in Central America*, and also Victor Bulmer-Thomas, *The Political Economy of Central America since 1920*, Cambridge 1987, both of which I draw on liberally in several sections of the present study.
3. Carlos M. Vilas, *Between Earthquakes and Volcanoes: Market, State, and the Revolutions in Central America*, New York 1995.
4. Jeffrey M. Paige, *Coffee and Power: Revolution and the Rise of Democracy in Central America*, Cambridge, MA 1997.
5. Carlos Vilas provides a good analysis of class and family lineage in Central America using the case of Nicaragua. "Family Affairs: Class, Lineage and Politics in Contemporary Nicaragua," *Journal of Latin American Studies*, vol. 24, part 2, 1992, pp. 309–41. See also Samuel Stone, *The Heritage of the Conquistadores: Ruling Classes in Central America from the Conquest to the Sandinistas*, Lincoln 1990; Paige, *Coffee and Power.*
6. This section draws liberally from William I. Robinson, "A Case Study of Globalisation Processes in the Third World: A Transnational Agenda in Nicaragua," *Global Society*, vol. 11, no. 1, 1997, pp. 61–92; Robinson, "Nicaragua and the World: A Globalization Perspective," in Thomas W. Walker (ed.), *Nicaragua Without Illusions: Regime Transition and Structural Adjustment in the 1990s*, Wilmington 1997.
7. See, *inter alia*, Robert A. Pastor, *Condemned to Repetition: The United States and Nicaragua*, Princeton 1987.
8. Literature on the US war and on the Sandinista attempt at popular democracy is voluminous. See, e.g., Robinson, *A Faustian Bargain*, Boulder 1992; William I. Robinson and Kent Norsworthy, *David and Goliath: The US War Against Nicaragua*, New York 1987; Thomas W. Walker (ed.), *Reagan Versus the Sandinistas: The Undeclared War on Nicaragua*, Boulder 1987; Harry E. Vanden and Gary Prevost, *Democracy and Socialism in Sandinista Nicaragua*, Boulder 1993; Vanessa Castro and Gary Prevost (eds.), *The 1990 Elections in Nicaragua and Their Aftermath*,

Lanham, MD 1992; José Luis Corragio, *Nicaragua: Revolucion y Democracia*, Mexico City 1985.

9. On the relationship between the capitalist class, fractions therein, and the revolution, see Rose Spalding, *Capitalists and Revolution in Nicaragua: Opposition and Accommodation, 1979–1993*, Chapel Hill 1992; Mark Everingham, *Revolution and Multiclass Coalition in Nicaragua*, Pittsburgh 1996.

10. On Sandinista economic policies and the class alliances they involved, see *inter alia*, Carlos Vilas, *Perfiles de la Revolucion Sandinista*, Buenos Aires 1985; Richard Stahler-Sholk, "Stabilization, Destabilization, and the Popular Classes in Nicaragua, 1979–1988," *Latin America Research Review* vol. 25, no. 3, 1990, pp. 55–88.

11. See Robinson, *A Faustian Bargain*, p. 36, on the destruction of the contra war, and also see Paul Oquist, "The Sociopolitical Dynamics of the 1990 Nicaraguan Elections," in Castro and Prevost, *The 1990 Elections in Nicaragua*. On the destruction of the war against Somoza, see Thomas W. Walker, *Nicaragua: The Land of Sandino*, Boulder 1981, pp. 41–2.

12. Robinson, *A Faustian Bargain*.

13. For discussion on *Grupo de Las Palmas* see Oscar René Vargas, *Á Donde Va Nicaragua: Perspectivas de una Revolution latinoamericana*, Managua 1991. For a largely descriptive account of the Chamorro years, see David Close, *Nicaragua: The Chamorro Years*, Boulder 1999.

14. See, *inter alia*, Laura Enriquez, *Harvesting Change: Labor and Agrarian Reform in Nicaragua, 1979–1990*, Chapel Hill 1991. In fact, the landed or latifunda oligarchy was shattered by the revolution. Holdings of over 850 acres dropped from 36.2 percent of all farmland in 1978 to 9.5 percent in 1988. But an agrarian bourgeoisie remained largely intact throughout the revolutionary period. Holdings of 86–850 acres represented 46.3 percent of farmland in 1978 and 42.0 percent in 1988. See Charles Brockett, *Land, Power, and Poverty: Agrarian Transition and Political Conflict in Central America*, second edition, Boulder 1998, p. 161, table 7.1.

15. See, *inter alia*, Alejandro Bendana, *Una Tragedia Campesina*, Managua 1991; Orlando Nunez (ed.), *La Guerra en Nicaragua*, Managua 1991; Enriquez, *Harvesting Change*.

16. Jon Jonakin, "Agrarian Policy," in Walker, *Nicaragua Without Illusions*, under the title "Agrarian Policy."

17. For discussion, see Vargas, *Á Donde Va Nicaragua?*; William I. Robinson and Kent Norsworthy, "The Nicaraguan Revolution Since the Elections," *Crossroads*, no. 6, 1991, pp. 21–7; George Vickers and Jack Spence, "Two Years After the Fall," *World Policy Journal*, Summer 1992, pp. 533–62; Robinson, *A Faustian Bargain*; *Promoting Polyarchy: Globalization, Hegemony and U.S. Intervention*, Cambridge, 1996, chapter five.

18. See Deputy Foreign Minister José Bernard Pallais, Speech to Students of the *Universidad Autonoma Americana*, Managua, May 10, 1995, distributed by the Nicaraguan Foreign Ministry.

19. Pallais, *ibid.*

20. United States Agency for International Development (AID), *Country Development Strategy Statement: USAID/Nicaragua 1991–1996*, Washington, D.C.: June 14, 1991, pp. 62–3.

21. Angel Saldomando, *El Retorno de la AID: El Caso de Nicaragua*, Managua 1992.

22. For the $541 million figure, see AID, *Strategy Statement*, "Resource Table,"

appearing on an unnumbered page following the last numbered page (63). For detailed analysis, see Saldomando, *El Retorno de la AID.*

23. Robinson, *A Faustian Bargain,* p. 164.

24. AID, *Strategy Statement,* pp. 47–8.

25. Vargas, *Á Donde Va Nicaragua?*

26. For details on the AID textbooks, see Midge Quandt, "US Aid to Nicaragua: Funding the Right," *Z Magazine,* Nov. 1991, pp. 47–51. For detailed discussion on the aforementioned political-ideological endeavor, see Robinson, *A Faustian Bargain,* chapter four.

27. For details, see Robinson, *A Faustian Bargain;* AID, *Strategy Statement;* Robinson, *Promoting Polyarchy,* chapter five.

28. AID, *Strategy Statement,* p. 20.

29. On these pressures, and explicit US demands to purge the EPS, see US Department of State, Office of the Assistant Secretary Spokesman, press release, "Statement by Richard Boucher, Spokesman," dated April 2, 1993.

30. See, e.g., Adolfo José Acevedo Vogl, *Nicaragua y el FMI: El Poso Sin Fondo del Ajuste,* Managua 1993; José Luis Medal, *Nicaragua: Políticas de Estabilizacion y Ajuste,* Managua 1993; Oscar Neira Cuadra (ed.), *ESAF: Condicionalidad y Deuda,* Managua 1996.

31. See, *inter alia,* Roberto Larios, "Bowing Before Financial Organizations," *Barricada Internacional,* vol. XIII, no. 367–8, Nov./Dec. 1993, pp. 8–9; "What's Behind the IMF Pressure," *ENVIO,* vol. 18, no. 220, Nov. 1999, pp. 3–11.

32. For these figures, see Anne Larson, "Foreign Debt: Where Have All the Dollars Gone?," *Envio,* vol. 12, no. 143, 1993, pp. 4–10; "President Arnoldo Alemán Between the Fund and the Front," *ENVIO,* vol. 16, no. 194, 1997, pp. 3–10. See also Oxfam International, "Debt Relief for Nicaragua: Breaking Out of the Poverty Trap," *Position Paper,* Oct. 1998, posted at http://www.oxfaminternational.org/advocacy/papers/Nicaragua2.html, and retrieved on February 21, 1999, and "So Poor, So Indebted, So Vulnerable," *ENVIO,* vol. 18, no. 219, 1999, pp. 3–12.

33. For these details, see AID, *Strategy Statement.* This AID report was explicit: "*Private banks will dramatically increase their lending to the agribusiness sector.* Producers will increasingly depend upon production loans from input suppliers, processors, and exporters rather than banks [in this way, agricultural producers are linked to the global market, not only through marketing, but through commercial intermediaries who import productions inputs]. The role of the BANADES [*Banco Nacional de Desarrollo,* the principal state bank catering to peasant producers] will diminish" (p. 40, emphasis in original).

34. See Larios, "Bowing Before Financial Organizations"; AID, *Strategy Statement,* pp. 36–7.

35. See Scarlet Cuadra, "Feeding the Big Fish," *Barricada Internacional,* vol. 15, no. 381/January 1995, pp. 12–13.

36. See Larson, "Foreign Debt: Where Have All the Dollars Gone?"; Medal, *Nicaragua: Políticas.*

37. AID, *Strategy Statement,* p. 39.

38. AID, *Strategy Statement,* Resource Chart; Saldomando, *El Retorno de la AID,* pp. 88–9.

39. Saldomando, *El Retorno de la AID,* p. 92; Medal, *Nicaragua: Politicas,* pp. 141–57. The 1994 ESAF agreement signed with the IMF on behalf of multilateral and Paris Club lenders prohibited the government from replenishing remaining state banks. By the end of that year, private banks handled 53 percent of

internal savings and 33 percent of credits. See AID, "Nicaragua 2000: Vision for the Year 2000," Managua March 1995, p. 19. This issue is discussed in more detail in chapter five.

40. Larios, "Bowing Before . . ."

41. See various entries in Mario D. Tello and William Tyler (eds.), *La Promoción de Exportaciones en Nicaragua, 1997–2010: Experiencias y Alternativas*, Managua 1997.

42. Saldomando, *El Retorno de la AID*, pp. 74–8.

43. Saldomando, *El Retorno de la AID*, p. 80.

44. See Rose Spalding, "The Economic Elite," in Walker, *Nicaragua Without Illusions*, for highly illuminating discussion on fractionation among the economic elite and the predominance of these new externally linked sectors.

45. For varied viewpoints on this issue, see e.g., discussion in Spalding, "The Economic Elite," Vargas, *Á Donde Va Nicaragua?*; William I. Robinson, "Sandinistas Face the 'Brave New World'," *Crossroads*, Sept. 1995, pp. 19–21; Oscar René Vargas, *El Sandinismo: Veinte Años Despues*, Managua 1999; interview with Sandinista leader Henry Ruiz in *El Nuevo Diario*, 30 June 1995, pp. 1 and 14.

46. See, e.g., discussion in Robinson, "A Case Study of Globalization Processes . . ."

47. On this point, see, e.g., Oscar Neira Cuadra, "El ESAF y la Transicion Politica en Nicaragua," in Cuadra (ed.), *ESAF: Condicionalidad y Deuda*, Managua, CRIES 1992. Key transnationally oriented economic groups associated with the Chamorro government that developed ties with Sandinista economic groups included the Mántica Group, the MIL Group, the Lacayo family, and the Roberto Terán Corporation Group. See *ibid.*, p. 3.

48. On the pact, see "Is the Game All Sewn Up? Questions and Contradictions," *ENVIO*, vol. 18, no. 218, Sept. 1999, pp. 3–12; "First Impacts of a Devil's Pact," *ENVIO*, vol. 18, no. 217, Aug. 1999, pp. 3–15.

49. AID, *Strategy Statement*, p. 63.

50. "Why Social Conflict," *Envio*, vol. 12, no. 138, 1993, p. 18.

51. *Ibid.*

52. Susanne Andersson, "New National Health Care Policy: Undercover Privatization," *Barricada Internacional*, vol. XIII, no. 367/8, Nov. Dec. 1993, pp. 12–13.

53. Close, *Nicaragua: The Chamorro Years*, p. 94.

54. AID, *Strategy Statement*, p. 8.

55. See, *inter alia*, "Nicaragua: President Arnold Alemán is Under Investigation in New Battle with Comptroller General," *Noticen*, vol. 5, no. 3, January 27, 2000, Latin America Data Base, Latin American Institute, University of New Mexico, Albuquerque.

56. The London-based *Economic Intelligence Unit* gave Nicaragua a "D" rating for political and policy risk in 1994, for the fourth post-electoral year straight, and forecast an *increase* in political instability. See *The Economic Intelligence Unit*, "Country Risk Service: Nicaragua," 4th Quarter, 1994, London.

57. On low-intensity warfare and its doctrinal emergence, see Robinson and Norsworthy, *David and Goliath*, particularly chapter one; Deborah Barry, Jorge Vargas, Raul Leis, *et al.*, *Centroamerica: La guerra de baja intensidad*, Managua 1986; Michael T. Klare and Peter Kornbluh (eds.), *Low Intensity Warfare: Counterinsurgency, Proinsurgency, and Antiterrorism in the Eighties*, New York 1988, and especially the chapter by Daniel Siegel and Joy Hackel, "El Salvador: Counterinsurgency Revisited." For a thorough documentation of low-intensity warfare and US counterinsurgency in El Salvador in the 1980s, see Michael McClintock, *The American Connection, Vol. I: State Terror and Popular Resistance in El Salvador*, London 1985.

58. James Dunkerley, in *Power in the Isthmus: A Political History of Modern Central America*, London 1988, p. 351, notes that the Salvadoran elite "was completely unprepared for the scale of US intervention in economic as well as political terms following the crisis of 1979." This fact is all the more significant since the Salvadoran elite did not have a tradition of political dependency on the United States as did, for example, its Nicaraguan or Honduran counterparts. Moreover, to be sure, the Salvadoran oligarchy put up much resistance to the US reform program and frictions between it and Washington persisted throughout the 1980s.

59. See: Benjamin Schwarz, *American Counterinsurgency Doctrine and El Salvador*, Washington, D.C. 1992; Kevin Murray, with Tom Barry, *Inside El Salvador*, Albuquerque 1995. Schwarz (p. 2) provides the following breakdown: some $4.5 billion in formal military and economic transfers; an estimated $500 million in covert monies; and $850 million in unsubsidized credits. See also, Breny Cuenca, *El poder intangible: La AID y el estado salvadoreño en los anos ochenta*, San Salvador 1992.

60. Cuenca, *ibid.*

61. For a year-by-year breakdown of US aid between 1980 and 1989, see table 13 in Mario Ucles Lungo, *El Salvador in the Eighties: Counterinsurgency and Revolution*, Philadelphia 1996, p. 101.

62. Cuenca, in *El poder intangible*, provides extended documentation and analysis on the different US aid programs. See also Tom Barry and Deb Preusch, *The Soft War: The Uses and Abuses of US Economic Aid in Central America*, New York 1988, esp. pp. 21–32.

63. On P.L. 480, see Rachael Garst and Tom Barry, *Feeding the Crisis: US Food Aid and Farm Policy in Central America*, Lincoln 1990.

64. Cuenca, *El poder intangible*, p. 92.

65. For this figure, see Murray, *Inside El Salvador*, p. 152. For excellent analyses of the role of the FUSADES and its relation to the AID, see Herman Rosa, "El Papel de la Asistencia de AID en el Fortalecimiento de Nuevas Instituciones del Sector Privado y en la Transformacion Global de la Economia Salvadorena: El Caso FUSADES," paper presented at the XVII Congress of the Latin American Studies Association (LASA), Los Angeles, September 1992; Michael W. Foley, "Laying the Groundwork: The Struggle for Civil Society in El Salvador," *Journal of Interamerican Studies and World Affairs*, vol. 38, no. 1, 1996, pp. 67–104. See also, Geske Dijkstra, "The Limits of Economic Policy in El Salvador," in Wim Pelupessey and John Weeks (eds.), *Economic Maladjustment in Central America*, New York, 1993, pp. 53–66.

66. On the clashes between the traditional private-sector groups and new ones, see Benjamin L. Crosby, "Crisis y Fragmentación: Relaciones Entre los Sectores Publico-Privado en America Central," *Occasional Paper Series*, No. 10, Miami: Latin American and Caribbean Center, Florida International University, May 1985.

67. For general discussion on this period, see *inter alia*: Tommie Sue Montgomery, *Revolution in El Salvador: From Civil Strife to Civil Peace*, second edition, Boulder 1995; Enrique Baloyra, *El Salvador in Transition*, Chapel Hill 1982; William Stanley, *The Protection Racket State: Elite Politics, Military Extortion, and Civil War in El Salvador*, Philadelphia 1996; McClintock, *The American Connection*; Dunkerley, *Power in the Isthmus*. To be sure, the PDC became so pliable because its more independent-minded and progressive elements were forced out and formed an alliance with the FMLN. See, e.g., Rubén Zamora, "Democratic

Transition and Modernization? The Case of El Salvador Since 1979," in Jorge I. Dominguez and Marc Lindenberg (eds.), *Democratic Transition in Central America*, Gainsville 1997, pp. 165–79.

68. On "demonstration elections", see Edward S. Herman and Frank Brodhead, *Demonstration Elections: US-Staged Elections in the Dominican Republic, Vietnam, and El Salvador*, Boston 1984.

69. Charles D. Brockett, *Land, Power, and Poverty: Agrarian Transformation and Political Conflict in Central America*, second edition, Boulder 1998, p. 138.

70. For these details, see Brockett, *ibid.*, pp. 141–6; Wim Pelupessey, "Agrarian Reform and Anti-Reform in El Salvador," in Pelupessey and Weeks, *Economic Maladjustment in Central America*, pp. 164–84; Murray, *Inside El Salvador*, pp. 96–101; and see Cuenca, *El poder intangible* for discussion on the AID's role and objectives.

71. See, e.g., the following US AID documents released to the author under Freedom of Information Act requests: "Country Development Strategy Statement: FY 1990–1994," USAID/El Salvador, June 1989, Agency for International Development, Washington, D.C.; AID, "US Agency for International Development El Salvador: Program Objectives Document, FY 1993 to FY 1997 and Action Plan, FY 1993 and FY 1994"; USAID/El Salvador, "Action Plan, FY 1992–1993," dated February 1991; USAID/El Salvador, "Action Plan, FY 1991–1992," dated March 1990. On the transition to capitalist agriculture, see Pelupessy, "Agrarian Reform and Anti-Reform"; also see Stanley's discussion, *The Protection Racket State*, pp. 234–8.

72. For these details, see, *inter alia*, Geske Dijkstra, "The Limits of Economic Policy in El Salvador," in Pelupessey and Weeks (eds.), *Economic Maladjustment in Central America*, esp. p. 56; Cuenca, *El poder intangible*, p. 115; Alexander Segovia and William Pleitez, "Politica de Promoción de Exportaciones No Tradicionales de El Salvador a Terceros Mercados en la Decada de los Ochenta," *Cuadernos de Investigación*, no. 4, San Salvador: FUSADES, Sept. 1990.

73. For these details, see Foley, "Laying the Groundwork," pp. 71–3.

74. Calculated on the basis of table 4.2, Dijkstra, "The Limits of Economic Policy in El Salvador," p. 57. See also Segovia and Pleitez, "Politica de Promoción de Exportaciones No Tradicionales . . ."

75. For discussion, see Pelupessy, "Agrarian Reform and Anti-Reform."

76. Pelupessey, "Agrarian Reform and Anti-Reform . . ." reports that 22.8 percent of the country's agricultural land was affected, as was 35 percent of the potential target group (pp. 170–71).

77. Lungo's conclusion that the ARENA government that came to power in 1989 was "none other than the traditional agro-export oligarchy" (*El Salvador in the Eighties*, p. 108) is simply untenable. (Tommie Sue Montgomery, in *Revolution in El Salvador: From Civil Strife to Civil Peace* (Boulder, second edition, 1995), among others, reaches a similar conclusion.) Moreover, the reforms were significant because they helped to accelerate the transition to capitalist agriculture even if they did not alter the essential class power of the dominant groups.

78. Stanley, *The Protection Racket State*, p. 235.

79. For details, see Cuenca, *El poder intangible*, pp. 92–112; Rosa, "El Papel de la Asistencia de la AID . . ."; the AID documents listed in note 71 above.

80. In 1990 much of the state banking system was privatized, as discussed further in chapter five. The Central Bank was also granted autonomy from the government and began to sign agreements directly with the AID (Cuenca, *El*

poder intangible, p. 177). In this way we see the externalization and transnationalization of key branches of the Salvadoran state.

81. For detailed discussion on this point, see Rosa, "El Papel de la Asistencia de la AID ..."; Lungo, *El Salvador in the Eighties*; Dunkerley, *Power in the Isthmus*; Dijkstra, "The Limits of Economic Policy."

82. Actually, research in the 1980s placed the size of the oligarchy at 184 family groupings encompassing 1,309 members. See Montgomery, *Revolution in El Salvador*, p. 69. On this period, and the issues raised here, see, *inter alia*, Dunkerley, *Power in the Isthmus*; Lungo, *El Salvador in the Eighties*; Montgomery, *ibid.*; Zamora, "Democratic Transition and Modernization? The Case of El Salvador since 1979," in Jorge I. Dominguez and Marc Lindenberg (eds.), *Democratic Transition in Central America*; Baloyra, *El Salvador in Transition*.

83. Baloyra, *El Salvador in Transition*. See also Zamora, *ibid.*; Dunkerley, *Power in the Isthmus*.

84. Lungo, *El Salvador in the Eighties*, p. 113.

85. *Ibid.*, pp. 120–21.

86. For details, see Rosa, "El Papel de la Asistencia de la AID." Among the first FUSADES Board of Directors were: Alfredo Cristiani, who became President of the Republic; Roberto Murray, who became President of the Social Investment Fund in the Cristiani government; Roberto Orellana Milla, who became the Central Bank President under Cristiani; Oscar Santamaria, who became the Minister of the Presidency; and so on. We see again for the case of El Salvador how transnational fractions come to capture key state ministries that link the country to the global economy and the transnational state.

87. Stanley, *The Protection Racket State*, p. 233.

88. For details, see Rosa, "El Papel de la Asistencia de la AID ...". The plan, as summarized and reiterated by the AID, included 1) economic stabilization; 2) structural adjustment; 3) increase of exports (including Free Trade Zones, NTAEs, coffee, and the promotion of foreign investment); and 4) market-oriented/private-sector programs to increase employment. See AID, "Program Objectives Document, FY 1993 to FY 1997," p. 13.

89. For these details, see Rosa, "El Papel de la Asistencia de la AID ..."; Murray with Barry, *Inside El Salvador*, esp. pp. 12–14, 82–5; Cuenca, *El poder intangible*, esp. pp. 71–81, 114–16, 138–40, and 173–4; Alexander Segovia, "Macroeconomic Performance and Policies Since 1989," in James K. Boyce, *Economic Policy for Building Peace: The Lessons of El Salvador*, Boulder 1996, pp. 51–72; AID documents cited in note 71.

90. For these details, see Murray, *Inside El Salvador*, pp. 82–3; Cuenca, *El poder intangible*, p. 74. On AID's discussion of the transition from bilateral to multilateral funding, see AID, "Country Development Strategy Statement, FY 1990–1994," pp. 70–71. On the role of the IFIs more generally in the peace process and restructuring in El Salvador, see Boyce (ed.), *Economic Policy for Building Peace*.

91. See USAID, "US Agency for International Development El Salvador, Program Objectives Document, FY 1993 to FY 1997, and Action Plan, FY 2993 and FY 1994," p. 73. Also see Eva Paus, "Exports and the Consolidation of Peace," in Boyce (ed.), *Economic Policy for Building Peace*, pp. 246–78.

92. Cited in Murray, *Inside El Salvador*, p. 245; World Bank, *El Salvador: Meeting the Challenge of Globalization*, Washington, D.C. 1996, p. 1.

93. See, e.g., Ismael Moreno, "El Salvador: 'End' of ARENA and Future of FMLN," *ENVIO*, vol. 16, no. 196, Nov. 1997, p. 14–19.

94. This paragraph draws on Spence, *et al.*, *Chapultepec: Five Years Later: El Salvador's Political Reality and Uncertain Future*, Cambridge, MA: Hemispheric Initiatives, Jan. 16, 1997, esp. pp. 22–3; Tommie Sue Montgomery, "El Salvador's Extraordinary Elections," *LASA Forum*, vol. XXVIII, no. 1, Spring 1997, pp. 4–8.

95. See Ismael Moreno Coto, "El Salvador: Left and Right in the Pre-Electoral Winds," *ENVIO*, vol. 17, no. 203, June 1998, pp. 11–15, citation from p. 13.

96. See Ismael Moreno Coto, "El Salvador: Absent Government and Opposition," *ENVIO*, vol. 18, no. 219, October 1999, pp. 14–19; and Moreno's analysis of possible future scenarios, "ARENA's Victory and the Predictable Disenchantment," *ENVIO*, vol. 18, no. 212, March 1999, p. 13–17.

97. Spence, *et al.*, *Chapultepec: Five Years Later*, pp. 4–5.

98. See Pelupessey, "Agrarian Reform and Anti-Reform . . .", pp. 178–9, and see discussion in chapter five.

99. The World Bank, *El Salvador: Meeting the Challenge of Globalization*, pp. 36, 77.

100. Baloyra, *El Salvador in Transition*, pp. 22–32, 62–3.

101. For these details on the reconstruction program, see Murray, *Inside El Salvador*, esp. pp. 228–32; Foley, "Laying the Groundwork," although the interpretation advanced here is my own.

102. See, e.g., Terry Lynn Karl, "El Salvador's Negotiated Revolution," *Foreign Affairs*, vol. 71, no. 2, 1992, pp. 147–64.

103. This section draws from William I. Robinson, "Neo-Liberalism, the Global Elite, and the Guatemalan Transition: A Critical Macrosocial Analysis," *Journal of Inter-American and World Affairs*, Winter 2000.

104. On the 1954 coup, see Stephen Schlesinger and Stephen Kinzer, *Bitter Fruit: The Untold Story of the American Coup in Guatemala*, New York, 1983; Richard H. Immerman, *The CIA in Guatemala*, Austin 1982. On the aftermath and the construction of a "counterinsurgency state," see, *inter alia*, Jonathan, L. Fried, Marvini E. Gettleman, Deborah T. Levenson, and Nancy Peckenham, *Guatemala in Rebellion: Unfinished History*, New York 1983; Michael McClintock, *The American Connection, Vol. 2: State Terror and Popular Resistance in Guatemala*, London 1985; Susanne Jonas, *The Battle for Guatemala: Rebels, Death Squads, and US Power*, Boulder 1991; George Black, *Garrison Guatemala*, New York 1984.

105. Jonas, *The Battle for Guatemala*, p. 64.

106. See, *inter alia*, various entries in Robert M. Carmack (ed.), *Harvest of Violence: The Mayan Indians and the Guatemalan Crisis*, Norman, Ok., and London 1988; Fried, *et al.*, *Guatemala: Unfinished Revolution*; McClintock, *The American Connection*; Black, *Garrison Guatemala*; Victor Perera, *Unfinished Conquest: The Guatemala Tragedy*, Berkeley 1993.

107. Jonas, *The Battle for Guatemala*, p. 149.

108. See, e.g., Carol A. Smith's excellent essays, "Destruction of the Material Bases for Indian Culture", pp. 206–4, in Carmack (ed.), *Harvest of Violence*; "The Militarization of Civil Society in Guatemala: Economic Reorganization as a Continuation of War," *Latin American Perspectives* vol. 17, no. 4, 1990, pp. 8–41.

109. Jonas, *The Battle for Guatemala*, p. 150.

110. For detailed studies, see various entries in Carol A. Smith (ed.), *Guatemalan Indians and the State: 1540–1988*, Austin 1990. By 1975, some 60 percent of the economically active rural population of the highlands migrated to work on the agro-export plantations, notes Charles Brockett, which made it, according to Jeffrey Paige, the world's largest migratory labor force as a percentage of total

population. Brockett, *Land, Power, and Poverty*, p. 86 (Paige as cited in Brockett). Brockett also points out that in the late 1970s, the largest 2.6 percent of land holdings in Guatemala had 56 percent of the land (p. 73).

111. Jeffrey M. Paige, "Social Theory and Peasant Revolution in Vietnam and Guatemala," *Theory and Society*, vol. 12, no. 6, Nov. 1983, pp. 699–736.

112. Smith, "The Militarization of Civil Society in Guatemala," pp. 12–13. See also, "Destruction of the Material Bases for Indian Culture."

113. Smith, "The Militarization of Civil Society in Guatemala," pp. 32–3.

114. See Jorge Escoto and Manfredo Marroquín, *La AID en Guatemala*, Managua 1992, esp. pp. 60–5; Tom Barry, *Inside Guatemala*, Albuquerque 1991, esp. pp. 101–110; United States Agency for International Development, "USAID/ Guatemala CDSS Update FY 1990—FY 1994," Washington, D.C. December 1988.

115. Cited in Barry, *Inside Guatemala*, p. 114.

116. Edgar Gutierrez, "Los Eligidos," *Pensamiento Propio*, vol. x, no. 92, 1992, pp. 28–30.

117. See, e.g., Kurt Petersen, *The Maquiladora Revolution in Guatemala*, Occasional Paper Series 2, 1992, New Haven: Yale Law School, Orville H. Schell Jr. Center for International Rights, 1992; Barry, *Inside Guatemala*, p. 114; and next chapter for further discussion.

118. See, e.g., Smith, "The Militarization of Civil Society in Guatemala," and discussion in next chapter.

119. Barry, *Inside Guatemala*, p. 56; Smith, "The Destruction of Civil Society in Guatemala," p. 12.

120. For Gramajo's own account of this process, see Hector Alejandro Gramajo Mora, "Political Transition in Guatemala, 1980–1990: A Perspective from Inside Guatemala's Army," in Jorge I. Dominguez and Marc Linderberg, *Democratic Transitions in Central America*, Gainsville 1997, pp. 111–38.

121. See, e.g., Bulmer-Thomas, *The Political Economy of Central America*, pp. 237–44; Jonas, *The Battle for Guatemala*, pp. 82–3.

122. Escoto and Marroquín, *La AID en Guatemala*, p. 34.

123. Escoto and Marroquín, *ibid.*, pp. 50, 69–70; AID, "USAID/Guatemala CDSS Update FY 1990—FY 1994," December 1988; AID, "USAID/Guatemala: FY 1991–1992 Action Plan", Washington January 1990.

124. See AID, "USAID/Guatemala: FY 1991–1992 Action Plan", Washington January 1990; Barry, *Inside Guatemala*; Escoto and Marroquín, *La AID en Guatemala*.

125. For these details, see Escoto and Marroquín, *La AID en Guatemala*, pp. 107–130.

126. As cited in Petersen, p. 58.

127. Escoto and Marroquín, *La AID en Guatemala*.

128. See Escoto and Marroquín, *La AID en Guatemala*, pp. 69–70.

129. *Ibid.*, p. 41.

130. See, *inter alia*, Thomas R. Dye, *Who's Running America?*, fourth edition, Englewood Cliffs 1986; G. William Domhoff, *Who Rules America?*, Englewood Cliffs 1967; Domhoff, *The Powers that Be*, New York 1978.

131. See Escoto and Marroquín, *La AID en Guatemala*, diagrams on pp. 119, 126, and 129, for the interlocking organizational structure of these New Right groups, the old Right, the Guatemalan state, and the AID and World Bank.

132. For these details, and on the development of non-traditional exports and diverse liberalization measures to promote them, see AID, "USAID/Guatemala: FY 1991–1992 Action Plan," January 1990, esp. Annex A, pp. 28–37; Escoto and Marroquín, *La AID en Guatemala*, p. 70, and Table 6, p. 71; Ana Maria

Colindres, "Non-Traditional Exports in Guatemala," in Pelupessey and Weeks (eds.), *Maladjustment in Central America,* pp. 111–27; Philip E. Karp, "Guatemala," in Eva Paus (ed.), *Struggle Against Dependence: Non-Traditional Export Growth in Central America and the Caribbean,* Boulder 1988, pp. 65–83; Juan Alberto Fuentes K., "The Systemic Weakness of Guatemala's Competitiveness," in Rudd Buiteluan and Pitou van Dijck (eds.), *Latin America's Insertion in the World Economy,* New York 1996, pp. 207–23.

133. For discussion, see Escoto and Marroquín, *La AID en Guatemala.*

134. Serrano's economic program was drafted by the ASIES and spelled out in an ASIES document titled "Strategic Outline for Social and Economic Development of Guatemala, 1991–1995." This document was drafted under the tutelage of US advisor Arnold Harberger, who headed the "Chicago Boys" team that drew up General Augusto Pinochét's second economic plan for Chile in the late 1970s. Harberger was first brought to Guatemala by the Pyramid Group. The ASIES document, "Compartiendo Costos y Beneficios: Lineamientos de Estrategia para el Desarrollo Social y Economico de Guatemala, 1991–1995," was released on June 8, 1990 by the ASIES, and published in three installments by *La Hora,* on January 12, 13, and 14, 1991. For background on the ASIES, see Raul Marin, "El Poder de los Empresarios," *Pensamiento Propio,* no. 69, Sept. 1990, pp. 9–14.

135. For these details, see, *inter alia,* Barry, *Inside Guatemala,* Raul Marin, 'La Nueva Derecha en Centroamerica', *Pensamiento Propio,* vol. VIII, no. 71, June 1990, pp. 30–7; Marin, "Guatemala: Sin Lugar para la Paz," *Pensamiento Propio* vol. VIII, no. 69, April 1990, pp. 14–17; Gutierrez, "Los Eligidos"; Gonzalo Guerrero, "President Arzu: A New Stage Begins," *ENVIO,* vol. 15, nos. 175–176, Feb/March 1996, pp. 11–15.

136. On the peace negotiations, the 1996 accord, and subsequent events regarding the peace process, see Jonas' detailed study, *Of Centaurs and Doves: Guatemala's Peace Process,* Boulder 2000. Also see Jack Spence *et al., Promise and Reality: Implementation of the Guatemalan Peace Accords,* Cambridge, MA August 1998.

137. Jonas, *Of Centaurs and Doves,* dedicates chapter three, pp. 69–92, to a detailed description of the peace agreement.

138. On the active participation of the IFIs, see James K. Boyce, "Reconstruction and Democratization: The International Financial Institutions and Post-Conflict Transitions," paper presented at the XXI International Congress of the Latin American Studies Association, Chicago, Sept. 24–26, 1998. See also Jonas, *Of Centaurs and Doves,* pp. 51–2.

139. On the reconstruction funds, see Latin America Data Base, "International Community Pressures Guatemala to Move Faster on Reforms Mandated by Peace Accords," *Ecocentral,* vol. 3, no. 40, Oct. 29, 1998, Latin American Institute, University of New Mexico, Albuquerque. On "peace conditionality," see Boyce, "Reconstruction and Democratization."

140. Jonas, *Of Centaurs and Doves,* pp. 169–74; Boyce, "Reconstruction and Democratization," pp. 10–15.

141. Latin America Data Base, "Guatemala: Government Sends New Tax Bill to Congress," *Ecocentral* vol. 2, no. 39, October 30 1997, Latin American Institute, University of New Mexico, Albuquerque.

142. AID, "USAID/Guatemala: FY 1991–1992 Action Plan," Washington, January 1990.

143. See, e.g., Philip McMichael, *Development and Social Change.*

144. Smith, "The Militarization of Civil Society in Guatemala," p. 26.

145. Jonas, *Of Centaurs and Doves*, p. 96.

146. Spence *et al.*, *Promise and Reality*, p. 6.

147. See Jonas, *Of Centaurs and Doves*, chapter eight, pp. 89–216. See also Juan Hernández Pico, "Guatemala: Why Was the Referendum Defeated?," *ENVIO*, vol. 18, no. 216, July 1999, pp. 12–17.

148. Boyce, "Reconstruction and Democratization," p. 10. See also Spence, *et al.*, *Promise and Reality*, p. 8.

149. See Jonas, *The Battle for Guatemala*, pp. 177–80; and Juan Hernández Pico, "Guatemala: Poverty: Protagonist of the Post War," *ENVIO*, vol 16, no. 193: August 1997, pp. 10–15.

150. Brockett, *Land, Power, and Poverty*, p. 122.

151. See Spence *et al.*, *Promise and Reality*, 1998; Latin America Data Base, "International Community Pressures Guatemala to Move Faster on Reforms Mandated by Peace Accords," *Ecocentral*, vol. 3, no. 40, October 29 1998, Latin American Institute, University of New Mexico, Albuquerque.

152. Jonas, *ibid.*, pp. 222–4.

153. Jonas, *Of Centaurs and Doves*, p. 224.

154. See, e.g., the special issue of *NACLA Report on the Americas*, "The Politics of Corruption and the Corruption of Politics," vol. xxvii, no.3, Nov/Dec 1993.

155. See: Torres Rivas, *History and Society in Central America*; Hector Perez Brignoli, *A Brief History of Central America*, Berkeley 1989; Donald E. Schultz and Deborah Sundloff Schulz, *The United States, Honduras, and the Crisis in Central America*, Boulder 1994; Lowell Gudmundson, "Lord and Peasant in the Making of Modern Central America," in Evelyn Huber-Stephens and Frank Safford, *Agrarian Structures and Political Power in Latin America*, Pittsburgh 1995.

156. For expositions on the banana enclave from this perspective, see Antonio Murga Frassinetti, *Enclave y Sociedad en Honduras*, Tegucigalpa 1985; Wilma Lainez and Victor Meza, "El Enclave Bananero en Honduras," in Medardo Mejia (ed.), *Historia de Honduras, Vol. 6*, Tegucigalpa 1990. See also Darío A. Euraque, *Reinterpreting the Banana Republic: Region and State in Honduras, 1970–1972*, Chapel Hill 1996.

157. On caudillismo more generally in Latin America, see Hugh M. Hamill, "Introduction," in Hamill (ed.), *Caudillos: Dictators in Spanish America*, Norman 1992, and on Honduran caudillismo, see James A. Morris, *Honduras: Caudillo Politics and Military Rulers*, Boulder: 1984.

158. Dunkerley, *Power in the Isthmus*, p. 524.

159. See, *inter alia*, on militarization in Honduras in general, and on the US role, Margarita Oseguera de Ochoa, *Honduras Hoy: Sociedad y Crisis Política*, Tegucigalpa 1987; Kent Norsworthy, with Tom Barry, *Inside Honduras*, Albuquerque 1993; Schultz and Schultz, *ibid.*; various contributions in Nancy Peckenham and Annie Street (eds.), *Honduras: Portrait of a Captive Nation*, New York 1985; various entries in Mark B. Rosenberg and Philip L. Shepherd (eds.), *Honduras Confronts its Future: Contending Perspectives on Critical Issues*, Boulder 1986; Dunkerley, *Power in the Isthmus*.

160. Kent Norsworthy, with Tom Barry, *Inside Honduras*, pp. xix, 155.

161. *Ibid.*, p. 163.

162. *Ibid.*, p. 119.

163. See Acker, *Honduras . . .* , p. 116.

164. See, *inter alia*, Norsworthy, p. 14; Acker, pp. 124–5; Richard Lapper and James

Painter, *Honduran State for Sale*, London 1985, pp. 113–15; Oseguera, *Honduras Hoy*, pp. 28–34; Dunkerley, *Power in the Isthmus*, pp. 580–81.

165. Oseguera, *Honduras Hoy*, p. 43. See also Andy Thorpe, "Honduras, the New Economic Model and Poverty," in Victor Bulmer-Thomas, *The New Economic Model in Latin America and Its Impact on Income Distribution and Poverty*, New York 1996.

166. See, e.g., Raul Marín, "La nueva derecha en Centroamerica," Pensamiento Propio, vol. VIII, no. 71, June 1990, pp. 30–33; Benjamin L. Crosby, "Crisis y Fragmentación: Relaciones Entre Los Sectores Public-Privado en America Central," *Occasional Paper Series*, no. 10, Miami: Latin American and Caribbean Center, Florida International University, May 1985.

167. Some of these APROH figures who would play prominent roles in the development of a New Right, in addition to Callejas himself, were Benjamin Villanueva, Oswaldo Ramos Soto, Gilberto Goldstein, and Emin Abufele. See Norsworthy, *Inside Honduras*, p. 18, and p. 184, nt. 26.

168. See Marin, "La nueva derecha en Centroamerica"; Crosby, "Crisis y Fragmentación."

169. For detailed discussion and analysis, see Crosby, "Crisis y Fragmentación." See also Norsworthy, *Inside Honduras*.

170. Norsworthy, *Inside Honduras*, p. 163.

171. *Ibid.*, p. 192.

172. *Ibid.*, pp. 163–71, and see Figure 6b, p. 164 for a year-by-year breakdown of US economic aid between 1977 and 1992.

173. On the rise of Callejas and MONARCA, see, e.g., Norsworthy, *Inside Honduras*, pp. 9–11; Oseguera, *Honduras Hoy*, pp. 110–11. The old guard in the National Party became known early on as the "politicos" and the New Right as the "tecnicos."

174. For details, see Marin, "La nueva derecha en Centroamerica"; Norsworthy, *Inside Honduras*, pp. 119–21; 163–71; Tom Barry, *Rain of Dollars*, Albuquerque 1986; Crosby, "Crisis y Fragmentatión."

175. Marin, *ibid.* and "Con las riendas en la mano," *Pensamiento Propio*, vol. VIII, no. 7, June 1990, p. 36.

176. Crosby, pp. 34–5.

177. See, e.g., Norsworthy, *Inside Honduras*, pp. 15, 170, and p. 184, nt. 22.

178. *Ibid.*, p. 166.

179. See Kathleen D. Heffernan, "Honduras," in Eva Paus (ed.), *Struggle Against Dependence: Non-Traditional Export Growth in Central America and the Caribbean*, Boulder 1988, pp. 124, 132–3. Chapter runs from pp. 123–43. On these laws, see also Thorpe, "Honduras, the New Economic Model and Poverty," in Bulmer-Thomas, *The New Economic Model in Latin America*, pp. 223–48.

180. Acker, *Honduras*, p. 127; Norsworthy, *Inside Honduras*, p. 54.

181. *Ibid.*, p. 128.

182. Heffernan, "Honduras," pp. 123–43.

183. On the paquetazo (*Ley de Ordenamiento Estructural*) under Callejas and under the government of Carlos Roberto Reina that followed him, see Thorpe, "Honduras, the New Economic Model and Poverty."

184. Jesuit Reflection, Research and Communication Team (ERIC), "Maquila: The Swallow that Lays Golden Eggs," *ENVIO*, vol. 16, no. 194, September 1997, pp. 16–22.

185. "Honduras: Government Unveils Social and Economic Package," *Ecocentral*, vol. 3, no. 19, May 21, 1998.

186. Jesuit Reflection, Research and Community Team (ERIC) of Honduras, "Honduras: A Model of Poverty," *ENVIO*, vol. 16, no. 187–188, Feb.–March 1997, pp. 21–6 (citation on p. 24).

187. See, e.g., Norsworthy, *Inside Honduras*, p. 60; Heffernan, "Honduras . . ."

188. Mario Posas, "President Reina: No Seller of Dreams," *ENVIO*, vol. 13, no. 151–152, Feb.–March 1994, pp. 18–22; Jesuit Reflection, Research and Communication Team (ERIC), *ENVIO*, vol. 16, no. 187–188, February–March 1997, pp. 21–6.

189. On demilitarization in Honduras, see J. Mark Ruhl, "Redefining Civil-Military Relations in Honduras," *Journal of Interamerican Studies and World Affiars*, vol. 38, no. 1, 1996, pp. 33–67.

190. For details, see, e.g., Norsworthy, *Inside Honduras*, p. 73; Brockett, *Land, Power, and Poverty*, p. 195–8.

191. See, e.g., Norsworthy, *Inside Honduras*, p. 64.

192. On this rural democracy thesis, see, *inter alia*, Samuel Z. Stone, *The Heritage of the Conquistadores*, Lincoln 1991; Carlos Monge Alfaro, *Historia de Costa Rica*, 16th edition, San José 1980; Hector Perez Brignoli, *A Brief History of Central America*, Berkeley 1989; Mitchell A. Seligson, *Peasants of Costa Rica and the Development of Agrarian Capitalism*, Madison 1980. For a summary and critique, see Lowell Gudmundson, *Costa Rica Before Coffee: Society and Economy on the Eve of the Export Boom*, Baton Rouge 1986; Bruce M. Wilson, *Costa Rica: Politics, Economics, and Democracy*, Boulder 1998. John Booth, *Costa Rica: Quest for Democracy*, Boulder 1998. Gudmundson observes (pp. 1–24) that the most influential version of Costa Rican political mythology was developed by the ruling National Liberation movement and the post-1948 junta (see below) because it served their political goals (and we may add that these myths have been perpetuated because they continue to serve the goals of dominant groups).

193. Stone, *Heritage of the Conquistadores*. On colonial land tenure, see Carlos Melendez Chaverri, "Land Tenure in Colonial Costa Rica," in Marc Edelman and Joanne Kenen, *The Costa Rica Reader*, New York 1989.

194. See Wilson, *Costa Rica*, p. 22. Jacobo Schifter notes that "authoritarian paternalism" was the pattern of social relations that prevailed at all levels of Costa Rican society. "La Democracia en Costa Rica Como Producto de la Neutralizacion de Clases," in *Democracia en Costa Rica? Cinco Opiniones Polémicas*, San José 1978.

195. Wilson, *Costa Rica*, p. 35.

196. On the Costa Rican civil war, see, *inter alia*, Manual Rojas Bolaños, *Luchas Sociales y Guerra Civil en Costa Rica*, San Jose 1979; Jorge Mario Salazar, *Politica y Reforma en Costa Rica, 1914–1958*, second edition, San José 1981; Schifter, "La Democracia en Costa Rica . . .".

197. The 1948 civil war decisively mediated class conflict, both between dominant and subordinate classes and within the ruling class, in a way not seen in other countries. The "revolution" was as much—perhaps even more so—a result of conflict within the dominant classes as between them and the popular classes; between the oligarchy and rising reformist groups. See Dunkerley, *Power in the Isthmus*, chapter five, "Costa Rica: Stability at a Price," for a summary of the literature and debates on this issue. Also see Schifter's important thesis on "class neutralization," according to which different social classes "neutralized" each other in the events of 1948, leading to a stalemate, to *de facto* polyarchy, and to the triumph of the "transformationist" ideology of "restructuring

dependence to facilitate a more autonomous process of economic development" (p. 177).

198. See Wilson, *Costa Rica*, pp. 81–2, and discussion in chapters three and four.

199. Wilson, *Costa Rica*, p. 47. For detailed discussion on Costa Rica's formal political system and parties, see Manuel Rojas Bolaños and Carlos Sojo, *El Malestar Con La Politica*, San José. FLACSO, 1995; Booth, *Costa Rica: Quest for Democracy*.

200. Wilson, *Costa Rica*, p. 104.

201. See Carlos Sojo, *La Utopía del Estado Minimo*, Managua, CRIES, 1991, table on p. 34, for the $1.3 billion figure, and see Sojo, *ibid.*, and *La Mano Invisible del Mercado*, for detailed analyses of the US aid programs in the 1980s and early 1990s. See Karen Hansen-Kuhn, *Structural Adjustment in Central America: The Case of Costa Rica* (Washington D.C.: The Development Gap, June 1993), pp. 5–7, for a breakdown of IMF, World Bank, and Inter-American Development Bank loans during this period.

202. Dunkerley, *Power in the Isthmus*, p. 592.

203. *Ibid.*, p. 636.

204. *Ibid.*, p. 592. The $32 million figure is provided by Soto, *La Utopía del Estado Minimo*, p. 19.

205. For analysis of Costa Rican militarization and the Nicaraguan contra "southern front," see, *inter alia*, William I. Robinson and Kent Norsworthy, *David and Goliath: The US War Against Nicaragua*, New York 1987; Martha Honey, *Hostile Acts: US Policy in Costa Rica in the 1980s*, Gainsville 1994.

206. On the cabinet reshuffle and on Lizano, see, *inter alia*, Lara, *Inside Costa Rica*, pp. 14–16; Wilson, *Costa Rica*, pp. 117–18; Honey, *Hostile Acts*, pp. 85–6. More generally, on the rise of new economic groups tied to commerce, finances, and other services and non-traditional exports, and their penetration of both parties, see Bolanos and Sojo, *El Malestar con la Política*.

207. Lara, *Inside Costa Rica*, p. 33; Andrew Zimbalist, "Costa Rica," in Eva Paws (ed.), *Struggle Against Dependence: Non-Traditional Export Growth in Central America and the Caribbean* (Boulder: Westview 1988), p. 37.

208. Sojo, *La Utopia del Estado Minimo*, pp. 15–16.

209. The following discussion on the neo-liberal restructuring, the transition to a new economic model, the role of the AID and the IFIs and the rise of a "parallel state" draws, among other excellent studies, on: Carlos Sojo, *La Utopía del Estado Minimo: Influencia de AID en Costa Rica en los Años Ochenta*, Managua 1991; Carlos Sojo, *La Mano Visible del Mercado*, Managua/San José 1992; Carlos Sojo, *La Gobernabilidad en Centroamerica: La Sociedad Despues del Ajuste*, San José 1995; Honey, *Hostile Acts*; Wilson, *Costa Rica*; Lara, *Inside Costa Rica*; Michael E. Conroy, Douglas L. Murray, and Peter M. Rosset, *A Cautionary Tale: Failed US Development Policy in Central America*, Boulder 1996; Booth, *Costa Rica*; Mary A. Clark, "Non-Traditional Export Promotion in Costa Rica: Sustaining Export-Led Growth," *Journal of Interamerican Studies and World Affairs*, vol. 37, no. 2, 1995, pp. 181–223. Hansen-Kuhn, *Structural Adjustment in Central America*; Alicia Korten, *Ajuste Estructural en Costa Rica: Una Medicina Amarga*, San José 1997.

210. On these autonomous institutes, see Wilson, *Costa Rica*, chapter four, "The Creation and Consolidation of the Social Democratic Model."

211. Wilson, *Costa Rica*, p. 126; Honey, *Hostile Acts*, pp. 105–10.

212. Clark, "Nontraditional Export Promotion in Costa Rica," p. 194. See Sojo, *La Mano Visible del Mercado*, chapter three, pp. 41–84, for detailed discussion on CINDE.

213. Honey, *Hostile Acts*, p. 120.

214. Conroy, *et al.*, *A Cautionary Tale*, p. 80.

215. Lara, *Inside Costa Rica*, p. 150; Honey, *Hostile Acts*, pp. 101–102.

216. Sojo, *La Mano Visible del Mercado*, pp. 46–7. An internal AID audit of the CINDE observed, for instance, that the organization was used "as a temporary resting place or springboard for aspiring politicians." Cited in Conroy, *et al.*, *A Cautionary Tale*, p. 86.

217. See, *inter alia*, Sojo, *La Mano Visible*, pp. 42–6 on the CINDE founding members and their prior and subsequent posts in the state.

218. Sojo, "En el Nombre del Padre: Patrimonialismo y Democracia en Costa Rica," in Bolaños and Sojo, *El Malestar con la Política*.

219. Clark, "Non-Traditional Export Promotion in Costa Rica," pp. 190–91; Sojo, *La Mano Visible del Mercado*, p. 56; USAID/Costa Rica, *FY 1992–1996 Project Objectives Document/FY 1993–94 Action Plan*, San José, Feb. 1992, p. 65.

220. Conroy, *et al.*, *A Cautionary Tale*, p. 70; Sojo, *La Mano Visible del Mercado*, pp. 33–5.

221. Conroy, *et al.*, *A Cautionary Tale*, p. 76.

222. For these details, see Wilson, *Costa Rica*, pp. 127–32.

223. Sojo, *La Mano Invisible del Mercado*, p. 30. In 1984, the private banks controlled less than 12 percent. By 1987, this figure had risen to 34.5 percent, and then to 54.2 percent in 1991. *Ibid.*

224. Lara, *Inside Costa Rica*, p. 149; Sojo, *La Mano Visible del Mercado*, pp. 12–13.

225. Conroy, *et al.*, *A Cautionary Tale*, p. 78.

226. On the new ministry, see, e.g., Wilson, *Costa Rica*, pp. 122–3; Honey, *Hostile Acts*, pp. 120–23. The broad programs to promote non-traditional exports and the new economic model are discussed, *inter alia*, by Robert Hallauer, *Export Promotion Policies in Costa Rica: The Works of CENPRO and Development Problems of the Agro-industrial Sector*, Technical Papers Series No. 51, Austin, Institute of Latin American Studies/University of Texas, 1985; Sojo, *La Utopía del Estado Minimo*, *La Mano Visible del Mercado*, and *La Gobernabilidad en Costa Rica*; Zimbalist, "Costa Rica,"; Conroy, *et al.*, *A Cautionary Tale*.

227. Clark, "Non-Traditional Export Promotion in Costa Rica," p. 183. This figure excludes tourism—technically not an "export"—which I am considering in this study as one of the central globalized economic activities of the new transnational model.

228. Lara, *Inside Costa Rica*, p. 47.

229. Sojo, *La Mano Visible del Mercado*, p. 62.

230. Conroy, *et al.*, *A Cautionary Tale*, p. 72.

231. See, *inter alia*, Hallauer, *Export Promotion Policies in Costa Rica*, p. 10.

232. Sojo, *La Mano Visible del Mercado*, p. 89.

233. For detailed discussion and data on these Agreements, see Sojo, *La Utopía del Estado Minimo*. Conroy, *et al.*, *A Cautionary Tale*, summarize these covenants in a table on p. 71.

234. Sergio Ruben Soto, *Ajuste Estructural en Centroamerica*, San José: 1988, pp. 38–40.

235. Wilson, *Costa Rica*, p. 128. Wilson goes on to note that "many important politicians from the PLN have argued that even without any international pressure, 90 percent of neo-liberal reforms during the Monge administration [1982–86] would have been implemented." *Ibid.*, p. 124.

236. Honey, *Hostile Acts*, p. 79.

237. As cited in Sojo, *La Utopía del Estado Minimo*, p. 82.

238. *Ibid.*, p. 69.

239. Sojo, *La Mano Visible del Mercado*, p. 2.

240. Dunkerley, *Power in the Isthmus*, p. 592
241. Lara, *Inside Costa Rica*, p. 58.
242. Wilson, *Costa Rica*, p. 138.
243. Lara, *Inside Costa Rica*, p. 63.
244. Honey, *Hostile Acts*, pp. 136–7.

3 The New Transnational Model in Central America: I: Incorporation into the Global Economy

1. See, *inter alia*, Victor Bulmer-Thomas, *The Political Economy of Central America Since 1920*, Cambridge 1987; Charles D. Brockett, *Land, Power, and Poverty: Agrarian Transformation and Political Conflict in Central America*, second edition, Boulder 1998; Robert G. Williams, *Export Agriculture and the Crisis in Central America*, Chapel Hill 1986; William Durham, *Scarcity and Survival in Central America*, Stanford 1979.
2. Brockett, *Land, Power, and Poverty*, demonstrates the dramatic concentration of land following successive waves of agro-export expansion.
3. On the general developmental experience in Latin America and Asia during this period see, *inter alia*, Gary Gereffi and D. L. Wyman (eds.), *Manufacturing Miracles: Paths of Industrialization in Latin America and East Asia*, Princeton 1990. In India the whole program was driven by a powerful national bourgeoisie to break loose from peripheral status in the world-system. Within the "Asian Tigers," the process was part of a far-reaching break with the pre-World War II structure of classes and property relations, and gave way, before ISI had become exhausted, to new models of capitalist development.
4. For discussion on the "lost decade" in Central America, see, *inter alia*, Richard Fagen, *Forging Peace: The Challenge of Central America*, New York, 1987 Hector Perez-Brignoli, *A Brief History of Central America*, Berkeley 1989; Trevor Evans (ed.), *La Transformación Neo-liberal del Sector Publico: Ajuste Estructural y Sector Public en Centroamerica y el Caribe*, Managua 1995.
5. Bulmer-Thomas, *The Political Economy of Central America Since 1920*, p. 251.
6. On these broader structural factors for Latin America as a whole, see William I. Robinson, "Latin America and Global Capitalism," *Race and Class*, vol. 40, no. 2/3, 1998/9, pp. 111–31.
7. Elizabeth Dore and John Weeks, "Up From Feudalism," *NACLA Report on the Americas*, vol. 36, no. 3, 1992, pp. 38–45.
8. AID, *Economic Assistance Strategy for Central America 1990 to 2000*, Washington, D.C., January 1991, p. i.
9. For discussion on the CBI and the strategy of non-traditional export promotion, see Eva Paus (ed.), *Struggle Against Dependence: Non-Traditional Export Growth in Central America and the Caribbean*, Boulder 1988.
10. Victor Bulmer-Thomas (ed.), *The New Economic Model in Latin America and its Impact on Income Distribution and Poverty*, New York 1996, and see in particular, chapter one, Bulmer-Thomas, "Introduction."
11. *Ibid.*, p. 10.
12. AID, *Economic Assistance Strategy for Central America 1991 to 2000*, p. 14, 27.
13. On the CBI, see R. Feinberg and R. Newfarmer, "The Caribbean Basin Initiative: Bold Plan or Empty Promise?", in R. Newfarmer (ed.), *From Gunboats to Diplomacy: New US Policies for Latin America*, Baltimore 1984. On the Kissinger Commission Report, see *Report of the National Bipartisan Commission on Central*

America, Washington, D.C. 1984. For discussion on early adjustment programs in the region, see Bulmer-Thomas, *The Political Economy of Central America Since 1920*, esp. pp. 244–94.

14. See Philip McMichael, *Development and Social Change*, Thousand Oaks 1996, p. 90.

15. See, *inter alia*, Folker Frobel, Jurgen Heinrichs, and Otto Kreye, *The New International Division of Labour*, Cambridge 1980 [first published in German in 1977]; Peter Dicken, *Global Shift*, New York 1998, third edition; Mauricio Jenkins, Gerardo Esquivel, and Felipe Larrain B., "Export Processing Zones in Central America," *Development Discussion Papers* no. 646, August 1998, Central America Project Series, Harvard Institute for International Development, Harvard University.

16. Dicken, *Global Shift*, p. 131.

17. Frobel, *et al.*, *The New International Division of Labour*, p. 15.

18. *Ibid.*, p. 19.

19. Philip McMichael, *Development and Social Change*, p. 57.

20. Frobel, *et al.*, *The New International Division of Labor*, pp. 22–3.

21. Gary Gereffi and L. Hemple, "Latin America in the Global Economy: Running Faster to Stay in Place," *NACLA Report on the Americas*, vol. 29, no. 4, 1996, pp. 18–27.

22. In Costa Rica, 62 percent of maquiladora employment is in garments. In Honduras and Nicaragua the figure is 98 percent. In El Salvador it is 89 percent, and in Guatemala it is 63 percent. Jenkins *et al.*, "Export Processing Zones in Central America," p. 32–6.

23. On the textile-garment industry and global commodity chains, see Gary Gereffi and Miguel Korzeniewicz (eds.), *Commodity Chains and Global Capitalism*, Westport 1994, and specifically, Ian M. Taplin, "Strategic Reorientations of US Apparel Firms," in *ibid.*, p. 205–22. See also Dicken, *Global Shift*, chapter nine, "'Fabric-acting Fashion': The Textile and Clothing Industries." On Central America and garment production, see Hector Figueroa, "In the Name of Fashion: Exploitation in the Garment Industry," *NACLA Report on the Americas* vol. 29, no. 4, pp. 34–41.

24. Gary Gereffi, Miguel Korzeniewicz, and Roberto Korzeniewicz, "Introduction," in Gereffi and Korzeniewicz, *Global Commodity Chains*, p. 7.

25. US state managers operated under the equivocal assumptions that stagnation—rather than the dynamic capitalist growth that had occurred—was responsible for instability. For analysis of the CBI, see *inter alia*, Kathy McAfee, *Storm Signals: Structural Adjustment and Development Alternatives in the Caribbean*, Boston 1991, and on the transfer of textile production to Central America and the CBI, see Cecilia Green's excellent (although nation-state centric) article, "The Asian Connection: The US-Caribbean Apparel Circuit and a New Model of Industrial Relations," *Latin America Research Review*, vol. 33, no. 3, 1998, pp. 7–47; various entries in Edna Bonacich, Lucie Cheng, Norma Chinchilla, Nora Hamilton, and Paul Ong (eds.), *Global Production: The Apparel Industry in the Pacific Rim*, Philadelphia 1994; S. Cox, "The Rag Trade Goes South," *The New Internationalist*, no. 246, 1993, pp. 8–10.

26. Saskia Sassen, *The Mobility of Labor and Capital: A Study in International Investment and Labor Flow*, Cambridge 1988.

27. Mario D. Tello and William Tyler (eds.), *La Promotion de Exportaciones en Nicaragua, 1997–2010: Experiencias y Alternativas*, Managua 1997, p. 43. For a description of each country's legislation, see Jenkins, *et al.*, "Export Processing Zones in Central America," pp. 19–25. In fact, several republics enacted more

limited EPZ laws in the 1970s but the earlier legislation had become largely defunct and the industry did not get off the ground until the 1980s. Costa Rica enacted major legislation in 1984, followed by Honduras in 1987, Guatemala in 1989, El Salvador in 1990, and Nicaragua in 1991. *Ibid.* On the incentives, see Teresa S. Weersma-Haworth, "Export Processing Free Zones as an Export Strategy for Central America and the Caribbean," in Rudd Buitelaan and Pitou van Dijck (eds.), *Latin America's New Insertion in the World Economy*, New York 1996, table 6.1, pp. 91–2.

28. As compiled by Gary Gereffi, "Global Shifts, Regional Response: Can North America Meet the Full-Package Challenge?," *Bobbin*, Nov. 1997, table appearing on p. 2. The 1998 Department of Commerce figure for Nicaragua was reported in National Labor Committee (NLC, 275 7th Ave., 15th fl., New York), "Serious and Systematic Worker Rights Violations at Chentex Garment," *Press Statement*, May 31, 2000, retrieved on June 15, 2000, from http://www.nicanet.org/nicaragua/pressenglish.htm.

29. As reported by Larry Willmore, "Reflexiones Sobre la Promocion de Exportaciones en Centroamerica," in Tello and Tyler, *La Promocion de Exportaciones*, table 4, p. 61. Willmore's data is taken from the Economic Intelligence Unit's Country Reports, except for Costa Rica, which is his estimate. Other estimates place these figures much higher. One group of Honduran researchers working with women maquiladora employees estimated that by 1999 there were already 110,000 maquila workers in that country. See Nelly del Cid, Caria Castro, and Yadira Rodriguez, "Maquila Workers: A New Breed of Women," *ENVIO*, vol. 18., no. 218, Sept. 1999, p. 25. Moreover—and this may also explain in part such variation in estimates—official employment data does not include those employed in local subcontracting operations not directly involved in exporting (e.g., local suppliers or service providers). In their study, Jorge Nowalski, Pedro A. Morales, and Gregorio Berliavsky, *Impacto de la Maquila en la Economía Costaricense*, San José 1994, concur with Willmore's 50,000 figure for Costa Rica for *direct* maquila plant employment, but estimate more than 70,000 when subcontracting employment is included. In general, all figures for the maquila sector should be approached with great caution, given well-known difficulties in gathering reliable data, including the inaccessibility of firms and the lack of official controls in the EPZs.

30. Jenkins *et al.*, "Export Processing Zones in Central America," as calculated from tables 4–8, pp. 27–30.

31. International Labor Organization, *La Industria Maquila en Centroamerica*, Geneva 1998, as posted at http://www.ilo.org/public/spanish/dialogue/actemp/papers/1998/maquila/capi-2.htm, and retrieved on August 17, 2000, p. 15, graph 1.3.

32. See NLC, *Press Statement.* HR 343 Trade and Development Act of 2000, known as the CBI Parity Law, was signed into law by President Clinton on May 18, 2000 and went into effect on October 21, 2000. The law eliminated the average 10 percent tariff levied against CBI apparel entering the United States and allowed the fabric to be cut anywhere in the CBI region. The NLC *Press Release* cites a number of TNC apparel producers discussing their plans to expand in Central America.

33. ILO, complied from graphs on pp. 5–6. These figures should be approached with some caution, however, because, as the ILO study notes (p. 1), they do not necessarily include all plants. For Costa Rica, data is for plants in the EPZs; for Salvador, all maquiladora plants; for Guatemala, only garments operations;

for Honduras, all plants; for Nicaragua, plants in the EPZs. Moreover, such data tells us little about the size of operations in distinct plants. Nonetheless, Jenkins *et al.* report their own figures on maquiladora plant ownership as percentage of total firms *and* as percentage of total employment (pp. 33–7). With the exception of Costa Rica (where US firms own 56 percent of total plants [the Jenkins *et al.* figure differs slightly from the ILO's] yet employ 84 percent of maquiladora workers), there is in fact only a slight variation, suggesting that the operations of Central American-owned firms may be on a somewhat smaller scale than TNC firms. There is, however, a more serious limitation to the data presented in this table: it tells us nothing of deeper ownership structures entailed in mixed capital operations (joint ventures, etc.). For instance, in their study Nowalski *et al.*, *Impacto de la Maquila en la Economía Costaricense*, estimate that 51 percent of maquilas operating in Costa Rica involve participation by Costa Rican capitalists (p. 17).

34. The ILO notes that some Central American entrepreneurs who participate in the maquiladora industry come from older capitalist strata but there are also "many new businesspeople who were earlier professionals or engaged in other activities." *La Industria de la Maquila en Centroamerica*, pp. 6–7.

35. Paul Baran and Paul Sweezy, *Monopoly Capitalism*, New York 1966.

36. For discussion on local capitalist EPZ developers and on these new forms of collaboration in the maquiladora sector, see: Weersma-Haworth, "Export Processing Free Zones," ILO, *La Industrial de la Maquila en Centroamerica*; Jenkins, *et al.*, "Export Processing Zones in Central America." On subcontracting arrangements, see Nowalski, *et al.*, *Impacto de la Maquila en la Economía Costaricense*, and Green, "The Asian Connection."

37. Terrence K. Hopkins and Immanuel Wallerstein, "Commodity Chains: Construct and Research," in Gereffi and Korzeniewicz, *Commodity Chains and Global Capitalism*.

38. Taplin, "Strategic Reorientations of US Apparel Firms."

39. *Ibid.*, pp. 210–20.

40. As reported by Kurt Petersen, *The Maquiladora Revolution in Guatemala*, Occasional Paper Series 2, 1992, New Haven: Yale Law School, Orville H. Schell Jr. Center for International Human Rights, pp. 39–40, for the Guatemalan maquiladoras. The ILO reported that total corporate profits for Fruit of the Loom, which has operations in Central America, were $60 million in 1994, of which a full $35 million came from its maquiladora plants. *La Industria de la Maquila en Centroamerica*, pp. 14–15.

41. Taplin, "Strategic Reorientations of US Apparel Firms," p. 208.

42. See Petersen, *The Maquiladora Revolution in Guatemala*, p. 1.

43. For these details see, e.g., Petersen, pp. 46–9.

44. Petersen, p. 139. Petersen spent two years researching the maquiladoras in Guatemala for his excellent 1992 study, which involves a major ethnographic component, including extensive interviews with Korean officials and fieldwork in the highlands.

45. *Ibid.*, p. 145.

46. Petersen, p. 28.

47. As cited in Petersen, p. 150.

48. Petersen, p. 39.

49. Petersen, pp. 49–50.

50. *Ibid.*, p. 212, endnote 55.

51. Kent Norsworthy, *Inside Honduras*, Albuquerque 1993, pp. 78–79.

52. The National Labor Committee, as cited in Green, "The Asian Connection," p. 28.
53. Karen Hansen-Kuhn, *Structural Adjustment in Central America: The Case of Costa Rica*, Washington, D.C., June 1993, p. 16.
54. See, *inter alia*, Nowalski, *et al.*, *El Impacto de la Maquila en la Economía Costaricense*.
55. This and the following paragraphs are based on Petersen's excellent 1992 study, including his detailed field research and ethnographic surveys. See chapters three ("The Market and the Players"), four ("Health and Safety Conditions"), five ("Working Hours, Compensation, and Labor Relations"), and six ("Unions and the Maquila: The Battle Against Impunity").
56. Some one fifth of workers were under the age of sixteen in Guatemala City. In the rural maquilas as many as half the workers were minors, and some were as young as six, according to Petersen's ethnographic survey (see p. 92).
57. See, *inter alia*, "Central America: Uproar Over US Investigation of Working Conditions in Maquiladora Plants," *Chronicle of Latin American Economic Affairs*, vol. 10, no. 47, Dec. 14, 1995, Latin America Data Base, Latin American Institute, University of New Mexico, Albuquerque. The description of Nicaragua's Las Mercedes *zona franca* is based on the author's visit in May 1999.
58. See Jenkins, *et al.*, "Export Processing Zones in Central America," pp. 39–40.
59. In Honduras and Nicaragua they appeared to be higher, but in Costa Rica, in the early 1990s, they were lower, between $80 and $120 a month. This was higher in absolute terms than in neighboring countries, but lower than the national monthly minimum wage of $150. Hansen-Kuhn, *Structural Adjustment in Central America*, p. 17.
60. See, NLC, *Press Statement*. The extreme difficulty in calculating maquiladora wages is well-known, and includes the difficulties in calculating bonuses and benefits, in fluctuating wage rates, the widespread practice of paying piecemeal, fluctuations in currency exchange rates, and so on. For example, the 48 cents an hour rate at the Chentex plant in Nicaragua may overstate actual pay. The Nicaraguan Human Rights Center (CENIDH) placed average hourly pay in the Las Mercedes *zona franca* in 1997 at only 20 cents. See Michael Sheridan, "Critics Say Profits Come at Workers' Expense," *Latinamerica Press*, vol. 29, no. 48, Dec. 25, 1997, p. 2.
61. "Cost Analysis of an Export Oriented Assembly Operation in Honduras," table attached to packet of promotional materials on the Honduran EPZs provided by FIDE to the author, March 1998.
62. For these details, see Geske Dijkstra and Carlos Rivera Alemán, "The Export Processing Free Zone of San Bartolo in El Salvador," in Rudd Buitelaan and Pitou van Dijck (eds.), *Latin America's New Insertion in the World Economy*, New York 1996.
63. For these details, see, *inter alia*, NLC, *Press Release*, "Dirigente Norteamericano Revela caso de Chentex: Datos Espantosos de Feroz Explotacion," *El Nuevo Diario*, June 1, 2000, p. 1; Witness for Peace, "From the Maquila to the Mall," Washington, D.C., 1997; Juan Hernandez Pico, "Labor Unrest and Organized Crime," *ENVIO*, vol. 14, no. 170, Sept. 1995, pp. 10–12; Reflection, Research and Communication Team (ERIC), "Maquila: The Swallow That Lays Golden Eggs," *ENVIO*, vol. 16, no. 194, Sept. 1997, pp. 16–22.
64. As cited in Nowalski, *El Impacto de la Maquila*, p. 57.
65. For these details, see Hansen-Kuhn, *Structural Adjustment in Central America*, pp. 16–18.

66. Larry Willmore, "Reflexiones Sobre la Promocion de Exportaciones en Centroamerica," in Tello and Tyler, *La Promocion de Exportaciones*, table 4, p. 61.

67. As cited in Richard Barnet and John Cavanagh, *Global Dreams: Imperial Corporations and the New World Order*, New York 1994, p. 325.

68. As cited in Petersen, *The Maquiladora Revolution in Guatemala*, pp. 42-3, 93. The Guatemalan Labor Code stipulated generous benefits and rights for pregnant women, including protection against dismissal, paid maternity leave, a right to lactation during working hours, and day care provisions for factories of more than thirty employees. These provisions existed on paper only. See *ibid.*, p. 92.

69. See Nelly del Cid, Caria Castro, and Yadira Rodriguez, "Maquila Workers: A New Breed of Women," *ENVIO*, vol. 18., no. 218, Sept. 1999, pp. 29-30. This excellent study runs from pp. 25-31.

70. *Ibid.*, p. 30. Nowalski, *et al.*, *Impacto de la Maquila*, found similar changes for Costa Rica, including a major transfer of formerly agricultural labor into the maquila sector.

71. This section draws on the excellent study by Michael E. Conroy, Douglas L. Murray, and Peter M. Rosset, *A Cautionary Tale: Failed US Development Policy in Central America*, Boulder 1996. It also draws on a number of other studies, among them: Bradford Barham, Mary Clark, Elizabeth Katz, and Rachel Schurman, "Non-Traditional Agricultural Exports in Latin America," *Latin America Research Review*, vol. 27, no. 2, 1992, pp. 43-82; Mary A. Clark, "Non-Traditional Export Promotion in Costa Rica: Sustaining Export-Led Growth," *Journal of Interamerican Studies and World Affairs*, vol. 37, no. 2, 1995, pp. 181-223; US Agency for International Development (AID), *Harvest of Progress: A Quiet Revolution in Latin America and Caribbean Agriculture*, Washington, D.C., December 1994; Eva Paus (ed.), *Struggle Against Dependence*; Brockett, *Land, Power, and Poverty*.

72. Economic Commission for Latin America and the Caribbean (ECLAC), *Economic Survey of Latin America and the Caribbean, 1993*, Santiago, Chile 1995.

73. These distinct meanings are detailed in Barham, *et al.*, "Non-Traditional Agricultural Exports in Latin America," p. 13, note 1.

74. The consumption of broccoli, for example, increased 300 percent in the United States in the 1980s. There are other related factors as well that account for the rise in consumption of these products, such as a new health consciousness, the increase of the Latino population in US cities who generate demand for tropical foodstuffs from their home regions, and so on. See, e.g., AVANCSO, *Apostando al Futuro Con los Cultivos No Tradicionales de Exportacion, Vol. I*, Guatemala 1994, pp. 9-10.

75. There is a growing body of literature on the globalization of food and agriculture that addresses the broader theoretical issues addressed in this section. See, *inter alia*, McMichael (ed.), *The Global Restructuring of Agro-Food Systems*, Ithaca 1994; McMichael (ed.), *Food and Agrarian Orders in the World Economy*, Westport 1995; Alessandro Bonanno, Lawrence Busch, William Friedland, Lourdes Gouveia, and Enzo Mingione (eds.), *From Columbus to ConAgra: The Globalization of Agriculture and Food*, Lawrence 1994; McMichael, *Development and Social Change*; D. Goodman and M. Watts (eds.), *Globalising Food: Agrarian Questions and Global Restructuring*, London 1997; L. A. Thrupp, *Bitter-Sweet Harvests for Global Supermarkets*, Washington, D.C. 1995.

76. See, e.g., McMichael, *Development and Social Change*, p. 65; Alain de Janvry, *The*

Agrarian Question and Reformism in Latin America, Baltimore 1981, p. 179; and more generally, Alain Revel and Christophe Riboud, *American Green Power*, Baltimore 1986.

77. McMichael, *Development and Social Change*, p. 100.

78. Harriet Friedmann, "Changes in the International Division of Labor: Agri-food Complexes and Export Agriculture," in Friedland, *et al.*, *Towards a New Political Economy of Agriculture.*

79. See, e.g., AID, *Harvest of Progress*; AID, *Economic Assistance Strategy for Central America 1991 to 2000*, Washington, D.C., January 1991; AID, *ROCAP Program Objectives, Documents and Action Plan 1992–1994*, Washington, D.C., December 1991.

80. On the relation of the CBI to NTAEs in Central America, see, *inter alia*, Paus, *Struggle Against Dependence*; Clark, "Non-Traditional Export Promotion in Costa Rica."

81. See, e.g., Roberto Codas Friedmann, *Exportaciones Agricolas No Tradicionales en El Salvador*, San Salvador 1991, p. 49; AID, *Economic Assistance Strategy for Central America* and *ROCAP Program Objectives.*

82. See Conroy, *et al.*, *A Cautionary Tale*, and especially chapter three, "Implementing The Strategy: USAID Creates a Parallel State"; Friedmann, *Exportaciones Agricolas No Tradicionales en El Salvador.*

83. See Barham, *et al.*, "Non-Traditional Agricultural Exports in Latin America."

84. Mary A. Clark, "Non-Traditional Export Promotion in Costa Rica: Sustaining Export-Led Growth," *Journal of Interamerican Studies and World Affairs*, vol. 37, no. 2, 1995, pp. 181–223. Costa Rica also specialized in cut flowers and ornamental plants. In 1993, the country's export sales from these products reached $82 million. See Clark, pp. 209–210.

85. AVACSO, *Apostando al Futuro*, p. 29.

86. See, e.g., Barham, *et al.*, "Non-Traditional Agricultural Exports in Latin America"; Friedmann, *Exportaciones Agricolas No Tradicionales en El Salvador.*

87. The following section draws heavily from Conroy, *et al.*, *A Cautionary Tale*, chapter five (pp. 91–109). See also Laura T. Raynolds, "Institutionalizing Flexibility: A Comparative Analysis of Fordist and Post-Fordist Models of Third World Agro-Export Production," in Gereffi and Korzeniewicz, *Commodity Chains and Global Capitalism*, pp. 143–61.

88. Conroy, *et al.*, *A Cautionary Tale*, pp. 97–103. See also Raynolds, "Institutionalizing Flexibility."

89. See David Glover and Ken Kusterer, *Small Farmers, Big Business: Contract Farming and Rural Development*, New York 1990; Peter D. Little and Michael Watts, *Peasants and Contracts: Contract Farming and Agrarian Transformation in Sub-Sahara Africa*, Madison 1995.

90. For a detailed analysis of the incorporation of family units into NTAE production in one region—the Guatemalan highlands—and the transformation of family and gender relations it engenders, see Claudia Dary Fuentes, *Mujeres Tradicionales y Nuevos Cultivos*, Guatemala 1991. On the general benefits to TNCs of contract farming, see Glover and Kusterer, esp. chapter one.

91. Conroy, *et al.*, *A Cautionary Tale*, p. 100. See also Fuentes, *Mujeres Tradicionales y Nuevos Cultivos*; Friedmann, *Exportaciones Agricolas No Tradicionales en El Salvador.*

92. Conroy, *et al.*, *ibid.*, p. 102.

93. Friedmann, *Exportaciones Agricolas No Tradicionales en El Salvador*, p. 59.

94. See Conroy, *et al.*, *A Cautionary Tale*, pp. 56–9. In his field study of melon

production in Western El Salvador, Friedmann found that, of seventy-five producers surveyed, twenty-six were forced to sell between three-fourths and 100 percent of their harvest on the local market. On this study, see Friedmann, *Exportaciones Agricolas No Tradicionales en El Salvador*, p. 59.

95. Conroy, *et al.*, *A Cautionary Tale*, p. 106.
96. Friedmann, *Exportaciones Agricolas No Tradicionales en El Salvador*, pp. 50–51.
97. Conroy, *et al.*, *A Cautionary Tale*, pp. 105–107.
98. For deeper discussion on these issues, see D. Goodman, B. Sorj, and J. Wilkinson, *From Farming to Biotechnology: A Theory of Agro-Industrial Development*, Oxford 1987. In this regard, NTAEs follow the model of industrial agriculture: energy and capital-intensive agriculture organized through agri-business and its upstream and downstream industries. On this model, see McMichael and Raynolds, "Capitalism, Agriculture, and World Economy."
99. Conroy, *et al.*, *A Cautionary Tale*, p. 96. See also Barham, *et al.*, "Non-Traditional Agricultural Exports in Latin America."
100. Fuentes, *Mujeres Traditionales Y Nuevos Cultivos*, p. 35.
101. Tom Barry, *Inside Guatemala*, Albuquerque 1991, p. 108.
102. See figure 1.5 in Conroy, *et al.*, *A Cautionary Tale*, p. 15.
103. *Ibid.*, p. 30.
104. Hansen-Kuhn, *Structural Adjustment in Central America*, p. 44.
105. See, e.g., Rachael Garst and Tom Barry, *Feeding the Crisis: US Food Aid and Farm Policy in Central America*, Lincoln 1990.
106. See, e.g, Conroy, *et al.*, *A Cautionary Tale*. The Central American agricultural ministries, which had serviced the peasant sector (credit, technical assistance, agrarian reform, etc.), were downsized under neo-liberal programs, as shown in chapter five, tables 5.3 and 5.4.
107. As cited in Hansen-Kuhn, *Structural Adjustment in Central America*, p. 13.
108. The AID report is discussed in Conroy, *et al.*, *A Cautionary Tale*, pp. 55–6. The AID had actually tried to suppress the report, which was provided to the authors by an anonymous dissident. See p. 63, note 5.
109. Calogero Carletto, Alain de Janvry, and Elisabeth Sadoulet, "Sustainability in the Diffusion of Innovations: Smallholder Non-Traditional Agro-Exports in Guatemala," *Economic Development and Cultural Change*, vol. 47, no. 2, January 1999, pp. 345–69.
110. AVANCSO, *Apostando al Futuro*, p. 27.
111. *Ibid.*
112. Laura Raynolds, "Harvesting Women's Work: Restructuring Agricultural and Industrial Labor Forces in the Dominican Republic," *Economic Geography*, vol. 74, no. 2, 1998, pp. 149–69.
113. A. Alberti, "Impact of Participation in Non-Traditional Agricultural Export Production on the Employment, Income, and Quality of Life of Women in Guatemala, Honduras, and Costa Rica." Report submitted to US AID, Guatemala/Washington, D.C.: Chemonics, as cited in Raynolds, "Harvesting Women's Work," p. 150.
114. See, e.g., Fuentes, *Mujeres Tradicionales y Nuevos Cultivos*; AVANCSO, *Apostando al Futuro*, p. 33.
115. Fuentes, *Mujeres Tradicionales y Nuevos Cultivos*.
116. Glover and Kusterer, *Small Farmers, Big Business*.
117. Fuentes, *ibid.*, chapter four, "Situación laboral y sociocultural de la mujer involucrada en el cultivo y procesamiento de los productos no tradicionales para la exportacion." Fuentes interviewed a random sample of 107 women,

but curiously did not indicate in her results the number for the total population.

118. By way of anecdote, the AID observes that "The need for instant communications in the produce business has led to sales of fax machines in isolated rural areas." AID, *Harvest of Progress*, p. 8.

119. On new forms of stratification and incipient class divisions among the highland indigenous, see also AVANCSO, *Apostando al Futuro.*

120. The role of local purchasing agents as commercial intermediaries is discussed by Fuentes, *Mujeres Tradicionales y Nuevos Cultivos*, esp. chapter three, "comercializacion de productos no tradicionales."

121. AVANCSO, *Apostando al Futuro*, pp. 66–7. In turn, behind the transnational fruit companies stands transnational capital more broadly. For example, transnational banks such as the Bank of America and Chase Manhattan, and food marketing transnationals such as Cargill, are major financiers and shareholders in the agri-business firms. See, e.g., Brockett, *Land, Power, and Poverty*, p. 57.

122. Lara, *Inside Costa Rica*, p. 52.

123. Conroy, *et al.*, *A Cautionary Tale*, p. 38.

124. *Ibid.*, p. 108.

125. *Ibid.*, pp. 95–6.

126. This is what Hoogvelt calls "global financial deepening." See Hoogvelt, *Globalization and the Postcolonial World.*

127. See, e.g., AVANCSO, *Postulando al Futuro*, pp. 45–6.

128. *Ibid.*, p. 56.

129. See, *inter alia*, Durham, *Scarcity and Survival in Central America*; Brockett, *Land, Power, and Poverty.*

130. E. Philip English, *The Great Escape? An Examination of North-South Tourism*, Ottawa 1986, p. 3.

131. There is a vast literature on world tourism and development, including a growing body of research on globalization and tourism. I am unable here to draw on all but a small sample of that literature, and cannot examine several sets of issues that have been central to the sociology of tourism, including tourism and representation, identity, and authenticity. For an overview of these issues, see Jozsef Borocz, *Leisure Migration: A Sociological Study on Tourism*, Oxford 1996, chapter one, "Leisure Migration." Also Dean MacCannell's classic post-structuralist sociological study *The Tourist: A New Theory of the Leisure Class*, New York 1976, which focuses on the dimensions of symbol, representation, and authenticity. The discussion here draws on Martin Mowforth's and Ian Munt's excellent critical study, *Tourism and Sustainability: New Tourism in the Third World*, London 1998, and on: David Harrison (ed.), *Tourism and the Less Developed Countries*, London 1992; Harrison, "Tourism, Capitalism and Development in Less Developed Countries," in Sklair (ed.), *Capitalism and Development*; E. Philip English, *The Great Escape?*; Marie-Françoise Lanfant, "Tourism in the Process of Internationalization," *International Social Science Journal*, vol. 32, no. 1, 1980, pp. 14–43; Winston Husbands (ed.) and Lynn C. Harrison (contributor), *Practicing Responsible Tourism: International Case Studies in Tourism Planning, Policy and Development*, New York 1996; Truong Thank-Dam, *Sex, Money, and Morality: Prostitution and Tourism in Southeast Asia*, London 1990; *The New Internationalist*, special issue on tourism, "Tourism: The Final Brochure," no. 245, July 1993; Vivian Kinnaird and Derek Hall (eds.), *Tourism: A Gender Analysis*, New York 1994; Martha Honey, *Ecotourism and Sustainable Development: Who Owns Paradise?*, Washington, D.C. 1999.

132. These estimates were provided by the World Travel and Tourism Council, an industry lobby group, as reported in *The Economist*, "A Survey of Travel and Tourism," special supplement, January 10, 1998, p. 3.

133. For this data, see Honey, *Ecotourism and Sustainable Development*, pp. 8–9.

134. Husbands and Harrison, "Practicing Responsible Tourism: Understanding Tourism Today to Prepare for Tomorrow," in Husbands (ed.), *Practicing Responsible Tourism*, table 1.1, p. 3.

135. Lanfant, "Tourism in the Process of Internationalization," p. 15.

136. Borocz, *Leisure Migration*, p. 13.

137. Both cites from Malcolm Waters appear in *Globalization*, London 1995, p. 154. On the "pleasure periphery," see L. Turner and J. Ash, *The Golden Hordes*, London 1975, as discussed by Waters in *ibid.*, pp. 153–4. See Mowforth and Munt, *Tourism and Sustainability*, on the analysis of the "new tourism," and in particular, p. 100, box 4.6, for a list of forms of "alternative" tourism.

138. See, e.g., World Tourism Organization, *Tourism Economic Report*, Madrid 1998, first edition, "Major Tourism Trends," pp. 6–7; Mowforth and Munt, *Tourism and Sustainability*.

139. See, e.g., World Tourism Organization, *Economic Review of World Tourism: Tourism in the Context of Economic Crisis and the Dominance of the Service Economy*, Madrid 1988.

140. Oscar Barrera Pérez, "Tourismo y Globalización: Un Reto para Nicaragua," *Encuentro*, vol. 30, no. 47, 1998, pp. 46–53.

141. Husbands and Harrison, "Practicing Responsible Tourism . . .", table 1.3, p. 4.

142. "Central American Presidents Draw Up Joint Plan to Develop Regional Tourism Industry," *Ecocentral*, vol. 1, no. 3, June 13, 1996, Latin America Data Base, Latin American Institute, University of New Mexico.

143. Barrera Peréz, "Tourismo y Globalización," p. 49. Barrera Perez's data includes tourist arrivals to Panama. I have modified the figures to include only the five Central American republics. These figures include intra- and extra-regional tourism. The approximate breakdown in regional earnings was: Costa Rica, $4.3 billion; Guatemala, $2.05 billion; Honduras, $559 million; El Salvador, $289 million; Nicaragua, $234 million. The 232,000 salaried workers is reported in World Tourism Organization, *Tourism Economic Report*, table 3.10, p. 92 (no country breakdown provided).

144. On Costa Rica, see *ibid.* On Nicaragua, see Barrera Pérez, "Tourismo y Globalización," p. 52. On Honduras, see World Tourism Organization, *Tourism Economic Report*, Madrid 1998, first edition, table 4.8, p. 108. On Guatemala, see "Guatemala," *International Tourism Reports*, no. 4, 1997, published by *Economist Publications*, p. 98.

145. See "Guatemala," *International Tourism Reports*, pp. 91–2. An increasing portion of tourists have traveled to Central America under the bracket of educational visits. An example are the thousands of visitors who travel annually to enroll in intensive courses in one of the many small, privately run Spanish-language schools.

146. Ecocentral, "Central American Presidents Draw Up Joint Plan." Regarding Costa Rica, see Deirdre Evans-Pritchard, "Mobilization of Tourism in Costa Rica," *Annals of Tourism Research*, vol. 20, no. 4, 1993, pp. 778–9.

147. Ecocentral, "Central American Presidents Draw up Joint Plan."

148. See Honey, *Ecotourism and Sustainable Development*, p. 131; Edward Orlebear, "Central America: Hopeful Hosts," *Business Latin America*, vol. 28, no. 34, p. 4.

The Costa Rican Tourist Board provides the following statistics, as reported in Honey, *ibid.*, p. 133, table 5.1:

	1976	1982	1984	1986	1989	1990	1992	1994	1995	1996
Arrivals (in thousands)	299	372	274	261	376	435	611	761	792	555
Gross Receipts (millions $)	57	131	117	133	207	275	431	626	718	654

149. World Tourism Organization, as cited by Barrera Pérez, "Tourismo y Globalización," table 2, p. 50. The WTO, in a separate report, *Tourism Economic Report*, first edition, 1998, table 1.3, p. 12, indicates that Nicaragua was in eighth place for tourist growth among all countries in the world, and Costa Rica was in nineteenth place. The same report, table 3.2, p. 68, indicated that tourism went from 1.71 percent of the region's GNP in 1985 to 3.31 percent in 1995.

150. See Barrera Pérez, "Turismo y Globalización," table 1, p. 49 and data presented on p. 50. Barrera Perez's table includes tourist arrivals to Panama. I have modified the figures to include only the five Central American republics. These figures include intra- and extra-regional tourism.

151. Barrera Pérez, "Turismo y Globalización," p. 51. See also Amanda A. Austin, "Nicaragua Offering Incentives to Hotel Investors," *Hotel and Motel Management*, vol. 209, no. 6, September 19, 1994, pp. 12–13.

152. Amanda A. Austin, "Guatemala Expects Tourist Boom," *Hotel and Motel Management*, vol. 21, no. 20, 1996, p. 8.

153. Orlebear, "Central America: Hopeful Hosts," p. 4.

154. As English shows, the degree of import content for the tourist industry and the degree of leakage may vary enormously and is exceedingly difficult to estimate with precision. See *The Great Escape?*, esp. pp. 22–8.

155. For these figures on the percentage of hotels in the Third World linked to TNC hotel chains, see Honey, *Ecotourism and Sustainable Development*, p. 38. On the five major contractual mechanisms used by the chains, see Mowforth and Munt, *Tourism and Sustainable Development*, box. 7.1, p. 192.

156. See, *inter alia*, S. Britton, "The Political Economy of Tourism in the Third World," *Annals of Tourism Research*, no. 9, 1982, pp. 331–58; Dennison Nash, "Tourism as a Form of Imperialism," in Valerie Smith (ed.), *Hosts and Guests: The Anthropology of Tourism*, Oxford 1989.

157. Austin, "Guatemala Expects Tourist Boom," p. 8.

158. Dinah A. Spritzer, "Nicaragua Seeks Investment to Expand Tourism Infrastructure," *Travel Weekly*, vol. 20, no. 76, September 24, 1994, pp. 94–5.

159. Latin America Data Base, "Honduras: Government Abandons Controversial Development Scheme After Police Fire on Protesters," *Notisur*, Latin American Institute, University of New Mexico, Albuquerque, vol. 4, no. 41, November 4, 1999.

160. For these details, see Honey, *Ecotourism and Sustainable Development*, pp. 14–21, and p. 17 for the $2 billion figure.

161. As cited in Honey, *Ecotourism and Sustainable Development*, p. 6.

162. See, *inter alia*, Honey, *Ecotourism and Sustainable Development*; Mowforth and Munt, *Tourism and Sustainability*; Deborah McLaren, *Rethinking Tourism and Ecotravel: The Paving of Paradise and What You Can Do To Stop It*, West Hartford 1998.

163. Honey, *Ecotourism and Sustainable Development*, p. 148.

164. For these details, see Honey, *Ecotourism and Sustainable Development*, pp. 3–4.

165. Carlos Vargas, as cited in Honey, *Ecotourism and Sustainable Development*, p. 155.

166. See Honey, *Ecotourism and Sustainable Development*, p. 150, for these figures, and see Carole Hill, "The Paradox of Tourism in Costa Rica," *Critical Survival Quarterly*, vol. 14, no. 1, 1990, pp. 14–19, who notes (p. 15) that confiscation of lands for reserves "has created conflicts between local communities and preservation policies" that have "been exacerbated by the presence of more and more tourists at national parks and reserve areas."

167. Guillermo Barquero, as cited in Honey, *Ecotourism and Sustainable Development*, p. 164.

168. S. Stonich, J. Sorenson, and A. Hundt, "Ethnicity, Class and Gender in Tourism Development: The Case of The Bay Islands, Honduras," *Journal of Sustainable Development*, vol. 3, no. 1, 1995, pp. 1–28.

169. On the Maya in Guatemala and Mexico, see, e.g., references and discussion by Mowforth and Munt, *Tourism and Sustainable Development*, pp. 239–42, and see *ibid.*, p. 262, for reference to the 1996 case.

170. See, e.g., Thank-Dam, *Sex, Money, and Morality*.

171. See Vivian Kinnaird, Uma Kothari, and Derek Hall, "Tourism: Gender Perspectives," in Kinnaird and Hall, *Tourism: A Gender Analysis*.

172. See *ibid.* for a summary of these findings.

173. Harrison, "Tourism, Capitalism and Development," p. 239.

174. Austin, "Guatemala Expects Tourist Boom," p. 8.

175. See, e.g., England's reference to the literature and summary discussion on this theme, in *The Great Escape?*, chapter six, "Culture at the Crossroads," and Mowforth and Munt's detailed discussion in *Tourism and Sustainability*.

176. See, e.g., Borocz, *Leisure Migration*.

177. Peter Stalker, *Workers Without Frontiers: The Impact of Globalization on International Migration* (Boulder: Lynne Rienner, 2000), p. 79.

178. See, e.g., Nigel Harris, *The New Untouchables: Immigration and the New World Worker*, London 1995, pp. 140–46; Stalker, *Workers Without Frontiers*, chapter six, pp. 75–92.

179. Stalker, *Workers Without Frontiers*, p. 81. Studies on remittances in Central America show how this income goes primarily for investment in family consumption and social capital. See, e.g., Mario Lungo and Susan Kandel, "International Migration, Transnationalism and Socio-Cultural Changes in El Salvador's Sending Towns," paper presented at the 1998 meeting of the Latin American Studies Association, Chicago, September 24–26, 1998.

180. Comision Economica para America Latina y el Caribe (CEPAL), "Informe Especial: Emigrantes: de la Sobrevivencia a Pilares de la Economia," as reproduced in *Inforpress Centroamericana*, no. 967, 23 January 1992 (special insert without page numbers), and as discussed in William I. Robinson, "The Global Economy and the Latino Populations in the United States: A World Systems Approach," *Critical Sociology*, vol. 19, no. 2, 1993, pp. 29–59.

181. Manuel Orozco, Rodolfo de la Garza, and Miguel Baraona, *Inmigración y Remesas Familiares*, San José 1997, p. 50.

182. See Stalker, *Workers Without Frontiers*, p. 80.

183. "Is the Game all Sown Up? Questions and Contradictions," *ENVIO*, vol. 18, no. 218, September 1999, p. 10.

184. As discussed in Jonas, *Of Centaurs and Doves*, p. 225.

185. See, e.g., Orozco, *et al.*, *Inmigración y Remesas Familiares*.

186. "Mitch, Foreign Debt, Disasters, Emigrants and Remittances in Central

America," *ENVIO*, vol. 18, no. 212, March 1999, p. 54 (article runs from pp. 46–54).

187. The study was conducted by Segundo Montes, as reported by Mario Lungo Ecles, *El Salvador in the Eighties*, Philadelphia 1996, p. 105. See also José Roberto Lopez and Mitchell A. Seligson, "Small Business Development in El Salvador: The Impact of Remittances," in Sergio Diaz-Briquets and Sidney Weintraub, *Migration, Remittances, and Small Business Development: Mexico and the Caribbean Basin Countries*, Boulder 1991, pp. 175–206; Gabriel Siri and Vilma de Calderón, "Uso Productivo de las Remesas Familiares en El Salvador," *Documento de Trabajo No. 42*, San Salvador January 1996.

188. José Itzigsohn, "Migrant Remittances, Labor Markets, and Household Strategies: A Comparative Analysis of Low-Income Household Strategies in the Caribbean Basin," *Social Forces*, vol. 74, no. 2, 1995, pp. 633–56.

189. Both the World Bank and the UN ECLAC studies are discussed in Orozco, *et al.*, *Inmigracion y Remesas Familiares*, p. 53.

190. Murray, *Inside El Salvador*, p. 89.

191. See, e.g., "US Efforts to Crack Down on Illegal Immigration Create Alarm in Central American Countries," *Ecocentral*, vol. 2, no. 9, March 6, 1997, Latin America Data Base, Latin American Institute, University of New Mexico, Albuquerque.

192. Brockett, *Land, Power, and Poverty*.

193. Willmore, "Reflexiones sobre la Promocion de Exportaciones en Central America."

194. On the reorientation of the Central American economic integration process, see, *inter alia*, José Manuel Salazar, "Present and Future Integration in Central America," *CEPAL Review*, No. 42, Dec. 1990, pp. 157–80; Romulo Caballeros Otero, "Reorientation of Central American Integration," *CEPAL Review*, no. 46, April 1992, pp. 125–37; Carlos Manuel Echeverria and Luis Alberto Chocano, "The New Direction of Integration in Central America," Center for International Private Enterprise, retrieved on July 15, 2000 from http://www.cipe.org/ert/e09/cent-3.html; Pedro Caldentey del Pozo and José Juan Romero Rodriguez, "Central American Integration: Open Agenda and Pending Dilemma," *ENVIO*, vol. 17, no. 201, April 1999, pp. 32–42.

195. See, e.g., Saskia Sassen, *The Global City: New York, London, Tokyo*, Princeton 1991.

196. See, e.g., Latin America Data Base, "Region: Trend Toward the Dollar Continues with New Law in Guatemala Permitting Use of Foreign Currency," Noticen: Central American and Caribbean Political and Economic Affairs, vol. 6, no. 1, January 11, 2001. Latin American Institute, University of New Mexico.

4 The New Transnational Model in Central America: II: Incorporation into Global Society

1. Jorge I. Dominguez, ed., *Technopols: Freeing Politics and Markets in Latin America in the 1990s*, University Park 1997.

2. This cite is from "Foreword" by Richard E. Feinberg, in Dominguez, *Technopols*, p. ix.

3. Dominguez, "Technopols," chapter one in Dominguez, p. 7.

4. See, *inter alia*, the very important essay by John Markoff and Veronica Montecinos, "The Ubiquitous Rise of Economists," *Journal of Public Policy*, vol. 13, no.

1, 1993, pp. 37–68. Markoff and Montecinos document the worldwide trend whereby economists have risen to the highest positions in government, and attribute this rise, beyond their technical knowledge, to the "legitimacy granting ceremonial aspect of their appointment" (p. 63).

5. See, e.g., José Luz Fiori, "Cardoso Among the Technopols," in *NACLA Report on the Americas*, vol. 27, no. 6, May/June 1995, pp. 17–22.

6. The official was Richard E. Feinberg, as stated in his "Foreword" to Dominguez (ed.), *Technopols*, p. x.

7. Peter Hakim, "Preface," in Dominguez, *Technopols*, p. xiii.

8. A well-researched case is the Bank of England, turned over to local British representatives of transnational capital and given near-complete independence by the Blair government in 1997. See, e.g., Simeon Kennedy, "New Labor and the Reorganization of British Politics," *Monthly Review*, vol. 49, no. 9, pp. 14–26. More generally on the trend towards Central Bank autonomy, see "The Central Bank as God," *The Economist*, Nov. 14, 1998, pp. 23–5.

9. Kathleen C. Schwartzman, "Globalization and Democracy," *Annual Review of Sociology*, 1998, vol. 24, p. 167.

10. Jorge Escoto and Manfredo Marroquín, *La AID en Guatemala*, Managua 1992, p. 38.

11. See, *inter alia*, David A. Gold, Clarence Y. H. Lo, and Erik Olin Wright, "Marxist Theories of the Capitalist State," in Marvin E. Olsen and Martin N. Marger, *Power in Modern Societies*, Boulder 1993.

12. Edelberto Torres Rivas, *History and Society in Central America*, Austin 1993, p. 106.

13. International programs were redesigned to facilitate the dismantling of nation-state development projects and integration into the emerging global economy under the local leadership of new transnationally oriented groups. According to the Initiative, governments were to be "encouraged" to "open their economies to a greater reliance on competitive markets and private enterprise" and "to foster the growth of productive, self-sustaining income and job producing private enterprises in developing countries." The Initiative identified "the possibility of a positive role for the public sector in the achievement of economic growth. That role [was] . . . the establishment of a favorable climate for private investment. Mission directors were instructed to identify government policy constraints to private enterprise development and seek to address these." This would involve, according to the AID, the following objectives: "economic policy reform"; "legal and regulatory changes"; "privatization of government services and parastatals"; "improved infrastructure in power, transport, and communications"; "access to credit for private enterprise"; the "creation of a trained labor force" for the private sector, and so on. Committee on Foreign Affairs, *The Private Enterprise Initiative*, pp. 6–7.

14. See Committee on Foreign Affairs, *The Private Enterprise Initiative*, p. viii–x.

15. See, e.g., *ibid.*, pp. 8–9, 14–15.

16. Benjamin L. Crosby, "Crisis y Fragmentacion: Relaciones Entre los Sectores Publico-Privado en America Central," Occasional Paper Series, No. 10, Miami: Latin American and Caribbean Center, Florida International University, May 1985, pp. 14, 18.

17. See FEDEPRICAP, "Posicion Empresarial Sobre los Grupos de Trabajo del ALCA," February 1998, presented at the "IV Foro Empresarial de las Americas" (IV Business Forum of the Americas), March 16–19, 1998, San José, Costa Rica.

18. Torres Rivas, *History and Society in Central America*, p. 107.

19. See, e.g., Robert Putnam, "Bowling Alone: America's Declining Social Capital," *Journal of Democracy*, vol. 6, no. 1, 1995, pp. 65–78; *Making Democracy Work: Civic Traditions in Modern Italy*, Princeton 1993. See also J. Burbridge, "Beyond Prince and Merchant: Citizen Participation and the Rise of Civil Society," R. Tandon Pact and Darcey de Oliveira M. (eds.), *Citizens: Strengthening Global Civil Society*, NY 1995.

20. Antonio Gramsci, *Prison Notebooks*, New York 1971, p. 263.

21. Sonia E. Alvarez, Evelina Dagnino, and Arturo Escobar (eds.), *Culture of Politics, Politics of Culture: Re-visioning Latin American Social Movements*, Boulder 1998, p. 17.

22. For discussion on the classical liberal conception, see *inter alia*, Adam Seligman, *The Idea of Civil Society*, New York 1992.

23. Martin Shaw, "Global Society and Global Responsibility: The Theoretical, Historical, and Political Limits of 'International Society'," *Millennium*, vol. 21, no. 3, 1992, p. 431. The other theoretical problem in Shaw's formulation is its nation-state centrism.

24. For discussion, see *inter alia*, Mustapha Kamal Pasha and David L. Blaney, "Elusive Paradise: The Promise and Peril of Global Civil Society," *Alternatives*, no. 23, 1988, pp. 417–50.

25. On the emerging regional civil society, see Abelardo Morales G. and Martha Isabel Cranshaw, *Regionalismo Emergente: Redes de la Sociedad Civil E Integración Centroamericana*, San José 1997.

26. See, e.g., William I. Robinson, *Promoting Polyarchy: Globalization, US Intervention, and Hegemony*, Cambridge 1996; *A Faustian Bargain: US Intervention in the Nicaraguan Elections and American Foreign Policy in the Post-Cold War Era*, Boulder 1992; "Promoting Capitalist Polyarchy: The Case of Latin America," in Inoguchi, Ikenberry, and Cox (eds.), *American Democracy Promotion*, New York 2000.

27. See, e.g., organizations listed in National Endowment for Democracy, *Annual Reports*, Washington, D.C., various years, 1988–96.

28. See, *inter alia*, Abelardo Morales G. and Cranshaw, *Regionalism Emergent*.

29. UNDP, *Human Development Report*, New York 1993, p. 86.

30. "Sins of the Secular Missionaries," *The Economist*, January 29, 2000, p. 25 (article runs from p. 25 to p. 27).

31. For diverse discussion on the NGO debate and the issues raised here, see, *inter alia*, David Hulme and Michael Edwards (eds.), *NGOs, States, and Donors: Too Close for Comfort?*, New York 1997; Alan Fowler, "Distant Obligations: Speculations on NGO Funding and the Global Market," *Review of African Political Economy*, no. 55, 1992, pp. 9–29; Peggy Antrobus, "Funding for NGOs: Issues and Options," *World Development*, vol. 15, Supplement, 1987, pp. 95–102; Charles Elliot, "Some Aspects of the Relationship Between the North and South in the NGO Sector," *World Development*, vol. 15, Supplement, 1987, pp. 57–68; Telmo Rudi Frantz, "The Role of NGOs in the Strengthening of Civil Society," *World Development*, vol. 15, Supplement, 1987, pp. 121–8; Rema Hammami, "NGOs: The Professionalization of Politics," *Race and Class*, vol. 37, no. 2, pp. 51–63; Paula R. Newberg and Thomas Carothers, "Aiding and Defining Democracy," *World Policy Journal*, no. 2, Spring 1996, pp. 97–108; John Clark, *Democratizing Development: The Role of Voluntary Organizations*, London 1991; Robinson, *Promoting Polyarchy*; Lester. M. Salamon, "The Global Associational Revolution: The Rise of the Third Sector on the World Scene," *Occasional Papers*, no. 15, 1993, Baltimore: Institute for Policy Studies, Johns Hopkins University.

32. See, e.g., Salamon, "The Global Associational Revolution."
33. *Ibid.*, p. 1.
34. "Sins of the Secular Missionaries," *The Economist*, January 29, 2000, pp. 25–6 (article runs to p. 27).
35. *Ibid.*, p. 26.
36. Hulme and Edwards, *NGOs, States and Donors*, p. 6.
37. Ankie Hoogvelt, *Globalization and the Postcolonial World: The New Political Economy of Development*, Baltimore 1997.
38. Hoogvelt, *Globalization and the Postcolonial World*, p. 179. Despite her critique, Hoogvelt speaks approvingly of the NGO phenomenon (e.g., pp. 233–4), seemingly oblivious to the link between it and the "politics of exclusion" under global capitalism that she simultaneously analyzes.
39. Committee on Foreign Affairs, *The Private Enterprise Initiative*, p. xii.
40. Cited in Laura MacDonald, "A Mixed Blessing: The NGO Boom in Latin America," *NACLA Report on the Americas*, vol. 28, no. 5, March/April 1995, p. 32.
41. World Bank, *Cooperation Between the World Bank and NGOs: FY96 Progress Report*, Washington, D.C.: World Bank, NGO Group, Social Development Department, August 1997, p. 23.
42. UNDP, *Human Development Report*, p. 93.
43. Petras, "A Marxist Critique of Post-Marxists," pp. 35, 38–9, 44.
44. UNDP, *Human Development Report*, p. 5.
45. *Ibid.*, p. 39.
46. See, *inter alia*, Hammami, "NGOs: The Professionalization of Politics"; Robinson, *Promoting Polyarchy*; Hoogvelt, *Globalization and the Postcolonial World*; Fowler, "Distant Obligations"; various contributions in Hulme and Edwards.
47. Fowler, "Distant Obligations," p. 25.
48. Tim Draimin, "Potential for Partnership: International Cooperation Institutions and Canadian and Latin American NGOs," discussion paper prepared for the International Development Research Center, Ottawa, Ontario, July 1994, p. 12, as cited in Laura Macdonald, "A Mixed Blessing: The NGO Boom in Latin America," p. 31.
49. The Albuquerque-based Inter-Hemispheric Resource Center produced a series of reports documenting AID support for NGOs in Central America. These include *Private Organizations with US Connections in El Salvador*, *Private Organizations with US Connections in Guatemala*, and *Private Organizations with US Connections in Honduras*, all published in Albuquerque, 1988.
50. Lisa Haugaard, "Development Aid: Some Small Steps Forward," *NACLA Report on the Americas*, vol. 31, no. 2, Sept/Oct. 1997, pp. 29–34.
51. Kevin Murray, *Inside El Salvador*, Albuquerque 1995, p. 246, nt. 41.
52. Adam Flint, "Social Movements, NGOs and the State: Contesting Political Space in the Transition to Democracy in El Salvador," paper presented at the Latin America Studies Association meeting, September 26, 1998, Chicago, p. 11.
53. Tom Barry, *Inside Guatemala*, Albuquerque 1992, p. 134.
54. Kent Norsworthy, *Inside Honduras*, Albuquerque 1993, p. 119.
55. See Robinson, *A Faustian Bargain*, esp. chapter six.
56. Macdonald, *Supporting Civil Society*, p. 107.
57. *Ibid.*, pp. 60, 64.
58. Silvia Lara, *Inside Costa Rica*, Albuquerque 1995, pp. 102–103. Lara notes: "The Private Agencies Collaborating Together (PACT) representative in Costa Rica confided that AID created ACORDE as a 'funding window' for NGOs and that

it is now 'the only show in town when it comes to getting big bucks for NGO work'." *Ibid.*, p. 103. See also Macdonald, *Supporting Civil Society*, pp. 63–4.

59. Macdonald, *Supporting Civil Society*, esp. pp. 23–4.

60. *Ibid.*, p. 24.

61. *Ibid.*

62. Cited in *ibid.*, p. 6. Jara concludes: "To what point does the situation of crisis lead to the justification of mechanisms which, fundamentally, allow groups to survive the crisis, and to perpetuate themselves, without really changing the mechanisms of domination?"

63. *Ibid.*, p. 88.

64. Cited in *ibid.*, p. 69.

65. Philip McMichael, *Development and Social Change*, Thousand Oaks 1996, p. 133.

66. *Ibid.* On privatization under neo-liberalism and globalization more generally, see the excellent study by Brendan Martin, *In the Public Interest? Privatization and Public Sector Reform*, London 1993.

67. On financial speculation and the Kodratieff cycles, see Giovanni Arrighi, *The Long Twentieth Century*, London 1994. On "casino capitalism," see Susan Strange, *Casino Capitalism*, Oxford 1986.

68. World Bank, *World Development Report 1989: Financial Systems and Development*, Washington, D.C., 1989.

69. Michel Camdessus, press conference, October 4, 1996, Washington, D.C., as cited in David Barkin, Irene Ortiz, and Fred Rosen, "Globalization and Resistance: The Remaking of Mexico," *NACLA Report on the Americas*, vol. 30, no. 4, Jan/Feb. 1997, p. 16.

70. World Bank, *World Development Report 1989*.

71. AID, *Economic Assistance Strategy for Central America 1991–2000*, Washington, D.C.: AID, January 1991, p. 17.

72. The first commercial bank was established in Costa Rica in 1864. A second, in Guatemala in 1874, followed in El Salvador, Nicaragua, and Honduras in 1880, 1887, and 1889, respectively. See Victor Bulmer-Thomas, *The Political Economy of Central America Since 1920*, Cambridge 1987, pp. 4–5, table 1.1. See *ibid.*, pp. 28–33 on the financial reforms carried out in the second and third decade of the twentieth century. See Trevor Evans, *Liberalización Financiera y Capital Bancario en America Central*, Managua 1998, p. 4, on the establishment of Central Banks. The following section draws heavily on Evans's superb study.

73. On this history, see Evans, *ibid.*, chapters one to three.

74. *Ibid.*, p. 12.

75. *Ibid.*, p. 13.

76. See *Ibid.*, pp. 14, and p. 14–20 on the following summary of the financial reforms.

77. The following table documents interest-rate liberalization:

	Initial Adjustments to Establish Real Rates	Complete Liberalization
Costa Rica	1983	1989
El Salvador	1989	1991
Guatemala	–	1989
Honduras	1990	1991
Nicaragua	1988	1992–93

Source: CEPAL, *El Regionalismo Abierto en America Central*, Mexico, January 1995, p. 13, as reported in Evans, *Liberalización Financiera*, p. 16, table 1.

78. See chapter three, and also Evans, *Liberalización Financiera*, pp. 24–5. The private banks' proportion of the supply of internal credit rose from 4.6 percent in 1983, to 15.3 percent in 1986, 29.1 percent in 1990, and 48 percent in 1995. Evans, *ibid.*

79. The Nicaraguan constitution approved under the Sandinista government in 1986 had actually stipulated that banks must be public, a stipulation that the Chamorro government skirted through dubious legality. The following table indicates the expansion of private banking activities in Nicaragua.

Participation in Nicaragua of Private Banks in Commercial Activity (in percentages)

Year	Deposits	Credits	Credit Flows (in millions $)
1991	17.2	1.1	2.6
1992	40.6	14.0	53.5
1993	53.4	18.6	22.7
1994	58.7	34.1	111.9
1995	60.0	46.5	152.8

Source: Central Bank of Nicaragua, *Informe Anual*, 1994 and 1995, as cited in Evans, *Liberalización Financiera*, p. 45, table 3.

80. For this data, see Evans, *Liberalización Financiera*, Annex 1.1 to 1.5, pp. 104–108. Evans reports that in 1995, the Salvadoran private banks had reserves of $4.2 billion; the Guatemalan banks, $4 billion; Costa Rican, $3.7 billion; Honduran, $1.3 billion; and Nicaraguan, $1 billion. (Pp. 18–19.) I am unaware of any study on the distribution of profits in Central America between banking and other sectors of capital. But Evans reports that the largest private bank in the region, El Salvador's *Banco Agricola Comercial* registered a 35 percent profit rate in 1985, while Nicaragua's largest private bank, the *Banco de America Central*, reported a 52 percent rate. (p. 17). In addition, private bank profit rates in Honduras went up from 18 percent before liberalization to 40 percent following liberalization in 1992, and had settled at 24 percent by 1995. Evans, p. 38.

81. *Ibid.*, p. 20, and pp. 50–65.

82. Evans, *Liberalización Financiera*, p. 37.

83. For these details, see Tom Barry, *Inside Guatemala*, Albuquerque 1992, pp. 88–91. In 1992, payments on the external debt represented 12 percent of government expenditure and domestic debt, 15 percent. *Ibid.*, p. 89. See also Evans, *Liberalización Financiera*, pp. 33–7.

84. Barry, *Ibid.*

85. Evans, *Liberalización Financiera*, pp. 17, 28

86. *Ibid.*, p. 17.

87. For all these details, see Evans, *Liberalización Financiera*, p. 74, who summarizes several studies by Central American researchers on these issues.

88. José Luis Velázquez, *Los Nuevos Grupos Empresariales en Nicaragua*, Managua 1994.

89. Mario Francisco Flores, *El Capital Financier en Honduras*, Master's Thesis, Economic and Development Planning Post-Graduate Program, Autonomous University of Honduras, Tegucigalpa, as cited and discussed in Evans, *Liberalización Financiera*, p. 71.

90. Carlos Sojo, "En El Nombre del Padre: Patrimonialismo y Democracia en Costa

Rica," in Manuel Rojas and Carlos Sojo (eds.), *El Malestar con la Política*, San Jose 1995, p. 65.

91. Evans, *Liberalización Financiera*, p. 73.

92. Evans, *Liberalización Financiera*, chapter six, and esp. p. 89. Real interest rates averaged between 10 and 20 percent in the first part of the 1990s.

93. Evans, *Liberalización Financiera*, p. 69.

94. Pablo Gentili, "The Permanent Crisis of the Public University," *NACLA Report on the Americas*, vol. 33, no. 4, Jan/Feb. 2000, pp. 12–18 (on delegation, see specifically, pp. 15–16). The AID's Private Enterprise Initiative called for the private sector to administer social services. See *The Private Enterprise Initiative of the Agency for International Development*, Committee on Foreign Affairs, US House of Representatives (Congressional Research Service, Library of Congress), September 1989, 101st Congress, 1st Session, Washington, D.C. 1989, pp. 13–14. On the issues in this section, also see Martin, *In the Public Interest?*.

95. Silvia Lara, *Inside Costa Rica*, Albuquerque 1995, pp. 66, 70.

96. See, e.g., Susanne Andersson, "New National Health Care Policy: Undercover Privatization," *Barricada International*, vol. 13, no. 367/8, Nov.–Dec. 1993, pp. 12–13.

97. Murray, *Inside El Salvador*, pp. 129–31.

98. Barry, *Inside Guatemala*, p. 172. See pp. 160–74 for a summary of the deterioration of health and welfare services under neo-liberal policies.

99. Antonio Ugalde and Jeffrey T. Jackson, "The World Bank and International Health Policy: A Critical Review," *Journal of International Development*, vol. 7, no. 3, 1995, p. 525. The article runs from pp. 525–41 and provides an excellent critique of the Bank's rationale in its neo-liberal health policies.

100. See Howeard Waitzkin and Celia Iriat, "How the United States Exports Managed Care to Third-World Countries," *Monthly Review*, vol. 52, no. 1, May 2000, pp. 21–35.

101. World Bank, *World Development Report 1993: Investing in Health*, New York 1993. Citation is from p. 46.

102. Economic Commission for Latin America and the Caribbean (CEPAL), *El Perfil de la Pobreza en America Latina a Comienzos de los Años 90*, Santiago November 1992, as cited in Carlos Vilas, "Neo-liberal Social Policy: Managing Poverty (Somehow)," *NACLA Report on the Americas*, vol. 29, no. 16, May/June 1996, p. 16.

103. See John Walton and David Seddon, *Free Markets and Food Riots: The Politics of Global Adjustment*, Oxford 1994.

104. See, *inter alia*, Karin Stahl, "Anti-Poverty Programs: Making Structural Adjustment More Palatable," *NACLA Report on the Americas*, vol. 29, no. 6, 1996, pp. 32–6; James Petras, "A Marxist Critique of Post-Marxists," *Links*, no. 9, 1997/1998, pp. 27–48; Henry Veltmeyer, "Latin America in the New World Order," *The Canadian Journal of Sociology*, vol. 22, no. 2, 1997, pp. 297–342.

105. Vilas, "Neo-liberal Social Policy," pp. 16, 18.

106. John Ruthrauff, "El Papel de Fondos de Inversion Social en Centro America," report by the Center for Democratic Education (CDE), Silver Spring, MD, 1996. The CDE is a Washington-based NGO that monitors IFI programs in Central America and provides consultation services to Central American development NGOs. On the FIS in each country, see Lael Parish, "Guatemala's Social Fund: Its Relationship with Non-Governmental Organizations and Poverty Alleviation," Silver Spring 1996; Joshua Lichtenseign and Richard Jones,

"El Salvador's Social Investment Fund: Its Role in Development and Poverty Alleviation," Silver Spring 1995; Maria Rosa Renzi, Mario J. Cangiani, and Sonia Agurto, "Impacto de los Proyectos FISE en las Condiciones de Vida de Los Nicaraguenses," Fundacion Internacional para el Desafio Economico Global (FIDEG), Managua 1994. On the World Bank's own assessment of these Funds more generally, see *Poverty Alleviation and Social Investment Funds: The Latin American Experience*, World Bank Discussion Papers, no. 261, Washington, D.C. 1994.

107. See, e.g., sources cited in *ibid.*

108. Murray, *Inside El Salvador*, p. 113.

109. See, e.g., Lester C. Thurow, "Poverty and Human Capital," in David M. Gordon (ed.), *Problems in Political Economy: An Urban Perspective*, Lexington 1969, pp. 457–77.

110. See Doeringer and Piore, *Internal Labor Markets and Manpower Analysis*, Lexington 1971.

111. David M. Gordon, Richard C. Edwards, and Michael Reich, *Segmented Work, Divided Workers: The Historical Transformation of Labor in the United States*, Cambridge 1982. For general discussion, see Paul A. Attewell, *Radical Political Economy from the Sixties*, New Brunswick 1984, chapter three, "Theories of Economic Segmentation and Poverty," pp. 40–92.

112. See, *inter alia*, Michael Porter, *The Competitive Advantage of Nations*, London 1990.

113. As cited in Doug Henwood, "Impeccable Logic: Trade, Development, and Free Markets in the Clinton Era," *NACLA Report on the Americas*, vol. 26, no. 5, 1993, p. 26.

114. As cited in Peter Stalker, *Workers Without Frontiers: The Impact of Globalization on International Migration*, Boulder 2000, p. 71.

115. Jeremy Brecher and Tim Costello, *Global Village or Global Pillage? Economic Reconstruction from the Bottom Up*, Boston 1994.

116. Juan Bautista Arrien, "Does a Trap Lurk Behind the Struggle for 6%," *ENVIO*, vol. 214, no. 16, Oct. 1997, pp. 18–22.

117. See Lucien O. Chauvin, "Future at Risk: Rethinking Education in Latin America," *Latinamerica Press*, vol. 29, no. 38, Oct. 16, 1997, p. 10.

118. *Ibid.*

119. See, e.g., World Bank, *World Development Report 1995: Workers in an Integrated World*, New York 1995; Interamerican Development Bank, *Economic and Social Progress in Latin America*, Baltimore 1993.

120. For critical discussion on these issues, see, *inter alia*, Chauvin, "Future at Risk"; Arrien, "Does a Trap Lurk Behind . . ." Arrien was an advisor to UNESCO on educational policy and coordinator of the Program to Promote Educational Reform in Latin America (PRESAL).

121. Paul Jeffrey, "Battle for the Soul of the Universities," *Latinamerica Press*, vol. 29, no. 38, October 16, 1997, p. 5.

122. Arrien, "Does a Trap Lurk Behind . . .", p. 20.

123. Murray, *Inside El Salvador*, pp. 121–24.

124. Lara, *Inside Costa Rica*, p. 68.

125. Harry Braverman, *Labor and Monopoly Capital: The Degradation of Work in the Twentieth Century*, New York 1974.

126. Pablo Gonzalez Casanova, "The Future of Education and the Future of Work," *NACLA Report on the Americas*, vol. 33, no. 4, Jan/Feb. 2000, p. 38.

127. Chauvin, "Future at Risk," p. 2.

128. For discussion on these issues, see Vilas, "Neo-liberal Social Policy," pp. 16–25.

129. *Capital*, Vol. I, New York 1967 [1867], p. 716.

130. Eric Hobsbawm, *The Long Twentieth Century*, New York 1994, p. 289.

131. It is not possible to revisit here these debates, but see, *inter alia*, Teodor Shanin (ed.), *Peasants and Peasant Societies*, New York 1987; Howard Newby, *International Perspectives in Rural Sociology*, New York 1987; David Goodman and Michael Redclift, *From Peasant to Proletarian: Capitalist Development and Agrarian Transitions*, New York 1982; and *Journal of Peasant Studies*.

132. See Farshad A. Araghi, "Global Depeasantization, 1945–1990," *The Sociological Quarterly*, vol. 36, no. 2, 1995, pp. 337–68, and esp. pp. 338–44 for a summary of these theses.

133. I tend to support De Janvry's contention that "there is no theoretical possibility for peasants to remain in their contradictory class position. However lengthy and painful the process may be, their future is full incorporation into one of the other of these two essential classes of capitalism." Alain De Janvry, *The Agrarian Question and Reformism in Latin America*, Baltimore 1981, p. 32. I support this disappearance thesis, not because it *has to* happen by some teleological *fiat* but because the historical evidence suggests that it *is* happening, and because *why* it is happening can be explained by the dynamics of capitalism. Also, the "peasant question" debate has been misrepresented by some advancing the permanence thesis with the conflation of the peasantry with the rural poor, such that the persistence of a poor and exploited rural population is taken as evidence of the persistence of a peasantry in class terms. Also, note that in the mid-1990s, the World Bank reported that for the first time in history less than half the world's labor force, 49%, worked in agriculture. Mark Edelman, "The Persistence of the Peasantry," *NACLA Report on the Americas*, vol. 33, no. 5, March/April 2000, p. 14.

134. William Durham, *Scarcity and Survival in Central America*, Stanford 1979.

135. Charles D. Brockett, *Land, Power, and Poverty: Agrarian Transformation and Political Conflict in Central America*, second edition, Boulder 1998, p. 73.

136. Brockett, *ibid.*, p. 3.

137. To reiterate, debate and theoretical complexity rage in the study of peasant societies and capitalist transformation and the theme cannot be adequately dealt with here. For summary discussion of key theoretical issues alluded to in this section, see Henry Bernstein, "Agrarian Classes in Capitalist Development," pp. 40–71, in Leslie Sklair (ed.), *Capitalism and Development*, London 1994.

138. José Luis Rocha, "On the Death of BANADES (r.i.p.)," *ENVÍO*, vol. 17, no. 200, March 1998, p. 25 (article runs from pp. 24–32).

139. See, e.g., Rocha, *ibid.*; Evans, *Liberalización Financiera*, pp. 47–8; Isabel Dauner, "Banks, Mini-Banks and Rural Producers," *ENVÍO*, vol. 17, no. 198, January 1998, pp. 23–9.

140. Evans, *Liberalización Financiera*, p. 26.

141. Evans, *Liberalización Financiera*, p. 42.

142. See, e.g., the entire special issue of *NACLA Report on the Americas* dedicated to this theme, "Adelante! The New Rural Activism in the Americas," vol. 33, no. 5, March/April 2000.

143. Marc Edelman, *Peasants Against Globalization: Rural Social Movements in Costa Rica*, Stanford 1999.

144. See, *inter alia*, David Harvey, *The Condition of Post-Modernity*, Oxford 1990; Robert Cox, *Production, Power, and World Order*, New York 1987; Jeremy Rifkin, *The End of Work: The Decline of the Global Labor Force and the Dawn of the Post-*

Market Era, New York 1995; Alain Lipietz, *Mirages and Miracles: The Crisis of Global Fordism*, London 1987; Dicken, *Global Shift*; Frobel, *et al.*, *The New International Division of Labor*; Hoogvelt, *Globalization and the Postcolonial World*.

145. On the hegemony of capital and political regimes of accumulation, see Buroway, *Manufacturing Consent: Changes in the Labor Process Under Capitalism*, Chicago 1979. On social structures of accumulation, see David M. Kotz, Terrence McDonought, and Michael Reich, *Social Structures of Accumulation: The Political Economy of Growth and Crisis*, Cambridge 1994.

146. For a summary of this neo-liberal line of reasoning, see Victor Bulmer-Thomas, "Introduction," and Jim Thomas, "The New Economic Model and Labor Markets in Latin America," in Bulmer-Thomas (ed.), *The New Economic Model in Latin America and its Impact on Income Distribution and Poverty*, New York 1996.

147. Rifkin, *The End of Work*.

148. In 1996 the ILO reported that chronic unemployment is worsening worldwide, that nearly one third of the world's EAP was unemployed, and that the phenomenon affects the rich as well as the poor countries. ILO, *World Employment Report 1996–7*, Geneva 1996.

149. Manuel Castells and Alejandro Portes (eds.), *The Informal Economy: Studies in Advanced and Less Developed Countries*, Baltimore 1989. Castells and Portes define the informal economy as "the unregulated production and distribution of licit products," "Introduction," p. 15.

150. McMichael, *Development and Social Change*, p. 195.

151. The ILO figure is cited in Henry Veltmeyer, "Latin America in the New World Order," *The Canadian Journal of Sociology*, vol. 22, no. 2, 1997, p. 220. For the 1990s figure, see Carlos Vilas, "The Decline of the Steady Job in Latin America," *NACLA Report on the Americas*, vol. 32, no. 4, Jan/Feb 1999, p. 15. See also Bulmer-Thomas, "The New Economic Model and Labor Markets," p. 88, table 2, for data on the increase in informal sector employment in Latin American countries between 1980 and 1992.

152. Veltmeyer, "Latin America in the New World Order," p. 22.

153. See: Juan Pablo Pérez Sáinz, "Mercado Laboral E Integraction Social en los Tiempos de la Globalization: Reflexiones Desde Centroamerica," paper presented to the 1999 meeting of the American Sociological Association, Chicago, August 6–10, 1999; Sáinz, *De la Finca a La Maquila*, San José 1996; Juan Pablo Pérez Sáinz and Allen Cordero, *Globalización, Empleo y Politicas Laborales en America Central*, San José 1997; Paul Bodson, Allen Cordero, and Juan Pablo Pérez Sáinz, *Las Nuevas Caras del Empleo*, San José 1995; various entries in Sáinz (ed.), *Globalizatión y Fuerza Laboral en Centroamerica*, San José 1994.

154. On these issues, see Sáinz, "Mercado Laboral E Integracion Social en los Tiempos de la Globalización," and on labor market reform, see Sáinz and Cordero, *Globalización, Empleo y Politicas Laborales*, esp. pp. 52–77.

155. John D. Abell, "The Neo-Liberal World Order: The View from The Highlands," *NACLA Report on the Americas*, vol. 33, no. 1, July/Aug. 1999, p. 39.

156. Manuel Angel Castillo, "Migration, Development and Peace in Central America," in Alan B. Simmons (ed.), *International Migration, Refugee Flows and Human Rights in North America: The Impact of Free Trade and Restructuring*, New York 1996, pp. 145–6.

157. Castells and Portes (eds.), *The Informal Economy*.

158. Alejandro Portes, "Latin America Class Structure," *Latin American Research Review*, vol. 2, no. 3, 1985, p. 15.

159. For these details, see Sáinz, *De la Finca a la Maquila*, pp. 186–91.

160. Sáinz, "Mercado Laboral e Integracion Social," p. 6.
161. This data by the United Nations Regional Employment Program for Latin America (PREALA), is summarized by Sáinz, in *De la Finca a la Maquila*, p. 108, table 12. The dramatic improvement of indicators for Honduras does not correspond to the country's economic performance and Sáinz attributes it to two factors. First is unidentified methodological flaws in the PREALA data collection and estimations. See also Sáinz and Cordero, *Globalización, Empleo y Políticas Laborales*, pp. 17–18. Second is the very rapid growth in maquila employment and, secondarily, in NTAE employment. In fact, according to the household survey administered by Sáinz and Cordero, employment in these two sectors, along with tourism, increased by an astounding annual average of 42 percent between 1989 and 1992. *Ibid.*, p. 29, and p. 31, table 4.
162. Sáinz, *De la Finca a la Maquila*, p. 131.
163. *Ibid.*, p. 134. Regarding the age brackets, "informality has been a gateway to the labor market for new members of the labor force as well as a mechanism to prolong participation in the market" in the face of the contraction of formal employment. *Ibid.*, pp. 131–2.
164. Sáinz, *De la Finca a la Maquila*, p. 133, table 17.
165. The AID's "Private Enterprise Initiative," for instance, called for funding micro-enterprise projects as part of the policy of expanding assistance to private business, and by 1989 had already invested $290 million in 87 projects around the world. See US House of Representatives, *The Private Enterprise Initiative of the Agency for International Development*, p. ix. The World Bank and the Intera-merican Development Bank also funded several micro-enterprise programs in Central America. See Sáinz and Cordero, *Globalización, Empleo y Políticas Labor-ales*, p. 77, table 16.
166. Hernando de Soto, *El Otro Sendero: La Revolución Informal*, Lima 1986. The micro-enterprise strategy has also become popular among First World Liberals following the experience of the Grameen Bank in Bangladesh, which has gained worldwide attention with its policies of making loans to poor women. While the issue cannot be explored here, the Grameen Bank does not deserve its reputation as a democratic and progressive form of liberation for the poor, and especially women, in that country, and has actually become an ideological bonanza for the transnational elite, including the World Bank and several TNCs that support the Grameen Bank (among them, Monsanto). The loan program serves to depoliticize the most oppressed sector of Bangladesh society, to fragment communities and draw them into a web of market relations. See Sarah Blackstock, "Bandaid Bandwagon," *New Internationalist*, no. 314, July 1999, p. 23, who notes that based on the Grameen experience, micro-loans promoted by the IFIs are increasing worldwide at a rate of 30 to 40 percent every year.
167. Sáinz, *De la Finca a la Maquila*, p. 135.
168. On the Sarchi case, see Sáinz, *De la Finca a la Maquila*, and also Sáinz, "Entre lo Global y lo Local: Economias Comunitarias en Centroamerica," *Sociologia de Trabajo*, no. 30, 1997, pp. 3–19.
169. Jorge Escoto and Manfredo Marroquín, *La Aid en Guatemala*, Managua 1992, p. 86.
170. Sáinz and Cordero, *Globalización, Empleo y Políticas Laborales*, p. 76.
171. On migration and globalization, and more generally on capitalism and migra-tion, see, *inter alia*, Peter Stalker, *Workers Without Frontiers*; Robin Cohen, *The New Helots: Migration in the International Division of Labor*, Avebury 1987;

Nigel Harris, *The New Untouchables: Immigration and the New World Worker*, London 1995; Stephen Castles and Mark J. Miller, *The Age of Migration: International Population Movements in the Modern World*, New York 1993; Lydia Potts, *The World Labor Market: A History of Migration*, London 1990. For an excellent discussion of current topics and new directions in the sociology of migration, see Alejandro Portes, "Immigrant Theory for a New Century: Some Problems and Opportunities," *International Migration Review*, vol. 3, no. 4, 1997, pp. 799–825.

172. Potts, *The World Labor Market*.

173. Alejandro Portes and Jozsef Borocz, "Contemporary Immigration: Theoretical Perspectives on its Determinants and Modes of Incorporation," *International Migration Review*, vol. xxiii, no. 3, 1990, pp. 606–30.

174. Portes and Borocz, "Contemporary Immigration: Theoretical Perspectives," p. 612.

175. Saskia Sassen, *The Mobility of Labor and Capital: A Study in International Investment and Labor Flows*, Cambridge 1988.

176. See, e.g., Alejandro Portes, "Transnational Communities: Their Emergence and Significance in the Contemporary World-System," *Working Papers #16*, April 1995, Department of Sociology, The Johns Hopkins University, Baltimore; "Global Villagers: The Rise of Transnational Communities," *The American Prospect*, no. 25, March–April 1996, pp. 74–7.

177. Portes, "Global Villagers," pp. 76–7.

178. Although the issue cannot be explored here, the politics of transnational communities are not neutral and they can be fomented by states in the interests of transnational capital. The Mexican government, for instance, created in 1990 the "Program for Mexican Communities Abroad" to facilitate projects cosponsored by the government and transnational communities, with the goals of getting NAFTA passed, pursing US–Mexico economic integration, and dampening support among Mexican immigrant groups for the presidential candidacy of opposition leader Cuahtémoc Cárdenas. See Robert C. Smith, "Mexican Immigrants, the Mexican State, and the Transnational Practice of Mexican Politics and Membership," *LASA Forum*, vol. 29, no. 2, 1998, pp. 19–21.

179. McMichael, *Development and Social Change*.

180. Sassen, *The Mobility of Capital and Labor*, p. 31.

181. Hence political borders *do* reproduce a global hierarchy, as Aristide A. Zolberg suggests. See "The Next Waves: Migration Theory for a Changing World," *International Migration Review*, vol. 23, no. 3, 1989, pp. 403–30. But that hierarchy is no longer nation-state ordered.

182. On these issues, see, e.g., the entire special issue of *NACLA Report on the Americas*, "The Immigration Backlash," vol. 29, no. 3, 1995; Susanne Jonas and Suzie Dod Thomas (eds.), *Immigration: A Civil Rights Issue for the Americas*, Wilmington 1999; Juan F. Perea (ed.), *Immigrants Out! The New Nativism and the Anti-Immigrant Impulse in the United States*, New York 1997.

183. Peter Stalker, *Workers Without Frontiers*, p. 45. See also Hector Figueroa, "In the Name of Fashion: Exploitation in the Garment Industry," *NACLA Report on the Americas*, vol. 29, no. 4, 1996, pp. 34–41.

184. See, e.g., Manuel Angel Castillo G. and Silvia Irene Palma C., *La Emigración Internacional en Centroamerica: Una Revision de Tendencias e Impactos*, Guatemala 1996, esp. chapter one, "Tendencias Recientes de la Migracion Internacional en Centroamerica," pp. 23–51. See also Castillo, "Migration, Development and Peace in Central America," in Alan B. Simmons (ed.), *International Migration,*

Refugee Flows and Human Rights in North America: The Impact of Free Trade and Restructuring, New York 1996, pp. 137–55.

185. Comisión Económica para America Latina y el Caribe (CEPAL), "Informe Especial: Emigrantes: de la Sobrevivencia a Pilares de la Economia," as reproduced in *Inforpress Centroamericana*, no. 967, 23 January 1992 (special insert without page numbers), and as discussed in William I. Robinson, "The Global Economy and the Latino Populations in the United States: A World Systems Approach," *Critical Sociology*, vol. 19, no. 2, 1993, pp. 29–59. For these figures on internal displacements and intra-regional migration, see Castillo, "Migration, Development and Peace in Central America," pp. 144–5. The US government estimated 2.2 million Central Americans in the United States in 1997, including those undocumented. See US Bureau of the Census, March 1997, Current Population Survey, table 3–4, "Country or Area of Birth of the Foreign-Born Population From Latin America and Northern America, 1997," at www.census.gov/population/ socdem/foreign/98/tab 03–4.pdf; and INS, "Illegal Alien Resident Population, Table 1", at http://www.ins.usdoj.gov/graphics/aboutins/statistics/illegalalien/index.htm.

186. See Alejandro Rincon, Susanne Jonas, and Nestor Rodríguez, "La Inmigración Guatemalteca en los EEUU: 1980–1996," manuscript prepared for and summarized in United Nations Development Program, *Guatemala: El Rostro Rural del Desarrollo Humano*, Guatemala City 1999, as discussed in Jonas, *Of Centaurs and Doves*, pp. 224–5.

187. See Stalker, *Workers Without Frontiers*, table 3.4, on p. 28. El Salvador and Guatemala were second and third, only behind Mexico, and Honduras and Nicaragua were seventh and ninth.

188. See, e.g., the discussion on this with regard to El Salvador by Mario Lungo and Susan Kandel, "International Migration, Transnationalism and Socio-Cultural Changes in El Salvador's Sending Towns," paper presented at the 1998 meeting of the Latin America Studies Association, Chicago, September 24–26, 1998; more generally, Orozco, de la Garza, and Baraona, *Inmigración y Remesas Familiares*.

189. Portes and Borocz, "Contemporary Immigration: Theoretical Perspectives," pp. 612–3.

190. Robinson, "The Global Economy and the Latino Populations in the United States," pp. 29–59.

191. Harris, *The New Untouchables*.

192. See Robinson, "The Global Economy and the Latino Populations," pp. 50–51; entire special issue of *NACLA Report on the Americas*, "On the Line: Latinos on Labor's Cutting Edge," vol. 30, no. 3, Nov/Dec. 1996. On Central Americans in the Washington, D.C. area, see Terry A. Repak's intriguing monograph, *Waiting on Washington: Central American Workers in the Nation's Capital*, Philadelphia 1995.

193. See Robinson, *ibid.*, and for general treatment of the theme of migration, ethnic relations, and minority group formation, see *inter alia*, Castles and Miller, *The Age of Migration*, esp. chapters two (pp. 18–42) and seven (pp. 168–94).

194. McMichael, *Development and Social Change*, p. 189.

195. As cited in Petersen, pp. 139–140.

196. Ian M. Taplin, "Strategic Reorientations of US Apparel Firms," in Gary Gereffi and Miguel Korzeniewicz, *Commodity Chains and Global Capitalism*, Westport 1994, p. 221, ft. note 4.

197. *Ibid.*, p. 208.

198. See, *inter alia*, Abelardo Morales and Carlos Castro (eds.), *Inmigración Laboral Nicaraguense en Costa Rica*, San José 1999; Abelardo Morales, *Los Territorios del Cuajipal: Frontera y Sociedad Entre Nicaragua y Costa Rica*, San José 1997; Abelardo Morales (ed.), *Las Fronteras Desbordadas*, San José 1997; Patricia Alvarenga Venutolo, *Conflictiva Convivencia: Los Nicaraguenses en Costa Rica*, San José 1997; Martha I. Cranshaw and Abelardo Morales, *Mujeres Adolescentes y Migración entre Nicaragua y Costa Rica*, San José 1998.

199. Morales and Castro, *Inmigración Laboral Nicaraguense en Costa Rica*, p. 31. The figure of 30 percent of the Costa Rican population is from Brockett, *Land, Power, and Poverty*, p. 206.

200. See table 17, p. 55 in Morales and Castro, *ibid.*

201. Morales and Castro, *Inmigración Laboral Nicaraguense*, p. 54.

202. *Ibid.*, p. 15.

203. *Ibid.*, pp. 12–13.

204. *Ibid.*, p. 17.

205. *Ibid.*, p. 18.

206. Patricia Alvarenga Venutolo, *Conflictiva Convivencia*.

207. *Ibid.*, p. 24.

208. *Ibid.*, pp. 17–18.

209. Morales and Castro, *Inmigración Laboral Nicaragueuse*, p. 25.

210. For detailed empirical treatment of the transborder region, see Morales, *Los Territorios del Cuajipal.*

211. Morales and Castro, *Ibid.*, p. 24.

212. Morales and Castro, *Ibid.*, p. 25.

213. Dicken, *Global Shift*, p. 64.

214. Morales and Castro, p. 27.

215. See, e.g., Castillo and Palma, *La Emigración Internacional en Centroamerica.*

216. See, e.g., Manuel Orozco, Rodolfo de la Garza, and Miguel Baraona, *Immigracion y Remesas Familiares*, San José 1997; Manuel Angel Castillo G. and Silvia Irene Palma C., *La Emigracion Internacional en Centroamerica: Una Revision de Tendencias e Impactos*, Guatemala City 1996; Mario Lungo and Susan Kandel, "International Migration, Transnationalism and Socio-Cultural Changes in El Salvador's Sending Towns," paper presented at the 1998 meeting of the Latin American Studies Association, Chicago, September 24–26, 1998; Stalker, *Workers Without Frontiers.*

217. Stalker, *Workers Without Frontiers*, p. 119.

218. Lungo and Kandel, "International Migration, Transnationalism, and Socio-Cultural Changes."

219. *Ibid.*, pp. 11, 13–14.

220. This literature is quite extensive. See, *inter alia*, June Nash and Maria Patricia Fernández-Kelly (eds.), *Women, Men, and the International Division of Labor*, Albany 1983; Diane Elson and Ruth Pearson, "Nimble Fingers Make Cheap Workers: An Analysis of Women's Employment in Third World Export Manufacturing," *Feminist Review*, Spring 1981, pp. 87–107; Maria Patricia Fernández-Kelly, *For We are Sold, I and My People: Women and Industry in Mexico's Frontier*, Albany 1983; Susan Joekes, *Women in the World Economy*, New York 1987; Susan Tiano, *Patriarchy on the Line: Labor, Gender, and Ideology in the Mexican Maquiladora Industry*, Philadelphia 1994. See also on the general issues addressed here, Maria Mies' well-known study, *Patriarchy and Accumulation on a World Scale: Women in the International Division of Labor*, London 1991.

221. For a good presentation of the WID literature, see Irene Tinker (ed.), *Persistent*

Inequalities: Women and World Development, New York 1990, and particularly, Tinker's own chapter, "The Making of a Field: Advocates, Practitioners, and Scholars," pp. 27–53; Maria Patricia Fernández Kelly, "Broadening The Scope: Gender and the Study of International Development," in Douglas Kincaid and Alejandro Portes (eds.), *Comparative National Development: Society and Economy in the New Global Order*, Chapel Hill 1994. See also Ester Boserup's famous 1970 study, *Women's Role in Economic Development*, New York.

222. See, *inter alia*, Lourdes Benería, "Gender and the Global Economy," in Arthur MacEwan and William K. Tabb (eds.), *Instability and Change in the World Economy*, New York 1989, pp. 241–58; Maria Mies, "Gender and Global Capitalism," in Leslie Sklair (ed.), *Capitalism and Development*, p. 107–22.

223. Lydia Potts, *The World Labour Market: A History of Migration*, London 1990, p. 291.

224. Guy Standing, "Global Feminization through Flexible Labor," *World Development*, vol. 17, no. 7, 1989, pp. 1077–95. Cite on p. 1077.

225. Valentine M. Moghadam, "Gender and Globalization: Female Labor and Women's Mobilization," *Journal of World-Systems Research*, http://csf.colorado.edu/wsystems/jwsr.html, vol. 5, no. 2, 1999, pp. 301–14. See p. 306.

226. United Nations Conference on Trade and Development (UNCTAD), *World Investment Report*, New York 1994, as cited in William I. Robinson, "Latin America in the Age of Inequality: Confronting the New 'Utopia'," *International Studies Review*, vol. 1, no. 3, Fall 1999, p. 55.

227. As cited in Maria Patricia Fernández-Kelly, "Political Economy and Gender in Latin America: The Emerging Dilemmas," Working Paper of the Latin America Program, No. 207, Washington, D.C. 1994, p. 17.

228. Standing, "Global Feminization through Flexible Labor."

229. Lourdes Beneria, "Gender and the Global Economy," in MacEwan and Tabb (eds.), *Instability and Change in the World Economy*, pp. 250–1.

230. See, *inter alia*, Lourdes Benería and Shelly Feldman (eds.), *Unequal Burden: Economic Crisis, Persistent Poverty, and Women's Work*, Boulder 1992; Giovanni Cornia, "Adjustment at the Household Level: Potentials and Limitations of Survival Strategies," in Giovanni Cornia, Richard Jolly, and Stewart Francis (eds.), *Adjustment with a Human Face*. New York and Oxford 1987, pp. 187–215; various entries in Christine E. Bose and Edna Acosta-Belen (eds.), *Women in the Latin American Development Process*, Philadelphia 1995; Helen Safa, *The Myth of the Male Breadwinner: Women and Industrialization in the Caribbean*, Boulder 1994; Moghadam, "Gender and Globalization."

231. Veltmeyer, "Latin America in the New World Order," p. 224.

232. World Bank, *Poverty and Income Distribution in Latin America: The Story of the 1980s*, Washington, D.C. 1997, p. 48.

233. Veltmeyer, "Latin America in the New World Order," p. 220.

234. Francesca Miller, "Latin American Women and the Search for Social, Political, and Economic Transformation," in Sandor Halebsky and Richard L. Harris (eds.), *Capital, Power, and Inequality in Latin America*, Boulder 1995, p. 182.

235. A. Alberti, "Impact of Participation in Non-Traditional Agricultural Export Production on the Employment, Income, and Quality of Life of Women in Guatemala, Honduras, and Costa Rica," report submitted to the AID, Guatemala (Washington, D.C. 1991), as cited in Laura T. Raynolds, "Harnessing Women's Work: Restructuring Agricultural and Industrial Labor Forces in the Dominican Republic," *Economic Geography*, vol. 72, no. 2, 1998, p. 150.

236. Moghadam, "Gender and Globalization."
237. For one discussion on gender and family dimensions of Central American migration to the US, see Christine Zentgraf, "Deconstructing Central American Migration to Los Angeles: Women, Men, and Families," Occasional Paper Series, 1995, *Central Americans in California: Transnational Communities, Economies and Cultures*, Los Angeles, The Center for Multiethnic and Transnational Studies, University of Southern California.
238. M. A. Faune, "Central America's Families and Women: What Does Reality Say?," *ENVIO*, vol. 14, no. 168, 1995, pp. 27–34.
239. Lara, *Inside Costa Rica*, p. 104.
240. Murray, *Inside El Salvador*, p. 145.
241. United Nations Development Program, *Estado de la Region en Desarrollo Humano Sostenible*, San José 1999, pp. 14–15.
242. For a sampling, see Michael Burawoy, *et al.*, *Global Ethnography: Forces, Connections, and Imaginations in a Postmodern World*, Berkeley 2000; Arlie Russell Hoschchild and Barbara Ehrenreich (eds.), *Global Women: Essays on Women and Globalization*, New York 2002; and Rhacel Salazar Parreñas (ed.), *Servants of Globalization: Women, Migration and Domestic Work*, Stanford 2000.
243. Safa, *The Myth of the Male Breadwinner*; Safa, "Where the Big Fish Eat the Little Fish: Women's Work in the Free Trade Zones," *NACLA Report on the Americas*, vol. 30, no. 5, March-April 1997, pp. 31–6.
244. Faune, "Central American Families and Women," p. 27.
245. Robinson, "Latin America in the Age of Inequality," p. 53.
246. See, *inter alia*, Jane S. Jaquette, *The Women's Movement in Latin America*, Boulder 1994; Elizabeth Jelin (ed.), *Women and Social Change in Latin America*, London 1990.
247. Kees van der Pijl, "The History of Class Struggle: From Original Accumulation to Neo-Liberalism," *Monthly Review*, vol. 49, no. 1, 1997, pp. 28–44.
248. *Ibid.*, p. 228
249. For one summary of this debate as regards in particular Latin American women, see Kathryn B. Ward and Jean Larson Pyle, "Gender, Industrialization, Transnational Corporations, and Development," in Bose and Acosta-Belen, *Women in the Latin American Development Process*.
250. For one detailed analysis on this point, see Safa, *The Myth of the Male Breadwinner*.
251. Fernández-Kelly, "Political Economy and Gender in Latin America," p. 7.
252. Safa, "Women's Social Movements in Latin America."

5   The Contradictions of Global Capitalism and the Future of Central America

1. These figures are from CEPAL, *Economic Survey of Latin America and the Caribbean*, Annual Report for 1998–99.
2. GDP per capita in Costa Rica in that year was $2,063. In El Salvador, it was $1,271; in Guatemala, $977; in Honduras, $652; and in Nicaragua, $466. IDB, *Economic and Social Progress of Latin America*, Annual Report, 1998–99.
3. IDB, *Ibid.*
4. Eva Paus, "A Critical Look at Non-Traditional Export Demand," in Paus (ed.), *Struggle Against Dependence: Non-Traditional Export Growth in Central America and the Caribbean*, Boulder 1988, p. 205.

5. As cited in Kurt Petersen, *The Maquiladora Revolution in Guatemala*, Occasional Paper Series 2, New Haven 1992, p. 34.

6. For discussion, see Gary Gereffi and Wyman, *Manufacturing Miracles: Paths of Industrialization in Latin America and East Asia*, Princeton 1990.

7. See Gary Gereffi and Miguel Korzeniewicz (eds.), *Global Commodity Chains and Global Capitalism*, Westport 1994.

8. More optimistically, one report has suggested that Central America could move up the value-added chain *within* the garments industry, from the current "basic market" output of T-shirts, interior wear, and so forth, to the next tier, the "fashion basic market" (ladies' fashionwear), or even the top tier, the "fashion market," which would include high quality and designer fashion. See ILO, *La Industria Maquila en Centroamerica*, p. 21.

9. See, e.g., Thomas T. Vogel, Jr., "Costa Rica's Sales Pitch Lures High-Tech Giants Like Intel and Microsoft," *The Wall Street Journal*, April 2, 1998, pp. A-18; Serge F. Kovaleski, "High Technology's Top Banana?," *The Washington Post*, March 11, 1998, pp. C10, C12.

10. See Tom Barry, *Inside Guatemala*, Albuquerque 1992, p. 107. On the issue of market saturation and other limitations to NTAE expansion, see also, Escoto and Marroquín, *La AID en Guatemala*, pp. 60–66; Friedmann, *Exportaciones Agricolas No Tradicionales en El Salvador*, Conroy, *et al.*, *A Cautionary Tale*, and other sources cited in chapter four.

11. See, e.g., Latin America Data Base, "Opening the Canopy: Central American Forests Face Threats of Globalization and Sustainable Development," and "Region: Plan Puebla Panama Hunting for Private Investment," *Noticen*, Latin American Institute, University of New Mexico. vol. 7, no. 29, Aug. 8, 2002.

12. On the environmental crisis in Central America, see Daniel Faber, *Environment Under Fire: Imperialism and the Ecological Crisis in Central America*, New York 1993.

13. See, e.g., Jeffrey Paige, *Coffee and Power in Central America*, Cambridge MA 1997.

14. Victor Bulmer-Thomas, *The Political Economy of Central America Since 1920*, p. 277, Cambridge 1987.

15. Steven Hymer, *The Multinational Corporation: A Radical Approach*, Cambridge 1979, see esp., pp. 54–75.

16. Samir Amin, *Maldevelopment*, London 1990.

17. On this point, see Bulmer-Thomas, *The Political Economy of Central America Since 1920*. Bulmer-Thomas presents a time scheme that is somewhat different from that which I have advanced. In his scheme, there have been five phases in the development of the export-led model. The first, based on coffee and bananas, survived into the late 1940s. The second phase ran until the early 1960s and was based on agro-export diversification. The third phase occurred in the 1960s and was marked by regional ISI through the CACM. The fourth occurred in the 1970s "as each republic sought to emphasize non-traditional exports outside the region" as well as an expansion of intra-regional and traditional exports. The fifth phase in Bulmer-Thomas' scheme began with the demise of the CACM after 1981 "and involves a shift of attention away from the regional market in favor of traditional and non-traditional exports to the rest of the world" (pp. 275–6). This fifth stage, although Bulmer-Thomas does not discuss it, constitutes the transnational model.

18. See Karl Polanyi, *The Great Transformation*, Boston 1944. It is difficult not to conclude that in the following passage Polanyi is referring to Central America in the 1990s: "Robbed of the protective covering of cultural institutions, human beings would perish from the effects of social exposure; they would die as the

victims of acute social dislocation through vice, perversion, crime, and starvation. Nature would be reduced to its elements, neighborhoods and landscapes defiled, rivers polluted, military safety jeopardized, the power to produce food and raw materials destroyed" (p. 73).

19. See, *inter alia*, the series of studies published by FLACSO on the spread of poverty and immizeration in the 1990s, including: Carlos Sojo, *Los de en Medio: La Nueva Pobreza en Costa Rica*, San José 1997; Maria Rosa Renzi and Kirk Kruijt, *Los Nuevos Pobres: Gobernabilidad y Política Social en Nicaragua*, San José 1997; Jose Rafaél del Cid and Dirk Kruijt, *Los Pobres Cuentan: Pobreza y Gobernabilidad en Honduras*, San José 1997.

20. Karen Hansen-Kuhn, *Structural Adjustment in Costa Rica: Eroding the Egalitarian Tradition*, Washington, D.C. 1995, p. 25.

21. Hansen-Kuhn, *Structural Adjustment in El Salvador: An Alternative Emerges*, Washington, D.C. 1995, p. 34.

22. UNDP, *Human Development Report*, New York 1997.

23. UNDP, Proyecto de Estado de la Region, *Estado de la Region en Desarrollo Humano Sostenible: Resumen*, San José 1999.

24. Apart from Costa Rica, adult illiteracy rates in the 1990s, after Haiti, were the highest in the Western hemisphere, one important social indicator of the severe levels of underdevelopment that continue to prevail in the region in the aftermath of the transitions, as shown below.

Adult Illiteracy Rates in Central America Compared to Other Latin American Countries, 1995 (percentage of total population)

Central America:	
Costa Rica	5.2
El Salvador	28.5
Guatemala	44.4
Honduras	27.3
Nicaragua	34.3
Select Other Countries:	
Argentina	3.8
Bolivia	16.9
Brazil	16.7
Colombia	8.7
Dominican Republic	17.9
Ecuador	9.9
Haiti	55.0
Mexico	10.4
Peru	11.3

Source: 1998 UNESCO Statistical Yearbook, as reported in "Education in Latin America and the Caribbean at a Glance," table appearing on p. 17 in *NACLA Report on the Americas*, vol. 33, no. 4, Jan/Feb. 2000.

25. UNDP, *Estado de la Region*, 1999.

26. This data is from UNDP, *Estado de la Region*, pp. 22–3.

27. For this and related data, see UNDP, *Estado de la Region en Desarrollo Humano Sostenible* (summary version), San José, 1999, pp. 12, 20; Chandrika Kaul and Valerie Tomaselli Moschovitis, *Statistical Handbook on Poverty in the Developing World*, Phoenix 1999, various tables.

28. UNDP, as cited in Stalker, *Workers Without Frontiers*, p. 139.
29. Roberto Patricio Korzeniewicz and Timothy Patrick Moran, "World Economic Trends in The Distribution of Income, 1965–1992," *American Journal of Sociology*, vol. 102, no. 4, January 1997.
30. See, *inter alia*, Will Hutton, *The State We're In*, London 1995; Ankie Hoogvelt, *Globalization and the Postcolonial World: The New Political Economy of Development*, Baltimore 1997.
31. Leslie Sklair, *Sociology of The Global System*, Baltimore 1995, p. 44.
32. As cited in Hoogvelt, *Globalization and the Postcolonial World*, p. 83. See also Jerry Harris, "Globalisation and the Technological Transformation of Capitalism," *Race and Class*, vol. 40, no. 2/3, Oct. 1998–March 1999, pp. 29–30.
33. See, *inter alia*, Edward J. Blakely and Mary Gail Snyder, *Fortress America: Gated Communities in the United States*, Washington, D.C.: Brookings and Cambridge, MA 1997 [citation from p. 30]; on the phenomenon in Istanbul, see A. Bartu, "Redefining the Public Sphere through Fortified Enclaves: A View from Istanbul," WALD International Conference, Istanbul 1999; in Bangalore, see A. King, "Suburb/Ethnoburb/Globurg: Framing Transnational Urban Space in Asia," WALD International Conference, Istanbul 1999; on Los Angeles, Mike Davis, *Ecology of Fear: Los Angeles and the Imagination of Disaster* (New York 1999).
34. These abstention rates are calculated on the basis of data provided by Central American national electoral institutes and compiled in a graph titled "Turning Off," in "Guatemala's Democracy of Chickens, Rabbits—and Locals," *The Economist*, October 16 1999, p. 36.
35. See, e.g., AID, *Economic Assistance Strategy for Central America: 1991 to 2000*, Washington, D.C. January 1991.
36. See, *inter alia*, Minor Sinclair (ed.), *The New Politics of Survival: Grassroots Movements in Central America*, New York 1995.
37. For an extended analysis of this new "social movement" unionism in the context of the restructuring of the global working class, see Kim Moody, *Workers in a Lean World: Unions in International Economy*, London 1997. Meanwhile, as a response to a new surge in union organizing within the Central American maquiladora plants in the 1990s, transnational firms, local business sectors, and governments have been promoting *solidarismo*, worker–employee associations designed as an alternative to class confrontation and collective bargaining. Over 90 percent of TNCs in Costa Rica sponsor *solidarista* associations. These associations do not place demands on companies and instead sponsor savings and collective self-help projects out of workers' own salaries and employee contributions through an ideology of worker–management conciliation and teamwork. *Solidarismo* became established in Costa Rica in the 1980s and has since spread to Guatemala, Honduras, El Salvador, and Nicaragua, promoted by TNCs and financially backed by the AID. See, *inter alia*, Silvia Lara, *Inside Costa Rica*, Albuquerque: The Resource Center, 1995 pp. 86–90.
38. Kees van der Pijl, "The History of Class Struggle: From Original Accumulation to Neo-Liberalism," *Monthly Review*, vol. 49, no. 1, 1997, pp. 28–44.
39. This was a general phenomenon of the Left in Latin America. For instance, the PRD in Mexico, the FREPASO in Argentina, the FSLN in Nicaragua, Lavalas in Haiti, and other groups, did not challenge neo-liberalism in their programs put forward during major elections in the late 1990s, and in fact were careful to allay the fears of transnational capital in these programs. Space constraints limit discussion, but the experience of Cuba in recent years—the survival of the revolution and its ongoing transformation even as it has been

forced to integrate into world capitalism and despite its internal problems—should be studied for the lessons it may offer, and I do not concur with the assessment of some progressives that the Cuban revolution should now be dismissed. For that assessment, see, e.g., Roger Burbach, "Socialism is Dead; Long Live Socialism," *NACLA Report on the Americas*, vol. 31, no. 3, Nov/Dec 1997, pp. 15–20.

40. See, *inter alia*, Abelardo Morales G. and Martha Isabel Cranshaw, *Regionalismo Emergent: Redes de la Sociedad Civil E Integración Centroamericana*, San José 1997; Marc Edelman, "Transnational Peasant Politics in Central America," *Latin American Research Review*, vol. 33, no. 3, 1998 pp. 49–86.

41. For example, see Fernando Calderón, *Movimientos Sociales y Politica: La Decada de los Ochenta en Latinamerica*, Mexico City: Siglo XXI, 1995.

42. On this issue, see Robinson and Harris, "Towards a Global Ruling Class."

43. Christopher Chase-Dunn, "Globalization from Below in Guatemala," paper presented at "Conference on Guatemalan Development and Democracy: Proactive Responses to Globalization," Guatemala City, March 26–28, 1998.

44. On cross-border union organizing, see, e.g., Ethel Brooks and Winifred Tate, "After the Wars: Cross-Border Organizing in Central America," *NACLA Report on the Americas*, vol. 32, no. 4, Jan/Feb 1999, pp. 32–6; Ralph Armbruster, "Cross-Border Labor Organizing in the Garment and Automobile Industries: The Phillips Van-Heusen and Ford Cuautitlan Cases," *Journal of World-System Research* vol. 4, no. 1, 1998, pp. 20–51.

45. For interesting discussion on this point, see Peter Evans, "Fighting Marginalization with Transnational Networks: Counter-Hegemonic Globalization," *Contemporary Sociology*, vol. 29, no. 1, 2000, pp. 230–41.

46. See, *inter alia*, Frans J. Schuurman, *Beyond the Impasse: New Directions in Development Theory*, London 1993; D. Booth, "Marxism and Development Sociology: Interpreting the Impasse," *World Development*, vol. 13, 1985; Booth, *Rethinking Social Development: Theory, Research and Practice*, London 1994; Colin Leys, *The Rise and the Fall of Development Theory*, Indianapolis, London, and Nairobi 1996; R. Peet, *Global Capitalism: Theories of Social Development*, London 1991.

47. See, *inter alia*, Arturo Escobar, *Encountering Development: The Making and Unmaking of the Third World*, Princeton 1995.

48. For a more detailed discussion and critique of these different theoretical approaches, see "Remapping Development in Light of Globalization: From a Territorial to a Social Cartography," *Third World Quarterly*, forthcoming, 2002.

49. David Harvey, *The Condition of Postmodernity*, Oxford 1990, p. 294.

50. See, e.g., Harvey, *The Condition of Postmodernity*; Allen J. Scott and Michael Storper, *Production, Work, Territory: The Geographic Anatomy of Industrial Capitalism*, Boston 1996.

51. McMichael, *Development and Social Change*, p. 173.

52. See Alejandro Portes's interesting comments on the relationship between typologies and theories, "Immigration Theory for a New Century: Some Problems and Opportunities," *Migration Review*, vol. 31, no. 4, 1997, p. 811.

53. See Portes's comments, "Immigration Theory for a New Century," p. 799–825 (esp. pp. 805–10).

Index